安藤忠雄の建築　3

Tadao

TADAO ANDO 3 Inside Japan

First published in Japan on October 10, 2008
Sixth published on June 15, 2023

TOTO Publishing (TOTO LTD.)
TOTO Nogizaka Bldg., 2F
1-24-3 Minami-Aoyama, Minato-ku
Tokyo 107-0062, Japan
[Sales]Telephone: +81-3-3402-7138 Facsimile: +81-3-3402-7187
[Editorial]Telephone: +81-3-3497-1010
URL: https://jp.toto.com/publishing

Author: Tadao Ando
Publisher: Akira Watai
Book Designer: Tetsuya Ohta
Printing Director : Noboru Takayanagi
Printer: Tokyo Inshokan Printing Co., LTD.

Except as permitted under copyright law, this book may not be reproduced, in whole or in part, in any form or by any means, including photocopying, scanning, digitizing, or otherwise, without prior permission. Scanning or digitizing this book through a third party, even for personal or home use, is also strictly prohibited.
The list price is indicated on the cover.

ISBN978-4-88706-296-2

Ando 3

Inside Japan

Tadao Ando 3 Inside Japan

目次
Contents

012
東京大学情報学環・福武ホール
Interfaculty Initiative in Information Studies
Fukutake Hall, the University of Tokyo

028
東急東横線渋谷駅
Tokyu Toyoko-Line Shibuya Station

044
東急大井町線上野毛駅
Tokyu Oimachi-Line Kaminoge Station

048
聖心女子学院創立100周年記念ホール
Sacred Heart School
100th Anniversary Hall

052
エッセイ Essay
安藤行基説序説
Tadao Ando, a Latter-day Gyoki?

鈴木博之 Hiroyuki Suzuki

080
TIME'S I + II
TIME'S I + II

090
渋谷プロジェクト
Shibuya Project

094
中之島プロジェクトII（アーバン・エッグ＋地層空間）
Nakanoshima Project II
(Urban Egg + Space Strata)

112
祈りの空間
Space for Prayers

114
水の教会
Church on the Water

128
光の教会
Church of the Light

140
光の教会／日曜学校
Church of the Light, Sunday School

148
兵庫県立こどもの館
Children's Museum, Hyogo

160
真言宗本福寺水御堂
Water Temple

176
JR京都駅改築設計競技案
The Reconstruction of JR Kyoto Station,
International Design Competition

184
ベネッセハウス ミュージアム
Benesse House Museum / Naoshima

204
ベネッセハウス オーバル
Benesse House Oval / Naoshima

220
大阪府立近つ飛鳥博物館
Chikatsu-Asuka Historical Museum, Osaka

230
サントリーミュージアム＋マーメイド広場
Suntory Museum + Plaza

240
大谷地下劇場計画
The Theater in the Rock, Oya

246
織田廣喜ミュージアム
Daylight Museum

256
風景の再生、建築の未来
Revival of Landscape,
Future of Architecture

258
淡路夢舞台
Awaji-Yumebutai (Awaji Island Project)

270
南岳山光明寺
Komyo-ji Temple

286
大阪府立狭山池博物館
Sayamaike Historical Museum, Osaka

300
司馬遼太郎記念館
Shiba Ryotaro Memorial Museum

312
国際芸術センター青森
Aomori Contemporary Art Centre

324
兵庫県立美術館＋神戸市水際広場
Hyogo Prefectural Museum of Art
+ Kobe Waterfront Plaza

336
国際子ども図書館
The International Library of Children's
Literature

348
加賀市立錦城中学校
Kinjo Junior High School, Kaga

362
野間自由幼稚園
Noma Kindergarten

376
20年越しの地中
The Subterranean Revisited
After Twenty Years

378
地中美術館
Chichu Art Museum / Naoshima

400
表参道ヒルズ
（同潤会青山アパート建替計画）
Omotesando Hills
(Omotesando Regeneration Project)

414
21_21 DESIGN SIGHT
21_21 DESIGN SIGHT

428
エッセイ Essay
建築の公共性
The Public Character of Architecture

安藤忠雄 Tadao Ando

462
六甲の集合住宅 I, II, III + IV
Rokko Housing I, II, III + IV

464
作品年表 Chronological Table of Projects

472
作品データ Projects Data

476
作品所在地マップ Map of Projects

478
略歴 Profile

TIME'S

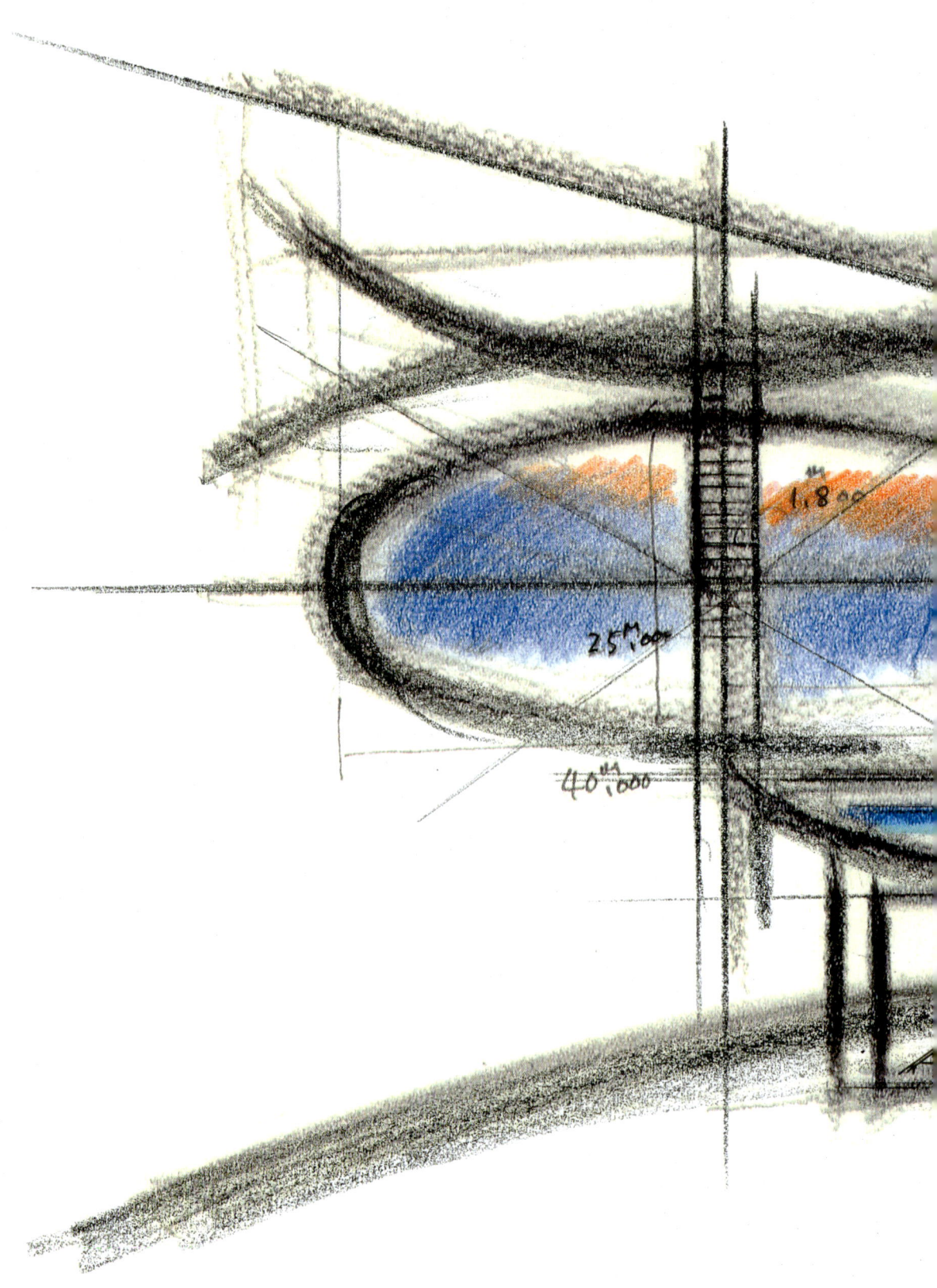

Water Temple

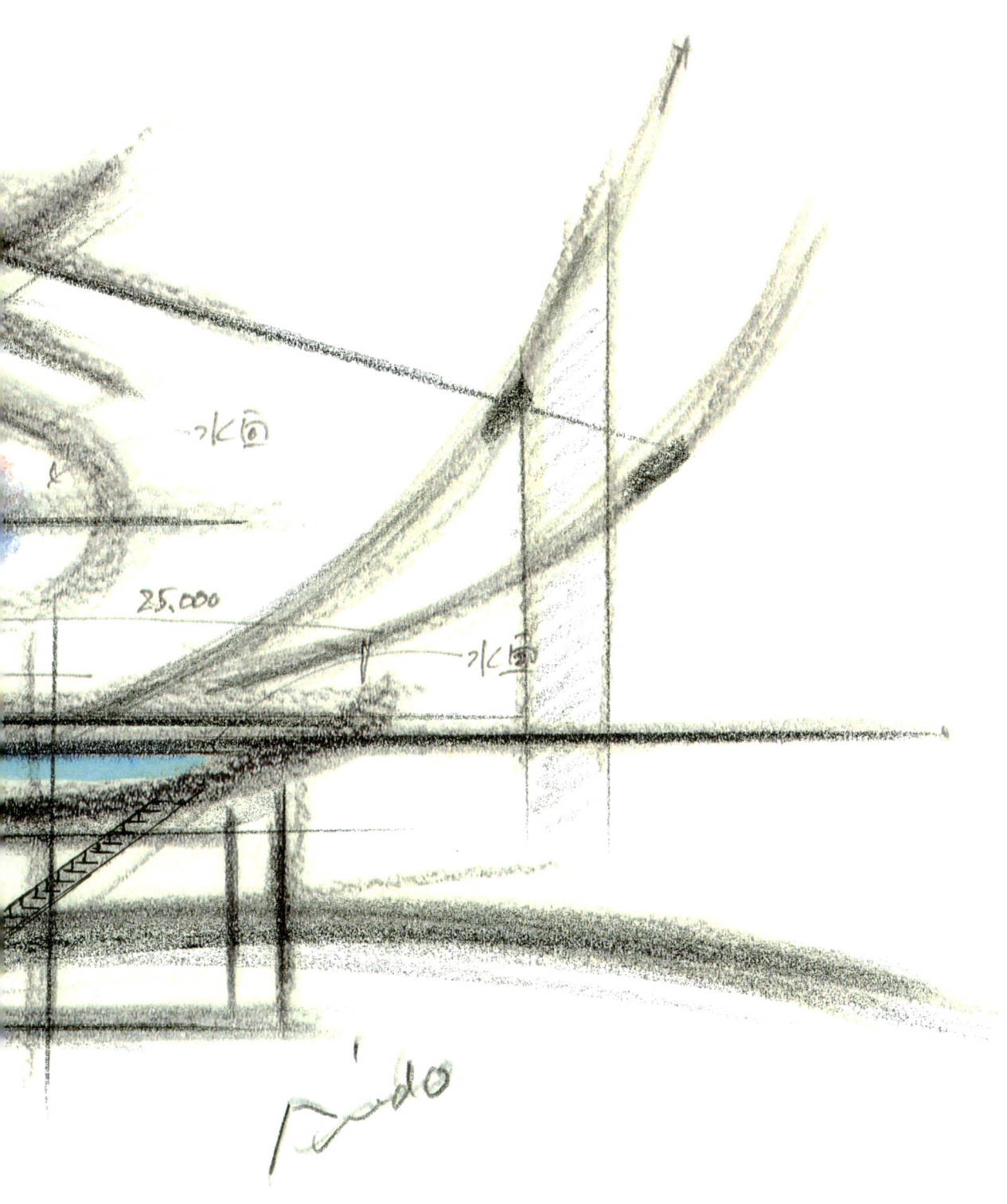

Chichu Art Museum / Naoshima

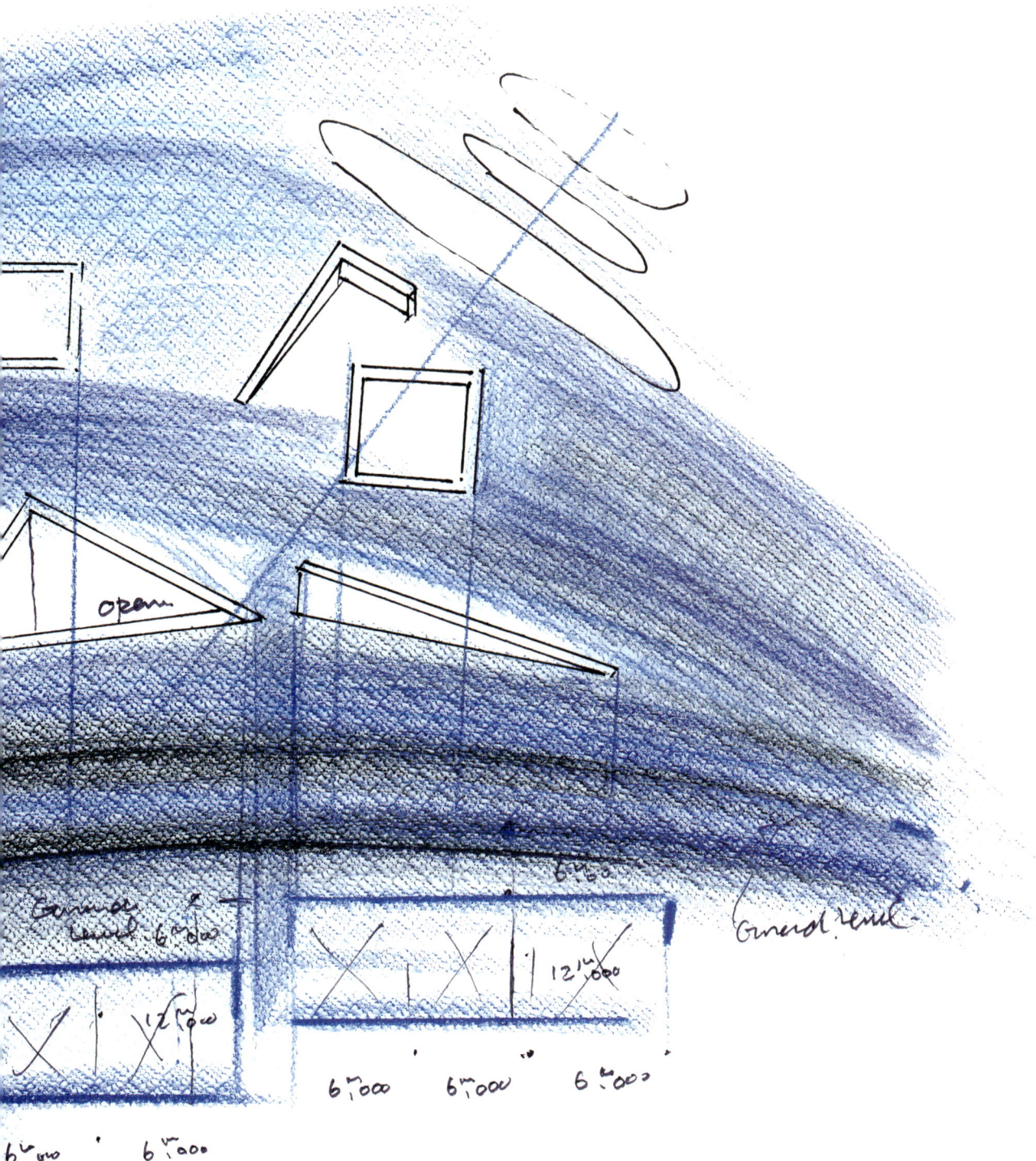

東京大学情報学環・福武ホール
Interfaculty Initiative in Information Studies Fukutake Hall, the University of Tokyo

2005-08　東京都文京区──Bunkyo-ku, Tokyo

　東京大学本郷キャンパス内に、大学創立130周年を記念してつくられた200人収容のホールをもつ校舎施設である。本郷キャンパスは、統一的にデザインされたゴシック風の建物を中心に、各時代の校舎が緑地軸に沿って建ち並ぶ、すぐれた歴史的環境を有している。随所に豊かな緑で覆われた余白の空間が設けられており、そのオープンスペースのネットワークによって、構内の各施設は緩やかに結ばれている。

　新たに加えられる建物の敷地は、キャンパス内最古の建造物である「赤門」に隣接する、本郷通りとキャンパスを隔てる緑地帯の一部に定められた。間口100m、奥行き15mの細長い敷地には、樹齢100年を超える見事なクスノキが繁っていた。キャンパスの緑地軸構成の踏襲、既存のクスノキの風景の継承を前提に、キャンパスの新たな刺激となるような〈場〉の創出を主題として計画に取り組んだ。そして生まれたのが、既存の樹木を避けて得られる矩形を2層分地下に沈め、その半分に4層分の高さのヴォリュームを配置し、もう半分を地下と地上をつなぐ階段状のドライエリアとする構成である。既存樹木と建物との一体感、すなわち建物の高さが樹木を超えないよう、低く抑えることを常に意識した。

　建物全長に及ぶ庇の水平線と呼応するように延びる前面のコンクリートの壁は、背後のオープンスペースの求心性を高めるのと同時に、キャンパス内に意図的な空白、内省の〈間〉が生まれることを期待してつくったものである。

　This is a school building containing a hall to accommodate 200 people, built on the Hongo campus of the University of Tokyo in commemoration of the 130th anniversary of the establishment of the university. Centered on buildings designed in a unified Gothic style, the Hongo campus has an excellent historical environment in which school buildings from different times are aligned along a green axis. Open spaces filled with abundant greenery have been established everywhere, and each facility on the premises is loosely linked through this network of open spaces.

　The site for the newly added building was determined to be adjacent to the Red Gate, the oldest structure on the campus, in a part of the green belt that separates the campus from Hongo Street. On this long and narrow site, 100m wide and 15m deep, magnificent camphor trees over a century old grow in abundance. Following the green axis composition of the campus, premised on inheriting the scenery of the existing camphor trees, I tackled the design with the theme of creating a "place" that would become a new stimulus for the campus. What emerged from this was a composition comprising a rectangular volume that avoids the existing trees with two stories buried underground. Half of this is arranged as a four-story-high volume, and the other half as a stair-shaped dry area connecting below ground to above ground. I was always conscious of the need to stay low to obtain a feeling of unity between the building and the existing greenery—in other words, for the height of the building to not exceed the trees.

　As if acting in concert with the horizontal line of the eaves that stretch along the entire building, the concrete wall of the extended facade heightens the concentricity of the open space to the rear, with the added intention of producing an intentionally empty "space" for introspection inside the campus.

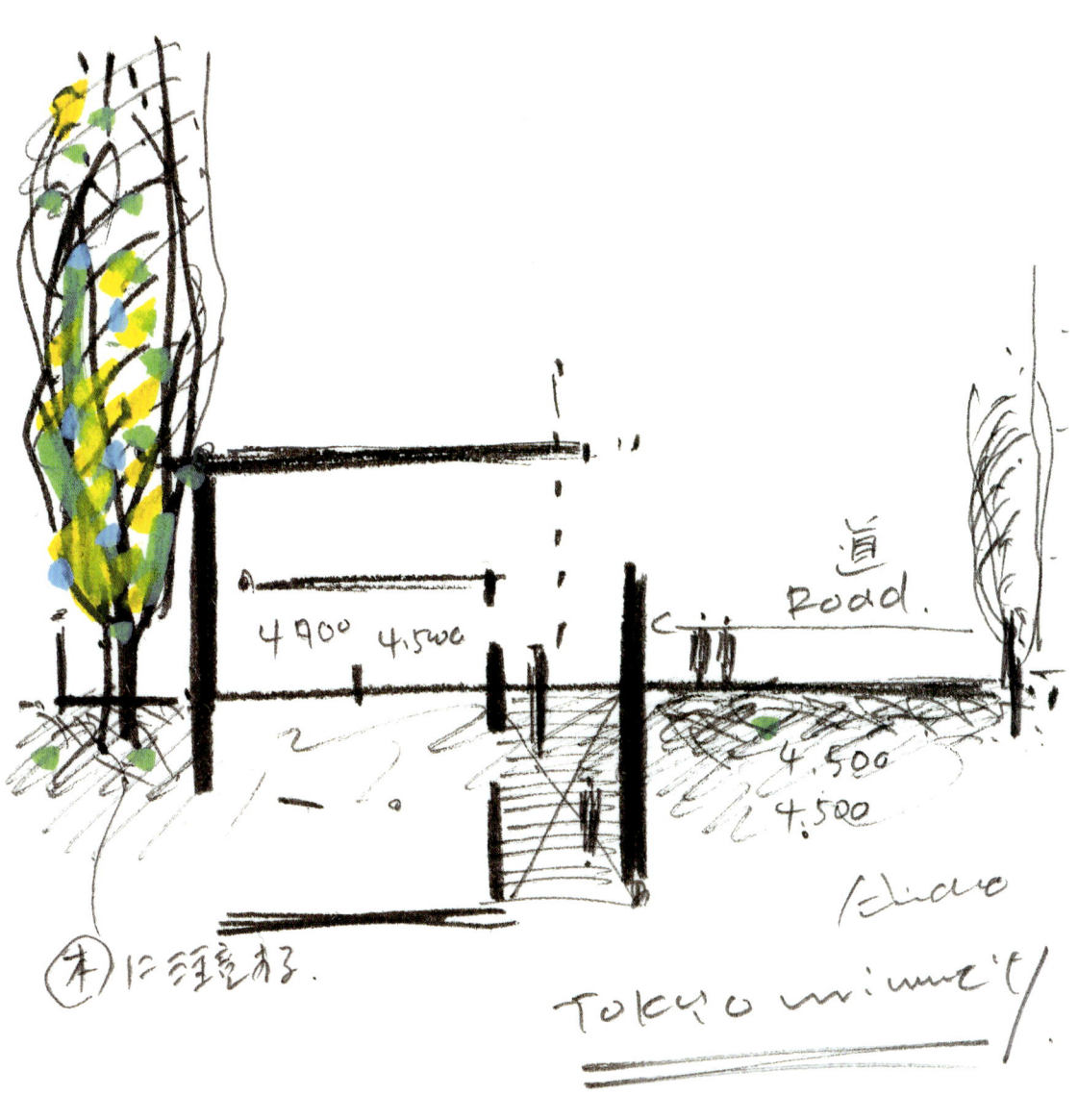

イメージスケッチ。建物背後のクスノキ、キャンパス側との関係を踏まえた建物断面のイメージが端的に描かれている。

Image sketch. Boldly drawn image of the building section, based on the relationship to the campus and the camphor trees behind the building.

建物と平行に延びるコンクリートの自立壁には、高さ30cmで横長のスリット開口が設けられている。建物内外を隔てつつ、つなげる壁の表現。

A 30cm-high rectangular slit has been made in the freestanding concrete wall that extends parallel to the building. Expression of a wall that connects while separating the interior and the exterior of the building.

京都の三十三間堂を思わせる、庇と自立壁の緊張感ある造形。
庇先端の見つけ寸法は20cm。

A form reminiscent of Sanjusangen-do Temple in Kyoto,
with a sense of tension between the eave and the freestanding wall.
The dimension of the eave edge is 20cm.

Section 1:800

Hongo Street

General Library

1 laboratory
2 meeting room
3 common space
4 studio

017 Fukutake Hall

福武ホールの向かいには東京大学総合図書館（設計：内田祥三／野田俊彦、1928年）が建つ。新旧の対話するキャンパス空間。

The University of Tokyo General Library (design: Yoshikazu Uchida / Toshihiko Noda, 1928) is located opposite Fukutake Hall. A campus space of dialogue between old and new.

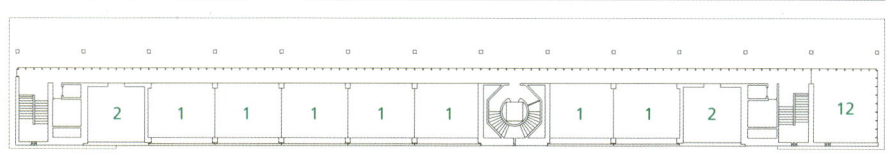
Second floor plan

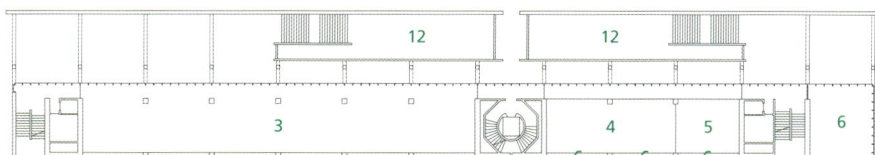
First floor plan

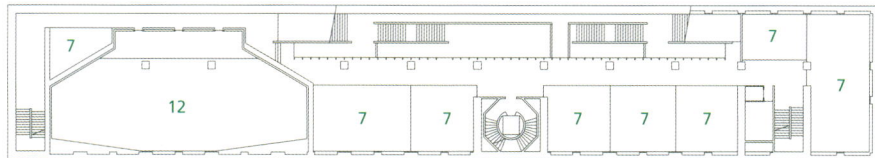
First basement plan

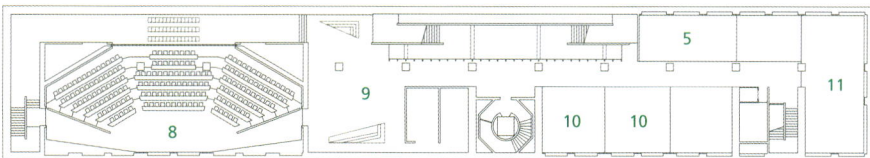
Second basement plan   1:800

1 laboratory
2 mechanical
3 multipurpose area
4 staff room
5 meeting room
6 café
7 common space
8 lecture hall
9 foyer
10 studio
11 workshop
12 void

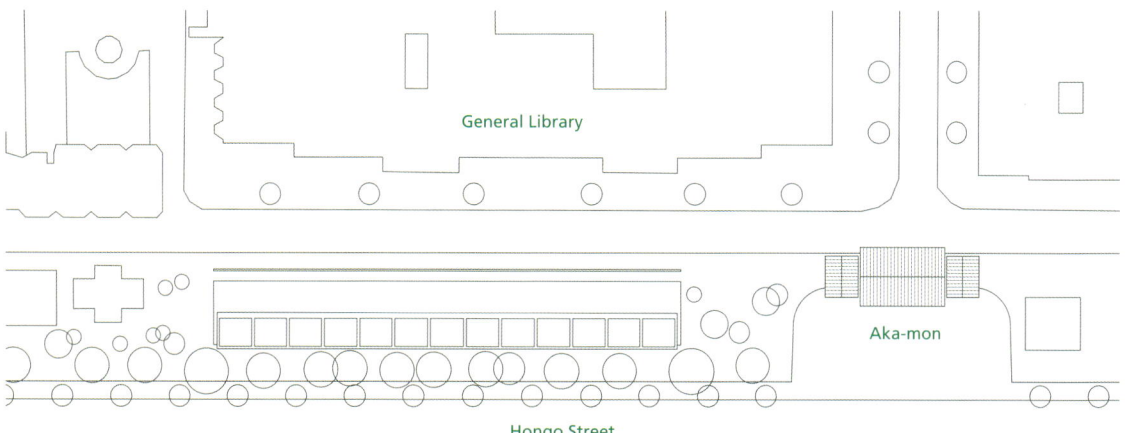
Site plan   1:1,500

019 Fukutake Hall

自立壁の背後に広がる地下2階へと続くオープンスペース。
The open space that extends behind the freestanding wall, leading to the second basement level.

鉄とガラスとコンクリート。限定された素材と表現手法による、簡素で清潔な空間。

Steel, glass, and concrete. A simple, clean space achieved by means of limited materials and expressive techniques.

023 Fukutake Hall

地下2階の大講義室。壁面は18mmのベイマツのリブをずらしながら重ねて不燃加工したもの。壁面は6度傾いている。

Large lecture room in the second basement level. The walls comprise layered offset 18mm ribs of bay pine with a fire-resistant treatment. The walls have a six-degree incline.

クスノキの大木群を背景に全長95.4mにわたって延びるファサード。自立するコンクリートの自立壁が、キャンパス内に新たな〈間〉をつくり出す。

Facade with a total length of 95.4m against the backdrop of a group of large camphor trees. The freestanding concrete wall creates a new "interval" in the campus.

東京メトロ副都心線、東急東横線が相互乗り入れする、新しい渋谷の地下駅の計画である。通常、地下駅の建築は、先行してつくられる土木躯体と切り離したかたちで計画されるが、ここでは、地下躯体の設計途中にプロジェクトがスタートしたため、建築と土木とをあわせた、より本質的な空間提案を行うことができた。

新しい地下駅は、〈地宙船＝地下深くに浮遊する宇宙船〉のイメージのもと、土木工事でつくられるコンクリート躯体に対し、まったく異なるフォルムに包まれた駅舎空間を入れ子状に挿入するかたちで計画されている。構成の中心は、地下躯体を貫いて、地下２階のコンコースから地下５階のホームへ至る楕円形の吹き抜けと、それを取り囲む卵型のシェルである。

かつて大阪・中之島で提案した「アーバン・エッグ」を思わせる造形は、都市の結節点たる渋谷に相応しい、ダイナミックな空間をつくり出す構成だが、一方で、現実の機能面においても重要な役割を担っている。

ひとつには、地上との位置関係がつかめず、方向の変化もわかりにくい地下空間にあって、〈卵〉の中心の吹き抜けが、利用者の空間認知を助ける、地下のランドマークとして機能するという点。もうひとつが、この〈卵〉のワンルーム構成が、隣地の東急文化会館跡地に設けられる地下までのドライエリアを利用した、地下駅舎内の自然換気のシステムに大いに供している点だ。

〈卵〉を形づくる材料にGRC素材を選択したことも、結果的に、このシステムの成功の一因となった。当初は、コンクリート打ち放しのイメージであったのを、構造・施工上の理由から、中身を空洞にして軽量化できるGRCにしたのだが、その〈卵〉の殻の中の空洞を利用して、自然換気と矛盾しない輻射冷房を実現することができた。

毎日数十万人の人間が往来する極めて公共性の高い都市施設だからこそ、消費されない強さと、環境の世紀に応える確かな視座をもった空間にしたいと考えた。

東急東横線渋谷駅
Tokyu Toyoko-Line Shibuya Station
2006-08　東京都渋谷区 —— Shibuya-ku, Tokyo

This is a design for a new subway station in Shibuya, through which the Tokyo Metro Fukutoshin Line and the Tokyu Toyoko Line will pass. Subway station buildings are usually designed in a form detached from the infrastructural framework that is constructed first, but because here the project began during the design of the underground framework, a more essential spatial proposal could be implemented, combining architecture and infrastructure.

Based on the image of a "hypogenous ship" (a space ship floating deep under the ground), the new subway station is contained in forms inserted as nested shapes entirely different from the concrete infrastructural frame. The center of the composition is an oval void that penetrates the underground frame and extends from the concourse at basement level 2 to the platforms on basement level 5, with an egg-shaped shell surrounding it.

Reminiscent of the Urban Egg proposed previously for Nakanoshima in Osaka, this shape is appropriate for the urban knot of Shibuya, as the composition produces a dynamic space, but on the other hand, it also bears an important role in terms of actual functions.

Firstly, it functions as an underground landmark in which the central void of the "egg" aids spatial recognition for the users of the underground spaces, in which changes in direction are hard to understand without above-ground positional relationships. Secondly, the single-space composition of this "egg" provides a natural ventilation system for the interior of the underground station by using an underground dry area established in the adjacent vacant lot formerly occupied by the Tokyu Bunka Kaikan.

The choice of glass fiber reinforced concrete as the material for forming the "egg" also led to the success of this system. The initial image was of bare, solid concrete, but for structural and technological reasons it was changed to glass fiber reinforced concrete to make the contents of the cavity lightweight, which enabled the cavity inside the shell of the "egg" to work as part of the radiant cooling panel system, consistent with the natural ventilation mechanism proposed for the station.

Precisely because this is an urban facility with a high degree of commonality through which hundreds of thousands of people pass every day, I wanted to make a space with a strength that cannot be consumed and an indisputable viewpoint that responds to the era of the environment.

断面コンセプト模型。3層にわたり卵型の地宙船が登場する。

Sectional concept model. The image of an egg-shaped space ship extending over three levels.

029 Shibuya Station

改札階からホームへと続くエスカレータを見る。卵型のGRCに包まれたような空間になっている。シェルには視認性を高めるためスリットが設けられている。

View of the escalator leading from the ticket gate level to the platform. The space is contained in an egg shape made of GRC. To improve visibility, slits have been made in the shell.

中間階(地下4階)から改札階(地下2階)を見る。
View of the ticket gate level (basement level 2) from the intermediate floor (basement level 4).

エスカレータの裏側。中間階から下階の線路が見える。

The underside of the escalator. The railway tracks on the lowest level are visible from the intermediate level.

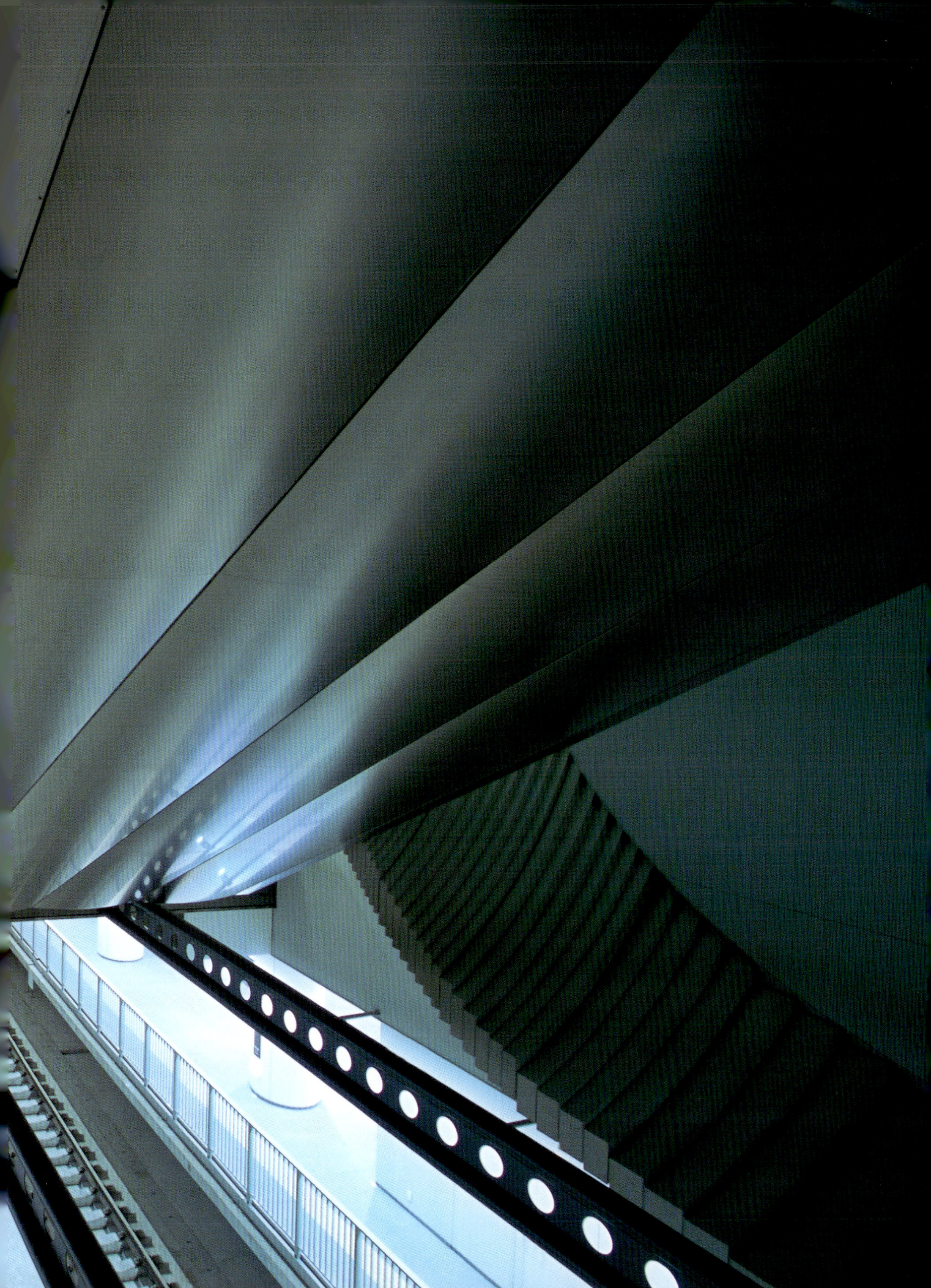

エスカレータ上部にあたる、卵型GRCシェルの先端部分。

The tip of the egg-shaped GRC shell meets the upper part of the escalator.

Site plan 1:5,000

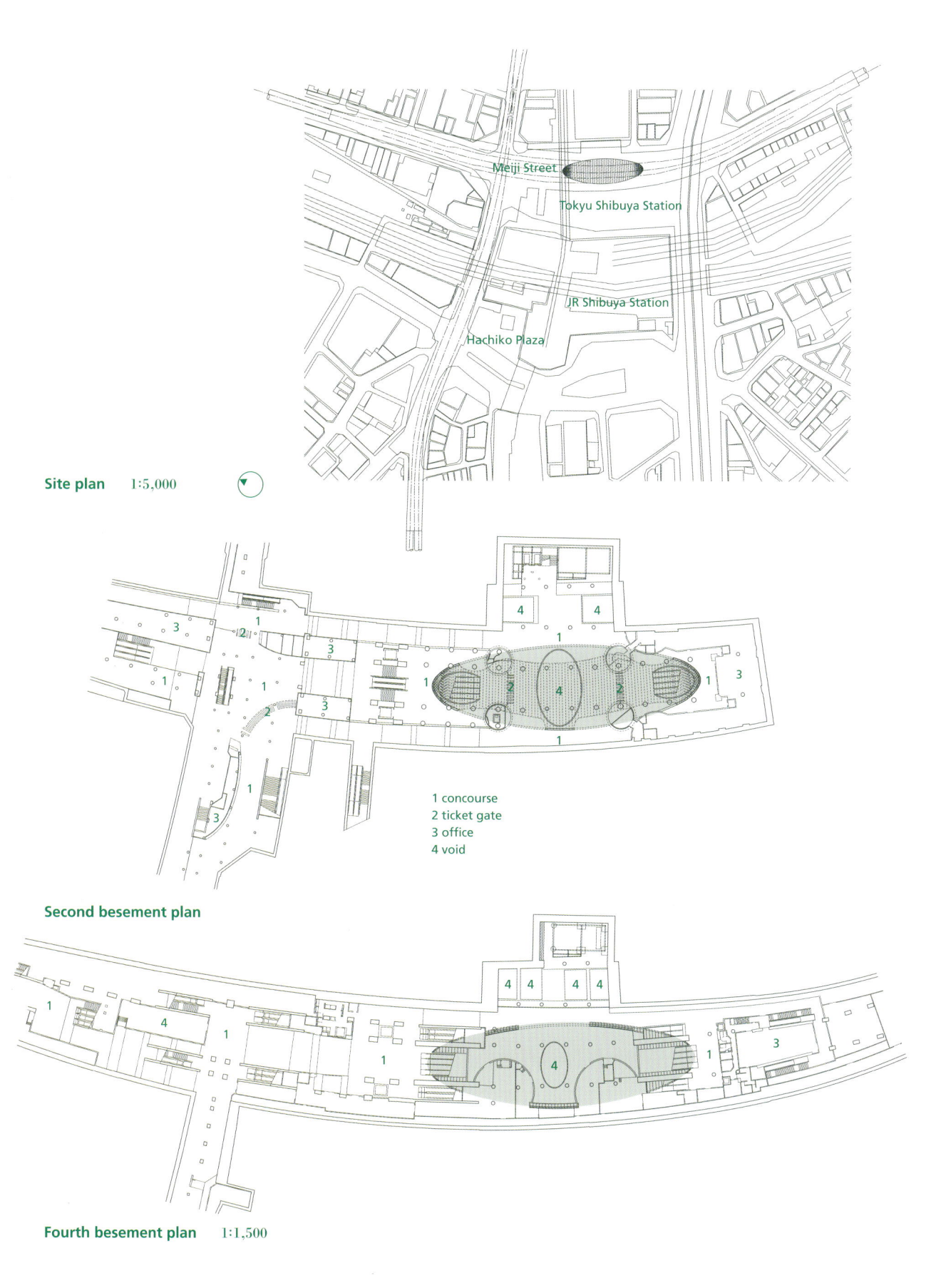

Second besement plan

1 concourse
2 ticket gate
3 office
4 void

Fourth besement plan 1:1,500

037 Shibuya Station

改札階から楕円形の吹き抜けを見下ろす。

Looking down at the oval void from the ticket gate level.

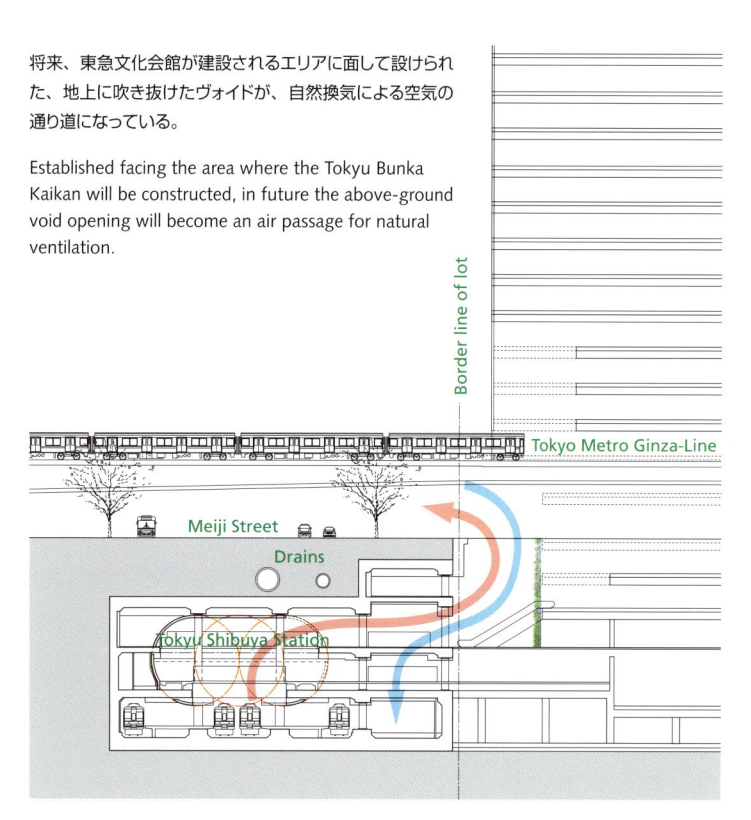

将来、東急文化会館が建設されるエリアに面して設けられた、地上に吹き抜けたヴォイドが、自然換気による空気の通り道になっている。

Established facing the area where the Tokyu Bunka Kaikan will be constructed, in future the above-ground void opening will become an air passage for natural ventilation.

Section 1:1,000

039 Shibuya Station

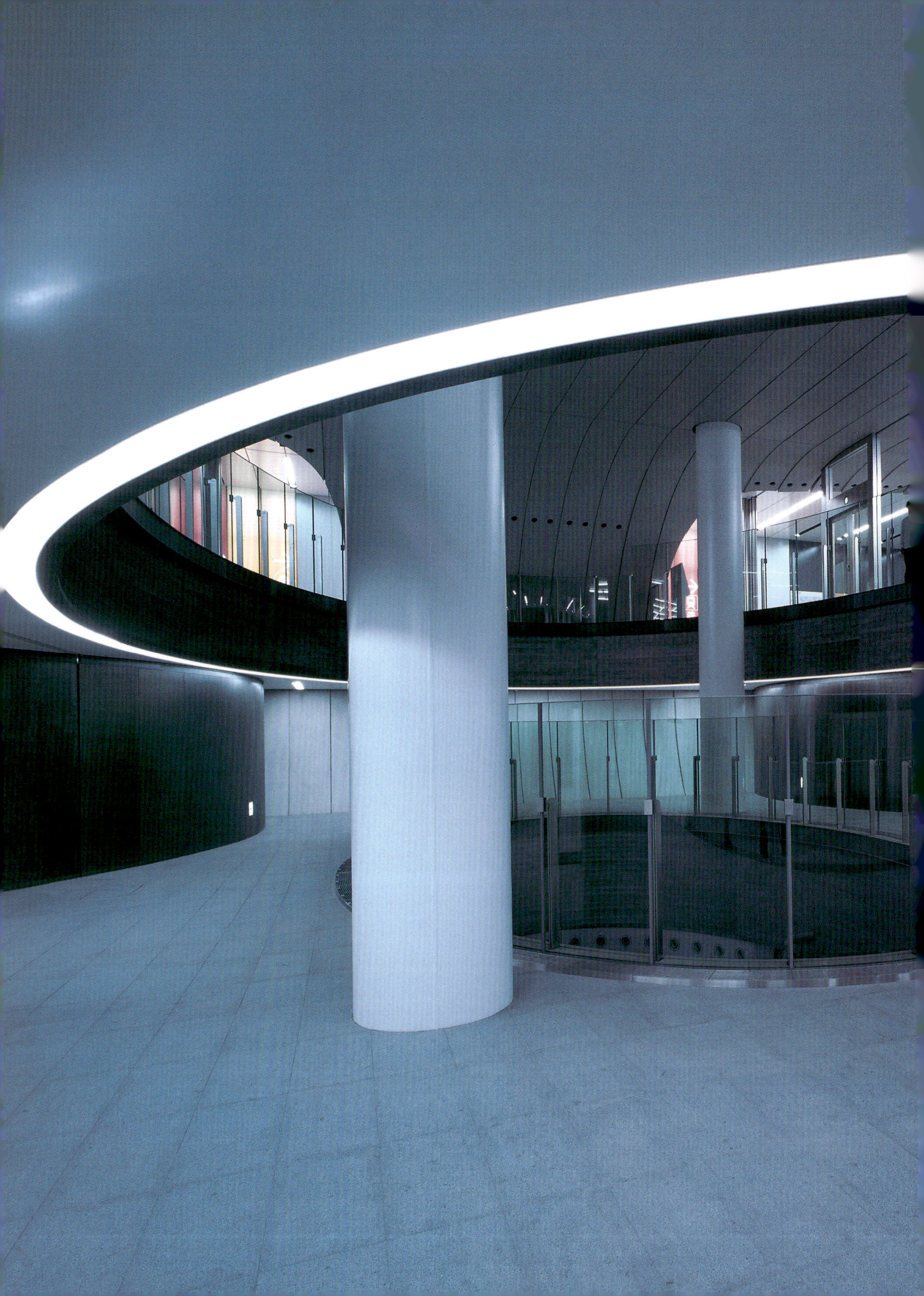

中間階から吹き抜けを見る。楕円形の吹き抜けが、駅舎内のスペースを立体的に結びつける。

The void seen from the intermediate level. The oval void three-dimensionally connects the spaces in the station.

地下5階のホーム階から楕円形の吹き抜けを見上げる。大胆に穿たれた垂直方向のヌケが、位置感覚を掴みにくくなりがちな地下空間の視認性を高める。

Looking up at the oval void from the platform at basement level 5. An underground space tends to cause difficulties in grasping one's sense of position, so visibility has been enhanced by boldly pierced vertical openings.

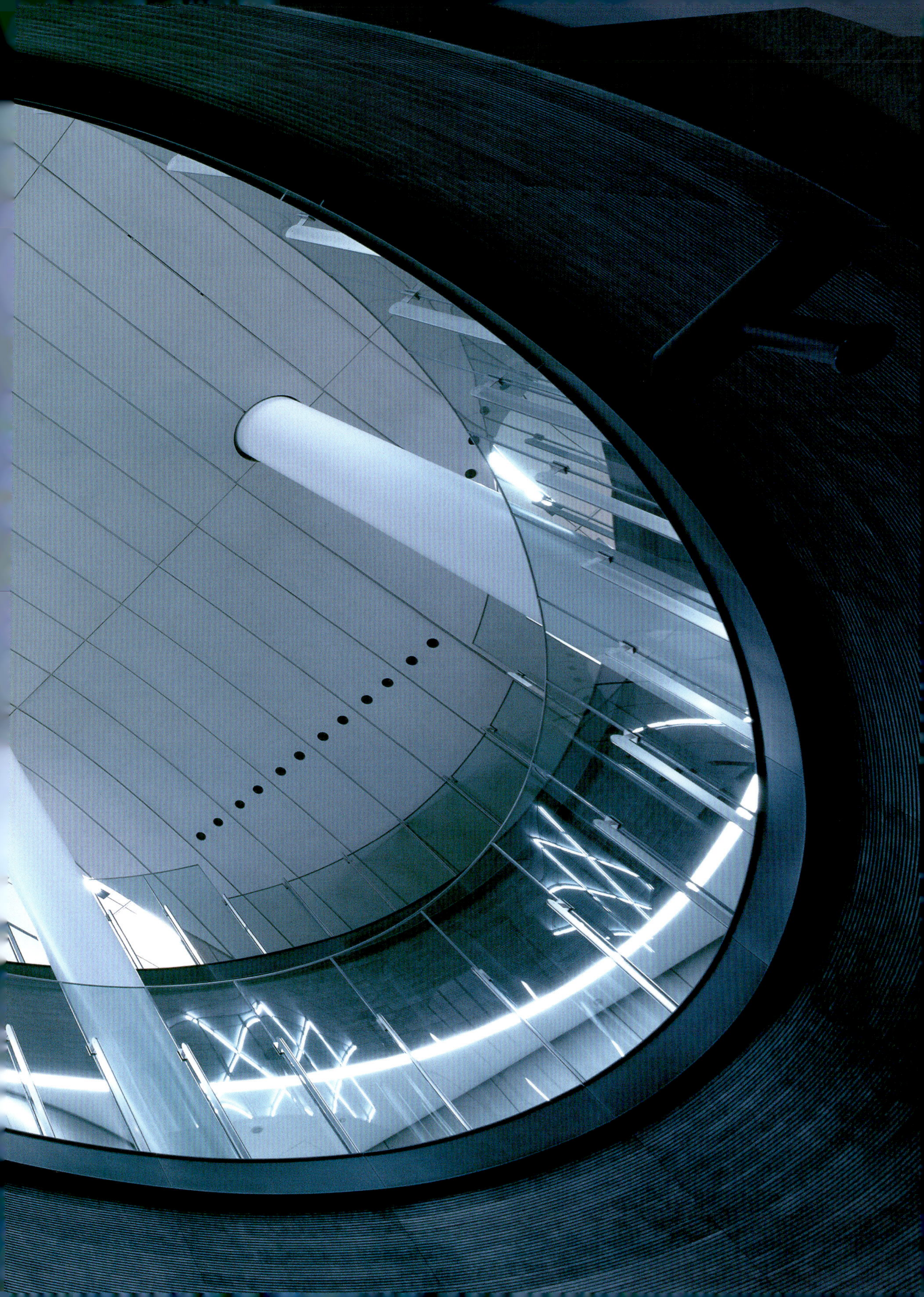

東急大井町線上野毛駅
Tokyu Oimachi-Line Kaminoge Station
2006- 東京都世田谷区 —— Setagaya-ku, Tokyo

東急大井町線上野毛駅の複々線化に伴う、路線拡張工事、及びバリアフリー化を含む駅舎の機能拡充計画である。上野毛駅は、鉄道敷が掘割りとなっており、プラットフォーム上部を環八通りから分岐した上野毛通りが横切っている。その立地特性を活かし、ここでは線路上空、上野毛通りのレベルにプラットホームの屋根を兼ねた人工地盤を設け、その上に駅の諸施設、テナント、バス停を含む駅前広場などを一体的に配置する提案をした。

地上部に現れる新しい駅舎は、上野毛通りを挟んで配されたヴォリュームと、それらを道路ごと覆う大屋根からなる。その北側に改札・託児所・駐輪場が、南側に同じく改札と駅務室を含むテナントが収められる。

バス停を含む駅前広場は、ふたつのヴォリュームが向き合う上野毛通りに面した部分に設けられる。頭上の大屋根には、円形のトップライトが穿たれ、内部化された広場に象徴的な光と影を落とす。歩行者・電車・バス・車・自転車といった多様な交通網をひとつの大屋根で覆い、一体化することで、都市インフラの合理的な統合とともに、地域の〈顔〉となる個性的な駅前風景の創出を意図した。

東急電鉄では沿線全体で壁面緑化・法面緑化を進めており、上野毛駅でも、積極的に法面緑化が行われている。次世紀に向けた都市再編を考える上で、都市に張り巡らされた駅と鉄道のネットワークには、大きなポテンシャルが秘められているように思う。

This is a project for the functional expansion of a station building, which includes making it barrier-free and the expansion work entailed by an increase in the number of tracks in Kaminoge Station on the Tokyu Oimachi Line. At Kaminoge Station the railway tracks are in a trench, and crossing above the platforms is Kaminoge Street, which branches from Kanpachi Street. Making good use of the characteristics of this location, this is a proposal in which the platform roof established above the tracks at the level of Kaminoge Street also acts as an artificial ground, on top of which are arranged the various station facilities, tenant spaces, and a bus stop unified with the station plaza.

The part of the new station building visible above ground comprises a large roof that covers the volumes arranged at either side of Kaminoge Street and each of the roads. On the north side is a ticket gate, a day nursery, and a bicycle parking area. On the south side is another ticket gate, and tenant spaces that include the station office.

The station plaza, including the bus stop, has been established in the area where the two opposing volumes face Kaminoge Street. A round skylight has been cut into the large roof overhead and symbolic light and shadow fall into the internalized plaza. In unifying the various transportation networks—pedestrians, trains, buses, cars, bicycles—by covering them with one large roof, the aim was to rationally integrate the urban infrastructure as well as create a characteristic space in front of the station that becomes the "face" of the area.

The greening of the wall surfaces and sloping banks along the entire Tokyu Railway network is progressing, and the greening of the sloping banks at Kaminoge Station is being actively undertaken. In considering urban reorganization for the next century, I think that there is huge latent potential in the network of stations and railways spread throughout the city.

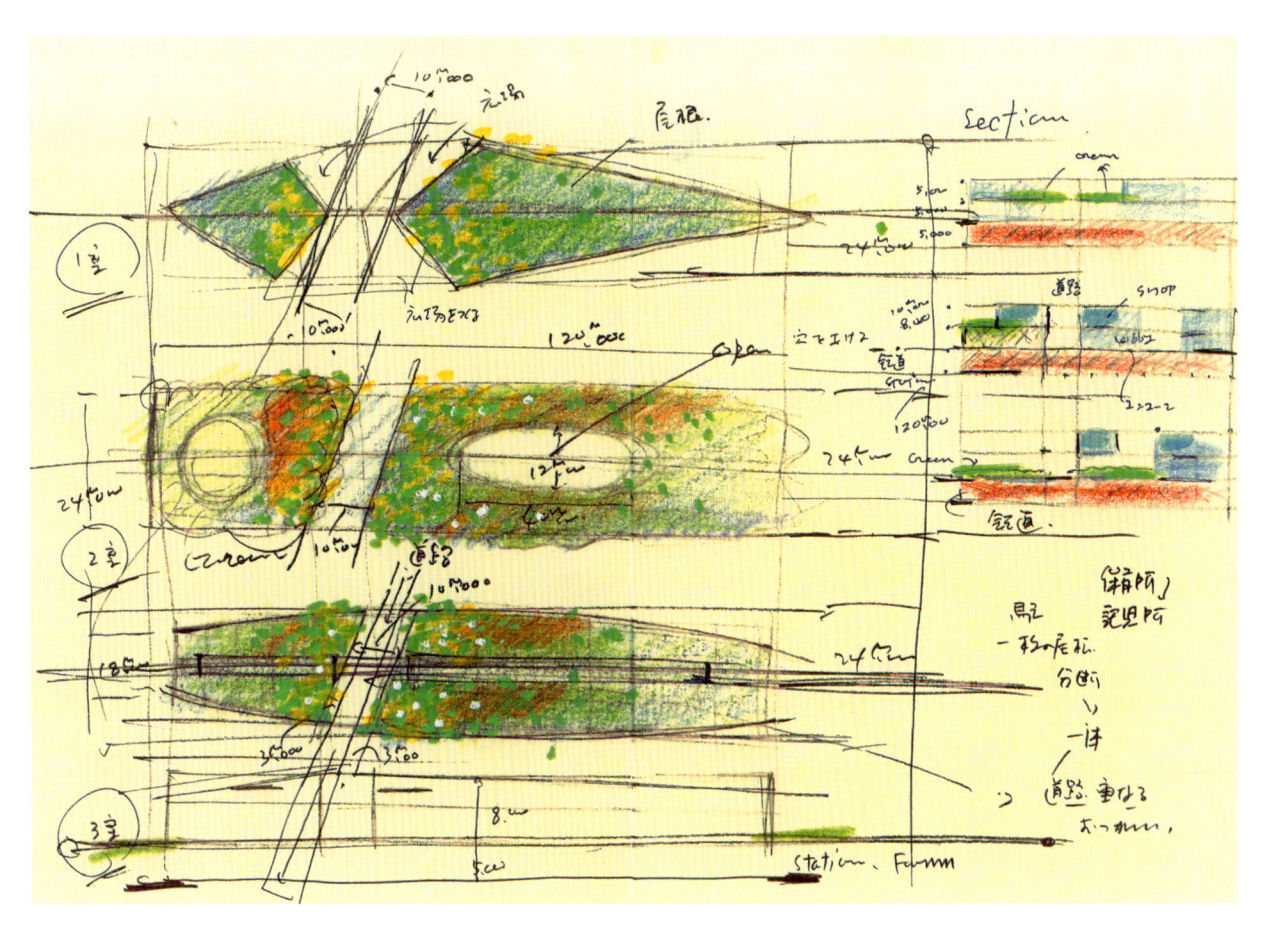

スタディスケッチ。線路に沿った全長120mの大屋根の下に、駅の施設と託児所、店舗などが一体的に計画されている。
Study sketch. A plan that unifies station facilities, a daycare center, stores, etc. below a large roof with a span of 120m following the railway line.

Elevation

Section

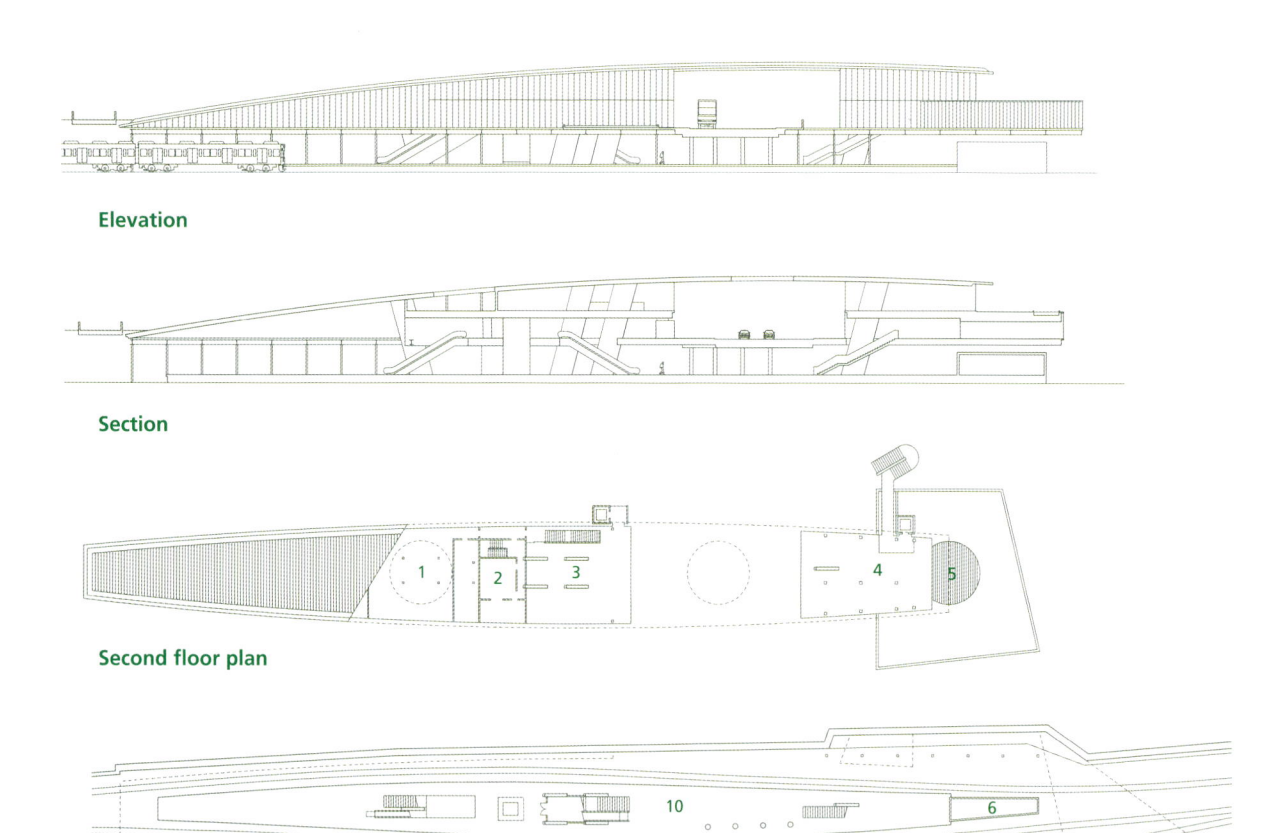

Second floor plan

Basement floor plan

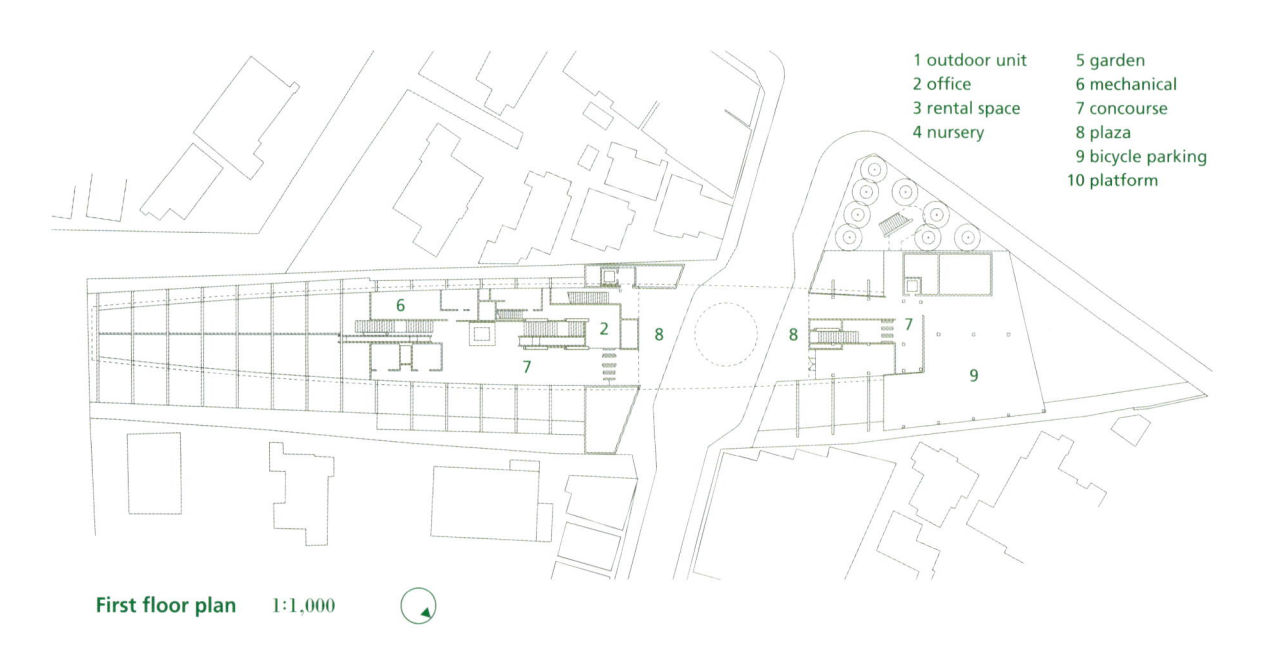

1 outdoor unit	5 garden
2 office	6 mechanical
3 rental space	7 concourse
4 nursery	8 plaza
	9 bicycle parking
	10 platform

First floor plan 1:1,000

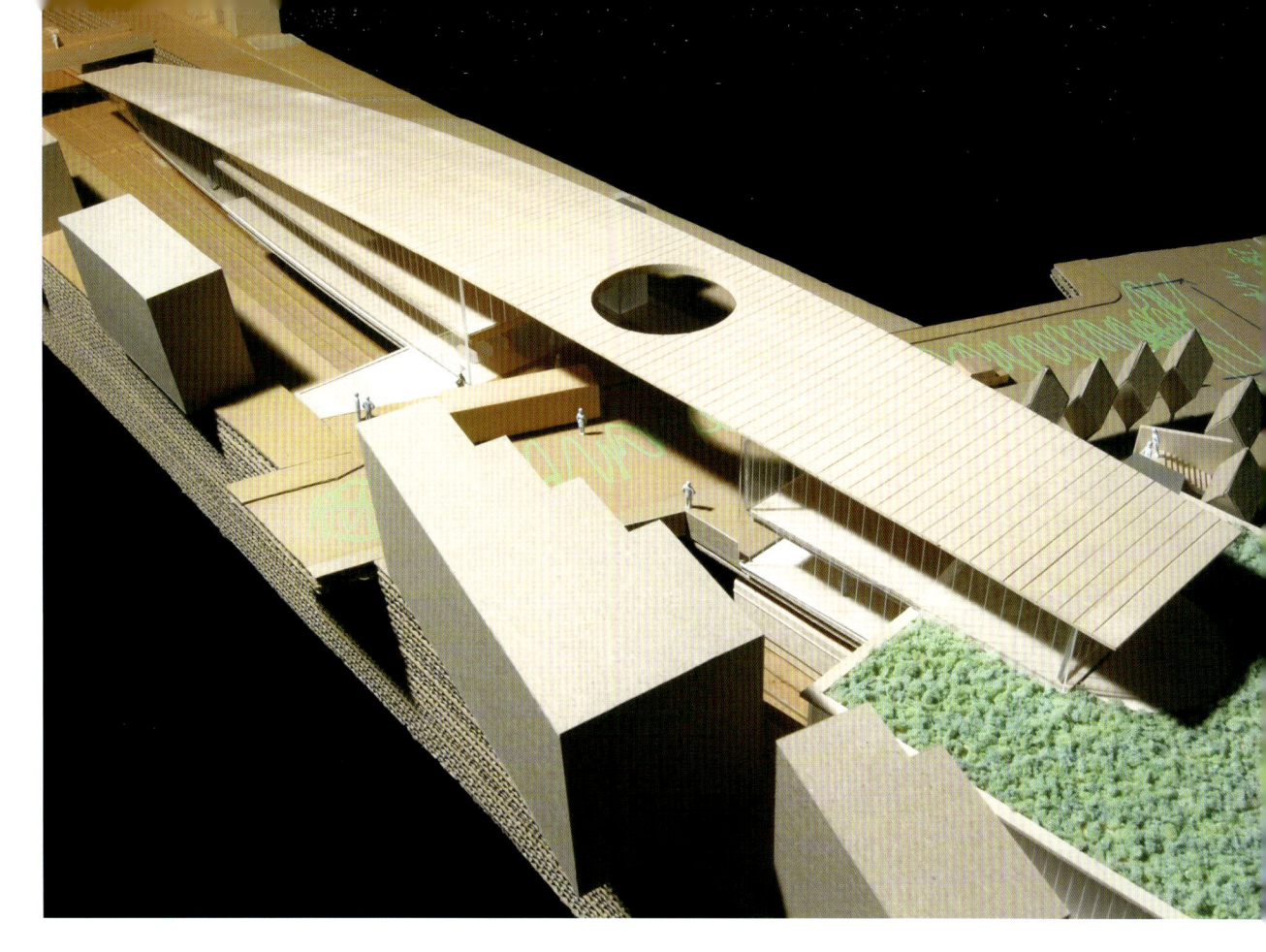

屋根に円形の開口が穿たれた部分が、線路を横切る上野毛通り。
通りを挟んで、屋根のある駅前広場が設けられる。

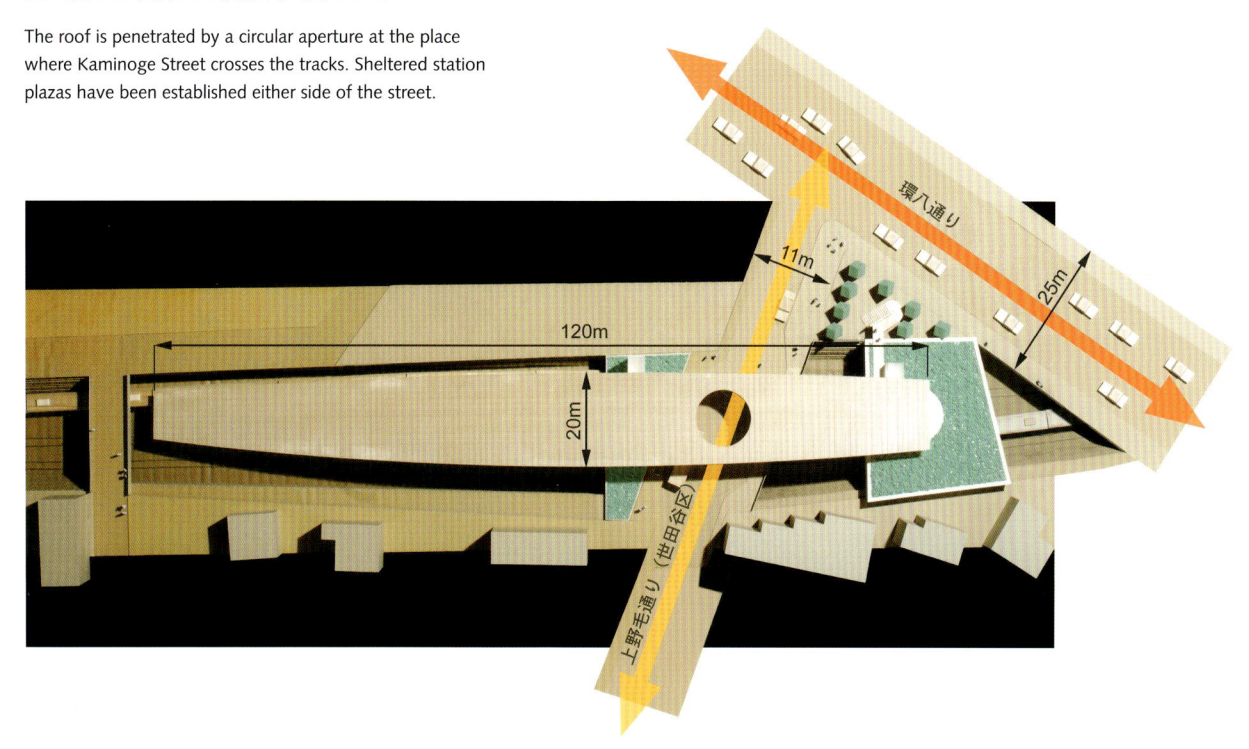

The roof is penetrated by a circular aperture at the place where Kaminoge Street crosses the tracks. Sheltered station plazas have been established either side of the street.

047 Kaminoge Station

東京都港区白金の閑静な住宅地に位置するカトリック系の私立校、聖心女子学院の創立100周年を記念するホールの計画である。聖心女子学院は、周囲を豊かな緑に包まれた中、アントニン・レーモンド設計の聖堂を中心とした校舎が中庭を囲んでコの字型に並ぶ、自然に恵まれた良好な環境をもつ。

今回のホールの計画場所は、中心部から外れた敷地北東端、既存の体育館と屋内プールの間のスペースで、敷地が限られていたために、屋内プールの屋上を利用した〈増築〉としてつくることとなった。1960年代につくられた旧い建物への増築は、法規的にも、また技術的にも、困難な問題を含んでいたが、一方で、そうした新旧にまたがった計画とすることで、ひとつの建築の挿入を、より広範な学校の環境再編の機会とする可能性が期待できた。そしてホールの新築と同時に、その下の屋内プール棟と隣接する体育館、さらにその周りの外構スペースの改修を含む、今回の計画が始まった。

体育館からプールへと至る経路は、従来の暗い〈裏側〉のイメージを払拭する、親しみやすいスケールの〈縁側〉つき広場として生まれ変わる。そこから階段を昇ってアプローチする屋内プールの屋上は、ウッドデッキを敷き詰めた空中のテラスとなる。そのテラスの上に、鉱物の原石のようなかたちのホールが浮かぶ。

金属パネルによる変形多面体の内部は、建物を支えるコアが形づくる円形平面のホールとその周囲のホワイエによる入れ子状の構成からなる。円形を象る壁の一部は、大型の可動建具となっており、壁に収納すると、ホワイエ越しに外の緑の風景がホール内部に取り込まれる。

環境と一体化した建築により、校内にもうひとつの中心をつくり出すことが主題だった。

聖心女子学院創立100周年記念ホール
Sacred Heart School 100th Anniversary Hall
2004-08 東京都港区——Minato-ku, Tokyo

This is a design for a hall commemorating the centennial of the founding of Sacred Heart School, a private school located in Shirogane, a quiet residential area in Minato-ku, Tokyo. Concealed by abundant greenery and centered on a church designed by Antonin Raymond, the buildings of Sacred Heart School are in a U-shape arrangement around a central courtyard in a favorable environment endowed by nature.

This hall is located away from the center, at the northeast end of the site in a space between the existing indoor pool and the gymnasium. Because the site is confined, the roof of the indoor pool has been used to make a "building addition." Making an addition to an old building constructed in the 1960s involved difficult legal as well as technical problems, but on the other hand, a design that straddles old and new suggests the possibility of a more comprehensive reorganization of the school environment by the insertion of a single building. This design began by including renovations of the indoor pool building below, the adjacent gymnasium, and the exterior spaces in the surroundings, at the same time as the construction of the new hall.

Surmounting the traditional gloomy image of an *uragawa* (backyard), the path leading from the gymnasium to the pool has been revived as a plaza with an intimately scaled *engawa* (verandah). Approached by climbing the stairs from there, the roof of the indoor pool is a sky terrace covered with a wood deck. The hall floats above the terrace, with a shape resembling a lump of raw mineral ore.

The interior of this deformed polyhedron made of metal panels has a nested composition comprising a foyer around a circular hall that forms the core supporting the building. The circular wall includes large moveable fittings, and when they are slid into the wall the green scenery visible outside across the foyer is brought into the hall interior.

The theme was to produce another center within the school by means of architecture integrated with its environment.

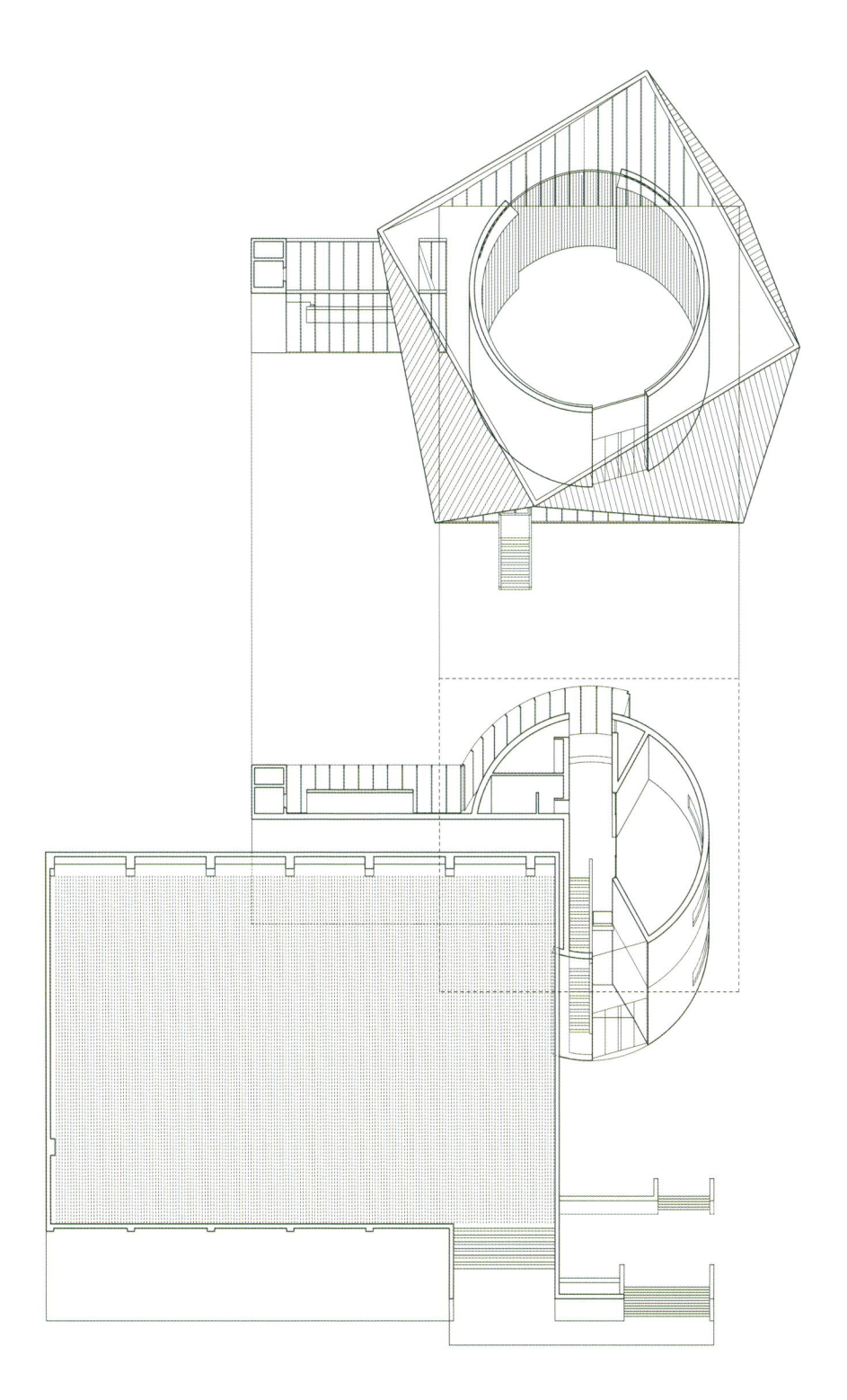

建築構成を表すアクソノメトリック。円形平面のコンクリートコアが傾斜壁に包まれたホールを支える。キャンティレバーでホールが重なる既存の屋内プールの屋上は、ウッドデッキのテラスとなる。

Axonometric drawing showing the architectural elements. The concrete core with a circular plan supports a hall enclosed by inclined walls. The hall is cantilevered from the roof of the existing indoor swimming pool, which becomes a wood deck terrace.

Third floor plan

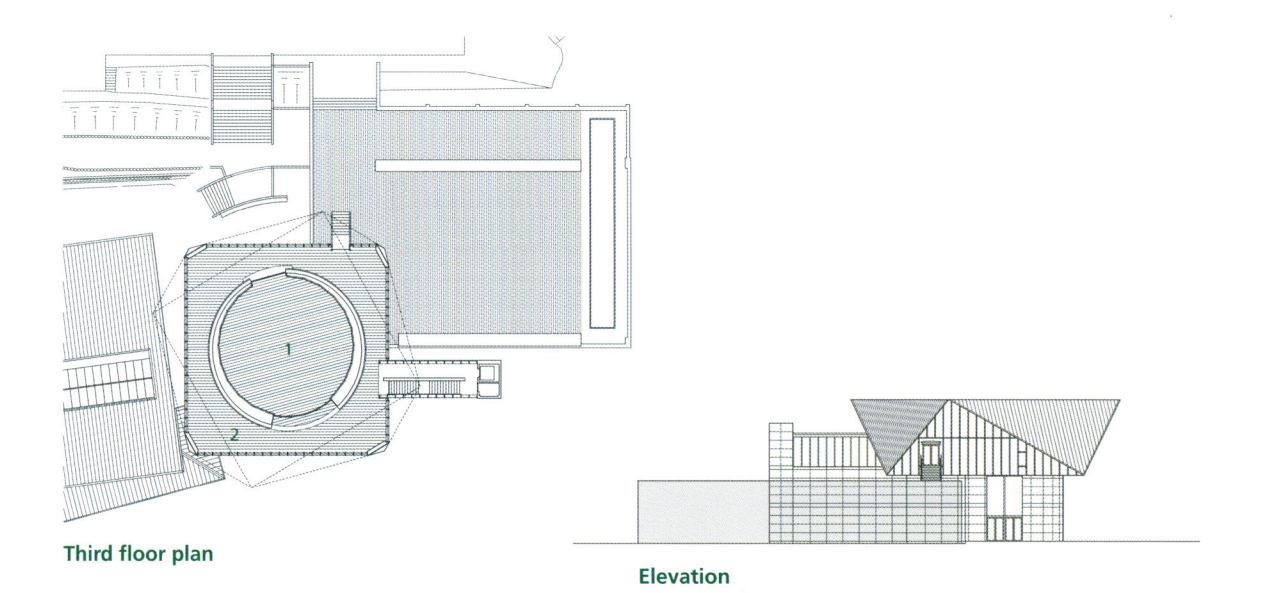

Elevation

不定形のホール外形は、鉄骨造（一部鉄骨鉄筋コンクリート造）でつくられる。

The amorphous hall exterior is made with a steel structure (in one part it is steel-framed reinforced concrete).

1 hall
2 foyer
3 classroom

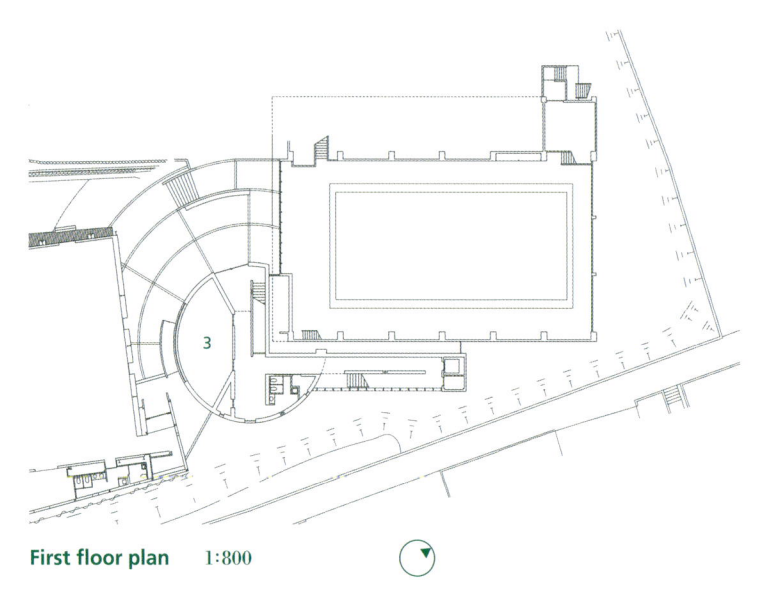

First floor plan 1:800

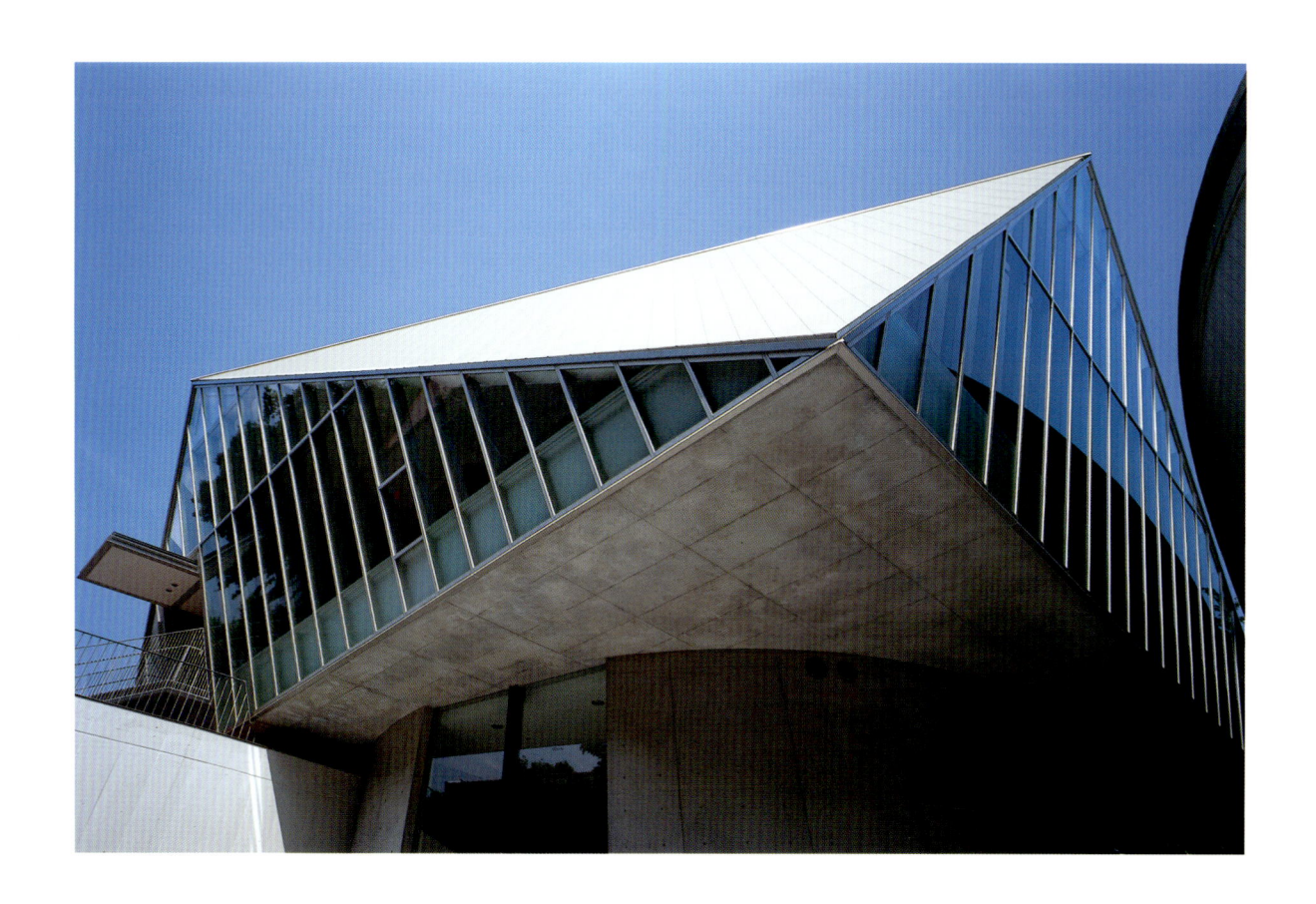

イメージパース。ホールを囲う円形の壁の一部は大きく開放され、ホワイエ越しに周囲の緑の風景が入り込んでくる。

Image perspective. Part of the curving wall that encloses the hall is wide open, and the scene of surrounding greenery enters across the foyer.

051 100th Anniversary Hall

安藤行基説序説

鈴木博之（建築史家）

大阪の都市・文化

　何時わたくしが安藤忠雄とはじめて会ったのか、それは記憶の彼方に消え去ってしまっていた。けれども、東京の佐賀町エギジビットという展示スペースで安藤の建築展が開かれたとき、わたくしは彼に大阪の都市事情を尋ねたことを鮮明に覚えている。その展覧会が、東京で安藤忠雄展が開かれる最初だったと思う。しかしながらそれも、いまでは不確かである。何はともあれ、その展覧会場で、彼にわたくしがしゃべったことは、はっきり覚えている。その年からわたくしは大阪大学に非常勤講師として集中講義をしに行くことになっていて、何日かを大阪で過ごさなければならなくなっていた。それで、大阪の建築家である安藤忠雄に、「大阪にこれから毎年、何日か行かなければならないのだけれど、どこに泊まったらいいのかねえ」というような、トンチンカンな質問をしたのであった。それが大阪の都市事情に関する質問というわけである。

　安藤忠雄は、いまも変らない、ものすごく人を安心させる笑顔を浮かべながら、「それなら、泊まるところあるから、そこに泊まったらええわ」ということを、洗練された大阪弁で請け合ってくれた。つまり、「大阪に来るなら、わたくしのところに来い」と言ってくれたのである。そこまで言ってくれるほど、そのときに彼と親しかったとは思えないのであったけれど、彼は事実として、そう言ってくれた。

　わたくしはそうして大阪との付き合いが始まったのだった。その関係は、2008年度末にわたくしが東京大学を定年になって、それを機会に大阪大学での非常勤講師も辞めることにするまで、20年以上に亙ってつづくことになった。安藤忠雄はわたくしが大阪に行くことになったとき、それを迎え入れてくれ、それを4半世紀近くつづけてくれたのである。わたくしは、大阪に彼が持っているマンションの1室に20年以上に亙って泊めてもらうことができたのである。それは通常であれば2DKくらいになる広さのマンションを、ワンルーム・マンション的に改造した部屋であった。はじめて泊めてもらった頃には、電話もテレビも冷房もなかった部屋であったけれど、かなり高層の1室だったので、夜はそれほど暑いということもなかった。テレビと電話は今にいたるまでないのだが、それらがないことは実に快適であった。

　この部屋のインテリア・デザインもまた4半世紀後の今にいたるまで、いっさい変っていないが、今みても古くさいところはまったくない。バス・トイレのある部分を、カー

ブを描いた合板の巨大な扉で覆い、その他のスペースと区別するだけで、部屋全体を開放的で広々した場所にしているのであった。ここで毎年、何日かを過ごせたことをわたくしは貴重な体験であったと感謝している。そうした好意を自然に施す安藤忠雄とは、どういう存在なのだろうか。

　大阪に行くことになったわたくしが、彼に大阪の宿泊事情を聞いてから、ずいぶん時間がたった後で、わたくしは彼に「われわれはいつ最初に会ったのかなあ」と聞いてみたことがある。

　彼は即座に、それが磯崎新の設計した「貝島邸」という東京の中央線沿線に建つ住宅の見学の折りであったと教えてくれた。それは磯崎新が若い建築家たちを連れていってくれた見学会だった。とすればそれは、1970年代末であろう。そこには伊東豊雄、石山修武らもいた。安藤忠雄は大阪から東京に出てきて、この見学会に参加していたのだろう。とすれば、こうした機会がわれわれ1940年代生まれの建築家や建築評論家たちが、互いに知り合う場であったのだろう。1970年代後半に、われわれは建築界での交流と交友を形成していったのである。

　安藤忠雄は、その頃、われわれ若い世代の建築関係者たちの間では、「関西三奇人（関西地方で活動するユニークな3人の建築家）」のひとりとして知られていた。他の2人は、すでに亡くなってしまった建築家毛綱毅曠と、現在は古代史の研究家としても知られる建築家渡辺豊和である。しかしながらこの3人のなかでは、安藤だけが正統なモダニズム建築のボキャブラリーを展開する建築家であった。毛綱も渡辺も、当時のポストモダニズムの典型というべき様式性と装飾性と物語性を、その作品に漂わせていた。しかしながら安藤は、鉄筋コンクリート構造によるモダニズムの表現を使って、20世紀末の建築の可能性を拡張しつづけていた。それなのに、何故、彼ら3人が「関西三奇人」という、ひとつのグループにまとめられていたかというと、このネーミングはデザインに関するものではなく、建築家としての個性にもとづくものだったからである。安藤忠雄はその個性の激しさによって知られていた。彼が若い頃、建築を独学で学び、ボクサーとして海外試合を体験してきたというエピソードが、彼を奇人のひとりに位置づけさせていた。しかし、そうした自己形成のなかで、安藤忠雄は建築の正統性を身につけていったのである。

　わたくしは数年前、安藤が設計した大阪府立狭山池博物館（1994-2001）を見学したとき、この池が行基菩薩によってつくられたという話を聞いて深く感銘を受けた。奈

良時代に行基（668-749）という僧侶がいたことをわれわれは知っている。彼は仏教の寺院を40カ所以上建設し、奈良の大仏殿の建設にも関わり、15のため池をつくり、13の水路や掘割を通し、6つの橋を架けたといわれている。彼は宗教家であるとともに偉大な組織者であり建設者であった。後の人は彼を行基菩薩とよんで、聖人とみなした。このような仏教僧は、土木工事を起こし、治水工事を行い、勧進につとめる勧進の聖（ひじり）なのである。弘法大師・空海もまた同じように多くの工事をおこなった聖（ひじり）である。安藤忠雄の活動は、こうした勧進の聖（ひじり）になぞらえることのできるものではないか。

都市は好奇心の場であり、好奇心をもつことが、人びとを生き生きさせると安藤忠雄はいう。その姿勢が現在、彼を美しい大阪づくりの運動に駆り立てている。これは造幣局の通り抜けの桜を15kmに亘って植えてゆこうという運動である。桜には寄贈者の氏名を付ける。このために1万円の寄付を募り、5万人から桜を寄贈してもらおうというのである。小泉元首相にも寄付をもらい、プロ野球の監督にも植樹してもらうといったイベントを織り込みながら、「町に桜を」というこの運動は現在3万5千人の寄付を得るところまで来たという。目標の5万人達成もそう遠いことではなさそうである。

安藤忠雄の建築は、機能性とともに一種の象徴性を備えている。これは上質な近代建築が見せる特質のひとつであるが、実際に機能性と象徴性を両立させる作品を実現させる建築家は少ない。

宗教建築のもつ普遍性

安藤の建築がもつ、機能性と象徴性の両立という特質を極めて印象的に実現した作品は、光の教会（1987-99）であろう。目覚ましいほどの規模ももたず、とりたてて印象的な場所に建つわけでもないこの小教会堂は、壁に穿たれたスリットによって十字架を浮き上がらせ、そこからの光によって堂内に超越的な息吹をもたらす。また、この教会堂には四角い空間に対して斜めに交わるエレメントが導入されており、閉じた箱ではなく、開かれた動きのある場が形成されている。限定的な具体物によってではなく、スリットによって教会の象徴を生み出すという手法こそ、機能性と象徴性の両立である。しばしば安藤忠雄の建築を、完結したコンクリートの箱を単位とするものと考えている人がいるが、そうではなく、彼の建築にはかならず開かれた要素が存在する。その開かれた要素が、物理的にも形而上学的にも、建築を拡げてゆく。

彼の出発点となった建築である住吉の長屋（1976）も、コンクリートの箱を木造の長屋のなかに挿入したように見えて、その実、コンクリートに開けられた中庭によってコンクリートの箱を開いているのである。

　彼が設計する宗教建築は仏教寺院もあればキリスト教教会堂もある。彼は宗教建築を教理によって設計するのではなく、個々の宗教の教理を越えて存在する超越性をダイレクトに表現して、宗教性を実現する。寺院を大きな池の下に沈めた真言宗本福寺（1987-99）は、仏教の浄土があるとされる西の方角に寺院を開き、自然な寺院の佇まいを生み出している。西の方角からの光によって仏像を浮かび上がらせる構成は、奈良の大仏殿を鎌倉時代に復興した勧進僧、俊乗坊重源が兵庫に建立した浄土寺の構成を思わせるところがある。安藤はおそらくこの名建築を参照しながら、本福寺を設計したのであろう。

　四国に設計したもうひとつの仏教寺院である光明寺（1998-2000）の場合、建築は池のなかに浮かぶ木造の抽象的構成となっている。日本の仏教寺院は、木造の大きな屋根をもち、軒の曲線が美しいところにその特徴がある。光明寺の場合、安藤は抽象化した軒の構成だけをつくり出すことによって、仏教寺院の図像を生み出している。木造の軒を支えるためには、複雑な組み物（木造の腕木のシステム）が用いられるが、安藤の軒の構成は抽象化された部材の組み合わせであり、歴史的様式のリヴァイヴァルを行なったりはしていない。抽象的な構成であることによって、この寺院は伝統的な寺院には見られない開放性を得ている。寺院が浮かぶ池の構成も抽象的であり、寺院は現代性と開放性を、抽象的構成によって獲得しているのだ。

　安藤が個々の宗教を超えた宗教性を目指していることは、彼がパリに実現したユネスコ瞑想空間（1994-95）に最もよく現われているといえよう。具体的な宗派的要素をもたず、瞑想するための抽象空間を用意することは、安藤にとって最も行ないたいことだったであろう。安藤忠雄の宗教建築は、普遍性と超越性を両立させた存在を目指しているのである。そのために彼は建築のなかに開かれた要素を必要とするのである。

別世界の構築

　安藤の建築の特徴をよく味わえるのは、美術館、博物館、図書館、記念館など、公共的な性格と、芸術的表現を要求される建築群においてである。彼は現代日本におい

て最も優れた美術館建築家であろう。建築自体の存在感が、その内部に収蔵されたり、その内部で行われたりする芸術作品に拮抗し得るからである。彼は美術館を設計するときにも、無色透明のホワイト・キューブの展示空間をつくるのではない。彼は建築作品が語りかけるべきだと考えている。

　1980年代末から、彼は瀬戸内海の小島である直島にミュージアム・コンプレックスというべき一群の現代美術館をつくり始める。これはベネッセという企業による美術コレクションの展示と芸術活動の舞台づくりであった。1992年、安藤忠雄が建築を設計したベネッセハウスミュージアム（直島コンテンポラリーアートミュージアム）が誕生した。これは直島の歴史にとって極めて重要な出来事であったが、同時にこの島の新しい未来への出発点でもあった。ベネッセハウスは、そこに多くの委嘱作品、すなわち美術館という場所を前提とした、サイト・スペシフィックな作品群を収める美術館として、個性的であった。直島という場所が生み出す芸術作品、そしてベネッセハウスという場所が触発する芸術作品が生み出されてゆく歴史が、ここに始まったのである。この試みはやがて、「家プロジェクト」とよばれる計画のなかで、直島の村落に残る住居や神社を舞台とする芸術作品の展開に拡がってゆく。すでに4棟の建築がこのプロジェクトのなかからあらたに生み出されている。2棟の民家、寺院跡、神社がこのプロジェクトのなかで生まれ変わった。安藤はここで闇と光をテーマにした南寺という建物をジェームズ・タレルと共同して創造している。「家プロジェクト」は伝統的な直島の集落のなかに潜む建築や場所の可能性を、現代の芸術家たちが再発見し、再創造してゆく試みである。このようにしてベネッセハウス設立に始まる創造活動は、直島全体に拡がる表現を生み出していったのである。安藤はホワイト・キューブとは対極に立つ美術館を目指していったのである。

　この直島に2001年から2004年までの時間をかけて彼は地中美術館をつくり上げた。地中に埋め込まれた建築は、われわれに神話的世界への想像を与えてくれる。世界には地中をたどる多くの神話がある。ギリシア神話に語られるエウリディーケとオルフェウスの物語、日本の神話に語られるイザナギとイザナミによる黄泉の平坂の物語はその代表であろう。ふたつの神話はともに、愛するものを追って黄泉の国まで出かけた主人公が、その愛によって死んだ恋人をよみがえらせるが、最後に後ろを振り返ってしまうために、すべてを失ってしまう悲話を伝えている。ふたつの神話のなかで、地中の世界はわれわれの存在の根源を問うのである。

地中美術館はわれわれを芸術作品への旅に誘うとともに、われわれ自身の内面への旅にも誘うのである。それがこの美術館が示す超越性であり、聖性である。また地中美術館はこれまでのベネッセハウスに対しても対話をもたらす。ベネッセハウスが、サイト・スペシフィックな作品を生み出す源であるのに対して、地中美術館は芸術作品の根源を示す試みなのである。そのことによって、直島に創造されたふたつのミュージアムは芸術作品を広く、深くしてゆく。それは芸術の自己相対化をもたらす行為だといってよいであろう。現代芸術の試みの場としての美術館が、できるだけ制約のない、自由な場を用意する方向を示すのに対して、ここでは現代芸術の試みをできるだけ1回限りの、ひとつだけの場に属するものとして提示する方法がとられている。地中美術館がアルカイックな相貌をもつことになるのは、以上述べてきたさまざまな糸が織りなされた結果である。すなわち、そこには神話的な構造が秘められているのである。

　このようなひとつの世界を形成してゆく仕事は、淡路島でも試みられている。明石大橋の完成によって、淡路島は大阪や神戸からおどろくほど近い世界になっている。神戸の向かいに横たわる、すぐそばの世界が淡路島だったことに気づくのである。ここにつくられた淡路夢舞台の世界は、現代建築の粋を集めた場所であり、どこか別世界のようである。夢舞台を訪れて、遠いと思っていた淡路島が、余りに近い存在になっているのに驚き、さらにその後で不思議な新しい建築世界に足を踏み入れた驚きに襲われる。遠いと思われた世界が近くて、しかしそこには、われわれを遠いはるかな世界に連れ込んでくれる夢舞台がある。人の心理的距離感をゆさぶる、感覚のゆらぎがおもしろい。

　淡路夢舞台の舞台は、土取り場の跡であるという。関西新空港など、巨大な埋め立て工事のために必要とされた土砂を提供した跡地なのだ。日本にはこのような開発の後遺症を残した場所が多いのだ。建設のために大量の土砂を取り去った跡地を整備し、緑化する事業として、この施設群は設けられた。安藤忠雄はそうした緑化計画を出発させる段階から、この仕事に関わっていった。敷地には、計画当初には土の肌がむき出しになった土地が拡がっていた。そこに樹木を植え、斜面を安定化しながら夢舞台の計画が始まる。樹木がどのように根付き、どのように成長してゆくのかを語るとき、彼は建築家というより庭師のオヤジといった顔になる。斜面に何種類かの樹木を混ぜ植えし、できるだけ早く斜面が自然の緑によって覆われるように、周到な計画が立てられた。

建築が計画されつつあるあいだも、樹木は育ちつづけ、やがて建物がその姿を現す頃、斜面はすでに緑に覆われている。工事の途中、何度かこの場所を訪れて、そのたびに確実に緑が成育していることに感動したものである。都市内の敷地に計画される建築とは明らかに違った建設工事の時間の流れ方がここにはあった。いくつもの時間の流れが重なり合いながら、この淡路夢舞台が生まれた。ここには複雑な建築群があるだけではなく、複雑でテンポの違う時間の流れが積層して隠されているのだ。

　直島での仕事、淡路島での仕事は、ともにひとつの別世界を形成する試みであったといえるだろう。それはかつて古代ローマ皇帝ハドリアヌスがローマ近郊のテヴォリにつくり上げた、ハドリアヌスのヴィラとよばれる離宮を思い起こさせる。いまは廃墟となって残るハドリアヌスのヴィラは、皇帝が生涯に旅した世界を写し込んだ縮図としての庭園であり、離宮であるといわれる。そこにはギリシアの画廊やアカデミア、エジプト、そしてローマやハデス（冥府）までもが写し込まれていた。現在訪れても、崩れかかった巨大な建築群の連なりのなかに、壮大な世界再構築の夢が息づいて感じられる。古代ローマ帝国が最大の版図を画した時代の皇帝にしてはじめて可能になった、世界の縮図作成の夢である。直島や淡路島での試みは、現代におけるハドリアヌスのヴィラではないかと、そんな気がするのである。

　ここには安藤忠雄が今日まで経巡ってきた世界が凝集されている。これほど大規模で多様な建築群を設計し切れる建築家はそうそう存在しないが、ここでの安藤の仕事は、大きな場所を埋め尽くす苦労よりは、彼がこれまで試みてきた広くて深く、しかも多様な建築的蓄積を、この限られた場所に凝集するための苦労の方が大きかったのではあるまいか。それほどの豊かな多様性がここには凝縮されている。時間をかけて完成した直島や淡路島には、広大な複合的世界が生まれていて、模型や写真では感じ取りにくい複雑な壮大さがある。

記念性の宿しかた

　安藤忠雄の出身地である大阪には、彼が設計した博物館や記念館が多い。大阪府立近つ飛鳥博物館（1990-94）、大阪府立狭山池博物館（1994-2001）は公立博物館であり、博物館が設けられた場所の古代以来の歴史を示す施設である。近つ飛鳥博物館は古代史の博物館であり、狭山池博物館はこの池を巡る土木史の展示を行って

いる。ふたつの博物館はともに場所の歴史を語る施設だといえるし、そこで語られる場所の物語は、わが国の大きな歴史と結びついている。とりわけ狭山池の築造には行基菩薩や俊乗坊重源などが関っており、建築の歴史とも交錯する。安藤は大規模なスケールの表現によってアルカイックな雰囲気を出現させ、一挙にその場所の時間を遡らせる。近つ飛鳥という古墳地帯の博物館を宏大なステップと幾何学的形態によって印象づけ、狭山池の断面を博物館のなかに取り込むことによって、ため池を巡る歴史の流れを現前させる。しかしながらそうした物理的構成のみによって、彼は場所の本質を開示するのではない。

　安藤は近つ飛鳥博物館の周囲には梅の木を植えつづけており、狭山池博物館の建つ狭山池の周囲には桜の木を植えつづけている。ふたつの博物館がそれぞれの場所の歴史を語る博物館であるから、梅の花と桜の花によってそれぞれの場所を祝福しつづけようというのが彼の意図であろう。こうして、これらの博物館の場合には、花々が彼の建築を周囲に対して開かれたものにしてゆく。彼の建築にはかならず開かれた要素が存在すると述べたが、このふたつの博物館を開かれた存在としてゆく梅や桜の木々が、物理的にも形而上学的にも、ふたつの博物館を拡げてゆくのである。

　東大阪に建つ司馬遼太郎記念館（1999-2001）では、直截明快に司馬遼太郎の世界が彼の蔵書によって表現される。司馬文学を蔵書によって示すという、これ以上はない直接性をデザインにしてしまうところが、いかにも安藤らしい。明快に本質を視覚化するところが、安藤忠雄の建築の勁さである。そして彼は司馬遼太郎の本質を書籍の壁だと喝破したのである。入館者は、湾曲する壁面全体を埋め尽くす蔵書のすがたに圧倒され、あたかも司馬遼太郎の脳髄のなかに入り込んだような興奮を覚える。しかしながらここでも、彼は緊張を解放し、建築を外に向かって開放するための要素を用意している。それは菜の花である。司馬の作品名に登場する菜の花を、司馬遼太郎のイメージに重ねて、記念館に菜の花を添えるというのが、安藤の手法である。

　植物によって都市や建築を囲むことは、都市を美しくし、環境を優しくする。安藤は植栽の大切さを若い頃から教え込まれたという。それは「平成の通り抜け」と名付けた桜並木を大阪に生み出す運動として進行しているし、瀬戸内海の廃棄物汚染の島であった豊島にドングリの種から育った苗を植えるオリーブ基金の運動など、さまざまに拡がっている。

　世界の最先端を行く安藤が、このような運動を生み出し、継続していることは彼の

建築に対する考え方が、自然環境に対する深い配慮に満ちたものであることの証拠だろう。こうした安藤忠雄のすがたが、行基菩薩のような、かつて存在した勧進の聖のすがたを彷彿とさせるのである。彼の建築には開かれた要素があると述べたが、それは建築作品を社会に開くということであり、最も広い意味での「公」の概念につながる。

東京での試み

　2008年の4月、東京大学本郷キャンパス内に東京大学情報学環・福武ホールが竣工した。本郷通りに沿って赤門と正門の間に配置された建物である。敷地は道路沿いの樹木地帯で、高木を残すためには細長い敷地をさらに細長く使わなければならない。敷地条件としては最悪といってよい場所である。しかも本郷通り沿いであるから、いやでも目に付く場所だ。

　建設が開始された建物は低層だが長大で、威圧感をもった建物が出現するのではないかと工事中には恐れたが、竣工して見ると低層であるために道路との間に残された楠の大木群はよく見えるし、建物自体、低いコンクリート壁に水平に開けられたスリットを通して気持ちよくその存在を感じられた。地上2階建てという低層の建物であるが、長大なので軒の部分がいやでも目に入る。そこにデザインの神経は集中されていて、あたかも京都の三十三間堂を思わせるような緊張感のある軒が、緩みなく、キリリと伸びている。わたくしはひそかにこの建物を本郷の三十三間堂と名付けた。

　低いコンクリート壁の内側には、地下2階まで人びとを導く階段が、ドライエリアを兼ねて開放的に降っている。建物を低層に抑えるために、地下2階にホールが収められているにもかかわらず、そこにも外光と通風が十分に確保されている。これほどダイナミックな空間構成は、いままで本郷キャンパス内には存在しなかった。本郷には歴代の建築設計担当教授の作品が並んでいるが、安藤建築はそこに新しい要素を確実に付け加えた。

　同時期、渋谷の地下で東急東横線渋谷駅の工事が進行中であった。東京メトロ副都心線相互直通運転化事業という工事の一環である。簡単にいうと、渋谷と池袋を結んで明治通りの地下を走る副都心線という新しい地下鉄と東急東横線を結ぶ新しい地下駅の建設現場である。安藤忠雄はここに巨大な繭あるいは卵のかたちをした駅舎の形態を挿入している。地下2階のコンコースから地下5階のホームに至る旅客通路

に、巨大な繭あるいは卵のかたちのシェルをもち込み、吹き抜け部分の殻にしようというのである。彼はこの形態を地宙船とよんでいる。この形態を中心とする吹き抜けが、地上部分へと連続し、自然換気が期待できる地下空間となるのである。

山手線の内側、バスターミナルの真下に当たる場所に建設されているこの新しい東急東横線渋谷駅は、すでに6月の開業を目指して骨格が完成し、内装の仕上げを急ピッチで進めているところだった。けれども巨大な地下工事現場は、すぐにわれわれの場所の感覚を失わせる。何階にいるのか、どちらの方向を向いているのか、すぐに解らなくなる。こうした巨大地下空間であっても、地宙船という名の繭あるいは卵のイメージが浮かべば、人びとは自分が使っている駅の全体像と、自分の位置を見失うことはないであろう。一見無駄な遊びのように見える地宙船は、現代の大都市に必要な安全性を確保するための、明快なサインなのである。工事中のこの現場には、すでに試運転中の地下鉄電車も入ってきていて、まるでダム工事のようなスケールと、都心とは思えない別世界の喧騒に満ちていた。

東京における安藤忠雄の現在を知る機会を得て、さまざまなことを考えた。近年の安藤建築には、明らかに地下への志向がある。地上に現れる部分を極力小さくして、地下に必要なヴォリュームを収めるのが彼の手法となっている。地下にはスケール感、開放性など、あらゆる要素をすべて計算した空間が用意される。渋谷駅に見られる繭あるいは卵のかたちは、かつて彼が大阪中之島の中央公会堂の改造計画案において挿入しようとした繭に起源をもつものだろう。自分のアイデアとイメージをあたため続けて、ここにその発現の場を見出したのである。持続するこころざしの賜物であろう。

安藤忠雄の建築の勁(つよ)さはここにある。彼の建築には持続するこころざしが流れている。神戸の六甲のアパートは何期にも亙って展開しつづけてきたし、地下に対するオブセッシブな心入れも、さまざまな機会に展開されている。そこに彼の建築の存在感が現れるのであり、それは背景を知らない人びとにも感じられるのである。

持続するメッセージ

2002年10月、日本人建築家としてはじめて京都賞を受賞した安藤忠雄は、その受賞の言葉のなかで、簡潔に次のようなポイントを指摘していた。

「自分は小さなころから物をつくることが好きであった。美しい町を生み出すために、

現在も自分の美学を追究しつづけようと考えている。一方、日本は大量生産・大量消費のシステムのなかでかつての社会がもっていたバランスを失ってしまった。そのなかで環境は破壊され、都市の美しさは失われた。これからも、自らの美学と、環境を考えた建築という、困難な課題をふたつながら追い求めたい」

　安藤の視点は明快であり、その発言も誤解の余地なく明瞭である。彼の建築は、そのような安藤の明快な視点から生まれる勁(つよ)さをもっている。多くの人びとに彼の作品が受け入れられ、支持されるのは、建築のなかに明確な世界観が込められているからである。彼は自らの建築について「建築単体で完結してしまうのでなく、都市との関わり、歴史との関わり、社会との関わり、といったさまざまなものとの関わりのなかで、場所に刺激を与えるべく、新たな関係を創り出す。ときにその試みは、敷地に刻まれた〈場所の記憶〉を掘り起こし、それを建築によって顕在化させる、環境の〈再生〉を実現する」と述べている。

　彼が「関わり」という言葉によって言おうとしているのは「関係性」であり、彼の建築はまずそれが計画される場所を読み解き、解釈するところから開始される。この方法は彼の処女作、「住吉の長屋」以来一貫しており、彼はまず場所からかたちを生み出してゆく。

　彼が連綿として継続的に発展させてきた六甲の集合住宅（I、II、III）は、急斜面を良好で安全な住宅に変える仕事であり、それは神戸の斜面についての解釈の歴史となっている。それらははるかに神戸の港を望む豊かな眺望をもった住まいを生み出し、同時に周囲や屋上にさまざまな植物が植えられることによって、緑を回復する試みともなっているのである。安藤がこの仕事に取り組んでいる時期、わたしは彼の口から、20世紀初頭の六甲の山並みの景観についての物語を聞いたことがある。その頃、燃料としての薪確保の乱伐の影響もあって、六甲の斜面は土の色の見える荒れた山肌だった、と。

　その頃ここに住宅を設計したフランク・ロイド・ライトが、アリゾナを思わせる景観に合わせてデザインを決定したという話が思い起こされた。その後の年月を通じて山に緑がよみがえってきた歴史を、安藤はこの場所の大切な記憶だと見抜いたのである。彼が六甲の集合住宅に多くの植物を導入したのは、「場所の記憶」を呼び覚ますためであった。「場所の記憶」とは、場所の解釈であり、その歴史の解釈であるからだ。

　彼の作品はすべて、こうした「場所の記憶」を解釈するところから出発している。し

かしながらそれは、「すべての作品は、それ以前のあらゆる作品群の再解釈である」というインター・テクスチュアリティという考え方とは、微妙に異なったものである。まずそれは、「場所の記憶」を「懐かしさ」という個人的でノスタルジックな領域に押し込めるものでもない。彼にとっての「場所の記憶」は、個人の感慨を越えて、社会的な広がりをもつものなのである。だからこそ彼の建築は多くの人びとの共感を得るのである。

だが、安藤は「場所の記憶」から何を生み出してゆくのか。

彼がコンクリート打ち放しによる建築表現を完成させたことはよく知られているが、それは「場所の記憶」から導き出されたものではない。それは彼の美意識、彼の建築イメージから生まれ、洗練されてきたものである。いわば「自分の美学」に根差した表現である。そうした強固な美学をもつからこそ、場所に対する彼の解釈は緊張感を漂わせる。「自らの美学と、環境を考えた建築という、困難な課題」があるからこそ、彼はひとつひとつの建築に固有の表現を与えられるのである。

しかしながらここで付け加えなければならないのは、安藤はそうしたオーソドックスな建築家の枠には嵌まりきらない部分をもっていることである。彼は「環境を考えた建築」を追い求める過程で、建築だけでない表現に到達している。彼の作品が多く建てられている神戸の町が大震災に襲われた後、彼は犠牲となった人びとへの鎮魂の思いと都市復興への願いを込めて、白い花の咲く樹木を植えつづける運動を起こしている。また、産業廃棄物によって瀬戸内海の環境が汚染されてしまった状況を回復するために、オリーブやドングリを植える運動を推進している。これらもまた建築家の仕事なのだろうか。

普通に考えれば、自然環境の回復を目指した彼の運動は、社会的活動であり、建築家の本業ではないと見なされる。安藤はすぐれた建築家であると同時に、すぐれた社会活動家なのだということになる。しかしながら安藤は、建築活動のかたわら社会活動を行っているのではあるまい。彼にとってふたつの活動は、密接に結びついている。そしてそこにこそ、安藤忠雄という建築家の本質がある。

この問題を考えるためには、現在の建築のすがた、あるいは現代の社会の仕組み全体を考えなければならない。ポスト近代といわれ、情報化の時代といわれる現代は、あらゆる仕組みが巨大化し複合化しており、相対的に個人の存在が小さなものになってしまっている。われわれは巨大な文化と技術のネットワークのなかで、自己の表現を奪い取られてしまっている。

われわれが建築家に興味を抱き、彼らの活動に喝采を送るのは、彼らが現代社会にあって極めて稀な、自己表現を許された存在だからだ。活躍する建築家は現代のヒーローである。安藤は人びとの抱くそうした憧れの対象となっている。けれど、安藤に喝采を送る人びとにも、彼らなりの表現意欲はある。自らの適わぬ表現意欲を彼の活動に託して、人びとは安藤に喝采を送るのである。このような建築と人びととの現代的構図を考えたときに、安藤の多面的な活動の全体像が見えてくる。

　安藤は建築作品を結晶させるときに、それらが建てられる場所のあらゆる可能性を読み取ろうとする。当然のことながら、その場所には人びとの抱いている願いもまた、折り重なるようにして積み重ねられている。彼はそれらの願いを解釈しながら建築をつくり上げてゆくが、同時にそれは白い花やオリーブやドングリとなって育ってゆきもするのである。彼にとってはそれらもまた、人びとの想いをかたちに表したという点で、建築なのである。

　2005年10月に、ラスキン文庫という財団の講演会に出席したときには、次のようなメッセージを発している。

　ラスキンと自分には共通性はないとしながらも、最近の仕事のなかで触れたイタリアやヴェネツィアの環境から安藤の話は始まった。彼は講演や仕事を依頼されたとき、その場所に自分が訪れたい、見てみたいと思う建築があれば引き受けることにしているという。ヴェネツィアにはマニエリスムの建築家アンドレア・パッラーディオの建築があるので、その地方での仕事に取り組むことにしたという。トレヴィソの町に建てられたベネトンのアートスクールは18世紀の建築を残しながら新しい要素を加えてゆくものであった。ここでは保存の専門家、建築史の専門家が改造する点を厳しくチェックしながら計画が進められたという。新発見の装飾などが出てくれば、丁寧に修復する。改造は最小限に抑える。屋根瓦も石材も、取り壊された建物から出たものを取っておいて、それを再利用する。そして調和を図るのである。石工の親子は「トレヴィソ積み」だという石積みの塀を楽しみながらつくり上げてくれた。伝統の材料、工法を生かして設計は実現された。こうした方針のもとに9年がかりでアートスクールができあがった。主要な施設は地下に埋め、浅い池を設けて建物のすがたが水辺に映るような効果を狙ったという。

　ヴェネツィアは商人の町であり、自分が育った大阪の町もまた商人の町である。そしてヴェネツィアもトレヴィソも水の町でもある。大阪もまた水の町だ。こうした共通の環

境のなかで彼は自分の仕事が行われる場所に対する親しみを増していったという。

　大阪では、現在桜宮にある桜宮橋、通称銀橋を増設する工事を行った。安藤は大阪に育ったので、小学生の頃この橋のたもとで撮った記念写真があるという。ここでのプロジェクトは今までの銀橋に平行して新しい橋を付けるものである。彼は従来の橋のデザインを変えずに同じシルエットの橋を設計し、ただその細部は現代の技術によってまとめるという手法がとられた。これによって新旧2本の橋が同じすがたで並びながらも、そこに時間の流れが感じられるデザインが生まれる。

　そしてこの銀橋のある桜宮には旧造幣寮の建物があり、そこからつづく桜の並木道は「通り抜け」の名で親しまれる花の名所となっている。その桜をつづけて大阪湾にまでつなげようという壮大な桜を植える運動を安藤は熱心に進めている。しかしその話に入る前に、彼は桜宮につづく大阪中之島の環境の問題に触れていった。中之島の風景は大阪の代表的な風景であり、昔から彼はスケッチや絵画にしてきたという。そのうちの1枚が映写されたのを見ると、端正なパステル画で、建築家としての片鱗が若い頃からすでに見られるのだった。

　中之島には大阪の中央公会堂、通称中之島公会堂が赤レンガのすがたを見せている。以前この建物が取り壊されようとしたとき、彼がこの歴史的な建物の内部に、新しい卵形のホールを挿入することによって建物をよみがえらせ、継承しつづけるという計画案を提出したことはよく知られている。これは、歴史的な建物とともに都市は生きつづけるべきだというメッセージであった。この計画は実現しなかったが、中央公会堂は保存が決定され、免震化されたうえで新しい公会堂として再生された。現在は重要文化財に指定されている。彼が渋谷地下駅でこの卵を実現しようとしていることは、すでに述べた。

　安藤忠雄の、行動力と独創性を備えた活動は、かつての勧進の聖、行基菩薩のようなものではないかと思われないだろうか。それが、冒頭に述べた安藤行基説とひそかに名付けるところの見方なのである。勧進の聖とは行い澄ました聖人ではなく、積極的に行動する快活なスポーツマンだったのではないか。安藤忠雄の建築が示すパブリックの精神は、こうした多様な行動と深く結びついている。

Tadao Ando, a Latter-day Gyoki?

Hiroyuki Suzuki (Architectural Historian)

Osaka, the City and Its Culture

I do not remember when I first met Tadao Ando. I did converse with him at an architectural exhibition he was holding at a gallery called Sagacho Exhibit Space in Tokyo. I asked him then what the situation was like in Osaka. I think that exhibition was his first in Tokyo, but I am no longer certain of the facts. Yet I clearly remember talking with him at the gallery. That was the year I was to begin giving intensive lectures at Osaka University. I was going to have to spend a number of days each year in Osaka, giving lectures at the university. Explaining my situation, I put a question to Ando that was completely beside the point as far as the exhibition was concerned. I asked the Osaka architect for suggestions on places to stay in that city. That is what I mean by my inquiring about the situation in Osaka.

 He smiled that smile of his that remains unchanged to this day, the one that puts people instantly at ease, and remarked in his refined Osaka dialect, "If that's the case, I have a place where you can stay. Why don't you use it?" That is, he offered me a place to stay when I visited Osaka. I do not believe we were on particularly close terms at the time, but the fact is that he made the offer.

 That is how my relationship with Osaka began. That relationship was to last more than 20 years, until I retired from the University of Tokyo at the end of 2008 and took the opportunity to quit my job as part-time lecturer at Osaka University as well. Ando put me up when I first began teaching in Osaka and continued to do so for a quarter-century. For more than 20 years I was able to stay in a unit in a condominium he owned in Osaka. It was about the size of a normal 2DK unit (i.e. two rooms and a dining area/kitchen) but had been converted into a one-room apartment. There was no telephone, television or air conditioner when I first stayed there, but being a single room on a fairly high floor, it was not that hot at night. There is still no television set or telephone, and it has been quite pleasant to do without them.

 The interior design of the room has not changed at all in the past quarter-century, but there is nothing old-fashioned about it, even today. A huge curved door of plywood screens the bath and toilet area and distinguishes it from the rest of the space. The entire room is thus made open and spacious. Being able to spend a number of days every year there has been for me a valuable experience, one for which I am grateful. What sort of person is this individual who spontaneously performs such acts of kindness?

 I once asked him when it was we first met. By then, considerable time had passed since my inquiry into the situation with respect to lodgings in Osaka.

He promptly informed me that it had been on the occasion of a visit to the Kaijima House, a house designed by Arata Isozaki and standing close to the Chuo Line in Tokyo. Isozaki took young architects on that visit. If that was the case, then it must have been at the end of the 1970s. Toyo Ito and Osamu Ishiyama had been there. Ando must have come from Osaka and participated in the visit as well. It must have been one of those opportunities we architects and architectural critics born in the 1940s had to get acquainted with one another. It was in the late 1970s that we formed our contacts and friendships in the architectural world.

At the time, Ando was known among those of us in the younger generation involved in architecture as one of "The Three Eccentrics of Kansai" (that is, three unique architects practicing in the Kansai region). The other two were Kiko Mozuna, the late architect, and Toyokazu Watanabe, the architect who is now also known as a student of ancient history. Among the three, only Ando used the architectural vocabulary of orthodox modernism. The works of both Mozuna and Watanabe had eclectic, ornamental and narrative qualities typical of postmodernism at the time. However, using reinforced concrete construction to achieve modernist forms of expression, Ando continued to expand the possibilities of late twentieth-century architecture. We grouped Ando and the other two architects together as "The Three Eccentrics of Kansai," not for any design reason, but because they were all individualistic architects. Ando was known for his intense personality. That he was self-taught as an architect and had experience boxing in an overseas bout in his youth established him in our minds as an "eccentric." However, through that process of self-formation, he had mastered architectural orthodoxy.

Several years ago, I visited Sayamaike Historical Museum, Osaka (1994-2001), which was designed by Ando, and was deeply impressed to learn that Sayamaike, the pond from which the museum takes its name, was created by Gyoki. We know that the monk named Gyoki (668-749) lived in the Nara period. He constructed over 40 Buddhist temples, was involved in the construction of the Great Buddha Hall of Nara and created 15 holding ponds, 13 aqueducts or canals and six bridges. He was not only a religious leader but a great organizer and builder. Later generations referred to him as Bodhisattva Gyoki and regarded him as a saint. He was a *kanjinnohijiri*, a peripatetic Buddhist monk who solicited funds for pious purposes, such as launching public works and carrying out flood-control projects. Kobo Daishi (also known as Kukai) was another monk who undertook many such projects. Perhaps the activities of Ando can be likened to those of a *kanjinnohijiri*.

Ando says that the city is a place of curiosity, and possession of curiosity gives people vitality. That belief is what is driving him now to campaign to make Osaka beautiful. Taking a hint from the famous cherry trees of the so-called "Passage" at the former Osaka Mint Bureau, the campaign aims to plant cherry trees along 15 kilometers of streets in Osaka. The name of a donor will be attached to each cherry tree. The goal is to have 50,000 persons donate ¥10,000 each. Former prime minister Jun'ichiro Koizumi has made a donation, and at one organized event, a professional baseball manager planted a tree. This campaign, called "Heisei-era Passages," has at present received donations from 35,000 persons. The goal of 50,000 donors should be reached in the not so distant future.

Ando's works possess both functionality and a kind of symbolic character. That is one of the hallmarks of excellent works of modern architecture, but there are few architects who actually realize works that possess both these qualities.

The Universality of Ando's Religious Architecture

Church of the Light (1987-99) was a work in which Ando succeeded in achieving both functionality and symbolic character in an especially impressive manner. This church, which is not imposing in size or located in a particularly impressive place, has a cruciform opening in one wall, and light entering through that opening endows the hall with a transcendental character. Furthermore, another wall is introduced at an angle relative to the square space of the church. As a result, the church is not a closed box but an open, dynamic place. It was precisely this approach—to generate a symbol of the church through, not some actual physical object, but an opening in the wall—that allowed him to achieve both functionality and symbolic character. People frequently believe Ando's buildings are based on box-like concrete units, each complete in itself. That is not the case. There is always an open element in his work. That open element expands the building, both physically and metaphysically.

Rowhouse in Sumiyoshi (1976), the work that became his starting point, seems like a concrete box inserted between a pair of rowhouses of wooden construction, but in reality, the concrete box is open to a courtyard in the middle.

His religious architecture includes both Buddhist temples and Christian churches. He does not base his designs on doctrine. Instead, he expresses directly the transcendental character that exists in all religions, whatever the doctrinal differences, and thus succeeds in giving the buildings a religious character. In Water Temple (1987-99), he oriented the Shingon-sect temple (created beneath a large pond) toward the west, the direction in which the Pure Land of Buddhism is believed to lie. As a result, the symbolism is quite natural. The way the image of Buddha is illuminated by light from the West reminds one of the composition of Jodo-ji, the temple founded in Okayama by Shunji-yobo Chogen, another *kanjinnohijiri* who reconstructed the Great Buddha Hall of Nara in the thirteenth century. Ando no doubt used Jodo-ji as a point of reference in designing Water Temple.

Komyo-ji (1998-2000), another Buddhist temple designed in Shikoku, has an abstract composition. It is a structure of wooden construction seemingly floating on a pool of water. Buddhist temples in Japan are characterized by large roofs that curve beautifully as they extend out. In the case of Komyo-ji, Ando has achieved the iconic effect of Buddhist temples by creating merely an abstract outward extension of the roof. A complex system of brackets was used to extend the eaves outward in a traditional temple of wooden construction, but in Ando's building, the eaves extension is a combination of abstract members. No attempt is made to revive a historical style. This temple has an openness not found in traditional temples because it is abstract in composition. The way the temple is built over a pool is also abstract. Ando succeeds in expressing through its abstract composition both contemporaneity and openness.

Mediation Space, UNESCO (1994-95) can be said to express best the transcendental religious character that is Ando's objective. It is an abstract space for meditation that possesses no actual religious feature. Ando's goal in religious architecture is to achieve both universality and transcendence. To do so, he requires in his architecture an open element.

The Construction of a World Apart

The distinctive character of Ando's architecture can be appreciated in buildings in which both public character and artistic expression are demanded, such as museums, libraries and memorial halls. He is probably the best architect of art museums in Japan today. That is because a building by him has such presence that it can compete with the artworks collected or created inside it. When he designs an art museum, he does not create galleries that are characterless white cubes. Ando believes that architectural works ought to speak, that is, to make their presence felt, as well.

Toward the end of the 1980s, he began creating a series of contemporary art museums, or more precisely a museum complex, on a small island called Naoshima in the Inland Sea of Japan. The aim was to create a stage for the exhibition of the art collection and art-related activities of a corporation called Benesse. Benesse House (Naoshima Contemporary Art Museum), designed by Ando, opened in 1992. That was an extremely important event in itself in the history of Naoshima, but it was just the start of a new future for the island. Benesse House, intended to house many commissioned works, that is, site-specific works premised on this particular museum, was quite unique. In this way, Naoshima began to generate, and Benesse House began to encourage the generation of, works of art. This experiment was eventually expanded in the so-called Art House Project to include the creation of artworks set in houses and shrines surviving in a village on Naoshima. Four buildings have already been newly produced, and two existing houses, the former site of a temple and a shrine have been transformed in this project. Ando has collaborated with James Turrell in creating a building called Minamidera (House Project No. 2) that has darkness and light as its theme. Art House Project is an attempt on the part of contemporary artists to rediscover and re-create possibilities in buildings and places in a traditional village on Naoshima. In this way, the creative activities that began with the establishment of Benesse House have been expanded to Naoshima as a whole. Ando's goal has been an art museum that is the polar opposite of a white cube.

From 2001 to 2004, he was involved in the creation of Chichu Art Museum on the island. A building buried underground evokes for us the world of myths. There are many myths about the underground in the world. Among the best known are the story of Eurydice and Orpheus in Greek myth, and the tale in Japanese myth of Izanagi and Izanami and the passageway called Yomotsu Hirasaka linking this world and an underground world of the dead. In both stories, the protagonist pursues his loved one into the world of the dead and brings her back to life with his love, only to lose her tragically when, at the last, she looks back. The underground world in both myths calls into question the origin of human existence.

Chichu Art Museum invites us to travel both to works of art and into ourselves. That is the transcendental and sacred nature of this museum. Chichu Art Museum also engages in a dialogue with the earlier Benesse House. Whereas Benesse House is a source generating site-specific works, Chichu Art Museum is an attempt to suggest the origin of works of art. In this way, the two museums created on Naoshima give the works of art broader and deeper meaning. They can be said to cause the self-relativization of art. Museums that are places for experiments in contemporary art tend to be free spaces, offering few constraints. Here, by contrast, the approach taken has been to present an experimental work of contemporary art as a unique thing belonging only to the one place. Chichu Art Museum appears archaic because it is the result of the weaving together of various strands that have already been mentioned. That is, a mythic structure is concealed there.

Ando has tried forming a world apart on the island of Awaji as well. The completion of Akashi Kaikyo Bridge has greatly eased access to the island from Osaka or Kobe. We have come to realize that the world glimpsed just across the water from Kobe is Awaji. The world of Awaji-Yumebutai, created on this island, represents the best of contemporary architecture and seems somehow a world apart. Visiting Awaji-Yumebutai, we are surprised to find the island, which had seemed such a distant place, so close at hand. We are surprised then to find ourselves in a strange new world of architecture. Thus, the island, once thought to be distant, is discovered to be close-by, but once we are there, Yumebutai leads us into a far-off world. The way our psychological sense of distance and our perception swing from one extreme to the other is intriguing.

The site of Awaji-Yumebutai is said to have once been used as a source of landfill. It provided soil required for enormous reclamation projects such as Kansai International Airport. There are many places in Japan that suffer the aftereffects of such development. The creation of the group of facilities at Awaji-Yumebutai was envisioned as a project to improve and reforest land from which large amounts of soil had been removed for construction. Ando was involved in this work from the start of the reforestation project. At the start of the project, land on the site was already laid bare. The Yumebutai project began with the planting of trees and the stabilization of hillsides on the site. When he speaks of how the trees have since taken root and grown, Ando seems less like an architect and more like a gardener. A careful plan was devised so that several varieties of trees could be planted in combination on the hillsides and cover the site with greenery as quickly as possible.

The trees continued to be nurtured while the buildings were being designed, and by the time the buildings were erected, the hillsides were covered in greenery. I visited this place several times during construction and was impressed each time by the steady growth of the trees. The pace of construction work here—that is, the flow of time—was clearly different from that of a project on an urban site. Awaji-Yumebutai was born of a combination of a number of different processes unfolding at different rates. This is not just a complex group of buildings. Diifferent currents of time layered in a complex way, each with its own tempo, are hidden here as well.

Both the work in Naoshima and the work in Awaji can be said to be attempts to form a world apart. They evoke the retreat known as Hadrian's Villa, which the ancient Roman Emperor Hadrian created in what is now Tivoli, a suburb of Rome. The villa, which survives as a ruin, was a vast network of gardens and palace buildings that is said to have been a miniature of the world through which the emperor had traveled in his lifetime. An art gallery and academia of Greece and structures from Egypt, Rome and even Hades were re-created there. Even today, a visitor can get a sense, in the series of enormous, crumbling structures, of his grand vision of reconstructing the world. An emperor of the ancient Roman Empire, ruling at a time when the empire stretched to its greatest extent, had been the first to be able to create a world in miniature. The attempts at Naoshima and Awaji seem to me to be contemporary versions of Hadrian's Villa.

Condensed there are the worlds Ando has envisioned to this day. There are not many architects who could have designed such a large and diverse group of buildings, but trying to condense the enormous, deep and diverse store of works he has attempted up to now in a limited area may have been a bigger problem for him than filling up the large site. Such is the richness of the diversity that is condensed there. Vast, complex worlds have been created over time in Naoshima and Awaji, and their complex grandeur is difficult to sense from just models or photographs.

Expressing a Commemorative Character

There are many museums and memorial halls designed by Ando in his native Osaka. Chikatsu-Asuka Historical Museum (1990-94) and Sayamaike Historical Museum are public museums—facilities that suggest the ancient history of the places where they have been built. Chikatsu-Asuka Historical Museum is a museum of ancient history and Sayamaike Historical Museum houses exhibits on the history surrounding the creation of the man-made pond from which it takes its name. The two museums can be said to be facilities that tell the history of their respective places, and the tales told are connected to the larger history of Japan. In particular, Gyoki and Chogen were involved in the creation of Sayama Pond. Thus the place intersects with the history of architecture as well. Ando produces an archaic atmosphere through the expression of scale and instantly turns back the time of the place. He makes the museum of an area of ancient burial mounds called Chikatsu-Asuka impressive by means of immense steps and geometrical form. By incorporating a section of Sayama Pond inside the museum dedicated to it, he makes manifest the history surrounding the holding pond. However, he does not disclose the essence of a place only through such physical compositions.

Ando continues to plant trees of Japanese apricot around Chikatsu-Asuka Historical Museum and cherry trees around Sayama Pond where Sayamaike Historical Museum stands. His intention seems to be to have Japanese apricot and cherry blossoms continue to bestow blessings on the places because the two museums are museums that tell the history of those places. Thus, in the case of these museums, flowers open his buildings to their surroundings. I have stated that there always exists an open element in his architecture. The apricot and cherry trees that open these two museums enlarge them both physically and metaphysically.

In Shiba Ryotaro Memorial Museum (1999-2001) in Higashi Osaka, Ryotaro Shiba's collection of books is used to express, clearly and directly, the world of the novelist. The work is very Andoesque in that the design could not be more direct. The strength of Ando's architecture lies in the way he clearly visualizes the essence of things. He astutely observed that Shiba's essence could be expressed by a wall of books. Overwhelmed by the sight of Shiba's collection of books that fills an entire curved wall, visitors feel an excitement as if they had entered the mind of the author. However, here too Ando has added an element that relieves the tension and opens the building toward the outside. That element is rapeseed. Ando has planted rapeseed on the grounds of the memorial museum—rapeseed, whose Japanese name (*nanohana*) appears in the title of a work by Shiba and which thus overlaps with the author's image.

Planting greenery around cities and buildings makes cities more beautiful and the environment more gentle. Ando says that he was taught at a young age the value of plants. That has led to various efforts such as the previously-mentioned campaign called "Heisei-era Passages" to plant cherry trees along streets in Osaka and to the Setouchi Olive Foundation 's campaign to plant saplings grown from acorns on Teshima, an island in the Inland Sea of Japan that was polluted by industrial waste.

That an international leading-edge architect would initiate and maintain such campaigns is proof that his ideas on architecture are deeply considerate of the natural environment. It is this aspect of Ando that reminds me of *kanjinnohijiri* of the past such as Gyoki. I explained that there is an open element to his architecture. I mean by that that his architectural works are open to society and imbued with a concept of what is public in a broad sense.

Attempts in Tokyo

Fukutake Hall (Interfaculty Initiative in Information Studies) was completed on the

Hongo campus of the University of Tokyo on April 2008. The building is situated along Hongo Avenue, between the university's Red Gate and Main Gate. The building is in a wooded zone along the street, and the long narrow site had to be further trimmed to save large trees. The site conditions can be said to have been the worst possible. However, the building cannot help but be conspicuous, situated as it is along the street.

I was afraid when construction began that the building would be intimidating because it is, though low-rise, extremely long. However, now that it is complete, it is obvious that the low-rise building shows to good effect the large camphor trees retained between the site and the street. The building itself, with its low concrete wall and horizontal slit, makes its presence felt but in a pleasant way. Though aboveground the building is only two stories high, its long roof cannot help but catch the eye. That was the focus of design. The resulting roof, possessing a tension that reminds one of the Sanjusangendo ("Thirty-Three Bay Hall," the main hall of Rengeoin) in Kyoto, is extended in a clean straight line, without any hitch or slack. I have secretly taken to calling it the Sanjusangendo of Hongo.

Behind the low concrete wall descends an open stairway that doubles as a dry area, leading people to the second basement floor. The hall has been accommodated on the second basement floor to keep the building low-rise, but there too natural light and ventilation have been sufficiently provided. Such a dynamic spatial composition had not existed before on the Hongo campus. There are works by successive professors in charge of architectural design at the University of Tokyo on the Hongo campus, and Ando's building has certainly added a new element.

Construction work on Shibuya Station on the Tokyu Toyoko Line was proceeding underground in Shibuya at the same time. The station is part of the so-called Tokyo Metro Fukutoshin Line Mutual Non-stop Service Operation Project. Simply put, it involves the construction of a new underground station linking a new subway line called the Fukutoshin Line (that runs underneath Meiji Avenue from Shibuya to Ikebukuro) with the Tokyu Toyoko Line. Ando has inserted here a station building in the shape of an enormous egg. The egg-shaped shell, introduced into a passageway for passengers extending from the second basement-floor concourse to the fifth basement-floor platform, is the envelope for a multi-level space. He calls this shape a "hypogenous ship." The multi-level space centered on this shape is continuous with the aboveground portion of the station, and the underground space is expected to be naturally ventilated.

Work on this new Shibuya Station on the Tokyu Toyoko Line, being constructed inside the Yamanote Line and directly under the bus terminal, had been largely completed—the station was to be opened in June—and interior finish work was proceeding at a rapid pace. We are apt to lose our sense of place on an enormous underground construction site; it is difficult to remember on which floor we are or in which direction we are facing. However, despite the enormous size of this underground space, people are not likely to lose sight of the overall image of the station they are using or their own positions in it, if they picture in their minds this egg called the hypogenous ship. The hypogenous ship, which may seem at first glance an extravagant amusement, is actually a clear sign that assures safety necessary in the contemporary metropolis. Subway cars on trial runs were already entering the construction site under construction, and the scene was characterized by the scale of a dam construction project and the tumult of a world apart, scarcely imaginable in the middle of the city.

Having had the opportunity to become acquainted with current works in Tokyo by Ando, I thought about various things. In recent years, Ando has clearly shown an underground orientation. His approach has become to minimize the portions that appear aboveground and to accommodate the required volume belowground as much as possible. A space in which every conceivable factor, from sense of scale to openness, has been carefully weighed is prepared underground. The egg-shape seen in Shibuya Station probably can be traced to the egg he tried to insert into the project to convert the Central Public Hall on the island of Nakanoshima in Osaka. He continued to mull over the idea and image and at last found in Shibuya a place to realize them.

The strength of Ando's architecture lies there. His architecture aspires to endurance. He has developed the Rokko Housing project in Kobe over a number of phases, and he has expressed his obsessive interest in the underground at every opportunity. That is what accounts for the presence in his buildings, a presence felt even by people who are not acquainted with the background to the works in question.

Perpetual Message

Ando, who became in October 2002 the first Japanese architect to receive the Kyoto Prize, made the following point in his concise remarks on that occasion.

"I have liked making things since I was child. I will continue to pursue my own aesthetic in order to produce a beautiful townscape. On the other hand, having adopted a system of mass production and mass consumption, Japanese society has lost the balance it once possessed. The environment has been destroyed and cities have lost their beauty. I want to continue to pursue these two difficult themes, my own aesthetic and an architecture that considers the environment."

Ando's viewpoint is clear, and his statement leaves no room for misunderstanding. His architecture has the strength that comes from being the product of such a clear point of view. Many people accept and support his works because his architecture expresses a lucid worldview. Concerning his own architecture, he has explained: "I do not create a building that is complete in itself. Instead, I create a building that, by its connections to various things such as the city, history and society, establishes new relationships aimed at stimulating the place. At times, the attempt is to uncover "the memory of place" and make it manifest in architecture, thereby achieving the "rebirth" of the environment."

By "connections," he surely means "connectedness." He first begins with the reading and interpretation of the place where the building is being planned. He has consistently taken this approach since Rowhouse in Sumiyoshi, his debut work. He first produces form from place.

Rokko Housing (I, II, II) which he has continually developed, has been a job of transforming a steep slope into favorable, safe housing. Its history has been a history of interpreting the slopes of Kobe. It has also been an attempt to produce dwellings affording views of the harbor of Kobe and, at the same time, to restore greenery by growing various plants in surrounding areas and on rooftops. While he was engaged in this work, I heard from his lips a story about the landscape of the Rokko mountain range at the start of the twentieth century. At that time, the slopes of Rokko had been laid bare by indiscriminate felling of trees for fuel.

I was reminded of the story of how Frank Lloyd Wright, when designing a house there, decided to design it to suit a landscape that then resembled that of Arizona. Ando perceived that the subsequent history of recovery of greenery by the mountains was a valuable memory of this place. It was to reawaken "the memory of place" that he introduced an abundance of plants into the Rokko Housing projects. That is because "the memory of place" is the interpretation of place and the interpretation of its history.

A work by him always starts from such an interpretation of "the memory of place." However, that is subtly different from the idea of intertextuality that every work is a reinterpretation of all works before it. First of all, his is not an attempt to impose a personal sense of nostalgia and call it "the memory of place." For him, "the memory of place" transcends personal emotion and has a social dimension. That is precisely why so many people are sympathetic to his architecture

But what does Ando produce from "the memory of place"?

He is well known for perfecting the architectural expression of exposed concrete, but that was not something elicited from "the memory of place." That is something that was born of and refined by his aesthetic, his architectural image. It is an expression rooted in a "personal aesthetic." It is because he possesses a strong aesthetic that his interpretation with respect to place has about it an air of tension. He is able to give each building a distinctive expression because he pursues "two difficult themes, [his] own aesthetic and an architecture that considers the environment."

Nevertheless, it needs to be added here that there is an aspect to Ando that does not fit the framework of an orthodox architect. In the process of pursuing "an architecture that considers the environment," he arrives at an expression that is not just architectural. After Kobe, a city where he has built many works, was visited by a major earthquake, he began a campaign to continue to plant trees bearing white blossoms as an expression of hope for the repose of the souls of the victims and for the reconstruction of the city. He is also promoting a campaign to plant olives and acorns to restore the environment in the Inland Sea of Japan which has been polluted by industrial wastes. Are these too the works of an architect?

Ordinarily, his campaign to restore the natural environment would be viewed as social activism, not as the true occupation of an architect. Ando would by such lights be considered a superb architect and at the same time a superb social activist. However, Ando is not engaging in social activism in addition to practicing architecture. To him, the two activities are closely related. And that is precisely where the essence of Ando as an architect lies.

To consider this question, it is necessary to consider the present state of architecture, or the system of society as a whole today. In the present age, referred to as postmodern or information-oriented, every conceivable system has become enormous and complex, and the individual has become in relative terms a smaller presence. Living in an enormous network of culture and technology, we have been robbed of the possibility of self expression.

We take an interest in architects and applaud their activities because they are the extremely rare individuals in contemporary society who are permitted self expression. Active architects are contemporary heroes. Ando is an object of admiration. The people who applaud Ando have their own, unfulfilled desire to express themselves, but they see him as their proxy. This helps explain the nature and overall image of Ando's multifaceted activities.

In crystallizing an architectural work, Ando attempts to read every possibility of the place where it is to stand. Naturally, people's aspirations too have accumulated in that place. He interprets those aspirations while creating the work, but at the same time, he also grows white flowers, olives and acorns. To him, those too are architecture in the sense that they express people's hopes.

On October 2005, in addressing the Ruskin Library, he conveyed the following message.

Though he said he had nothing in common with Ruskin, Ando began his talk with comments about the environment of Venice with which he had dealt in a recent work. He states that, when he is asked to lecture or to design, he accepts if there is a building in that place he would like to visit or see. He said he decided to take on the work in Venice because works by Andrea Palladio, the Mannerist architect, are in the region. FABRICA (Benetton Communication Research Center) built in the town of Treviso called for the retention of an eighteenth-century building and the addition of new elements. There, as the project proceeded, experts in preservation and architectural history rigorously checked any areas to be remodeled. Any ornamentation that was newly discovered was carefully restored. Remodeling was kept to a minimum. Objects from a dismantled building, such as roof tiles and stones, were kept and reused. An attempt was made to achieve harmony in that way. A father-and-son pair of masons enjoyed laying a stone wall in a pattern called the Treviso style. The design used to advantage traditional materials and construction methods. A new art school was created, based on such a policy, after nine years of work. The main facilities were buried underground, and a shallow pool was built so that the building would be reflected on the water.

Venice is a city of merchants, and he himself grew up in Osaka, another city of merchants. Both Venice and Treviso are cities on the water. Osaka too is a city on the water. His empathy for these places where he was doing work increased as he discovered things their environment and the environment of Osaka had in common.

He is presently involved in building an addition to Sakuranomiya Bridge, more commonly referred to as Ginbashi (Silver Bridge), in the district of Sakuranomiya in Osaka. Ando grew up in Osaka and says that there is a souvenir photograph taken at the foot of this bridge when he was an elementary school student. This project involves adding a new bridge parallel to the old Ginbashi. His approach is to design a bridge with the same silhouette as the old one but to use contemporary technology in the details. The result will be the juxtaposition of two bridges, the old and the new, that are similar in appearance but express the intervening passage of time.

The former Osaka Mint Bureau is also in the Sakuranomiya district, and the tree-lined road leading from the building, familiarly known as the Passage, is famous for its cherry blossoms. Ando is enthusiastically promoting an ambitious cherry tree-planting campaign aimed at extending the trees all the way to Osaka Bay. However, before embarking on that story, he touched on the problem of the environment of Nakanoshima, an island in Osaka that connects to Sakuranomiya. The landscape of Nakanoshima is representative of Osaka, and he has long drawn sketches and pictures of it. One can get a glimpse of the future architect in a good pastel drawing done in his youth.

Osaka Central Public Hall, commonly referred to as the Nakanoshima Public Hall, is a red brick building standing on Nakanoshima. When this building was once threatened with demolition, Ando presented a by-now well-known project to convert the building by introducing a new egg-shaped hall inside this historic building and thus to preserve it. This was a message that a city should coexist with its historic buildings. This project was not realized, but it was decided nevertheless to preserve the Central Hall. Having been made earthquake-resistant through base-isolation, the building has been reborn as a new public hall. It is now designated an Important Cultural Property. I have already explained how Ando is now realizing this egg in the underground Shibuya Station in Tokyo.

The fact that Ando, the design genius active internationally on the leading edge, initiates and maintains diverse campaigns is proof that his ideas of architecture are profoundly considerate of the natural environment. This aspect of Ando evokes the *kanjinnohijiri*, the peripatetic monks of old who worked for the public good. His activities, characterized by energy and originality, evoke those of the *kanjinnohijiri* Gyoki. That is the reason behind the thesis I explained at the outset—that is, my belief that Ando is a latter-day Gyoki. A *kanjinnohijiri* may not have been a saint who assumed a serene, detached attitude but a cheerful sportsman who took vigorous action. There is a close connection between the public spirit suggested by Ando's architecture and his diverse activities.

TIME'S I + II
TIME'S I + II
1983-84, 84-91　京都府京都市中京区 —— Nakagyo-ku, Kyoto, Kyoto

敷地は京都市中心部、高瀬川に架かる三条小橋のほとりに位置する。II期にわたって建設された商業施設の計画である。近代都市化の進む京都の市街地にあって、ここでは、人々の日常から遠ざけられていた川を都市に取り戻すこと、即ち川と一体化する建築空間の創出を主題としている。

建物は、高瀬川に面する敷地の親密なスケール感に応えるよう、敷地全体を水面レベルまで掘り下げ、地下1階、地上2階の高さに抑えて計画されている。川に沿って延びるヴォールト屋根を冠した整形のヴォリュームを中心とする単純な構成だが、その周囲を取り巻く〈余白〉を階段や通路として建築化し、店舗間を内外空間の入り組む立体的な路地空間でつないでいくことで、さまざまな視点で〈川〉と出会える複雑多様な空間のシークエンスを生み出そうと考えた。

水際に緩やかな弧を描く、水面上30cmレベルのテラスは、「護岸に手を加えてはならない」という行政側との粘り強い交渉の末、実現したものである。道行く人々に、「そこに川が流れている」当たり前の事実を伝え、都市の水際を公共空間として取り戻していく、きっかけとなるような建築を意図した。

I期からII期へ、7年越しに行われた拡張計画の際には、建築を介しての、三条通りと竜馬通りを結ぶ〈通り抜け〉も実現した。70年代から一貫して〈閉じる〉ことで、都市の建築を組み立ててきた私が、建築を都市に〈開き〉、街の文脈を建築化するという主題に取り組んだ最初の仕事であった。

The site is in the center of Kyoto, in the vicinity of the Sanjo Kobashi bridge spanning the Takasegawa River. This is a design for a commercial facility, constructed in two phases. Located amid the ongoing modernization and urbanization of Kyoto's downtown, the theme was to reclaim the river, which had become alienated from the everyday life of people—that is to say, the creation of architectural spaces integrated with the river.

Responding to the intimate sense of scale on a site facing Takasegawa River, the entire site has been excavated to the water level and the building designed with its height restricted to two stories above ground and one story below ground. It has a simple composition centered on a smooth regular volume extending along the river and capped by a vaulted roof, but the "blank spaces" surrounding it are made architectural, in the form of stairs or passages. By connecting the shops with complex three-dimensional alley spaces of intertwined interior and exterior spaces, I tried to create a diverse spatial sequence in which the river can be encountered from various viewpoints.

Describing a gentle arc at the water's edge 30cm above water level, the terrace was achieved only after prolonged discussions with the administration, who said, "do not touch the river embankment." I aimed at an architecture that took the opportunity to reclaim the water's edge in the city as a public space that conveys to pedestrians the obvious fact of "a river flowing here."

For the expansion plan carried out in phase II, seven years after phase I, a "passage" was implemented that connects Sanjo dori to Ryoma dori through the medium of architecture. Having consistently constructed "closed" architecture since the 1970s, this was the first project in which I tackled the theme of architecture "open" to the city and turned the town context into architecture.

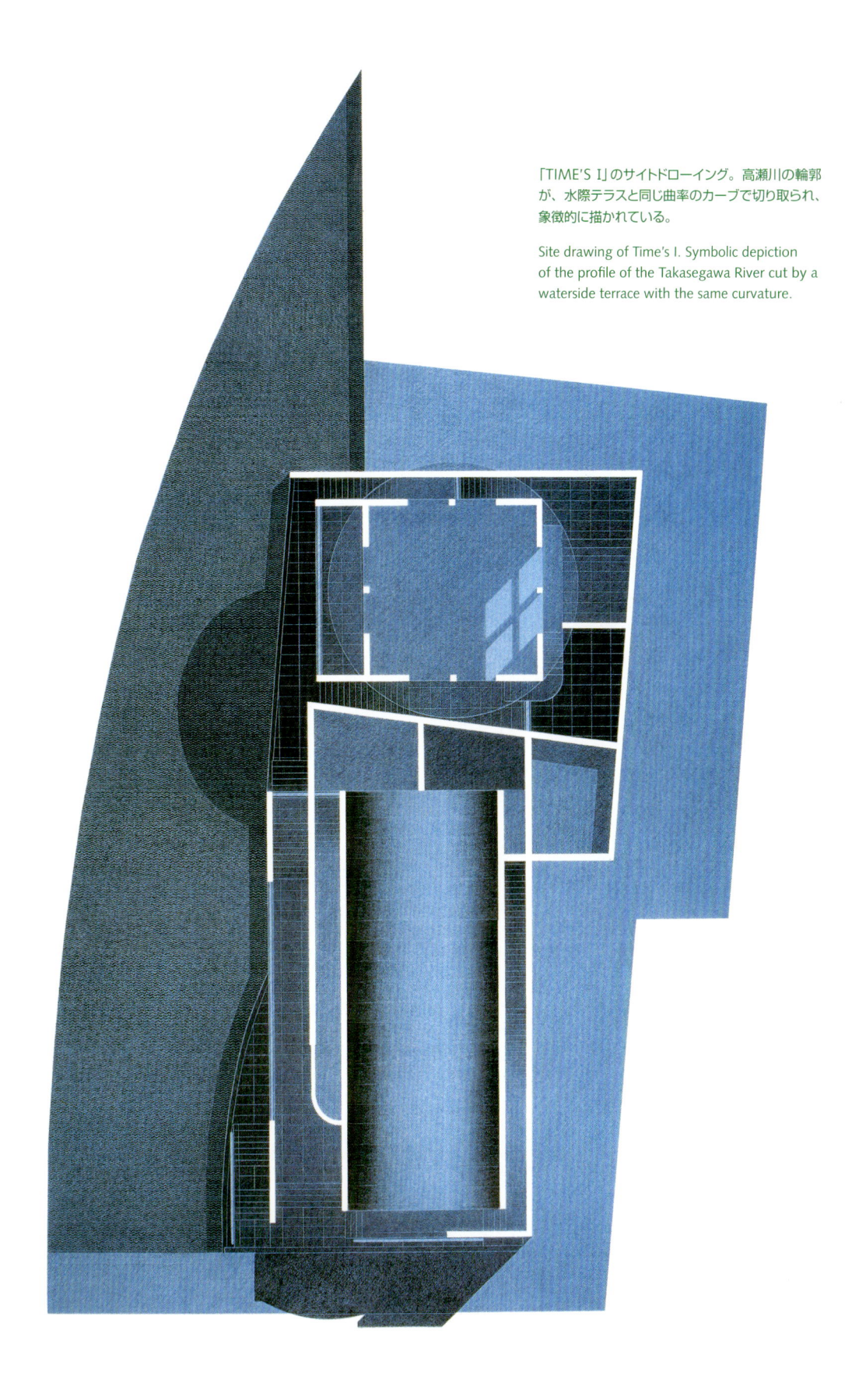

「TIME'S I」のサイトドローイング。高瀬川の輪郭が、水際テラスと同じ曲率のカーブで切り取られ、象徴的に描かれている。

Site drawing of Time's I. Symbolic depiction of the profile of the Takasegawa River cut by a waterside terrace with the same curvature.

水面レベルに設けられた1階のテラスから、3層の建物がセットバックしつつ建ち上がる。川に向けられた、柔らかな建築のファサード。

From the first floor terrace at water level, the three-storied building rises as it steps back. A subdued architectural facade faces the river.

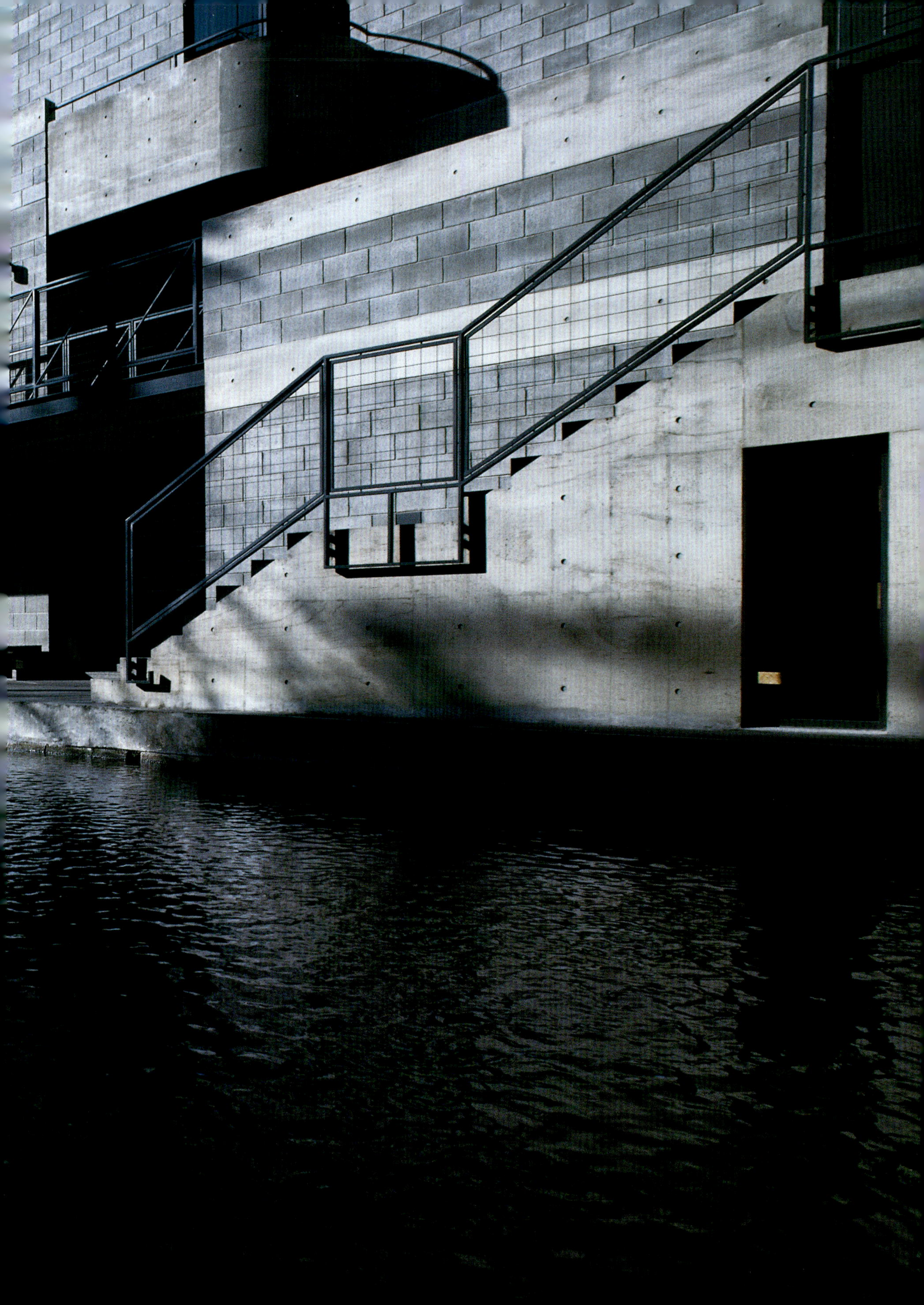

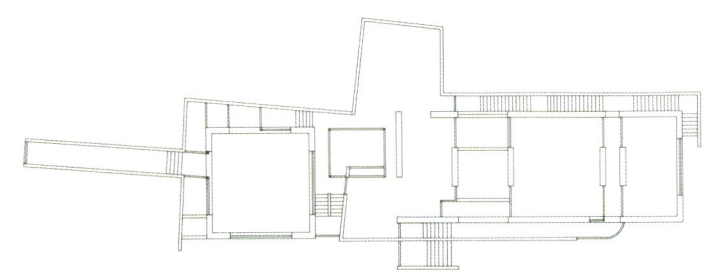

Third floor plan

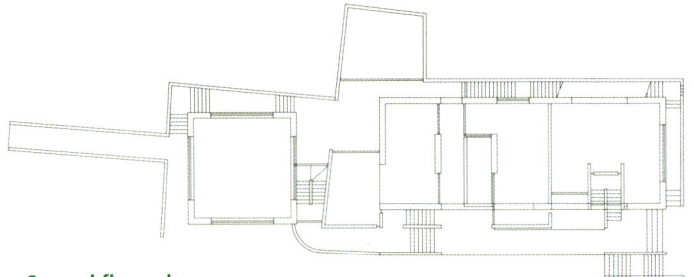

Second floor plan

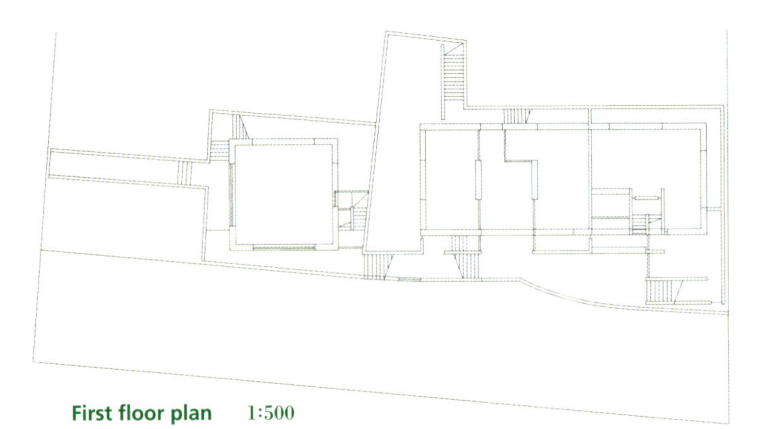

I期完成から7年を経てII期が完成。水際の立体路地を拡張するとともに、表通りと裏通りを結ぶ〈通り抜け〉を実現させた。

Phase II was completed seven years after the completion of phase I. As well as expanding the three-dimensional alley along the water's edge, a "walk-through" was implemented to connect the main street with a side street.

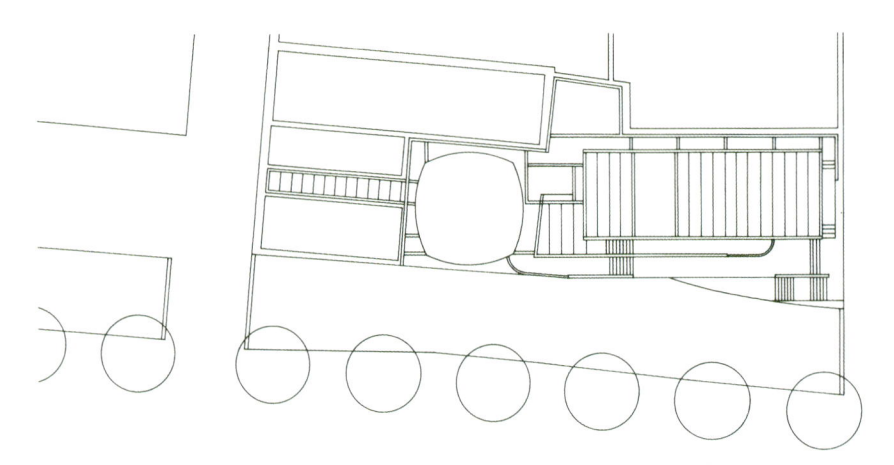

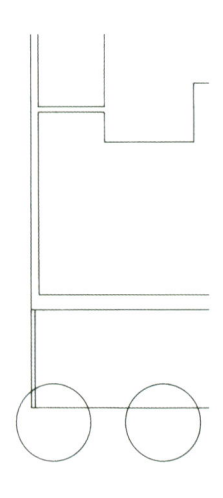

First floor plan   1:500

Site plan   1:600

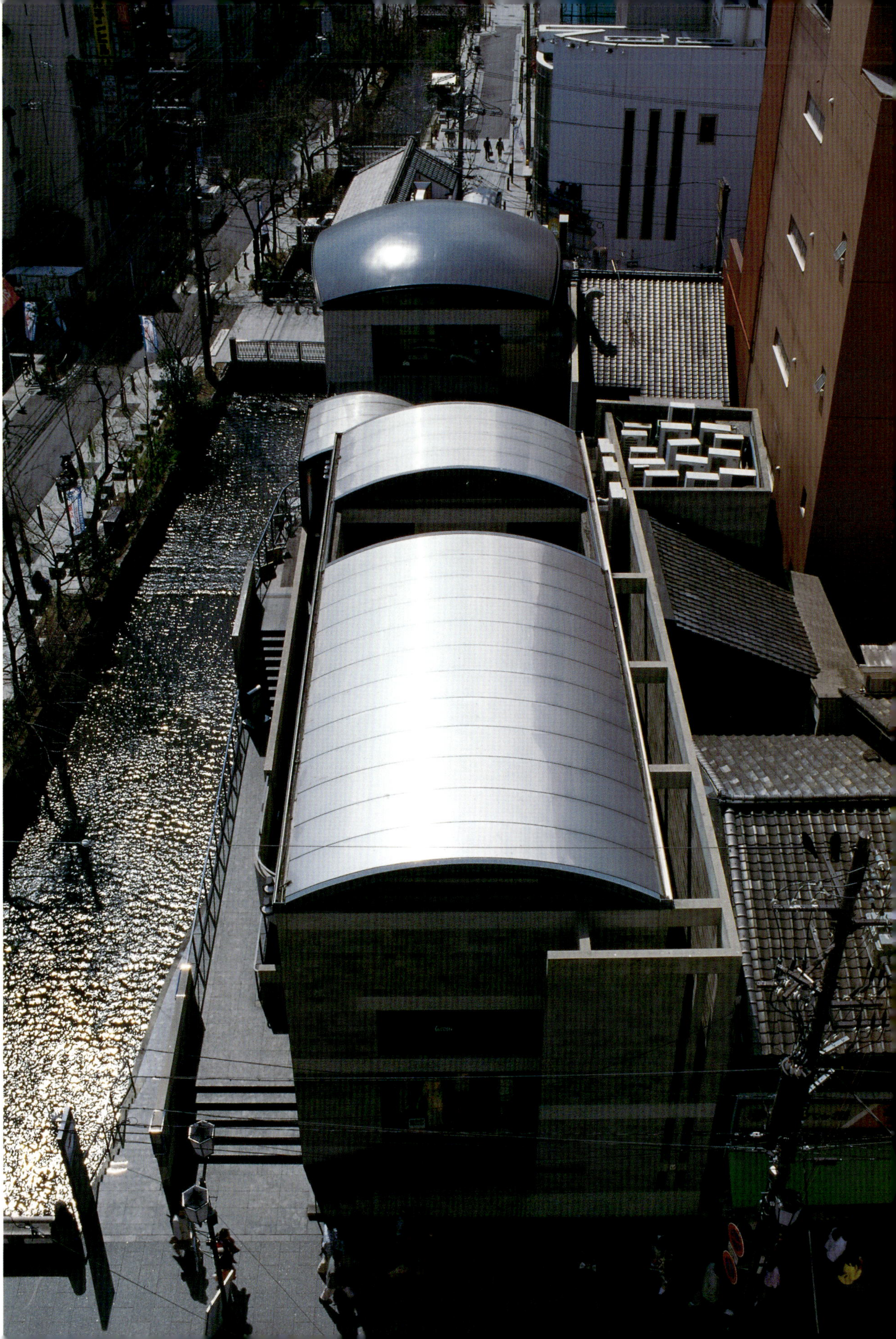

三条小橋の傍らの階段を降りると、高瀬川の水辺に緩やかなカーブを描くテラスが待ち受ける。
Descending the stair adjacent to Sanjo Kobashi, there awaits a terrace that traces a gentle arc across the edge of the Takasegawa River.

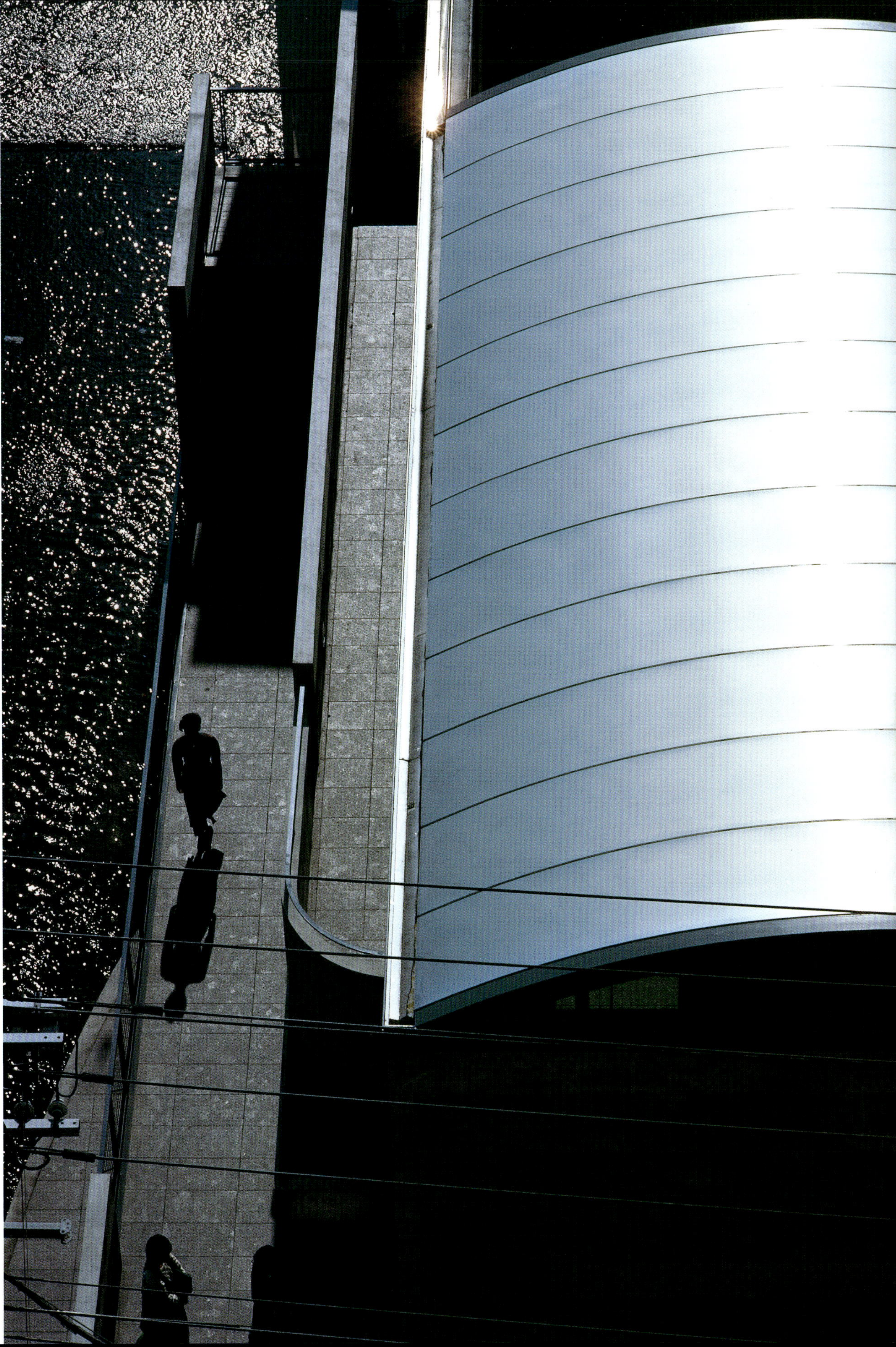

高瀬川に面する各店舗は、路地的な通路と随所に設けられた光庭により立体的に結びつけられている。
Each of the shops facing the Takasegawa River is connected three-dimensionally by means of alley-like paths and light gardens placed everywhere.

外壁に用いられているのはコンクリートブロック。自然とともに朽ちて、古都の町並みに溶け込む建築が主題とされた。

Concrete blocks are used for the exterior walls. The theme is an architecture that blends in with the townscape of the former capital, and ages together with nature.

渋谷プロジェクト
Shibuya Project
1985-87 　東京都渋谷区 —— Shibuya-ku, Tokyo

　非実現に終わった、東京渋谷の中心街に商業コンプレックスをつくる計画である。後に南青山につくった「COLLEZIONE」の原型ともいうべきこの計画案には、大規模化、複合化する都市施設に対する私の基本的な考え方が端的に表れている。

　高地価の立地ゆえに要求される巨大な容積を、地上ではなく、地下に展開する建築をもって確保しようという、地下建築への志向性。その〈深さ〉を活かした立体的空間構成による、劇的なパブリックスペースの獲得──。

　渋谷プロジェクトにおいては、不定形の敷地形状に沿って立ち上がる壁と、その中に角度を振って配された直方体とシリンダーによる幾何学ヴォリュームの間に生まれる余白を、地下まで続く階段状の屋外広場として、積極的な意味を与えている。

　前面道路に沿う壁は、沖縄に実現した「フェスティバル」と同様の、ガラスブロックによるスクリーンの表現としている。建物の内包するパブリックスペースと雑多な都市空間とを緩やかに隔てる〈閾〉の役割を果たす壁だ。

　立地、規模含め、つくられた状況はまったく異なるが、都市に対する建築の関わり方という意味では、2006年に完成した「表参道ヒルズ」もまた、この「渋谷プロジェクト」の延長上にあるといえるかもしれない。

This is an unrealized design for a commercial complex on a street in the center of Tokyo's Shibuya district. It should also be considered a prototype for Collezione, later constructed in Minami-Aoyama. This design proposal is a frank expression of my fundamental way of thinking about large-scale, mixed-use urban facilities.

Going below ground rather than above ground to try and meet the demand for a huge capacity due to the high cost of the land, I focused my attention on the underground architecture. Making use of this "depth" in a three-dimensional spatial composition produced a dramatic public space.

In the Shibuya Project, the blank space that arises between the walls that line the amorphous site, and the geometrical volumes of the cylinder and the rectangular volume placed at an offset angle between those walls, is given a positive value as a stepped outdoor plaza that descends underground.

Similar to Festival, constructed in Okinawa, the wall along the front road is a screen of glass blocks. This wall plays the role of a "threshold" that gently shuts out the incoherent urban spaces from the public spaces within the building.

Although the location and scale conditions are entirely different, perhaps Omotesando Hills, completed in 2006, could also be called an extension of the Shibuya Project in terms of the way the architecture relates to the city.

シリンダーを軸として、垂直動線が立体的に交錯する構成は、後に南青山の「COLLEZIONE」で具現化されることとなった。

This composition of three-dimensionally intersecting vertical circulation routes, with a cylinder as their axis, was later realized at Collezione in Minami-Aoyama.

091 Shibuya Project

Elevation

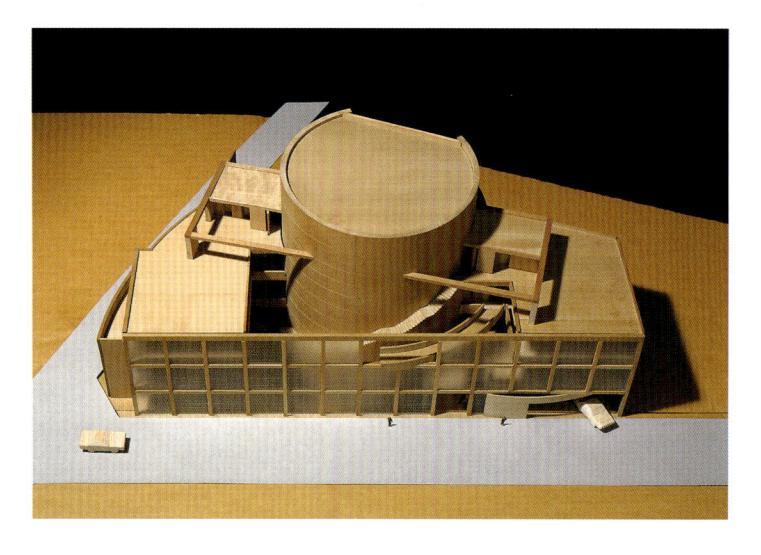

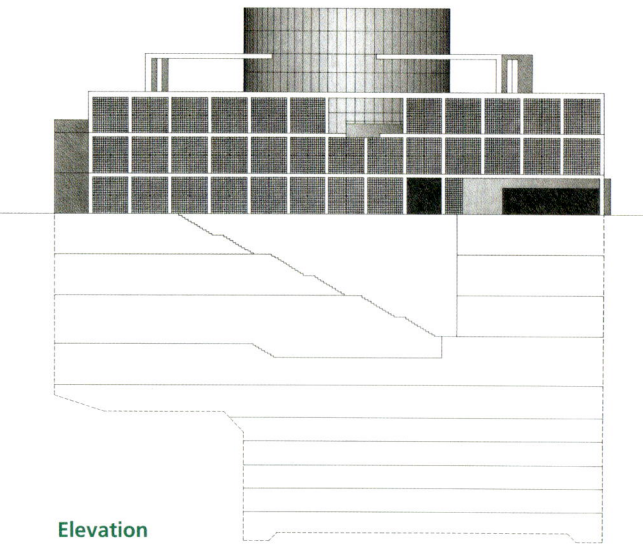

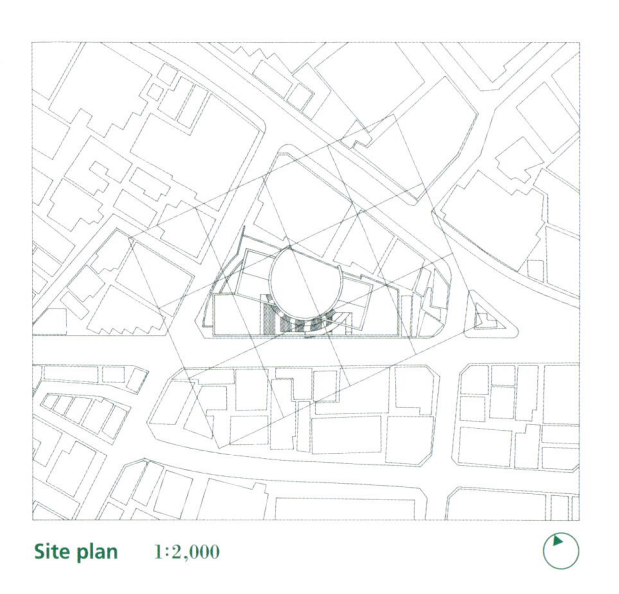

Site plan 1:2,000

092 TADAO ANDO 3

街路に沿って建ち上がるガラスブロックのスクリーン壁と、角度を振って配された矩形と円形の組み合わせによるヴォリューム。その余白のスペースが階段広場として地下深くまで掘り下げられ、地下4階から地上4階に至る、立体的なパブリックスペースが生まれる。

The volume combines a glass-block screen wall erected along the road, and a circle and a rectangle set at an angle. The interstitial space is dug deep into the ground as a stair-shaped plaza, producing a three-dimensional public space from the fourth level below ground to the fourth level above ground.

093 Shibuya Project

中之島プロジェクト II（アーバン・エッグ＋地層空間）
Nakanoshima Project II (Urban Egg+Space Strata)

1988-　大阪府大阪市北区 —— Kita-ku, Osaka, Osaka

　1989年、自ら企画した展覧会で、大阪・中之島を敷地とするふたつのプロジェクトを発表した。中之島とは、大阪中心部を流れる川の中州であり、両側を川に挟まれた島内には市役所や図書館、公会堂など、旧くから地域の文化、行政の中枢を担う施設が建ち並ぶ。

　「アーバン・エッグ」は、その島の史的建造物のひとつ、1918年につくられた中之島公会堂の改造計画である。老朽化のため「解体か、保存か」と議論の揺れていた建物に対し、私が提案したのは、建物の外郭はそのままに、内部に卵型のシェルに包まれた新たなホールを挿入するというアイディアだった。完全な入れ子状の構成をとることで、既存のホール内壁も一切手を加えず残すことができ、またその形状を1点でのみ接地する球形とすることで、既存建物の構造補強も、最小限の範囲に留めることができる。技術的問題も踏まえた上での、新旧の対立的共存をはかる〈再生〉提案だった。

　もうひとつのプロジェクト「地層空間」は、「アーバン・エッグ」を含む、中之島全体を一大文化ゾーンとする構想である。パリのシテ島になぞらえられる中之島の地理的・文化的ポテンシャルを最大限活かすべく、文化施設を充実していこうという都市開発戦略――その方法論として、私は新たな施設の建設を地上ではなく、すべて地下に行うことを提案した。この敷地の〈重層化〉が叶えば、中之島は、既存の歴史的景観、緑溢れる都市公園の雰囲気はそのままに、それ自体が都市を刺激する巨大な文化コンプレックスとして生まれ変わることができる。

　かたちの見えない地中の空間に無意識に惹かれる私の生来の感性が、幼少の頃から身近にしてきた中之島の風景への思いと結びつき、この大規模な都市提案を企てるに至った。

In 1989, I produced an exhibition in which I presented two projects sited on Nakanoshima, Osaka. Nakanoshima is a sandbank in a river flowing through central Osaka. Municipal offices, a library, and the public hall, as well as other facilities supporting the administrative center and old local culture, are arrayed on this island contained by river on either side.

　The Urban Egg is a remodeling scheme for one of the island's historical buildings, the Nakanoshima Public Hall constructed in 1918. During the debate over whether to "destroy or preserve" due to its dilapidated state, I proposed preserving the building's exterior unchanged and inserting within it a new hall enclosed in an egg-shaped shell. With a completely nested composition, the inner walls of the existing hall could be preserved entirely untouched. Furthermore, with a globular shape that only touches the ground at one point, the structural reinforcement of the existing building could also be kept to a minimum. Beyond its basis in technical issues, this is a "regeneration" proposal aimed at a confrontational coexistence of new and old.

　Space Strata, the other project, incorporates Urban Egg in a plan to turn the entire island of Nakanoshima into a large cultural zone. We should make maximum use of the cultural and geographic potential of Nakanoshima, which resembles Paris's Ile de la Cité, in an urban regeneration strategy for the enrichment of cultural facilities. As a methodology, rather than building all the new facilities above ground I proposed to put them underground. If this "stratification" of the site were to be realized, leaving the existing historical scenery and the atmosphere of a lush green urban park unchanged, Nakanoshima itself could be transformed into a huge cultural complex that stimulates the city.

　My natural sensitivity has a subconscious attraction toward underground spaces, the forms of which cannot be seen. The decision to make this large-scale urban proposal is related to the sentiments I have had for the nearby scenery of Nakanoshima since I was a child.

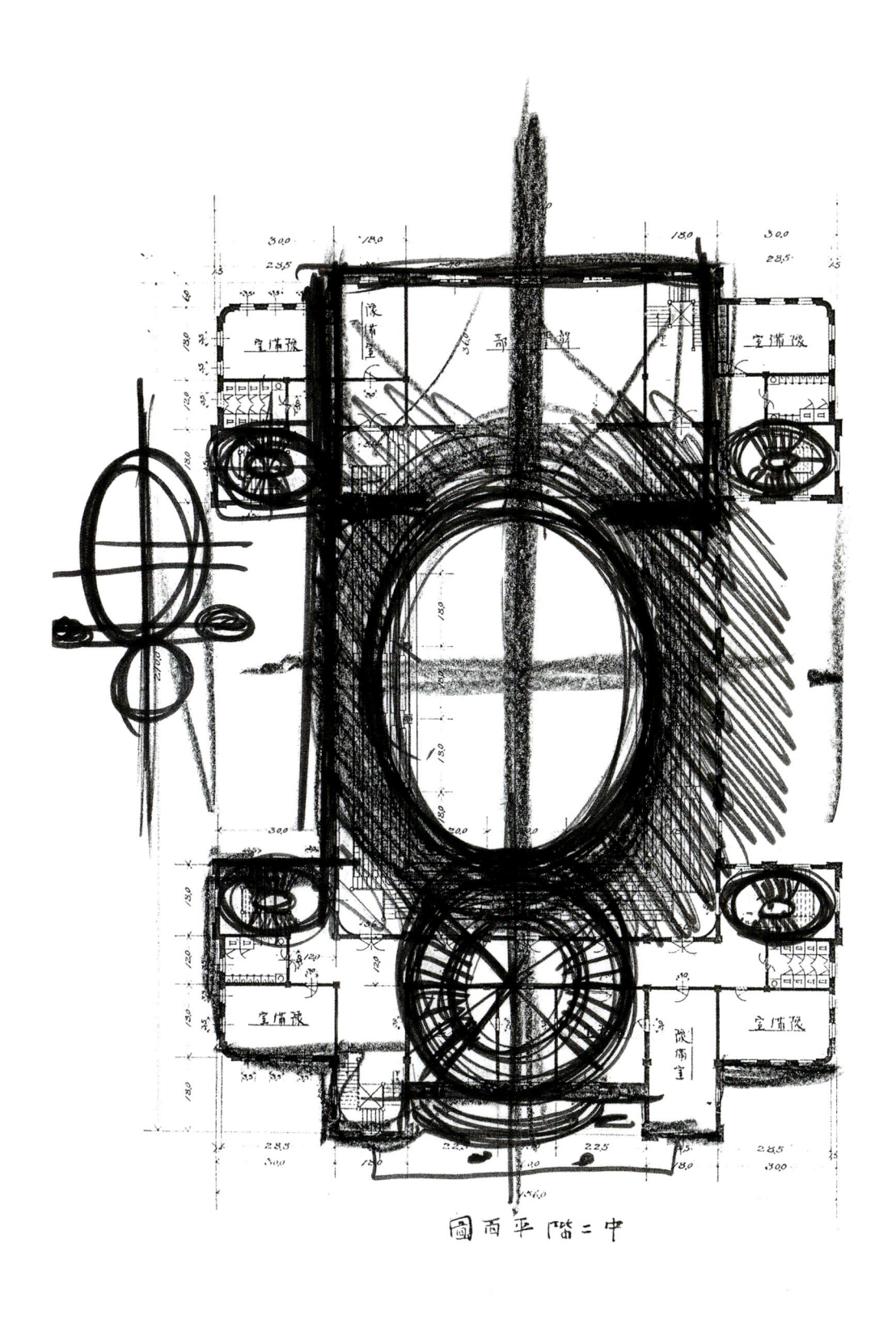

既存の中之島公会堂のプランの上に重ねて描かれたアーバン・エッグの初期イメージスケッチ。
An early image sketch of Urban Egg, drawn on top of a plan of the existing Nakanoshima Public Hall.

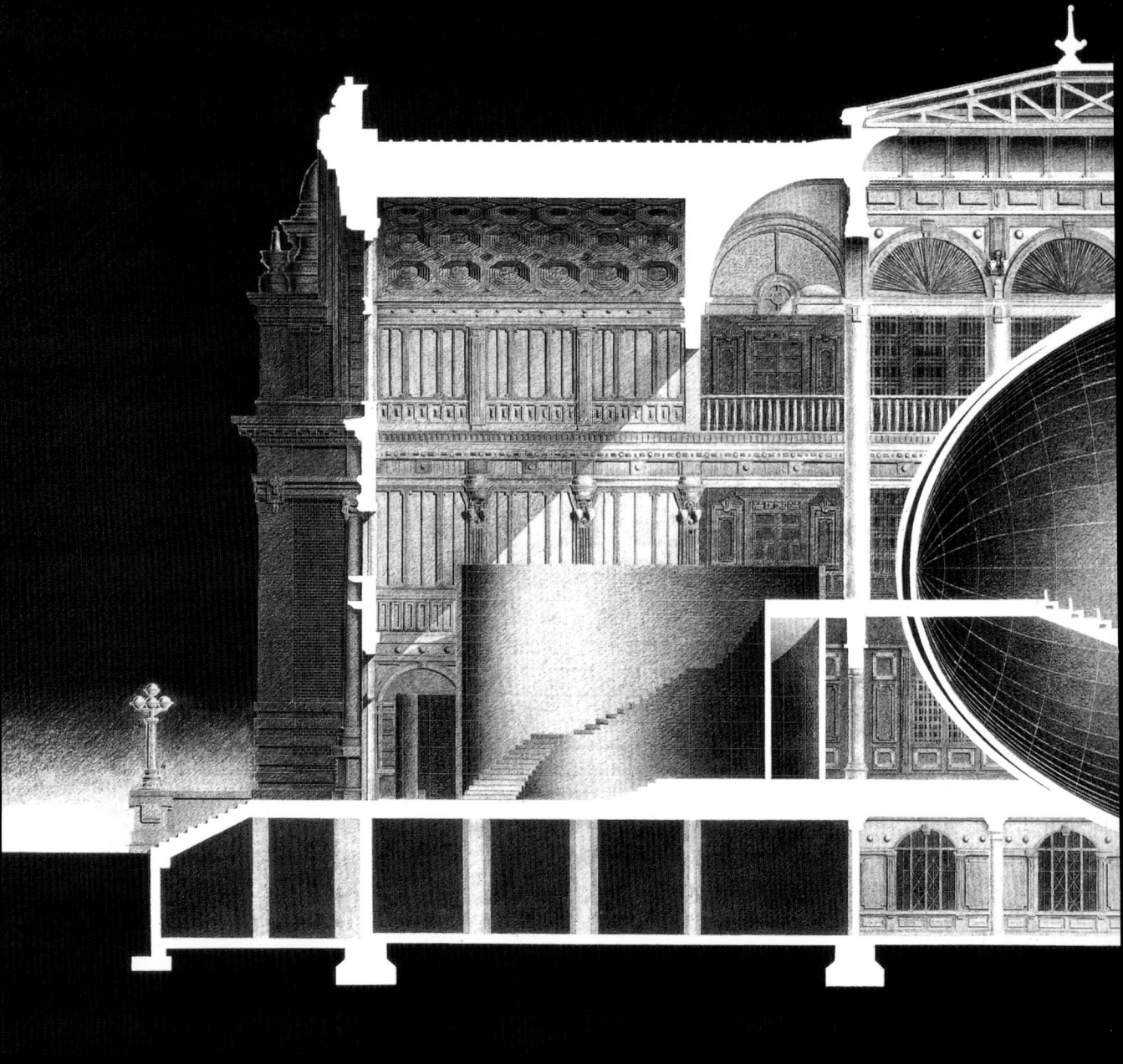

リトグラフをベースに作成された「アーバン・エッグ」の断面ドローイング。〈卵〉を囲う既存建物の精緻な表現に、
新旧の対話を主題とする計画の意図がうかがわれる。

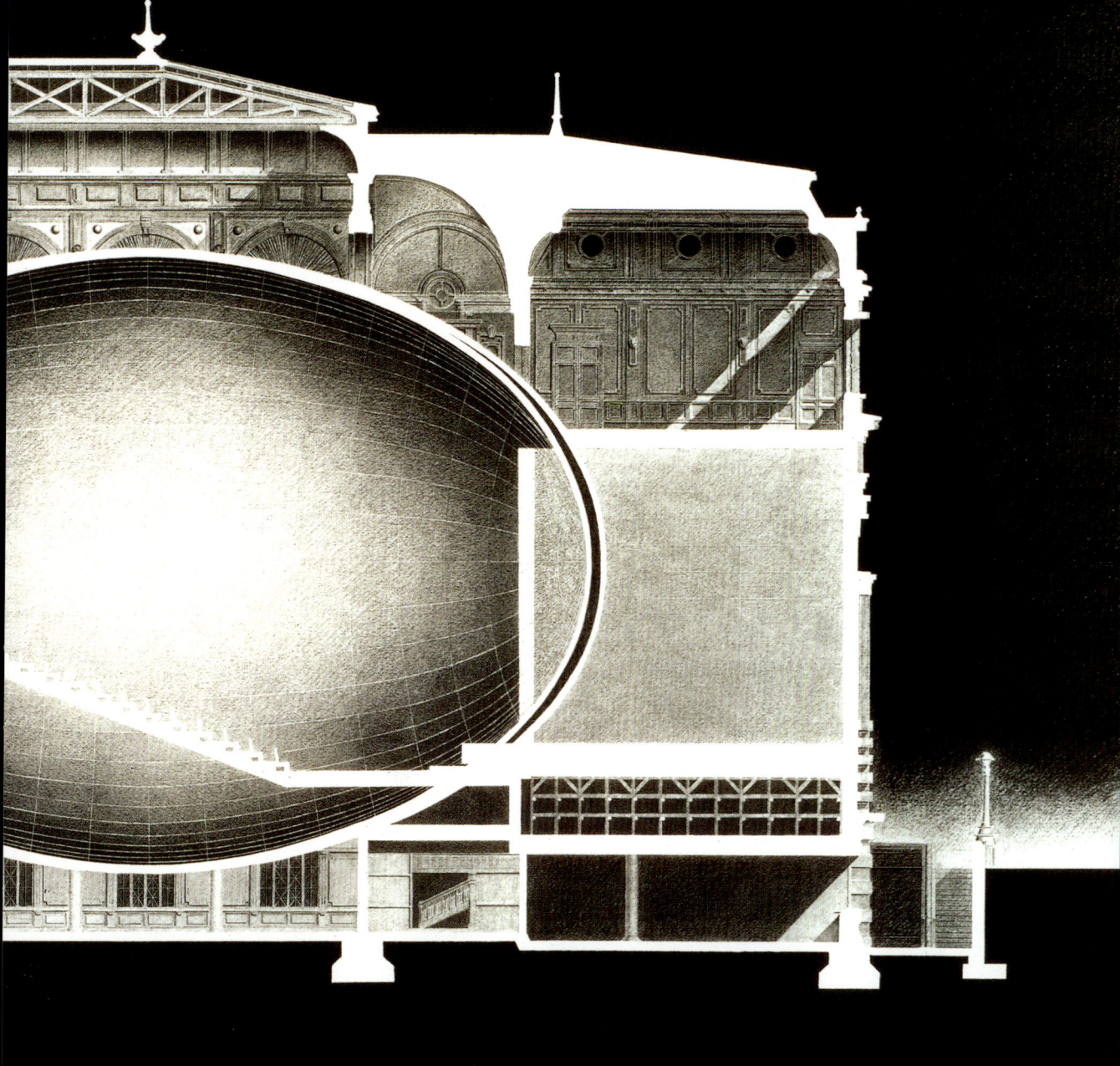

Cross-section drawing of the Urban Egg, based on a lithograph. Attention was paid to designing on the theme of a dialogue between old and new, in the delicate expression of the existing building surrounding the "egg."

097 Nakanoshima Project

リトグラフをベースに作成された「アーバン・エッグ」の平面ドローイング。入れ子状に卵型のシェルを挿入することで、新たなホール機能をもたせつつ、旧い建物の保存を図る。

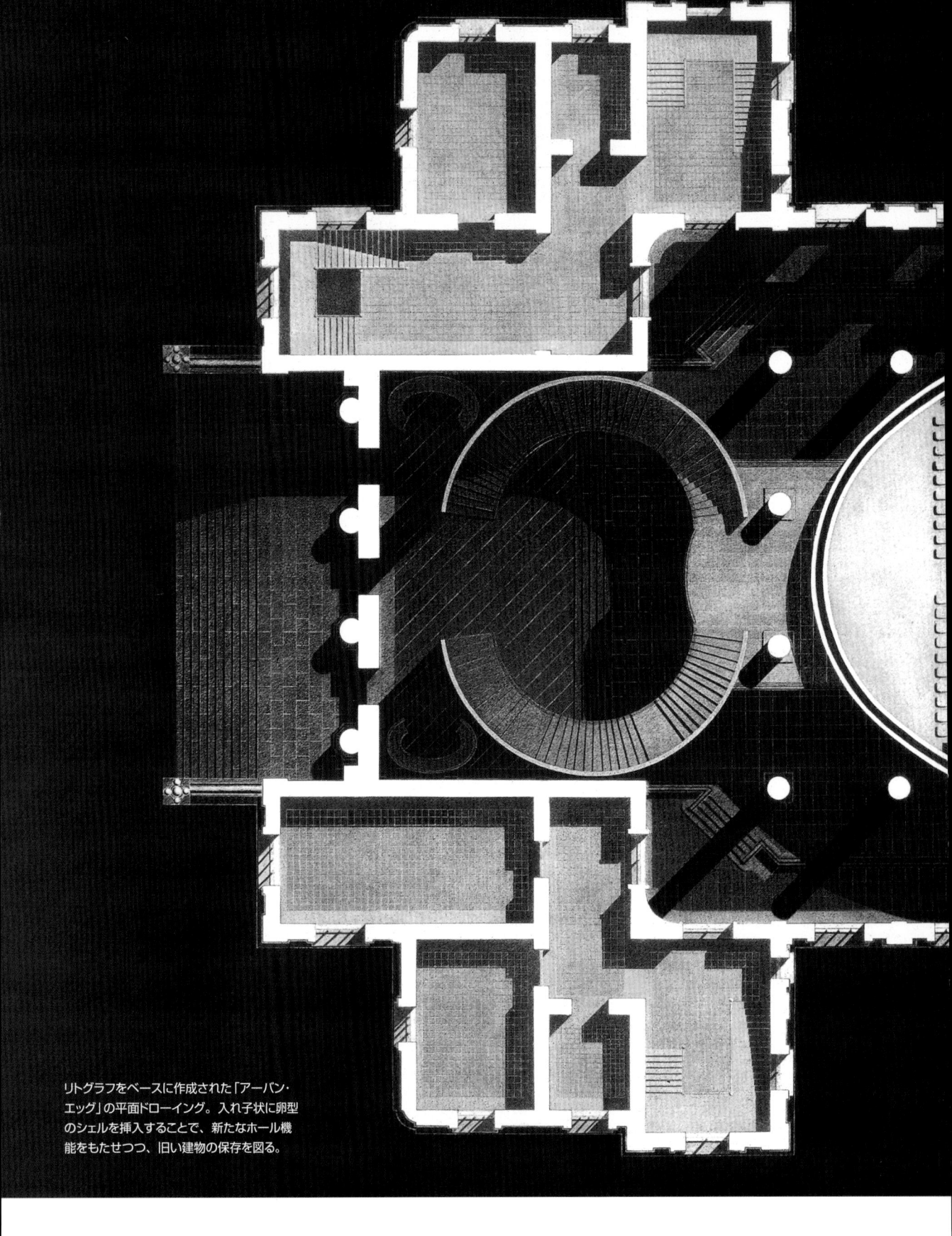

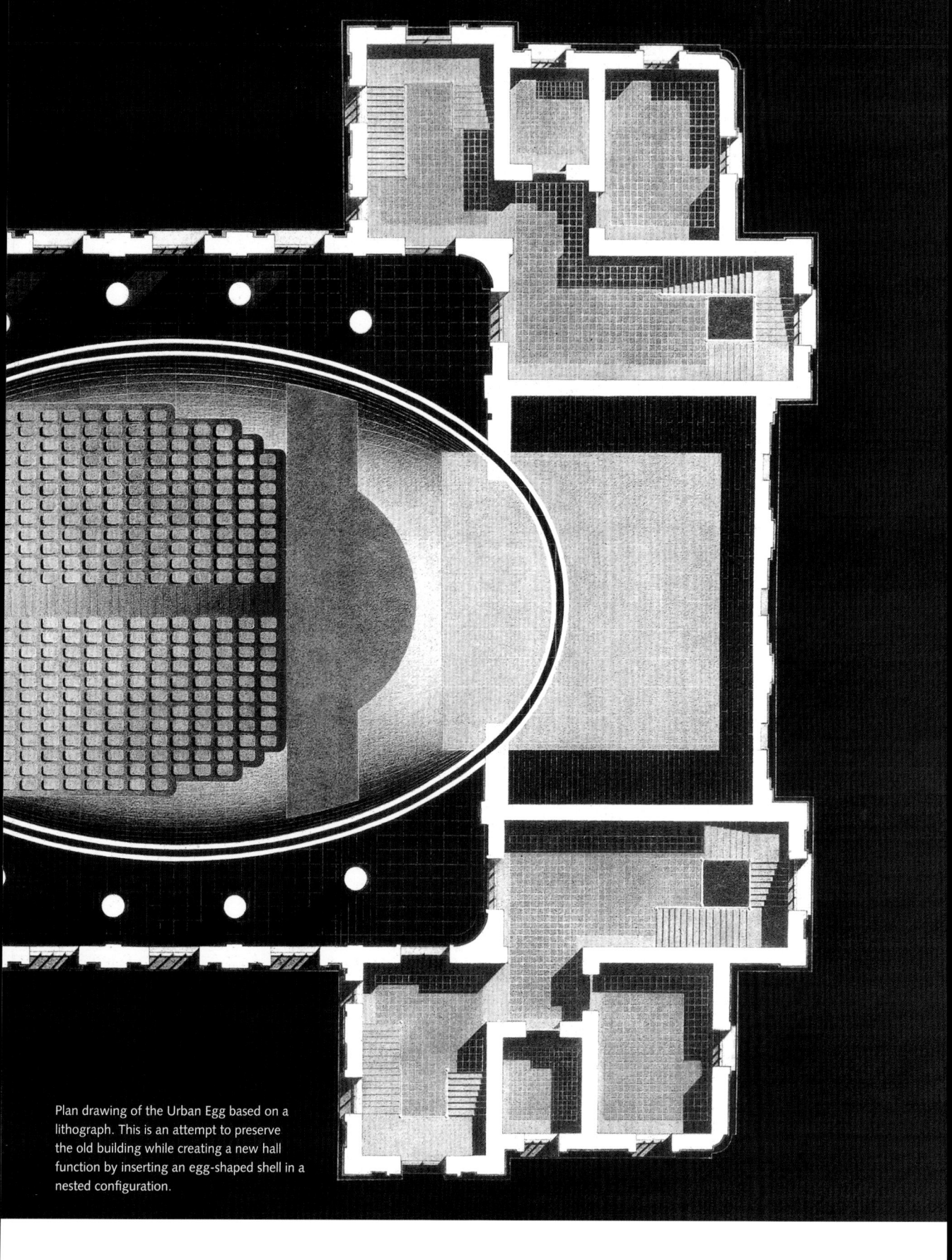

Plan drawing of the Urban Egg based on a lithograph. This is an attempt to preserve the old building while creating a new hall function by inserting an egg-shaped shell in a nested configuration.

099 Nakanoshima Project

リトグラフをベースに作成された「地層空間」のドローイング。最大幅150m、全長920mの中之島全域を建築化し、一大文化ゾーンとする壮大な計画。地上の風景をそのままに、地下へと展開するドラマチックな空間の複合体が描かれている。

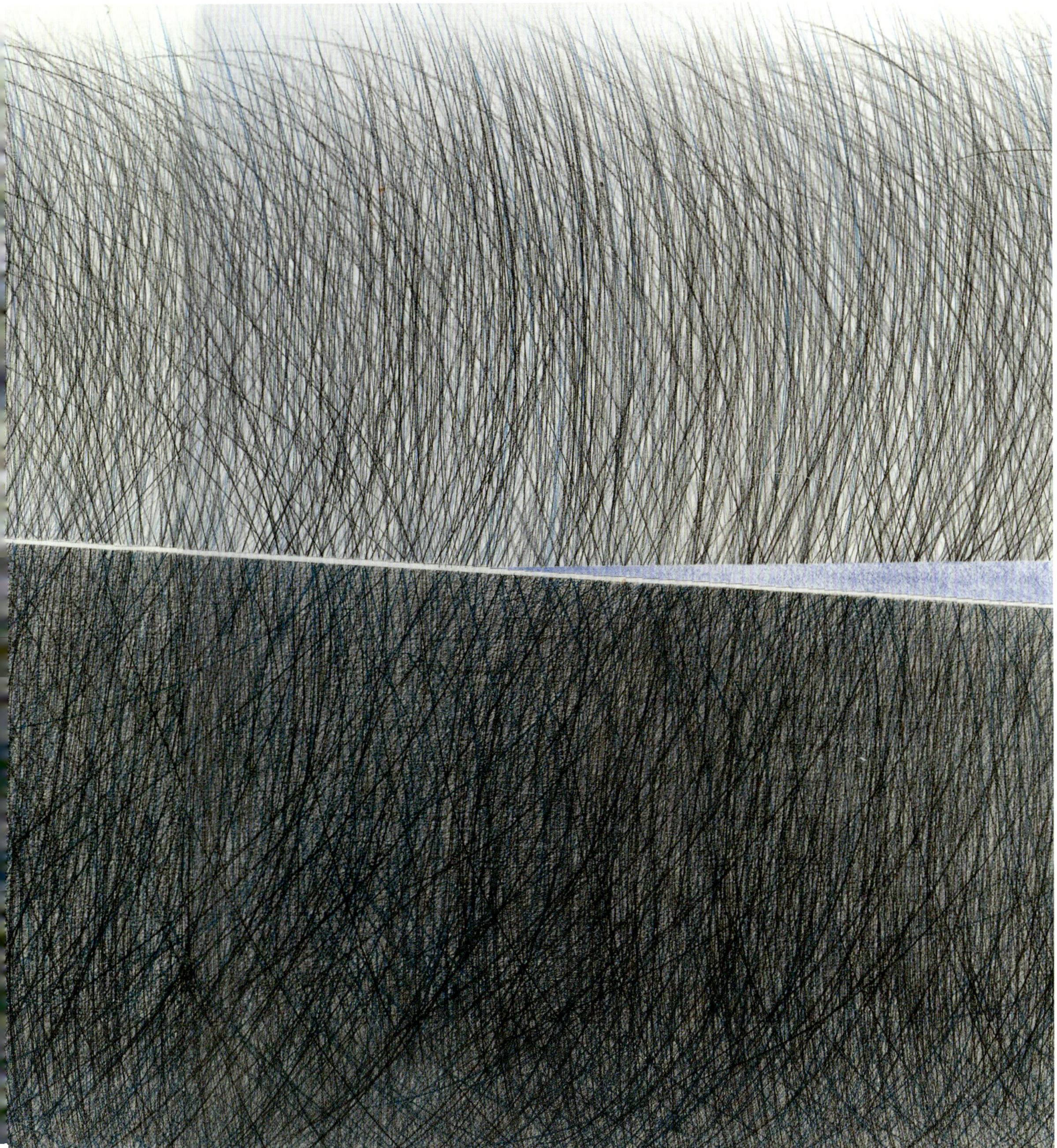

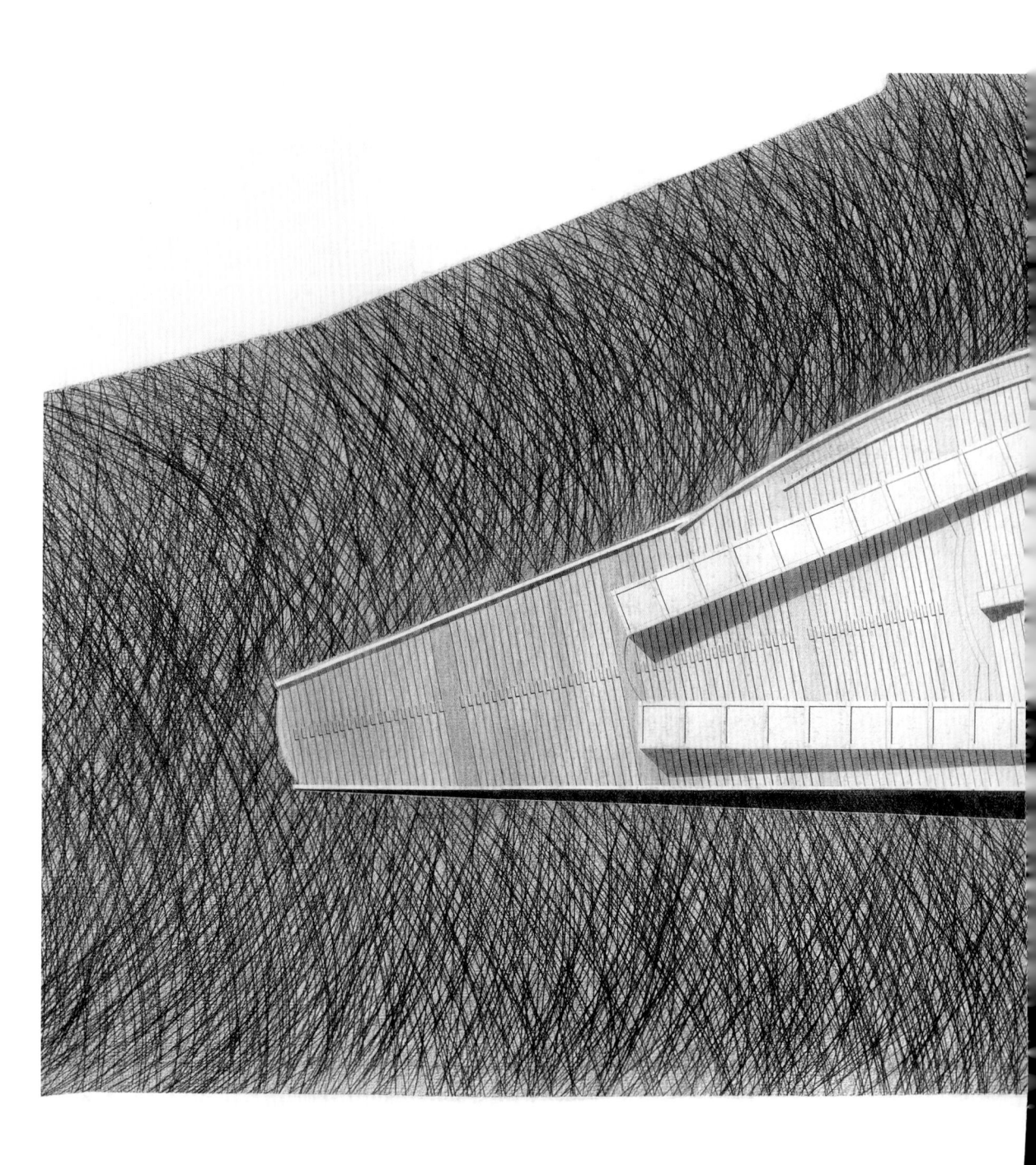

Drawing of the "Space Strata" based on a lithograph. With a maximum width of 150m and a total length of 920m, the entire island of Nakanoshima is turned into architecture, a grand plan for single large cultural zone. Depicting a dramatic spatial complex developed underground while the scenery above the ground remains unchanged.

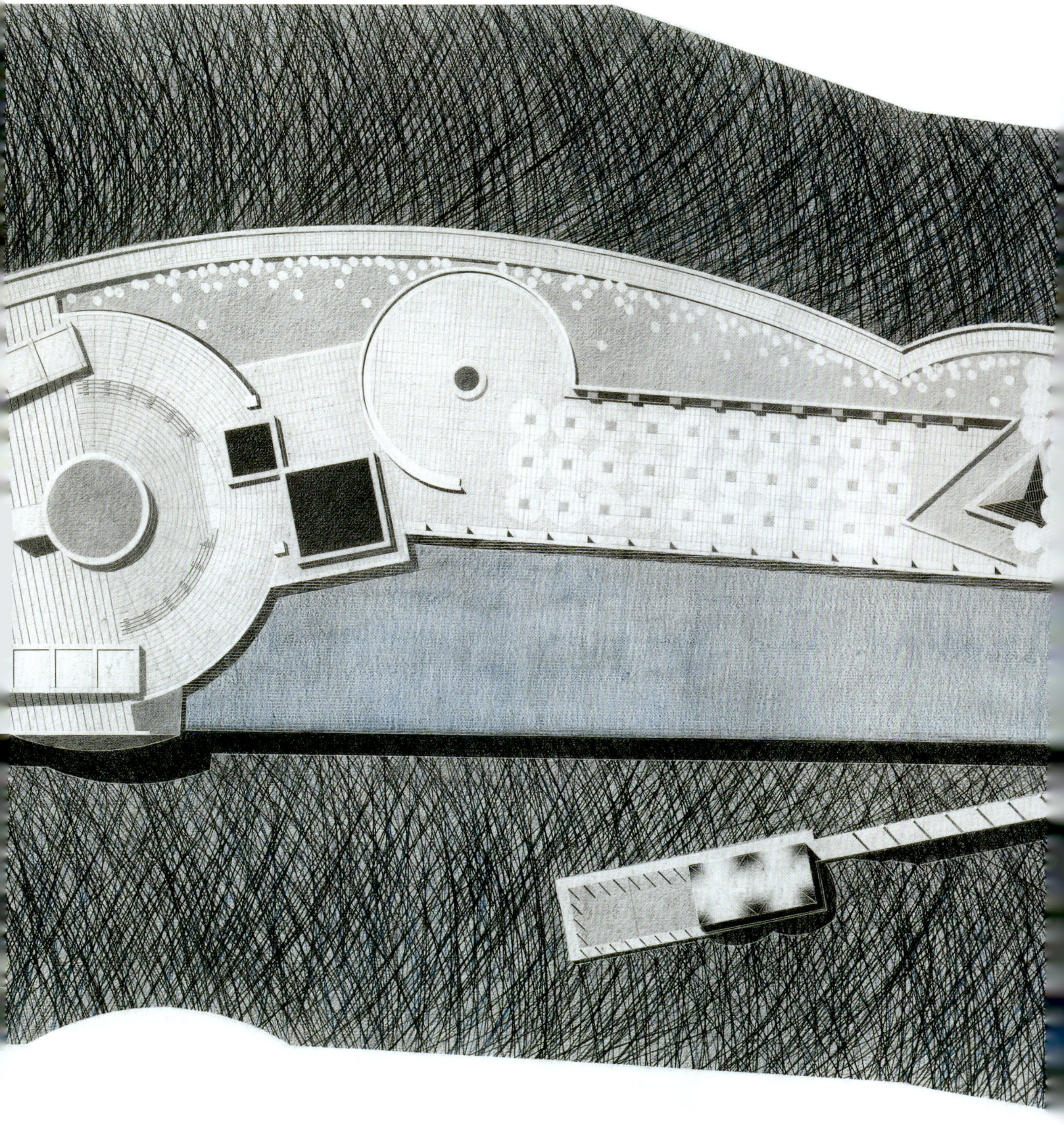

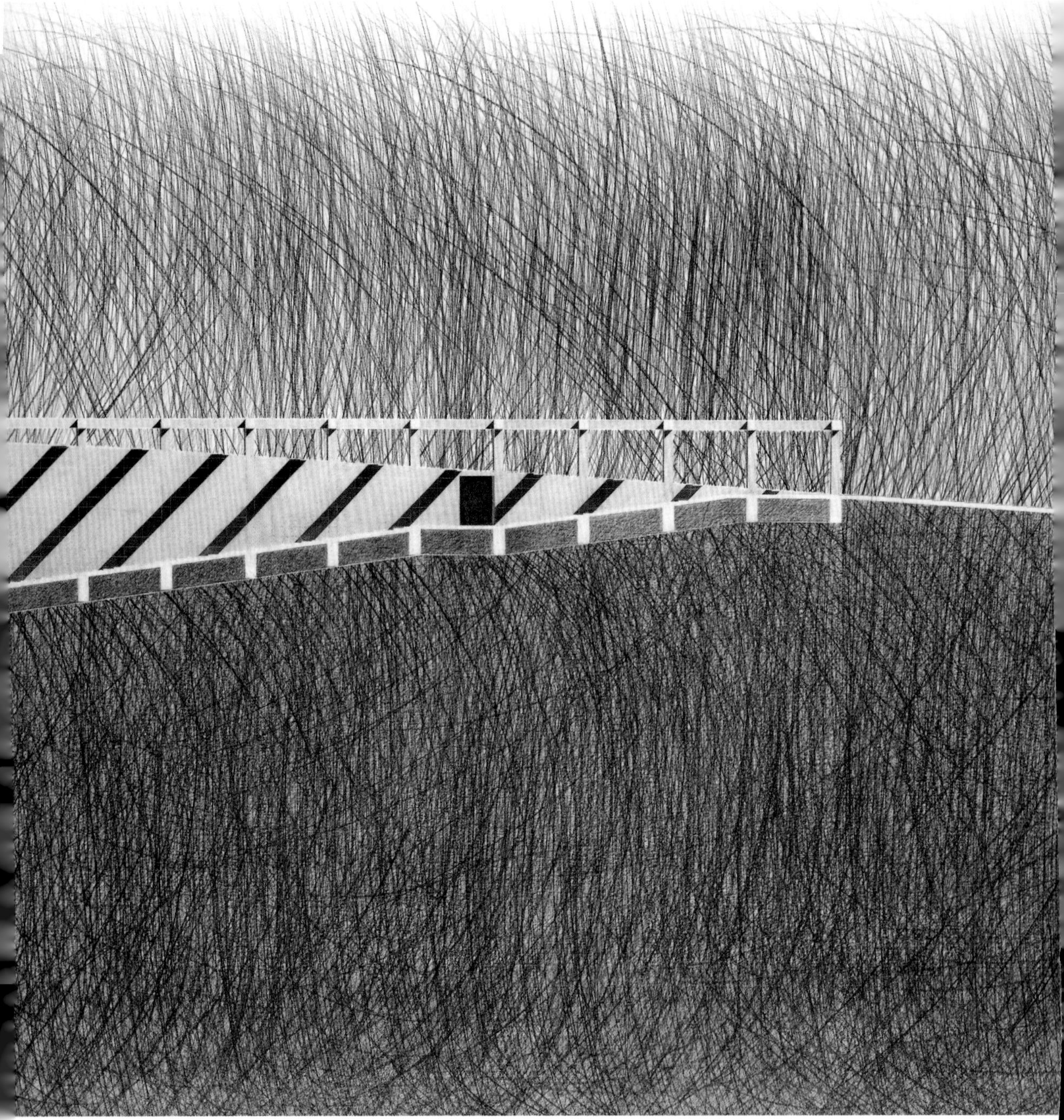

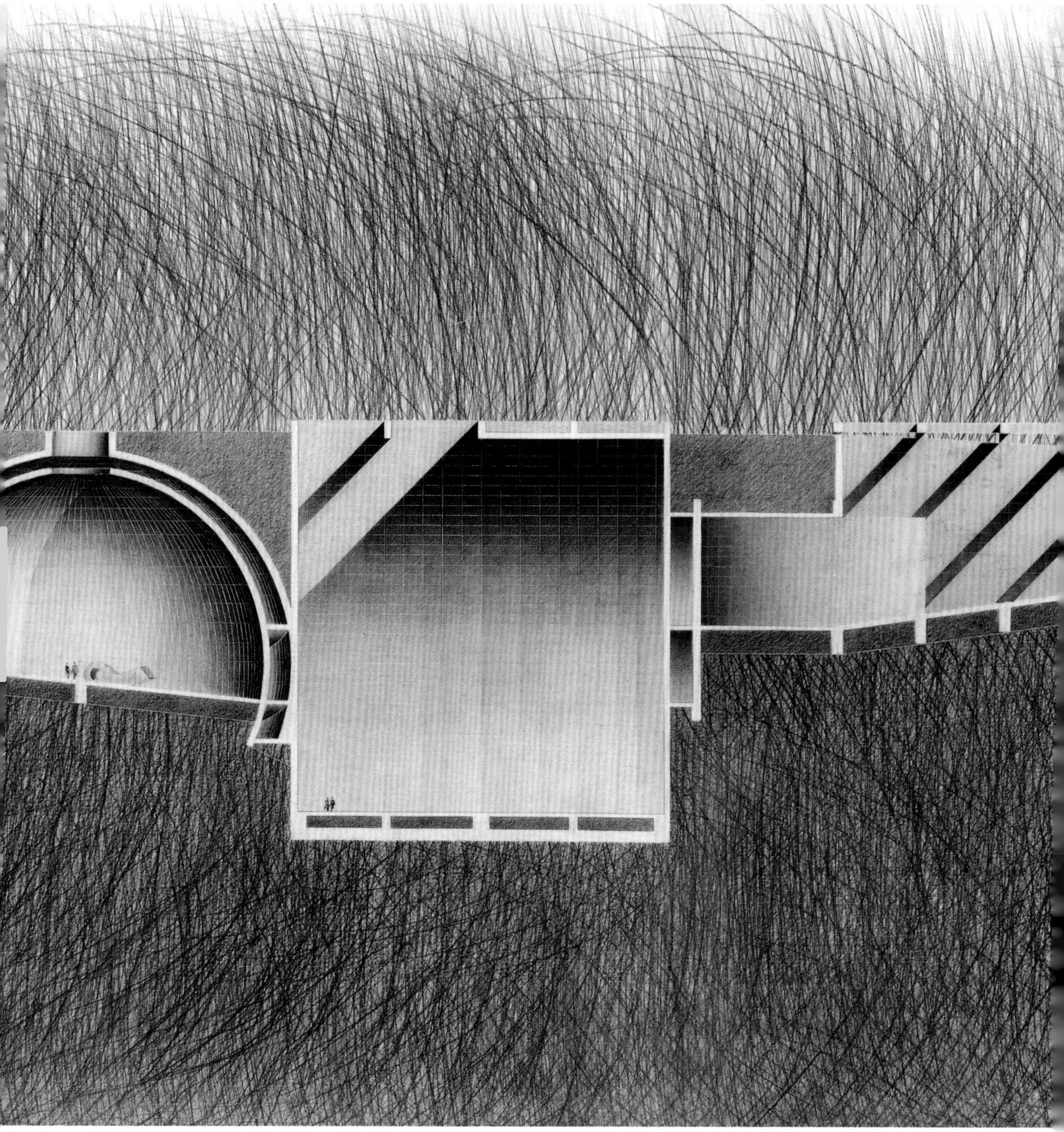

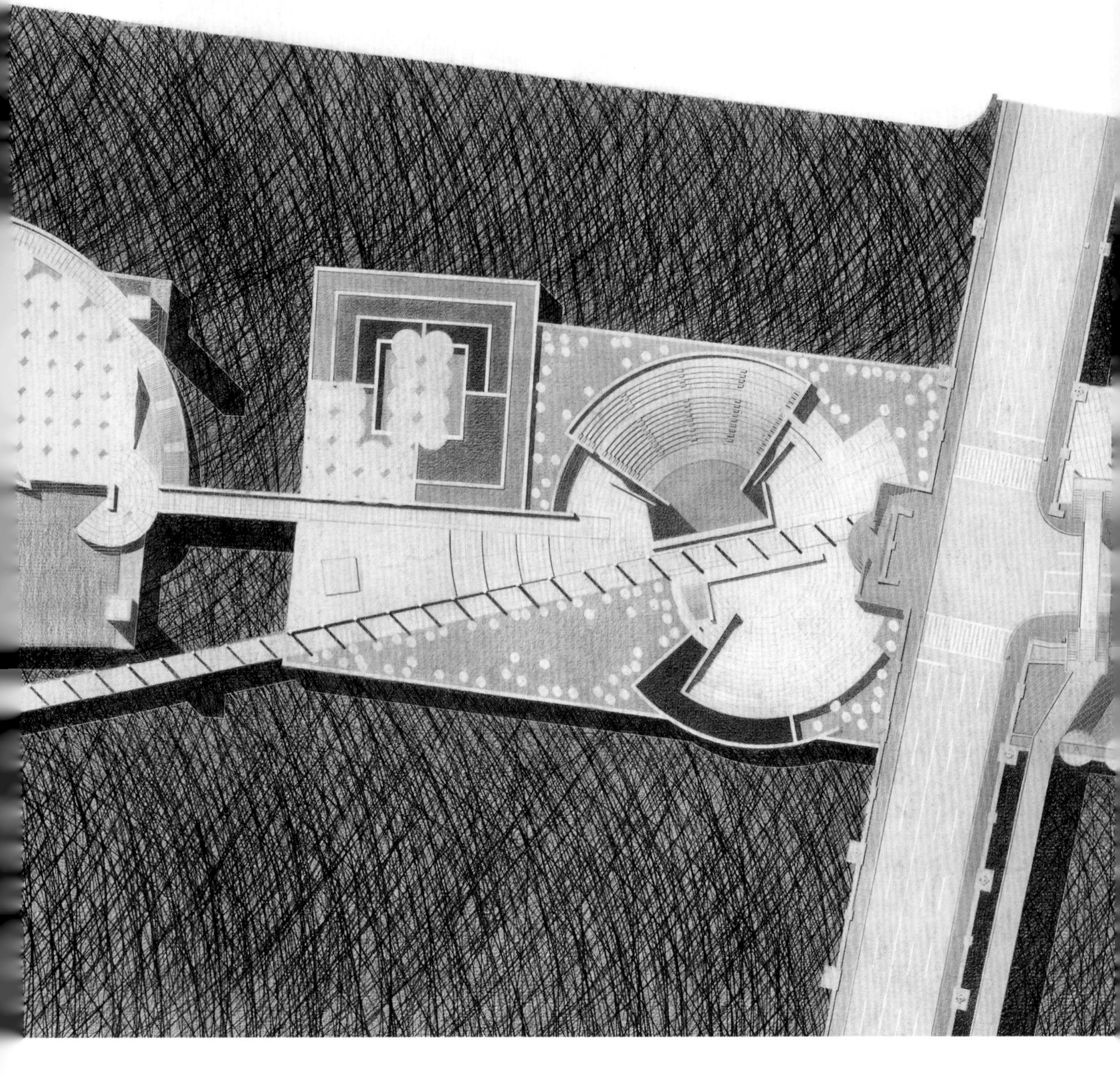

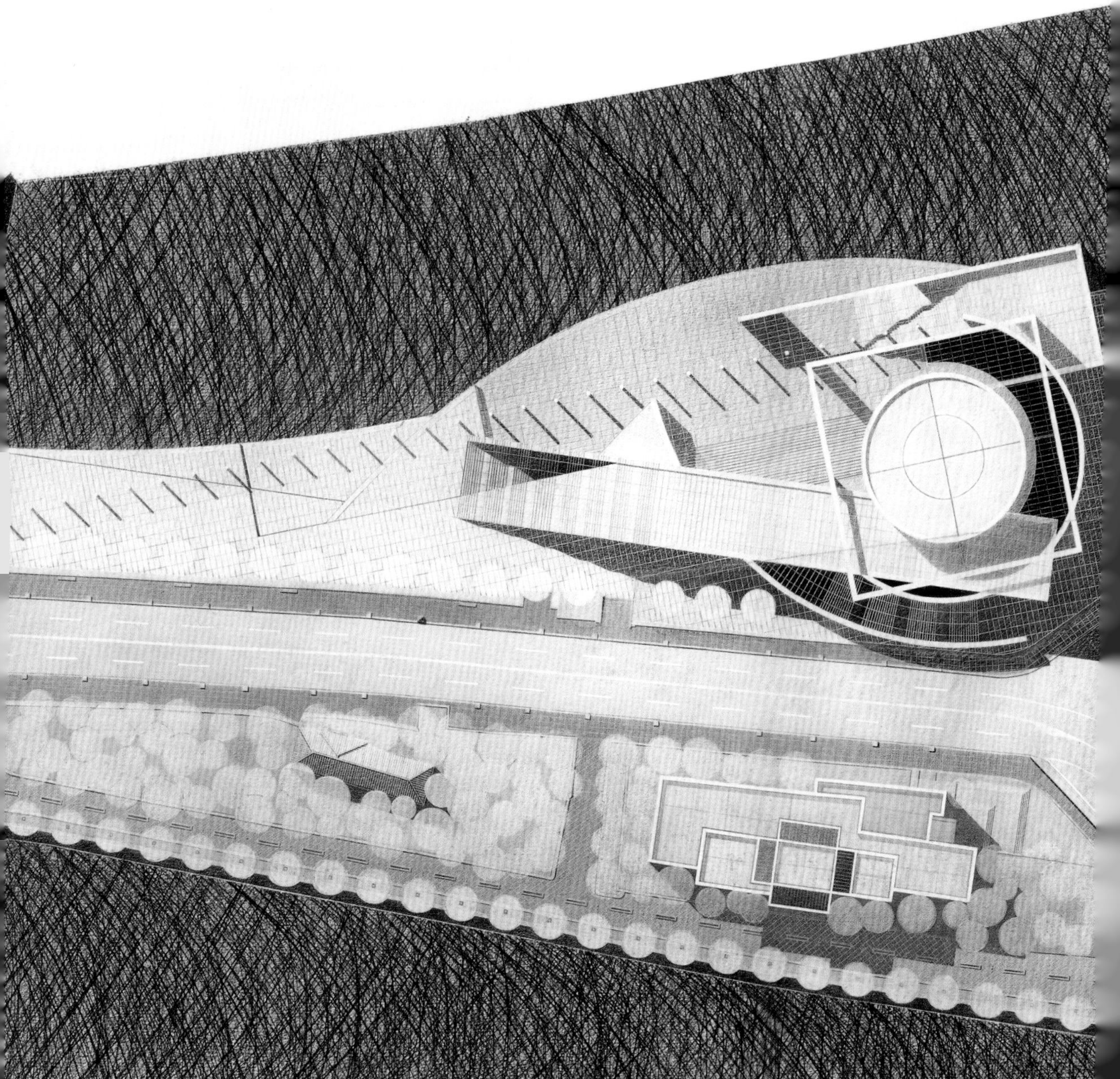

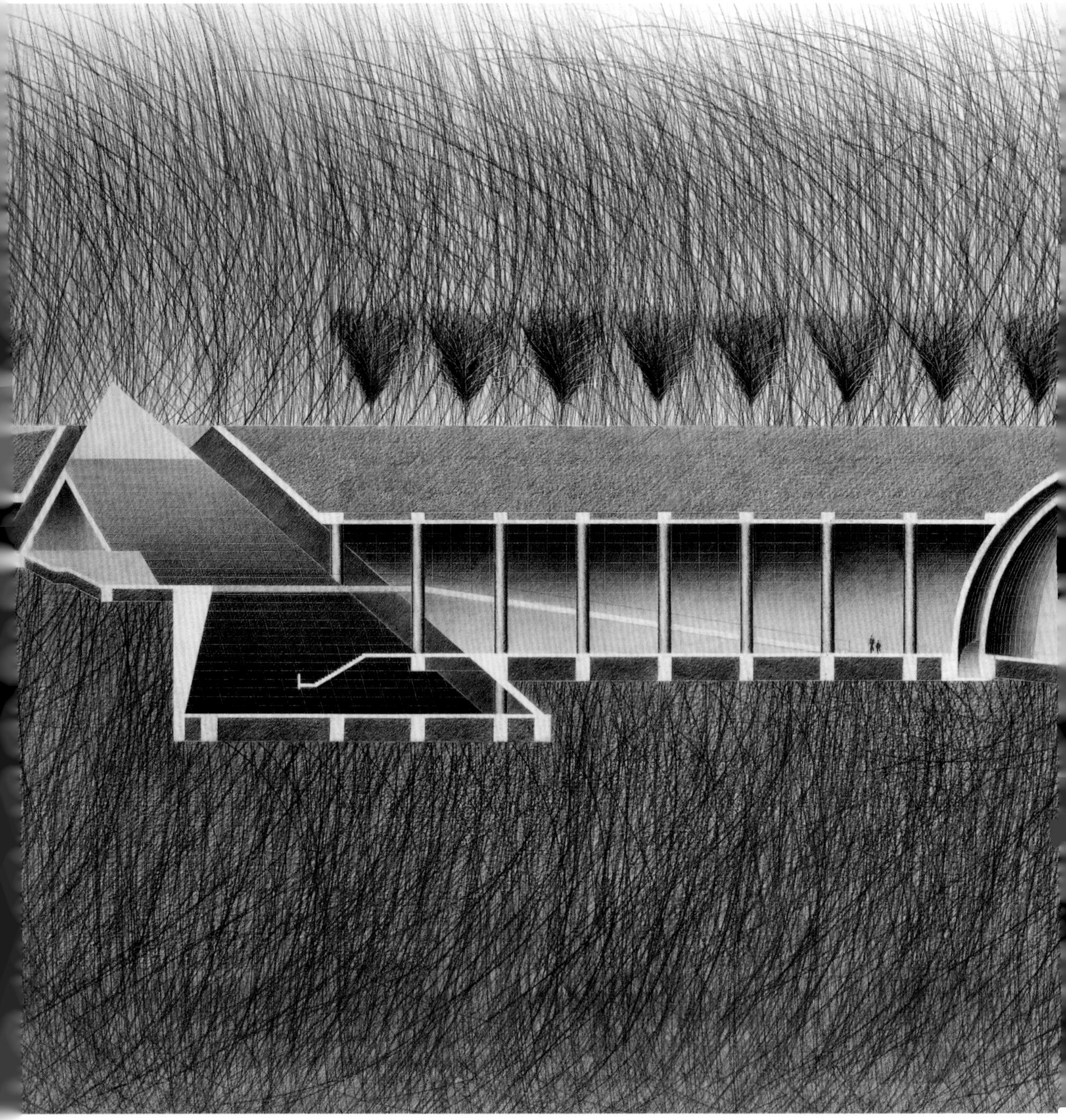

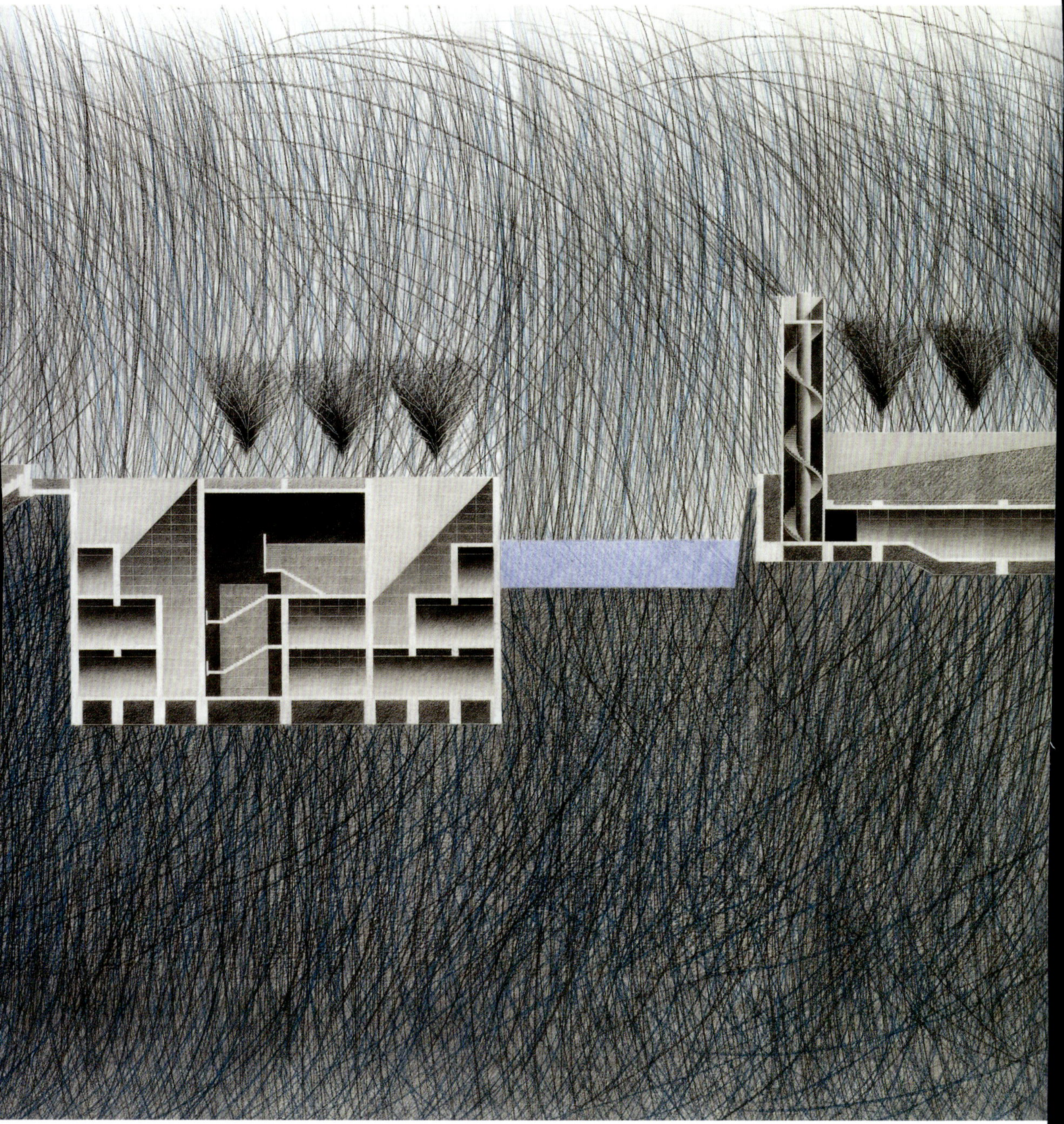

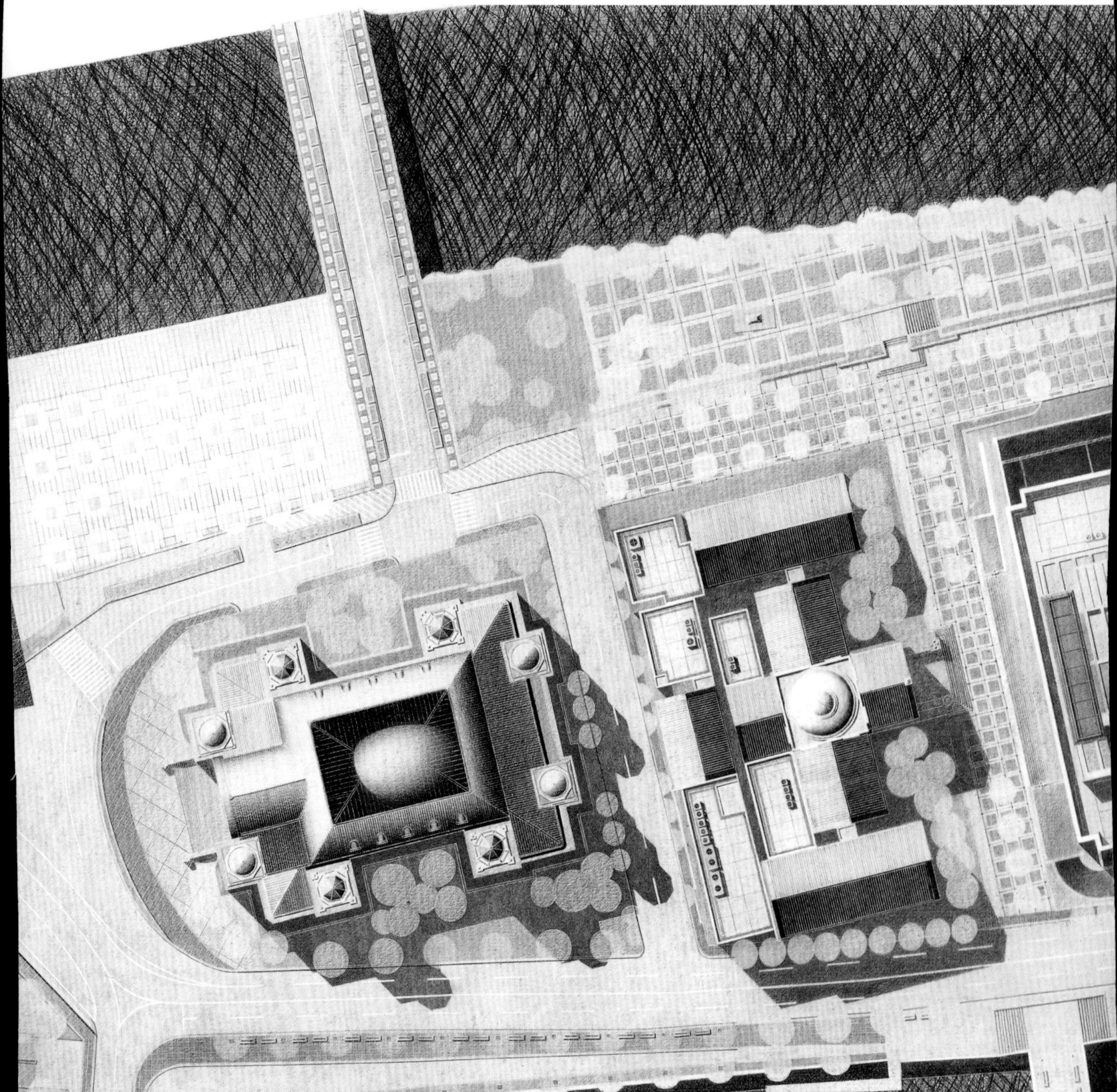

111 Nakanoshima Project

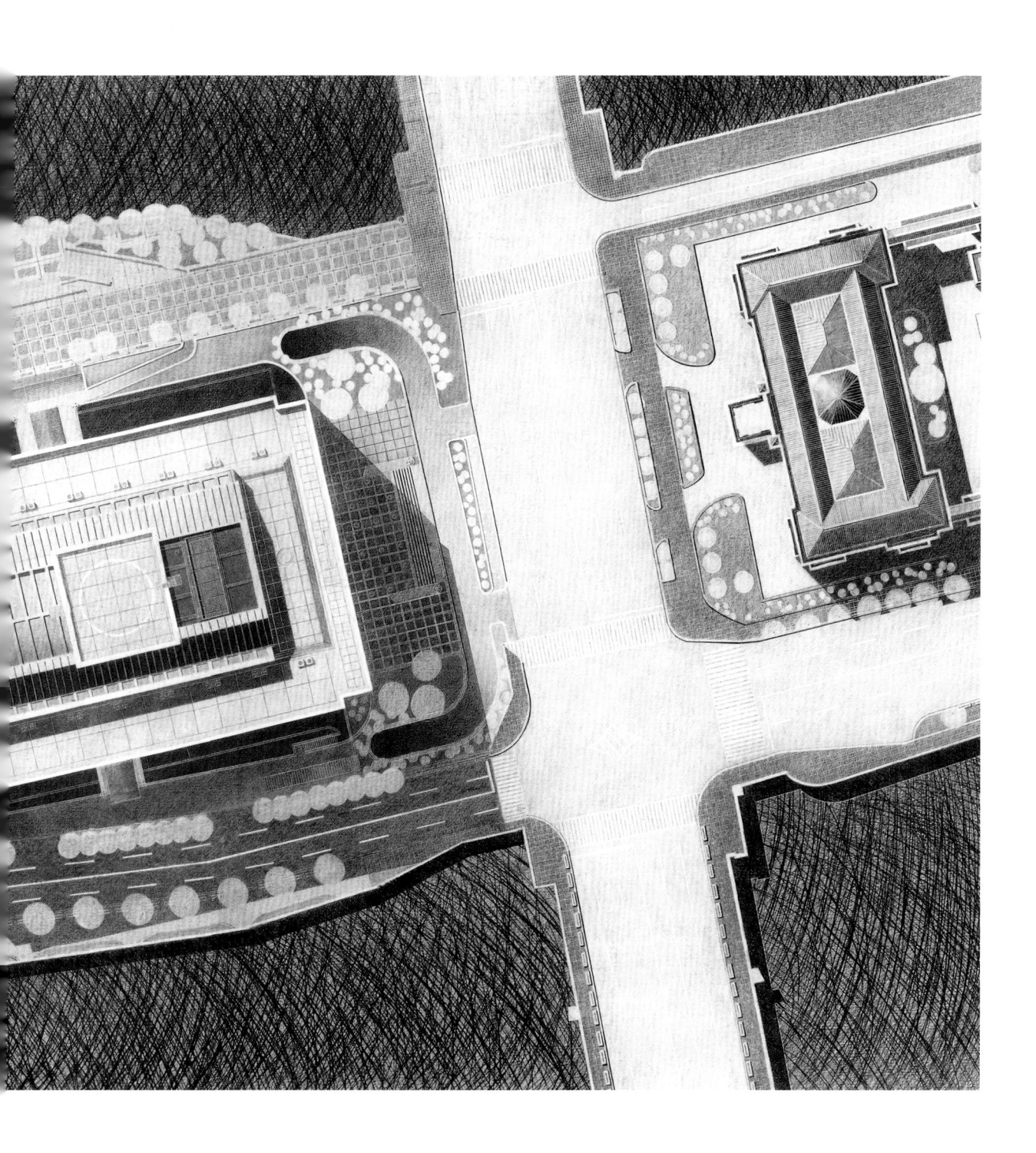

祈りの空間

20代の頃、建築を学ぼうと世界を旅していたとき
フランスでル・コルビュジエのロンシャン礼拝堂を
フィンランドでヘイッキ・シレンのオタニエミ工科大学付属礼拝堂を訪ねた。
建築家の構想力が生んだ"空間"で
人々が心をひとつにして一心に祈っている
その光景は、若い日の私に、大きな感動と、夢を与えてくれた。

「自分もいつか、人々の心に訴える、祈りの空間をつくりたい」

80年代末、ついにその"夢"に挑戦する好機が訪れた。
既成の形式、概念には一切こだわるつもりはなかった。
イメージとして抱いていたのは、ロマネスクの修道院の礼拝堂である。
修道士が、命を削り、つくりあげた石積みの建築。
その簡素極まりない空間に
ガラスもない開口部から、強い光がダイレクトに差し込み
床の石の表情を静かに照らす。
あの厳しくも美しい世界を、いかにして
コンクリートの箱の中に生み出すか——目指したのは
モノを削り落としていった先に見えてくる空間の原型
人々の心をひとつにする精神の空間である。

Space for Prayers

When, in my twenties, I traveled around the world to study architecture, I visited Le Corbusier's Notre-Dame-du-Haut Chapel at Ronchamp in France as well as the Chapel of the Technical University in Otaniemi, Finland, designed by Heikki Siren. What I saw there was people offering a devout prayer in the "space" conceived by an architect—a sight that greatly moved me and encouraged me to dream for the future.

"Someday I'd like to create prayer spaces myself that touch people's hearts."

Finally, at the end of the 1980s, I got a great opportunity to realize this "dream." I had absolutely no intention to stick to any preexisting forms and concepts. The image that I had in my mind was that of a Romanesque chapel: an architecture built by monks who devoted their lives to their mission as they laid stones. There, strong light pours directly into an extremely simple space through unglazed openings as it quietly illuminates the face of its stone floor. How could I create that space, so austere and beautiful, inside a concrete box? What I aimed at was the prototypical space that reveals itself as we shave off stuff, the space for spirit that binds people's hearts together.

水の教会
Church on the Water
1985-88　北海道勇払郡 —— Yufutsu-gun, Hokkaido

　敷地は北海道、中央山岳部の平原に位置する。水を主題とした教会の計画である。野生の樹木が生い茂る敷地周辺は、春から夏にかけては瑞々しい緑に、秋には美しい木々の紅葉に包まれ、冬には一面真っ白な銀世界となる。この豊かな自然の営みをありのままに体感できる、自然と一体化する装置として建築を考えた。

　建物は、大小ふたつの正方形を重ねたプランをもつ教会本体と、その前面に広がる人工の湖、さらに、その全域を取り囲むように配されたL字型のコンクリートの壁によって構成される。

　アプローチは、L字型の壁に沿って進む。視界を遮る長大な壁のために、はじめはかすかなせせらぎの音でしか湖の存在を確認できない。そのまま歩を進め、壁の端部で穿たれた開口部をくぐったとき、初めて視界一面に広がる水面との対面が叶う。この劇的なアプローチの演出が、日常から非日常へ、訪れる人々の意識を切り替える。

　水際を歩いて建物に辿り着き、ガラスボックスを冠した光溢れるエントランスを経て、円弧状の暗い階段を降りてゆくと、そこが礼拝堂である。黒御影石の貼られた床の先には、わずかな風にもさざなむ水面が広がり、その中央には、そこが礼拝堂の一部であることを告げる十字架がひっそりと打ち立てられている。壮大な自然の風景の中に身体が溶け込んでいくような、不思議な感動が人々を包み込む。

　宗教建築という聖なる空間の主題とともに、当時考え始めていた〈環境と一体化する建築〉を存分に試み得た、稀有の仕事の機会だった。

The site is located on a plain in a mountainous area in central Hokkaido. This is a proposal for a church in which the main theme is water. The site environment is overgrown with wild trees and shrubs. It is covered in fresh green from spring to summer, and in the beautiful changing colors of leaves in autumn. In winter, it becomes a snowscape with a single, pure white surface. I conceived the architecture as an installation unified with nature, allowing this abundant natural life to be sensed directly.

　The building comprises the church itself, which is planned as a small square overlapping a large square, an artificial lake that extends in front, and an L-shaped concrete wall placed as if enclosing the entire area.

　The approach route follows the L-shaped wall. Because this very long wall obstructs the field of view, the existence of the lake can only be ascertained at first by a faint murmuring sound. Walking further and passing the opening that pierces the end of the wall, one is confronted for the first time with a broad body of water filling the view. This dramatic approach route shifts the consciousness of visitors from ordinary to extraordinary.

Walking along the water's edge and finally reaching the building, passing the light-filled entrance crowned with glass blocks, and descending the dark, curving stairs, one reaches the worship hall. Beyond the black granite-paved floor extends the water surface, ruffled by slight breezes, in the center of which stands a solitary cross denoting that this is also part of the worship hall. People are enveloped in a mysterious sensation, as if their bodies are melting into the magnificent natural scenery.

　Together with the theme of sacred space in religious architecture, this was a rare opportunity for free experimentation in "architecture unified with nature," a topic I started to think about at that time.

サイトドローイング。北国の大自然の中に、静寂な空白の場を切り取る純粋幾何学の建築。
Site drawing. A simple geometric architecture framing a silent, empty space within the natural environment of this northern region.

礼拝堂前面の大型ガラス戸越しに望む。吹きすさぶ雪で霞む真冬の北海道を背景に、水上の十字架が揺らぐ。

View through the large glass doors at the front of the worship hall. The cross shimmers above the water in the midwinter Hokkaido scenery, made hazy by gusts of snow.

plan 1:1,000

雪に覆われた大自然と対峙する礼拝堂。前面開口部から7.5mの位置にスチール型鋼の十字架が象徴的に浮かぶ。

The worship hall confronts the natural world covered with snow. A cross of steel beams floats symbolically at a location 7.5m from the front opening.

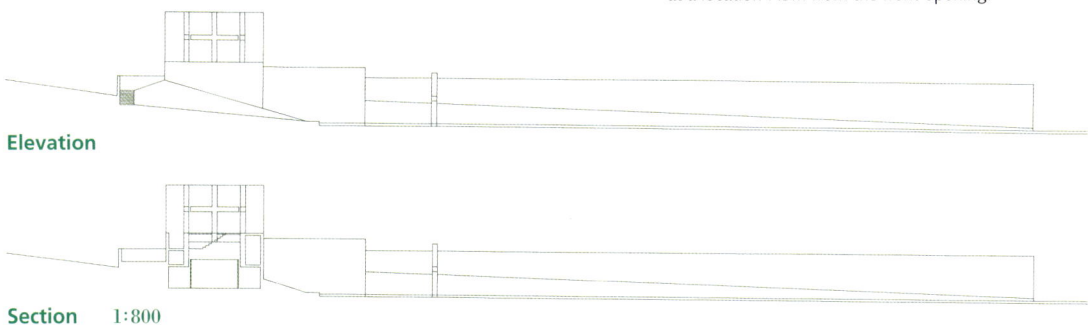

Elevation

Section 1:800

Church on the Water

黒御影石張りの床と、三方コンクリート打ち放しの面に囲まれた、最小限の空間。
厳しい寒冷地での内外打ち放しコンクリートの表現を可能にする二重壁構造や床暖
房の設えなど、結晶のような空間の背後には、多大な技術的工夫が隠されている。

The smallest space has a black granite lined floor and is surrounded on
three sides by exposed concrete. To allow an exposed concrete expression on
the inside as well as the outside in this extremely cold region, various technical
devices are concealed behind this crystal-like space, such as floor heating
equipment and a two-layered wall structure.

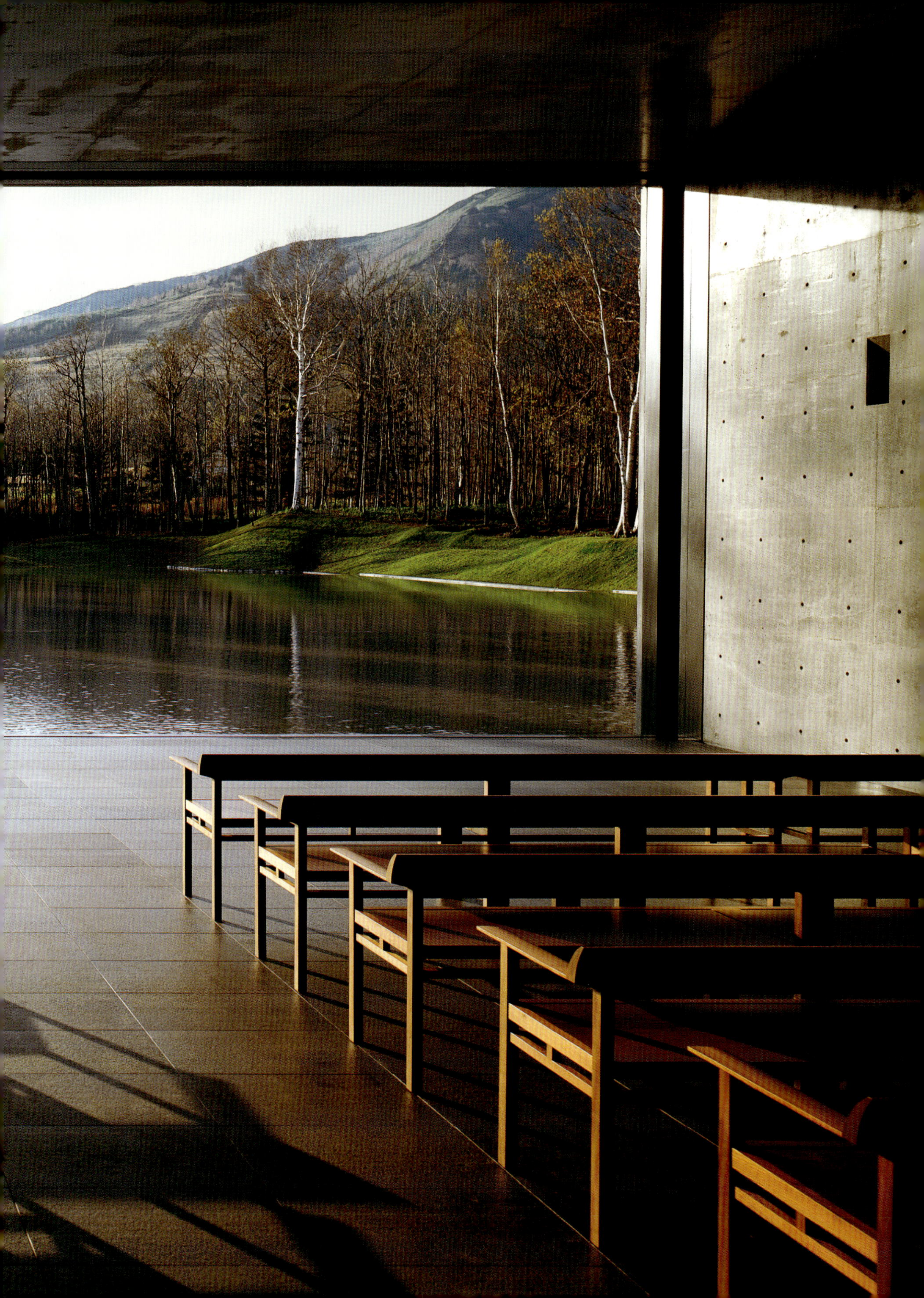

人工湖越しに建物を見る。礼拝堂前面のガラス開口部は巨大な吊戸となっており、水上に架けられたフレーム方向に引くと、全面開放が可能である。

Looking at the building across the artificial lake. The glazed opening in the facade of the worship hall is a huge hanging door, which can be opened entirely by pulling it toward the frame suspended above the water.

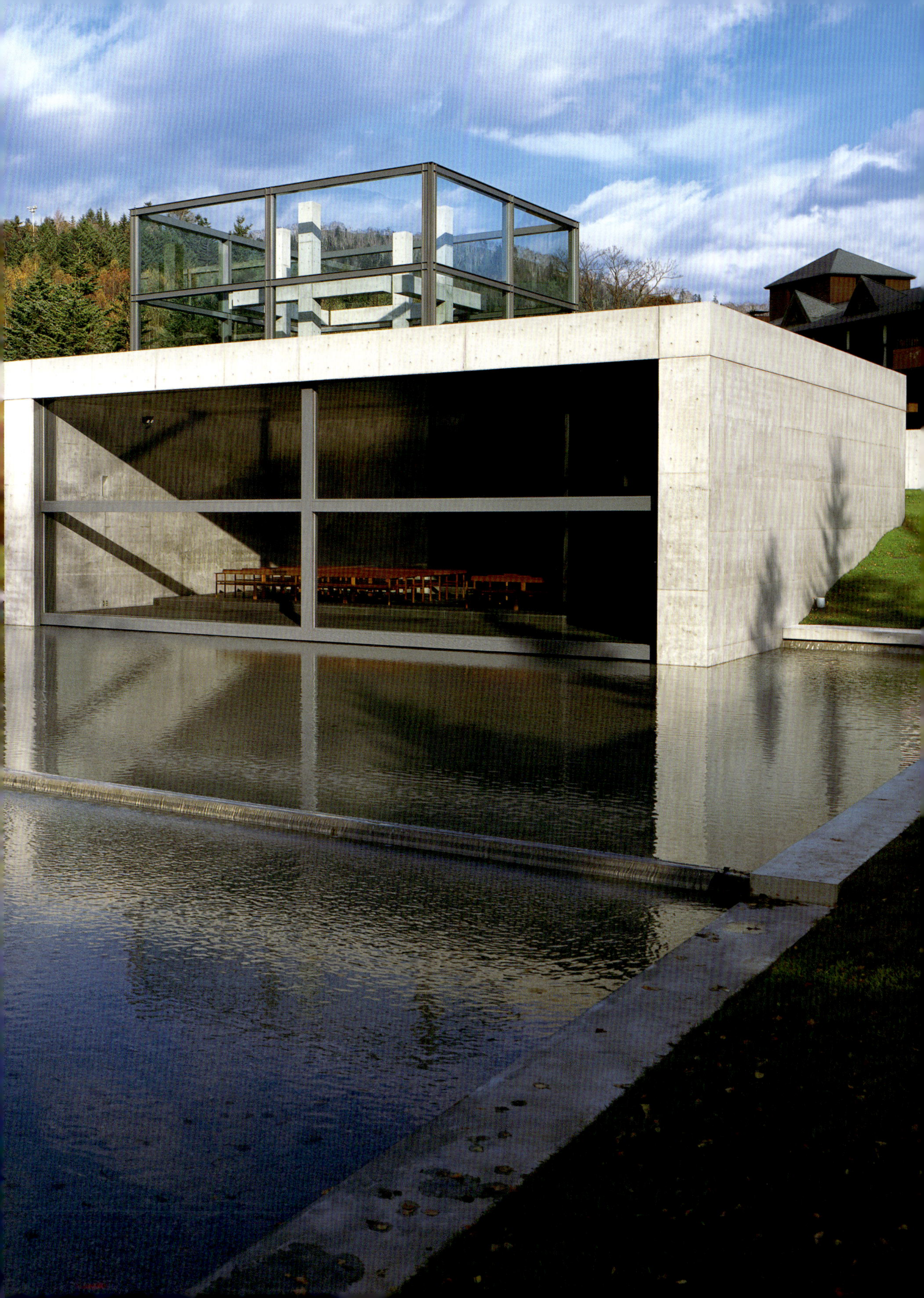

訪問者は四方に自立する十字架に囲まれたガラスの箱を経て、円弧の壁で囲われた階段を降り、そしてついに礼拝堂に辿り着く。聖俗領域の境を告げる、空間の明暗のコントラスト。

The visitors pass through a glass box enclosing a cross that is freestanding on all four sides, descend the steps contained within an arc-shaped wall, and finally arrive at the worship hall. The contrast of light and dark spaces indicates the boundary between the sacred and the profane realms.

Axonometric

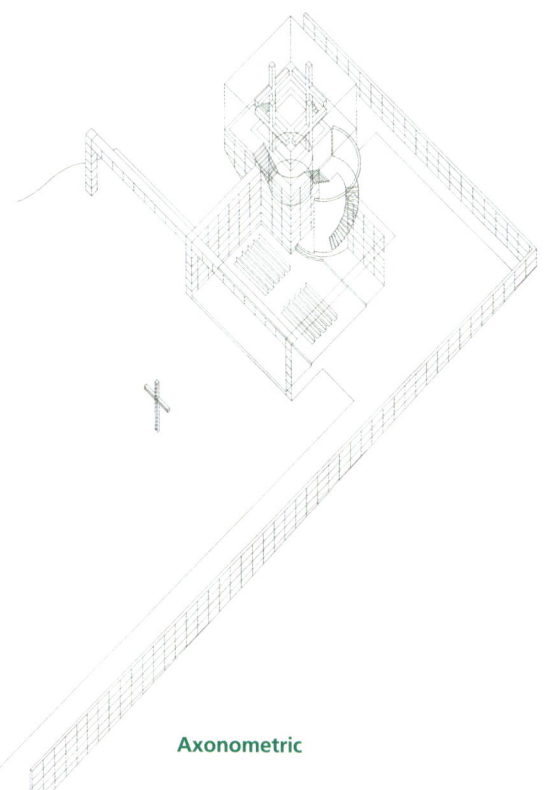

大小ふたつの正方形平面と、領域を囲い取るL字型の自立壁による構成。延々と続くアプローチを導く壁が、大自然の只中に静寂な空白の場を切り取る。

A composition comprising two square planes of different sizes and a freestanding L-shaped wall surrounding the area. The wall guides the meandering approach route, and sequesters a silent, empty space in the midst of nature.

Church on the Water

2枚のスラブが、さざなむ水庭越しに雄大な秋の風景を切り取る。礼拝堂との一体感、微妙な水面の表情を出すために、人工湖の水深設定には細心の注意が払われている。

Two slabs frame the magnificent autumn scenery across the tranquil water garden. In order to draw out the subtle expression of the water surface and a sense of unity with the worship hall, careful attention was paid to setting the depth of the water in the artificial lake.

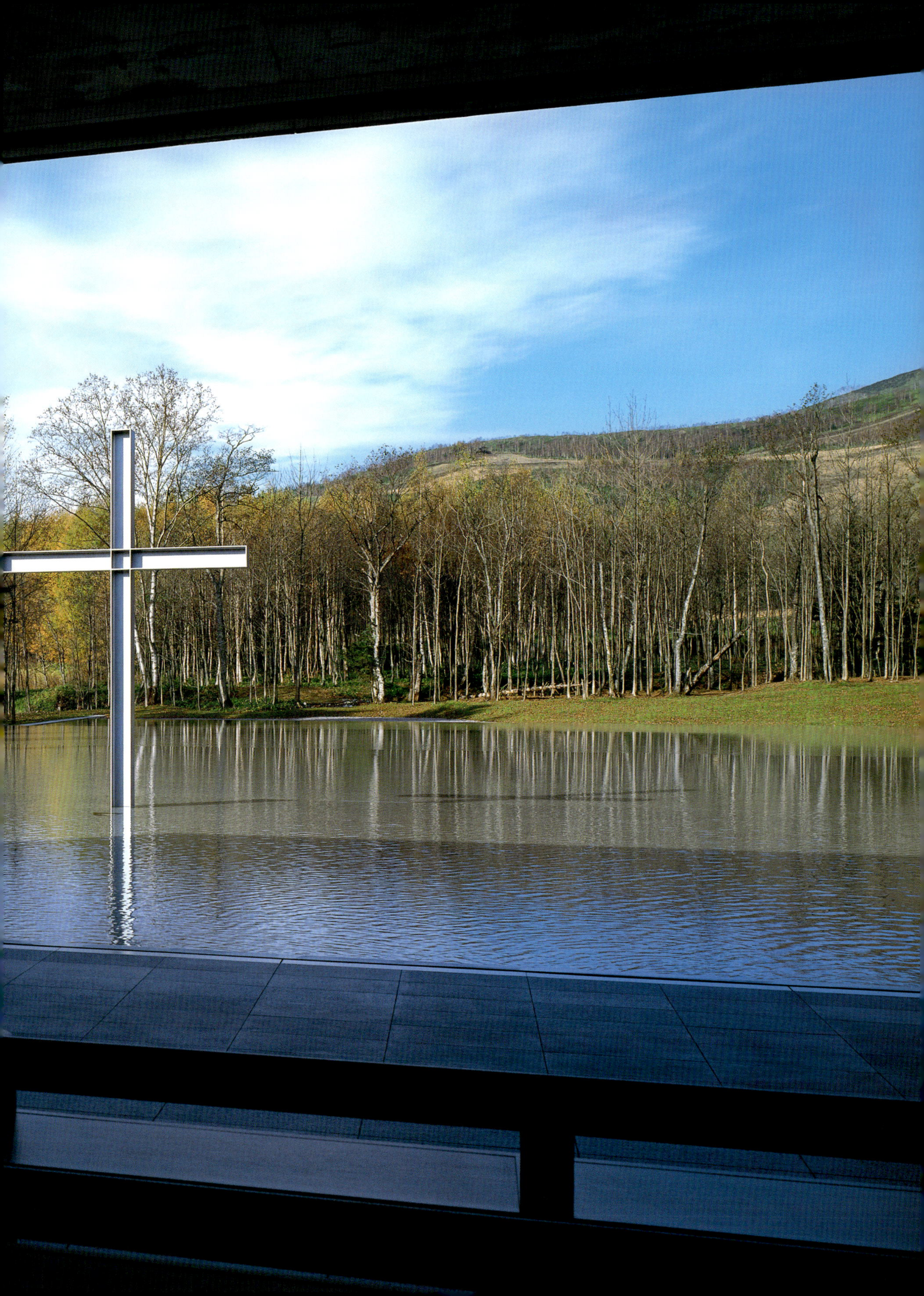

光の教会
Church of the Light

1987-89　大阪府茨木市——Ibaraki, Osaka

　依頼を受けたのは1987年、ちょうど「水の教会」の計画のスタートと同じ時期である。北海道の大自然に包まれた景勝地で、プログラムも比較的自由に考えることが許された「水の教会」に対し、大阪・茨木市に建設を依頼された教会は、規模は小さく、立地環境もごく普通の郊外住宅地、予算も実に心許ない。厳しい条件であったが、新たな建築を願う信者たちの強い思いに打たれ、仕事を引き受けた。

　限られた予算のため、建物は単純な箱型とせざるを得なかった。ならばその箱の中に、いかにして人々が集い、祈りを捧げる場所に相応しい、神聖な空間を生み出すか。1年間余り考えた末に辿り着いたのが、1枚のコンクリートの壁が箱を斜めに貫き、内部を階段状に床を掘り下げたワンルームの礼拝堂とエントランス部分とに分節する構成である。

　冷暖房の設備もない、内外コンクリート打ち放しの堂内に置かれるモノは、素朴な素材感の説教壇とベンチのみ。装飾的な要素は一切ない、極限まで削ぎ落とされた裸形の空間にあって、唯一正面の壁に穿たれた十字の切り込みが、薄暗い空間に教会のシンボルを映し出す——光の教会。

　与条件の厳しさを逆手に取ったアイディアだったが、プロジェクトの真の困難は、その次の段階、現実に建物をつくり上げていく建設の過程にあった。何とか工事をスタートしたものの、資金不足は決定的であり、ついには、壁までで工事を終え、屋根のない野外礼拝堂とする代案まで考えるに至った。

　だが、信者の熱意と、それに応えるべく奮起した建設会社のモノづくりとしての誇りによって、工事は完遂された。
　この小さな建築のプロセスは、人間の思いが、時に経済をも乗り超え得るという偉大な事実の証明であった。

I received this commission in 1987, at exactly the same time that I started the design of the Water Chapel. Compared with the Water Chapel, which is surrounded by the abundant picturesque natural scenery of Hokkaido and for which I was permitted to think about the program with relative freedom, the church design commissioned for Ibaraki in Osaka is small in scale, with a generic suburban residential district as the site environment, and a truly precarious budget. These conditions were severe, but I was struck by the strong wills of the faithful who were requesting the new building, so I took on the job.

Because of the limited budget, the building was unavoidably a simple box shape. How to bring forth a sacred space within this box, appropriate for a place where people gather and pray? After thinking hard for more than a year, I arrived at a composition in which a concrete wall diagonally cuts through the box, dividing the entrance from the single-space worship hall, which has a descending stepped floor.

Without heating or cooling equipment, the bare concrete hall contains only pews and a pulpit made of simple, untouched materials. With absolutely no ornamental elements, it is a naked space reduced to the limit. Only a cross-shaped incision in the front wall projects the symbol of the church into this gloomy space: Church of the Light.

The idea was to take advantage of the severity of the given conditions, but the real difficulty of the project was in the next stage, the process of actually constructing the building. Somehow, once construction had started the lack of funds became conclusive, and construction was finally stopped after the walls had been completed. I even had to consider an alternative plan for an open-air worship hall without a roof.

However, construction was completed due to the enthusiasm of the believers and the response this drew from the construction company, who have produced something worthy of pride.

The process of producing this small work of architecture is great proof that human will can sometimes transcend economic issues.

礼拝堂の平面ドローイング。厳格な幾何学の支配する緊張感に満ちた〈簡素〉な空間。
Plan drawing of the worship hall. A "simple" space imbued with a sense of tension dominated by a strict geometry.

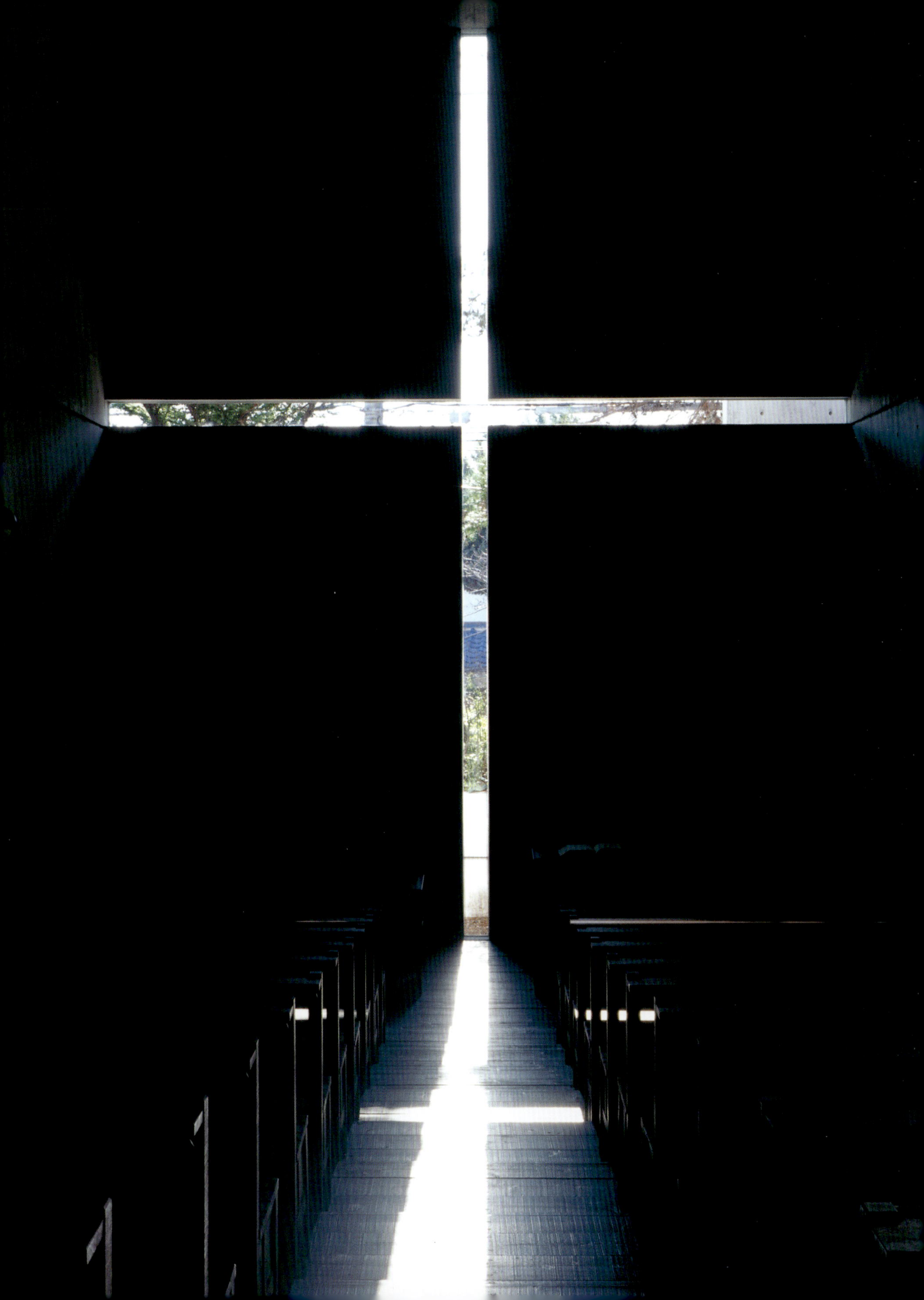

箱に貫入する壁がつくり出す開口部からの光。

Light from the opening created by the wall piercing the box.

時とともに移ろう自然の光が、単純なコンクリートの箱に
多様な表情を与える。

The natural light moves as time passes, giving varying
expressions to the simple concrete box.

黒のオイルステインで塗り込められた荒々しい
足場板の床に、光の十字架が描かれる。

A cross of light is delineated on the floor of rough
wooden planks coated with a black oil stain.

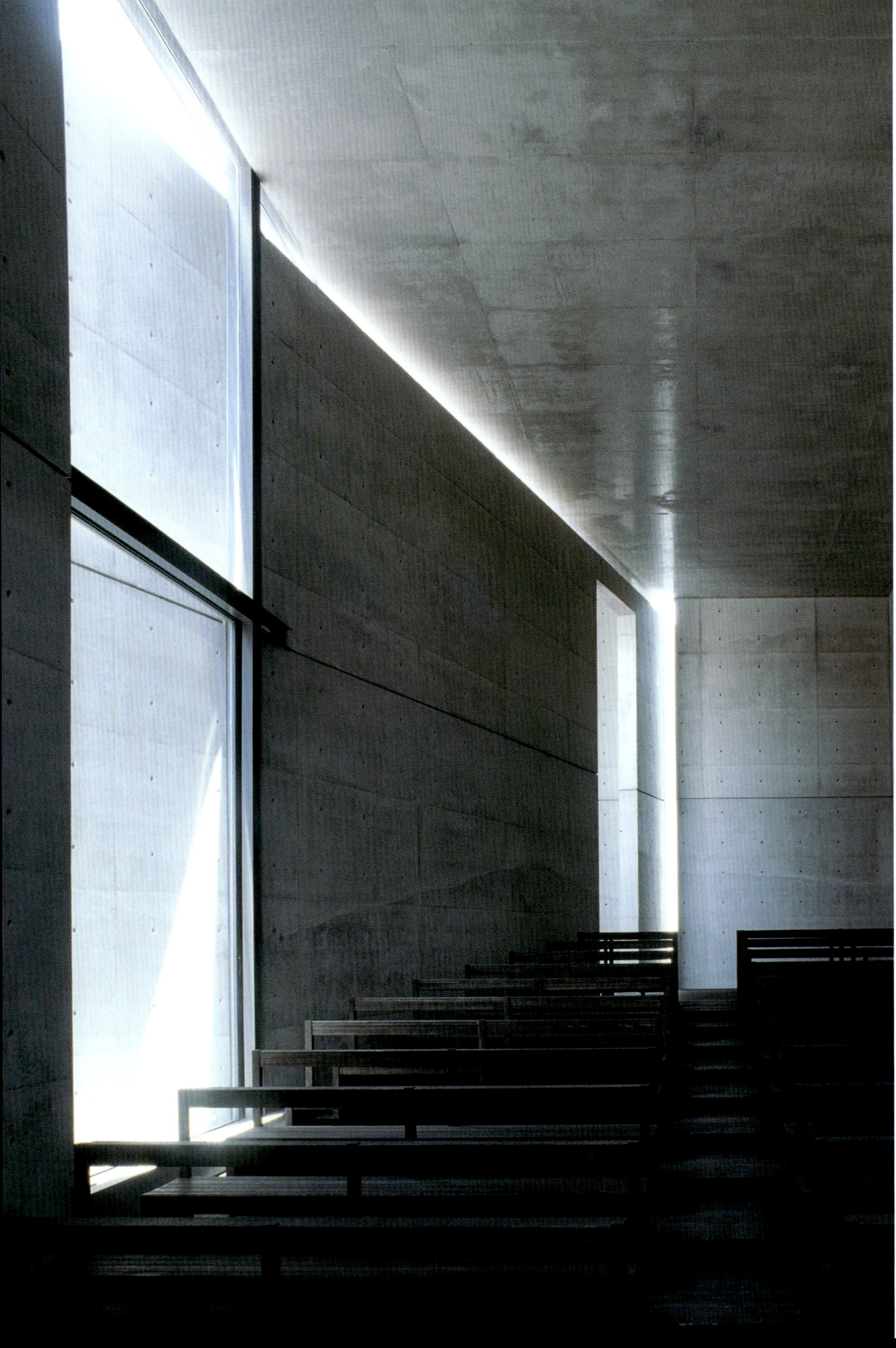

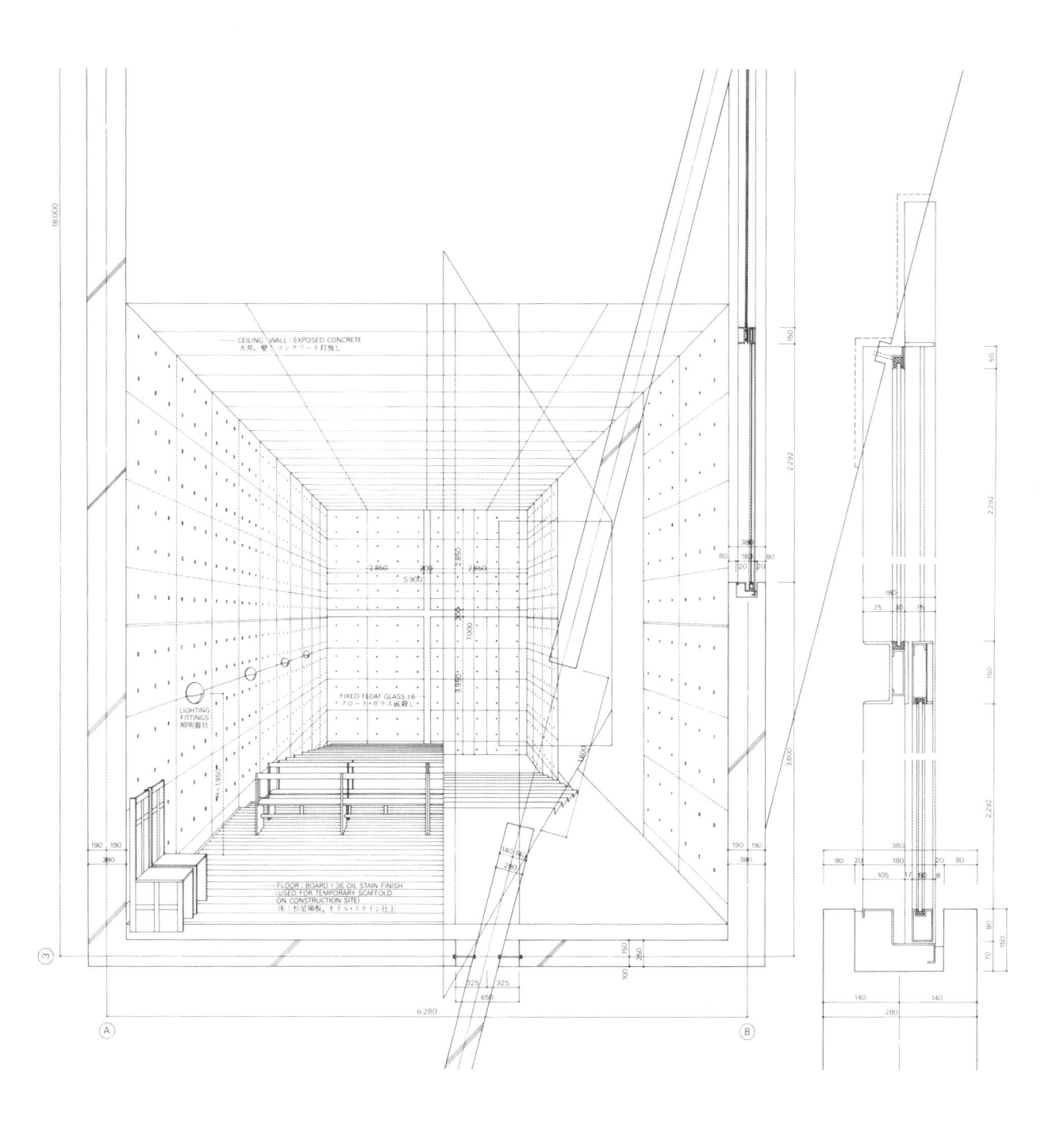

コンクリートの箱を、闇と光の聖なる空間へと劇的に変身させる、1枚の壁。最小限に抑えられた開口部からの光が、構成の幾何学を浮かび上がらせる。

A single wall dramatically transforms the concrete box into a sacred space of light and dark. The light from the minimal openings emphasizes the geometry of the composition.

135 Church of the Light

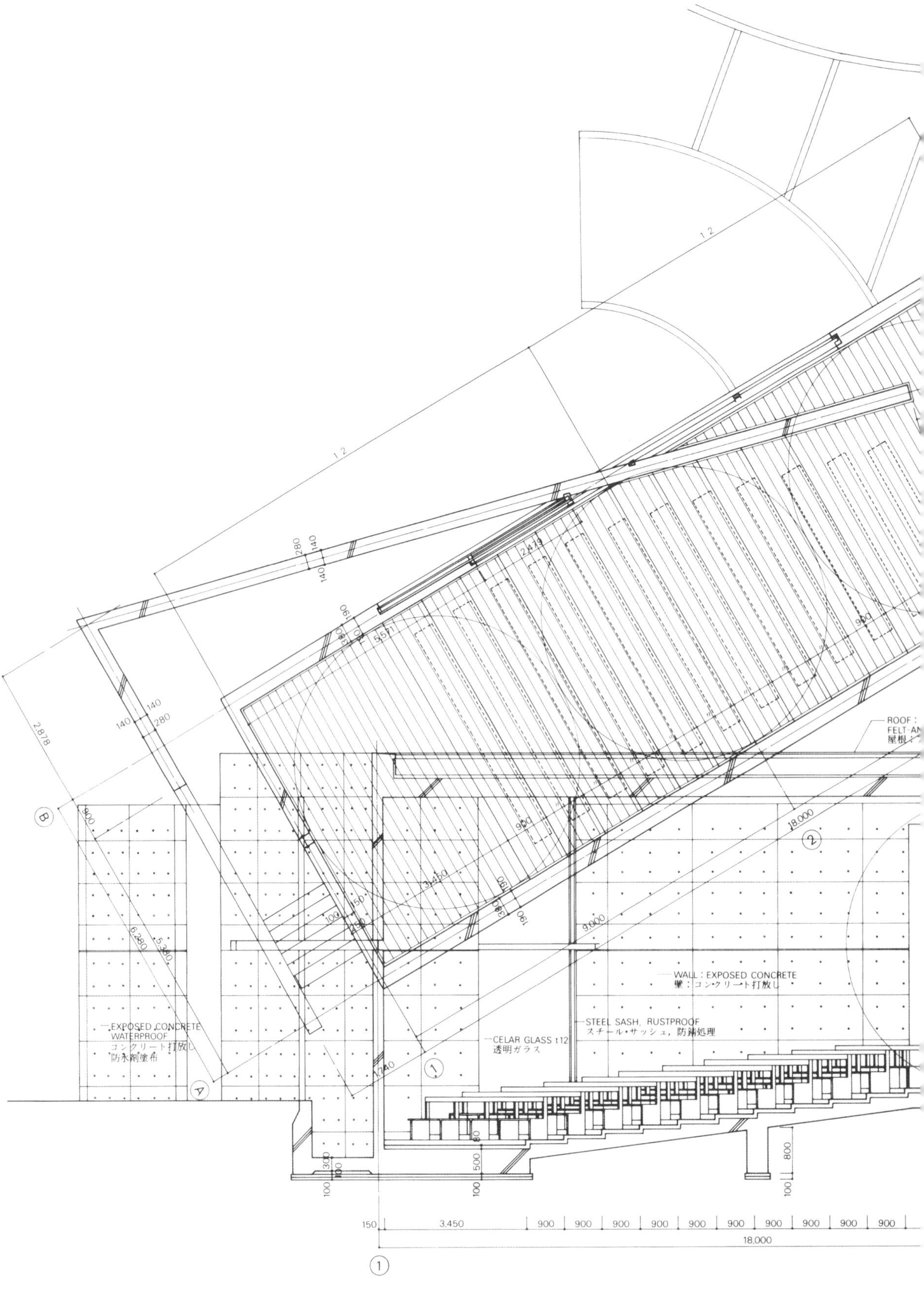

ROOF :
FELT-AN
屋根：
WALL : EXPOSED CONCRETE
壁：コンクリート打放し
STEEL SASH, RUSTPROOF
スチール・サッシュ，防錆処理
CELAR GLASS t12
透明ガラス
EXPOSED CONCRETE
WATERPROOF
コンクリート打放し
防水剤塗布
150
3,450
900
18,000

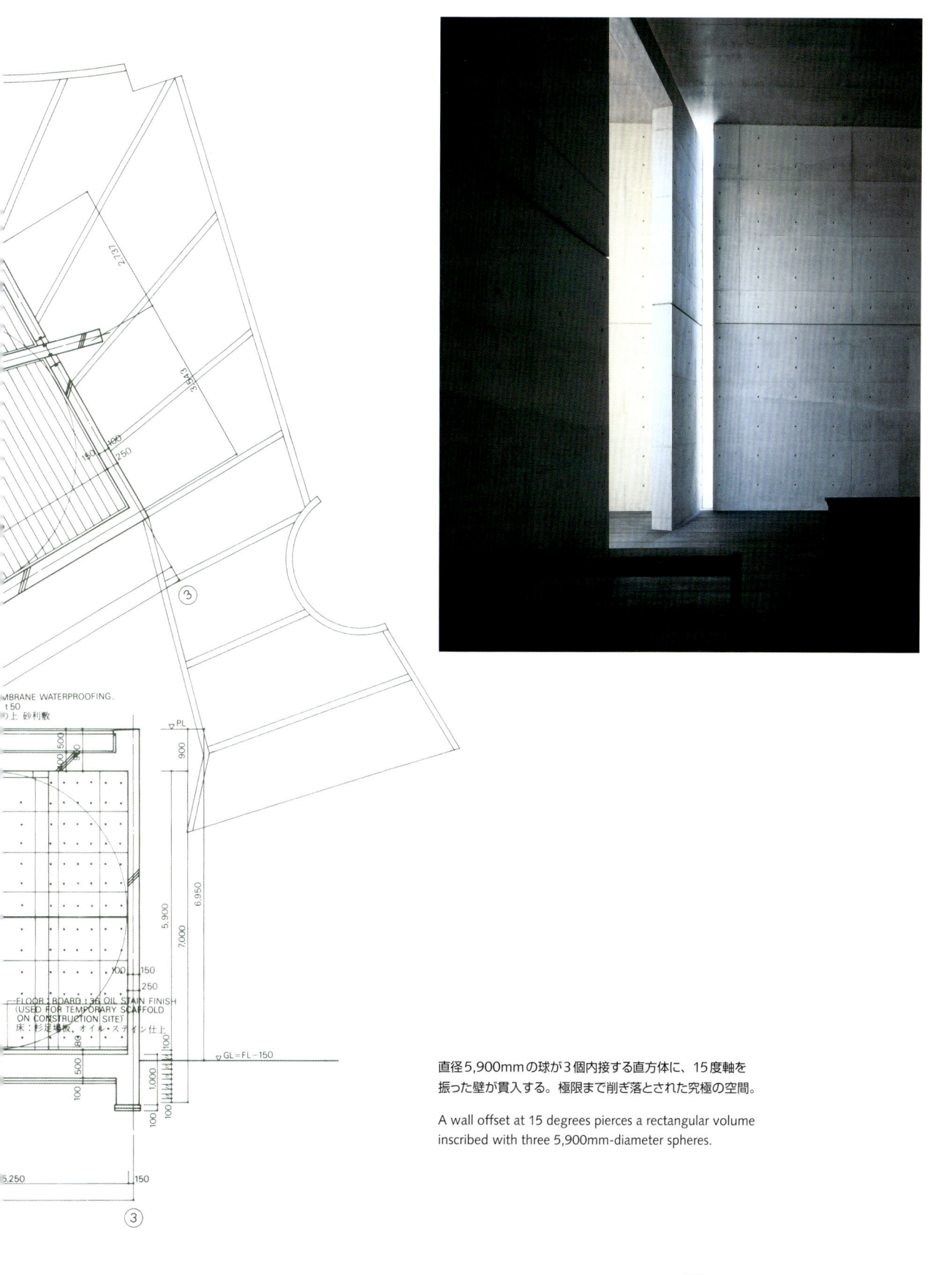

直径5,900mmの球が3個内接する直方体に、15度軸を
振った壁が貫入する。極限まで削ぎ落とされた究極の空間。

A wall offset at 15 degrees pierces a rectangular volume
inscribed with three 5,900mm-diameter spheres.

137 Church of the Light

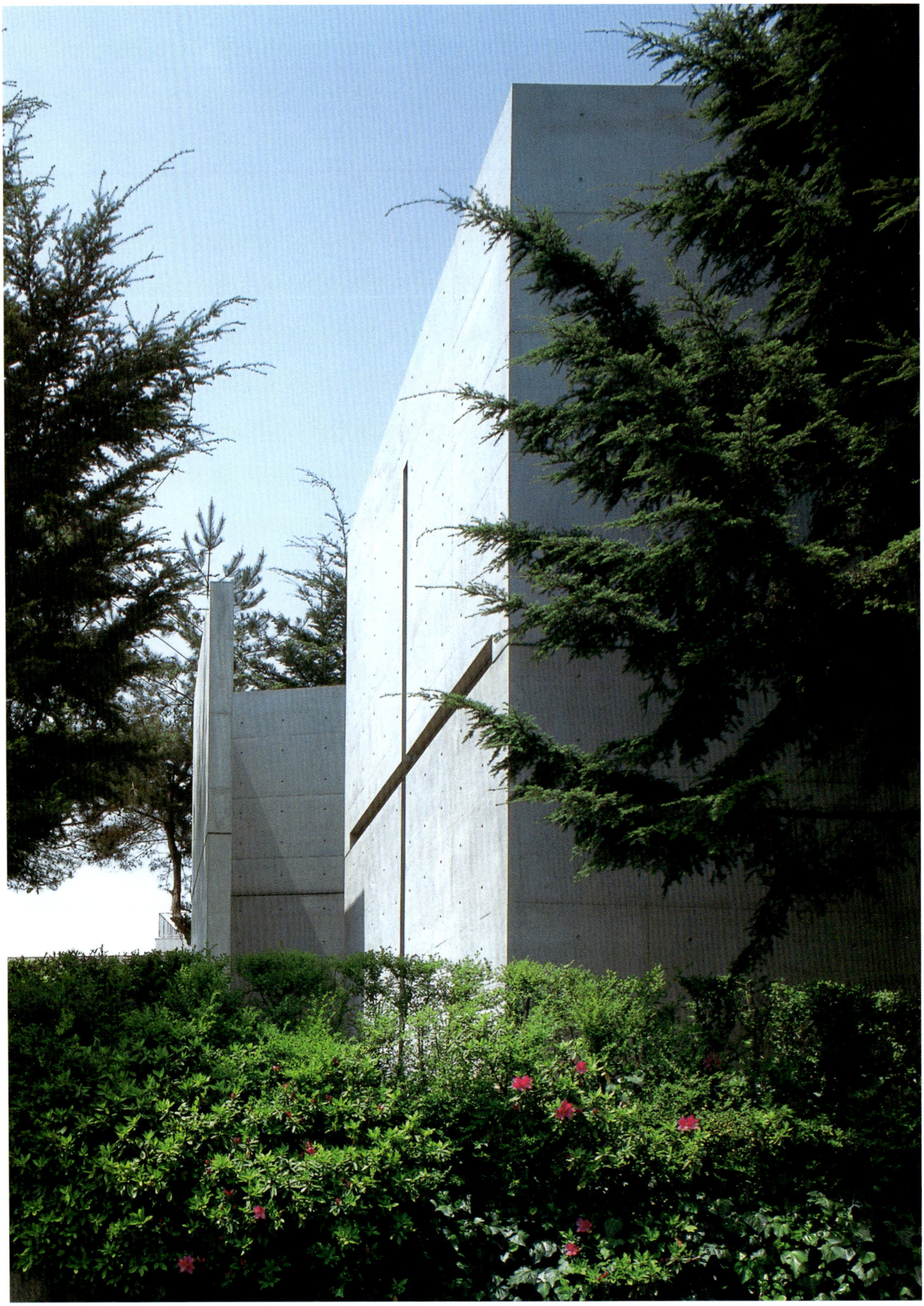

日曜日の礼拝の風景。光の十字架を道標に人々は集い、祈りを捧げる。
Scene of the Sunday church service. People gather and pray with the cross of light as a guide.

光の教会／日曜学校
Church of the light, Sunday School
1997-99

「光の教会」完成から10年を経て増設された、教会付属の集会施設である。ここでは、単なる継ぎ足しの増築ではない、緊張感ある新旧建物の関係性の創出を主題としている。

まず、規模、構成ともに、既存の礼拝堂のそれを踏襲したコンクリートの箱を、礼拝堂と〈対〉となるようなかたちに配置することを考えた。その結果生じるふたつの建物の間の余白のスペースを積極的に活用し、新旧の建物を関係づける緩衝領域として、新旧の壁に挟まれた外部階段、角度をなす2棟を円弧でつなぐポーチなどの共用空間を設けた。

そうして外観においては徹底して〈礼拝堂の反復〉を演出しつつ、建物内部においては、あえてその印象を覆すような光の空間を志向した。象徴的な十字の光を浮かび上がらせる礼拝堂の闇の空間とは好対照をなす、コンクリートの壁を燦々と照らす、明るい光に満ちた「日曜学校」の空間である。

その指向を、家具においても貫徹させた。礼拝堂では、闇の深度を深めるよう、すべてを黒のオイルステインで塗り込めたが、「日曜学校」では、杉板の床材、シナベニヤの家具とも生成りのまま仕上げている。これらの造作の存在が、一層内部を明るい印象にしている。

一旦完結させた建築に新たな機能を付加することは、建築家にとって困難だが、やりがいのある挑戦である。この教会ではさらにもうひとつ、敷地に残る牧師邸の改築の話が出ている。いまだ〈建築〉は終わっていない。

This is a meeting facility attached to the Church of the Light ten years after the latter's completion. Here the theme is not only the addition of an annex to a building but also the production of a tense relationship between old and new buildings.

I first thought to place a concrete box that followed the scale and organization of the existing worship hall in a shape "opposed" to that of the worship hall. Actively making use of the resulting empty space between the two buildings, I created a communal space as a buffer area that makes a relationship between the new and old buildings, comprising a curved porch in the angle between the two buildings and an exterior stair held between the old and the new walls.

While producing a full "repetition of the worship hall" in the exterior appearance, the inside of the building is intended as a space of light that completely reverses that impression. In a pleasing contrast with the symbolic light of the cross floating in the gloomy space of the worship hall, the space of the Sunday School is suffused with bright light and the concrete walls are brilliantly illuminated.

This shift was also achieved in the furniture. In the worship hall, everything was painted with a black oil stain in order to deepen the gloom, but in the Sunday School the Japanese cedar floor boards and plywood furniture are left in their natural state. The presence of these fixtures gives an even lighter impression to the interior.

Adding a new function to a provisionally completed building is stressful for an architect, but is a rewarding challenge. There is now talk of reconstructing the pastor's residence for this church, which remains on the site. The "architecture" is still unfinished.

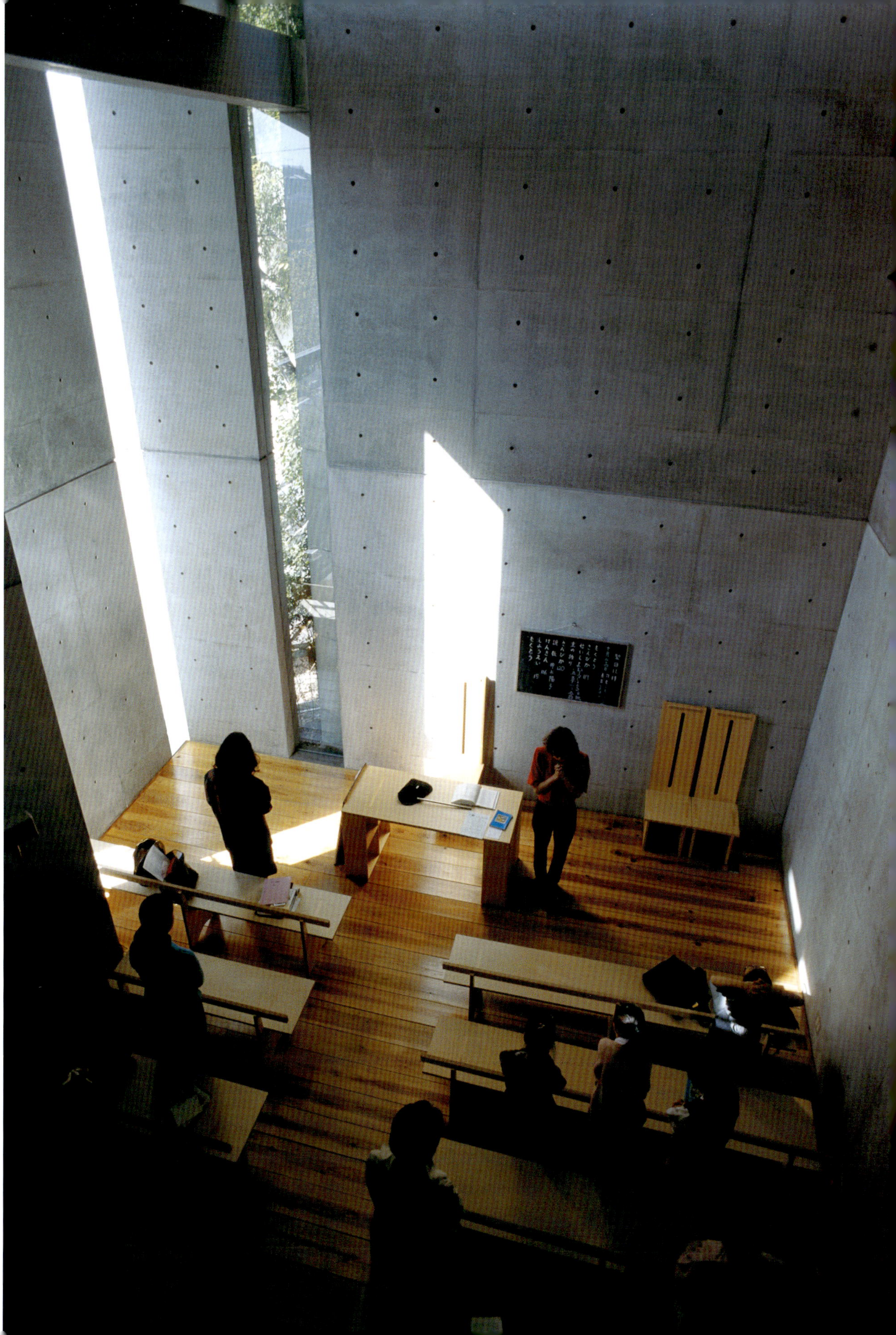

Second floor plan

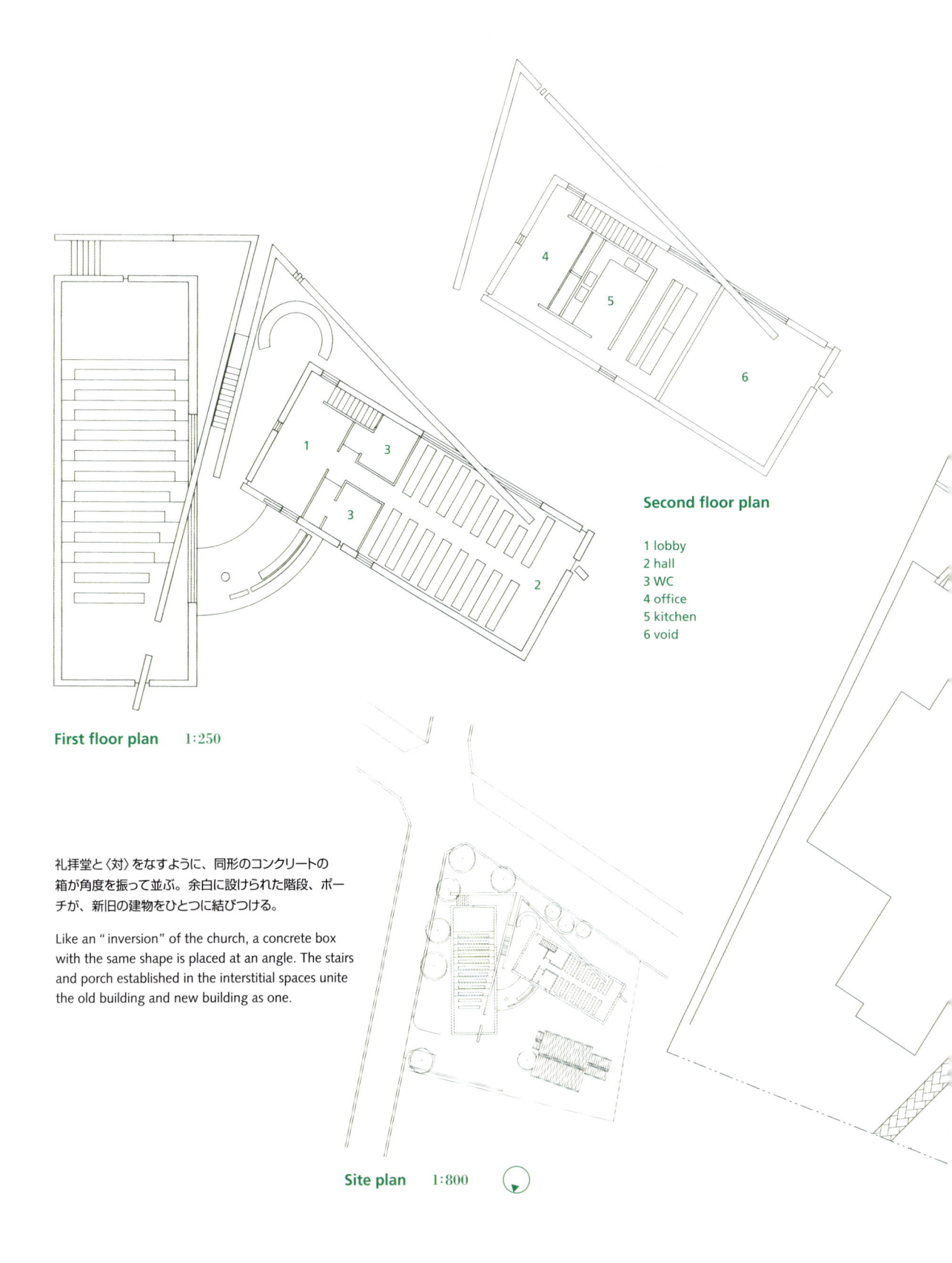

1 lobby
2 hall
3 WC
4 office
5 kitchen
6 void

First floor plan 1:250

礼拝堂と〈対〉をなすように、同形のコンクリートの箱が角度を振って並ぶ。余白に設けられた階段、ポーチが、新旧の建物をひとつに結びつける。

Like an "inversion" of the church, a concrete box with the same shape is placed at an angle. The stairs and porch established in the interstitial spaces unite the old building and new building as one.

Site plan 1:800

axonometric

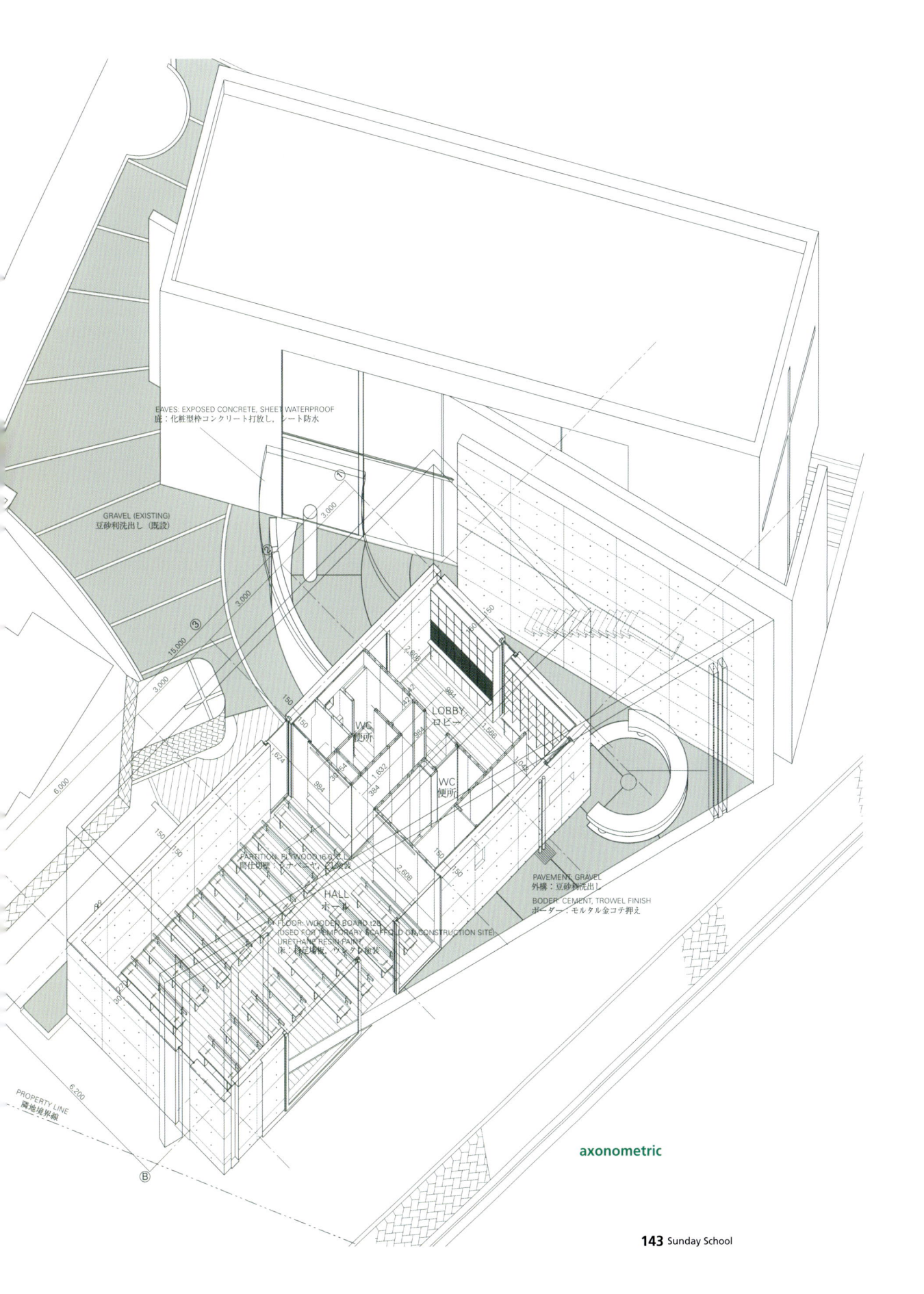

143 Sunday School

礼拝堂と同じ杉足場板の床に、シナベニヤの造作家具が並ぶ。
闇の深度を深めるためすべて黒で塗られた礼拝堂の家具とは対
照的に、ここではすべてが生成り色のまま仕上げられている。

Plywood furniture is arrayed on the floor of Japanese cedar planks, similar to the church. Here it is all finished in a natural color so as to contrast with the furniture of the church, which was painted entirely black in order to deepen the gloom.

集会室正面の壁をスリットからの光が燦々と照らす。礼拝堂と同様の構成が、まったく異なる光の空間として再現されている。

Light shines brightly through the slit in the front wall of the meeting room. A composition identical to that of the church is repeated as an entirely different space of light.

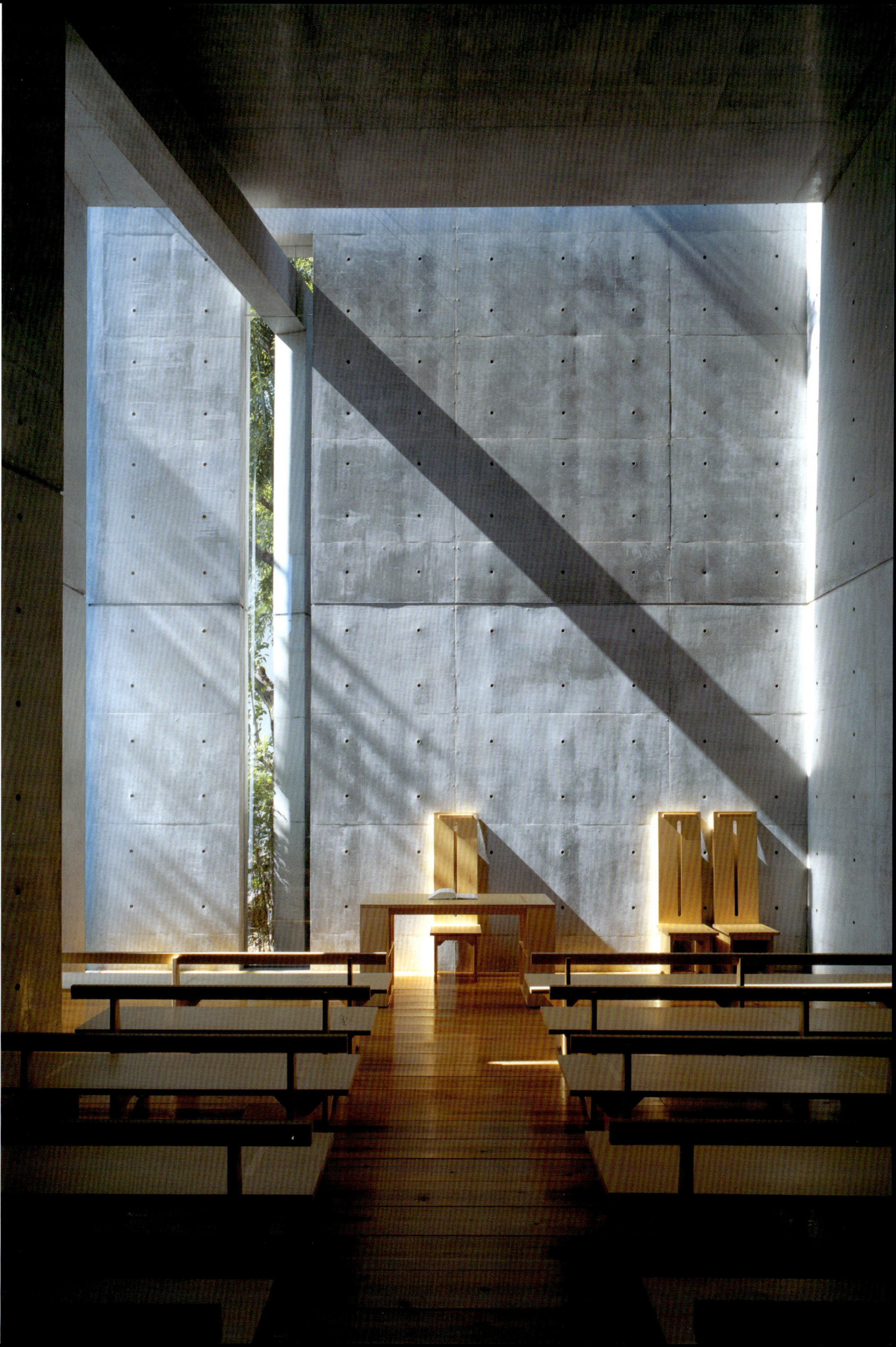

兵庫県立こどもの館
Children's Museum, Hyogo

1987-89　兵庫県姫路市——Himeji, Hyogo

　敷地は兵庫県姫路市郊外、緑深い山の裾野に広がる約32ヘクタールの広さの貯水池に面してつくられた、子供のための文化教育施設である。初めての大規模な公共施設への挑戦となったこのプロジェクトにおいて、私は〈スケールの拡大〉、〈自然環境への応答〉という新たなテーマに取り組み、自身の建築の次なる展開を試みることとなった。

　ここで考えたのは、建物を自然環境の中に溶け込ませ、場所全体をもって要求される施設のプログラムに応えること、即ち環境造形としての建築である。

　建物は、施設のエントランスとなるメインの本館と、16本のコンクリート柱の並ぶ野外の中間広場、その先の工房という、3つの部分から構成される。貯水池に沿って、全長500mの範囲いっぱいに配置されたそれらの施設の間を、地形に沿って設けられた大地の切り込みのような屋外通路が結ぶ。施設を利用する子供たちを、知らず内に水と緑に囲まれた敷地の散策に誘い出す〈庭園〉のイメージである。

　図書館、ホールといった機能を収め、大きなヴォリュームをもつ本館部分においては、そのスケール感を和らげ、周囲に馴染ませる手立てとして、〈水〉を用いた。建物を取り巻くように配された人工の水盤は、建物の内側においては遠くの風景を引き込む装置として働き、建物の外側においては、人工と自然との間を緩やかにつなぐ、緩衝領域の役割を果たす。

　「ハコモノ行政」と批判されるよう、えてして日本の公共建築は内容の伴わない、利用者におもねるばかりの無個性な〈箱〉になりがちである。「こどもの館」では、立地を活かし大きく自然に開いた建物と同時に、その外構を舞台とした「子供の彫刻アイディアコンペ」など、ソフトの提案も積極的に行っている。

Constructed at the foot of green mountains and facing a reservoir extending over approximately 32ha on a site in the outskirts of Himeji City, Hyogo Prefecture, this is a cultural and educational facility for children. This project was my first attempt at a large-scale public facility, and I employed the new themes of "enlarged scale" and "response to the natural environment" with the ambition of further developing my own architecture.

　Here I conceived a building that blends into the natural environment, supporting a program of required functions with the entire place. In other words, this is architecture as an environmental form.

　The building is composed of three parts: a main building that acts as the entrance to the facility, an outdoor central plaza in which sixteen concrete columns are arrayed, and a workshop beyond. Distributed along the full length of the 500m-long reservoir, these elements are connected by outdoor pathways seemingly cut into the ground and arranged along the topography. It has the image of a "garden" that subconsciously invites the children using the facility to stroll through the site surrounded by water and nature.

　The main building is a large volume containing the functions of library and hall, in which the sense of scale is reduced, and "water" is used as a method for involvement with the surroundings. Artificial basins, distributed as if surrounding the building, act as installations that draw the distant scenery inside the building, whereas outside the building they play the role of a buffer zone gently connecting nature with artifice.

　Like a critique of *hakomonogyousei* (literally "box administration," a phrase that refers to the waste of public funds on unnecessary public facilities), Japanese public architecture tends to comprise characterless "boxes" unrelated to their content, merely flattering their users. In order to make best use of its location as well as being a building that is wide open to nature, the Children's Museum also actively makes proposals such as a "children's sculpture competition" on the outdoor stage.

工房・中間広場・本館と3つのエリアに分けられた施設が、
屋外通路で結ばれて500mにわたり展開する。

Divided into three areas (workshop, central plaza, and main
building) this facility is linked by a 500m-long exterior pathway.

工房から中間広場へと訪問者を導く壁の造形。
Sculpting of the walls that guide visitors from the workshop to the central plaza.

緑深い山に囲まれた32ヘクタールの広さの貯水池の
ほとりに、自然に溶け込むように配された建物。

Extending over 32ha surrounded by deep green
mountains in the vicinity of a reservoir, the building
is arranged as if melting into nature.

グリッド上に16本の柱が並ぶ中間広場。
A grid of sixteen columns in the central plaza.

151 Children's Museum

本館の四周を人工の水盤が取り巻く。貯水池へとつながるかのごとく、階段状に下降する
水面の先に、雄大な水と緑の風景が広がる。建築と自然をつなぐ緩衝帯としての水。

Artificial water basins surround the main hall. As if connected to the reservoir, the water
surface descends in a stepping shape that extends to the magnificent scene of water and
greenery beyond. Water as a buffer zone linking architecture and nature.

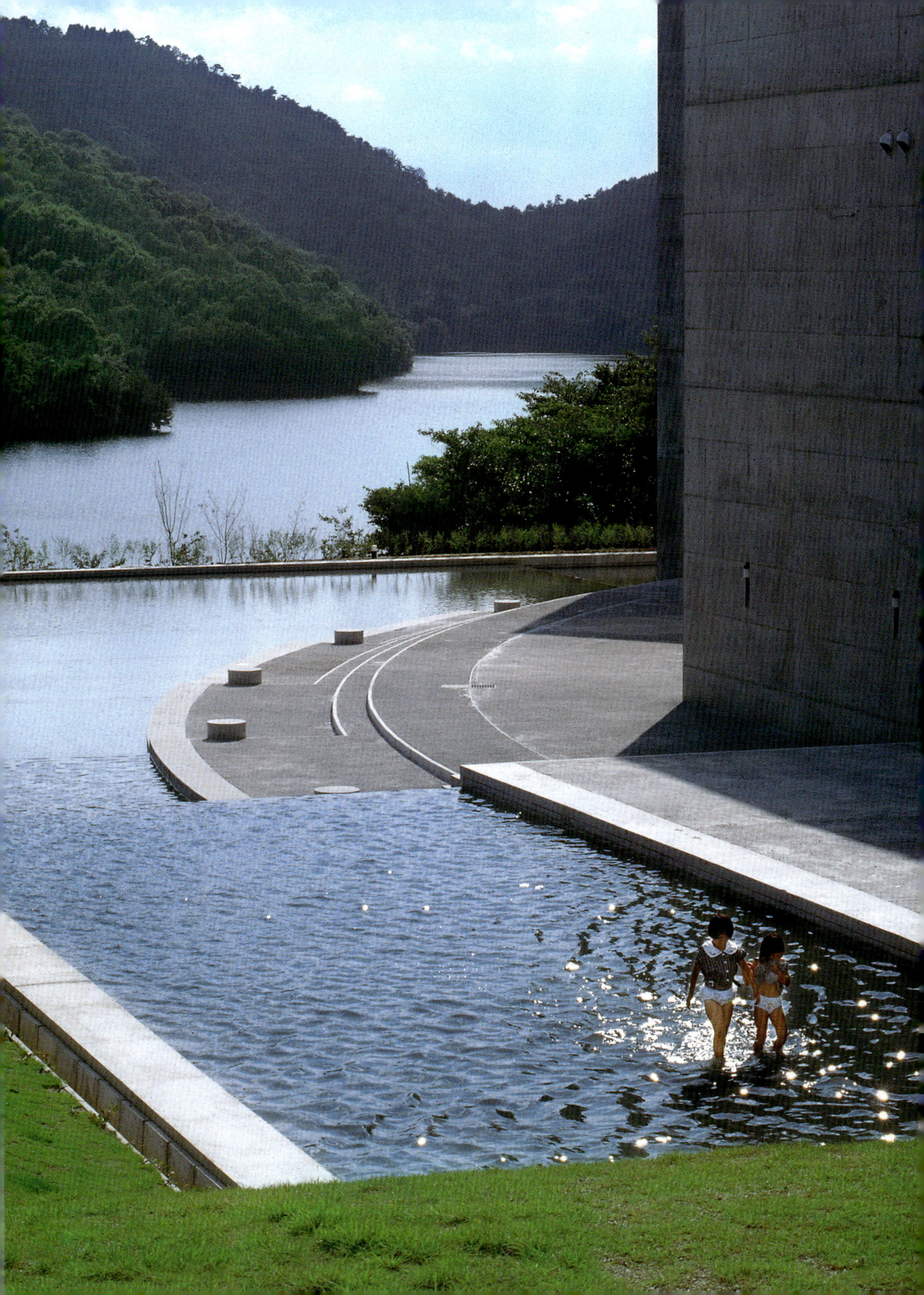

本館部分、2棟をつなぐ建物前面の水池と、貯水池側、2階レベルに設けられたデッキ。2本の直方体のボックスを基調とする単純な構成の中に、内外空間の入り組む複雑多様な空間のシークエンスが展開する。

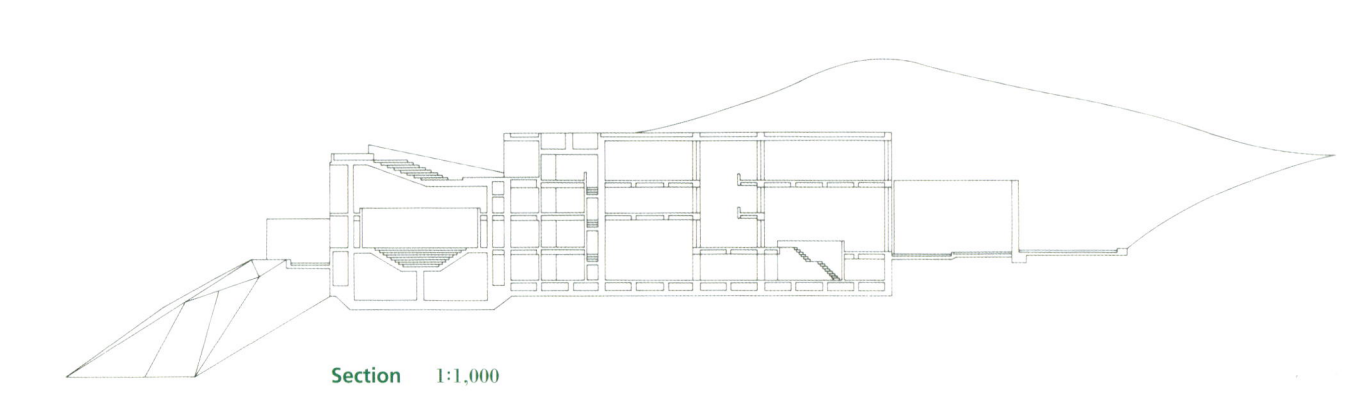

Section　1:1,000

A deck has been established at the second floor level, facing toward the reservoir and the pond in front of the building that connects the two wings of the main hall. With this simple composition, based on two rectangular boxes, a complex and diverse spatial sequence has been developed in which interior and exterior spaces are interwoven.

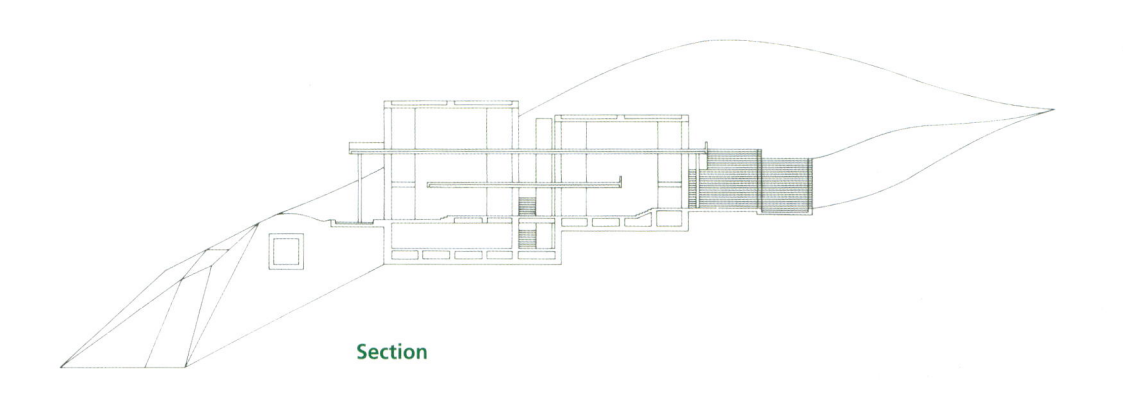

Section

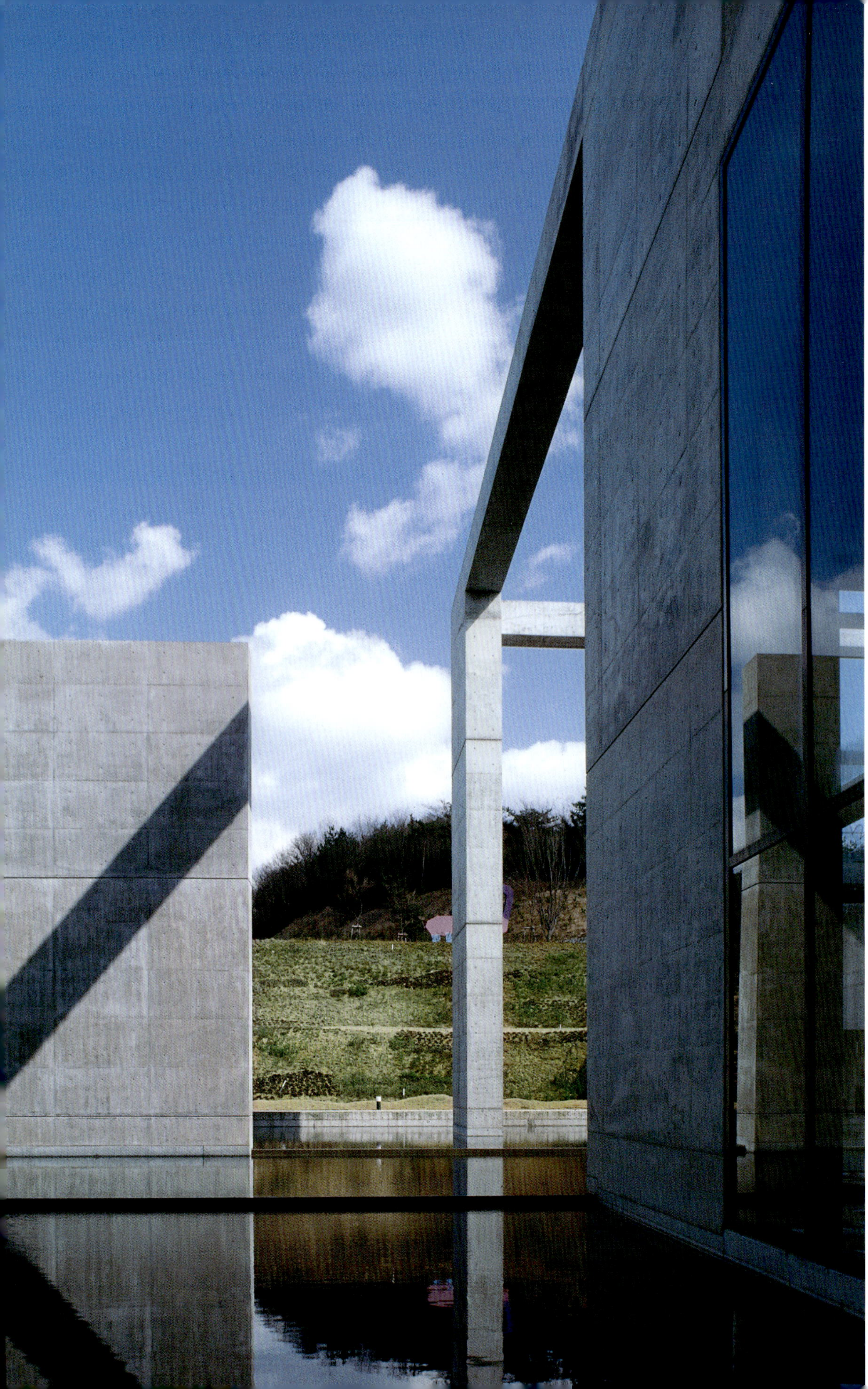

Third floor plan

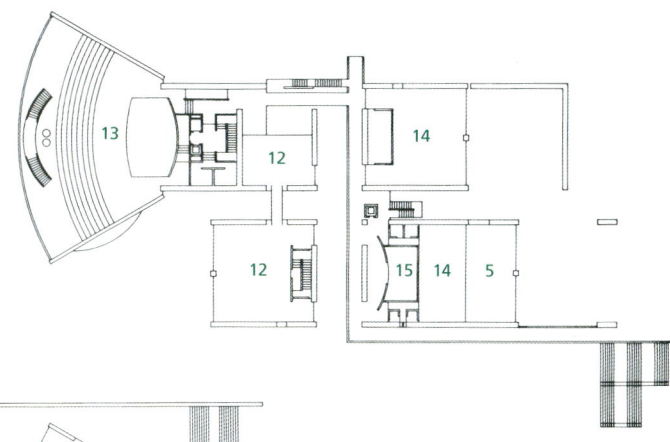

Second floor plan

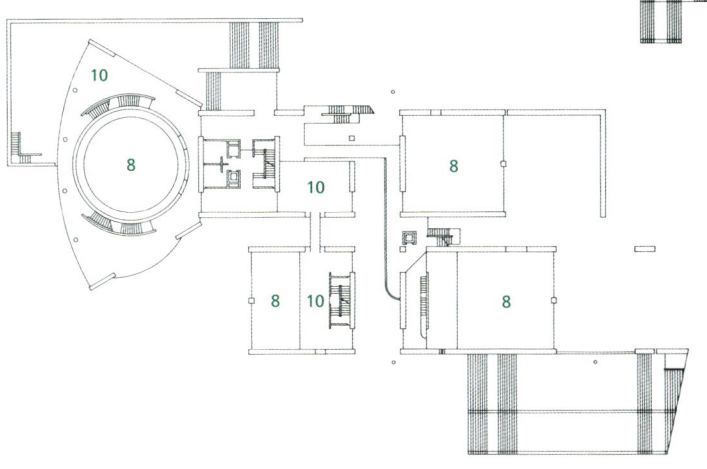

First floor plan

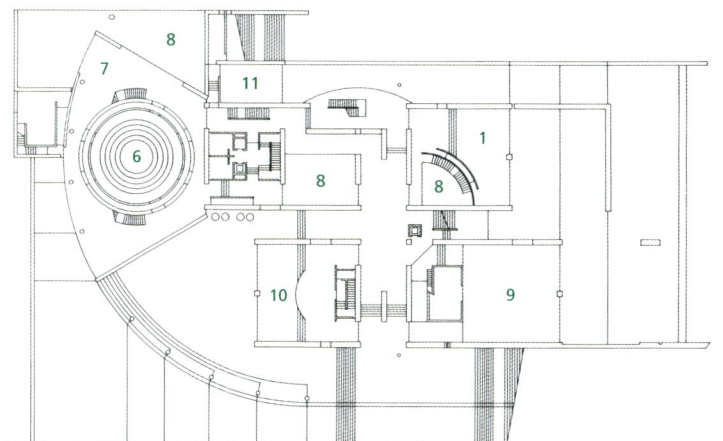

1 library
2 restaurant
3 mechanical
4 stack room
5 terrace
6 theater
7 foyer
8 void
9 multipurpose hall
10 gallery
11 meeting room
12 office
13 outdoor theater
14 seminar room
15 information office

Basement floor plan
1:1,300

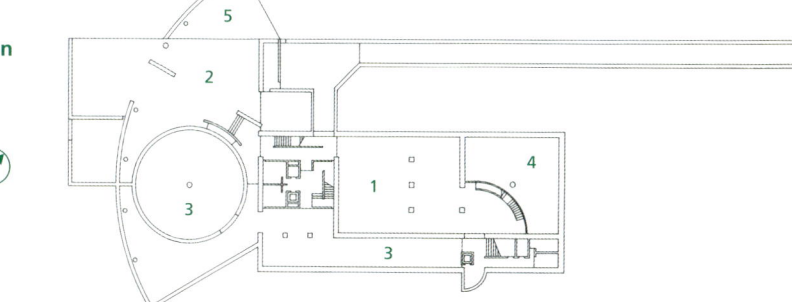

157 Children's Museum

空中に力強い幾何学を描く建築のフレームが、雄大な
自然の風景を大胆に切り取る。
The architectural frame delineates a strong geometry
in the sky, boldly framing the magnificent scenery.

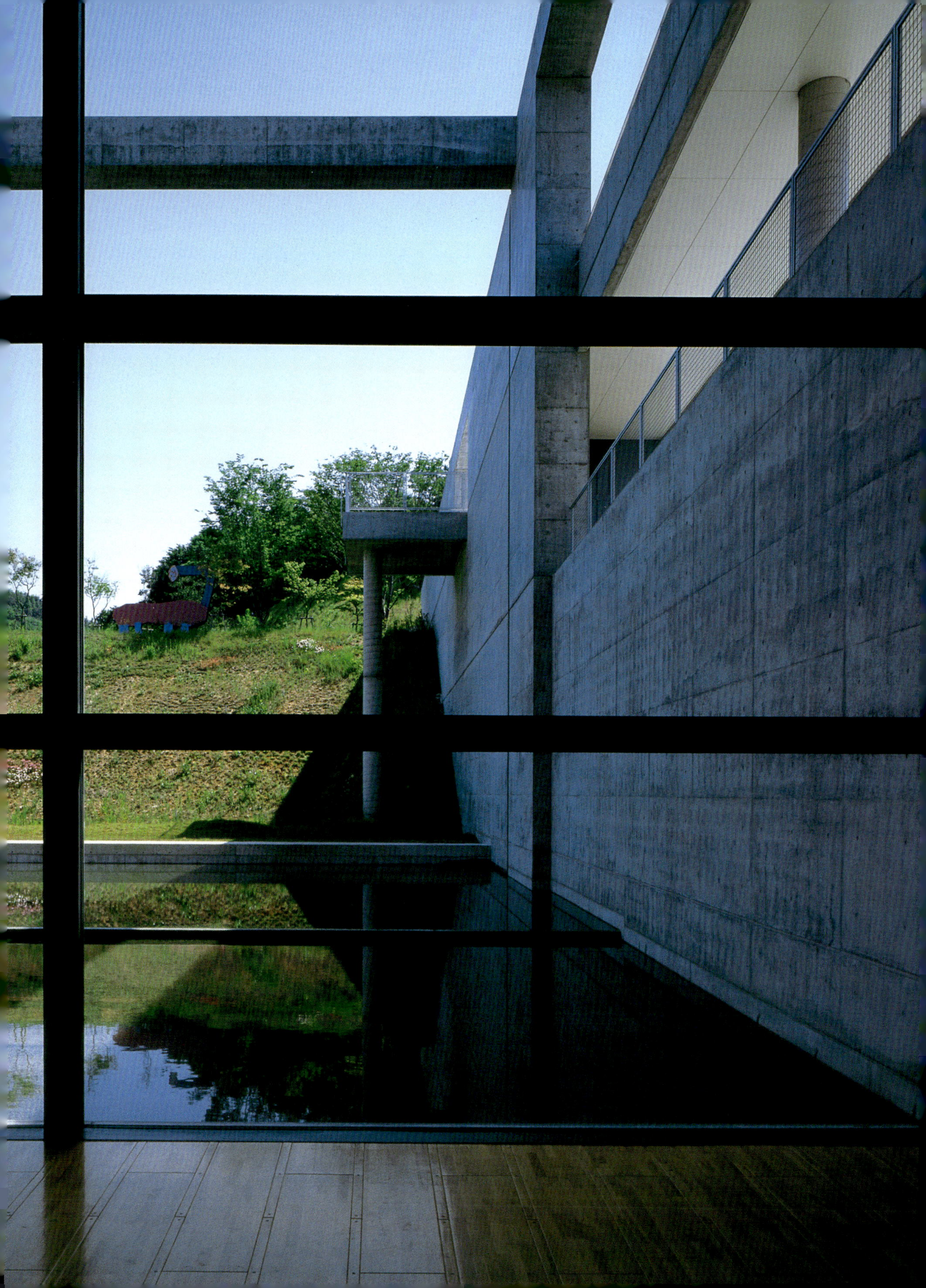

真言宗本福寺水御堂
Water Temple

1989-91　兵庫県淡路市 ── Awaji, Hyogo

敷地は、淡路島北東部の大阪湾を一望する小高い丘の上に位置する。真言宗仁和寺派に属する本福寺の本堂である。ここでは、日常世界から非日常の聖域へ、その劇的な移行の時間と空間による表現に、主題を集約している。

御堂へのアプローチは、丘の裾の小道を進むところから始まる。緑の中を迂回しつつ、昇り詰めると、直立するコンクリートの壁を背景とする、白砂を敷き詰めた前庭が現れる。この壁に穿たれた開口部をくぐり抜けると、さらにもう1枚のコンクリートの壁が、緩やかな弧を描いて迎える。

青空と足下の白砂以外何もない、2枚の壁に切り取られた空白の空間を、白砂を踏みしめる自身の足音を聞きながら進んで行く。円弧の壁の端部で折れ上がると、突如視界が開け、楕円形の蓮池が現れる。

蓮は仏教を開いた釈迦の姿の象徴といわれる。その中央に切り込まれた階段を、蓮池に吸い込まれるような感覚を味わいながら下降すると、ついに目指していた御堂との対面が叶う。

円形の室の中の内陣と外陣の構成それ自体は、宗派の慣習的な形式に則ったかたちであるが、ここではそのすべてが朱色に塗られている。意図したのは、背後の格子窓からの自然光を受けて赤く輝く、〈西方浄土〉のごとき光の空間である。

聖俗領域を切り替える通過装置ともいうべき建築の位置づけは、地形を巧みに利用した配置、迂回する露地のアプローチなど、日本の伝統的建築に顕著に見られる傾向である。初めての寺院建築の設計に際し、私はかたちや形式ではなく、その背後にある精神の継承をもって、伝統という主題に応えようと考えた。

The site is located in the northeast of Awaji Island, on top of a slightly elevated hill that has an unobstructed view over Osaka Bay. This is the main hall of Honpukuji, a temple attached to the Ninnaji School of Shingon Buddhism. The theme here was to express a dramatic shift in time and space from the ordinary world to an extraordinary sacred precinct.

The approach route to the hall starts with the continuation of a small road at the foot of the hill. Ascending and turning in the greenery, a front garden covered with white gravel appears, with a perpendicular concrete wall as the backdrop. Through an aperture cut in this wall is another concrete wall that describes a gentle curve.

With nothing but blue sky and the white gravel below, one continues through the empty space defined by the two walls while listening to the sound of one's own feet treading on the white gravel. Walking around the end of the curved wall, the field of view suddenly expands and an elliptical lotus pond appears.

The lotus is said to symbolize the figure of Siddhartha Gautama, the founder of Buddhism. Descending the stairs that slice through the center while savoring the sensation of being immersed in the lotus pond, one finally arrives at the hall.

The composition of the apse and the nave inside the circular room conforms to the conventions of this sect, but everything here is painted vermilion. The intention was to bring in the red glow of natural light from behind the lattice windows, creating a space of light like the "Western Pure Land."

The placement of the architecture in an arrangement making skilful use of the topography and the indirect path of the approach route, which could be called a transitional path between the sacred and the profane realms, can obviously be seen as similar to traditional Japanese architecture. On the occasion of my first Buddhist temple design, I thought about responding to the theme of tradition and to the spirit behind it, not to the shape or form.

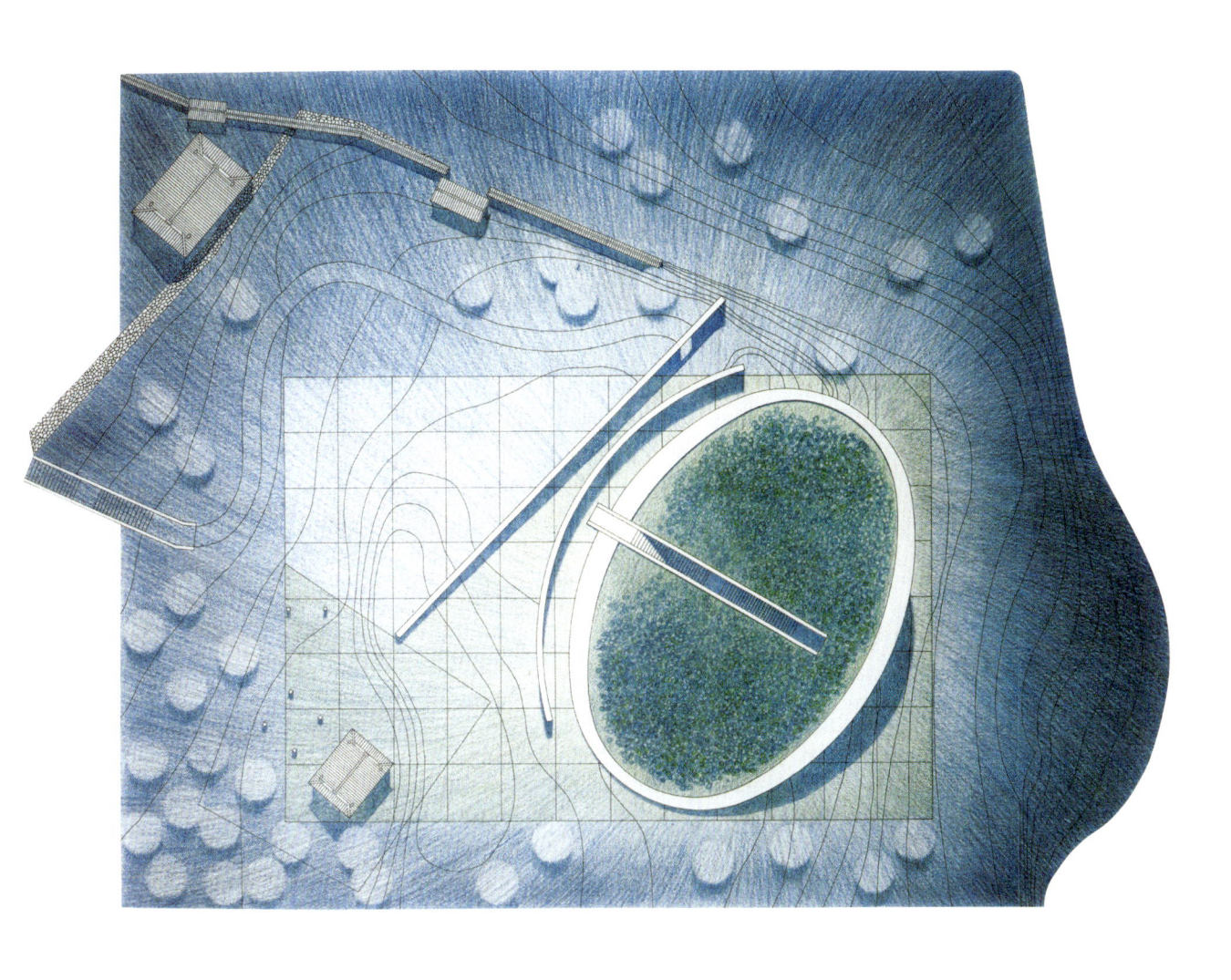

丘の頂にそっと置かれた楕円の蓮池と、直線・弧を描く2枚の壁。人々を水面下のお堂へと誘う階段が、楕円の中央に切り込まれている。

An elliptical lotus pond gently placed at the summit of a hill, together with two walls, one straight, the other describing an arc. A stair inviting people to the hall below the water slices through the center of the ellipse.

池の中央を切り裂き下降する階段は、日常から
非日常の聖域への劇的な移行の空間。

The stair cutting down through center of the
pond is a space of dramatic transition from the
everyday world to the extraordinary sacred realm.

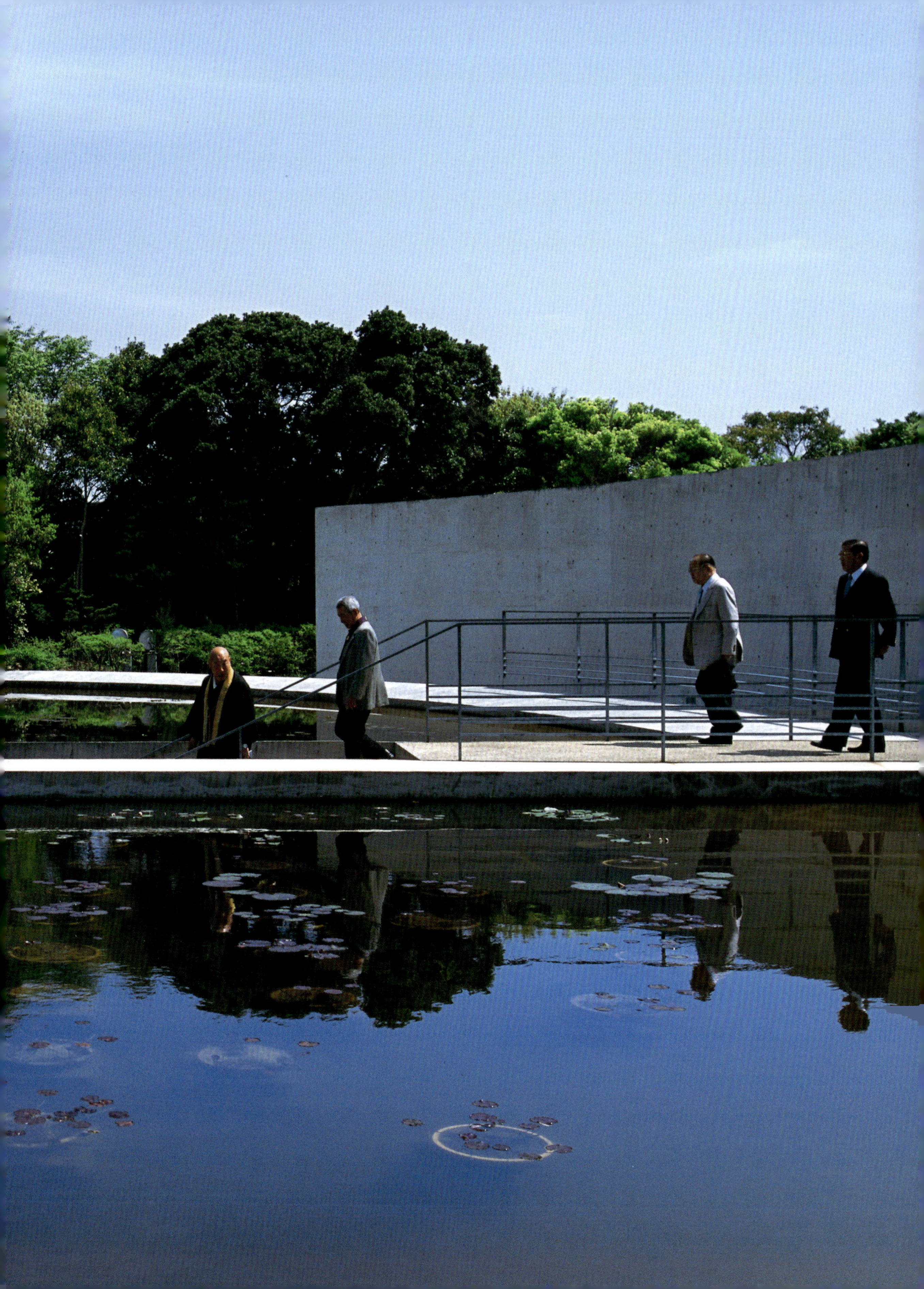

楕円形の水面は蓮に覆われる。蓮は悟りを開いた釈迦の姿の象徴といわれる。
The elliptical water surface is covered with lotus flowers. The lotus symbolizes the enlightened Buddha.

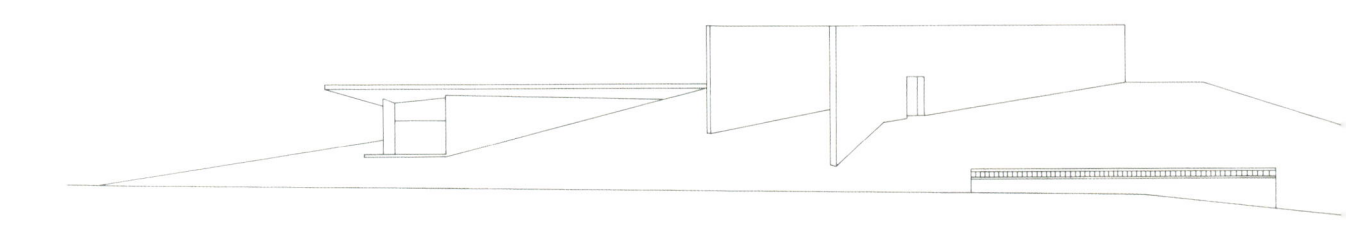

Elevation 1:400

165 Water Temple

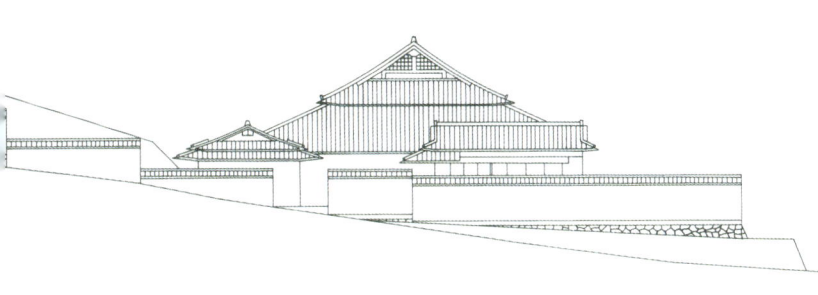

蓮池の屋根の下、建物は斜面に半ば埋もれるかたちで計画されている。斜面方向に穿たれた開口部から、地下のお堂に光と風が導かれる。
Below the lotus pond roof, the building is designed in a shape half buried into the slope. Light and wind are brought into the underground hall through an opening aligned with the direction of the slope.

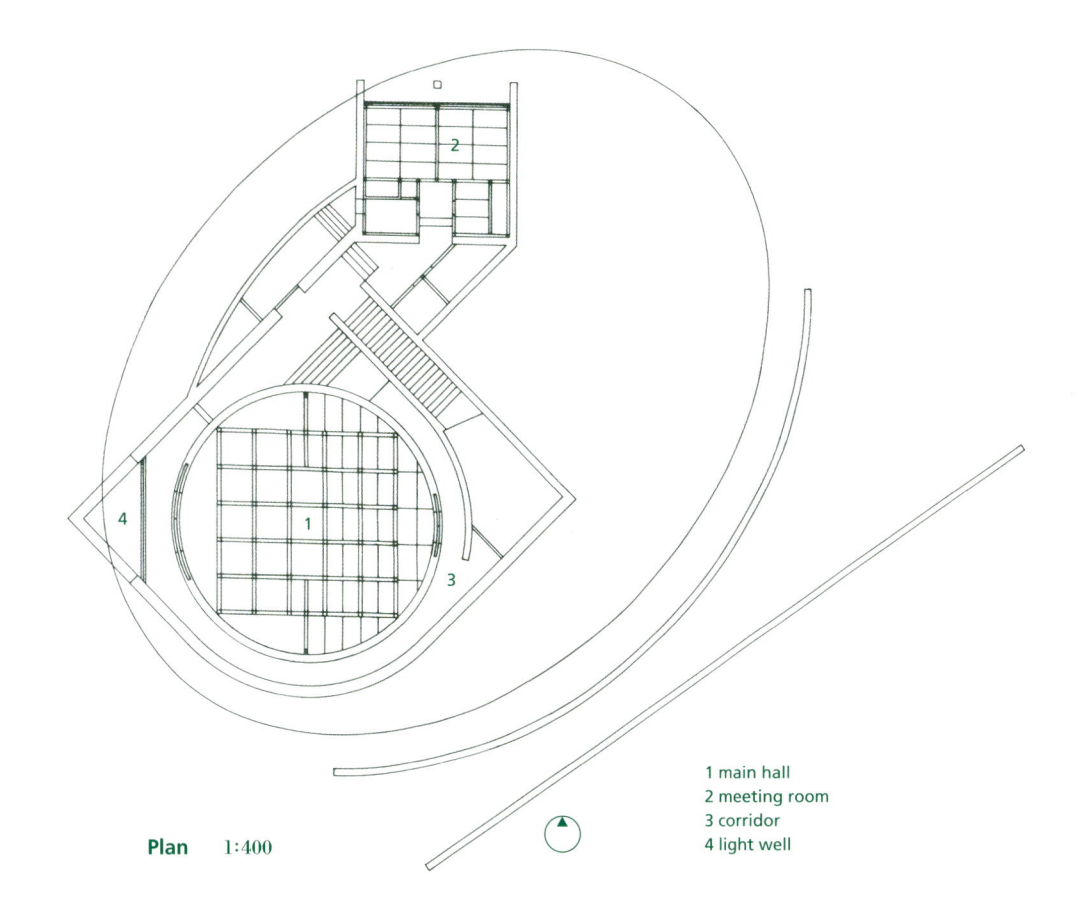

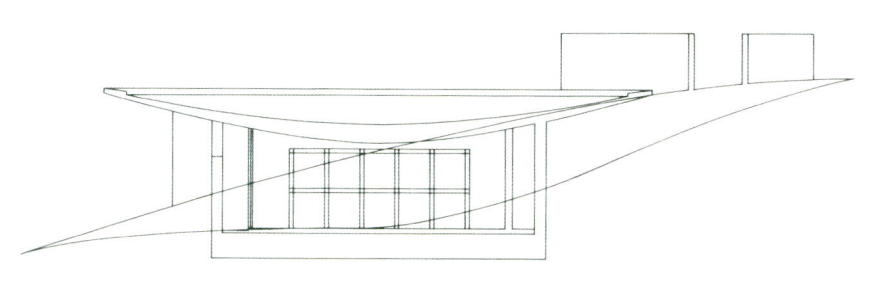

1 main hall
2 meeting room
3 corridor
4 light well

Plan 1:400

Seciton

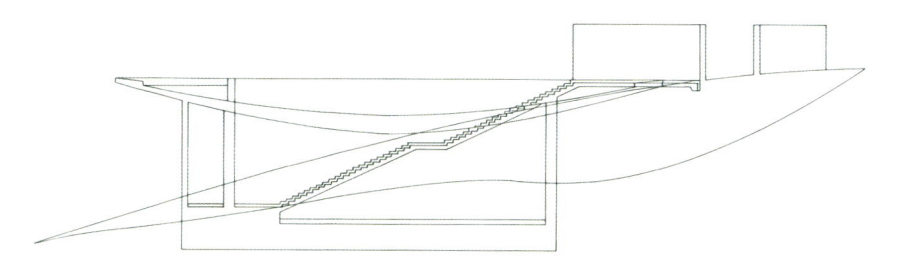

Seciton 1:400

167 Water Temple

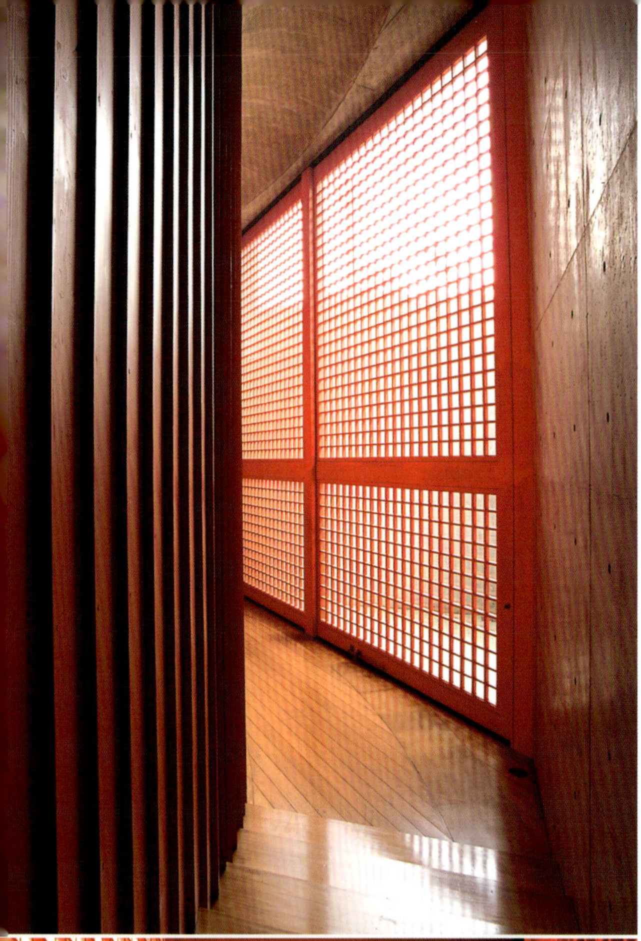
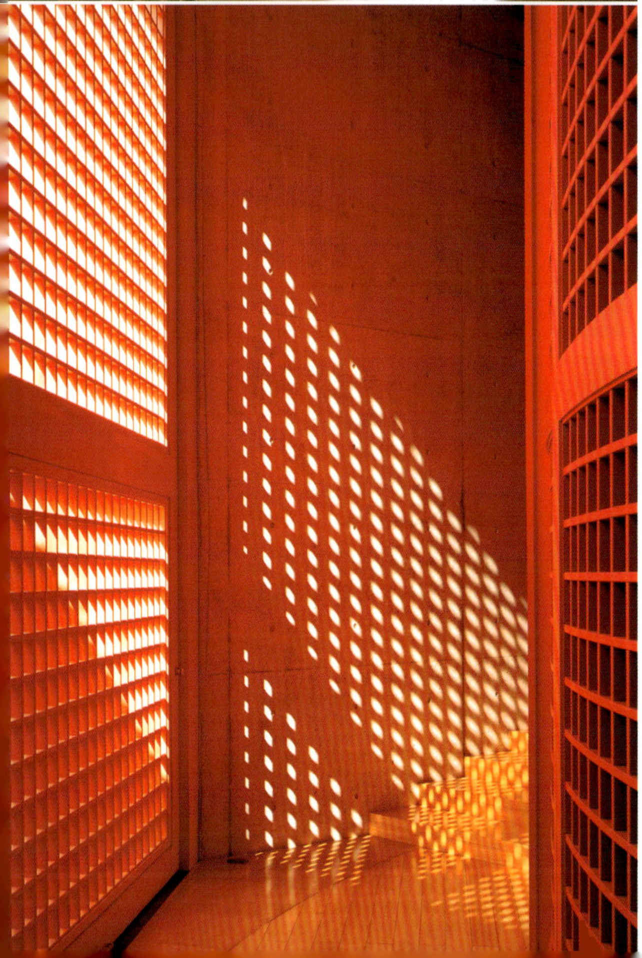
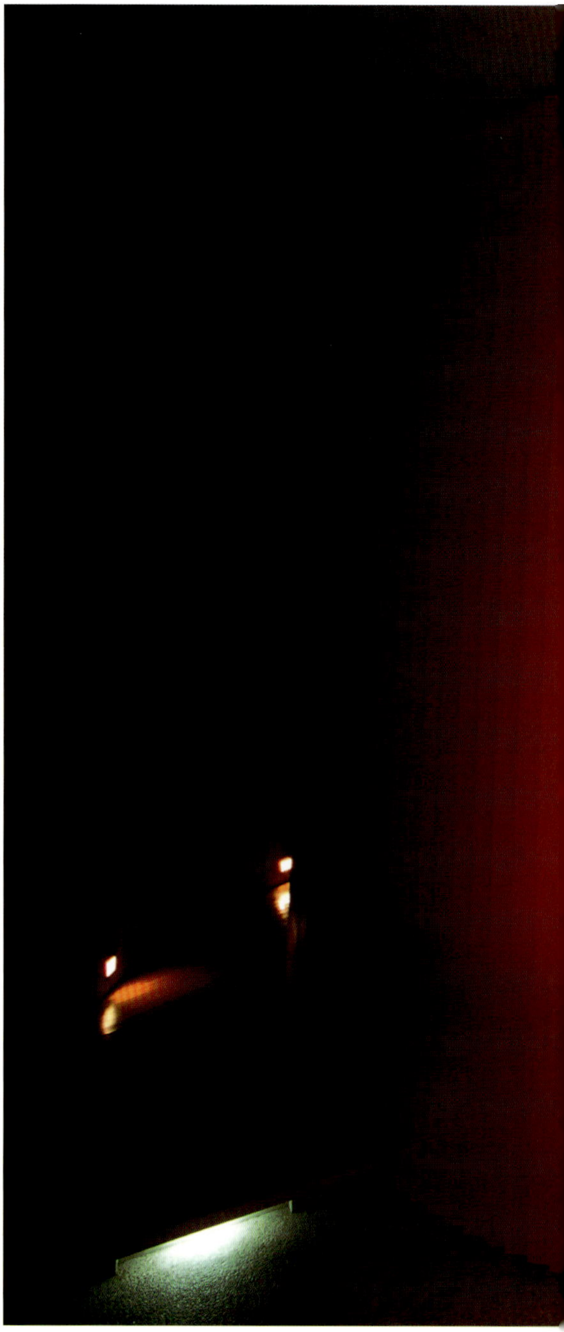

本堂の真西に光庭が設けられ、内陣に背後から光をもたらす。円形平面の本堂は、朱色に塗られた杉板に囲まれている。

A light garden has been established due west of the main hall, and light is brought into the inner sanctum from the rear. The circular main hall is enclosed by Japanese cedar boards painted vermilion.

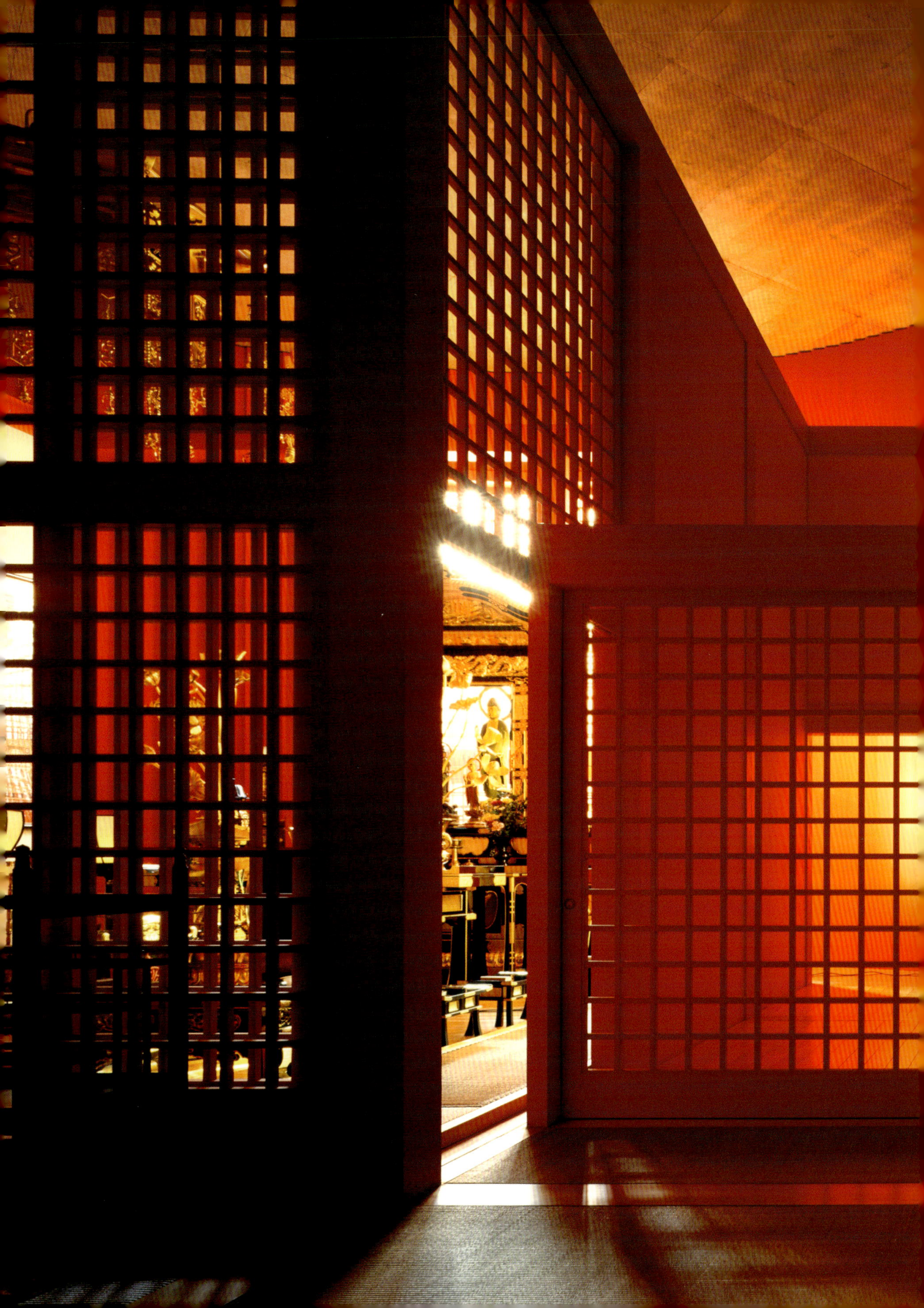

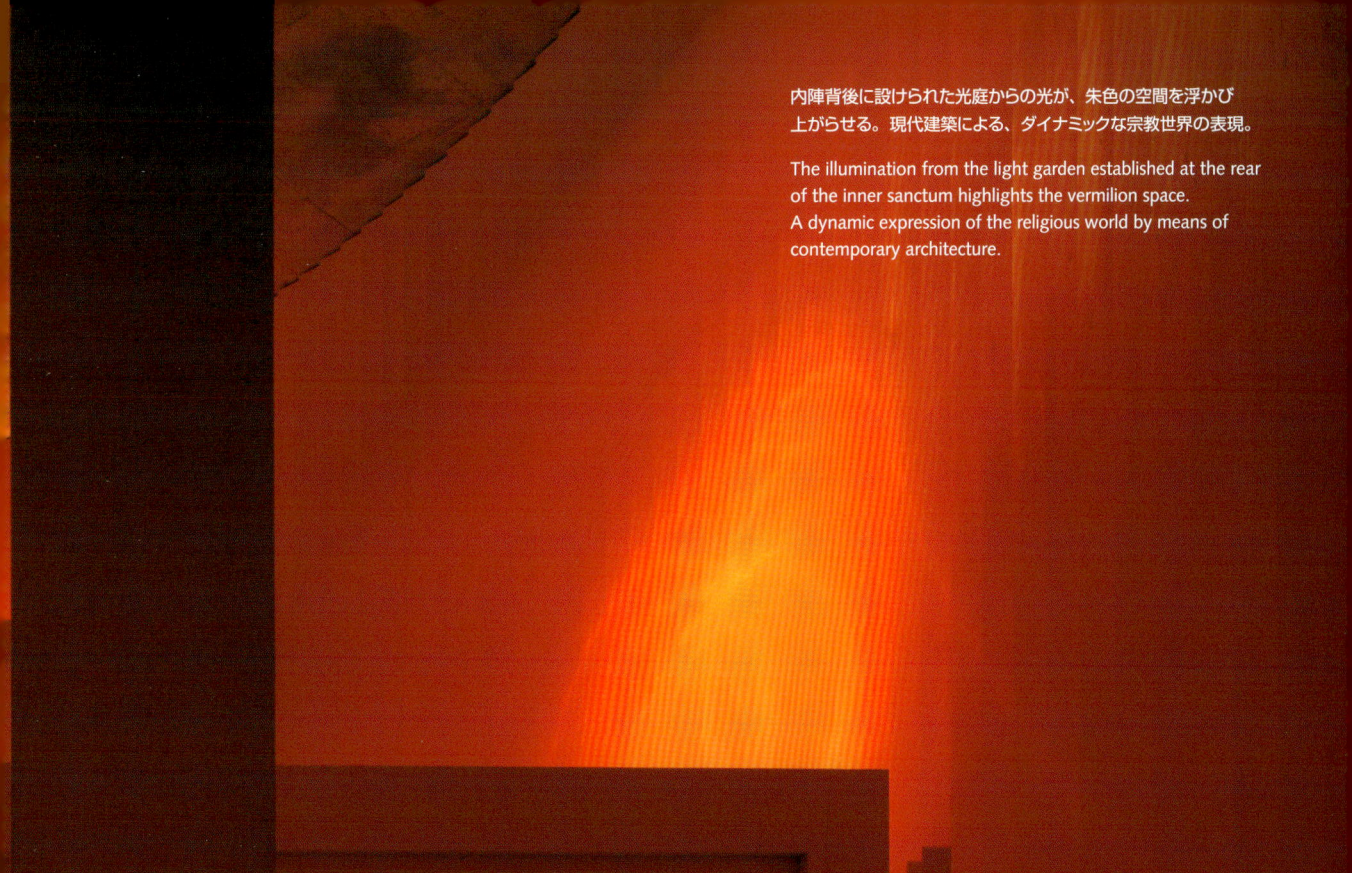

内陣背後に設けられた光庭からの光が、朱色の空間を浮かび上がらせる。現代建築による、ダイナミックな宗教世界の表現。

The illumination from the light garden established at the rear of the inner sanctum highlights the vermilion space.
A dynamic expression of the religious world by means of contemporary architecture.

円形の壁に囲まれた本堂内部。グリッド状に林立する柱と格子の
スクリーンが内陣と外陣を分割する。

The interior of the main hall is enclosed by a circular wall.
The inner sanctum and the outer chamber are divided by
a lattice screen and closely spaced columns in a grid pattern.

階段を見上げる。壁が切り取る空の光景が、
水面下の空間の深度を伝える。

Looking up at the stairs. A scene of sky
framed by walls conveys the depth of the
space below the water.

西側から見る。蓮池を囲う壁の向こうに瀬戸内海が広がる。

Looking from the west side. The Inland Sea extends
beyond the wall surrounding the lotus pond.

JR京都駅改築設計競技案
The Reconstruction of JR Kyoto Station, International Design Competition

1990-91　京都府京都市下京区 —— Shimogyo-ku, Kyoto, Kyoto

　平安建都1200年の記念事業として企画された、JR京都駅改築設計競技の提出案である。駅施設のほか、文化施設、商業空間、ホテルなどを含む複雑なプログラムに応えつつ、京都の玄関口となる建物にどのような〈顔〉を与えるか、建物と都市とをいかに関係づけるか——困難な課題に際し、私は羅生門を形象化したような計画案をもって、自身の抱く未来の京都への視座を表明した。

　建物は地中深く掘り込まれた円形の広場を中心として、東西に直列する3つのヴォリュームと、それを南北に貫いて架けられた人工地盤によって構成される。中央のヴォリュームが、一対の門型を象るガラスの「ツインゲート」である。建物内の各施設エリアは、円形のヴォイド、ゲートの間のクレバスといった、光と風を引き込む立体的な外部空間によって緩やかに接続され、〈都市の中の都市〉ともいうべき、変化に富んだ公共空間を形成する。その一方で、風景を映し出すガラスのゲートは、威圧的ではないシンボル性を場に付与しつつ、東海道線によって分断されていた都市の南北の風景を再びつなぎあわせる。

　ゲートをまたぐ人工地盤は、駅と都市空間とを一体化するアプローチ広場である。緩やかな階段を上ると、ゲートの真下に穿たれた円形の広場、その先に広がる桜の大庭園が目に飛び込んでくる。この桜並木と、ツインゲートが形づくるダイナミックな建築のフレームにより、借景として、遠く東山や北山の自然を引き寄せることを考えた。

　歴史都市で真剣にコンペを闘った経験は、その後の自身の建築に大いに活かされている。ちなみに「桜の大庭園」のアイディアは、15年後、幕張の「さくら広場」として実現している。

This is a proposal submitted to the international design competition for the reconstruction of JR Kyoto Station, planned as a commemoration project for the 1200th anniversary of the founding of Heian (the original name of Kyoto). While responding to a complex program that included cultural facilities, business spaces, and a hotel in addition to the station facilities, with regard to the difficult theme of how to give a "face" to a building that would become the entrance hall to Kyoto, I proposed a design modeled on Rashomon Gate as a declaration of my personal views on the future of Kyoto.

　The building is composed of three volumes aligned east-west and pierced north-south by a suspended artificial ground plane, surrounding a circular central plaza dug deep into the ground. The central volume is a glazed "twin gate," shaped like a pair of gates. All the functional areas inside the building are gently connected by means of a three-dimensional exterior space that draws in wind and light, including the crevasse between the gates and the circular void. This forms a public space filled with variation that could be called "a city within a city." On the other hand, the scenery-reflecting glass gates give the place an understated symbolism, reconnecting the north-south scenery of the city divided by the east-west train lines.

　The artificial ground plane straddling the gate is an approach plaza that unifies the station and the urban space. Ascending the long stair gives a view of the circular plaza incised directly below the gate and the large cherry-tree garden extending beyond. I considered drawing in the distant nature of the Higashiyama mountains and Kitayama mountains as "borrowed scenery" through the dynamic architectural frame formed by the twin gates and the rows of cherry trees.

　The experience of sincere engagement in a competition for a historic city greatly influenced my later architecture. The idea of the "large cherry-tree garden" materialized fifteen years later as Sakura Hiroba in Makuhari.

矩形のヴォリュームの組み合わせからなる構成の中に、突如登場する純粋幾何学形態。
ダイナミックな造形が、長大な施設内部に変化に富んだ空間のシークエンスを与える。

Pure geometric shapes suddenly emerge from a composition comprising rectangular volumes. This dynamic sculpting gives the long interior of the facility a spatial sequence rich in variation.

177 Kyoto Station

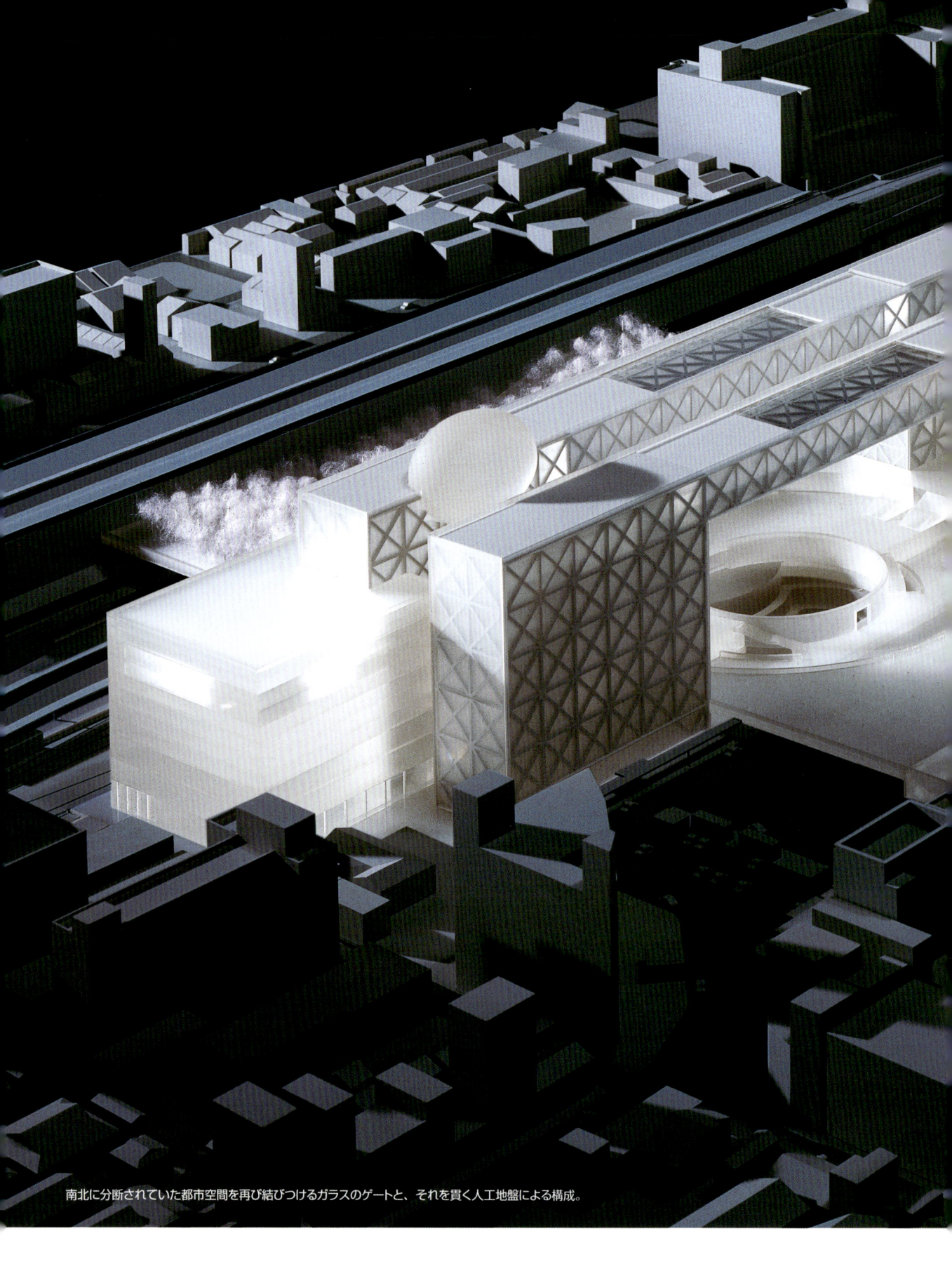

南北に分断されていた都市空間を再び結びつけるガラスのゲートと、それを貫く人工地盤による構成。

The urban space divided north-south is reconnected by a glazed gate, which is penetrated by an artificial ground surface.

180 TADAO ANDO 3

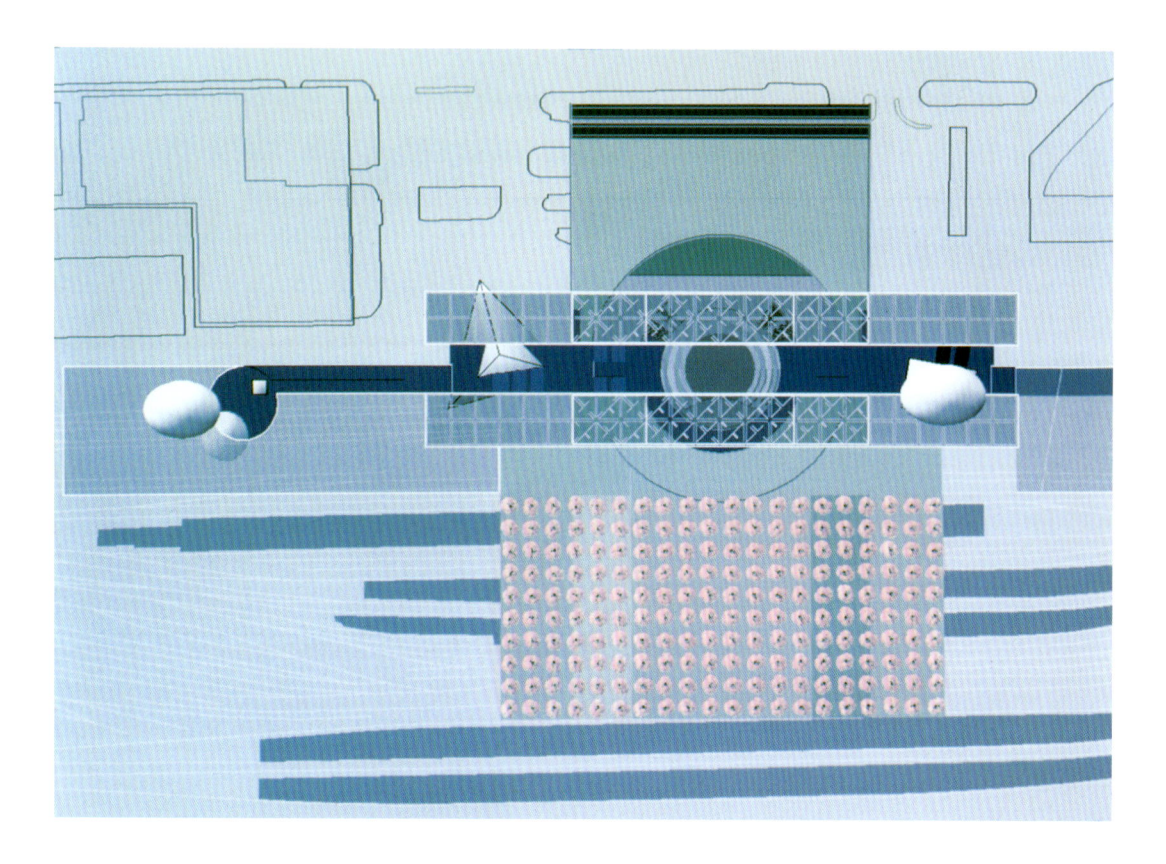

ツインゲートの真下に穿たれた円形のヴォイド空間。光と風を引き込む立体的なパブリックスペースが、建物内にもうひとつの〈都市〉をつくり出す。

A circular void space has been excavated directly below the twin gates. This three-dimensional public space draws in light and air, creating another "city" inside the building.

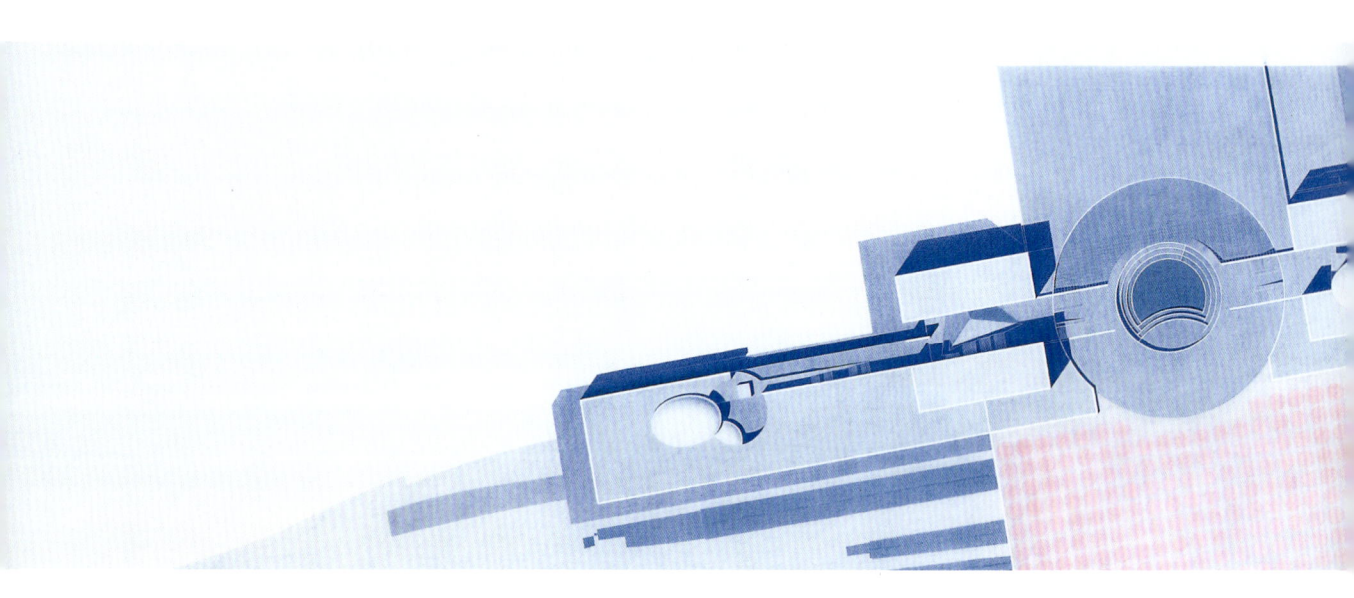

和紙に描かれたドローイング。都市を刺激する装置として考えられた建築空間。

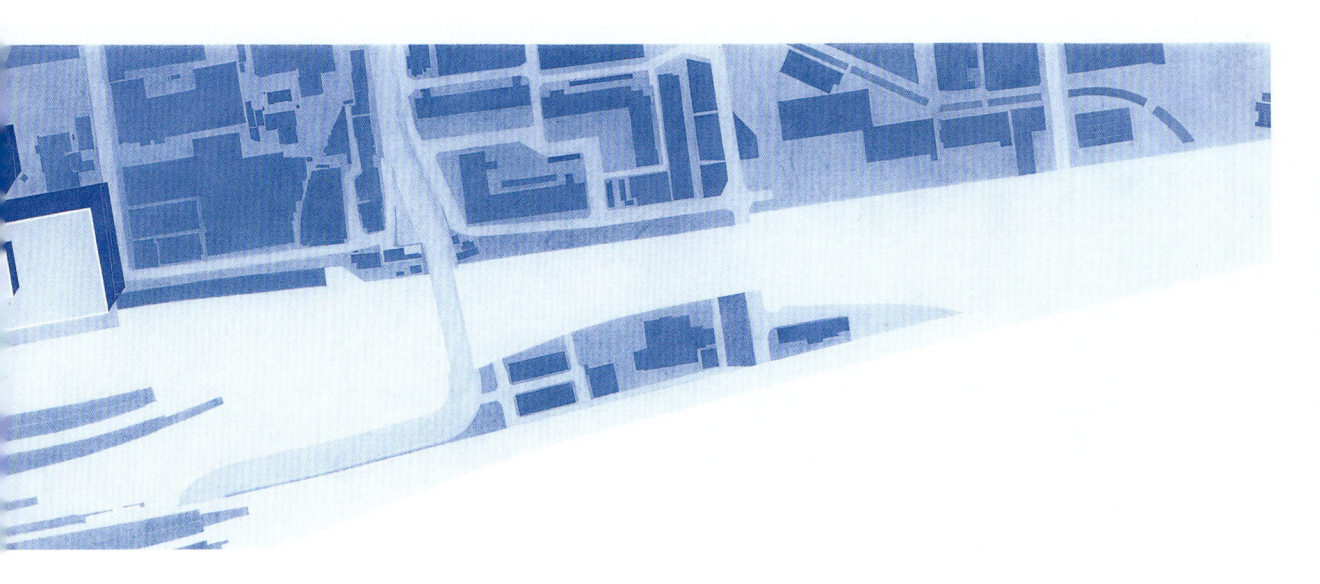

Drawing on Japanese paper. Architectural space conceived as a device to stimulate the city.

ベネッセハウス ミュージアム
Benesse House Museum/Naoshima
1988-92　香川県香川郡── Kagawa-gun, Kagawa

　80年代後半、瀬戸内海に浮かぶ小島、直島を〈自然あふれるアートの島〉として再生すべく、文化プロジェクトがスタートした。その最初の建築である「ベネッセハウス ミュージアム」は、島の南端部、三方を海に囲まれた岬の上につくられた、宿泊施設を伴う〈滞在型〉美術館である。

　この美術館には、船に乗って海からアプローチする。桟橋に降り立った人々は、階段状の広場を経て、木々の間に見える建物の自然石を積んだ壁に向かい歩を進める。大地に切り込む壁の軌跡、丘の上に載せられた1枚のスラブなど、アプローチに散りばめられた建築のエレメントが、豊かな自然の風景をさらに際立たせている。

　眼下に瀬戸内の海景の広がる緑の丘にあって、建物は自然の風景を侵さぬよう、注意深く地形の中に沿うように配置されている。結果、その半分の部分が地中に埋め込まれたかたちになっているが、その内に展開される空間は明るく開放的である。単純な幾何学形態の組み合わせの中で、垂直方向のヴォイドを軸とした立体的な空間分節が行われており、その節々に設けられたテラスを介して、内外空間は大胆に交流する。

　建物は1992年に完成したが、それは同時に、アートディレクターによるアートスペースの獲得という闘いの〈始まり〉だった。建物内外に展開するひとつひとつの場所の可能性を読み解きながら、建築とアートの緊張関係を構築していく──その過程で、アーティスト自身が場所を選び、その場所をテーマに制作された作品も生まれた。建築とアート、自然のコラボレーション。地道な取り組みの積み重ねによって、ひっそりと時間を刻んできた内海の小島は、いつしか世界に発信するアートの聖地と呼ばれるに至った。

　The regeneration of Naoshima, a small island floating in the Seto Inland Sea, into an "island of nature filled with art" is a cultural project that was initiated in the second half of the 1980s. The first building is the Benesse House Museum, an "overnight stay" museum that includes lodging facilities built on top of a cape surrounded on three sides by the sea.

　This museum is reached from the sea by boat. People alight at the pier, traverse a stepped plaza, and continue walking toward the building wall of stacked natural stones, visible between the trees. The architectural elements scattered along the approach, such as the line of the wall cut into the ground and the single slab placed on top of the hill, are even more conspicuous within the lush natural landscape.

　On a green hill from which the scenery of the Seto Inland Sea unfolds below, the building is arranged as if invading the natural scenery and following the remarkable topography. As a result, half of it is buried into the ground, but the spaces that unfold inside are open and bright. Between the collection of simple geometric shapes are vertical voids forming the axis of the three-dimensional spatial articulation. There is a bold intermingling of interior and exterior space in the terraces established at their joints.

　The building was completed in 1992, which coincided with the start of the struggle for the acquisition of art space by the art director. Tense relationships between architecture and art were constructed while interpreting the possibilities of each of the places created inside and outside the building. Within this process, the artists themselves could choose a place and create a work that took the place as its theme. A collaboration between architecture, art, and nature. Through steadily accumulating efforts, this quiet island in the Seto Inland Sea, sculpted by time, has surreptitiously become known as a sacred spot for art conveyed to the world at large.

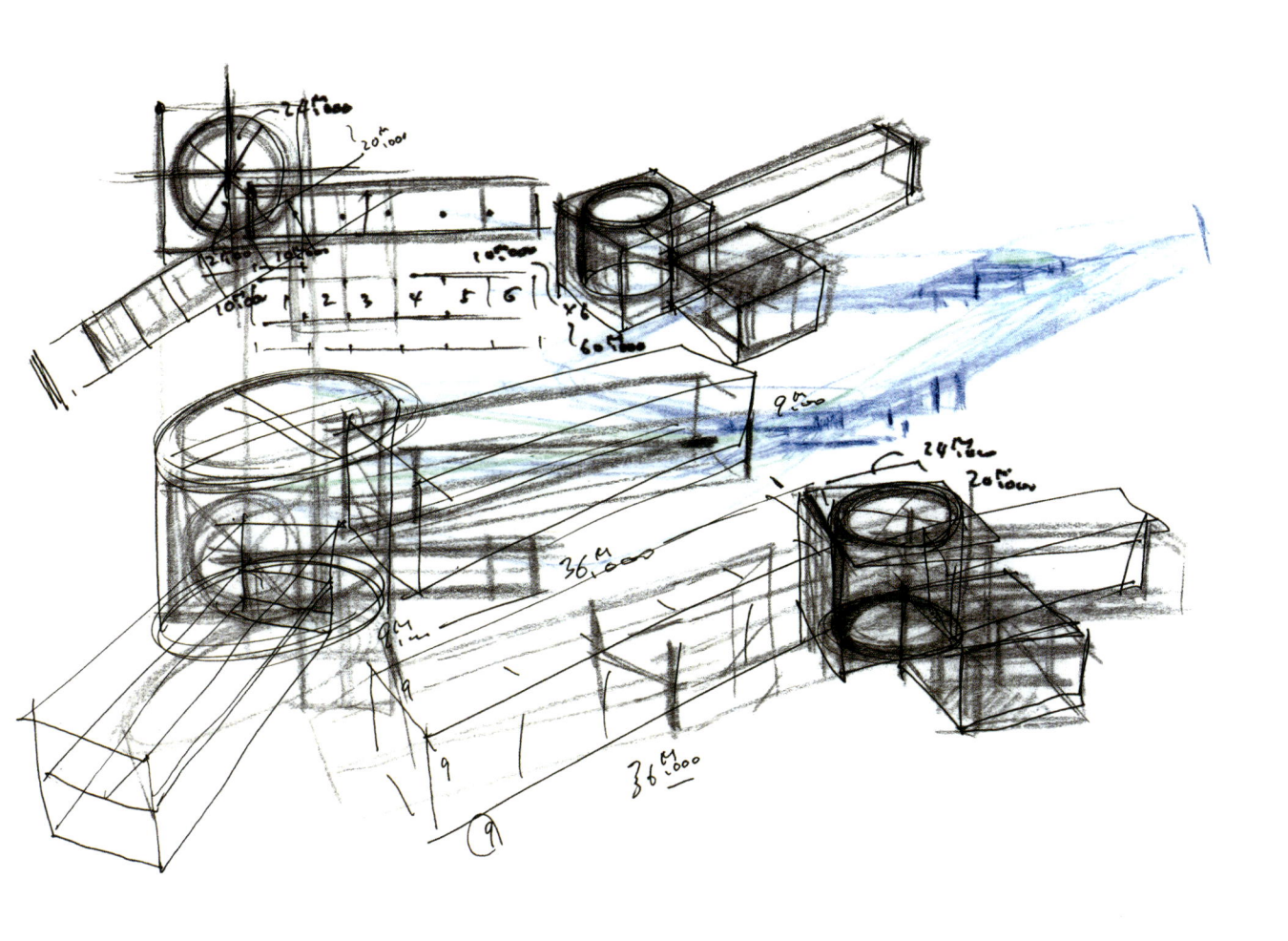

ミュージアムの初期イメージスケッチ。シリンダーや直方体といった単純な
幾何学形態の重なりの中に、立体的な空間を生み出すべく検討がなされている。

Early image sketches of the museum. An investigation into how
three-dimensional spaces can be produced from the overlapping of simple
geometrical forms such as cylinders and rectangular volumes.

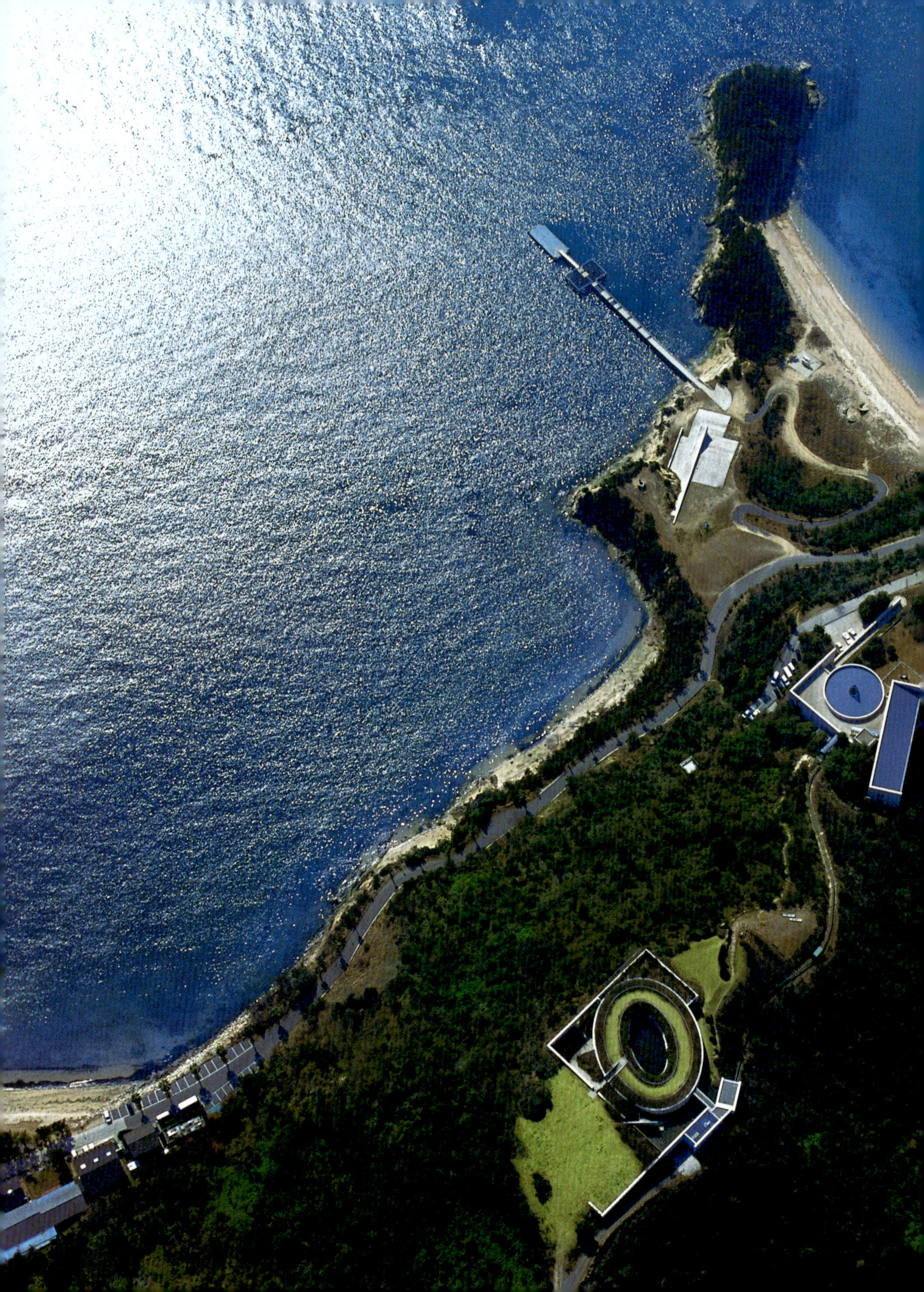

海に突き出た緑の丘に埋め込むように配された建築の幾何学。ミュージアムと後に増築されたオーバルとはケーブルカーで結ばれている。

The architectural geometry is distributed as if buried into green hills and projecting out to the sea.
The later addition of the Oval is connected to the museum by a cable car.

海からアプローチする人々を迎える、階段状のテラス。
雄大な海景の中に差し込まれる建築の断片が、自然を感得
するための装置としての役割を果たす。

Stair-shaped terrace that welcomes people approaching
from the sea. The building fragments inserted in a
magnificent seascape act as devices for
perceiving nature.

Site plan 1:2,500

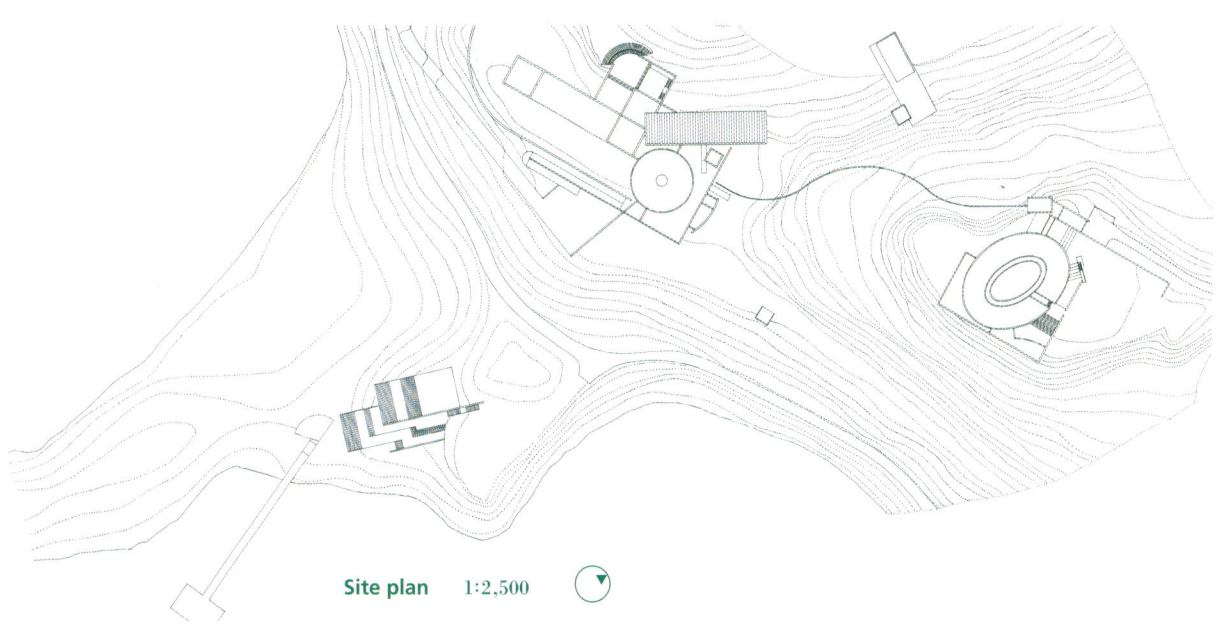

189 Benesse House Museum

Section 1:1,000

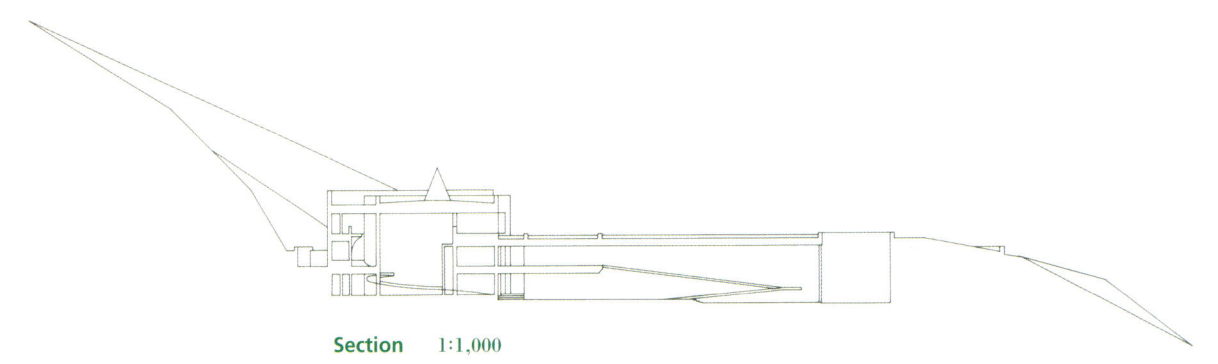

背後の斜面から、ミュージアム越しに瀬戸内海を望む。ヴォリュームの大半は地下に埋め込まれ、屋根は周囲の緑と連続する屋上庭園となっている。風景と一体化する建築の風景。

View of the Inland Sea across the museum from the rear slope. The majority of the volume is buried under the soil, and the rooftop is a garden continuous with the surrounding greenery. A scene of architecture unified with landscape.

主要な外壁には白大理石の乱石積みの表現が与えられている。瀬戸内の青い空と海、木々の緑に呼応する建築。

An expression of irregular white marble has been applied to the main exterior walls. Architecture that acts in concert with the blue sky and water of the Inland Sea and the green of the trees.

Second floor plan

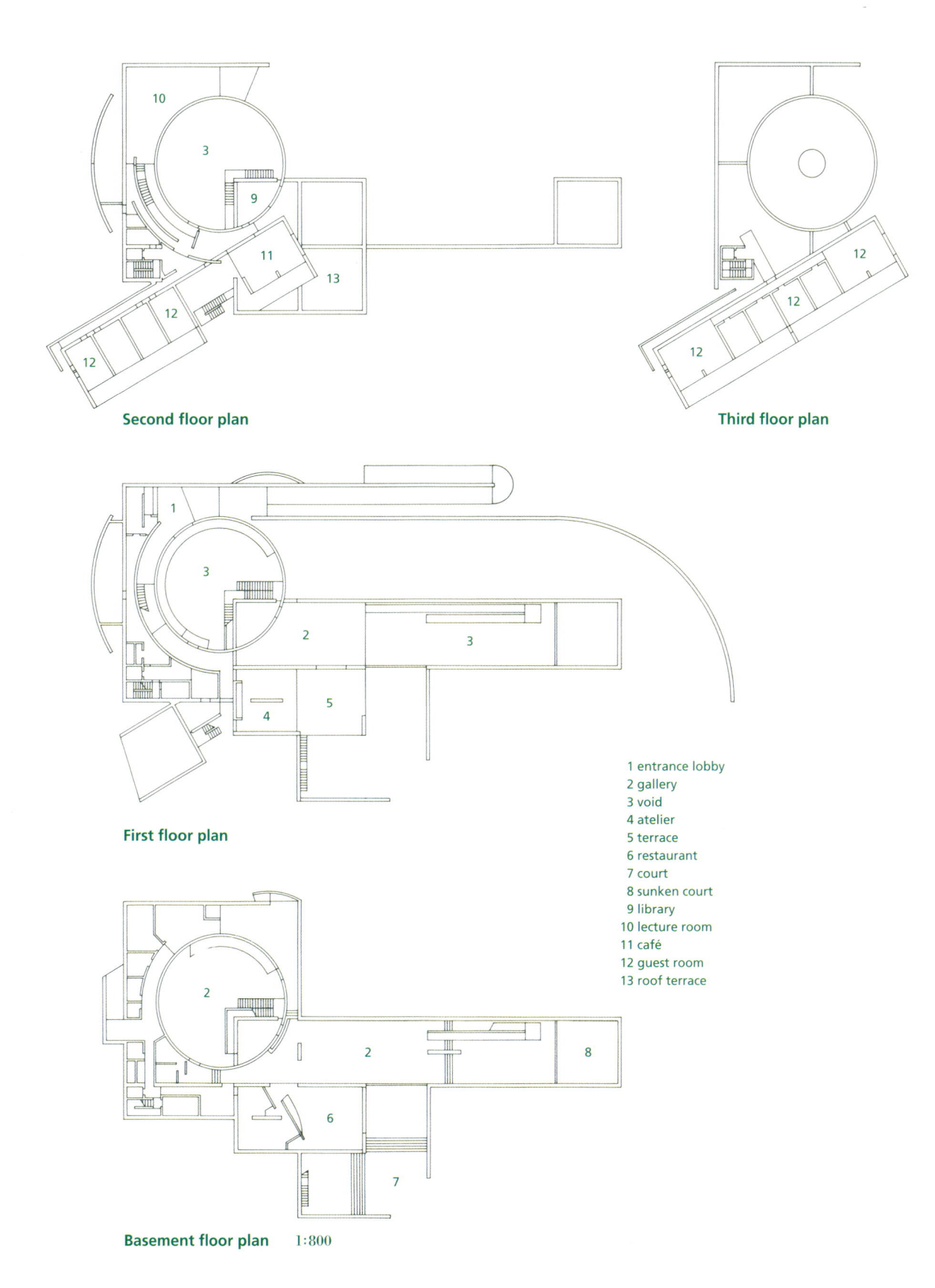

Third floor plan

First floor plan

1 entrance lobby
2 gallery
3 void
4 atelier
5 terrace
6 restaurant
7 court
8 sunken court
9 library
10 lecture room
11 café
12 guest room
13 roof terrace

Basement floor plan 1:800

193 Benesse House Museum

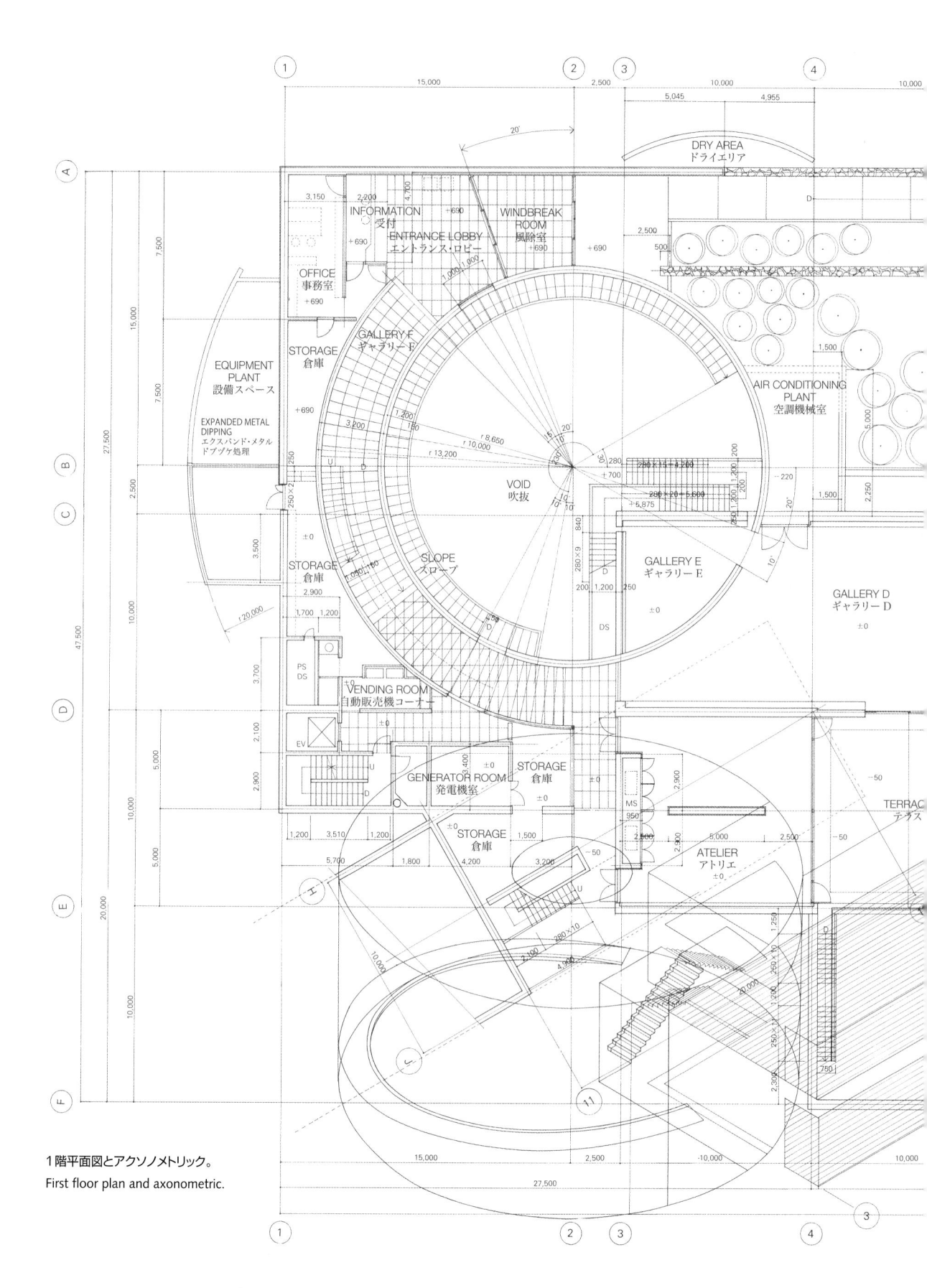

1階平面図とアクソノメトリック。
First floor plan and axonometric.

195 Benesse House Museum

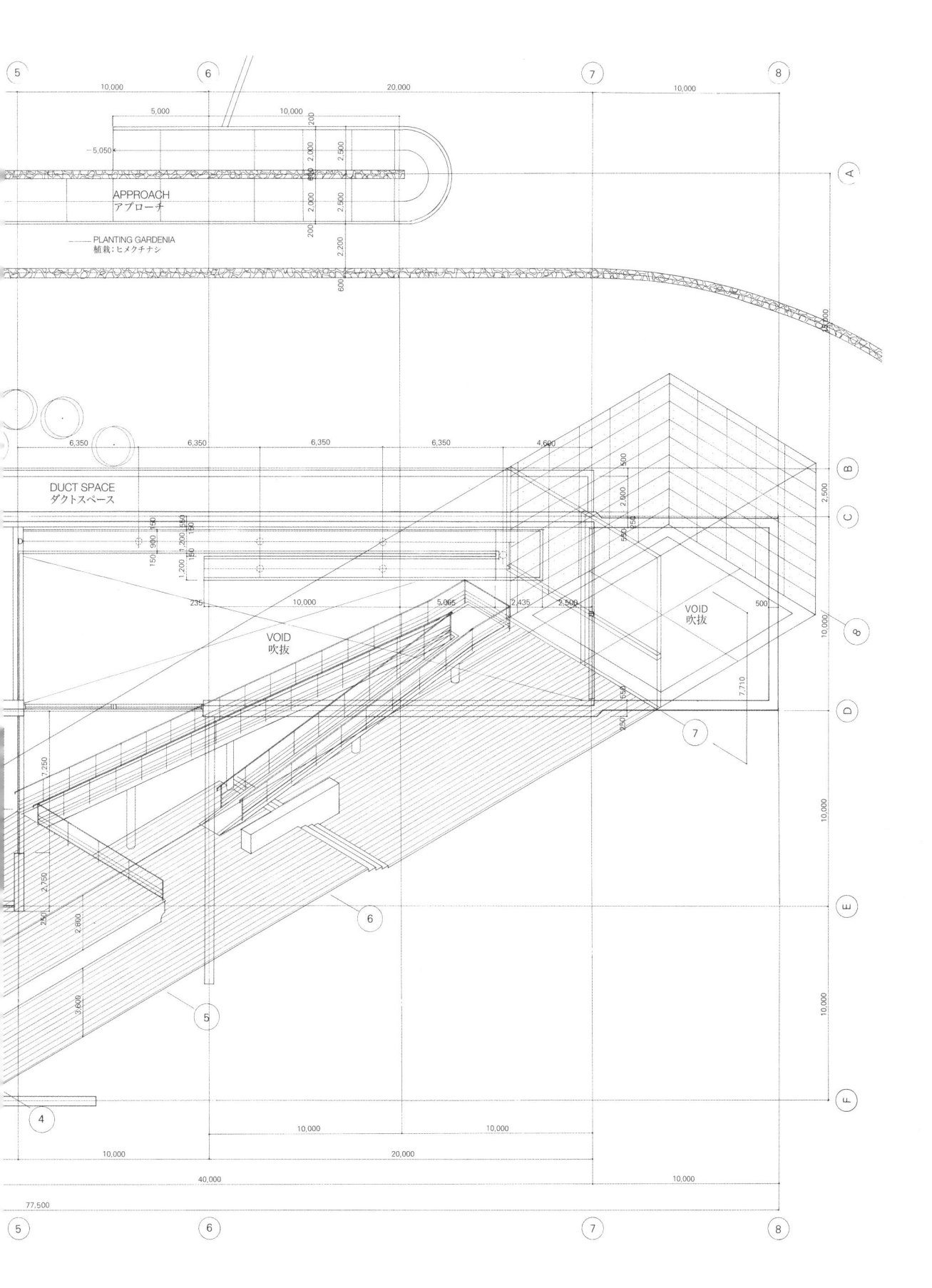

地形を活かした巧みな断面計画により、シンプルな幾何学であ
りながら多様な、自然光に満ちた内部空間を実現している。

By means of a sectional scheme intended to make use of
the topography, diverse light-filled internal spaces have
been achieved within simple geometries.

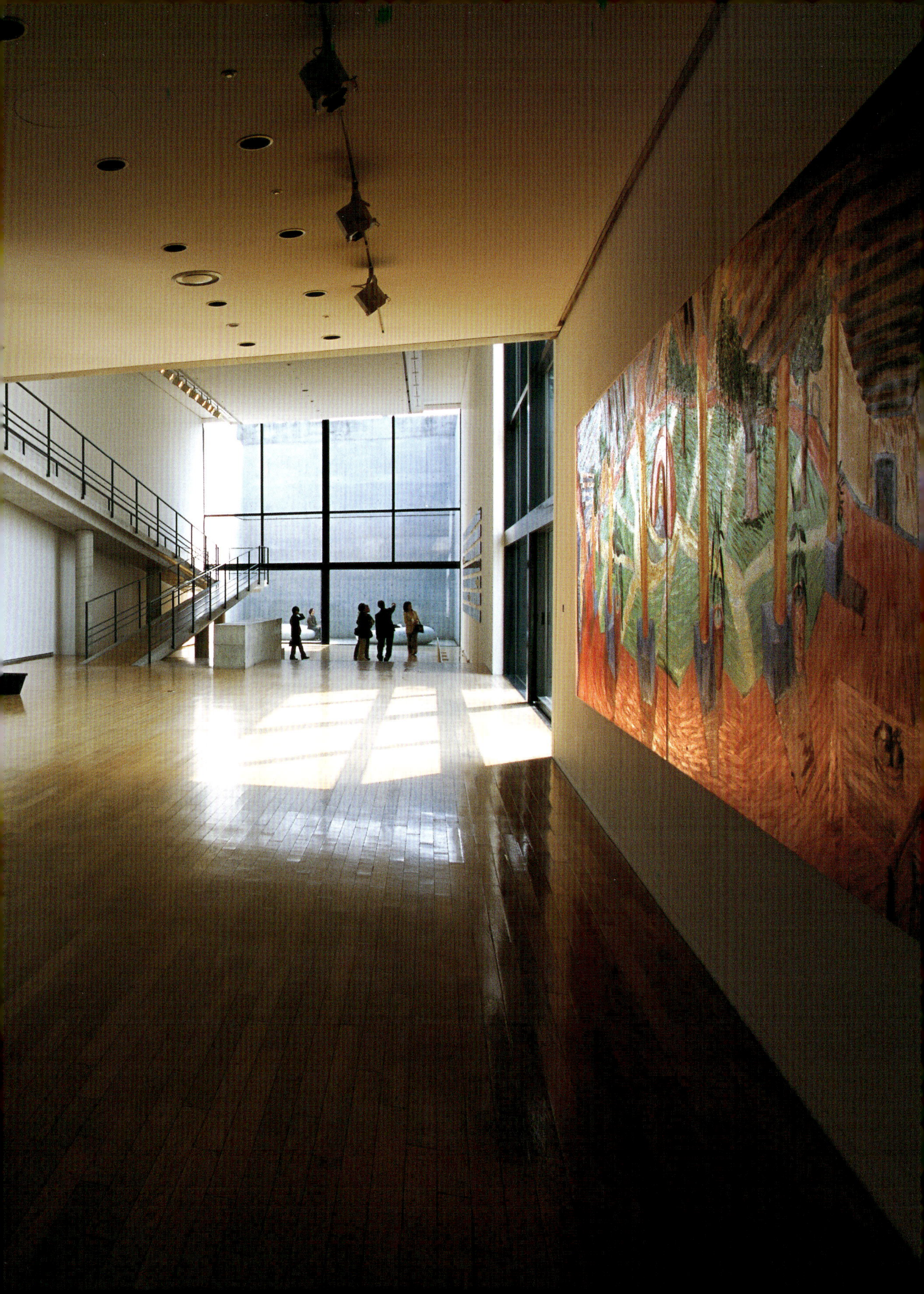

建物に入った人々を待ち受ける、採光を天井の円形スカイライトに絞ったシリンダー状の吹き抜け空間。直径20m、高さ10.7m。薄暗闇の中、ブルース・ナウマンの「100生きて死ね」が明滅する。

Light is drawn through a round skylight in the ceiling of the cylindrical void space that awaits people entering the building. It is 20m in diameter and 10.7m in height. Bruce Naumann's 100 Live and Die is blinking in the gloom.

199 Benesse House Museum

直方体の展示室のドライエリアに設置された安田侃の「天秘」、海に開かれたコートに設置されたアレキサンダー・カルダーの「mobile」、リチャード・ロングによる「瀬戸内の流木の円」。内外の区別なく、現代アート作品が予期せぬ場所で人々を迎える。

Kan Yasuda's The Secret of the Sky has been installed in the dry area of the rectangular volume exhibition room. A mobile by Alexander Calder installed in a courtyard open toward the sea, and Richard Long's Inland Sea Driftwood Circle. Making no distinction between inside and outside, people are invited into unexpected places for contemporary artworks.

201 Benesse House Museum

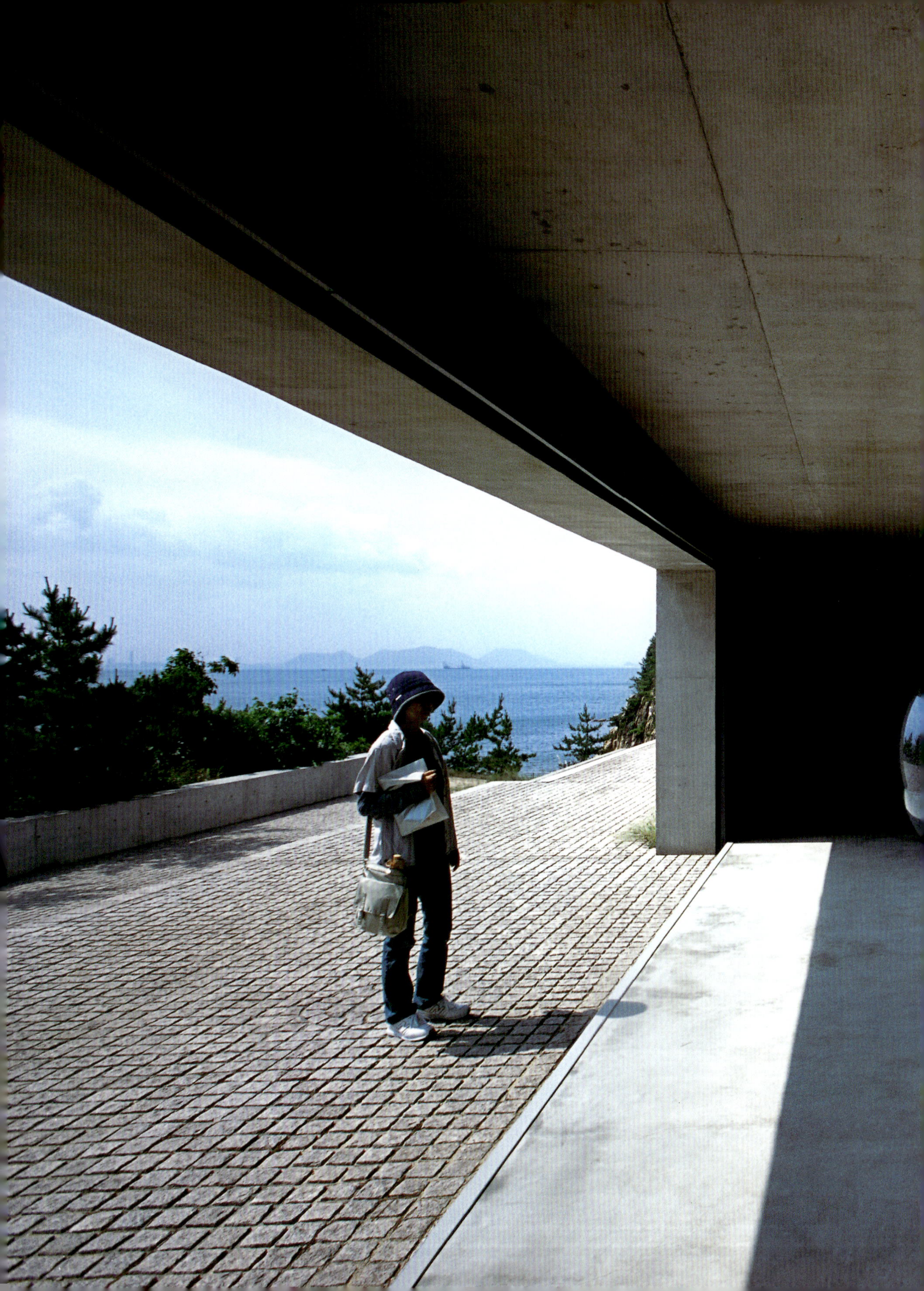

アプローチの階段広場の側面に設けられた屋外展示スペース。
ウォルター・デ・マリアの地中美術館での作品の序章とも言うべき
「見えて／見えず　知って／知れず」が置かれている。

An outdoor exhibition space located in the side of the
approach plaza stair. Placed here is Walter de Maria's
Seen/Unseen Known/Unknown, which could be called a
prologue to his work at the Chichu Art Museum.

ベネッセハウス オーバル
Benesse House Oval / Naoshima
1993-95

　ミュージアムの完成から3年後、その背後の丘の上にアネックスとして宿泊棟「オーバル」がつくられた。ミュージアムとは斜面を這うように進むケーブルカーで結ばれている。

　「オーバル」は、その名の通り楕円をモチーフとした建築である。楕円形は、円と同じくある種の完結性を呈しながら、その偏心性ゆえに、不思議な奥行き感を空間にもたらす強い幾何学形態である。

　建物は、領域を象る正方形と、その中心に軸を振って配置された楕円という構図でできている。楕円の内側には、同じく楕円の中庭が設けられており、それを取り囲むように宿泊室が並べられている。楕円形の中庭には水が張られており、その水面には楕円形に切り取られた青空の輪郭が、静かに時を刻むよう映し出されている。楕円の外側の大らかな自然の海景と好対照をなす、抽象化された自然と幾何学による異世界の創出を意図した建築である。

　ミュージアム本館同様、宿泊棟の屋根は屋上庭園とされており、連続する自然の風景の中に、構成の幾何学は埋没している。予定外の増築ではあったが、逆にその時間のズレが、自然な建築の展開につながったように思う。

　以降、直島の文化プロジェクトは、旧市街・本村地区での古民家再生を主題とする「家プロジェクト」、3人のアーティストの作品を永久展示する「地中美術館」、さらにベネッセハウス新館「パーク／ビーチ棟」と、生物が増殖するように段階的・継続的な建築の拡張を続けている。現代の高度に管理化された社会生産システムの中では望み得ない、マスタープランなき、〈成長する建築〉の試みである。

Three years after the completion of the museum, the lodging building Oval was constructed as an annex on the hill to the rear. It is connected to the museum by means of a cable car that seems to crawl along the slope.

As its name indicates, Oval is a building with an elliptical motif. While providing a kind of completeness like a circle, the ellipse is a strong geometric shape that has a mysterious sense of depth due to its eccentricity.

The building is composed of a square defining the shape of the area, in the center of which is an ellipse with an offset axis. Within the ellipse is an inner courtyard of the same elliptical shape, around which the guestrooms are arrayed. Water is spread in the elliptical inner courtyard and blue sky framed by the elliptical shape is reflected in the water surface, peacefully marking the passage of time. This is an architecture intended to create another world by means of geometry and abstracted nature, in a pleasing contrast to the generous natural seascape outside the ellipse.

Like the main building of the museum, the roof of the lodging building is a rooftop garden, and the geometry of the composition is embedded in the continuous natural scenery. Although this was an unexpected addition to a building, conversely I think that the shift in time is connected to the natural development of the architecture.

With the House Projects themed on regenerating old houses in the historical town district of Honmura, the Chichu Art Museum containing permanent installations of works by three artists, and the Park/Beach Building as a new annex to Benesse House, the Naoshima culture project gradually continues to expand the architecture, like the propagation of living things. This is an experiment in "cultivating architecture" without a master plan, something that is unexpected in our highly controlled contemporary social production system.

205 Benesse House Oval

緩やかなカーブを描く水盤に、刻々と姿を変える光が映し出される。
大自然の只中に現出する抽象化された自然の風景。

Light changing in appearance from moment to moment is
reflected in the water basin, which traces a gentle curve. A scene
of abstracted nature appearing in the middle of real nature.

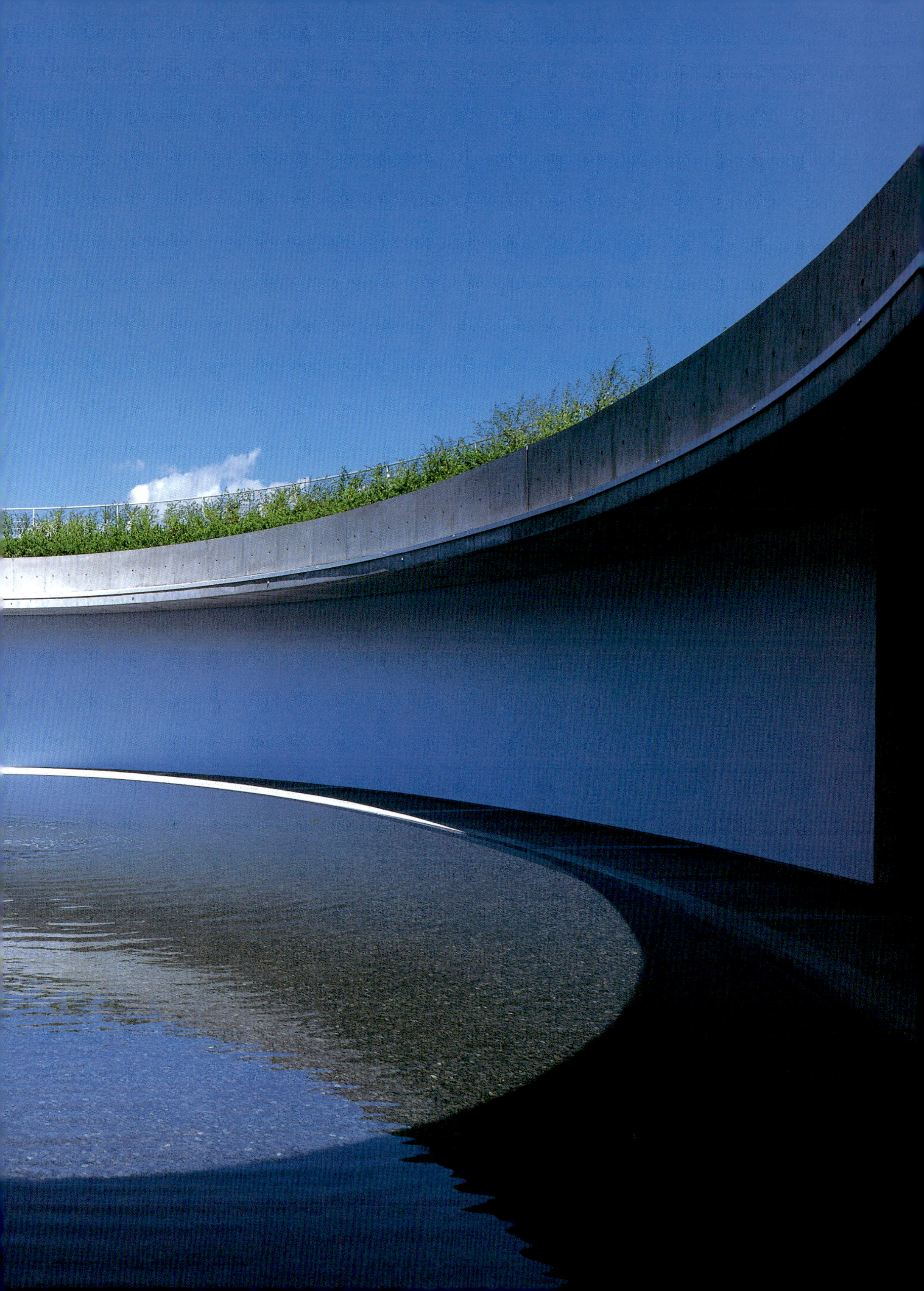

楕円形に切り取られた青空と水盤に挟まれた空間。
楕円がもつ偏心性が不思議な奥行き感を生み出す。

Space interposed between the water basin and
the blue sky framed in an oval shape.
The eccentricity of the oval creates a mysterious
sense of depth.

上空から見るオーバルの夜景。光が水面に反射し、幻想的な雰囲気を醸し出す。

Night view of the oval seen from above. Light reflects in the water surface, producing a magical atmosphere.

外に開かれたアプローチのカスケードと、中庭の静寂な水盤の空間は
対照的である。薄いブルーの壁面はベネチアン・スタッコ塗。

There is a contrast between the cascade in the approach route,
open to the outside, and the silent water basin space in the courtyard.
The pale blue wall has been coated with Venetian stucco.

211 Benesse House Oval

1 cafeteria
2 guest room

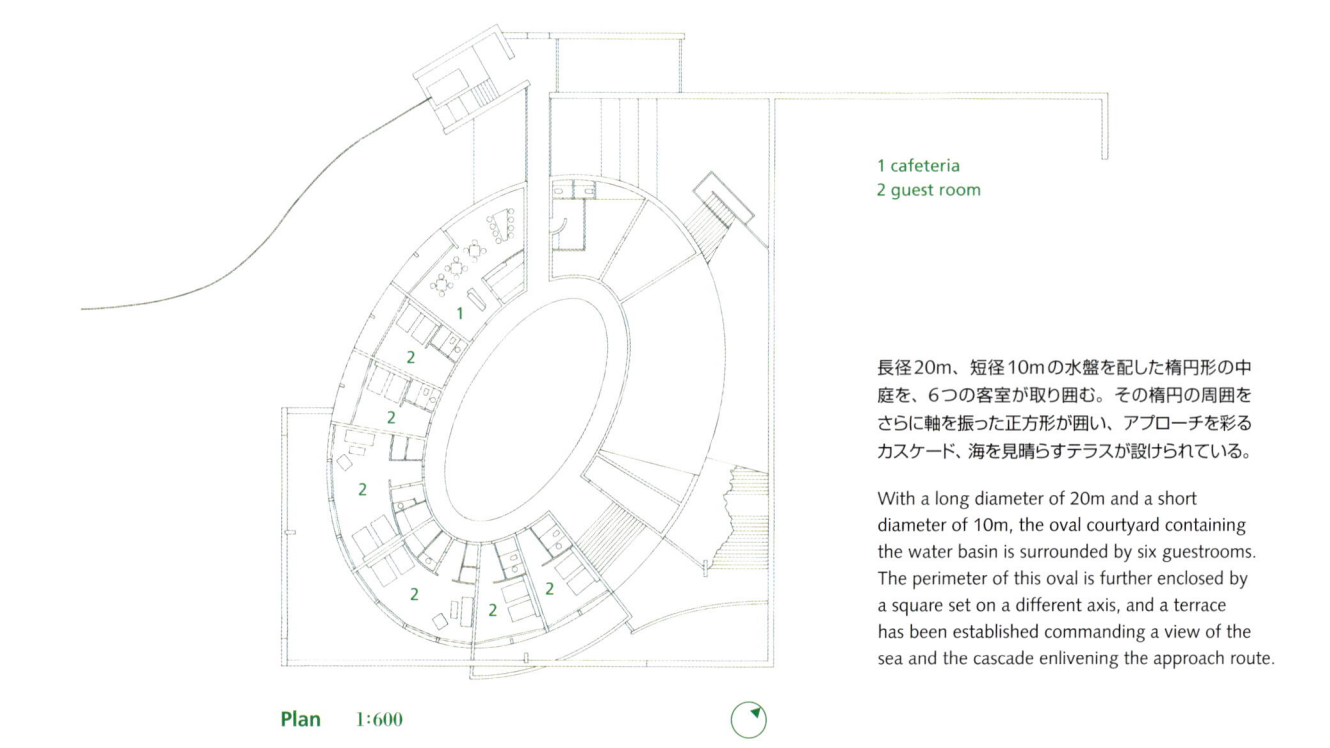

長径20m、短径10mの水盤を配した楕円形の中庭を、6つの客室が取り囲む。その楕円の周囲をさらに軸を振った正方形が囲い、アプローチを彩るカスケード、海を見晴らすテラスが設けられている。

With a long diameter of 20m and a short diameter of 10m, the oval courtyard containing the water basin is surrounded by six guestrooms. The perimeter of this oval is further enclosed by a square set on a different axis, and a terrace has been established commanding a view of the sea and the cascade enlivening the approach route.

Plan 1:600

Section / roof plan　1:1,500

213 Benesse House Oval

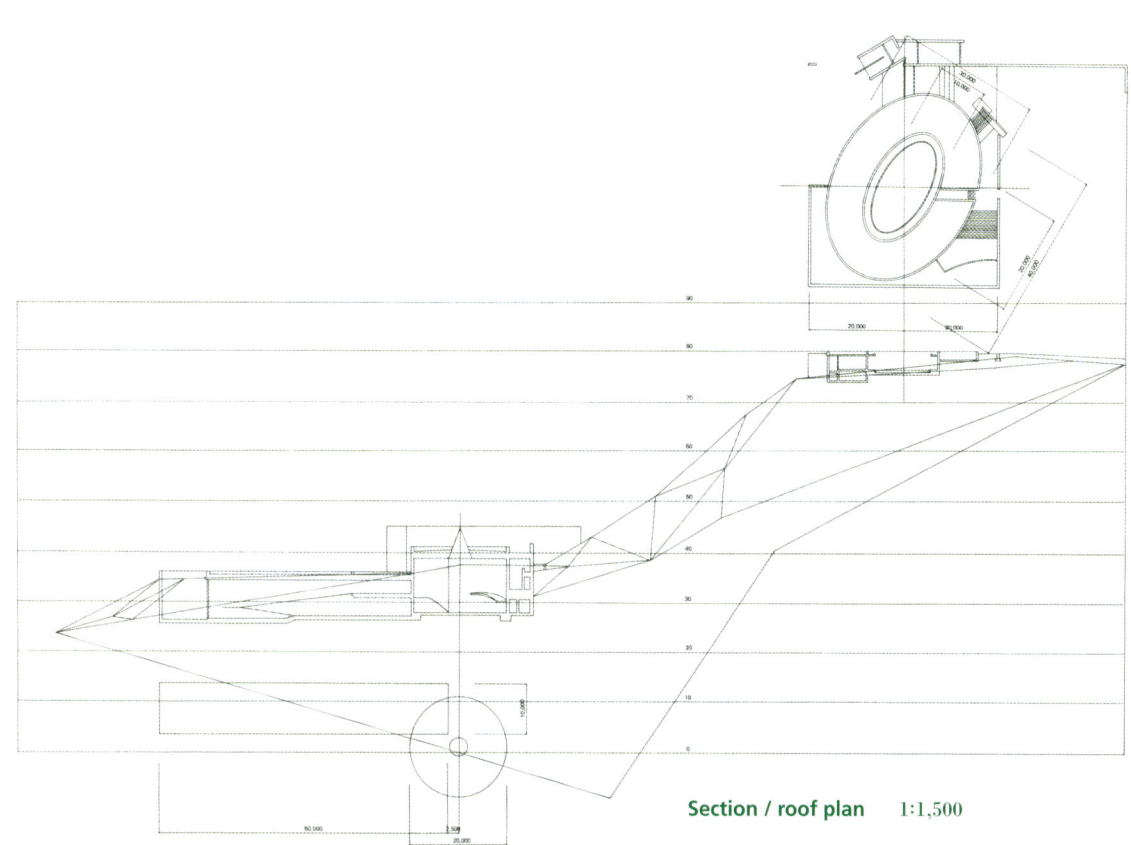

楕円と正方形の隙間の庭には植物が生い茂り、時とともに建築が自然に融和していく。
Plants grow in abundance in the garden located in the interstitial space between the oval and the square, and the building harmonizes with nature as well as with time.

楕円の外に向かって開かれた客室。雄大な海景を一望できる。
Guest room open toward the outside of the oval. A magnificent seascape is visible.

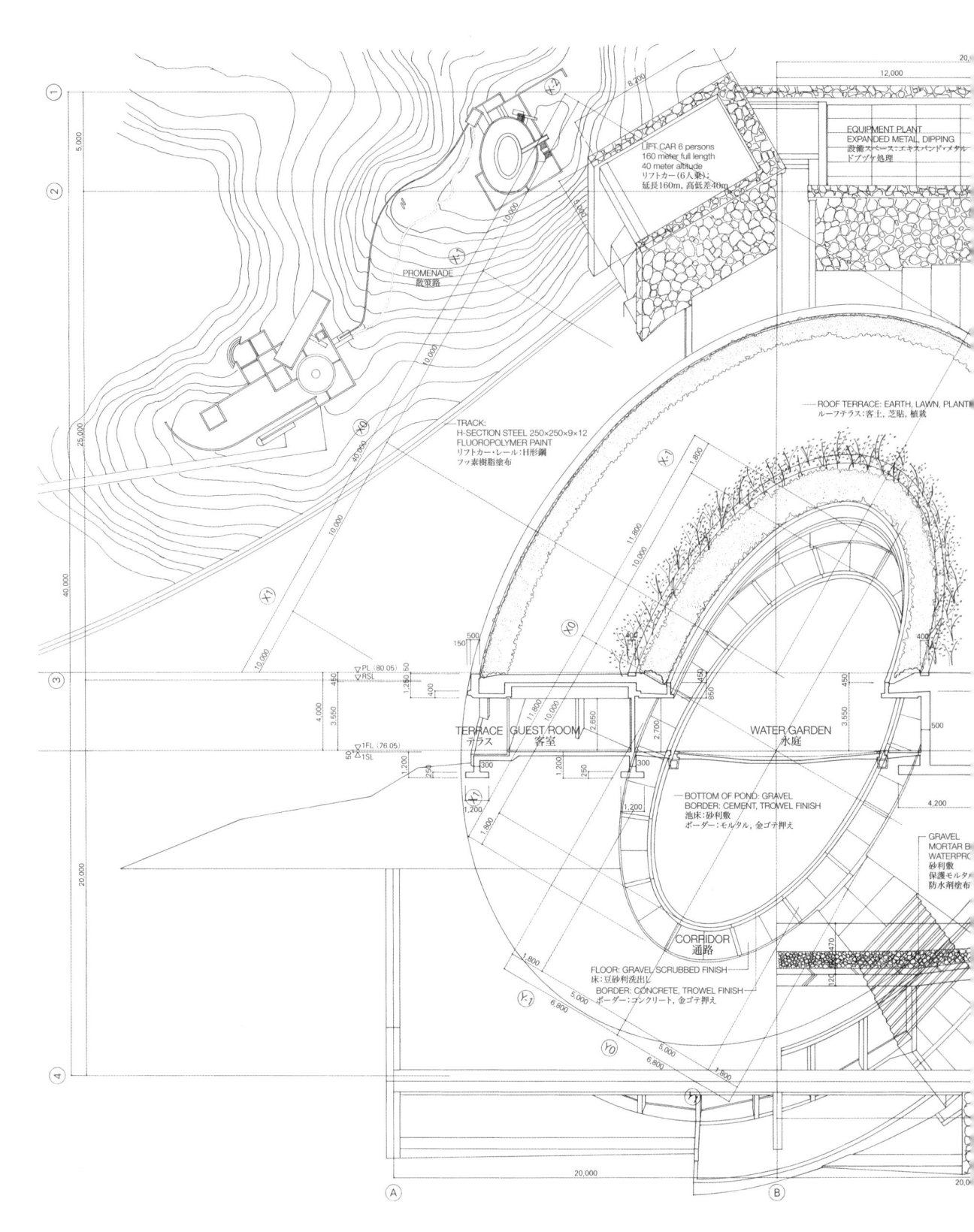

配置図、アクソノメトリック及び断面詳細図。
Site plan, axonometric and sectional detail.

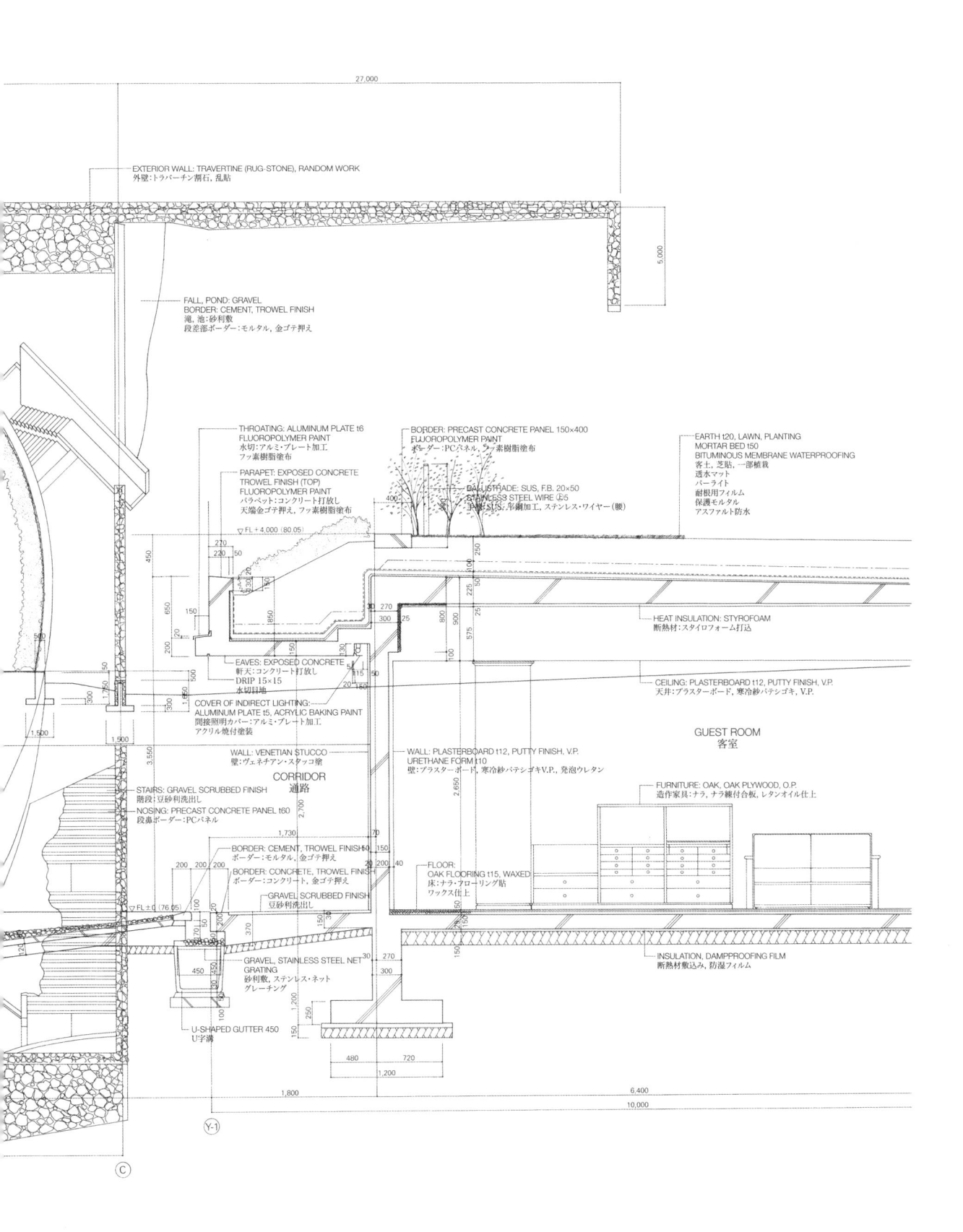

217 Benesse House Oval

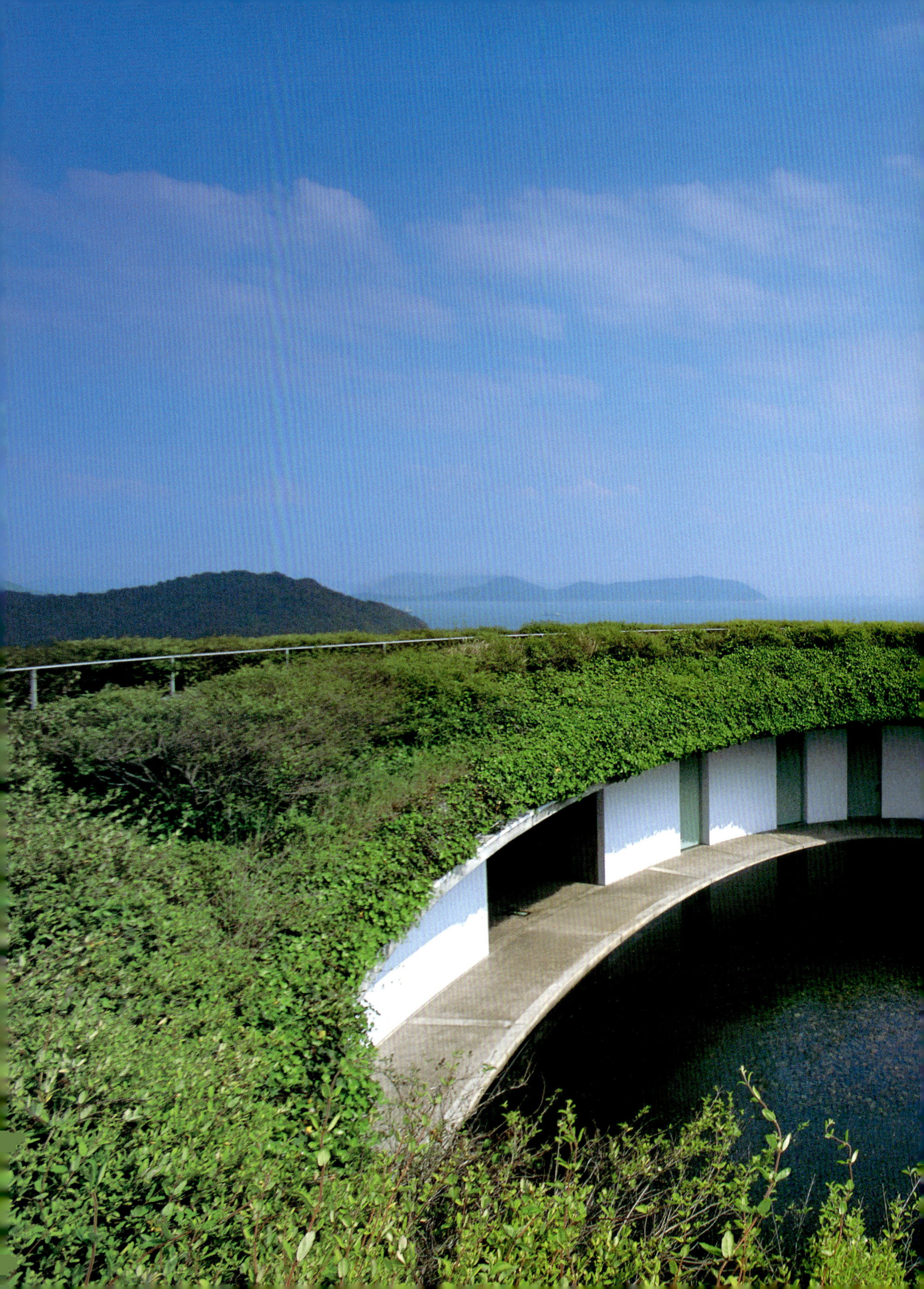

ミュージアム同様、屋根には屋上植栽が施されている。
海・空と一体となる丘の頂に置かれた建築。

Planting has been applied to the rooftop, similar to the museum. Architecture placed on top of a hill, uniting sea and sky.

敷地は、日本有数の古墳密集地として知られる大阪府南河内郡の、緑深い谷間に設けられた史跡公園内に位置する。古墳文化の展示と研究を目的としてつくられた博物館である。30万m²の広さをもつ公園内には、100基余りの古墳の石組みが残されており、周囲には、4基の天皇陵のほか、さらに100基以上の古墳が点在する。

日本黎明期からの悠久のときの流れを体感できる、このすぐれた歴史的環境の只中で、私は既成の博物館の概念とは異なる方向の建築を試みた。即ち、緑の谷間に埋め込むように配した建物の屋上をすべて階段広場とし、歴史の刻まれた風景との対峙を第一義とする、環境体験型博物館という構想である。

階段に覆われた博物館内部は、墳墓内さながらの〈地下の闇〉を思わせる空間となっている。中心は、前方後円墳を模したようなかたちの2層吹き抜けの常設展示室で、来館者はエントランスのある1階レベルから、室形状に沿って配された出土品を眺めつつ、緩やかな弧を描くスロープを下降し、展示のクライマックスとなる地階の巨大な古墳模型のスペースへと導かれる。物語性に富んだ、劇的な空間演出を意図した構成である。

「兵庫県立こどもの館」以降、恵まれた自然環境の中での建築のランドスケープ化が、自身の建築のひとつのテーマとしてあった。だが、幾何学性の強いかたちと自然との〈融和〉を意図したそれらの建物に対し、「近つ飛鳥」では、構成の幾何学は地形に同調して、より曖昧なかたちに崩されている一方、構築物と自然との境目は植栽で覆ったりせず、ぶしつけなほど直裁に表現されている。

これは恐らく、私の中にこの建築を〈現代の古墳〉とする思いがあったからだろう。大地に標された、壮大な人間の意志の表現——何十万個の白い花崗岩の葺石で覆われた階段は、古墳と同じく空に向けたファサードの表現だった。

大阪府立近つ飛鳥博物館
Chikatsu-Asuka Historical Museum, Osaka
1990-94　大阪府南河内郡——Minamikawachi-gun, Osaka

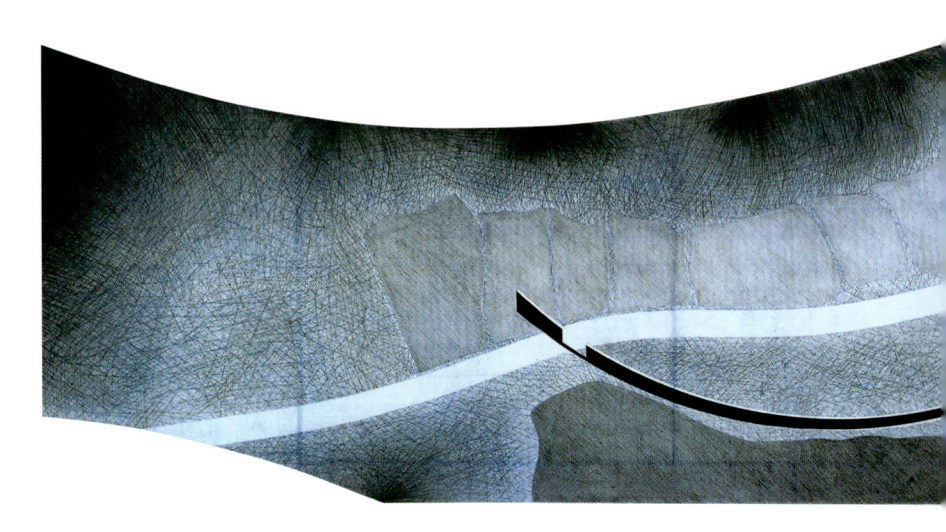

サイトドローイング。池に面した長く緩やかな壁など、環境と一体化する建築の意図が、サイトに強く表れている。

The site is located in a historical park established in a deep green valley in Osaka's Minamikawachi district, well known in Japan as an area containing a cluster of *kofun* (mounded tombs). This is a museum constructed with the aim of researching and displaying *kofun* culture. The stone arrangements of more than a hundred tombs remain inside the park, which extends over some 30,000m², and the vicinity is dotted with at least another hundred tombs in addition to four Imperial tombs.

Right in the middle of this extraordinary historical environment, wherein the ceaseless flow of time since the dawn of Japan may be sensed, I attempted an architecture that takes a direction different from conventional museum concepts. That is to say, the entire rooftop of the building, arranged as if buried into the green valley, has been turned into a stepped plaza. The concept is an environmental experience museum, with its first principle being a confrontation with scenery carved by time.

The interior of this museum covered by stairs is a space of "underground gloom" that brings to mind being inside a tomb. At the center is a permanent exhibition room, a double-height void shaped as if imitating a *zenpo koen kofun* (keyhole-shaped mounded tomb). From the guest entrance on the first floor level, visitors descend a slope describing a gentle arc while looking at excavated artifacts distributed along the room shape, and are guided to an underground space containing an enormous model of a mounded tomb that is the climax of the exhibition. This composition is intended to produce a dramatic space filled with narrative.

Since the Hyogo Prefecture Children's Museum, turning architecture into a landscape within a lush natural environment has become one of the themes of my architecture. However, in contrast with buildings aimed at a "harmony" between nature and strong geometrical shapes, the compositional geometry of the Chikatsu-Asuka Historical Museum is aligned with the terrain in a more ambiguous shape. On the other hand, the borders between nature and the structure are expressed with a direct boldness, not overwhelmed by planting.

This is perhaps because I conceived this architecture as a "contemporary *kofun*." A mark on the earth as a majestic expression of human will—covered with hundreds of thousands of white granite tiles, the roof is expressed as a facade turned to the sky, just like a *kofun*.

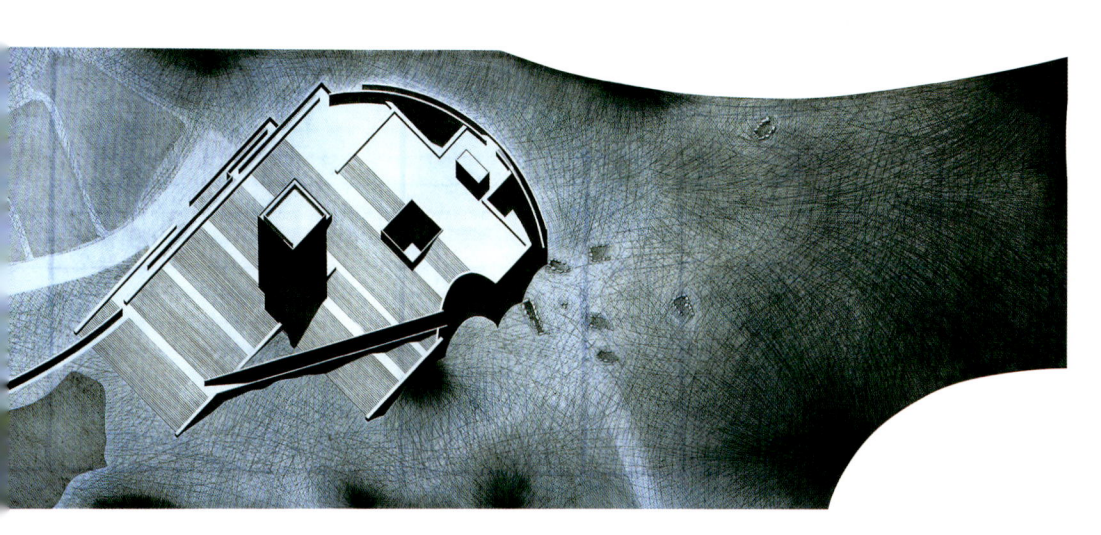

Site drawing. Through features such as the long gentle wall facing the pool, the intention of integrating architecture with the environment is expressed strongly on the site.

背景の緑と鮮烈な対比をなす、石を敷き詰めた大階段と
コンクリートの塔。

The concrete tower and large stone-paved stair produce
a vivid contrast with the background greenery.

西側から池越しに見る。周辺に点在する古墳群と呼応する、
〈現代の古墳〉としての建築。

Looking across the pond from the west side. Architecture as a "contemporary *kofun*," fitting in with the *kofun* that dot the surroundings.

建物へのアプローチとなる古墳公園「風土記の丘」の散策路から、梅林越しに建物を見る。
Looking at the building across the plum grove from the walking path on the "Fudoki hill" in the *kofun* park, which is the approach route to the building.

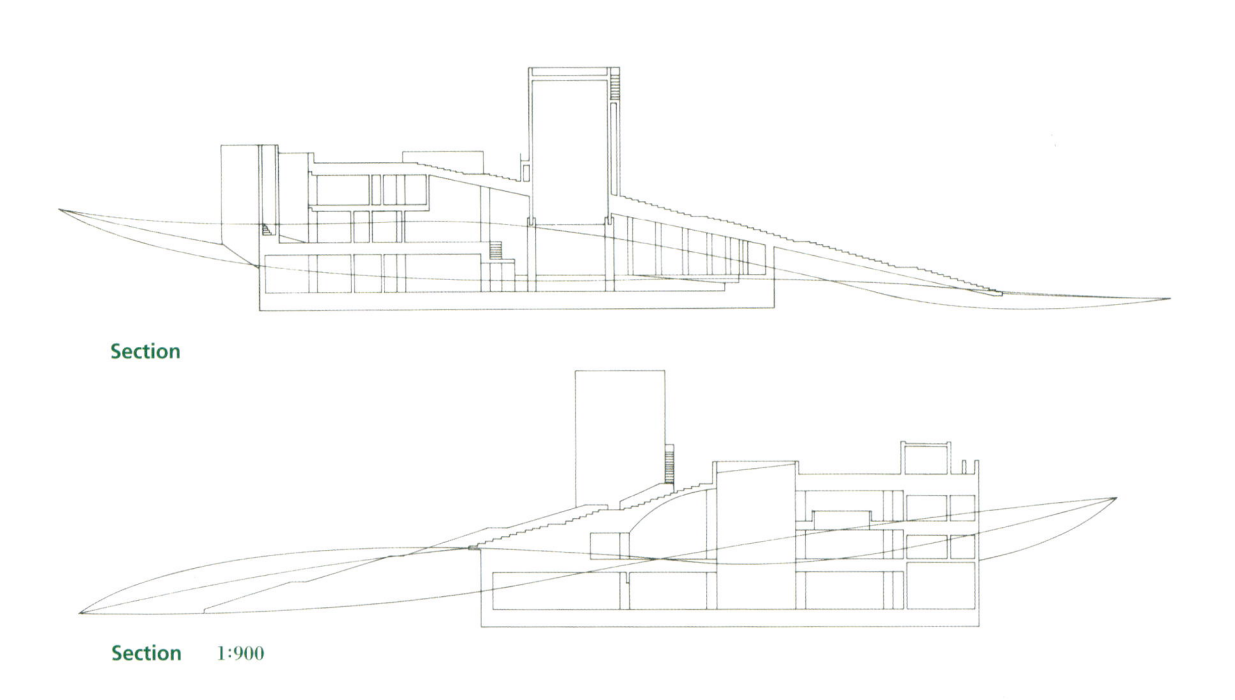

Section

Section 1:900

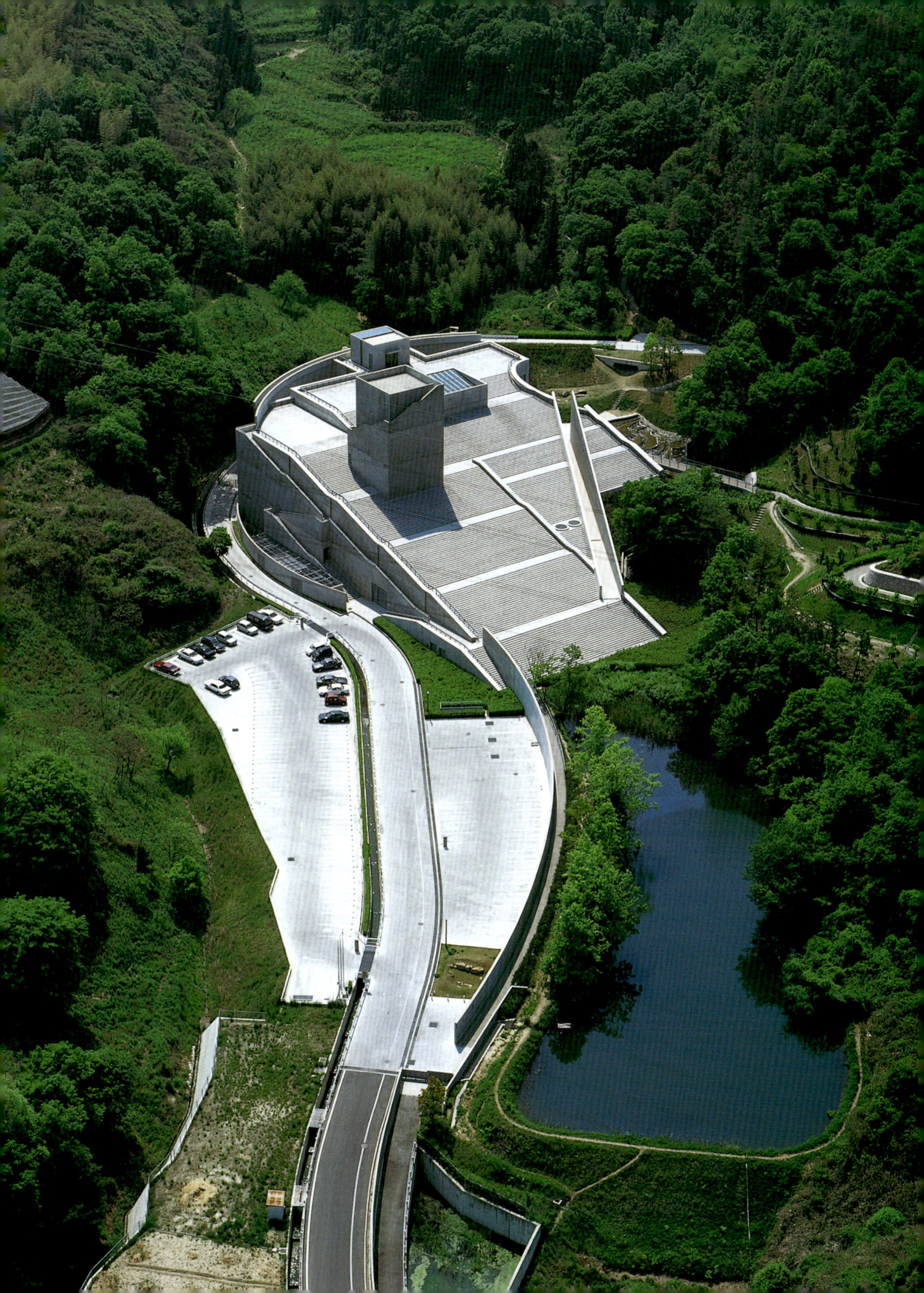

地階ホワイエ。トップライトから光が差し込む３層吹き抜けの
底には、高さ８ｍの十三重塔が展示されている。

Basement foyer. An 8m-high, thirteen-story tower is
exhibited in a three-storey-high void with light flooding in
through a skylight.

地下の常設展示室。円形の展示室の中央には、縮尺1/150の仁徳天皇陵の復元模型が展示されている。

Underground permanent exhibition room. Exhibited at the center of the circular exhibition room is a model of Emperor Nintoku's mausoleum reduced to 1/150 scale.

Roof plan

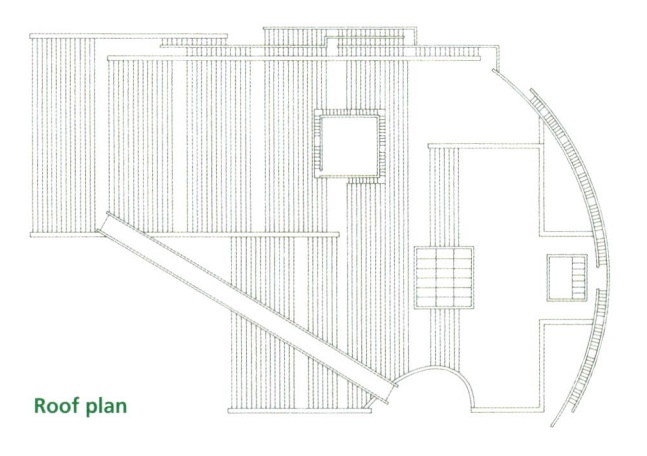

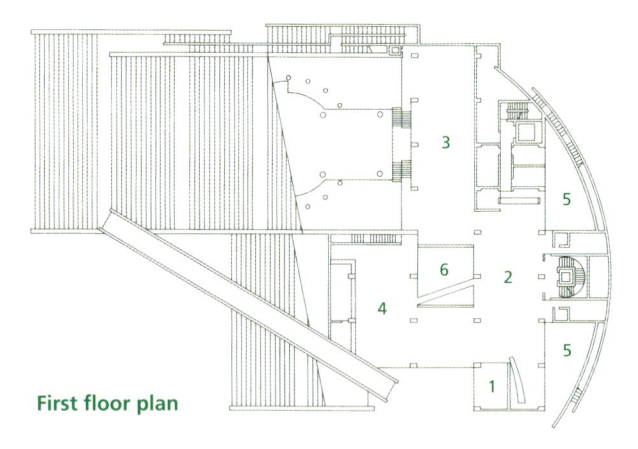

First floor plan

1 entrance
2 lobby
3 exhibition space
4 library
5 court
6 void
7 foyer
8 auditorium
9 storage

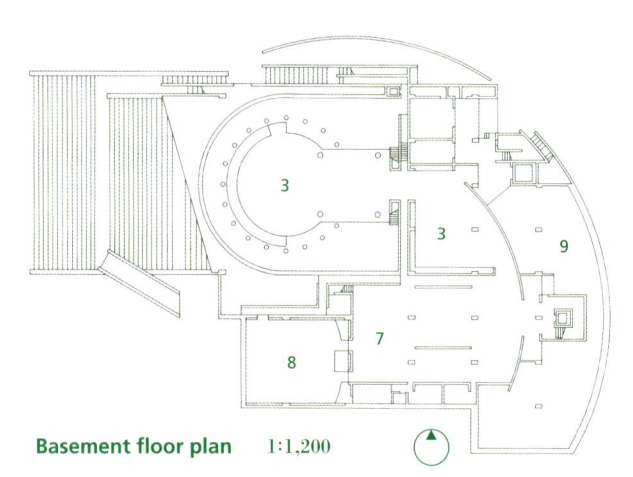

Basement floor plan 1:1,200

御影ピンコロ石で覆われた大階段。周囲の風景を見渡す展望広場で
あるのと同時に、野外劇場として演劇祭、音楽祭などにも利用される。

Large stairs paved with granite. An outlook plaza for viewing the
surrounding scenery, which can simultaneously be used as an
open-air theater for plays and music performances.

229 Chikatsu-Asuka Museum

サントリーミュージアム＋マーメイド広場
Suntory Museum+Plaza

1989-94　大阪府大阪市港区 —— Minato-ku, Osaka, Osaka

敷地は大阪南港、天保山に位置する。天保山は、1980年代からいわゆるウォーターフロント開発の進められてきた場所であり、その「天保山ハーバービレッジ」のいわば最後の仕上げとして、この美術館はつくられた。

ここでは、与えられた敷地の範囲をいわば越境して建築を考え、そこから海に至るまでの水際空間、即ち大阪市の所有する護岸、国の所有する海上をも含めた、公共の空間全体の再編を試みた。

美術館本体は、球形の3Dシアターを内包する逆円錐型のシリンダーを軸に、2本の直方体が角度とレベルを違えて海に突き出す、極めて単純な幾何学的構成による。湾岸部のあっけらかんとした風景にあって、海と対峙して負けないスケール感と象徴性をもった強い建築表現が意図されている。

その美術館と海の水際線との間に、幅100m、奥行き40mの親水広場が設けられている。広場は海に向かって降りていく階段とスロープで、緩やかに海と接続する。水際に屹立する5本のコンクリート柱が、海側から眺める広場の視覚的なアクセントになっているが、逆にその柱の下から前方の海を眺めると、数10m先の堤防の上に、同じく5本の柱の痕跡が標されていることに気づくだろう。

都市空間に〈海〉との交流を取り戻す——テーマは極めて率直であったが、その実現のためには行政との折衝を重ね、防災上のさまざまな規制をひとつひとつクリアしていく困難なプロセスを闘わねばならなかった。

〈境界〉を超えてつくるという、この「TIME'S」から「サントリーミュージアム」へと続いたテーマは、その後より大きなスケールの「兵庫県立美術館＋神戸市水際広場」へと発展していく。

The site is located in Tempozan, Nanko Port, Osaka. Tempozan is a so-called waterfront development that has been ongoing since the 1980s, and this museum was made to finally complete the Tempozan Harbor Village.

I conceived here an architecture that somehow transgresses the extent of the given site in an attempt to reorganize the entire public space itself, including the waterfront space up until the sea—that is to say, the embankment owned by Osaka City as well as the nationally owned sea area.

The museum itself is based on an extremely simple geometric composition, consisting of two rectangular volumes projecting toward the sea at different levels and different angles from the axis of an inverted cone-shaped cylinder containing a spherical 3D theater. Standing in the indifferent waterfront scenery, the intention is a strong architectural expression with a sense of scale and symbolism confronting the sea.

A 100m-wide and 40m-deep water plaza has been established between the museum and the sea edge. The plaza is gently connected to the sea by descending ramps and steps. The five concrete columns standing at the water's edge are a visual accent in the plaza when looking back from the sea edge, but conversely, looking out toward the sea from below the columns it may be noticed that traces of these same columns are imprinted on the bank about 10m ahead.

To reclaim the mingling of "sea" into the urban space—the theme is extremely straightforward, but its implementation entailed a great deal of negotiation with the administration and struggles in the difficult process of meeting all the various regulations for disaster prevention.

The theme of crossing "boundaries," which has been ongoing from TIME'S until the Suntory Museum, was later developed at an even larger scale in the Hyogo Prefectural Museum and the Kobe Waterfront Plaza.

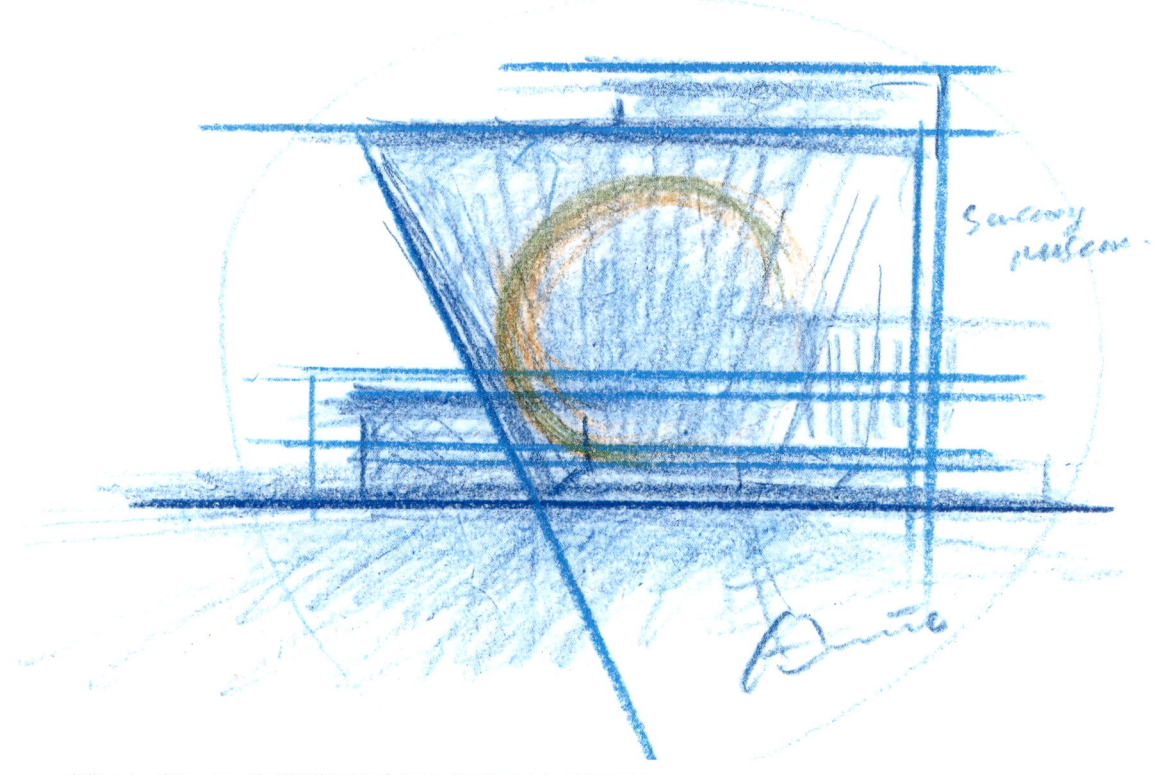

初期イメージスケッチ。球と逆円錐によるダイナミックな造形イメージとともに、
その建築を敷地境界を超えて海までつなげていこうとする建築家の意思が、直裁に描かれている。

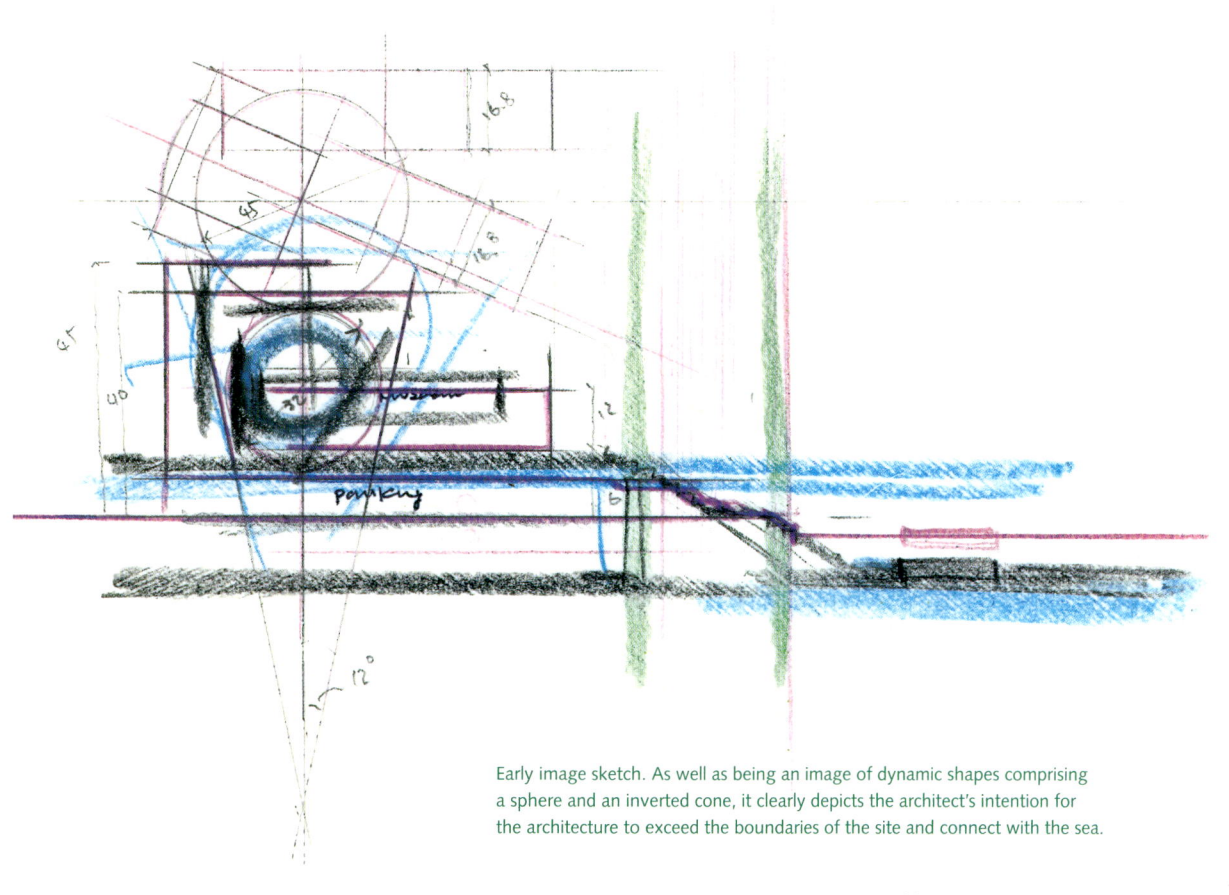

Early image sketch. As well as being an image of dynamic shapes comprising
a sphere and an inverted cone, it clearly depicts the architect's intention for
the architecture to exceed the boundaries of the site and connect with the sea.

231 Suntory Museum

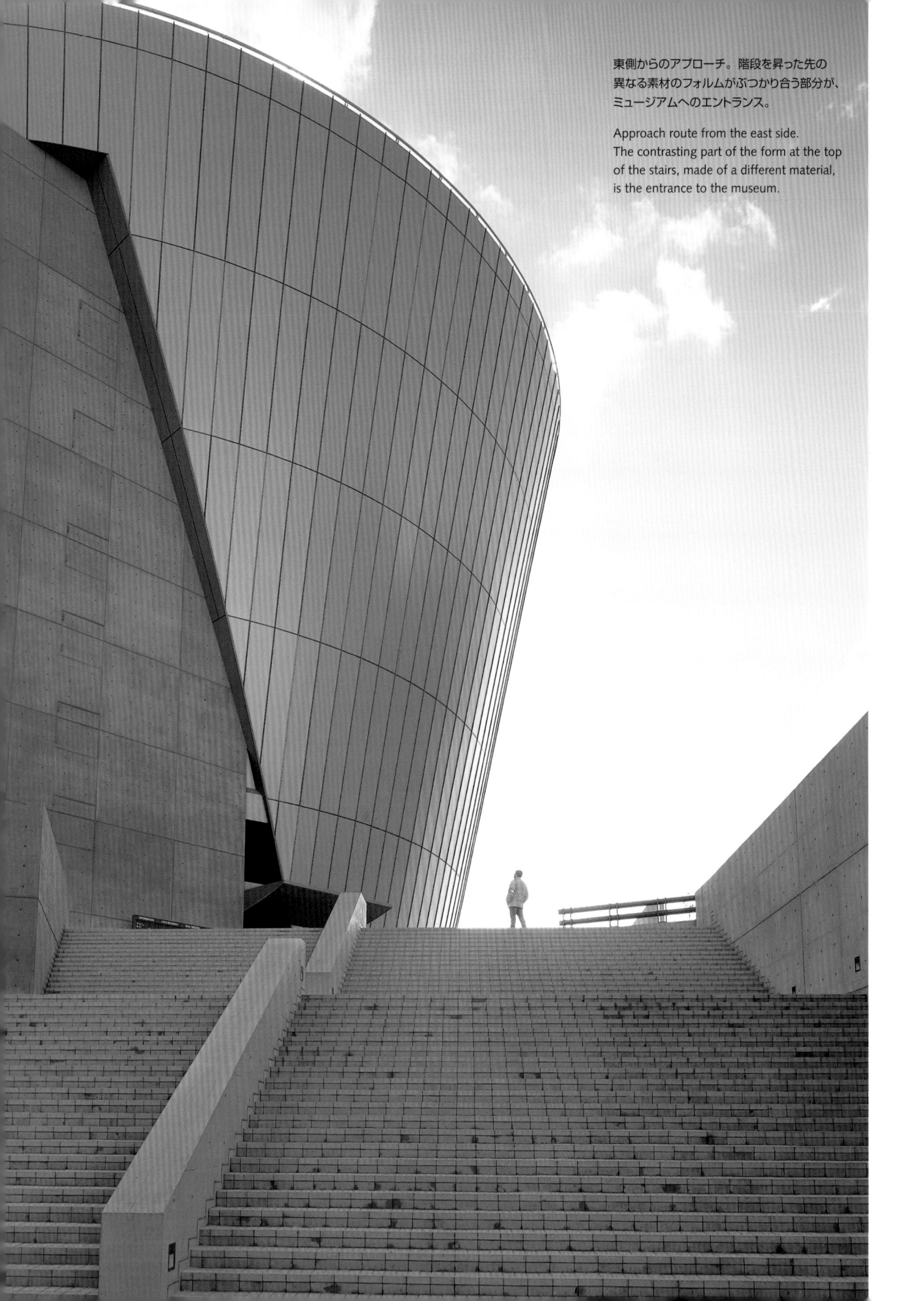

東側からのアプローチ。階段を昇った先の
異なる素材のフォルムがぶつかり合う部分が、
ミュージアムへのエントランス。

Approach route from the east side.
The contrasting part of the form at the top
of the stairs, made of a different material,
is the entrance to the museum.

西側からの空撮。境界を超えてつくられた水際の建築空間。

Aerial view from the west. Architectural space made at the water's edge, beyond the site boundary.

海上の防波堤から見るミュージアムの夜景。逆円錐の
フォルムの中に球体が浮かび上がる幻想的な都市光景。

Night view of the museum seen from the sea
breakwater. A magical urban scene of a sphere floating
within the form of an inverted cone.

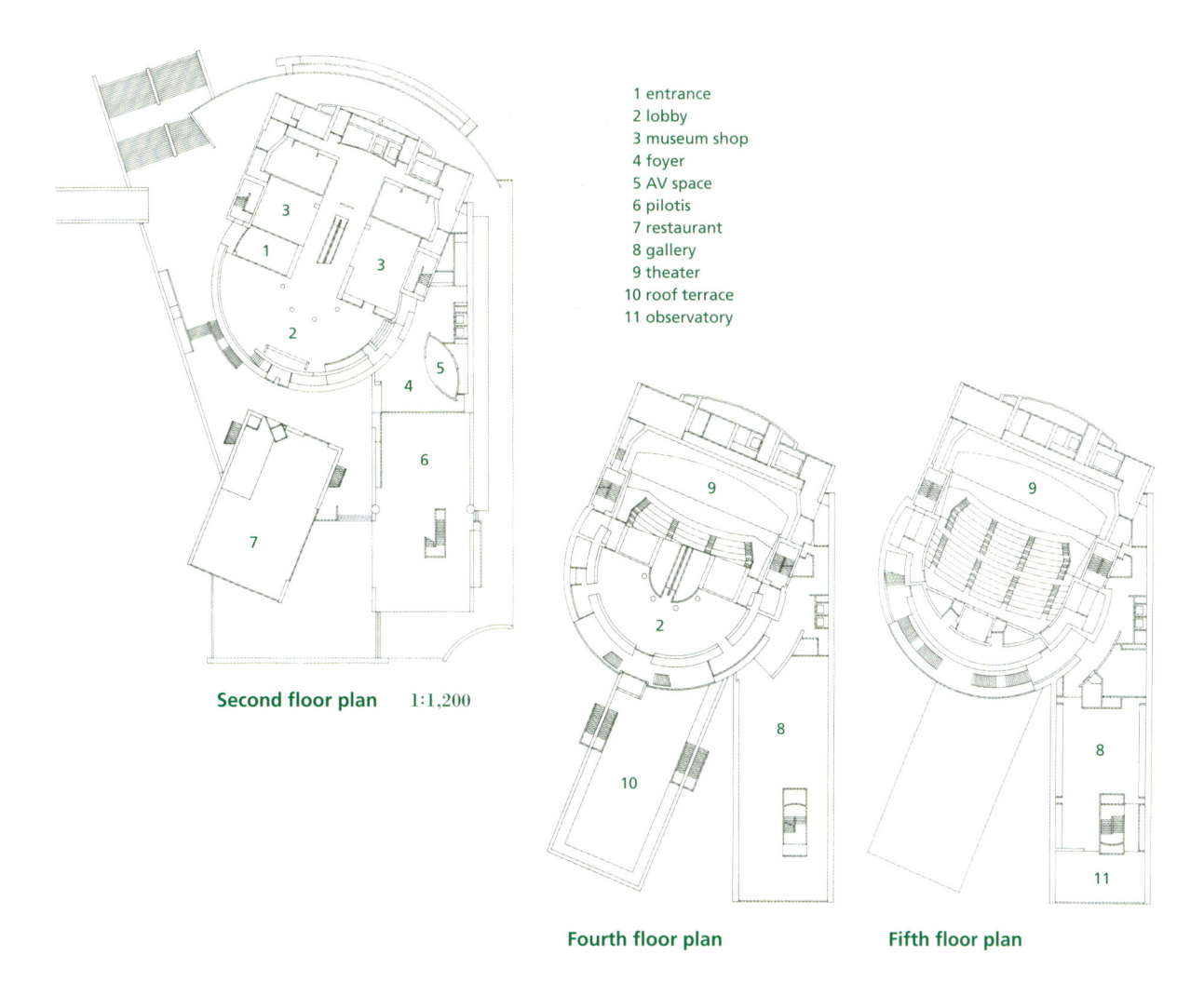

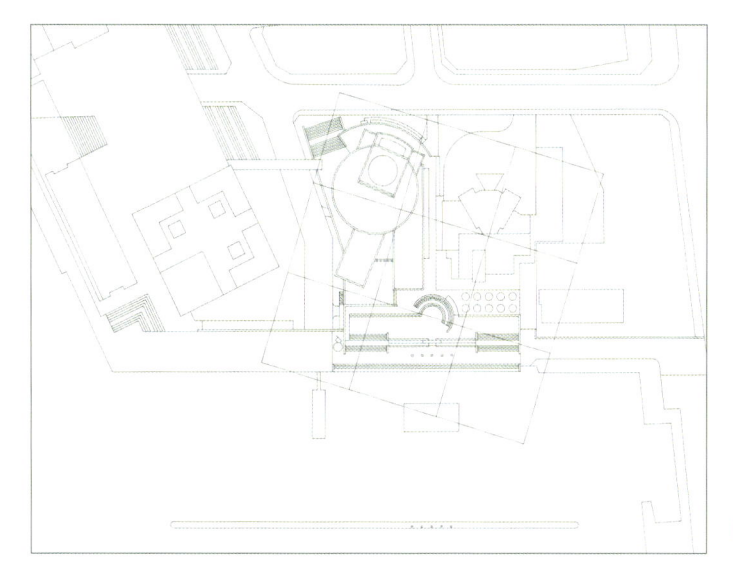

1 entrance
2 lobby
3 museum shop
4 foyer
5 AV space
6 pilotis
7 restaurant
8 gallery
9 theater
10 roof terrace
11 observatory

Second floor plan 1:1,200

Fourth floor plan

Fifth floor plan

Site plan 1:4,000

235 Suntory Museum

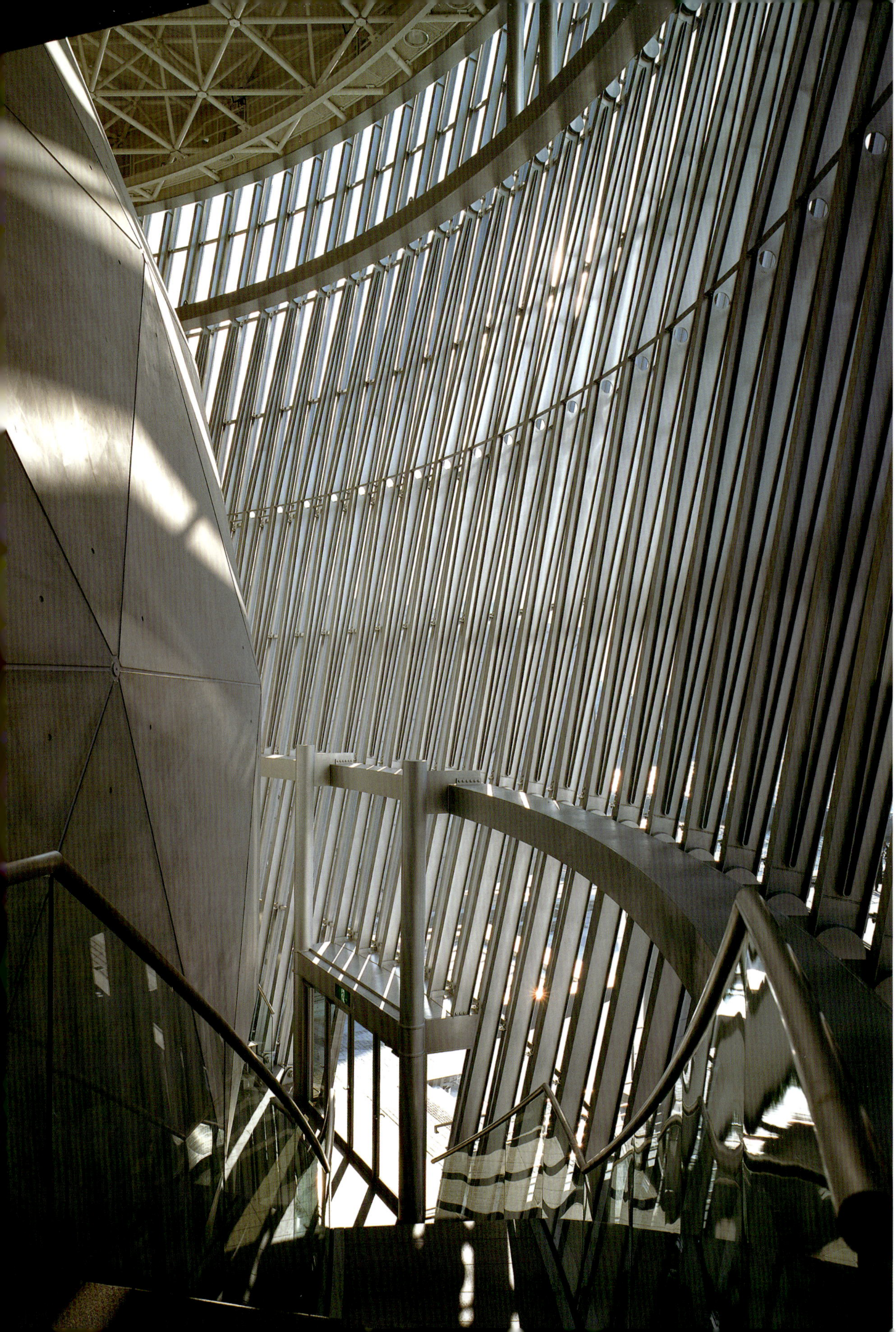

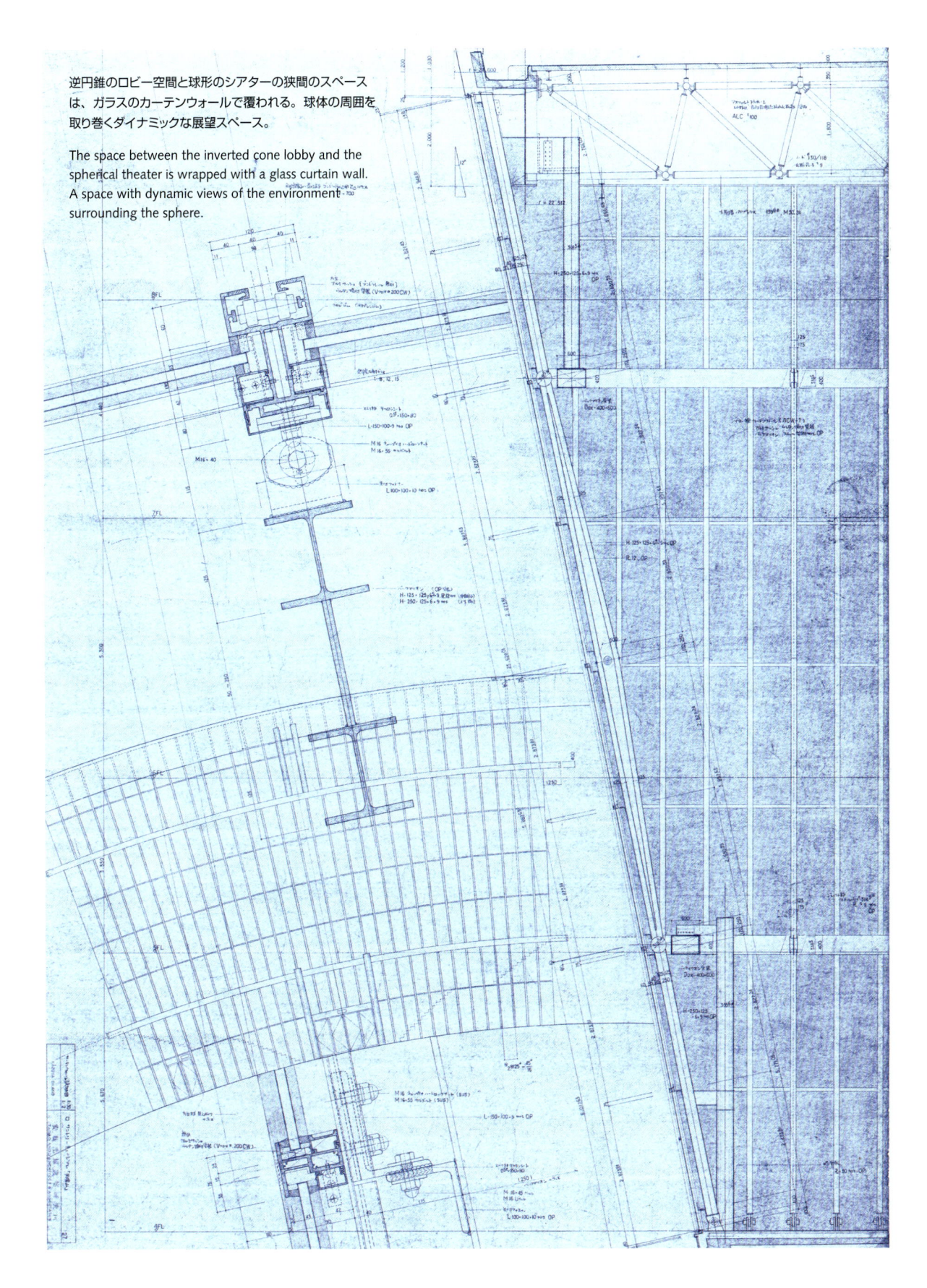

逆円錐のロビー空間と球形のシアターの狭間のスペースは、ガラスのカーテンウォールで覆われる。球体の周囲を取り巻くダイナミックな展望スペース。

The space between the inverted cone lobby and the spherical theater is wrapped with a glass curtain wall. A space with dynamic views of the environment surrounding the sphere.

Elevation

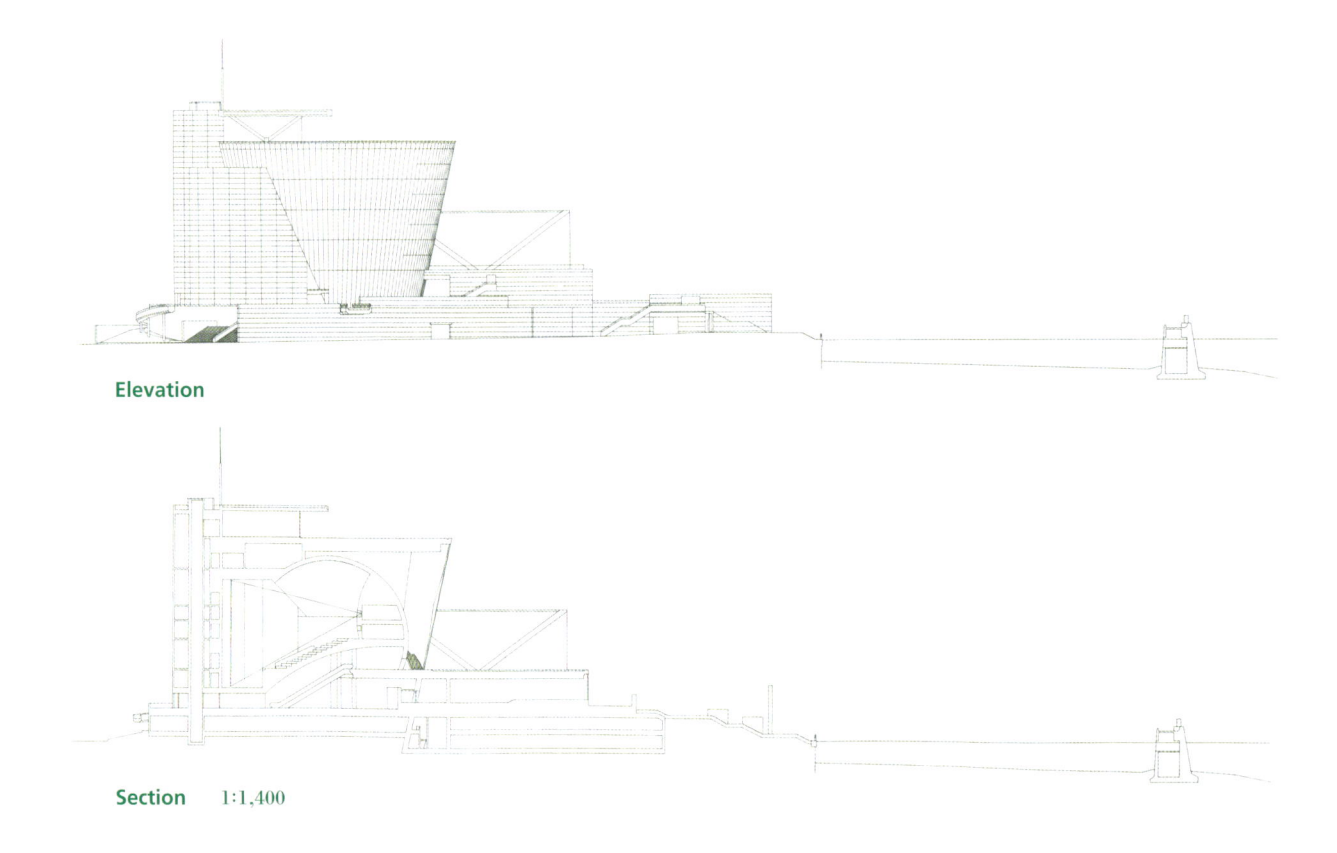

Section　1:1,400

レストラン上部のルーフテラスから見下ろす「マーメイド広場」。階段、スロープ、列柱に石床のパターン。控えめに配された建築のエレメントが、人々を水際へと誘う。

The Mermaid Plaza seen from the roof terrace above the restaurant. The stone floor pattern has been applied to the stairs, the ramps, and the rows of columns. These unobtrusively arranged architectural elements invite people to the water's edge.

湾岸の場所が有するスケール感に、単純で力強い建築のフォルムが呼応する、新しい都市の水際の風景。

A new urban waterfront scene, in which simple and powerful architectural forms respond to the sense of scale at this coastal location.

大谷地下劇場計画
The Theater in the Rock, Oya

1995-　栃木県宇都宮市──Utsunomiya, Tochigi

　敷地は栃木県宇都宮市、フランク・ロイド・ライトの帝国ホテルに用いられたことで有名な、大谷石の地下採掘場に対し行った建築提案である。大谷石の採掘は、10m四方の広さの堅坑を軸に、碁盤目状に横坑を走らせるかたちで行われる。深いところで地下80mにも及ぶ地下坑の空間を偶然に訪れた私は、その荘厳な空間に大いに触発され、ついに自主提案としてこの計画を構想するに至った。

　「大谷地下劇場計画」は、既存の地下杭の再利用計画ではない。計画的に切り出す石の残余として残される空隙を劇場にするという提案である。平面的には10m間隔で〈柱〉を残すこと、その深さは、石を地表から15m残した上で、地下30mまでの範囲に留めること。ふたつの構造条件を手がかりに、既成の建築の枠組みから完全に解き放たれたような、自在な地下空間のイメージを描いた。

　このプロジェクトの最大の意義は、建築を目的としたものではない開発行為の結果を、そのまま建築空間として読み替えるという逆転の発想にある。石切職人による通常の採掘事業が、即ち地下劇場の建設過程となるわけだから、高度な建築技術も工事監理も必要なく、掘削土の処理に悩まされることもない。採掘事業としての採算性が確保されれば、結果的に建設に費やされるエネルギーは〈ゼロ〉ということになる。工期は石が切り出されるまで──未定ということになるが、これこそ究極の〈エコロジー〉建築ではないか。

　法規的な問題から計画は見送りとなり今日に至るが、今なお私はあきらめていない。劇場と同時に、地下に十字を描く「石の教会」をつくるアイディアも温めている。

The site is in Utsunomiya City, Tochigi Prefecture. This is an architectural proposal for an underground mine of Oya stone, famous for the fact that it was used in Frank Lloyd Wright's Imperial Hotel. The quarrying of Oya stone is carried out in a grid pattern on an axis of vertical supports at 10m intervals in the horizontal direction. By chance visiting this underground space, which extends up to 80m at its deepest, I was greatly provoked by the solemnity of the space and finally conceived this design as an independent proposal.

The design for the Theater in the Rock is not a plan for reusing the existing underground pits. It is a proposal to make the spaces left after systematically quarrying the rock into a theater. In plan, "columns" are left at 10m intervals, the depth of which extends from the stone remaining up to 15m from the ground surface and from 30m below ground. With these two structural conditions as a key, I drew an image of a free underground space as if totally liberated from existing architectural frameworks.

The most significant aspect of this project is that it does not have building as its goal, but a reverse conception of directly reinterpreting the results of development as architectural spaces. Because this is an ordinary mining project done by stonemasons, in the construction process of the underground theater there is no need for advanced architectural techniques or construction supervision, and no trouble in with dealing with excavated materials. If its profitability as a mining project is ensured, the energy devoted to construction as a result becomes "zero." The construction period will last until the stone is excavated, the timing of which is as-yet undecided, but precisely for that reason this might be the ultimate "ecological" architecture.

Due to regulatory problems, today I must say farewell to the project, but I will not give up. At the same time as the theater, I am also warming to the idea of making a Stone Chapel that delineates an underground cross.

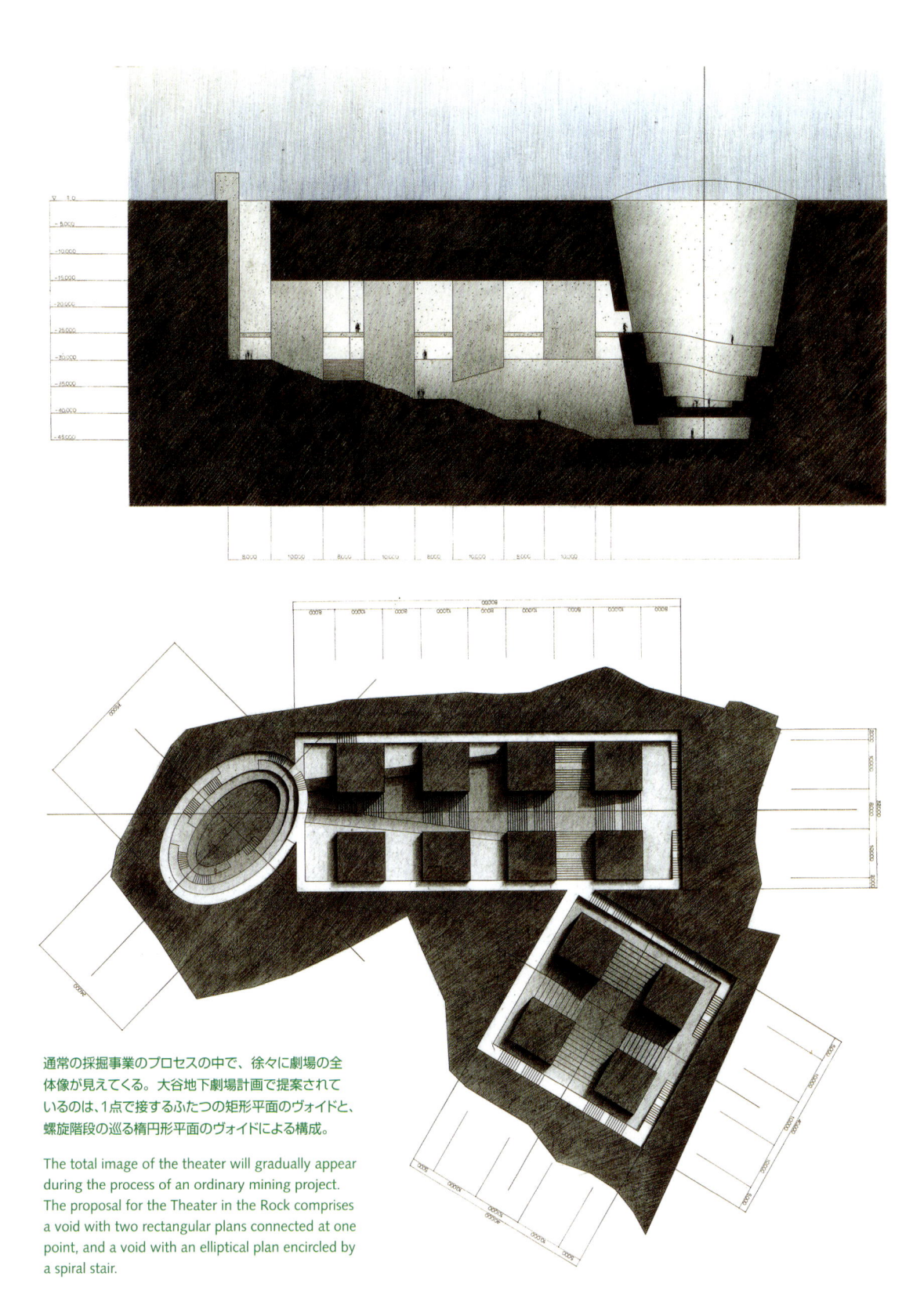

通常の採掘事業のプロセスの中で、徐々に劇場の全体像が見えてくる。大谷地下劇場計画で提案されているのは、1点で接するふたつの矩形平面のヴォイドと、螺旋階段の巡る楕円形平面のヴォイドによる構成。

The total image of the theater will gradually appear during the process of an ordinary mining project. The proposal for the Theater in the Rock comprises a void with two rectangular plans connected at one point, and a void with an elliptical plan encircled by a spiral stair.

241 Theater in the Rock

コルク板の積層によりつくられた模型。地中30mの深さに10m間隔でソリッドとヴォイドが連続する荘厳な空間。
Model made from laminated corkboard. A dignified space comprising a series of solids and voids at 10m intervals, located 30m underground.

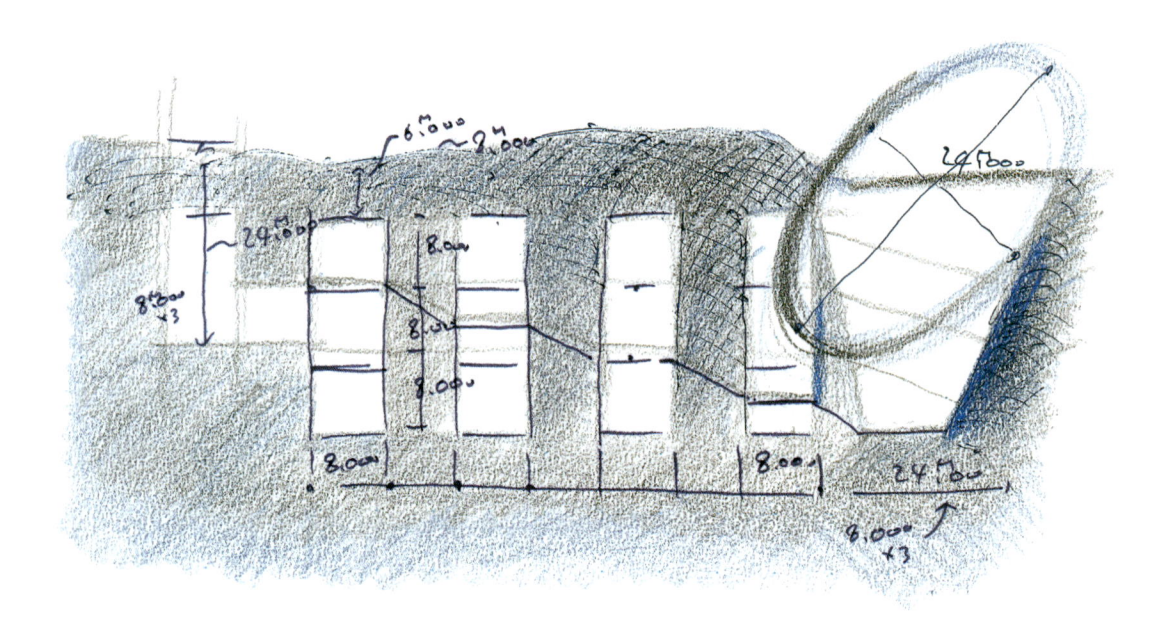

243 Theater in the Rock

かたちのない地下の特性を活かし、自在に展開する空間イメージ。地下を指向する建築家の想像力が存分に発揮されている。

An image of freely expanding spaces, utilizing the amorphousness that characterizes being underground. Directed underground, the imaginative powers of the architect may be exercised without restraint.

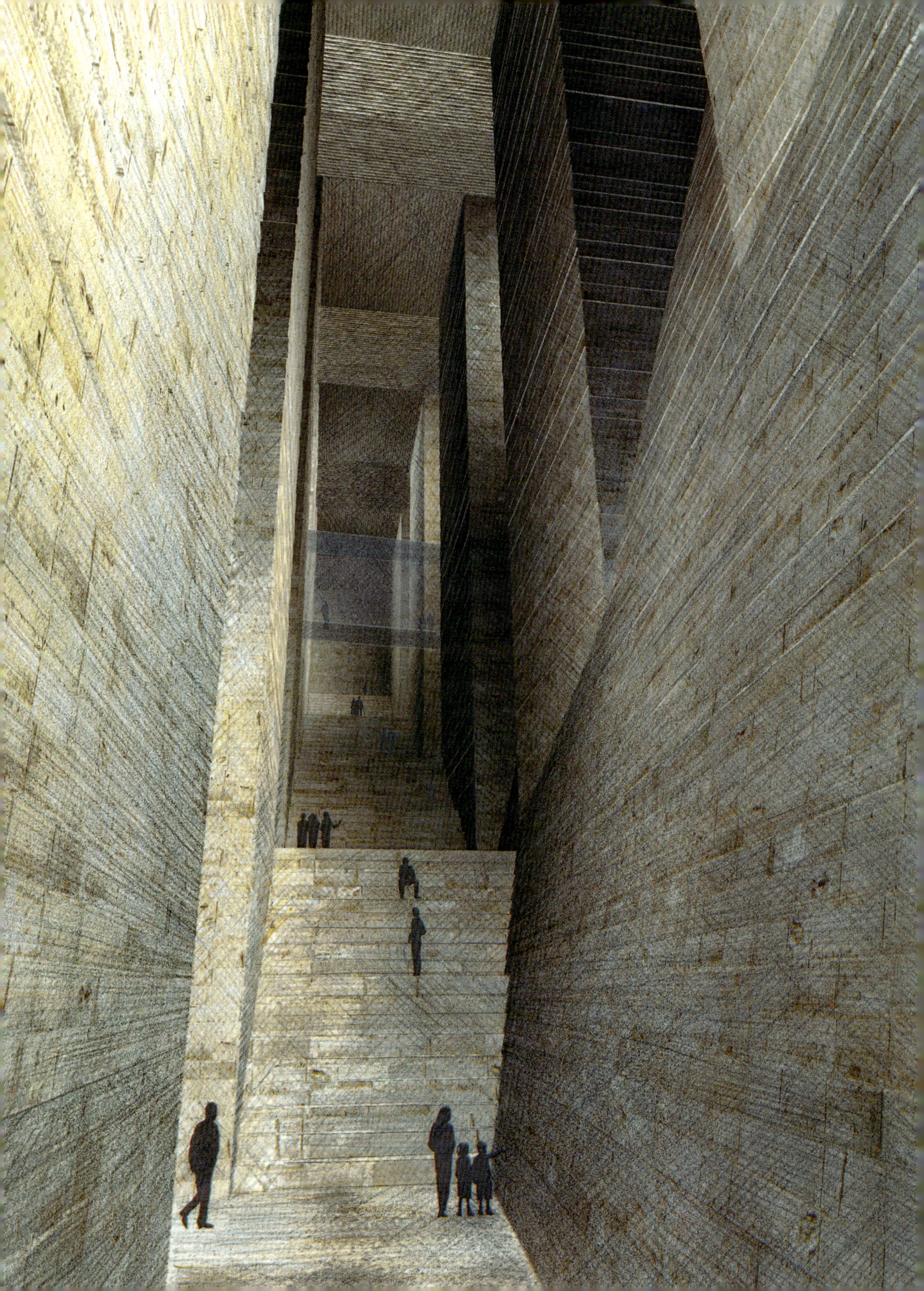

織田廣喜ミュージアム
Daylight Museum
1997-98　滋賀県蒲生郡——Gamo-gun, Shiga

　敷地は、滋賀県蒲生郡の緑豊かな自然公園内に位置する。画家織田廣喜の作品を展示する小さな美術館である。

　発想の原点は、戦後間もなくの画家とその家族の生活風景を写した写真だった。画家自身が廃材を用いてつくった粗末な家。電気もガスも水道も引かれていない、その家で「日のある間はひたすら絵を描き、日没と共に寝る」という画家の言葉通り、自然の中で慎ましく、健やかに生きる家族――。

　この画家が生きた証として描いた絵を、作品として標本にしてしまうのでなく、それが描かれた風景にそのまま留めておくことが、その作品を納める美術館の設計を任された私の役割だと考えた。そして生まれたのが、人工照明を一切使わない、自然光のみの美術館である。

　作品の保護を第一に考えるならば、展示室は一様に管理された人工的環境としてあるべきである。だがそれは、作品を仮死状態にしての延命措置であって、本当の意味で作品を「生かしている」とはいえない。より自然に近い環境に置かれることで、絵も人間と同じく老いていくが、そうした限りある時間の中だからこそ、確かに絵は「生きて」存在できる。模範解答とはなり得ない考え方かもしれないが、少なくとも、織田廣喜の絵には、そうした終の棲家としての建物のあり方が相応しい。

　建物は、公園の池沿いに緩やかな弧を描くように配されている。池に面したガラスの回廊の背後に設けられた展示室への採光は、壁に沿って穿たれたトップライトからの光のみ。季節や時間によって、光は変化し、空間と作品もその表情を変える。文字通りの自然とともにある美術館――閉館は日没時である。

The site is located in a lush green natural park in the Gamo district of Shiga Prefecture. This is a small museum for exhibiting artworks by the painter Hiroki Oda.

　The conceptual starting point was a photograph showing a scene of the daily life of the painter and his family shortly after World War II. In a crude house that the painter himself had built from scrap wood, with no electricity, no gas, and no plumbing, the family lived healthily and humbly within nature. According to the painter, in this house, "while there is light, I do nothing but paint, and I go to bed at sunset."

　The paintings made as evidence of the painter's life are not just specimens of his work. Having been entrusted with the design of a museum that would contain these works, I thought that the environment in which they were painted should also be preserved. What resulted was a museum that uses only natural light, with absolutely no artificial lighting.

　If primary consideration is given to the protection of the artworks, the exhibition rooms should have a uniformly controlled artificial environment. However, this longevity measure will stifle the artworks, and they cannot be said to "live" in a real sense. By placing them in an environment closer to nature, the paintings will age just like people, but precisely because of this limited time span, the paintings certainly have a "living" presence. This way of thinking probably will not become an exemplary solution, but at least in Hiroki Oda's paintings such an end is appropriate for the building that was his home.

　The building is arranged as if drawing a gentle arc along the park pond. The only illumination for the exhibition rooms located behind the glazed corridor facing the pond is light from a skylight incised along the wall. The light changes depending on season and time, changing the expression of the space and the artworks. It is a museum that literally exists with nature—it closes at sunset.

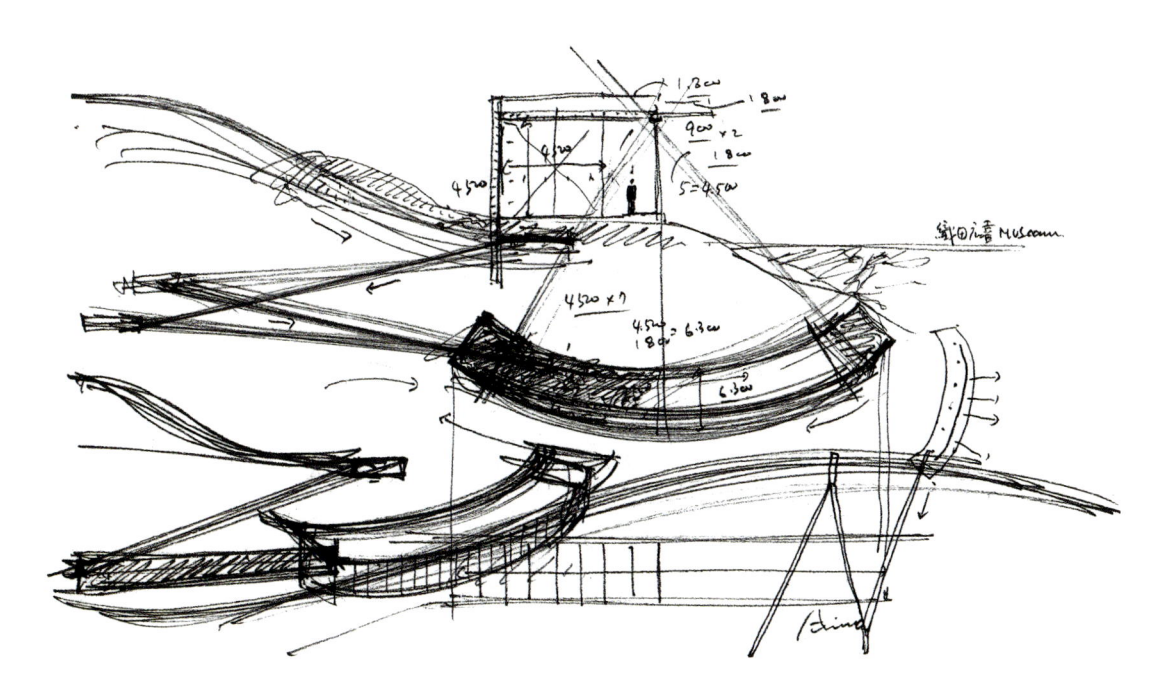

初期イメージスケッチ。ヒューマンスケールの〈ささやかな〉建築ゆえ、各部の寸法に細心の注意が払われている。
Early image sketches. Careful attention has been paid to the dimensions of each part, for a "humble" architecture at a human scale.

247 Daylight Museum

緑豊かな公園内の池のほとりに建つ、ひっそりとした建築の佇まい。
The solitary appearance of an architecture built near a pond in a park full of abundant greenery.

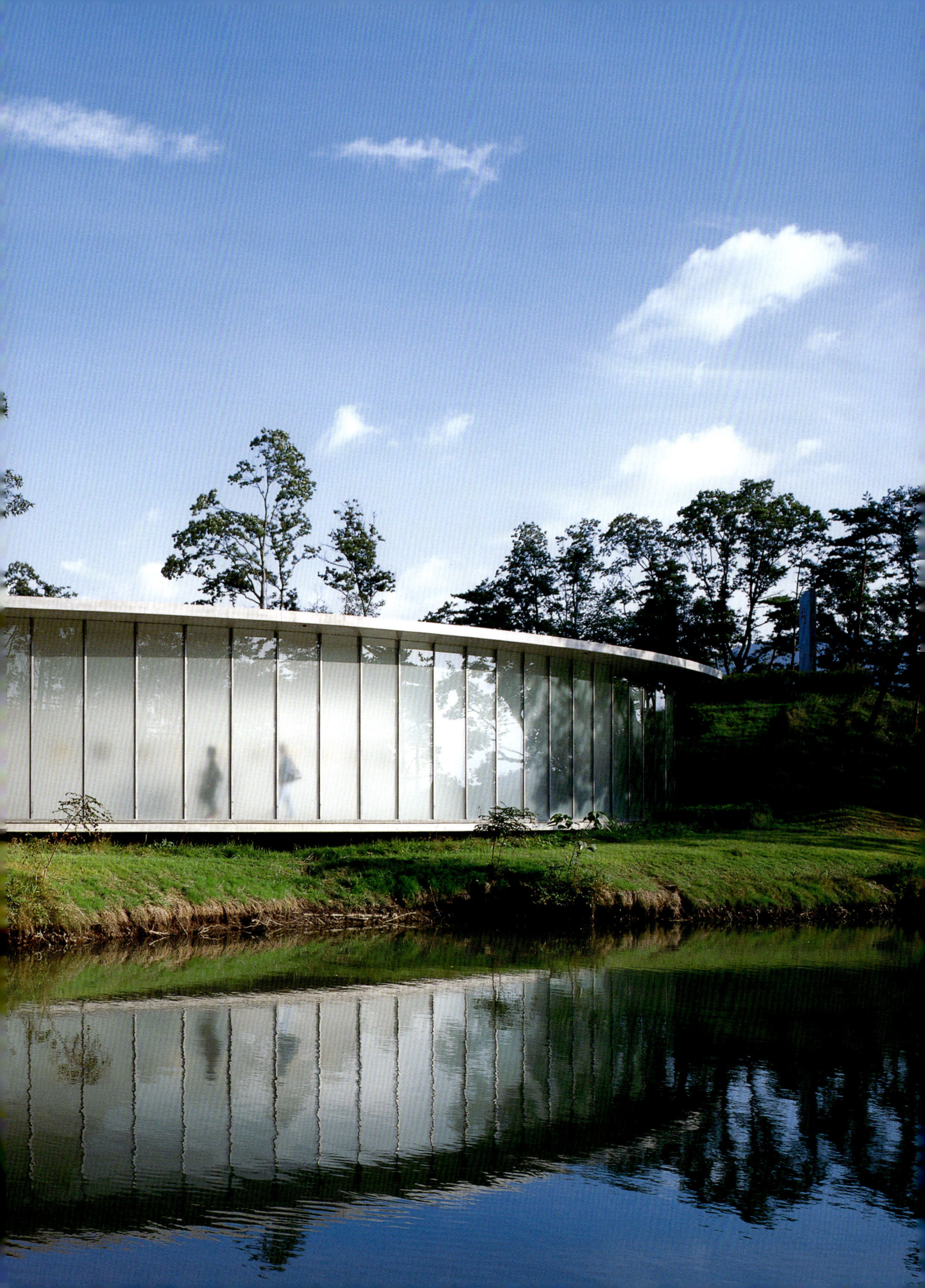

1/6円の緩やかなカーブを描く一層のヴォリュームと、その片方の
妻面に入り込むアプローチのスロープ。シンプル極まりない構成。

A one-story volume with a gentle curve that delineates
one-sixth of a circle, and an approach ramp penetrating the
wall on the other side. An extremely simple composition.

251 Daylight Museum

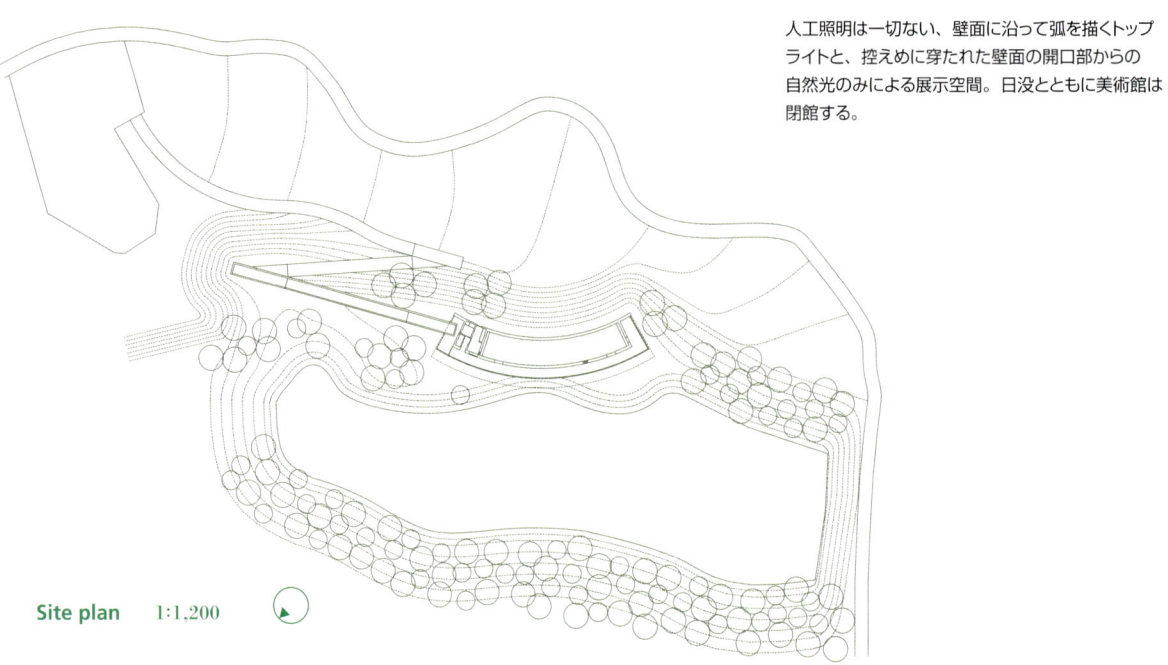

人工照明は一切ない、壁面に沿って弧を描くトップ
ライトと、控えめに穿たれた壁面の開口部からの
自然光のみによる展示空間。日没とともに美術館は
閉館する。

Site plan 1:1,200

An exhibition space without a single artificial light, lit only by natural light from an aperture that discreetly pierces the wall surface, and a skylight that traces an arc along the wall surface.

Section

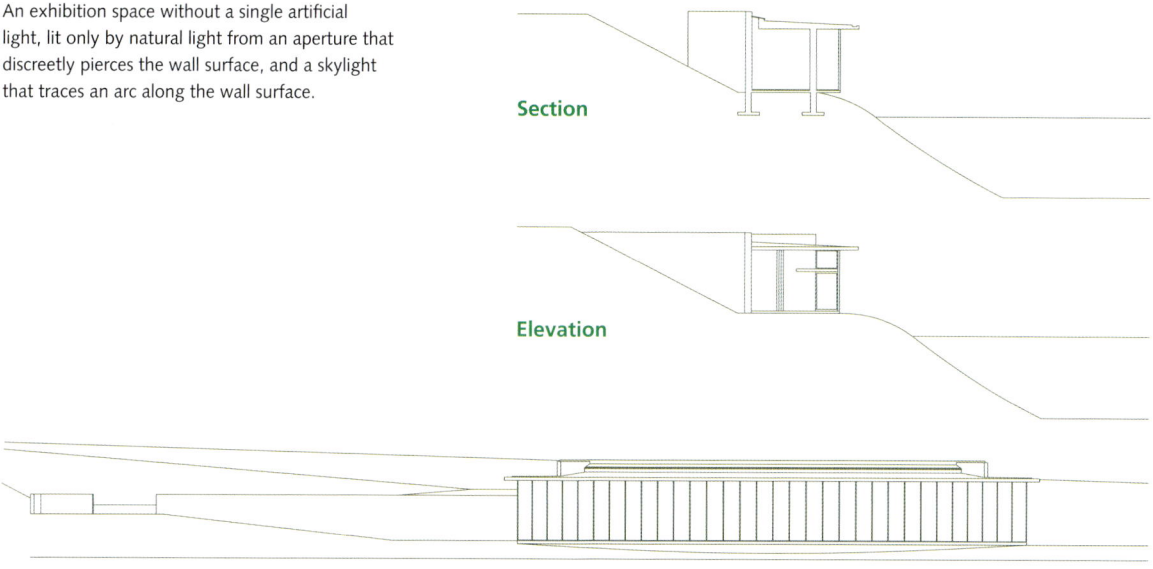

Elevation

Elevation 1:500

253 Daylight Museum

展示室西側に緩衝領域として設けられた回廊。すりガラスのはめ込まれた溶融亜鉛メッキ仕上げのスチールサッシ越しに、柔らかな光が入り込む。

The corridor established as a buffer zone on the east side of the exhibition room. Soft light comes in through galvanized steel frames inlaid with frosted glass.

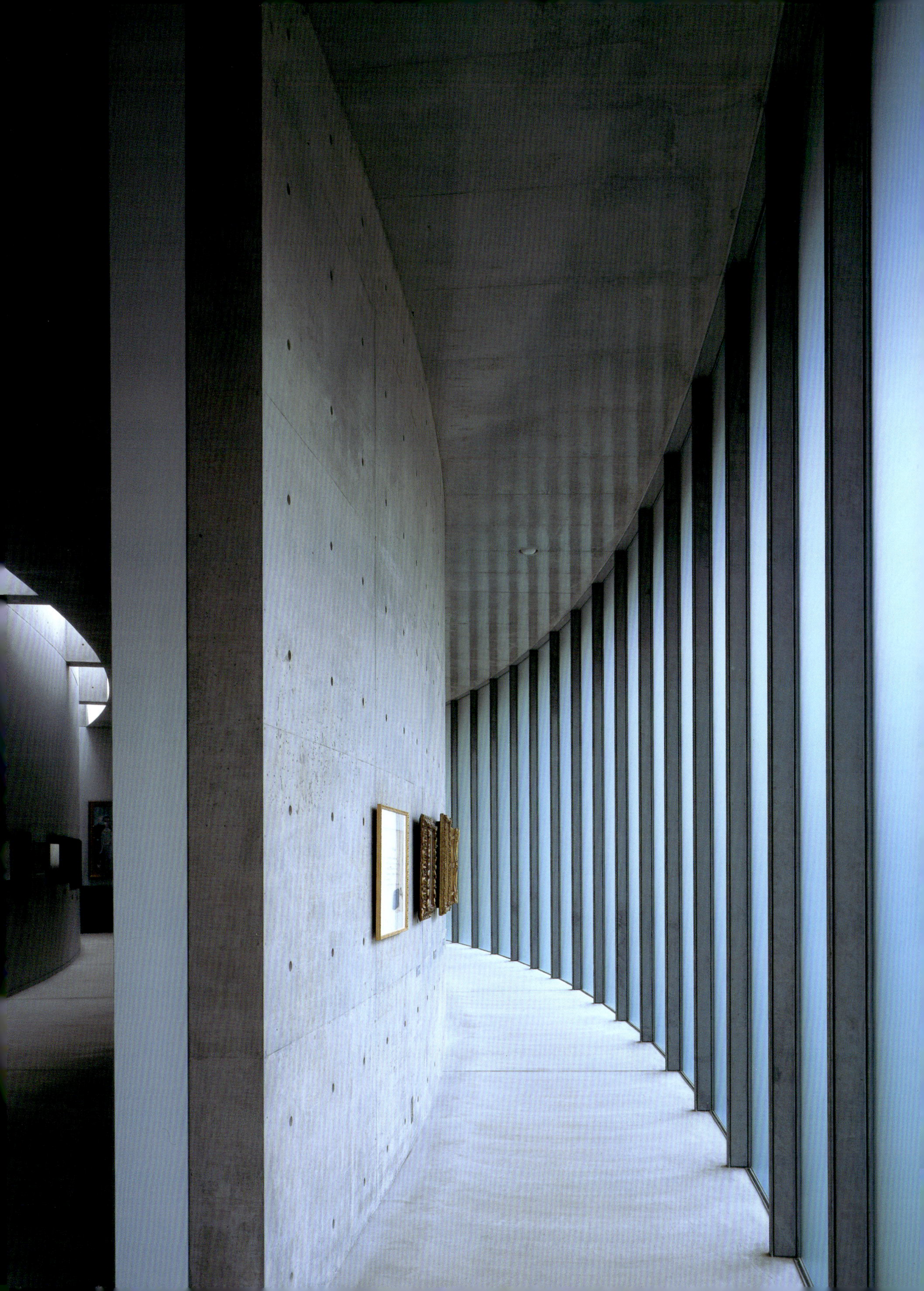

風景の再生、建築の未来

1995年1月17日、マグニチュード7.2の大地震が
淡路島から阪神地方一帯を襲った。
計画途中にあった淡路夢舞台の敷地は、震源の至近に位置していた。
計画中止は止むを得ない——私を含め、関係者の多くがそう考えた。
だが、被災地の創造的復興を目指す兵庫県の人々は
計画続行を決断、夢舞台は復興プロジェクトとして
再スタートを切ることになった。

地震に傷ついた人々が、それでも勇気ある決断を下したのは
プロジェクトの背後にあるのが
単純な再開発ではない、土砂採掘跡地として荒廃していた
大地の蘇生にあったからだろう。
夢舞台の成否は、施設単体ではなく、それを包む森を含めた
環境全体の再生にかかっていた。
斜面地に苗木を植えるところから始めた関係者の努力
淡路の風景の再生に復興の希望を託した被災者の思いが
この困難な事業を完遂させた。

環境とは、与え、与えられるものではない、育ち、育てるものである。
その"育てる"プロセスの中に
建築の未来を切り拓く手がかりがある。

Revival of Landscape, Future of Architecture

On January 17, 1995, the Kobe-Osaka region and Awaji Island were hit by an earthquake registering a magnitude of 7.2. The plan for Awaji Yumebutai (Awaji Island Project) was then underway, and its site was located close to the hypocenter. Cancellation is inevitable, many of those involved in the project, including myself, thought. People of Hyogo Prefecture, however, decided to go on with the plan, seeking creative recovery in the earthquake-affected region.
Thus, Awaji Yumebutai was restarted as a restoration project.

The reason why those people who had just suffered a huge earthquake made this courageous decision lies in the fact that this project was not just another simple redevelopment scheme but one aimed at resuscitation of land that had been devastated as a result of quarrying for earth and sand. The success of Yumebutai did not hinge upon the built facilities themselves but on the revitalization of the whole environment, including the woods that surround the buildings. Those involved in the project spared no effort, starting with planting saplings on the hillside, while the locals who had been hit by the earthquake projected their hope for recovery upon the resuscitation of the landscape of Awaji. Together, these factors made it possible to complete this difficult project.

Environment is not something one gives or is given. It's what we cultivate and are cultivated by. Hints for carving out the future of architecture exist in this process of "cultivation."

敷地は兵庫県淡路島、明石海峡寄りの海岸部に位置する。国営公園、県立公園を含む「淡路島国際公園都市」の中核施設として計画された、文化コンプレックスである。

全長1km、広さ28ヘクタールに及ぶ広大な「夢舞台」の敷地は、かつて大阪湾埋め立てに供する土砂採掘地としてあった場所だった。山を丸ごと削り取られた跡に残されていたのは、赤茶けた岩盤がむき出しの、無残な土地の風景——。

「夢舞台」は、この人間の営為により傷ついた大地の蘇生を主題として構想され、プロジェクトは建物より先に、まず周囲の斜面地に苗木を植えることから始まった。つくること自体を目的とした巷の再開発事業とは、その出発点からまったく異なる視座を「夢舞台」はもっていたのである。

そうして人間の手で回復された緑の斜面地に、会議場、ホテル、店舗、温室、野外劇場からなる全長800mの複雑な建築複合体が埋め込まれている。驚くべき大規模の計画であるが、中を歩く人々に、そのスケールを実感する機会は訪れない。それぞれの施設のヴォリュームが敷地内に分散して、地形をなぞるように控え目に配置されている上に、その間の余白が、徹底して分節された、人間的尺度の空間の重ね合わせとしてつくられているからだ。

私の建築の集大成ともいうべき建築群と、その間をつなぐ水庭が織りなす光景に、ローマ郊外のティボリの地にあるヴィラ・アドリアーナの遺跡を思い浮かべる人は多いだろう。この建築庭園のクライマックスは、斜面上に設けられた百区画の花壇である。

「百段苑」と名づけられた壮大な人工の丘は、1995年にこの地を襲った阪神淡路大震災で亡くなった人々に向けた鎮魂のモニュメントであり——同時にそれは、あの大災害に直面してなお建設を諦めずに、復興としてプロジェクトを完遂させた人々の意思の証である。

淡路夢舞台
Awaji-Yumebutai (Awaji Island Project)
1993-99　兵庫県淡路市 —— Awaji, Hyogo

右は1995年の阪神淡路大震災の後に描かれたサイトスケッチ。左は震災前のもの。
敷地内に活断層が見つかったため、計画は大幅に修正された。

The site is located on Awaji Island in Hyogo Prefecture, in a coastal area near the Meiseki Channel. This is a cultural complex designed as the central facility of Awaji Island International Park, which includes a national park and a prefectural park.

Extending 1km in total length and 28ha in area, the enormous Yumebutai site is a place previously mined for land reclamation in Osaka Bay. The traces left when the mountain was entirely scraped away formed a tragic scene of exposed reddish-brown bedrock.

Yumebutai was conceived with the theme of resurrecting this earth injured by human actions. Even prior to the building, the project began with the planting of saplings on the surrounding slopes. Yumebutai has a standpoint completely different from the starting point of the harbor regeneration project, wherein the act of making is itself the goal.

An 800m-long mixed-use architectural complex, containing conference rooms, a hotel, shops, a greenhouse, and an open-air theater, has been buried in the green slopes revived by human hands. It is an astonishingly large-scale design, but people walking through it have no opportunity to sense this scale. That is because the volumes of each facility are dispersed throughout the site, and in addition to a restrained arrangement that seems to trace the topography, the blank spaces between them are thoroughly articulated in a superimposition of human-scale spaces.

This scene of a collection of buildings, which could be called a compilation of my architecture, and the interwoven water gardens that connect them, probably reminds many people of the historic ruins of the Villa Adriana in Tivoli on the outskirts of Rome. The climax of this architecture garden is a flowerbed divided into one hundred sections, established on a slope.

This magnificent artificial hill, named Hyakudan-en, is a monument for the repose of souls of the people who died in the Hanshin-Awaji Earthquake, which devastated this area in 1995. At the same time, it evinces the intentions of the people who accomplished this revival project, confronting a large disaster without abandoning construction.

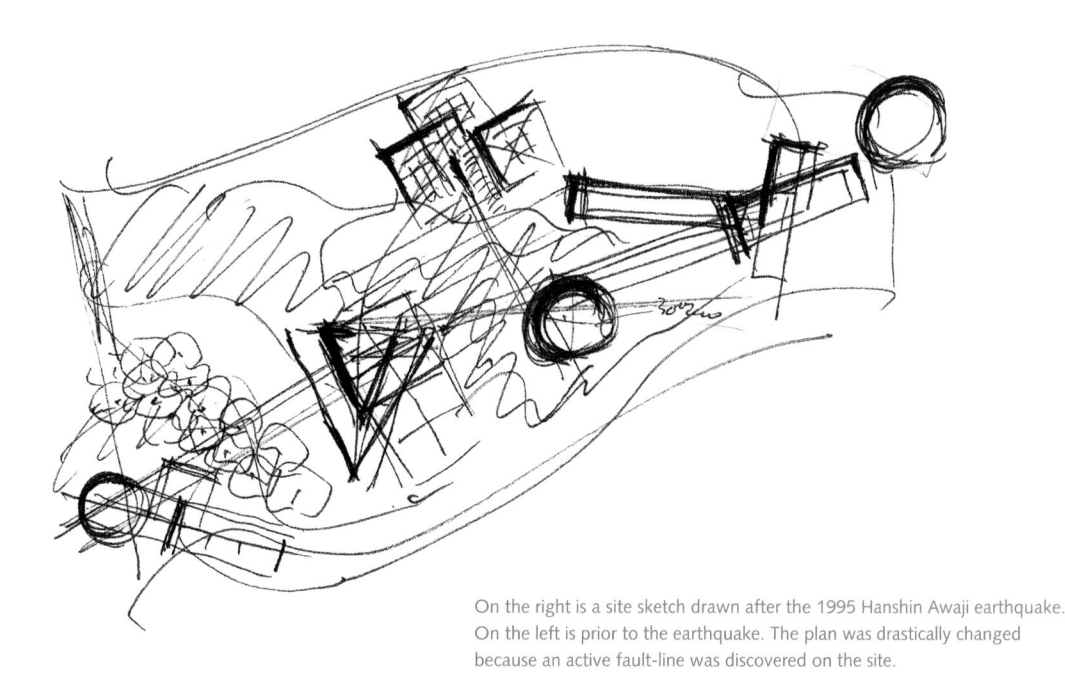

On the right is a site sketch drawn after the 1995 Hanshin Awaji earthquake. On the left is prior to the earthquake. The plan was drastically changed because an active fault-line was discovered on the site.

海と山に挟まれた28ヘクタールの敷地に散りばめられた壮大な建築群。相互にズレた軸線が水池を介して交錯する構成は、ローマ郊外のティヴォリに建つヴィラ・アドリアーナの遺跡を思わせる。

A grand architectural ensemble dispersed across a 28ha site interposed between the sea and the mountains. Comprising mutually offset axes blended through the medium of ponds, the composition is reminiscent of the historic ruins of the Villa Adriana, built in Tivoli in the outskirts of Rome.

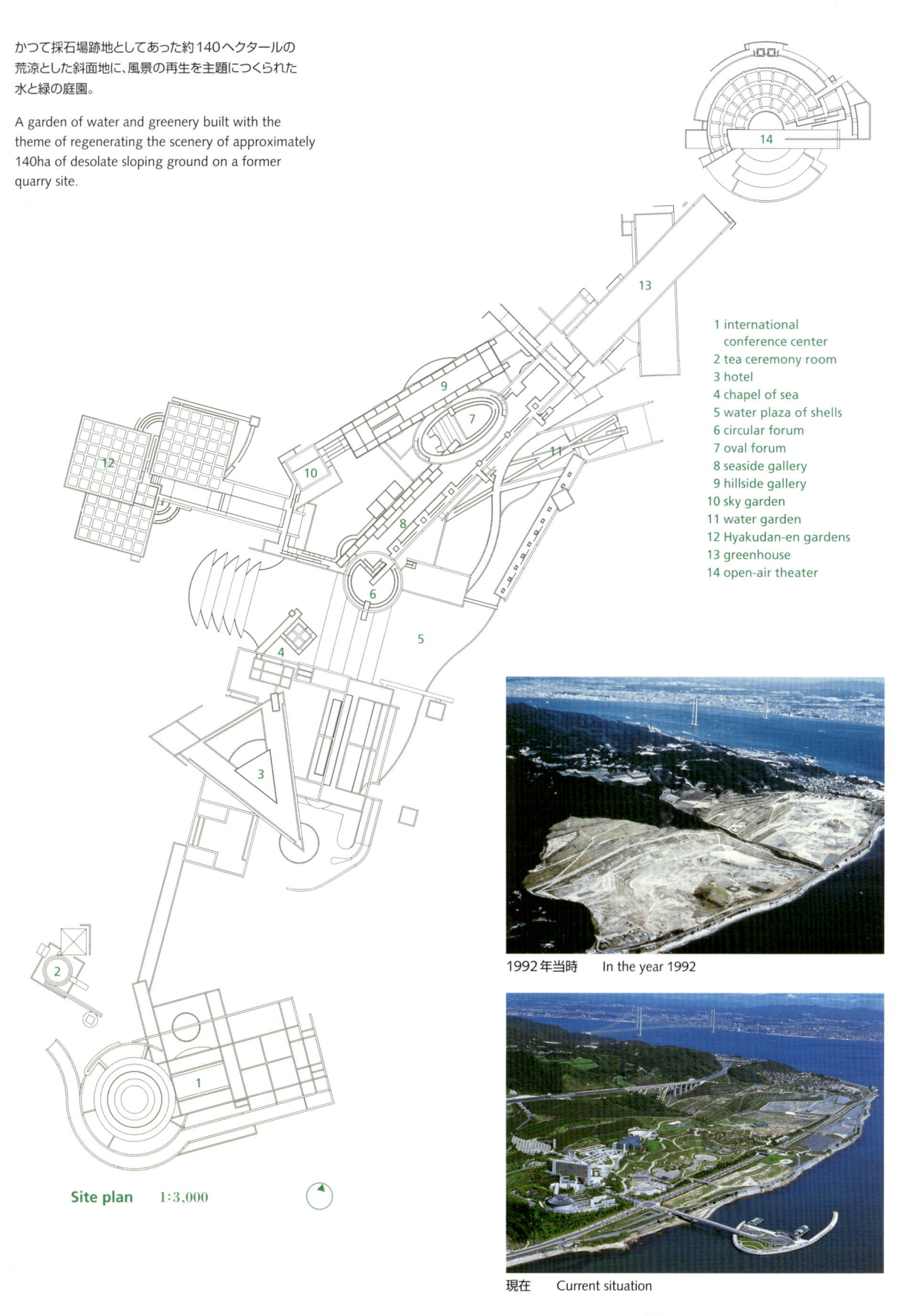

かつて採石場跡地としてあった約140ヘクタールの荒涼とした斜面地に、風景の再生を主題につくられた水と緑の庭園。

A garden of water and greenery built with the theme of regenerating the scenery of approximately 140ha of desolate sloping ground on a former quarry site.

1 international conference center
2 tea ceremony room
3 hotel
4 chapel of sea
5 water plaza of shells
6 circular forum
7 oval forum
8 seaside gallery
9 hillside gallery
10 sky garden
11 water garden
12 Hyakudan-en gardens
13 greenhouse
14 open-air theater

Site plan 1:3,000

1992年当時　In the year 1992

現在　Current situation

Awaji-Yumebutai

再生された緑の斜面に展開する建築庭園。地形に沿って配された幾何学的構成の建物が、ヴォイドと水庭を介して接続される。

An architectural garden developed within regenerated greenery on the sloping site. Geometrically composed buildings arranged along the topography are connected by means of voids and water gardens.

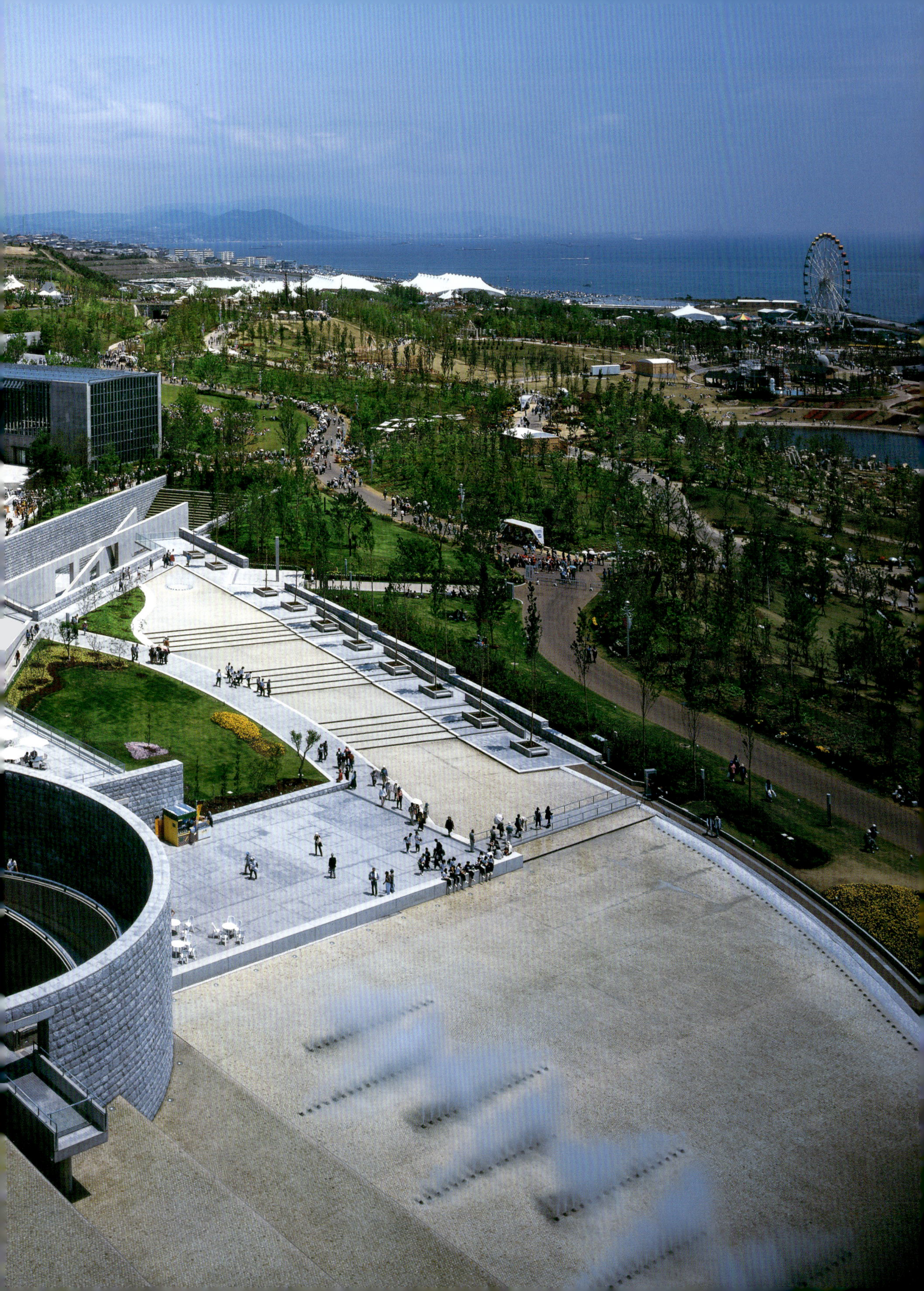

国際会議場。正方形と円を基調とした平面構成により、屋上には淡路産の瓦を用いた円環状屋根をもつ。
The international conference center. Based on a plan composition of a square and a circle,
it has a toroid roof using tiles produced in Awaji.

円形フォーラム。複雑に絡み合う建築の結節点で、訪問者を迎える水の造形。
Circular forum. A node point of the complex interwoven architecture, it shapes the water that greets visitors.

貝の浜。100万枚の帆立貝の貝殻を約1万m²の床一面に敷き詰めている。
表面を流れる水が凹凸に応じてさざなみを立てる。

The Water Plaza of Shells. One million scallop shells have been spread across a surface of approximately 10,000m². The water flowing on the surface ripples due to the unevenness.

上：全長108mの温室。コンクリート打ち放しの円柱列に支持された立体トラスがガラスの天井面を構成する。
下：楕円フォーラム。長径50m、高さ17mの楕円形平面を象る壁に囲まれた劇場空間。

Above: A greenhouse 108m in length. The glass-ceiling surface comprises three-dimensional trusses set along rows of bare concrete cylindrical columns.
Below: Oval forum. A theater space surrounded by walls modeled on an elliptical plan 50m in length and 17m high.

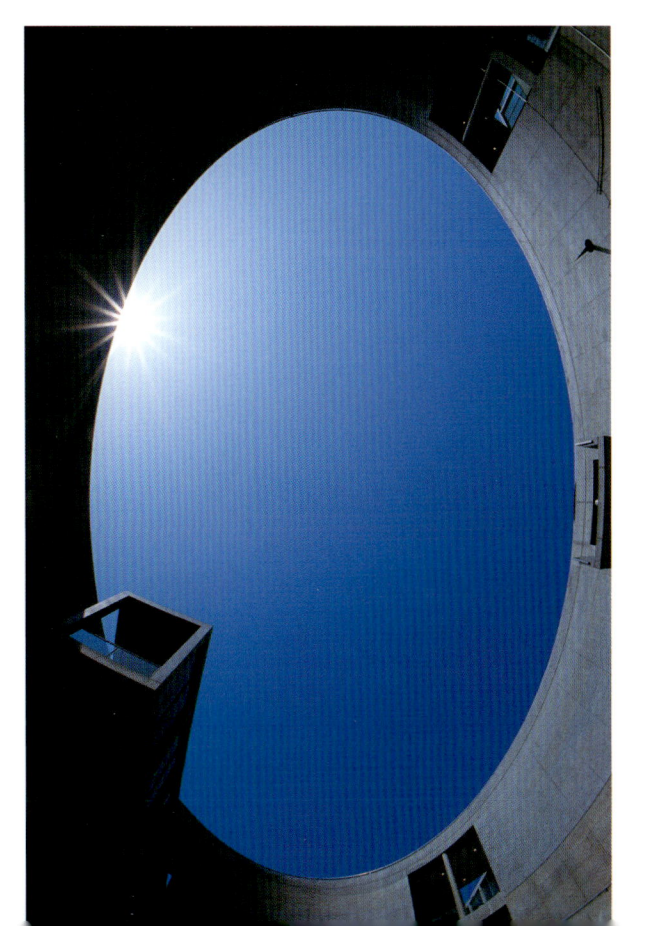

上：敷地の最北部に斜面の地形と一体化するようにつくられた野外劇場。古代ギリシャの円形劇場をモチーフに、海と空を背景としたステージを囲んで、約3,000人を収容する客席が設けられている。

Above: An open-air theater built as if unified with the sloping terrain at the northernmost part of the site. Taking the motif of an ancient Greek amphitheater, seating for approximately 3,000 people has been established surrounding a stage, with the sea and the sky as a backdrop.

267 Awaji-Yumebutai

百段苑。岩盤斜面地に設置された100区画の花壇。1辺4.5mの正方形平面が、上下の高低差約30mの地形に沿って段状にずれ重なる。1995年の阪神淡路大震災で亡くなられた人々に捧げる鎮魂のモニュメント。

The Hyakudan-en. A flowerbed in one hundred sections created on the sloping bedrock. Stepping layers of 4.5m-square planes, set across terrain with a 30m difference in height. This is a monument for the repose of souls, dedicated to the people who died in the 1995 Hanshin Awaji Earthquake.

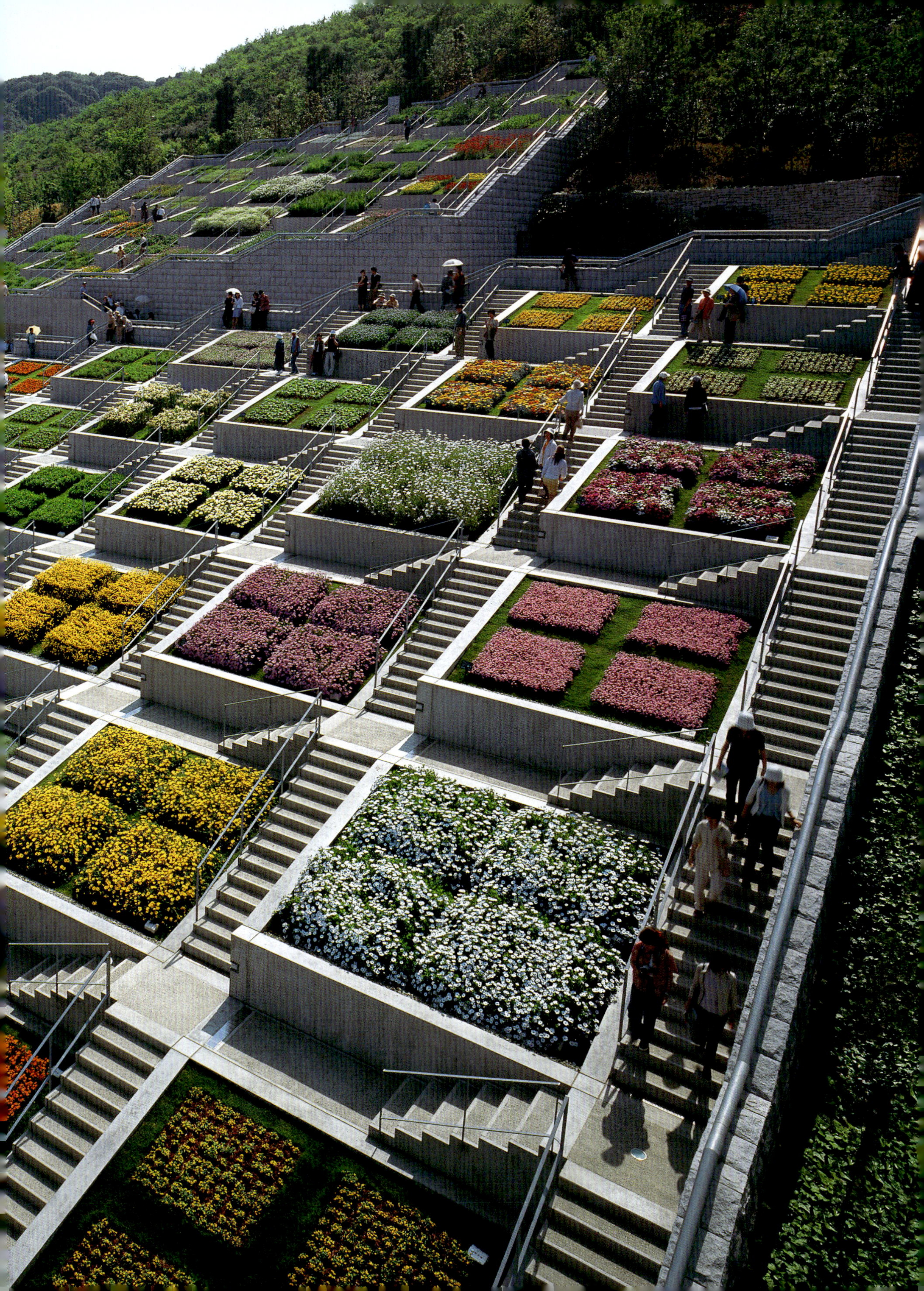

南岳山光明寺
Komyo-ji Temple
1998-2000　愛媛県西条市 —— Saijo, Ehime

　敷地は愛媛県西条市中心部の住宅地に位置する。250年余り続く浄土真宗寺院の建て替え計画である。この小都市は豊富な伏流水で知られており、街中至るところに清廉な水路を見つけることができる。そんな原風景をもつ地域の核となるべき〈お寺〉として、水面に浮かぶ柔らかな光に包まれた木のお堂を構想した。

　新しい寺院は、地下水を利用して設けられた池の中心に建つ木造の本堂と、池を取り巻くように配されたコンクリート打ち放しによる客殿、礼拝堂と庫裏から構成される。本堂は、集成材を用いたまったく現代的な工法による木造建築であるが、その空間構成は、ある部分で日本の伝統的建築のエッセンスを受け継いでいる。木部材の組み合わせとしてつくられる木造建築の、その力の流れを視覚化する簡素な構造美の表現である。

　100畳の広さをもつ本堂の空間を支えるのは、4本で1組をなす16本の柱と、その上部に井桁状に積み重ねられた梁の木組みによる力強い架構である。その本堂の周囲をすりガラスの木格子スクリーンが囲い、さらにその外側をピッチの細かい縦格子の外壁で池の水面と緩やかに隔てられた回廊が巡る。外陣から回廊へ連続する天井垂木は、縦格子の外壁を越えて水上に大きくせり出し、深い庇を形づくっている。

　すべてが線状部材の集積に還元された、この現代的〈組物〉の架構の下、日中の堂内は、二重のスクリーンを経て入り込む柔らかな自然光で満たされ、逆に夜間は、内部の光が散乱して池に反射し、幻想的な雰囲気を醸し出す。

　古い山門と鐘楼はあえて建て替えずにそのまま残し、池を挟んでの穏やかな新旧の対話が生まれるよう意図した。場所と歴史と伝統と向き合う中で、人の集まる場としてつくった〈お寺〉である。

The site is located in a residential district in the center of Saijo City, Ehime Prefecture. This is a design for the reconstruction of a Jodo Shinshu (True Pure Land School) Buddhist temple that has been here for over 250 years. This small city is known for its abundant spring water, and pure waterways can be found throughout the town. As a "temple" that should become the nucleus of an area with such primal scenery, I conceived a wooden hall floating on water and wrapped in gentle light.

　The composition of the new temple comprises a wooden main hall at the center of an artificial pond created using spring water, with a bare concrete reception hall, worship hall, and monastery quarters arranged as if surrounding the pond. The main hall is a wooden building of glue-laminated timber using entirely modern construction techniques, yet the spatial composition partly retains the essence of traditional Japanese architecture. As an assemblage of timber components, this wooden architecture has a simple structural beauty that visualizes the flow of forces and gravity.

　Sixteen columns made up of four posts each support the 100-tatami-mat main hall space, on top of which is a strong frame construction comprising an assemblage of beams layered in a grid pattern. A wooden lattice screen of frosted glass encloses the main hall, beyond which are outer walls of closely spaced vertical wooden louvers that gently separate the cloister from the surface of the pond. The ceiling rafters continue from the nave to the cloister and past the vertical louver exterior walls, projecting above the pond to form deep eaves.

　Below this contemporary "braided" frame structure, entirely reduced to an accumulation of linear elements, the hall is suffused with soft natural light that comes in through a double screen during the day, and conversely by night the interior light is dispersed and reflects on the pond, creating a magical atmosphere.

　By preserving the old gate and belfry without rebuilding them, the aim was to produce a gentle dialogue between old and new with the pond interposed between. In confronting locale, history, and tradition, this "temple" has been made as a place where people may gather.

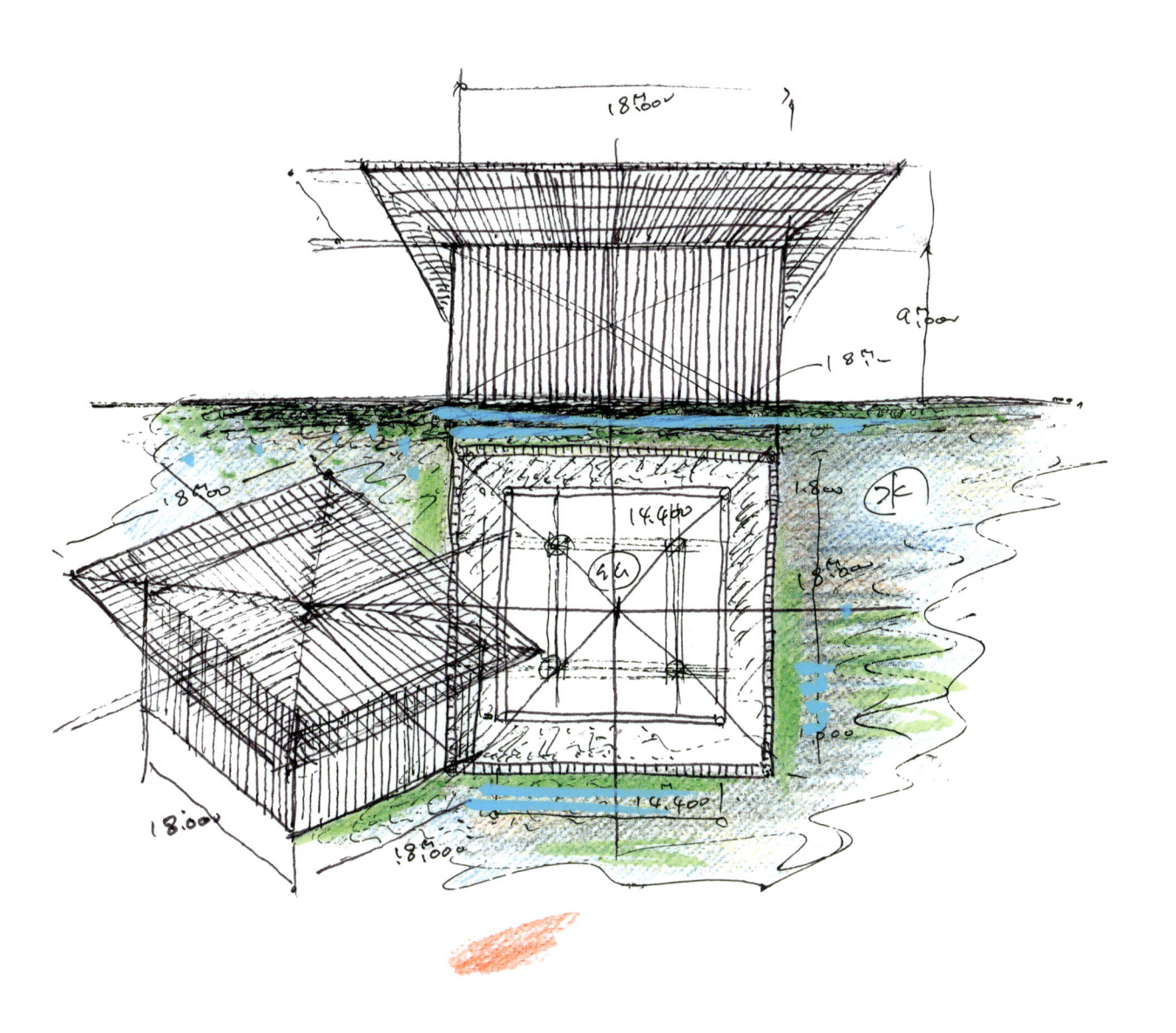

初期イメージスケッチ。架構のプロポーションが具体的な数値をもって検討されている。計算されつくした建築の構造美。

Early image sketch. The proportions of the composition were examined using actual numerical values.
The calculated beauty of the architectural structure.

石鎚山系の伏流水が絶えることなく湧き出る池の上に浮かぶ本堂。

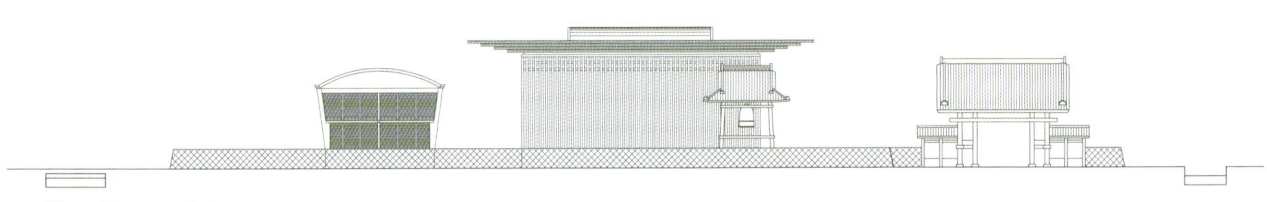

Elevation　1:500

The main hall floats above a pond into which the underground water of the Ishizuchi Mountains pours endlessly.

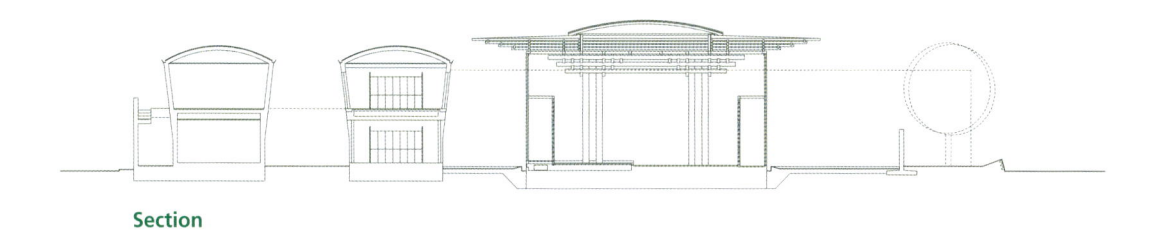

Section

273 Komyo-ji Temple

4層の垂木が約4m水上に迫り出し、大きな軒を支持している。
Four layers of rafters project approximately 4m out over the water, supporting large eaves.

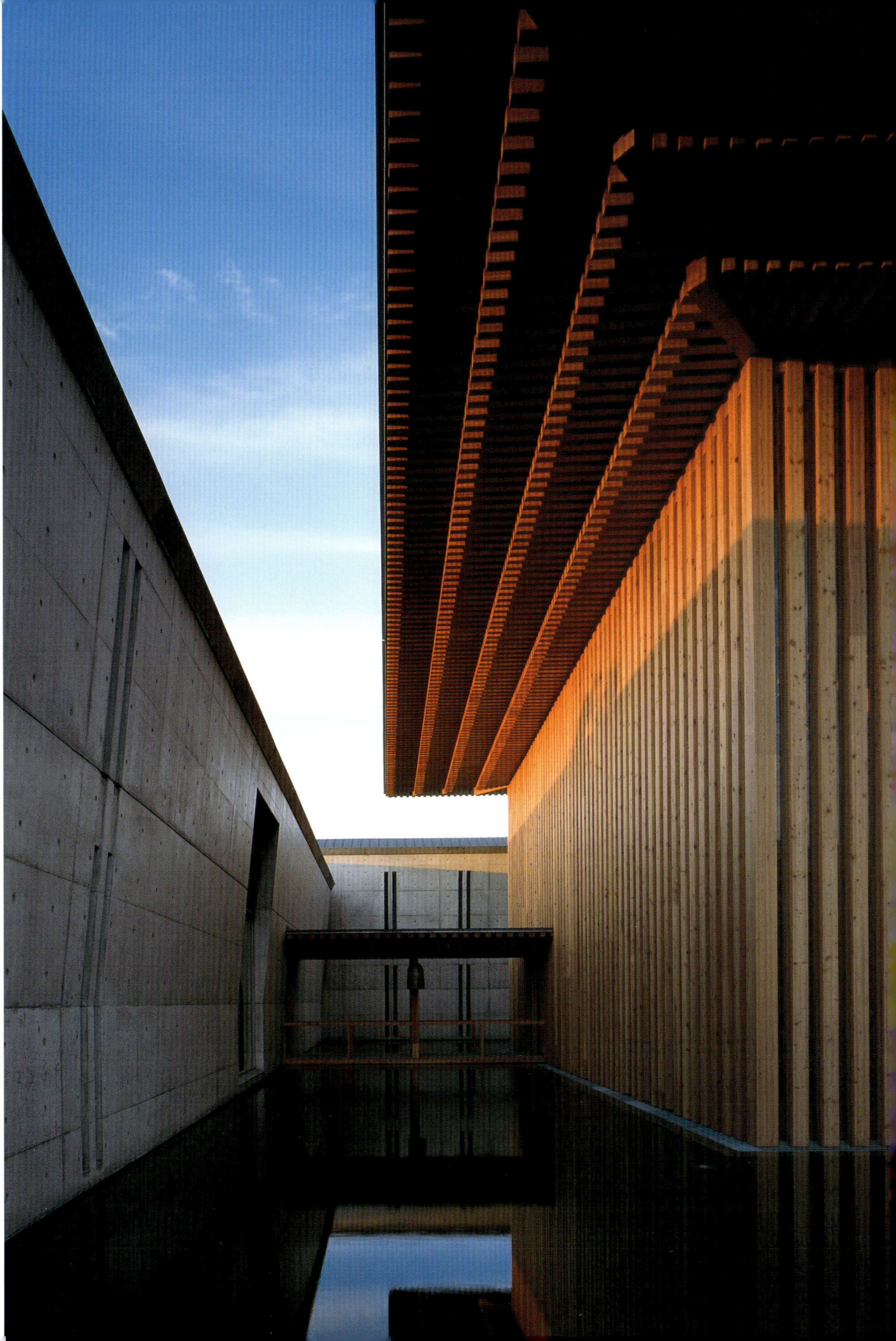

First floor plan 1:1,000

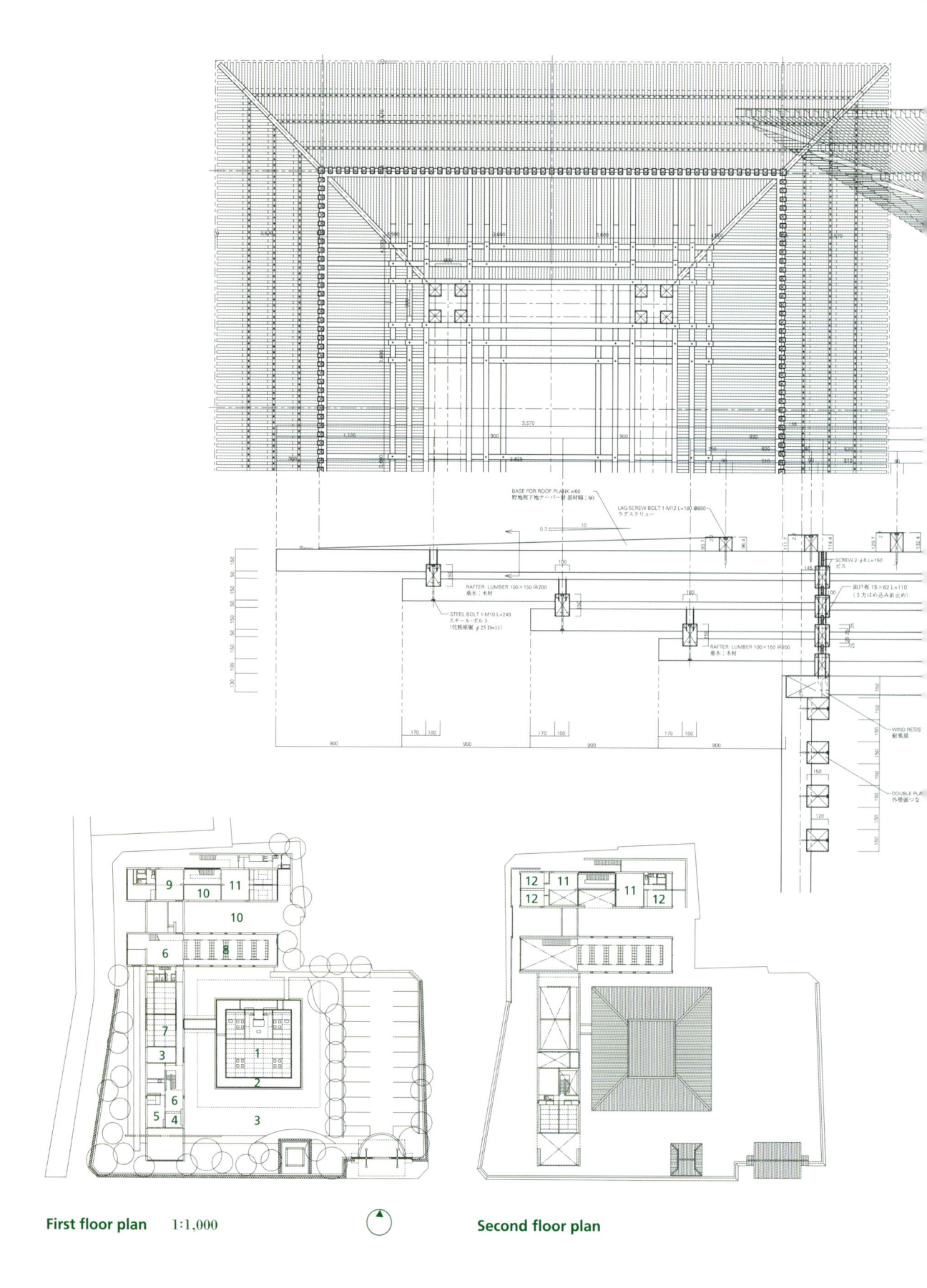

Second floor plan

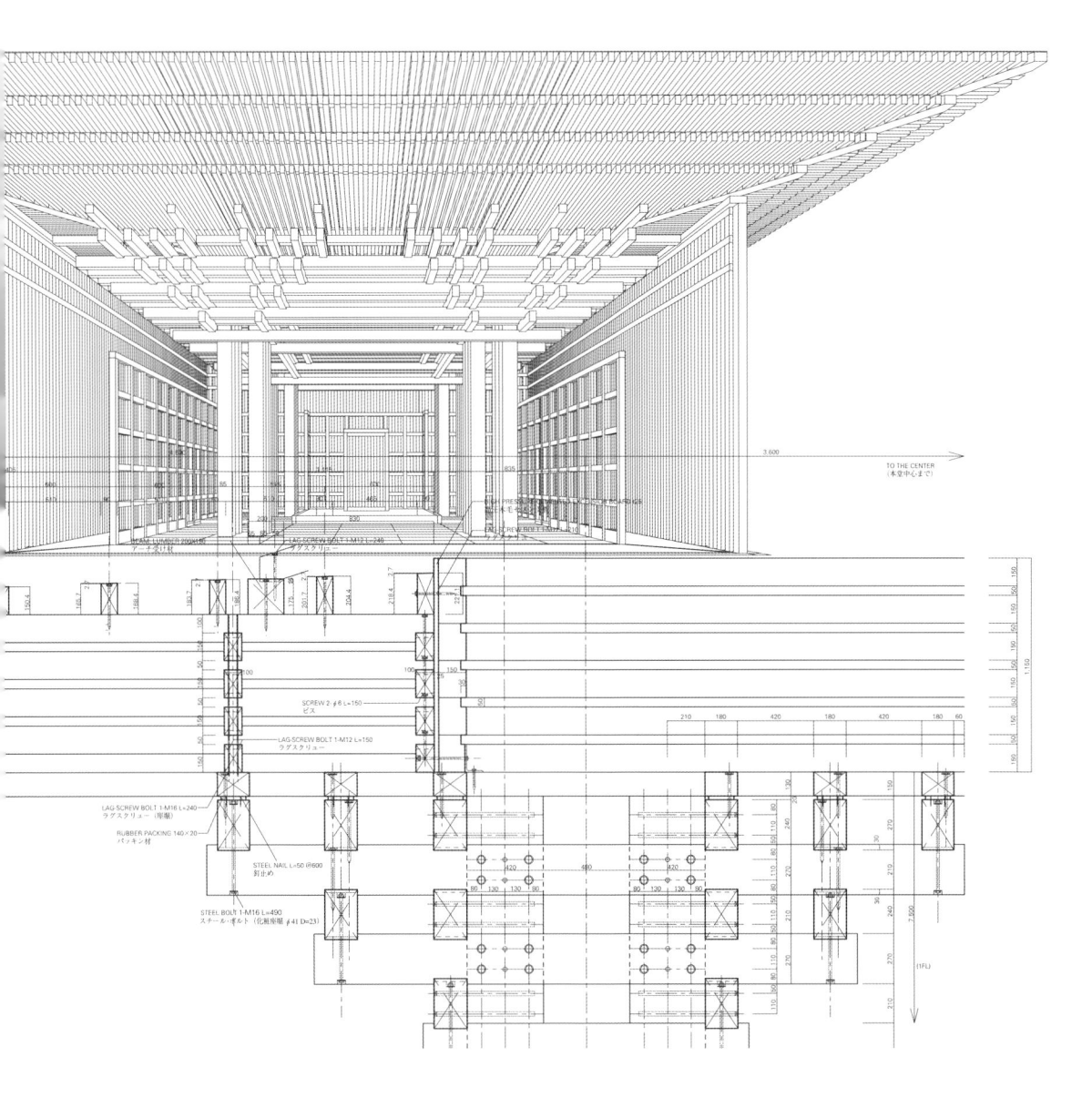

1 main hall
2 corridor
3 pool
4 entrance
5 office
6 lobby
7 hall
8 hall of worship
9 dining room
10 court
11 living room
12 bedroom

中心に木造の本堂を配した水池の周りを、コンクリート造の客殿、礼拝堂、庫裏が取り囲む構成。

A composition in which the wooden main hall is placed at the center of the pond, surrounded by the bare concrete reception hall, worship hall, and monastery quarters.

277 Komyo-ji Temple

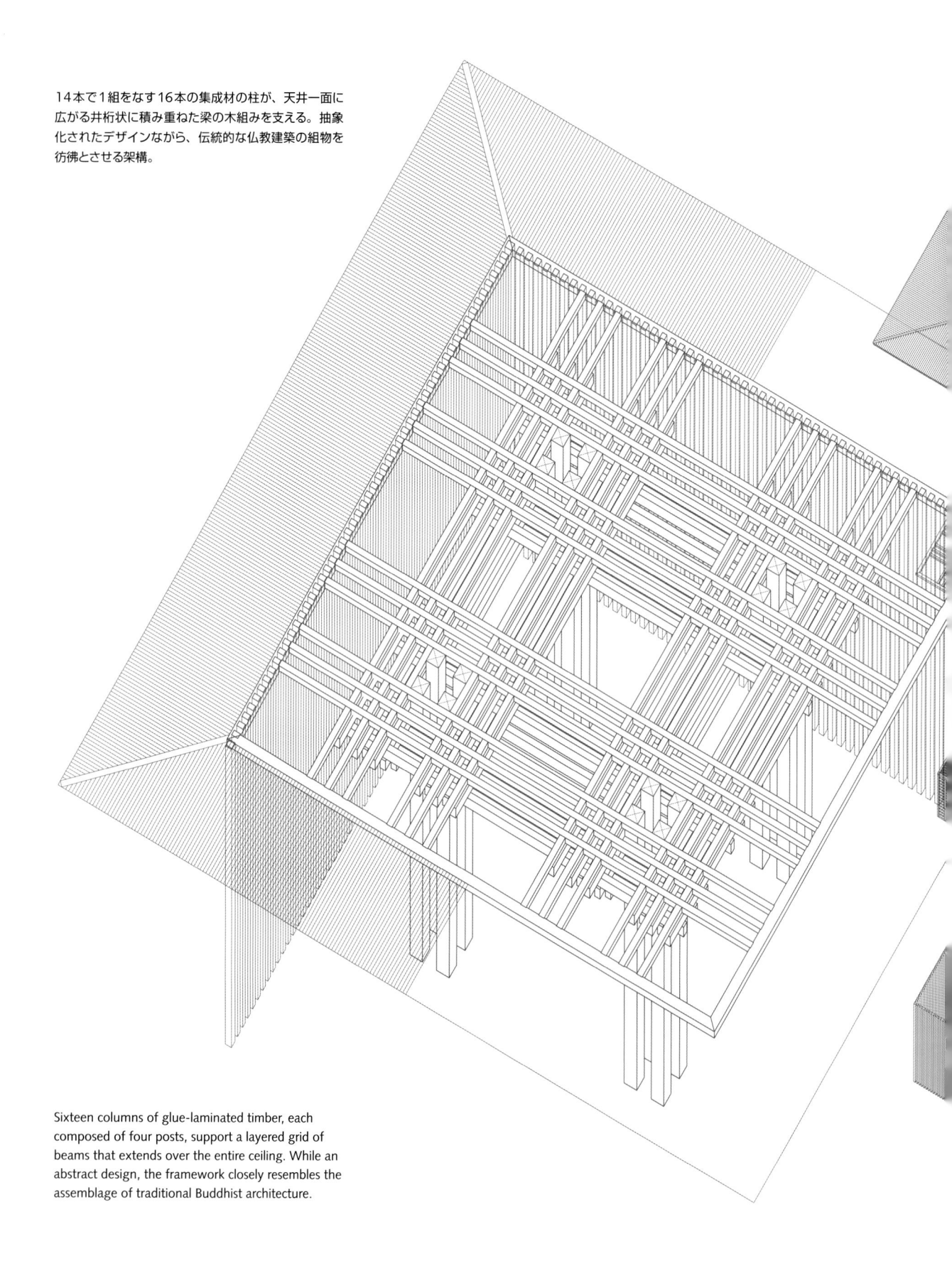

14本で1組をなす16本の集成材の柱が、天井一面に広がる井桁状に積み重ねた梁の木組みを支える。抽象化されたデザインながら、伝統的な仏教建築の組物を彷彿とさせる架構。

Sixteen columns of glue-laminated timber, each composed of four posts, support a layered grid of beams that extends over the entire ceiling. While an abstract design, the framework closely resembles the assemblage of traditional Buddhist architecture.

279 Komyo-ji Temple

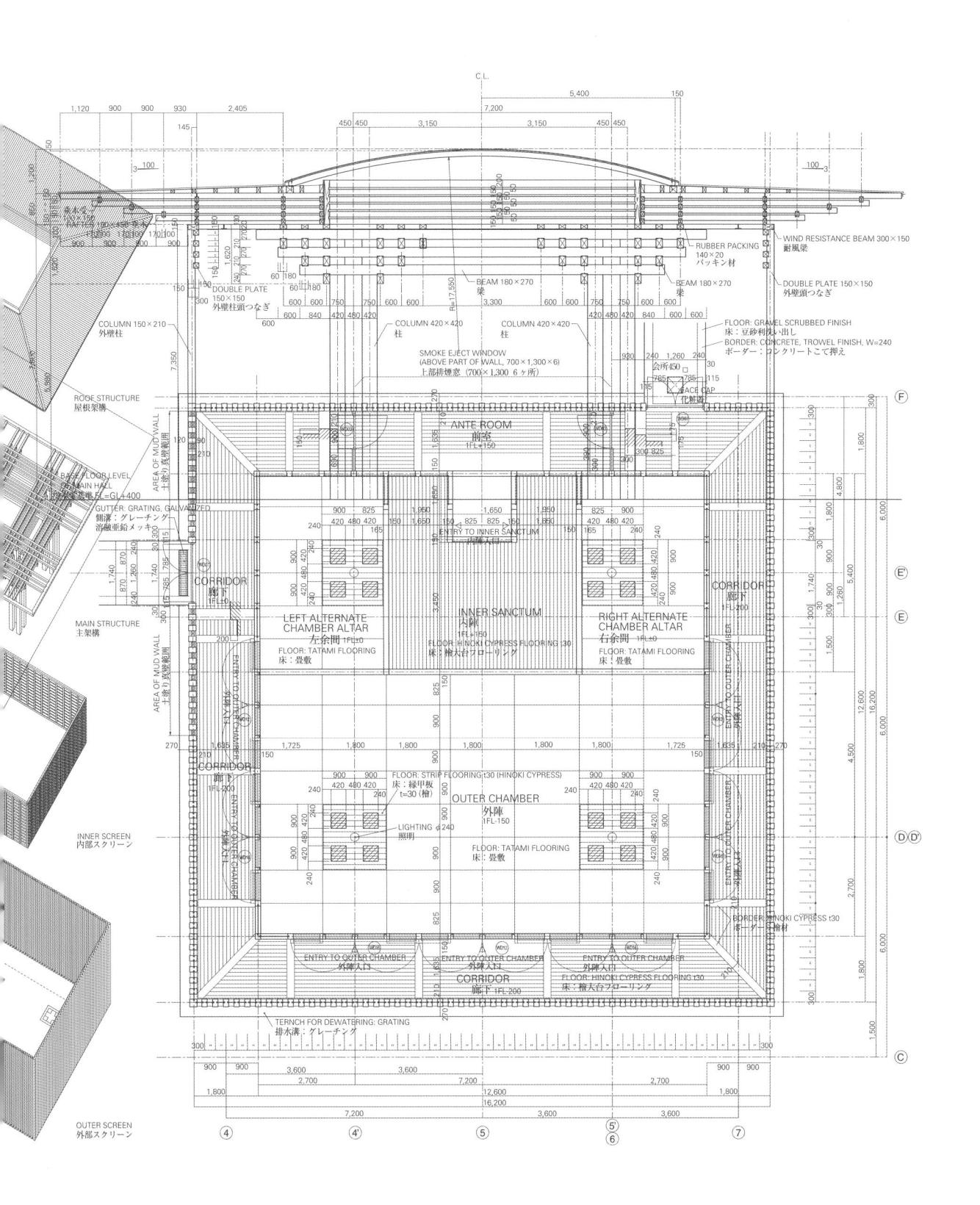

約100畳の本堂内部。すりガラスのはめこまれた内部スクリーンが四周を囲い、柔らかな光を内部に引き込む。

The interior of the main hall, approximately one hundred tatami mats in area. An interior screen inset with frosted glass surrounds it on all sides, drawing soft light into the interior.

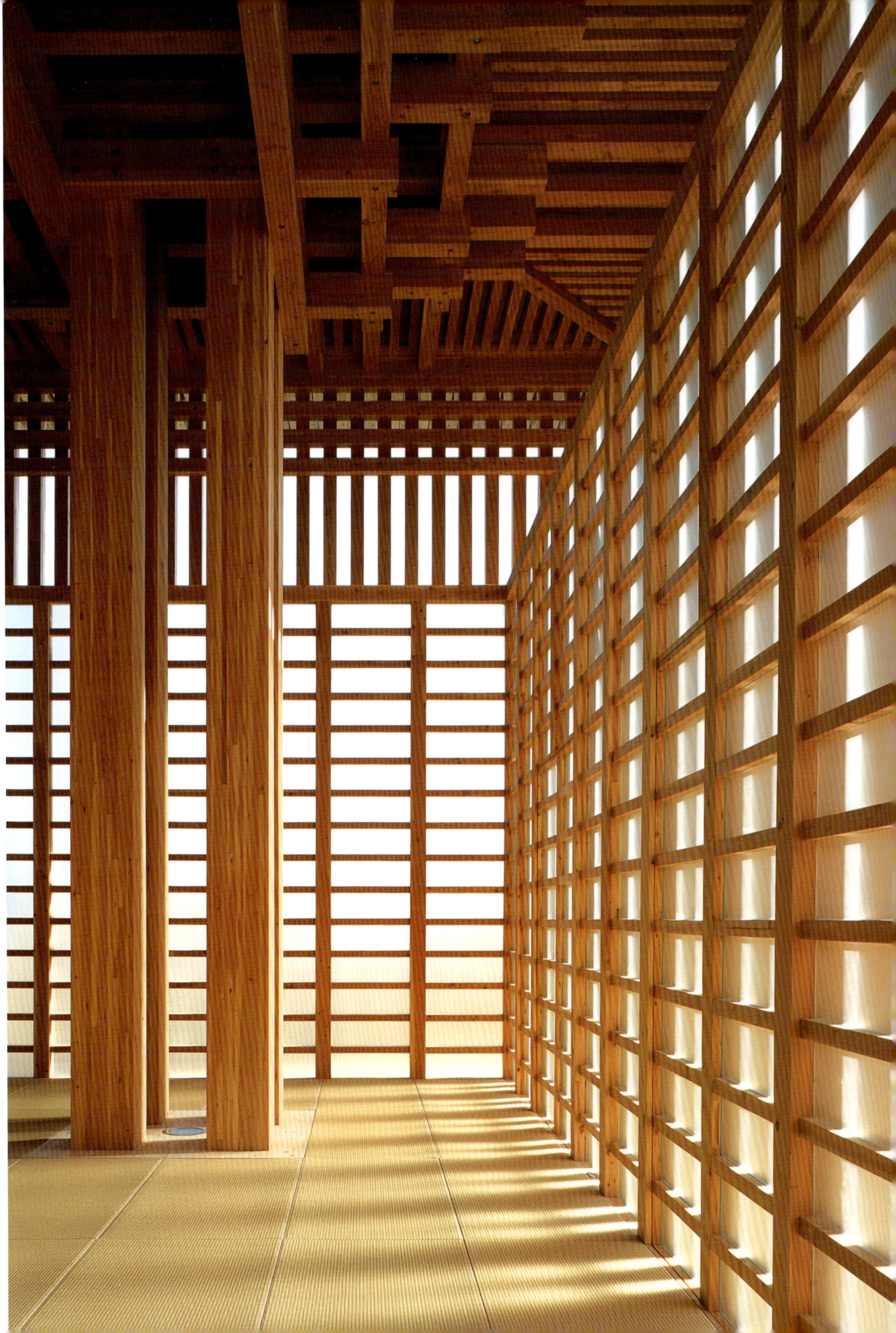

本堂の外側に濡れ縁として、竪格子を介して池と接する
内部廊下が設けられている。

An interior corridor connected to the pond
through vertical louvers has been established as an open
verandah on the outer edge of the main hall.

283 Komyo-ji Temple

水上に浮かぶ本堂の夜景。格子の隙間から漏れる内部の
光が水面に映し出され、幻想的な雰囲気を醸し出す。

Night view of the main hall floating above the water.
The interior light leaking through the gaps in the lattice
is reflected in the water surface, creating a magical
atmosphere.

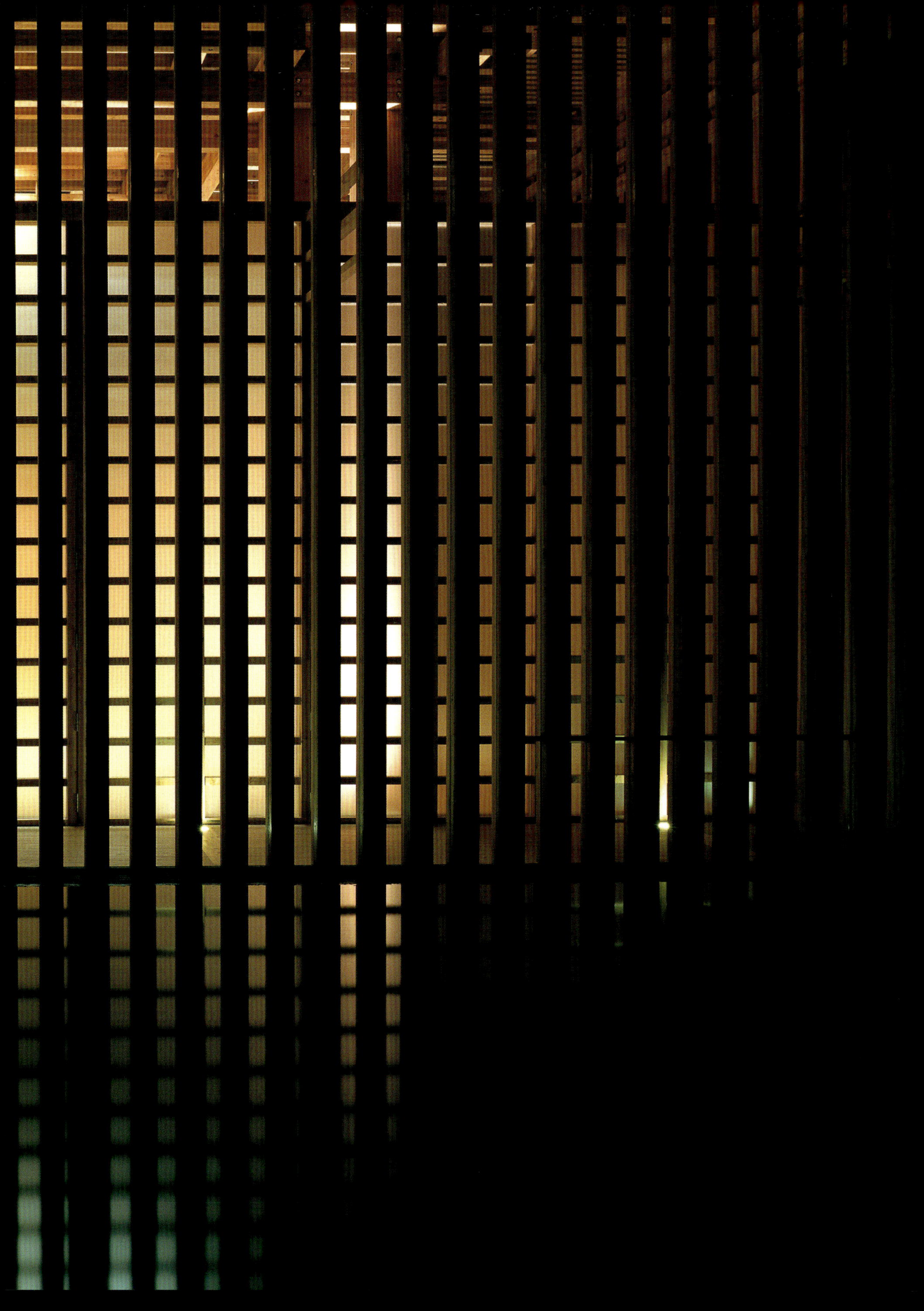

大阪府立狭山池博物館
Sayamaike Historical Museum, Osaka
1994-2001　大阪府大阪狭山市 —— Osakasayama, Osaka

　敷地は大阪南部、1994年に完成した「近つ飛鳥博物館」から西に10kmほど離れた位置にある。7世紀に築造された日本最古のため池「狭山池」のほとりにつくられた、日本の治水事業の歴史を伝える博物館である。

　事の始まりは、狭山池の治水工事中に鎌倉時代の樋の遺構が発見されたときにさかのぼる。再調査の結果、狭山池を囲う堤体(つつみ)の断面には、古代からの改修の痕跡が、重層構造として残されていることが判明、そして、その遺構の保存と周辺環境の整備を目的とする今回の博物館の計画がスタートした。

　「近つ飛鳥博物館」同様、ここでも考えたのは、狭山池という場所と一体化してある環境博物館という主題である。

　計画敷地は池の堤より15mほど低いレベルに位置する。その高低差を活かし、まず堤から緩やかに連続する基壇部を形づくる。露出する外壁部には、周囲の落ち着いた雰囲気に馴染むよう、石積みの表現を与える。建物主要なヴォリュームはすべてこの基壇部の中に埋め込まれ、その結果、高い天井高を必要とする展示棟と、地下に光を導くガラスの棟だけが地上に現れる。意図したのは、堤の延長としてある控え目な建築の構えである。

　堤から地下の博物館へと導くアプローチは、両側を滝面に挟まれた水庭となっており、さらにその先には、2層分の高さの壁に囲われた円形のコートが待ち受ける。流れ落ちる滝の水音、壁に切り取られる空の情景——ダイナミックな空間のシークエンスによって、人々を壮大な歴史の世界へと導くよう考えた。

　狭山池では、建物の竣工以来、地元住民の協力のもと、継続的に堤への桜の植樹が行われている。堤の全周を美しい桜並木が巡るまで、建築は完結しない。

The site is in south Osaka, approximately 10km west of the Chikatsu-Asuka Museum completed in 1994. This is a museum that displays the history of Japan's civil works, specifically flood control projects, and it is located on the shores of Sayamaike, Japan's oldest irrigation pond, constructed in the seventh century.

　The project began with the discovery of the remains of an ancient tub from the Kamakura period during flood control works at Sayamaike. As a result of further investigation, the traces of ancient repairs in the cross-section of the dam enclosing Sayamaike established that it survived as a multi-layered structure, so this museum project began with the aim of preserving the remains and maintaining the surrounding environment.

　Like the Chikatsu-Asuka Museum, the theme being addressed here is an environmental museum integrated with the Sayamaike locale.

　The project site is located approximately 15m lower than the bank of the pond. To make use of this difference in height, I first formed a base platform that gently extends from the bank. The exposed wall of the outcrop has been given a stone masonry finish in order to blend with the quiet atmosphere of the surroundings. The main volume of the building is buried entirely into this base platform, and as a result only the glass wing that brings light underground and the exhibition wing that requires a high ceiling appear above ground. The aim is a restrained architecture like an extension of the bank.

　The approach route to the museum under the bank is a water garden interposed between waterfalls on either side, beyond which awaits a circular court enclosed by a two-story wall. The sound of the water flowing down the waterfalls, the sight of the sky framed by the walls—I thought of guiding people to a magnificent historical world through a dynamic spatial sequence.

　With the cooperation of the local citizens, planting of cherry trees along the bank has been carried out at Sayamaike since the construction was completed. The architecture will not be finished until the entire bank is surrounded by a beautiful row of cherry trees.

初期イメージスケッチ。　　Early image sketch.

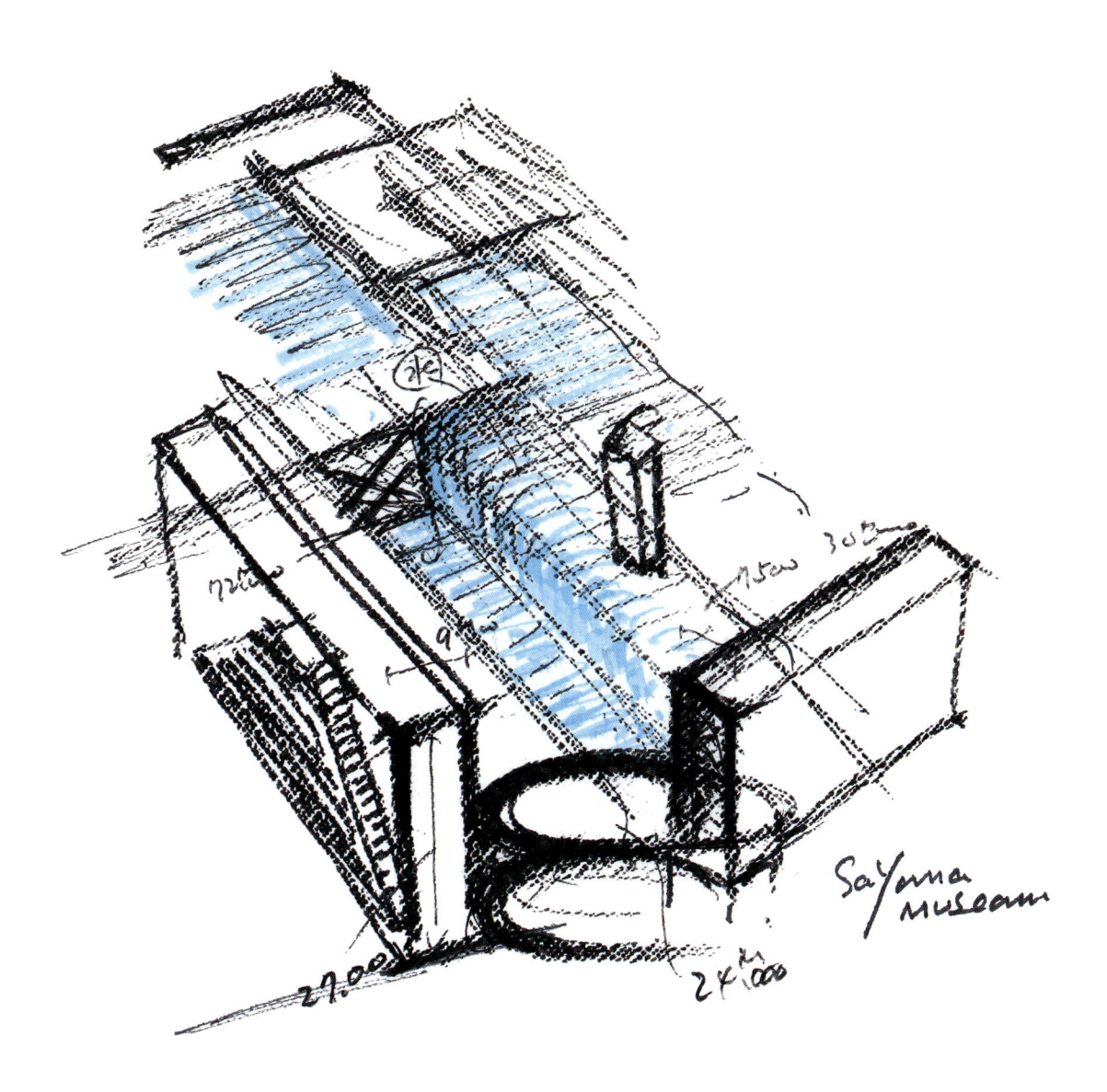

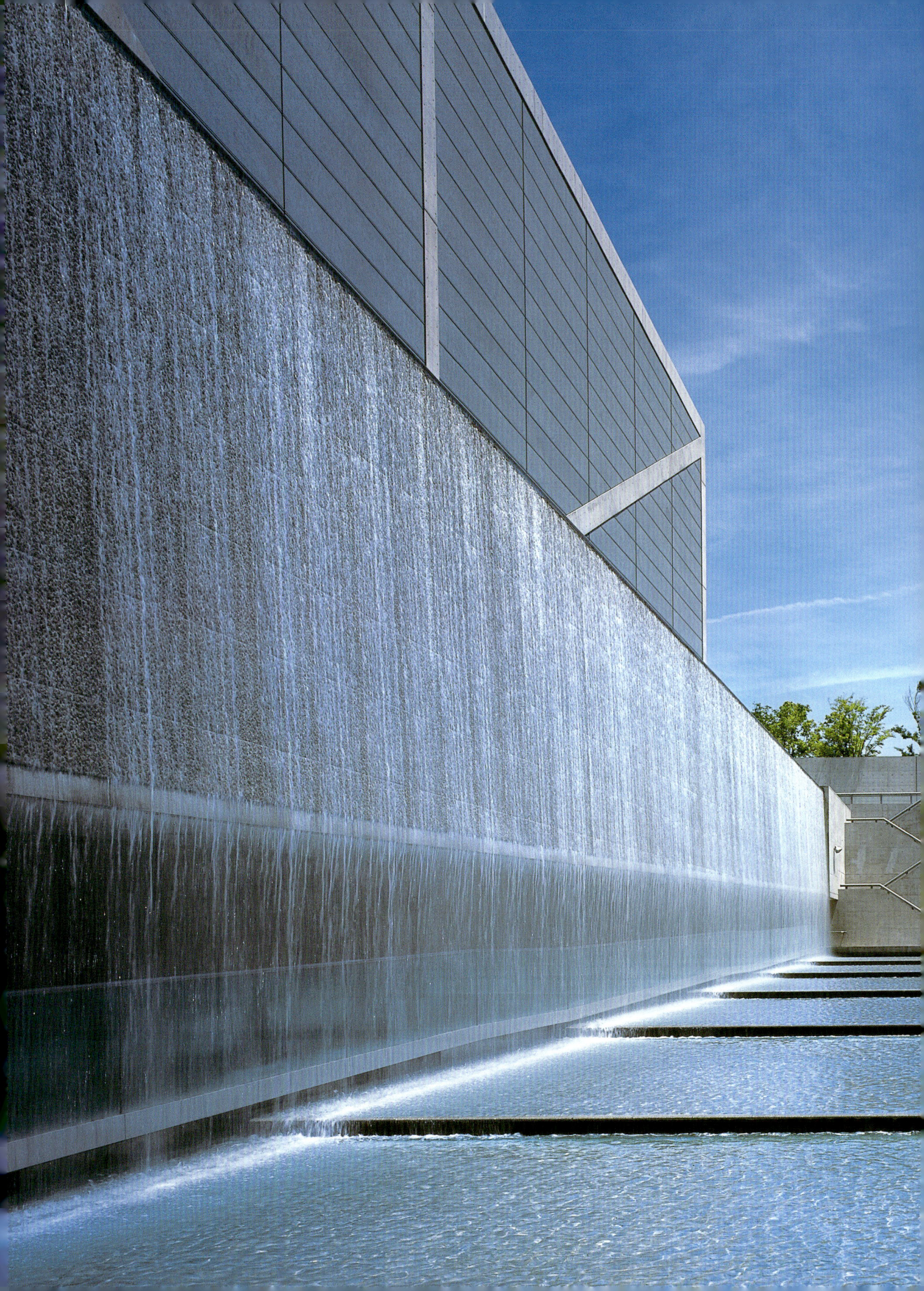

堤のレベルから、2層分掘り下げられたアプローチの水庭。奥行き25mにわたり段状に流れる水盤の両側を、地上レベルの水盤から流れ落ちる滝面が覆う。

Water garden approach route, excavated two stories below bank level. The water basin flows in a stepped shape for 25m, and both sides are lined by cascades falling from the ground-level water basins.

流れ落ちる水の音に包まれて、博物館内部へと歩を進める。治水を主題とした博物館に相応しい、壮大な建築の導入部。

One continues walking toward the museum interior while enveloped by the sound of falling water.
A grand entry to the building, appropriate for a museum with flood control as its theme.

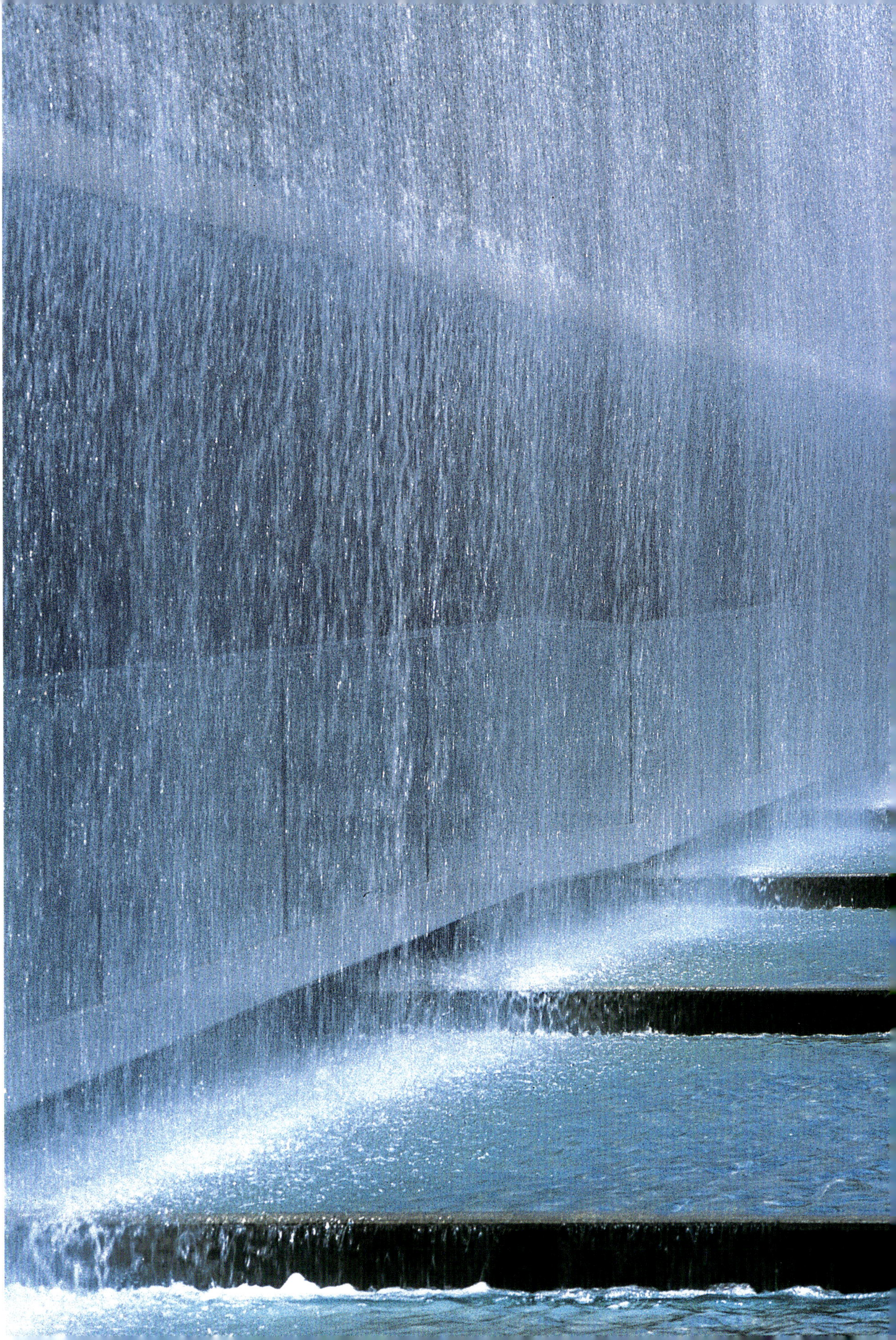

292 TADAO ANDO 3

Site plan 1:2,700

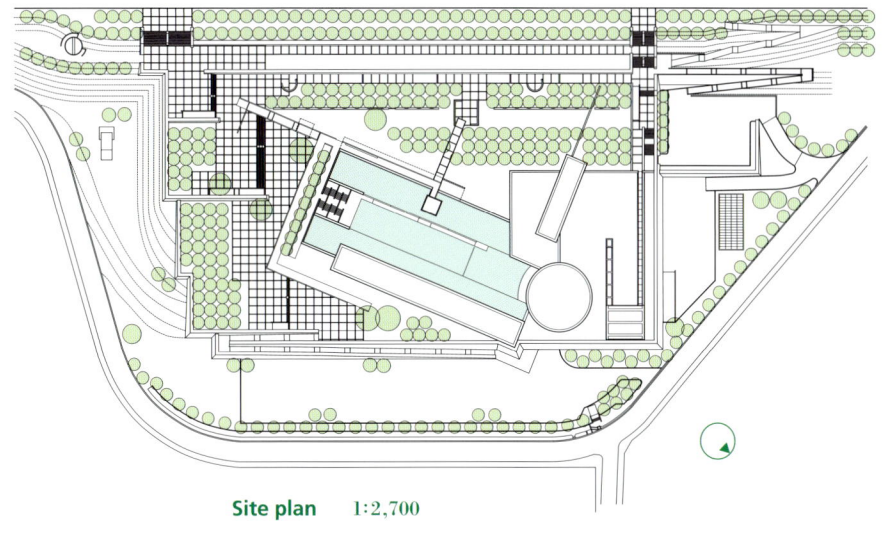

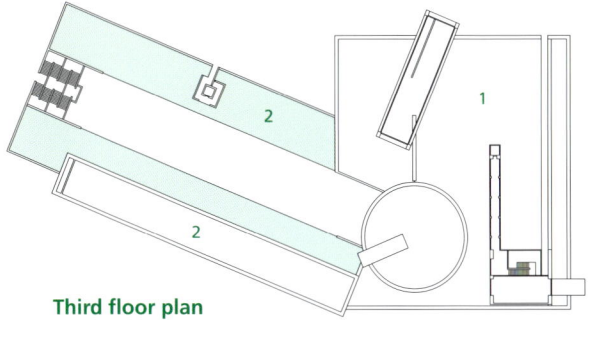

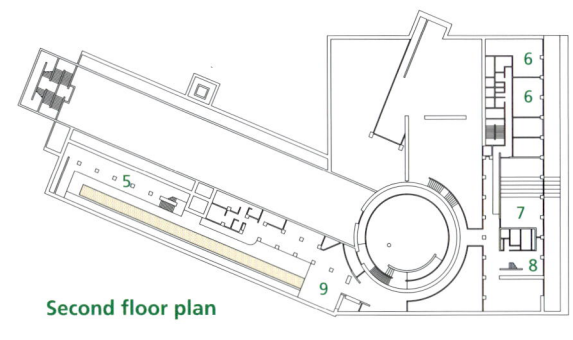

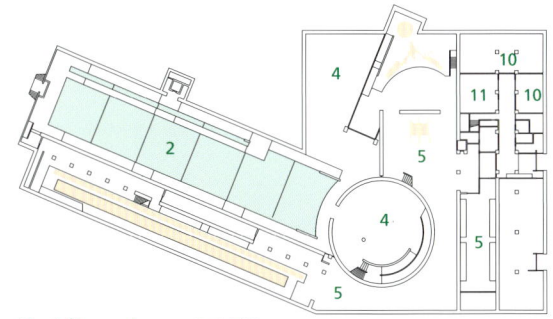

Third floor plan

Second floor plan

First floor plan 1:1,700

1 roof garden
2 cascade
3 café
4 court
5 exhibition room
6 office
7 auditorium
8 foyer
9 entrance hall
10 storage
11 stack room

狭山池堤を拡張したようなかたちでつくられた基壇部に、矩形に掘り込まれた水庭、円形の広場を取り巻くかたちで、堤体断面を収める展示棟と、地下の展示室に光を導くガラスボックスが埋め込まれている。

As an enclosure for the sunken rectangular water garden and the circular plaza, the exhibition wing containing a cross-section of the dam and glass boxes bringing light into the underground exhibition rooms are embedded in a podium formed as an extension of the Samayaike dam.

293 Sayamaike Museum

水庭の先で人々を待ち受ける円形のコート。
円形をなぞるスロープが、地上と地下を結ぶ。

A circular court awaits people beyond the water garden. The ramp tracing the circle connects below ground with above ground.

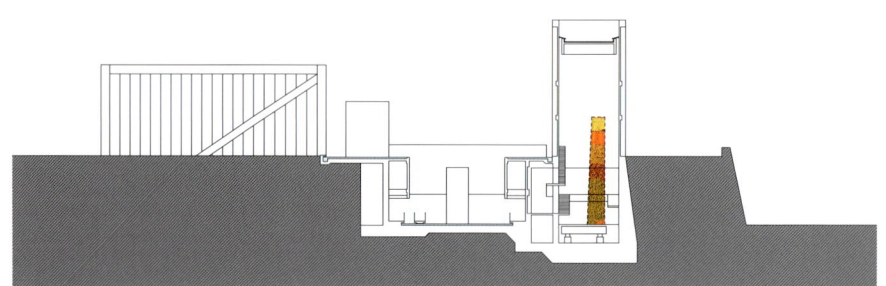

Section

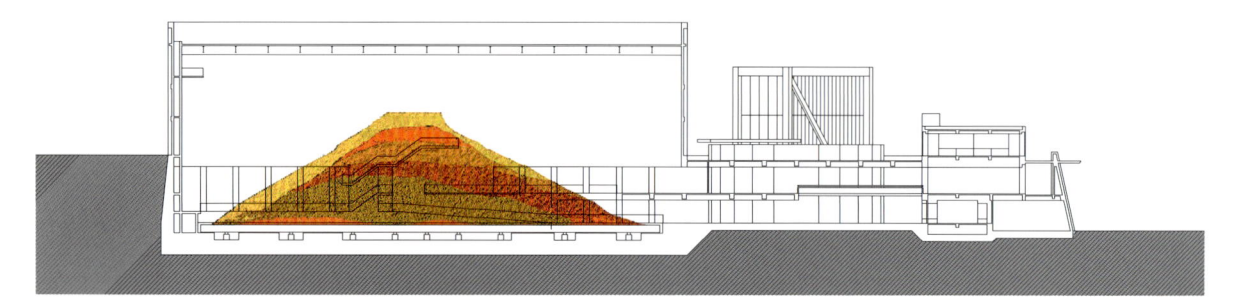

Section　1:1,000

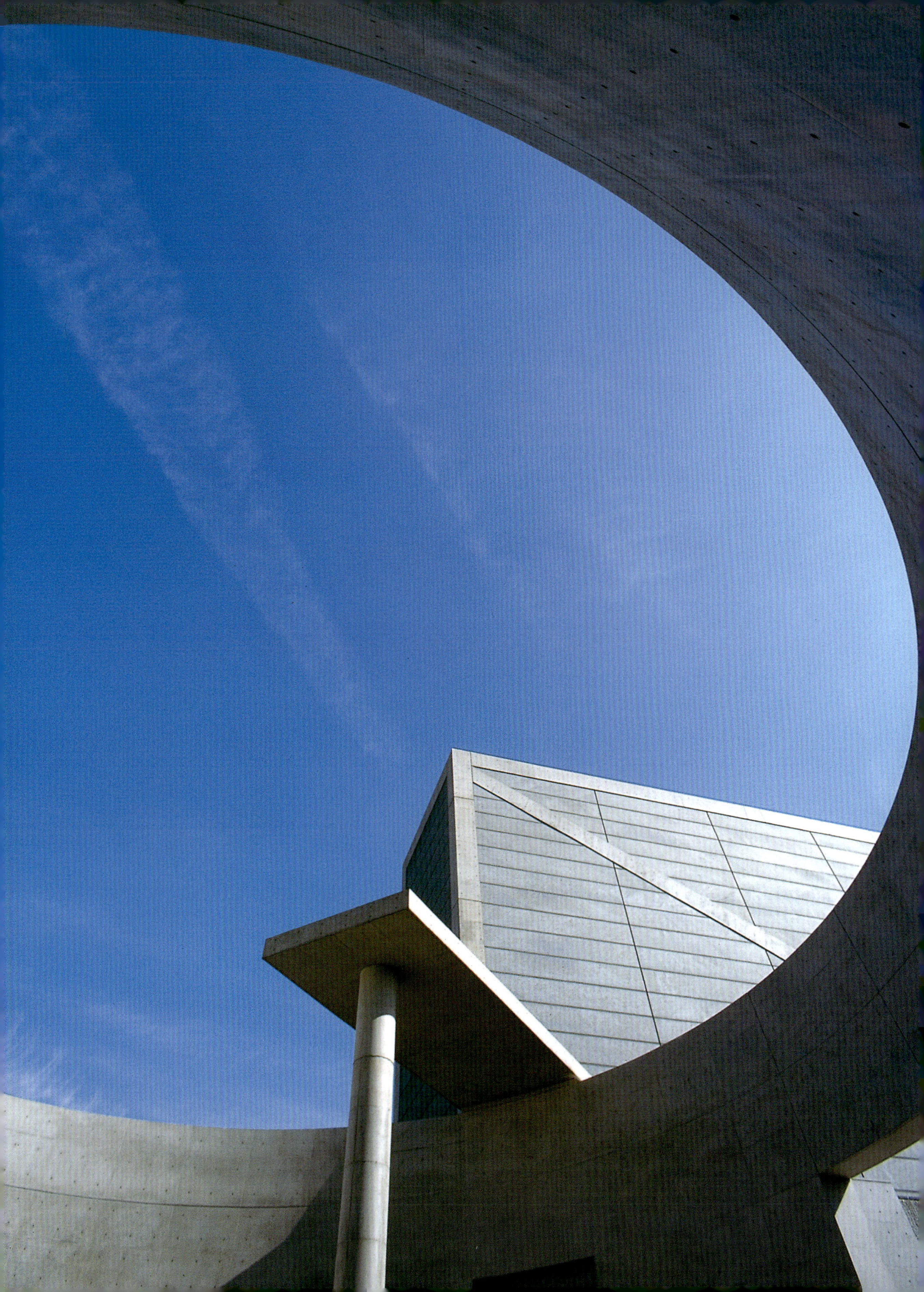

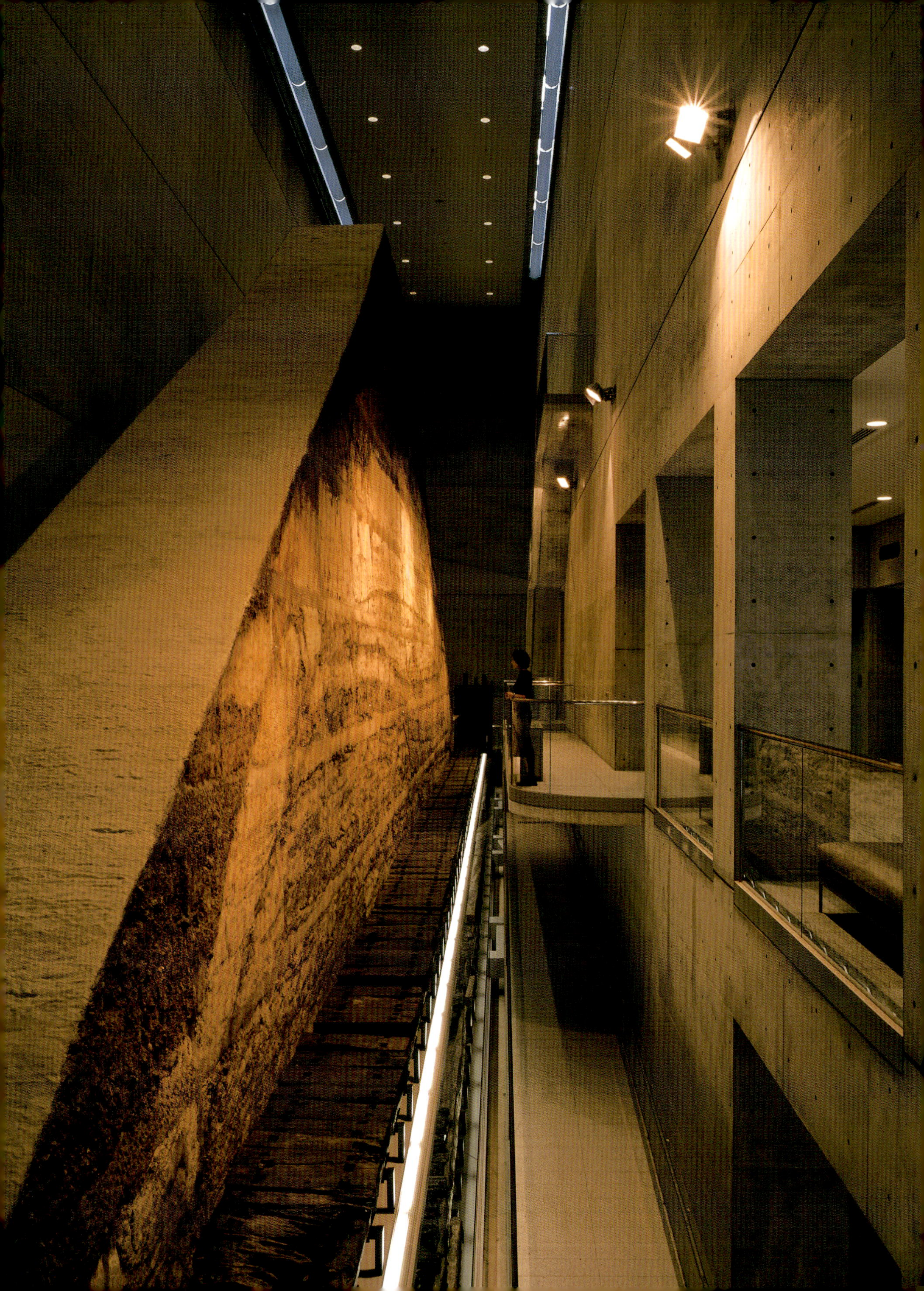

博物館のクライマックスとなる堤体断面を収める展示空間。天井高は22.5m。

Exhibition space containing a cross-section of the dam, which is the climax of the museum. The ceiling height is 22.5m.

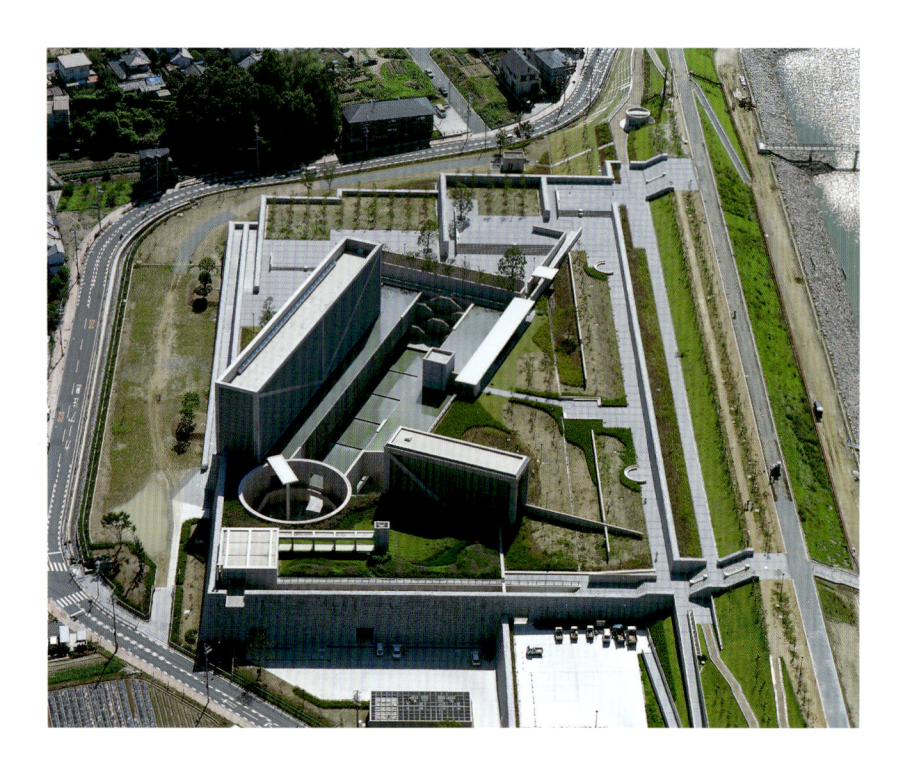

環境と一体化する博物館。建築の完成を期に、池の四周に桜の並木道をつくる住民活動が進められている。

A museum integrated with the environment. Since the completion of the building, the citizens have been making a road lined with cherry trees on the periphery of the lake.

Sayamaike Museum

司馬遼太郎記念館
Shiba Ryotaro Memorial Museum
1998-2001　大阪府東大阪市──Higashiosaka, Osaka

　戦後日本を代表する作家司馬遼太郎の記念館である。敷地は大阪郊外の閑静な住宅地、作家の自邸に庭続きで隣接している。

　建物は、敷地形状に沿った、同心の円弧を基準として構成されている。住宅地である周辺環境との調和のため、建物は1層分地下に埋め、地上に現れるのは2層分の高さのヴォリュームのみ。それによって生まれる敷地の余白のスペースは、建物を挟んでそれぞれ前庭と後庭に充てられている。

　記念館へは、司馬邸の門より親密なスケールの雑木の庭を通り抜け、その先に見える記念館の回廊を経てアプローチする。建物内部は、入口から奥に進むに従い、徐々に光が絞られていく、陰影深い空間となっている。

　その闇の奥に、施設の中心となる展示室「もうひとつの書斎」がある。3層吹き抜けの空間は、壁面のすべてが書架で覆われている。書架には、作家の小説執筆の手がかりにされたという膨大な量の書物が納められている。この空間に光を導くべく、棟の妻面に設けられた唯一の開口部には、白いステンドグラスがはめ込まれている。ステンドグラスは、さまざまな形状・色調のガラスで構成され、それぞれに異なる表情の光を室内に招き入れる。暗闇に灯る光は作家が作品に込めた未来への希望を、その多彩な表情はさまざまな個性をもった人間という存在の象徴である。

　人間と社会への深い愛情に満ちた作家の創造世界の奥行きを、細部から全体の構成に至る建築空間そのもので伝えることが、この建築の主題だった。司馬邸の庭をそのまま拡張したような、雑木で覆われた記念館の前庭も、普通は庭木には用いられない雑木を特に愛しんだという作家の温かい人間性を思い、つくったものである。

This is a memorial hall for writer Ryotaro Shiba, a figure representative of postwar Japan. The site is adjacent to a continuation of the garden of the writer's own residence, in a quiet residential area on the outskirts of Osaka.

The building composition is based around concentric arcs that follow the shape of the site. In order to harmonize with the surrounding environment of this residential area, the building is buried one level into the ground and only a two-storied volume appears above ground. The resulting blank space on the site is set aside for a front yard and a rear yard, between which the building is inserted.

The memorial hall is approached from the gate of the Shiba residence through an intimately scaled garden, from which one can see the corridor of the memorial hall beyond. Inside the building, the light gradually diminishes from the entrance to the rear, and it becomes a deeply shaded place. In the depths of this gloom, there is "another study room," which is the central exhibition room of the facility. The wall surfaces of this triple-height void space are entirely lined with bookshelves. On these bookshelves stand large quantities of books that could be said to give clues to the texts of this writer. The single aperture in the sloping roof surface contains white tinted glass, in order to let light into the space. The stained glass is composed of glass with various shapes and hues, and each brings light of a different expression into the room. The multicolored expressions of light illuminating the darkness symbolize the existence of people with varied personalities and future aspirations embedded by this writer in his works.

From the small details to the composition of the whole and architectural space itself, the theme of this building is to convey the depths of the creative world of this writer, who was filled with deep affection for humanity and society. Like a direct extension of the garden of the Shiba residence, the greenery-covered front yard of the memorial hall was also made while thinking about the warm humanity of the author, using only wild plants not usually used in gardens and arranging them in a way reminiscent of a truly natural environment.

イメージスケッチ。作家の人間性に近づくべく、本に囲まれた空間、雑木の森に佇む建築のイメージが描かれている。
Image sketches. Approaching the humanity of the author, these are images of a space surrounded by books and of architecture standing in a forest of various trees.

301 Shiba Ryotaro Museum

展示室を見上げる。作家の生涯をかけての創作活動に費やされた、膨大なエネルギーを象徴する空間。

Looking up at the exhibition room. A space symbolizing the enormous energy spent on creative activities during the author's life.

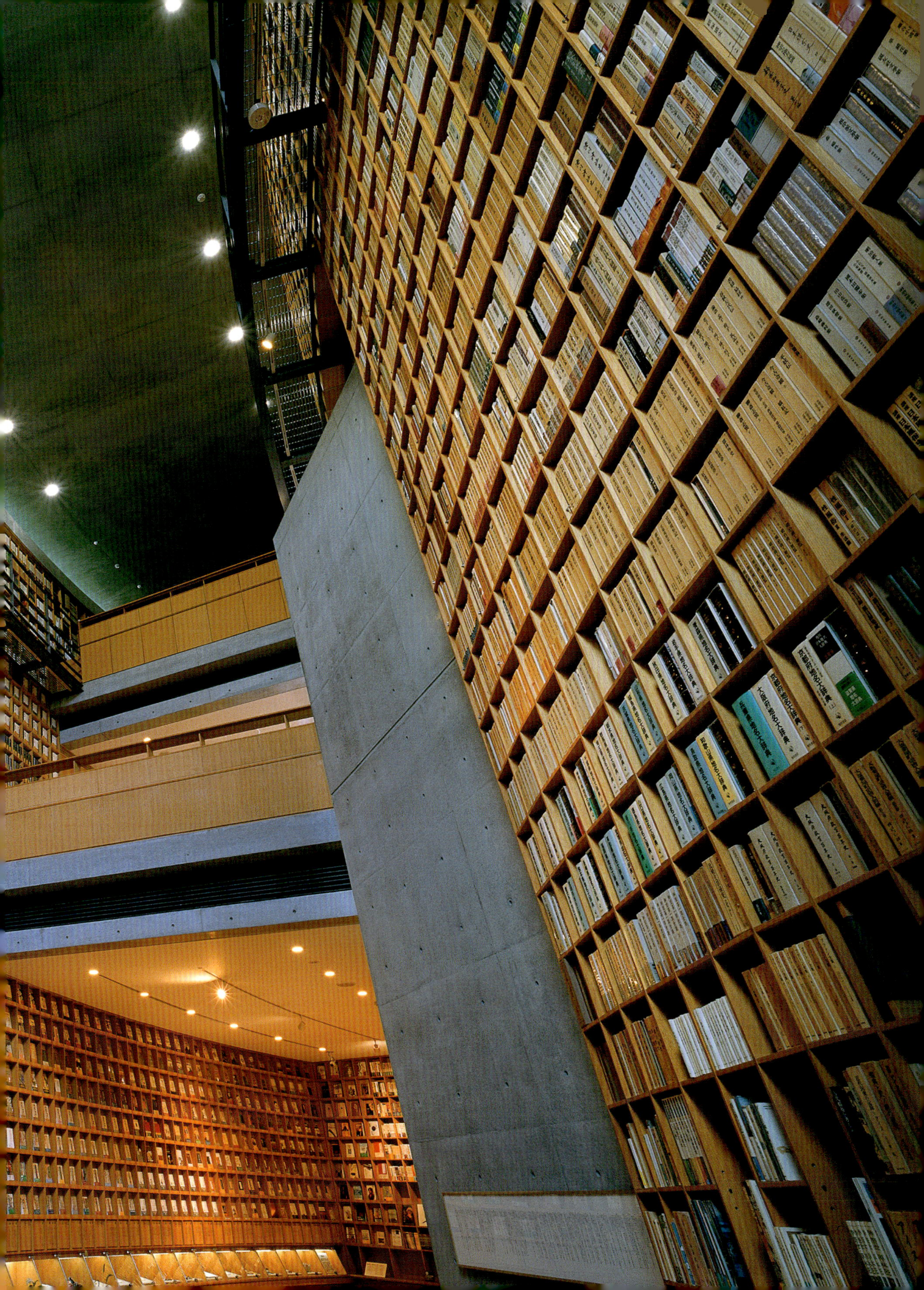

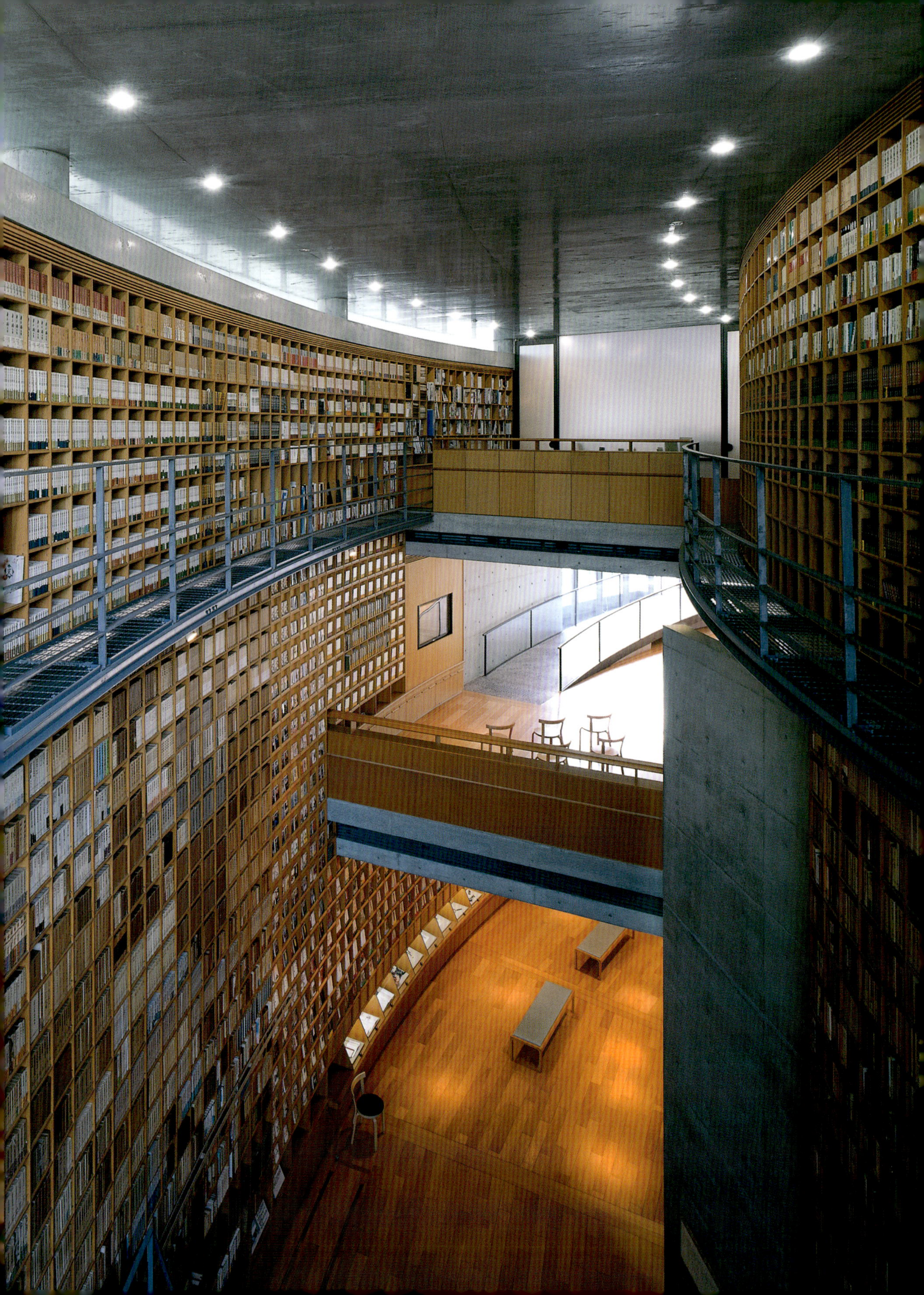

「もうひとつの書斎」と名づけられた3層吹き抜けの展示室。高さ11mの壁全面を、
生前作家が資料として保有していた2万冊の書物を収めた書架が覆う。

The three-storey-high exhibition room has been named "the other study." All the surfaces of the 11m-high walls are covered with bookshelves, holding 20,000 books accumulated by the author during his life.

Shiba Ryotaro Museum

巨大な吹き抜け空間を内包する建物の軒高は約7.2m。閑静な住宅地にある周辺環境との調和のため、ヴォリューム感は極力抑えるように計画されている。

The eaves height of the building encompassing the enormous void is approximately 7.2m. To ensure harmony with the surrounding environment of this quiet housing district, it is designed so that the volume feels as low as possible.

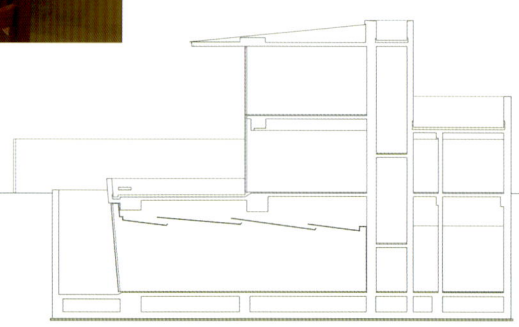

Section

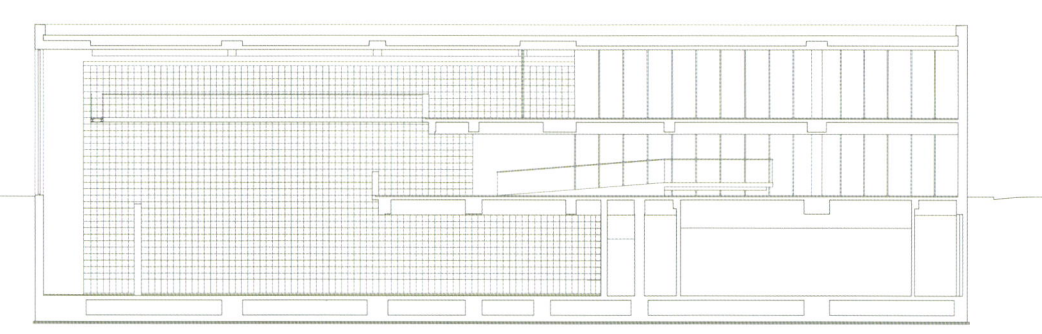

Section　1:350

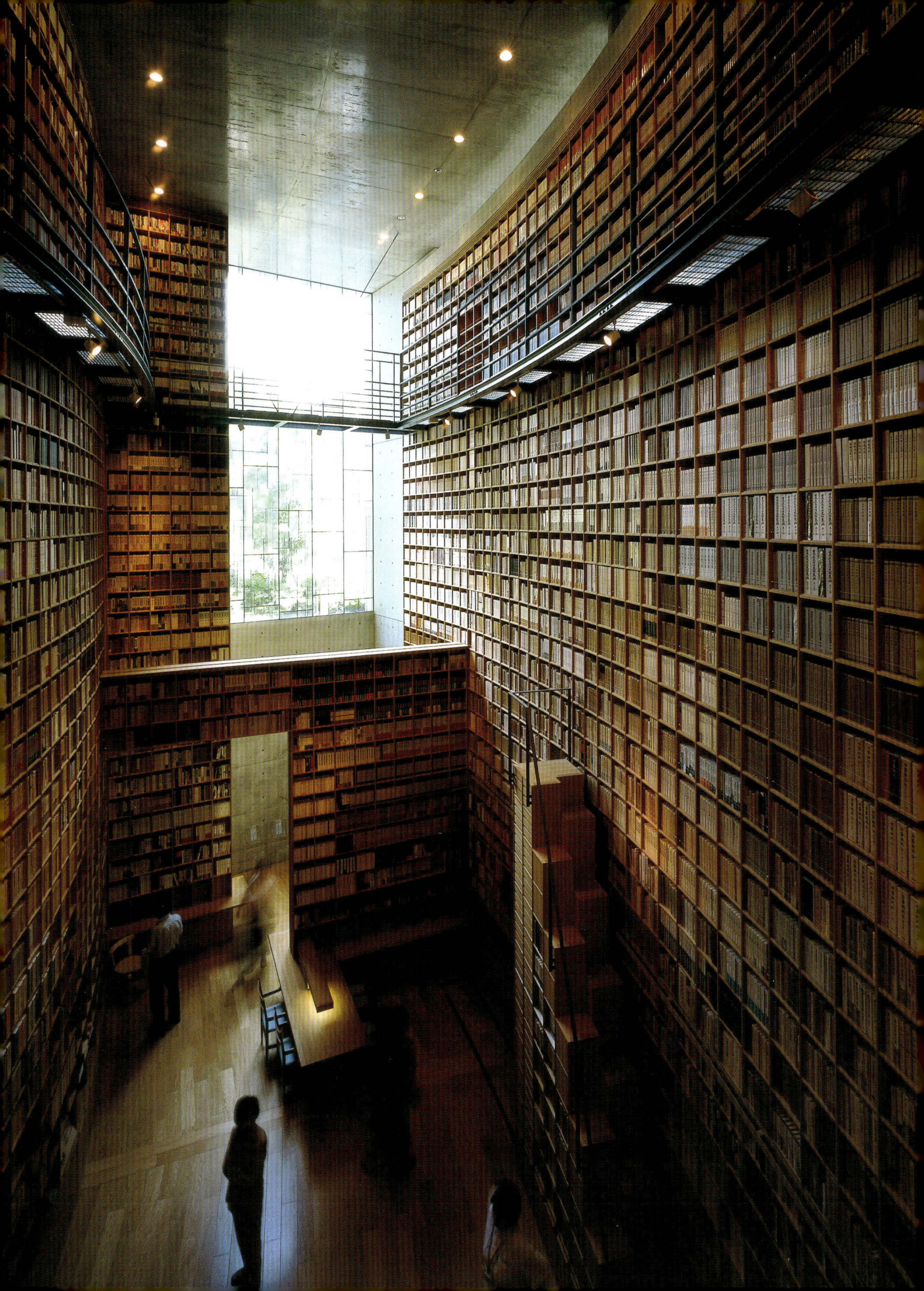

Site plan 1:1,000

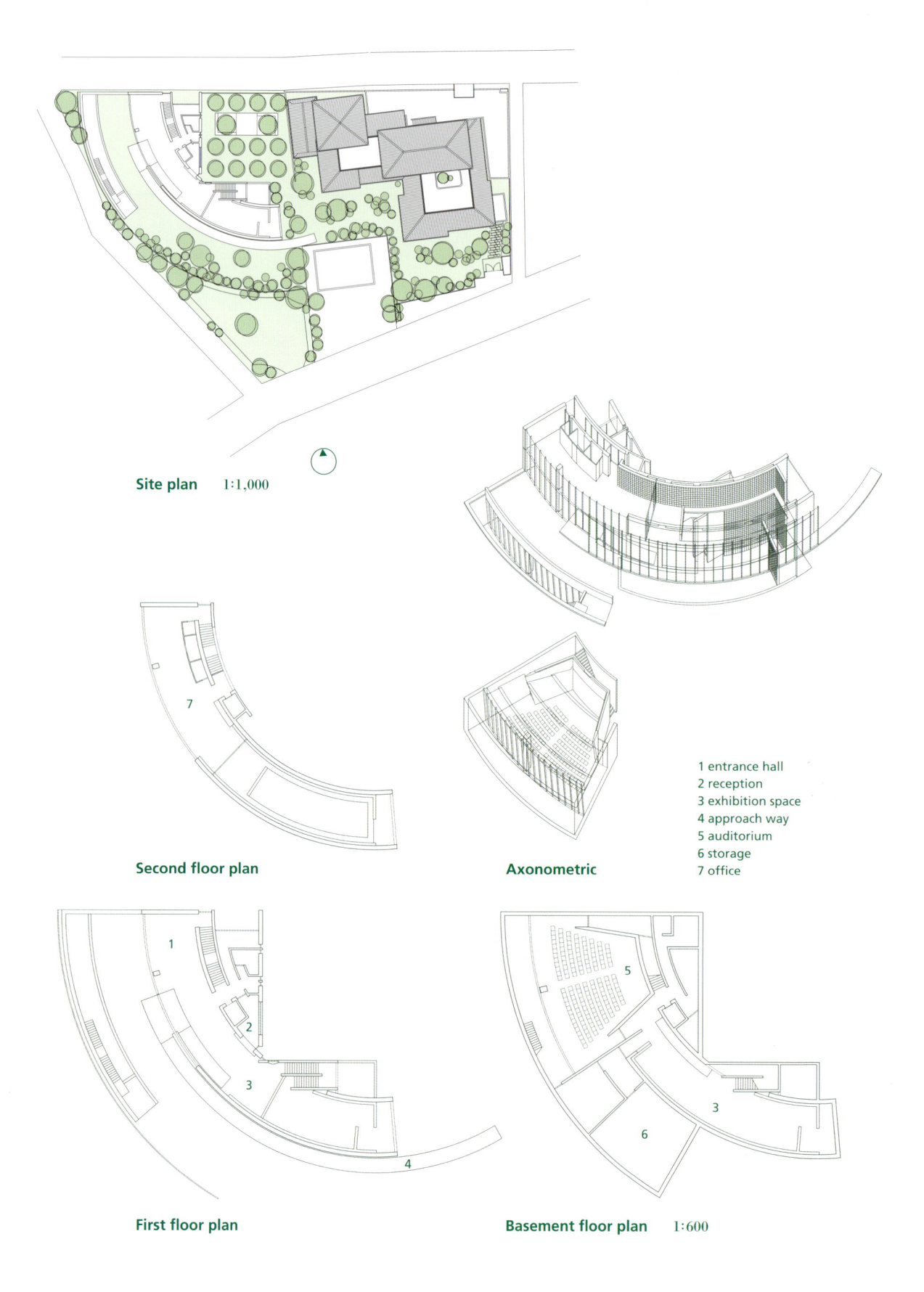

Second floor plan

Axonometric

1 entrance hall
2 reception
3 exhibition space
4 approach way
5 auditorium
6 storage
7 office

First floor plan

Basement floor plan 1:600

1階入口ロビーから地階の展示室へと人々を導く階段。開口部には多様な表情を見せるステンドグラスがはめ込まれている。

Stair leading people from the first floor lobby to the basement exhibition room. Stained glass showing a variety of expressions has been inserted in the openings.

司馬邸の庭から記念館へのエントランスを見る。ガラススクリーンに囲われた回廊の緩やかなカーブが、静かに人々を建物内部へと誘う。

Looking at the entrance of the memorial hall from the garden of the Shiba residence. The gentle curve of the corridor enclosed by a glass screen quietly invites people into the building.

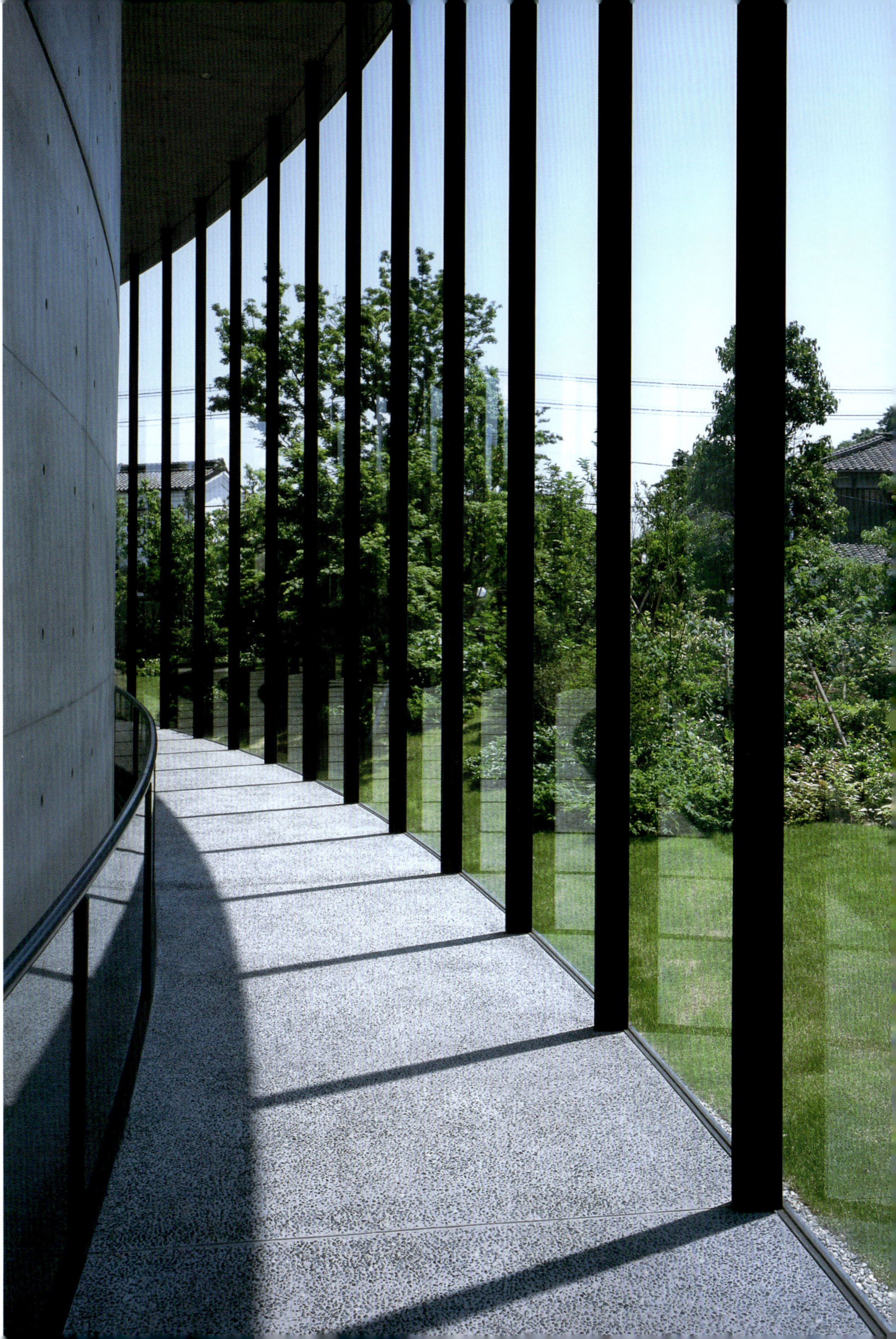

国際芸術センター青森
Aomori Contemporary Art Centre
2000-01　青森県青森市—— Aomori, Aomori

敷地は青森市郊外の緑深い山間部に位置する。通常の美術館の枠組みを超えて計画された、芸術家の制作活動を支援し、企画展示やワークショップなどを通じて広く国際交流と地域活動を行う、〈アーティスト・イン・レジデンス〉を主題とする施設群である。

コンペで勝ち取ったこの建物のアイディアの説明として、計画段階より、私は〈見えない建築〉という言葉を用いた。ここで言う〈見えない建築〉とは、即ち起伏の激しい丘陵地の豊かな自然の中にあって、自らの存在を主張するような建築ではない、既存の風景に溶け込み、大地と一体化する建築である。

自然とともに生きること——とりわけ、春夏秋冬、激しく四季の移ろう北国の敷地にあっては、その自然との直截な出会いこそが、アーティストの創造力を育てる最大の力ともなり得ると考えたのだ。

建物は2/3円を描く円弧型のギャラリー棟（展示棟）と、距離をおいて、異なる角度で配された宿泊棟、アトリエ棟（創作棟）からなる。緑の谷間に架かる2本の橋として、ひっそりと配された宿泊棟、アトリエ棟は、斜面地を活かした雄大な自然のヴィスタと、三方を自然の樹木で囲われた親密性をあわせもつ、内省的空間をアーティストに提供する。そのような〈ケ〉の場としての2棟に対し、ギャラリー棟は〈ハレ〉の場として位置づけられる。

完結しない円という特異な幾何学形態が地形に埋め込まれ、内部にはハイサイドライトからの光が連続する伸びやかなギャラリー空間が、外部には円形を補完する水庭を背景とする段状の野外劇場が形づくられる。

この地域にとって、最大の試練は冬の厳しさである。その不安と、次の季節への期待に満ちた時間は、そこで思索に耽るアーティストにどのような影響を及ぼすか——北国の自然が育む人間の創造力に期待したい。

The site is located in a deep green mountainous region on the outskirts of Aomori City. A project that exceeds the framework of an ordinary art museum, this is a group of facilities to support the creative activities of artists and to carry out a wide range of regional activities and international exchanges through planned exhibitions and workshops, with a theme of "artists in residence."

To explain the idea of this competition-winning building, throughout the design stage I used the phrase "invisible architecture." This "invisible architecture" is architecture that does not assert its own presence within the abundant natural environment of violently undulating hills, but architecture that merges into the existing scenery and is unified with the earth.

Living together with nature—particularly amid the tempestuous changes of the four seasons in this northern region, the creative power of an artist will be maximized by direct encounters with nature.

The building comprises a gallery wing (Exhibition Hall) in a shape that describes two-thirds of a circle, and set at distance are a lodging wing (Residential Hall) and an atelier wing (Creative Hall) placed at different angles. Distributed independently as two bridges spanning the green valley, the lodging wing and atelier wing offer the artists space for reflection, maximizing the slope for the magnificent natural vista and intimately surrounded on three sides by natural greenery. In contrast with these two buildings, which are places of "emptiness," the gallery wing has been designed as a place of "brightness."

The distinctive geometric shape of an incomplete circle is buried in the topography. Inside is a comfortable, continuous gallery space illuminated by clerestories, and outside, the circle is completed by a water garden with a backdrop of steps forming an open-air theater.

The biggest test for this region is the severity of winter. How will this time of anxiety, full of anticipation affect the artists absorbed in speculation? I hope to enhance their creative power in the natural environment of this northern region.

初期イメージスケッチ。　Early image sketch.

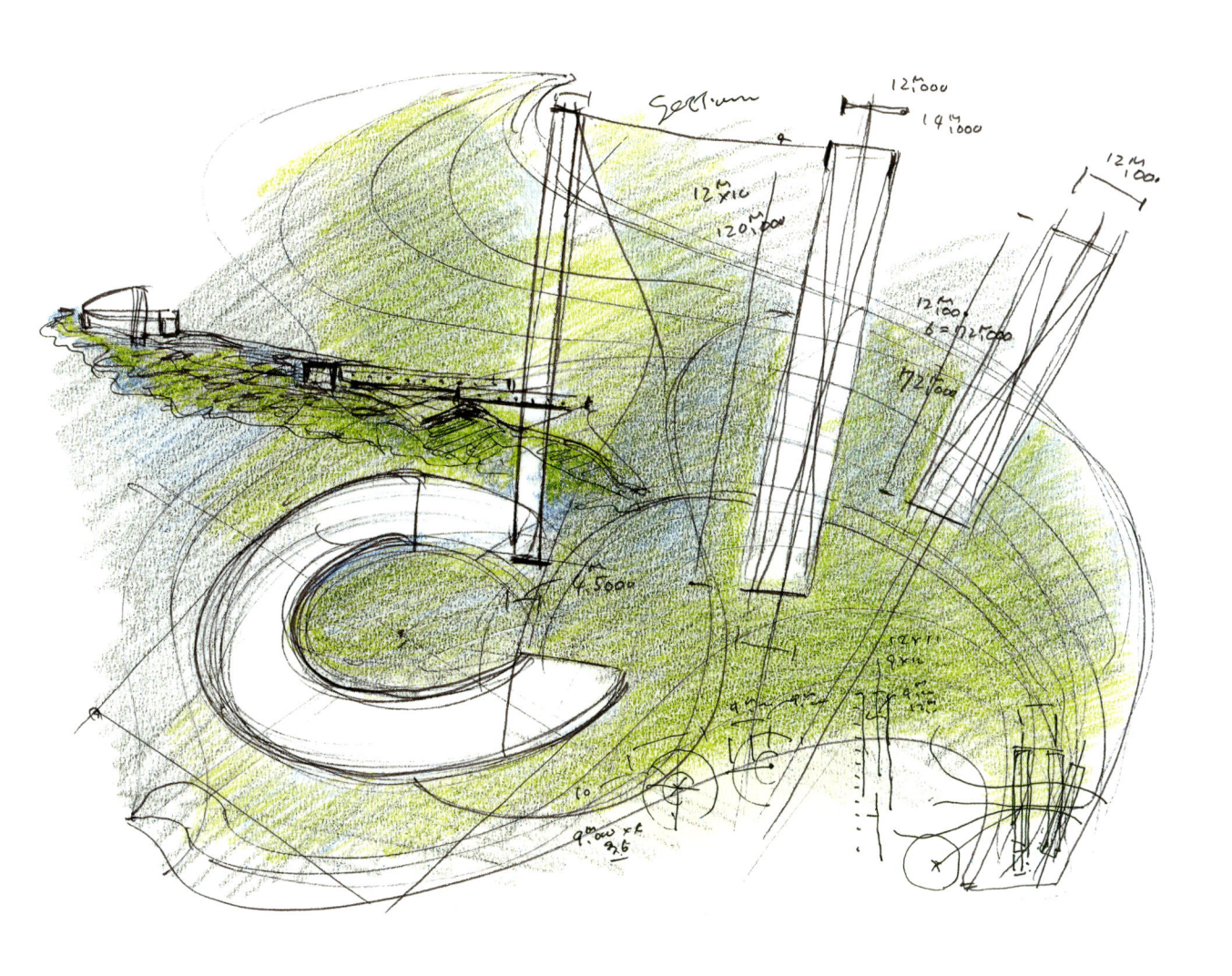

中央に円形の野外劇場を抱く展示棟。周辺の雑木林のスケールにあわせ、建物の高さは低く抑えられている。

Exhibition Hall containing a circular open-air theater in the middle. The building height is kept low to match the scale of the various shrubs and trees in the surroundings.

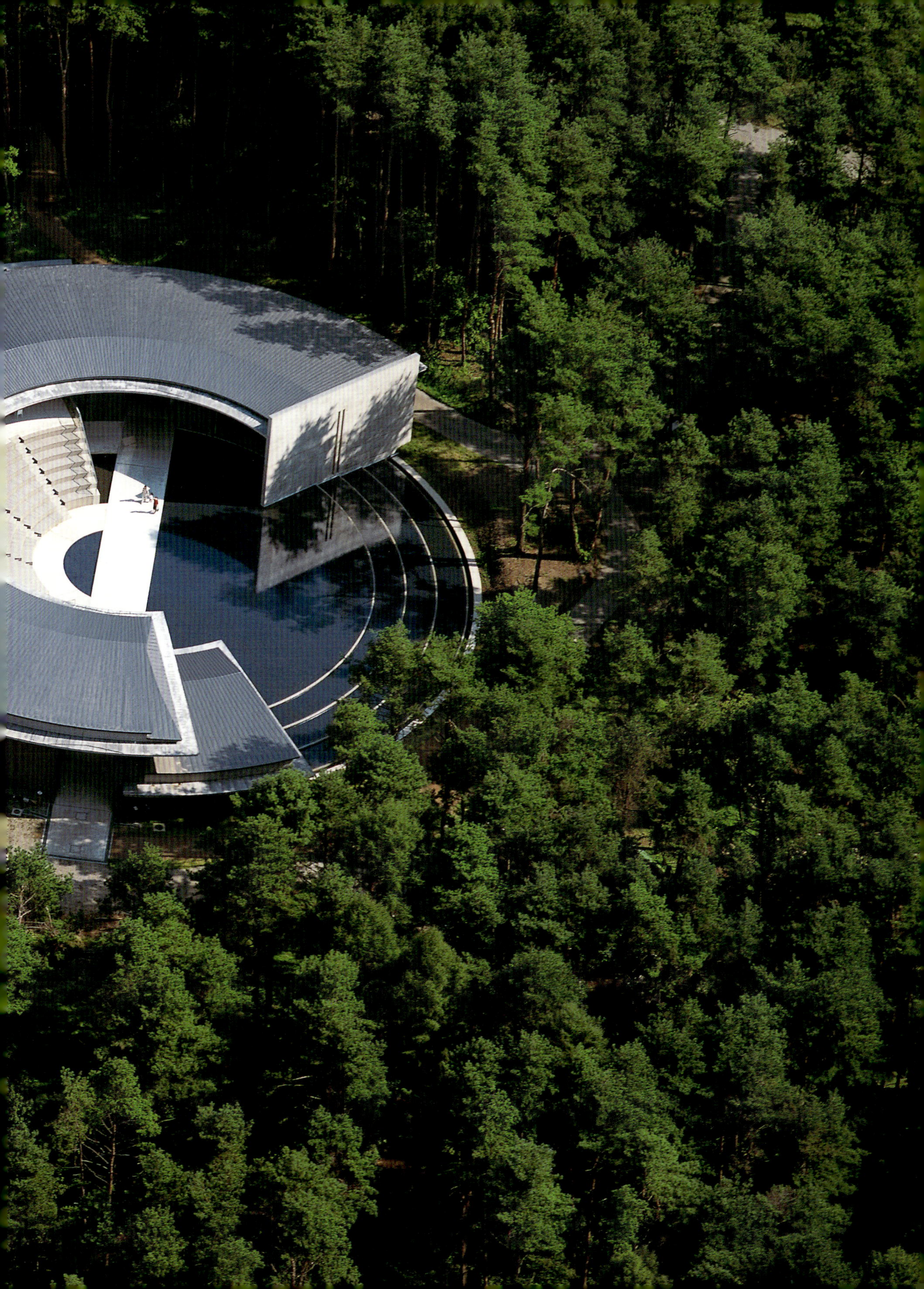

Site plan   1:6,000

展示棟の円形劇場の外観。建物と水庭で形づくられる
円形平面を貫いて、幅4.2mのステージが設けられている。

Exterior appearance of the circular open-air theater enclosed by the Exhibition Hall. A 4.2m-wide stage has been established through the circular plan formed by the building and the water garden.

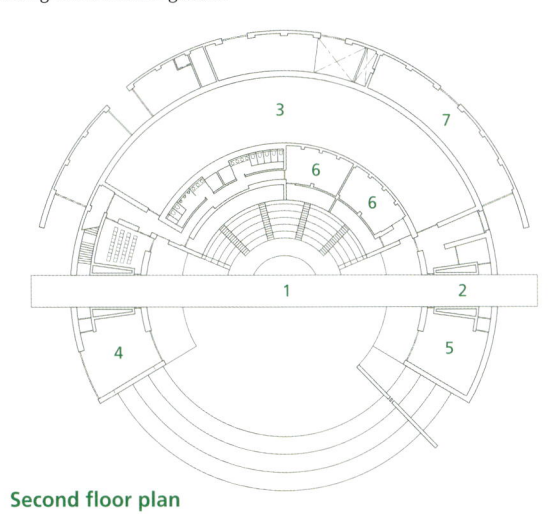

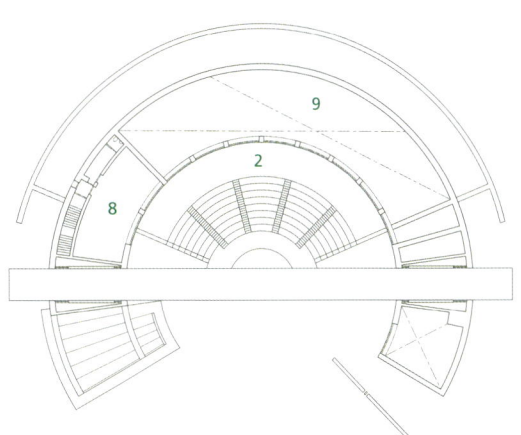

Second floor plan

Exhibition Hall first floor plan 1:1,000

1 Stage
2 terrace
3 exhibition gallery
4 library / café
5 sub gallery
6 storage
7 mechanical
8 office
9 void

317 Aomori Contemporary Art Centre

単純な幾何学と、限定された素材感による簡素な空間に、周囲の豊かな自然が入り込む。自然と共生する、アーティストのための創造空間。

The abundant nature of the surroundings penetrates
the unadorned space, comprising a simple geometry and
limited sense of materiality. A creative space for artists,
coexisting with nature.

319 Aomori Contemporary Art Centre

110m以上の長さをもつ創作棟西側外観。敷地の起伏に手を加えず、谷間の架け橋のイメージで建物は配置されている。

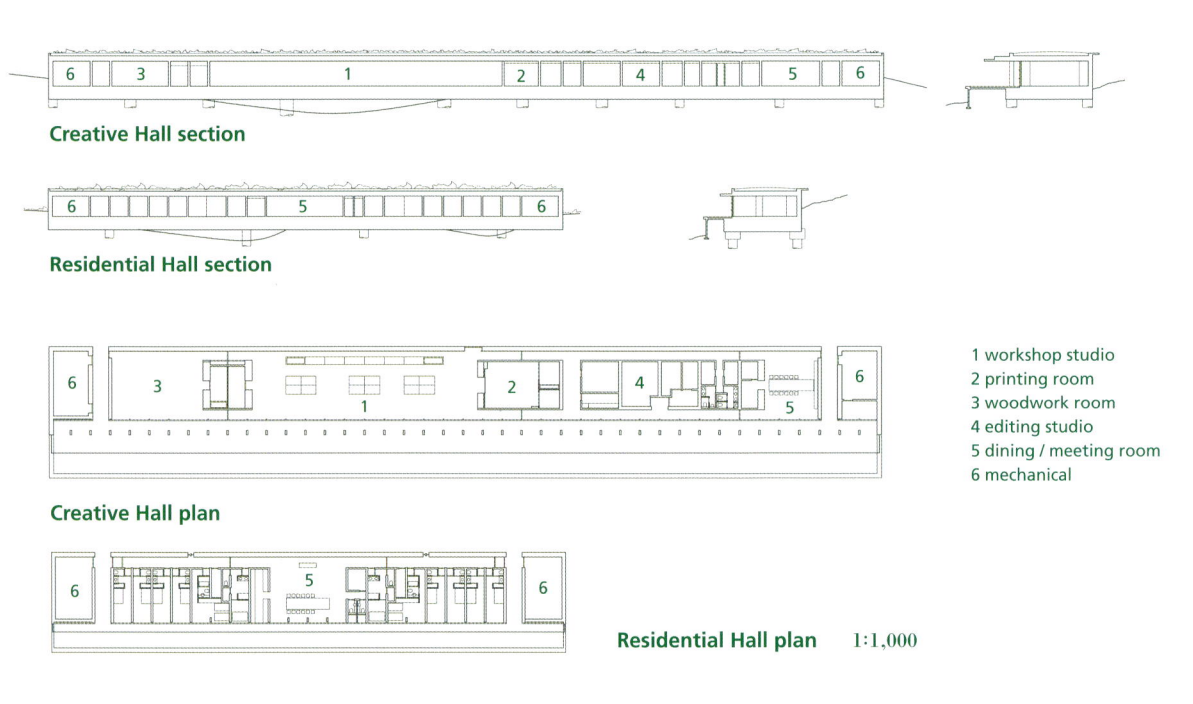

Creative Hall section

Residential Hall section

Creative Hall plan

Residential Hall plan 1:1,000

1 workshop studio
2 printing room
3 woodwork room
4 editing studio
5 dining / meeting room
6 mechanical

Western exterior of the Creative Hall, which has a length exceeding 110m. The building is arranged using the image of a bridge spanning the ravine, without altering the undulations of the site.

宿泊棟客室内観。創作棟同様、すべての室は、建物の長手方向いっぱいに延びる、奥行き深い軒下のテラスに面する。

Interior view of a guest room in the Residential Hall. Like the Creative Hall, all the rooms face the terrace under the deep overhang that extends along the entire length of the building.

321　Aomori Contemporary Art Centre

四季のアーケードと名づけられたアプローチの空間。
Approach space, named the arcade of the four seasons.

3棟の建物を俯瞰する。自然の地形に埋没して見えない建築。
An overview of the three buildings. Invisible architecture buried into the natural terrain.

敷地は兵庫県神戸市の臨海部、かつて製鉄や造船で栄えた工場地帯の跡に生まれた再開発地区「東部新都心」の中心に位置する。県立の美術館と、それに隣接する市の広場の計画である。

　1995年、阪神淡路大震災により地域一帯は壊滅的な打撃を受けた。それゆえ、震災後に建設が予定されていた東部新都心の計画には、単なる再開発事業を超えた、復興のシンボルとなるべく期待が寄せられていた。私も震災直後、その立地を活かした「海の集合住宅」を構想、自主提案として発表し、それがきっかけで新都心の中心部に、非常時の防災拠点としてつくられる水際の市民広場の設計に関わることになった。

　そして1997年、その広場に隣接する敷地に、さらに県の新しい美術館をつくる計画がもち上がり、建築コンペがプロポーザル形式で行われた。結果、設計者として私が選ばれた。このときから、発注者も工事期間も異なるふたつのプロジェクトを統合して、復興のシンボルに相応しい街の顔をつくるべく、新たな試みが始まった。

　美術館は、石壁に覆われた基壇部分と、その上に間隔を空けて3棟のボックスが並列する構えをもつ。主要な機能はすべて基壇部に収められている。その基壇部から建ち上がる3棟は、企画展示室を収めたコンクリートのボックスをさらにガラスが包み込む、入れ子状の構成になっている。展示室の周囲に海際の風景と対面する〈縁側〉をつくり出す仕掛けだ。その〈縁側〉から連続する基壇上の外部空間は、海側においては緩やかに下降する階段広場となり、また棟の間の部分においては、背後の山の手の風景に向かい立体的に展開する屋外展示スペースとなる。

　美術館閉館時も東部新都心の〈庭〉として開放される、この美術館のパブリックスペースの拡張として、隣接する敷地の「神戸市水際広場」がある。美術館の階段広場から、同様な色調のペイヴが、幾何学のパターンを描きつつ、眼前の海に沿って展開していく。緩やかにレベルを変える階段、円形のステージ、自立壁や列柱といった最小限の建築の要素が、美術館から連続する屋外展示空間のような多様な空間のシークエンスを演出する。

　美術館と広場が一体化し、機能を補完しあうことで、それぞれが単体では期待し得ない可能性が生まれる。復興を願う地域の強い意思が、市、県という制度上の枠組みを超えて、この大らかな水際の風景の創出を可能にした。

兵庫県立美術館＋神戸市水際広場
Hyogo Prefectural Museum of Art+ Kobe Waterfront Plaza

1997-2001　兵庫県神戸市中央区 —— Chuo-ku, Kobe, Hyogo

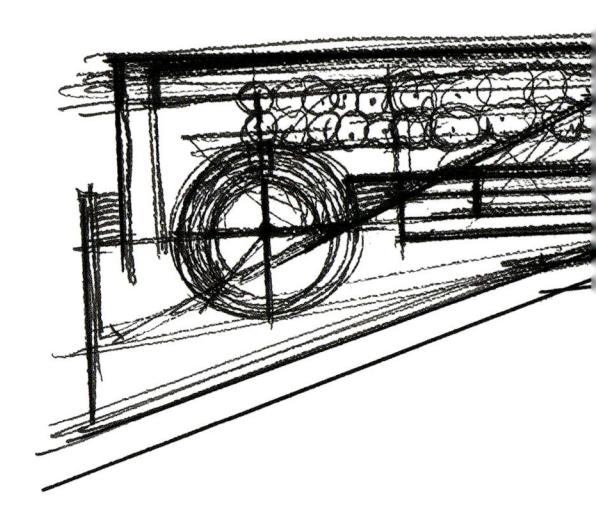

Facing the sea in Kobe City, Hyogo Prefecture, the site is located in the middle of New Eastern Center, a redevelopment area that emerged from the remains of a once-prosperous industrial area for the steel manufacturing and ship building industries. This is a proposal for a museum established by the prefecture and an adjacent urban plaza.

This whole area was devastated by the Hanshin-Awaji Earthquake in 1995. Moreover, the construction of the New Eastern Center, planned after the earthquake, exceeds a mere redevelopment project and is anticipated to become a symbol of revival. After the earthquake I also made a plan for "sea housing" that maximized the location, which I presented as an independent proposal. With this impetus I became involved in the design of a citizen plaza on the water's edge at the heart of this new center, also intended to serve as an evacuation area during extraordinary disasters.

In 1997 a plan to build a new prefectural art museum on the site adjacent to this plaza was announced, and an architecture competition was held for proposals. As a result, I was chosen as the designer. From that point on, I integrated the two different projects in terms of ordering materials and construction timing, beginning a new experiment to build a face for the city appropriate as a symbol of revival.

The art museum is composed of a platform part concealed by a stone wall, aligned on top of which are three separate boxes. The three buildings rising up from the platform are nested boxes containing the permanent exhibition rooms, which comprise concrete boxes wrapped in glass. This is a device that produces an *engawa* (verandah) facing the scenes of the water's edge around the exhibition rooms. The exterior space on top of the platform that continues from the engawa becomes a stepped plaza that gently descends towards the seaside, and the parts between the buildings becomes exterior exhibition spaces that develops in a three-dimensional way toward the scenery of the mountains to the rear.

Expanding the public space of this museum, the Kobe Waterfront Plaza is located on an adjacent site. From the stepped plaza of the art museum, a pavement of the same hue delineates geometric patterns and expands along the seaside in front. The camphor trees growing in the green area that cuts through the pavement were gifted as reconstruction assistance by each government ordinance city. The minimal architectural elements of the stairs gradually changing in level, the circular stage, and the rows of columns and independent walls produce various spatial sequences like exterior exhibition spaces contiguous with the art museum. By integrating the art museum and the plaza with complementary functions, possibilities emerged that would not be expected from either of them individually. The strong intentions of the desired regional revival exceeded the framework of municipal or prefectural systems, enabling the production of this generous waterfront scenery.

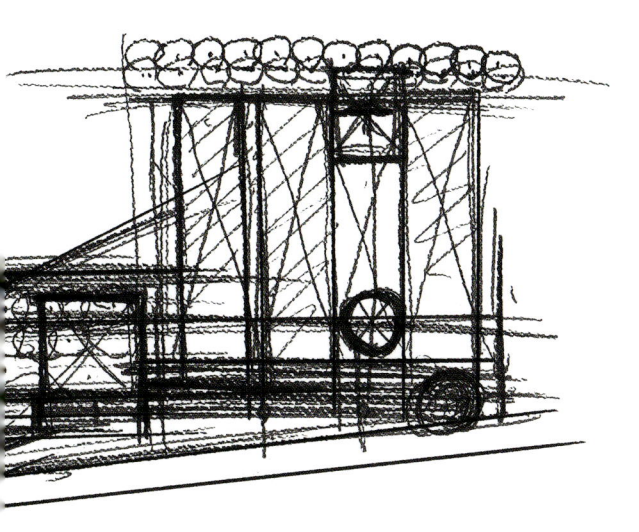

イメージスケッチ。境界を超えて、一体的に計画される美術館と広場。
Image sketch. The plaza and the museum have a unified design that exceeds the site boundaries.

Site plan 1:4,000

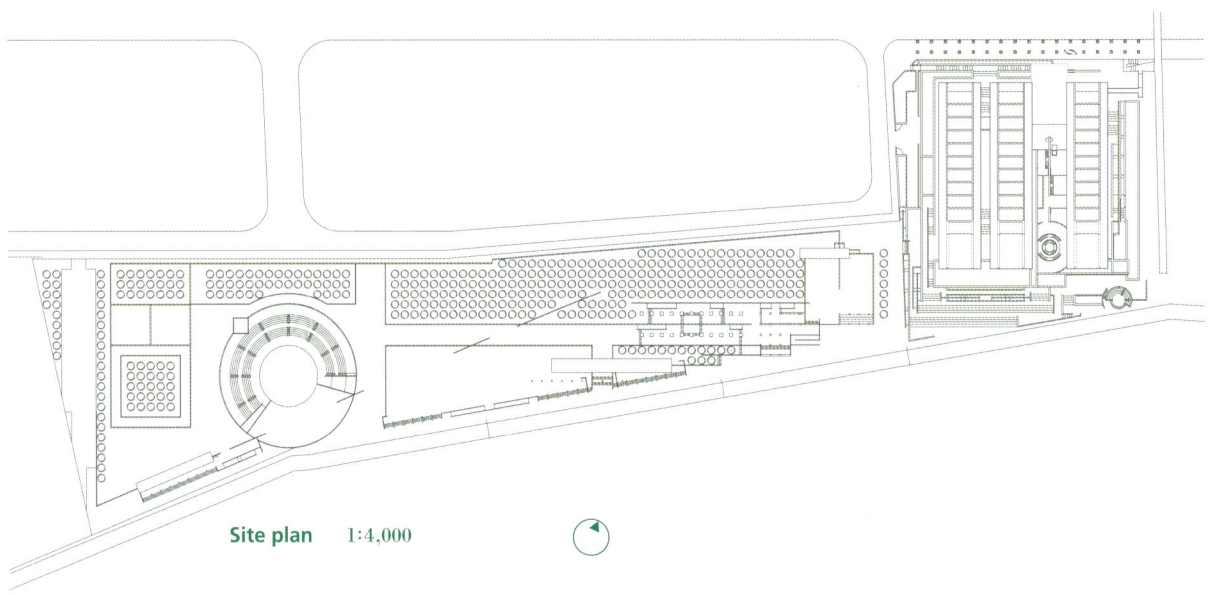

海へと連続する兵庫県の美術館の基壇部分と連続するかたちで、
神戸市の広場が計画されている。全長500ｍにわたる広場の北側
には、兵庫県の県木であるクスノキの森がつくられている。

The Kobe Waterfront Plaza has been designed in a shape continuous
with the podium of the Hyogo Prefectural Museum of Art,
continuing to the sea. On the north side of the plaza,
which extends over a total length of 500m, there is a grove
of camphor trees, the official tree of Hyogo Prefecture.

美術館夜景。御影石貼りの壁で覆われた基壇部の上に、コンクリートとガラスの二重皮膜構造のボックスが3棟並列する。

Night view of the museum. Three double-layer boxes of concrete and glass are aligned on top of the podium, which is concealed by a granite-clad wall.

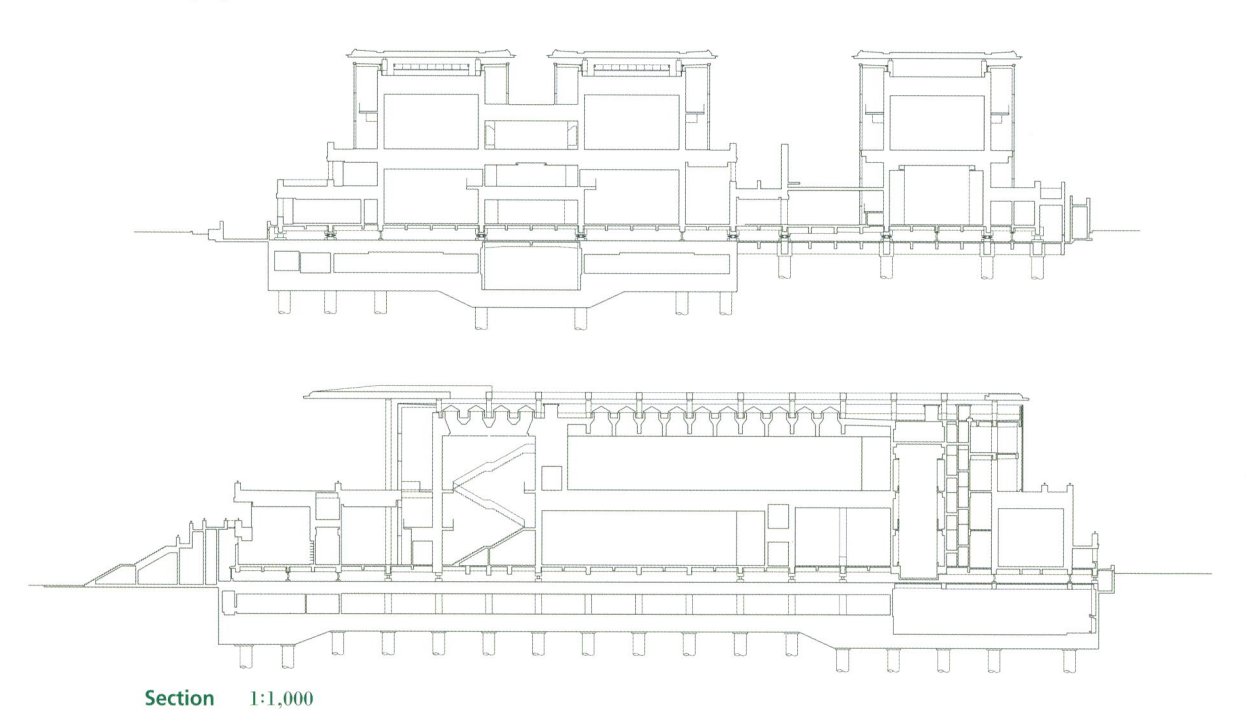

Section 1:1,000

3棟の隙間に内外空間の入り組むパブリックスペースがつくられている。

In the gaps between the three boxes, public spaces has been made that interweave interior and exterior.

3棟の並列するボックスを中心とする単純な構成の中に、さまざまなスケールの展示空間が立体的に展開する。
Exhibition rooms of various scales have been developed three-dimensionally
within this simple composition centered on three parallel boxes.

1 entrance
2 entrance hall
3 workshop
4 lecture room
5 exhibition room
6 shop
7 conference room
8 office
9 storage
10 atelier
11 auditorium
12 foyer
13 gallery

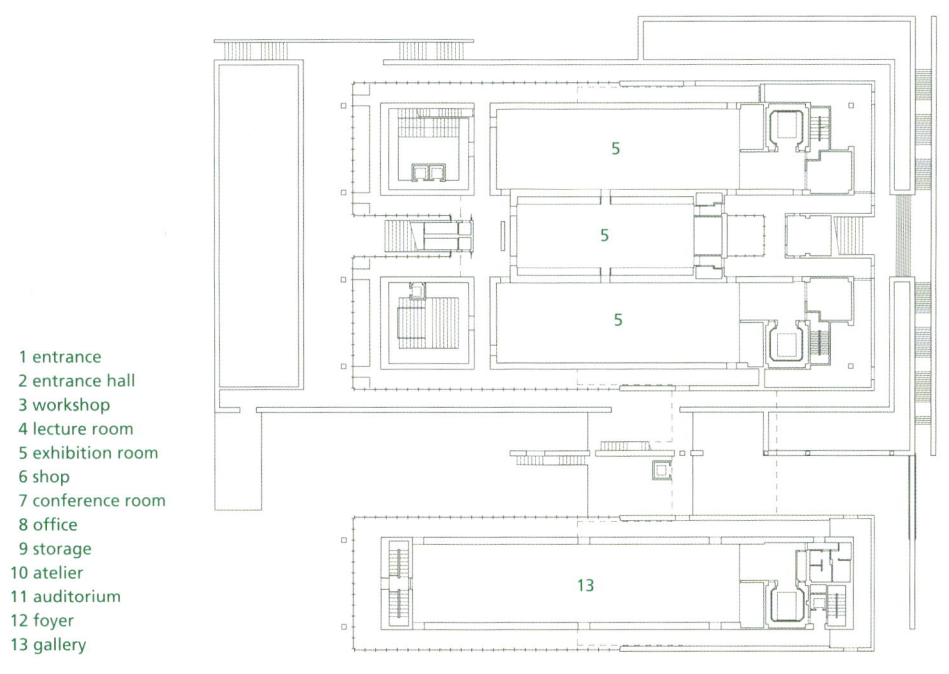

Third floor plan

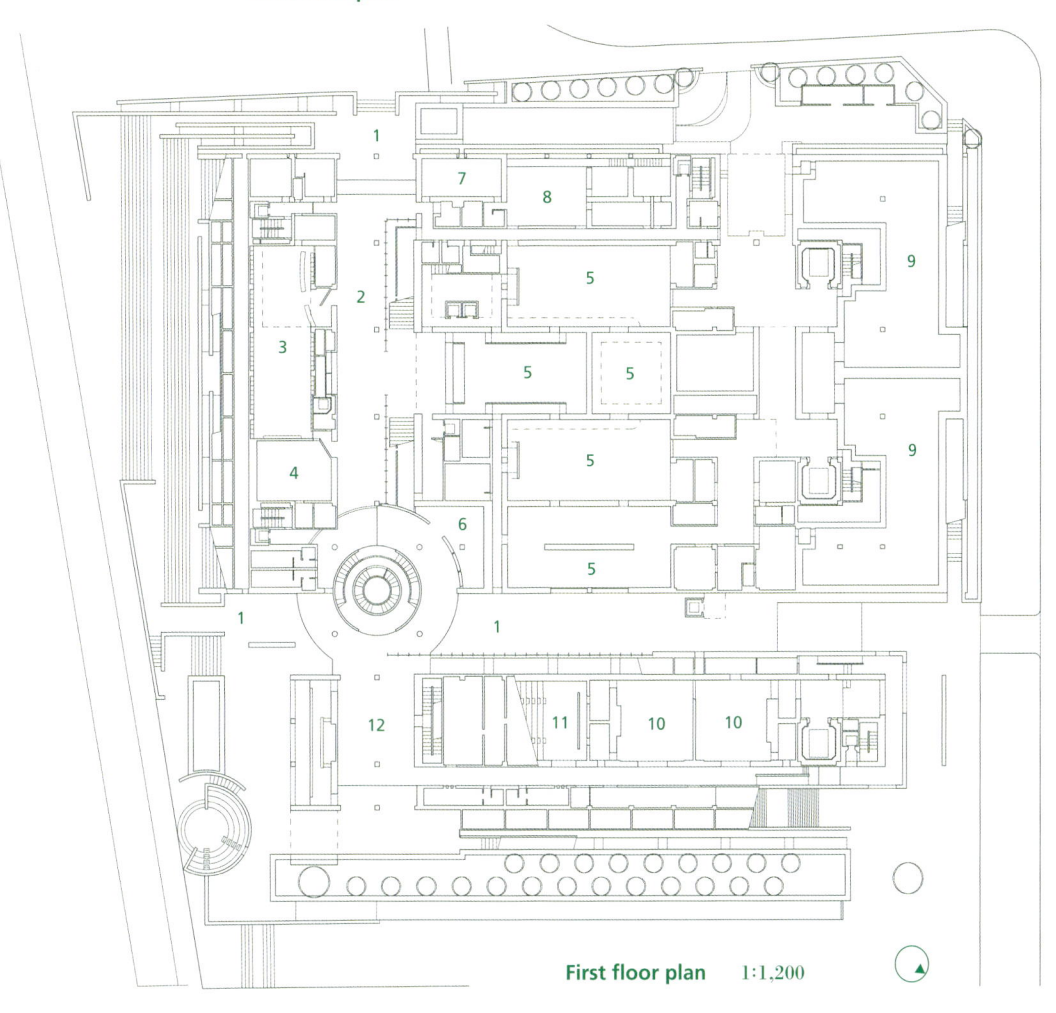

First floor plan 1:1,200

331 Hyogo Prefectural Museum of Art

エントランスホール。　Entrance hall.

333 Hyogo Prefectural Museum of Art

各エリアの結節点となる場所に、垂直動線と絡めたヴォイドが、ブリージングスペースとして設けられている。
At places that act as the node points for each area, the voids containing the vertical circulation routes have been established as breathing spaces.

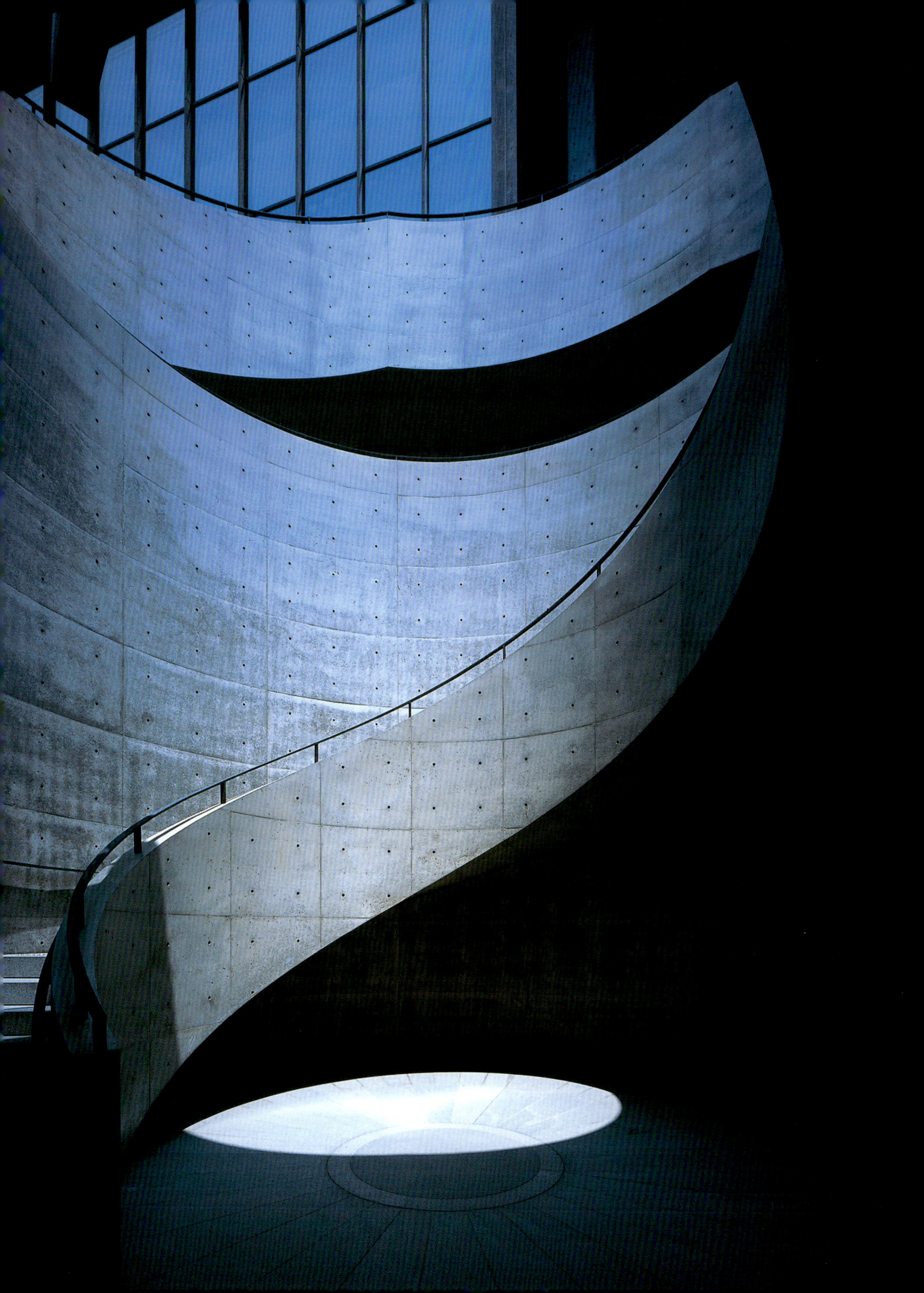

敷地は東京の上野公園内、明治39年竣工の旧国会図書館上野図書館を改修してつくられた子どものための図書館である。

旧図書館は、日本近代の西欧化を目指す機運の中でつくられた擬似洋風建築である。荘厳な雰囲気の佇まいは、文化施設の数多く建ち並ぶ上野公園内でも、際立った存在感を醸している。その改修にあたり目指したのは、旧い建物をただ凍結的に保存するのでない、その修復を前提とした、現代への〈再生〉である。

旧い建物の〈再生〉は、既に京都の「大山崎山荘美術館」やイタリア、トレヴィソの「FABRICA」、ミラノの「アルマーニ・テアトロ」などのプロジェクトで取り組んでいた。だが、どちらかといえば新旧の穏やかな対話を意図したそれらの建築に対し、「子ども図書館」ではより激しい、新旧の対話の創出を試みた。新旧の衝突するイメージの原型は、1995年の「テート・ギャラリー現代美術館国際設計競技案」かもしれない。

「子ども図書館」における〈衝突〉は、2本のガラスボックスの挿入によって実現されている。1本は地上レベルにおいて、図書館へのアプローチの用に充てられる。もう1本は3階レベルにおいて既存部を突き抜けるように配置され、新たなプログラムに対応する主動線として機能する。

既存の煉瓦壁と現代的なガラスに挟まれたスペースは、内においては新旧を緩衝する縁側空間となり、外に対しては新旧の対立的な共存を象徴する標となる。

既存部分については、竣工当時の状態の忠実な復元に徹したが、ミュージアムとして再利用される旧閲覧室については、空間を覆う内壁を旧いままに、あえて部屋のかたちと無関係な、展示用の円形シリンダーを中心に据え、新旧の入れ子状の空間を試みている。

過去の記憶の継承の上に、現代の視点が力強く介在してこそ、真の意味での、未来へとつながる再生がなされると考えている。

国際子ども図書館
The International Library of Children's Literature
1996-2002　東京都台東区——Taito-ku, Tokyo

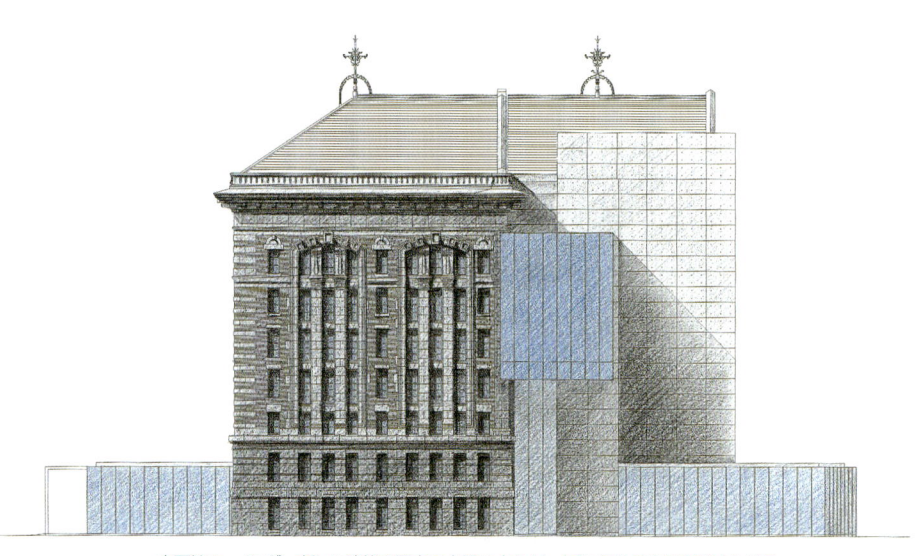

立面ドローイング。新しい建築の要素の大胆な介入が、旧い部分の表情を際立たせる。

On a site in Tokyo's Ueno Park, this is a renovation of the old Imperial Library into a library for children.

The old building has a pseudo-Western architectural style, built motivated by the dominant trends during the Westernization of modern Japan. Even among the many cultural facilities arrayed in Ueno Park, its solemn appearance has a prominent presence. The aim of this renovation was not merely a frozen preservation of the old building, but a "regeneration" toward the future based on these repairs.

I have tackled the "regeneration" of old buildings in projects such as the Oyamazaki Villa Museum in Kyoto, FABRICA in Treviso, and Teatro Armani in Milan. However, they were all intended to create a smooth dialogue between old and new. In contrast with those designs, the International Library of Children's Literature is an attempt at a more violent dialogue between old and new.

The image of conflict between old and new probably originates with my proposal for the 1995 international design competition for the Tate Gallery. The "collision" in the International Library of Children's Literature is manifest in the insertion of two glass boxes. One is at ground level and used as the approach route toward the library. The other is placed as if piercing the existing part at the third floor level, and functions as the main axis supporting the new program.

The space interposed between the modern glazing and the existing brick walls is an *engawa* (verandah) space that from inside is a buffer between old and new, while from outside it symbolizes the confrontational coexistence of old and new.

Regarding the existing part, when completed it was in a faithfully restored condition, but the old reading room that is now reused as a museum space is an attempt to nest old and new spaces by placing cylindrical exhibition spaces—a shape unrelated to the room—within the old inner walls wrapping the space.

Beyond the inheritance of memories of the past, precisely because this is a strong intervention with a modern-day viewpoint, I think it is truly a regeneration connected to the future.

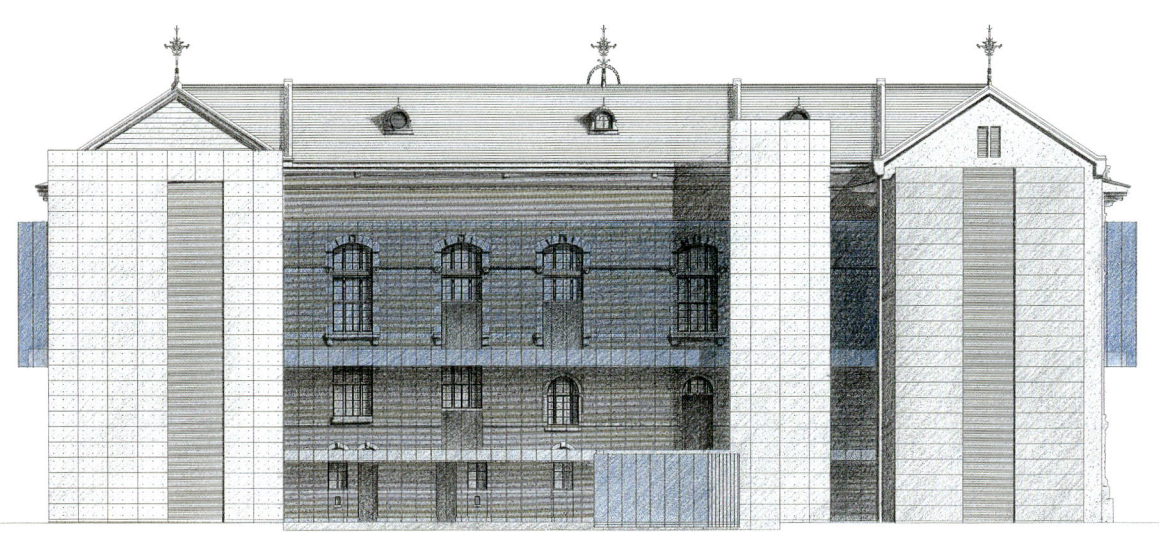

Elevation drawing. The bold imposition of new architectural elements enhances the expression of the old part.

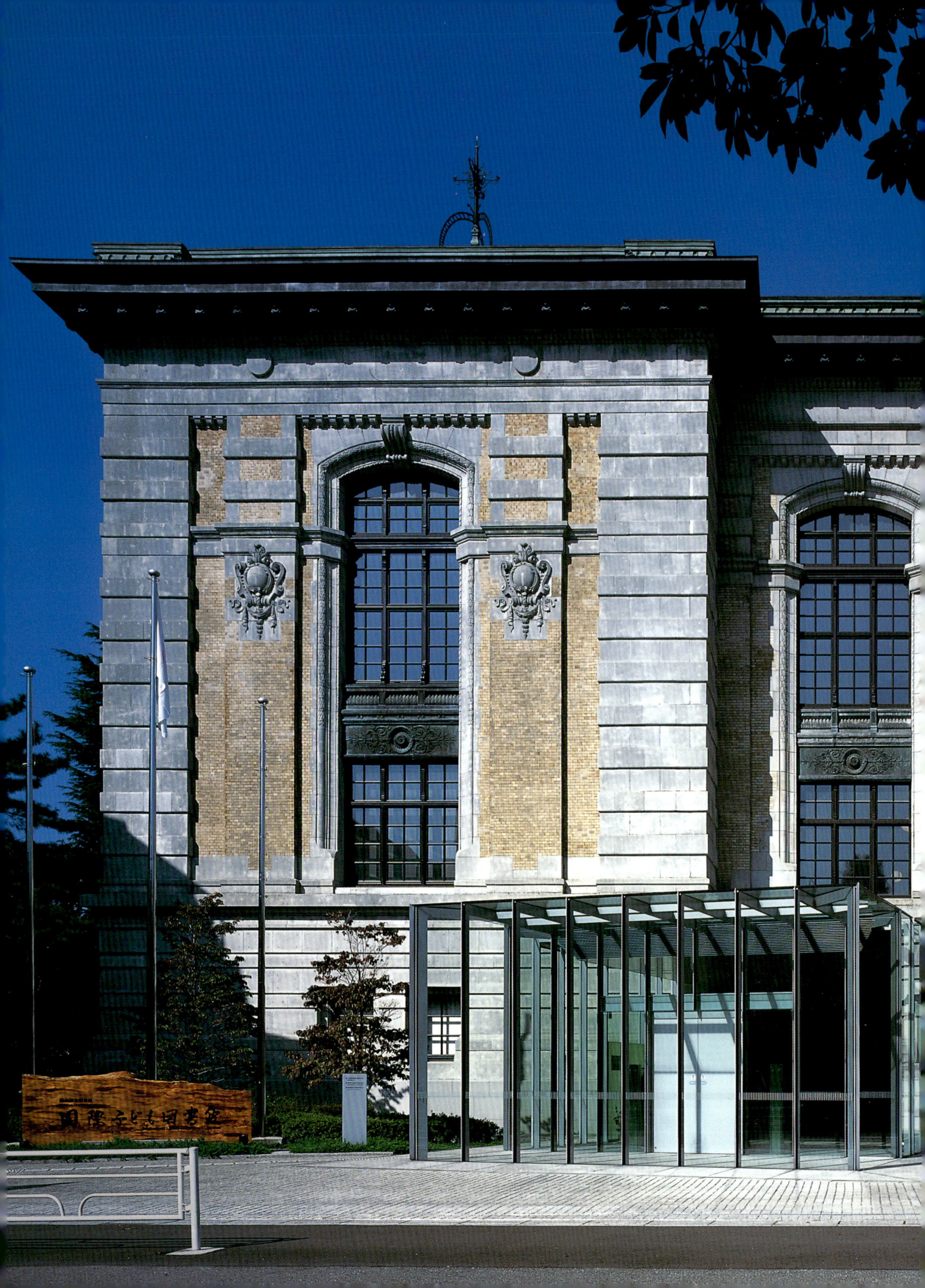
国際子ども図書館

東側外観。1906年に「帝国図書館」として完成した建物の外観をそのままに、それと15度角度を振ったガラスボックスが、新たにエントランスホールとして加えられている。

Exterior view of the east side. The outer appearance of the building, completed in 1906 as the Imperial Library, is unchanged, and a glass box set at a 15-degree angle has been added as the new entrance hall.

Section 1:400

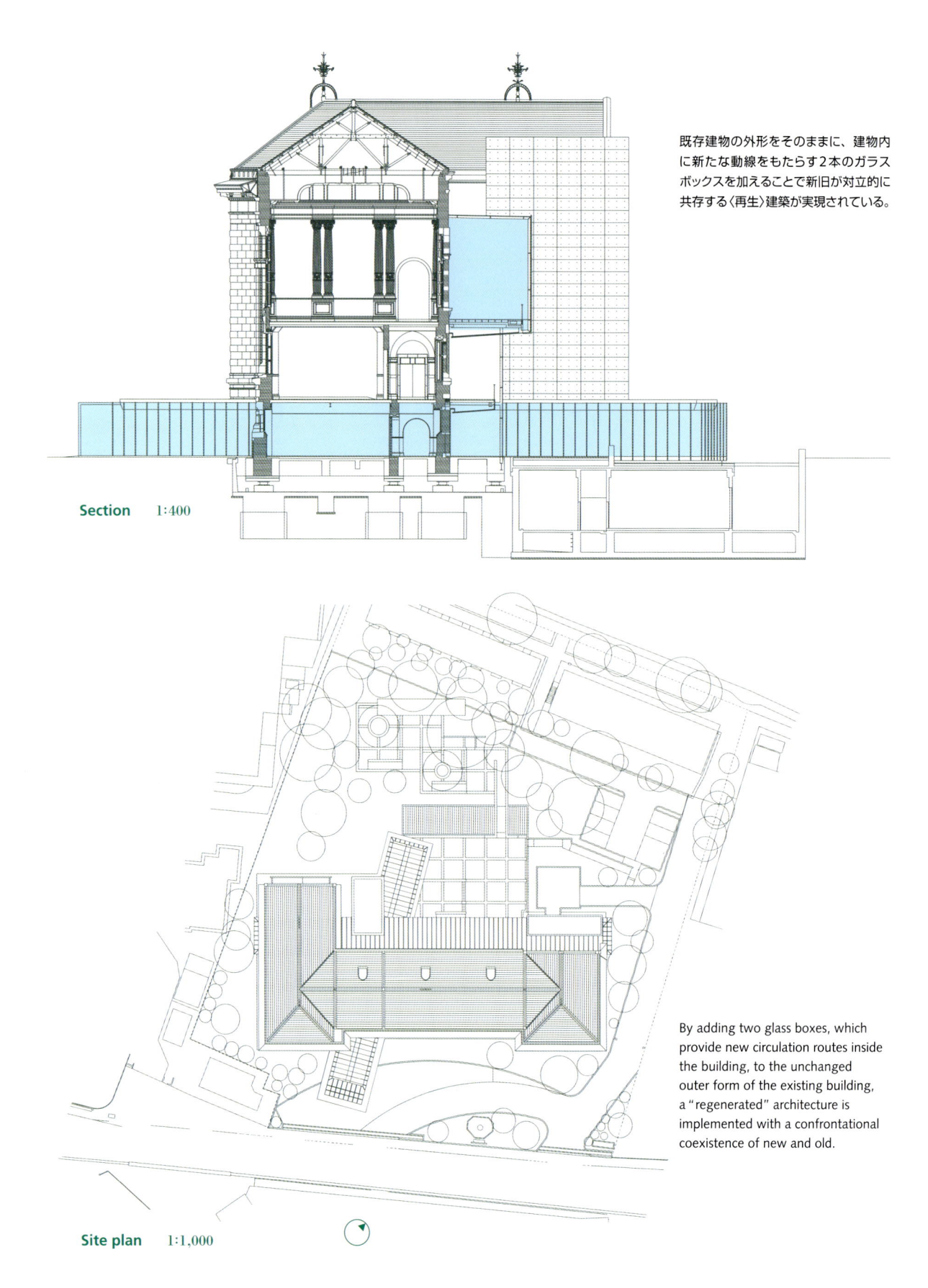

既存建物の外形をそのままに、建物内に新たな動線をもたらす2本のガラスボックスを加えることで新旧が対立的に共存する〈再生〉建築が実現されている。

Site plan 1:1,000

By adding two glass boxes, which provide new circulation routes inside the building, to the unchanged outer form of the existing building, a "regenerated" architecture is implemented with a confrontational coexistence of new and old.

Third floor plan

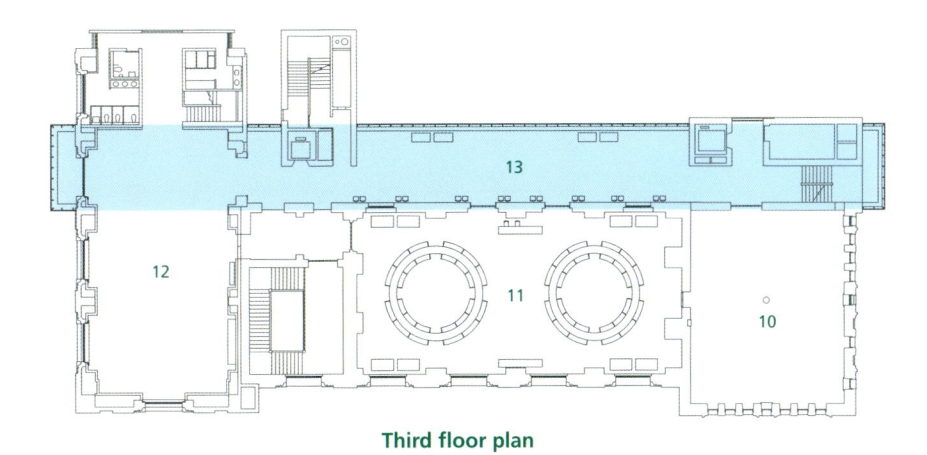

1 entrance hall
2 office
3 reading room
4 mechanical
5 corridor
6 kitchen
7 cafeteria
8 resources room
9 training room
10 bookstack
11 book museum
12 hall
13 lounge

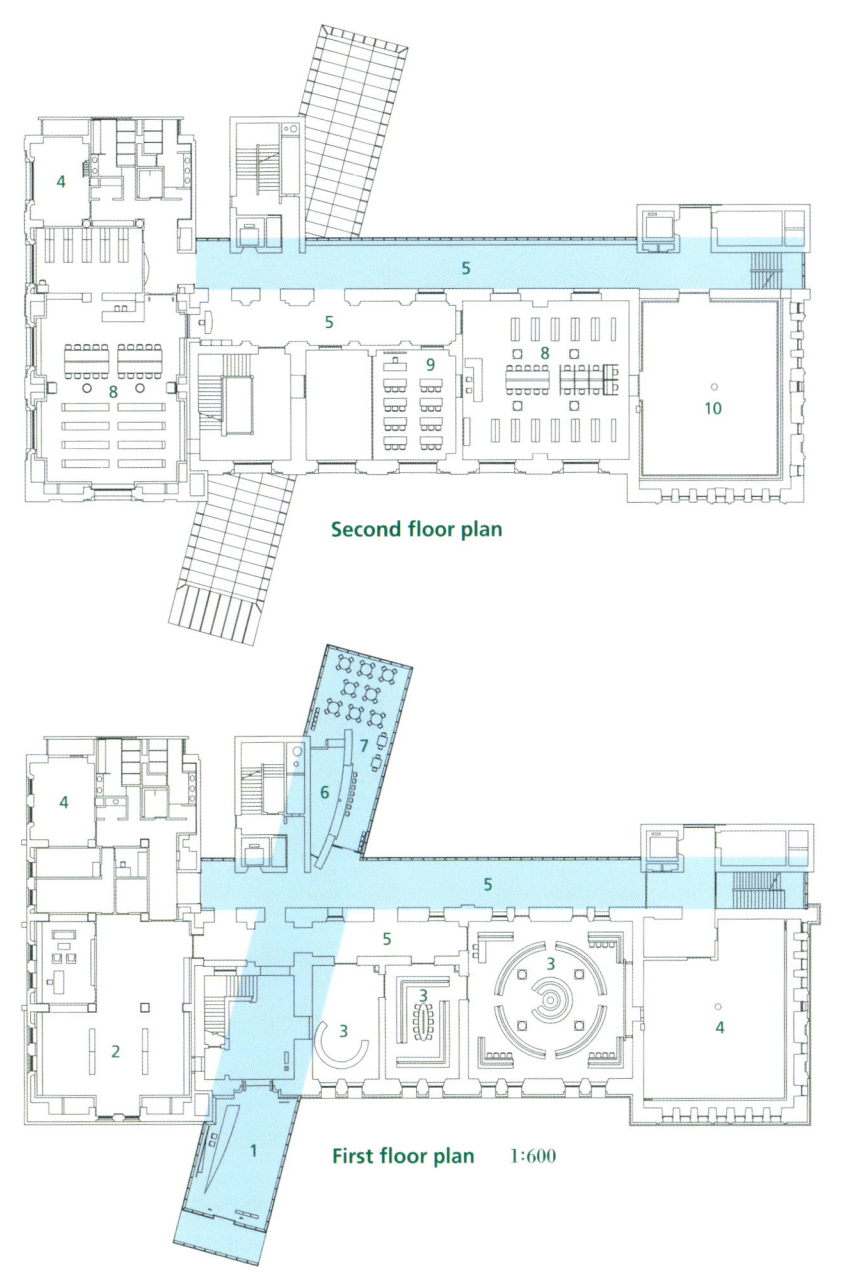

Second floor plan

First floor plan 1:600

341 Library of Children's Literature

3階、旧閲覧室は「本のミュージアム」として生まれ変わった。中央に置かれた円筒形の展示装置には空調機が組み込まれている。頭上には漆喰の見事な天井装飾を見ることができる。

On the third floor, the old reading room has been revived as a "book museum." Air-conditioning units have been inserted in the cylindrical exhibition units placed in the center. Magnificent plaster ceiling ornamentation is visible overhead.

1階に設けられた「こどものへや」。4本の漆喰の柱が復元されている。
"Children's room" established on the first floor. The four plaster columns have been restored.

2階、明治期のインテリアを復元した旧特別閲覧室。
On the second floor, the Meiji-period interior of the old special reading room has been restored.

343 Library of Children's Literature

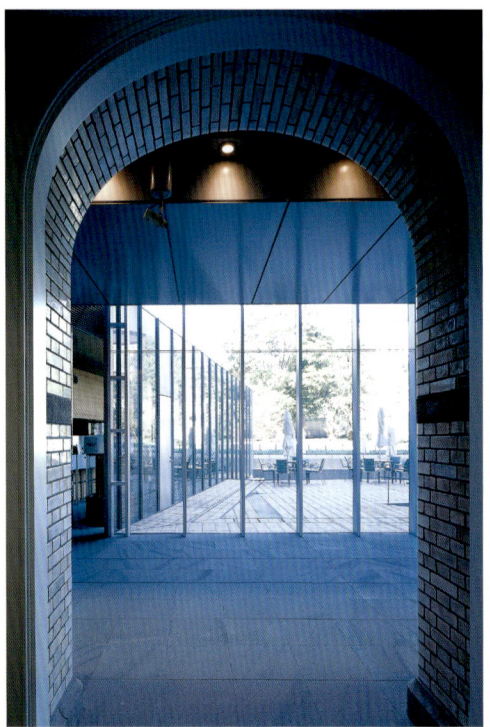

既存部分は、ディテール、素材に至るまですべて建設当初のデザインに復元されている。西側外観においては、
増築されたガラスのカーテンウォール越しに、かつての建物の表情を見ることができる。

The existing part has been restored to the design as originally built, right down to the details and materials.
In the exterior view from the west, the expression of the former building is visible through the added glass curtain-wall.

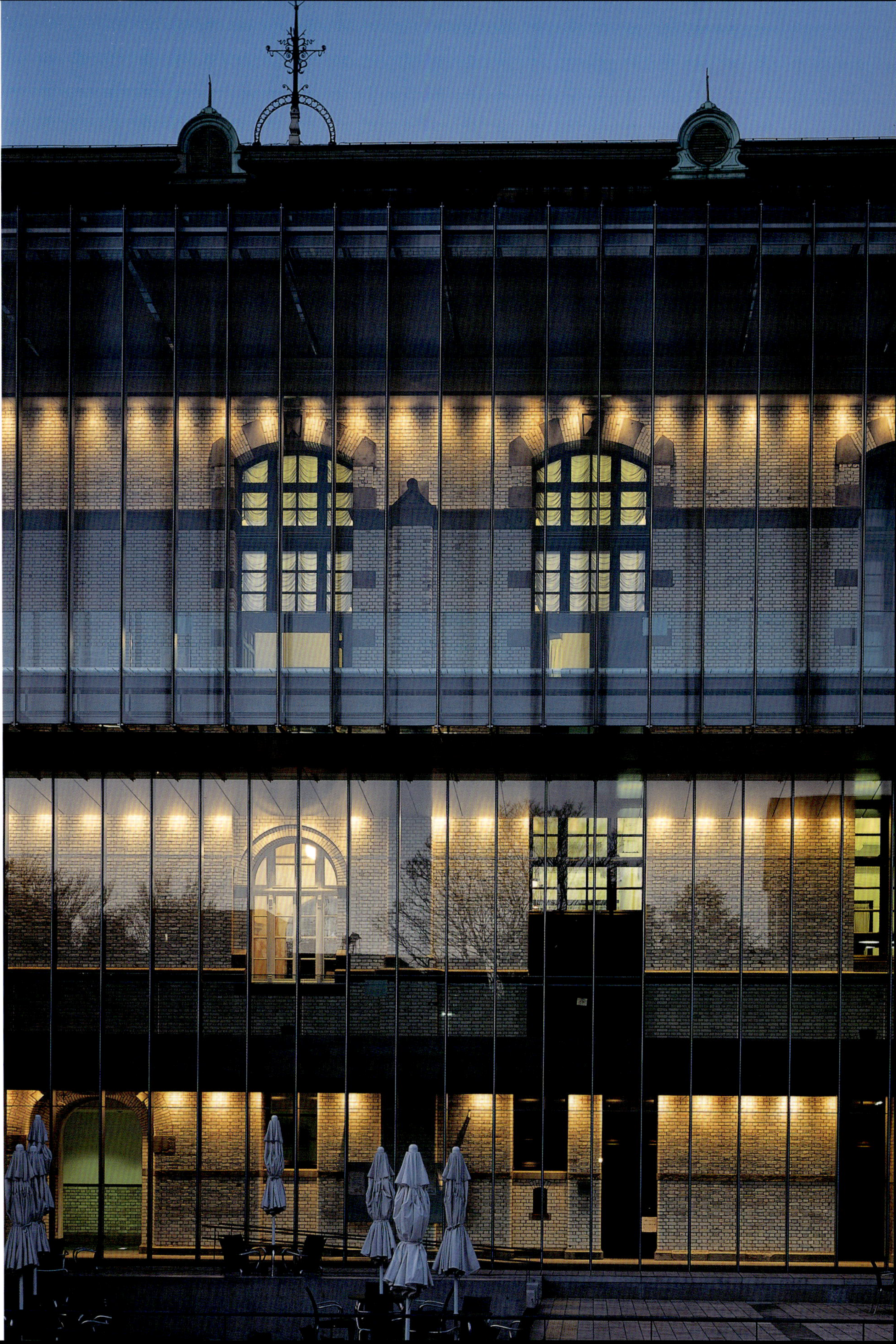

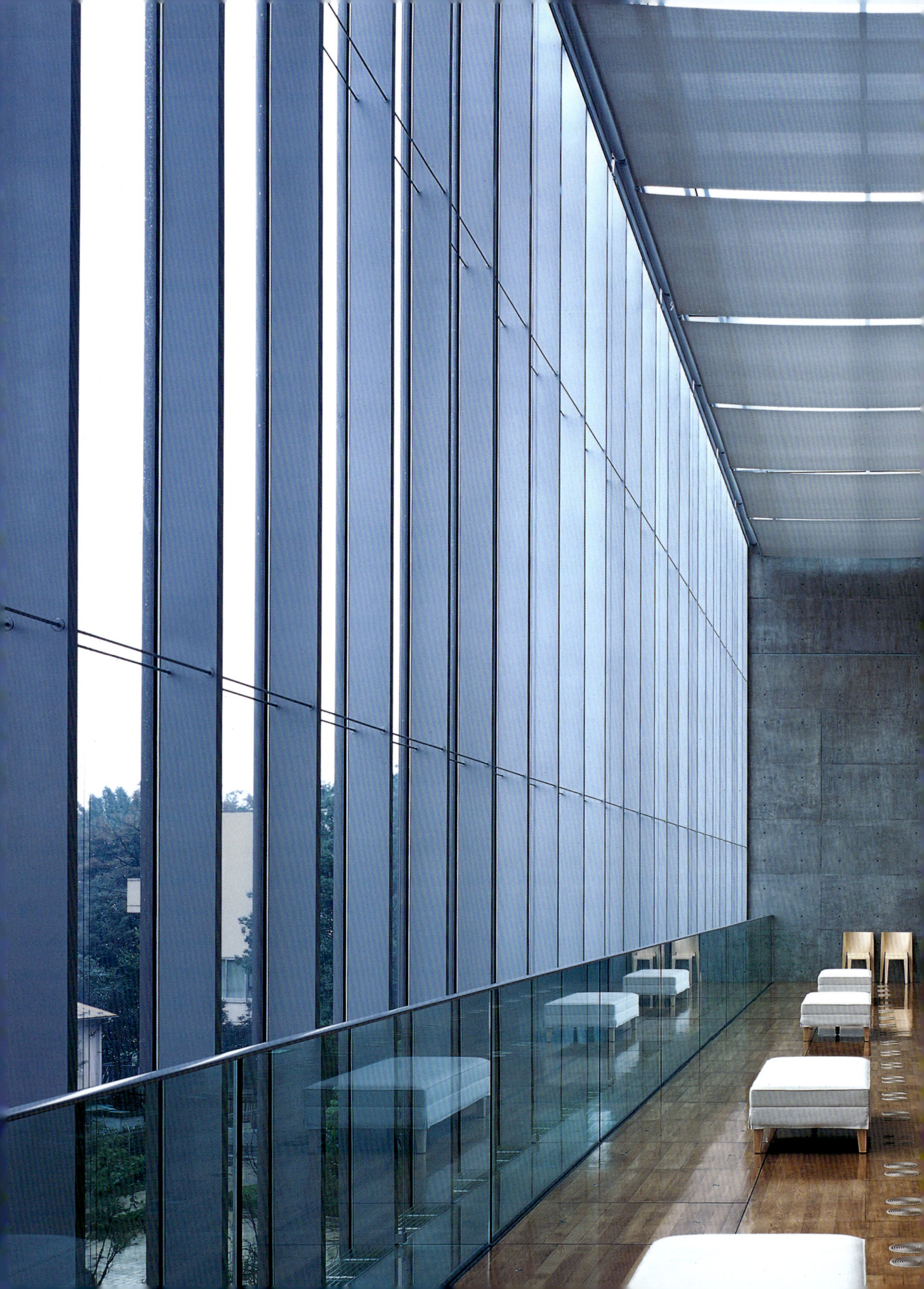

西側にラウンジとして増築されたガラスボックス内の様子。旧い建物の外壁と、現代的なガラスのカーテンウォールが対峙する、緊張感溢れる空間。

View inside the glass box added as a lounge on the west side. This is a space brimming with tension, in which the exterior wall of the old building and the modern glass curtain wall confront each other.

敷地は石川県加賀市郊外の緑豊かな場所にある。老朽化の進む中学校の新校舎として計画された建物である。全体は、東西方向に延びる楕円形平面の校舎棟と、それに30度軸を振ってかみ合う1階建て矩形平面の地域開放棟からなる。

　2層分の高さをもつ校舎棟は、外形に沿って南側に主に普通教室、北側に特別教室などが配されたホール型の構成をもつ。特徴的なのは、その中央に生まれるオープンスペースである。2階各室をつなぐ〈回廊〉を残すよう、建物と相似形の吹き抜けが穿たれ、両端に上下階をつなぐ階段が、中間に吹き抜けをまたぐ3本のブリッジが架けられている。その立体的な動線空間に、楕円形を描く天井のトップライトから、ルーバー越しに豊かな自然光が降り注ぐ——。

　学年間の隔たりなく、学校全体を一体化する、この吹き抜け空間で起こるさまざまな出来事が、子供たちの感性を刺激し、生き生きとした対話を喚起する。通常は二義的な意味合いしかもたない廊下、通路といった空間の接合部を集約し、空間化することで、制度にとらわれない、生徒たちの自由な活動を許容する〈もうひとつの教室〉をつくりたいと考えた。

　仕上げは、内外ともに木素材で統一し、特に空間を囲う壁面には、地元産の杉の間伐材を用いている。部材ひとつひとつが不揃いな間伐材はクセのある材料だが、ここでは逆に、その不揃いさが空間の意図に相応しかった。

　楕円の柔らかなフォルムの空間を包み込む間伐材がすべて異なる表情を見せるように、この場所で3年間を過ごす子どもたちが、それぞれの個性を大事に生きる力を育み、未来を創る人間として孵化していくことを期待している。

加賀市立錦城中学校
Kinjo Junior High School, Kaga
2000-02　石川県加賀市——Kaga, Ishikawa

イメージスケッチ。　　Image sketch.

The site is located in a place with abundant greenery on the outskirts of Kaga City, Ishikawa Prefecture. This building was designed as a new structure for a dilapidated junior high school. The whole complex comprises a schoolhouse with an elliptical plan that extends from east to west, and a one-story regional development building with a rectangular plan set at a 30-degree angle.

The two-story schoolhouse has a hall-shaped composition in which ordinary classrooms are mainly distributed on the south side following the external shape, and special classrooms are distributed on the north side. It is characterized by the open space created in the center. This void is similar in shape to the building, leaving a "corridor" linking each of the rooms on the second floor. The upper and lower floors are connected at either end by stairs, and three suspended bridges straddle the center of the void. From a ceiling skylight with an elliptical shape, abundant natural light pours through louvers into this thee-dimensional circulation space.

Unifying the entire school and not separating the grades, the various events that occur in this void space stimulate the sensitivity of the children and provoke lively interactions. Spatial connections that are usually regarded as secondary, such as paths and corridors, are intensified, and by turning them into spaces I wanted to make them into "alternative classrooms" permitting free activities by the pupils without being constrained by the system.

The interior and exterior finishes are unified with wood, and in particular the walls of enclosed spaces used locally produced Japanese cedar from forest thinning. With every piece slightly different, the thinned wood is an idiosyncratic material, but here this unevenness was appropriate for the spatial intentions.

Contained in a space with a gentle elliptical form, like the pieces of thinned wood that all show different expressions, children who spend three years in this place will each develop an important individuality, and I hope this place may incubate the people who will create the future.

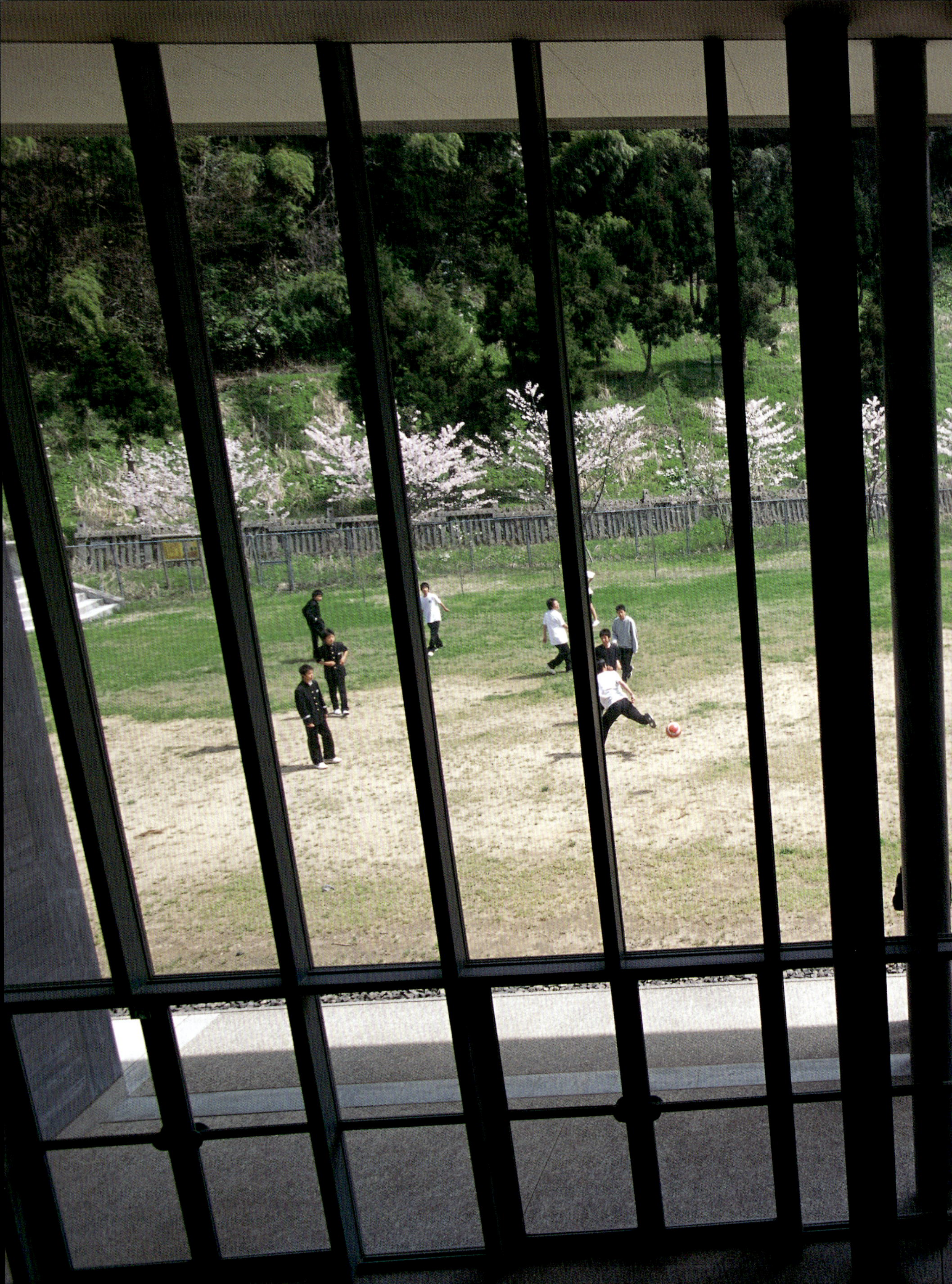

1階南側昇降口の見下ろし。ガラス越しに敷地を囲む豊かな自然が見える。

Looking down at the foyer on the south side of the first floor. The abundant nature surrounding the site is visible through the glass.

1階昇降口前から西側を見通す。天井高さ6.85m、2層吹き抜けの木質空間。
Looking west from the front of the foyer on the first floor.
The wooden space of the two-story void, with a 6.85m ceiling height.

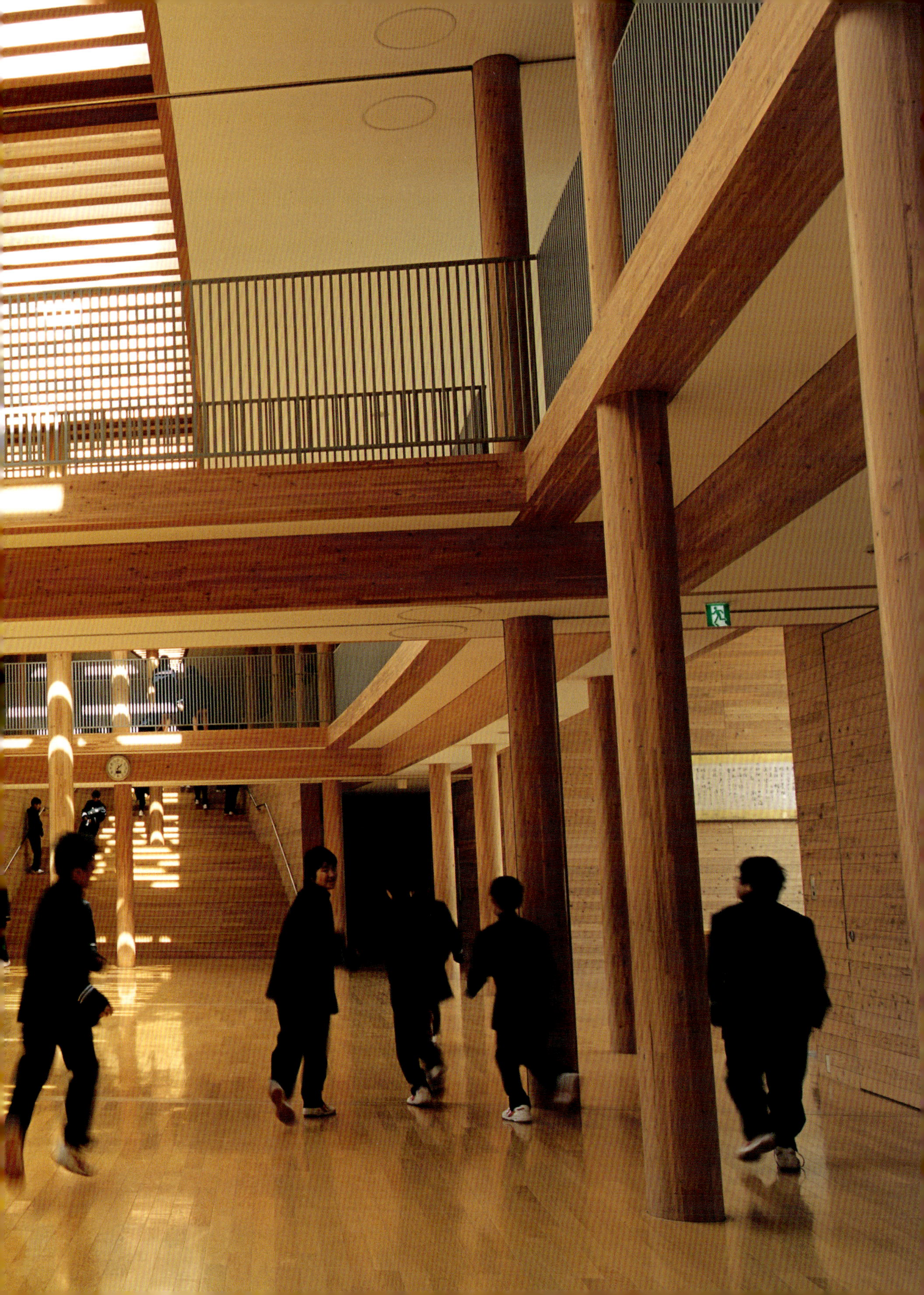

楕円形平面の外側に教室が並び、その内側に吹き抜けに面して回廊が巡る単純な構成。吹き抜けの空間は機能を限定しない〈もうひとつの教室〉として位置づけられる。

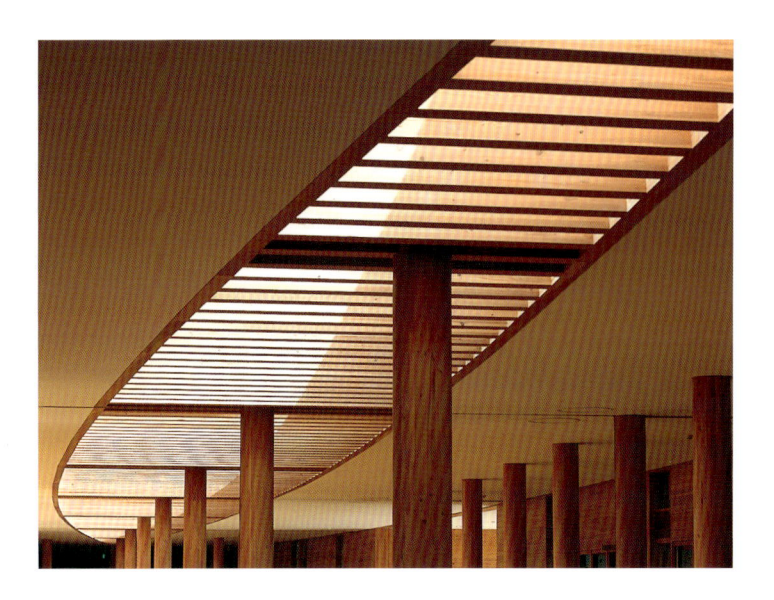

A simple composition in which the classrooms are aligned along the exterior edge of the elliptical plan, inside which is a loop corridor facing the two-story void space. The two-story void space is placed as "another classroom" with no defined function.

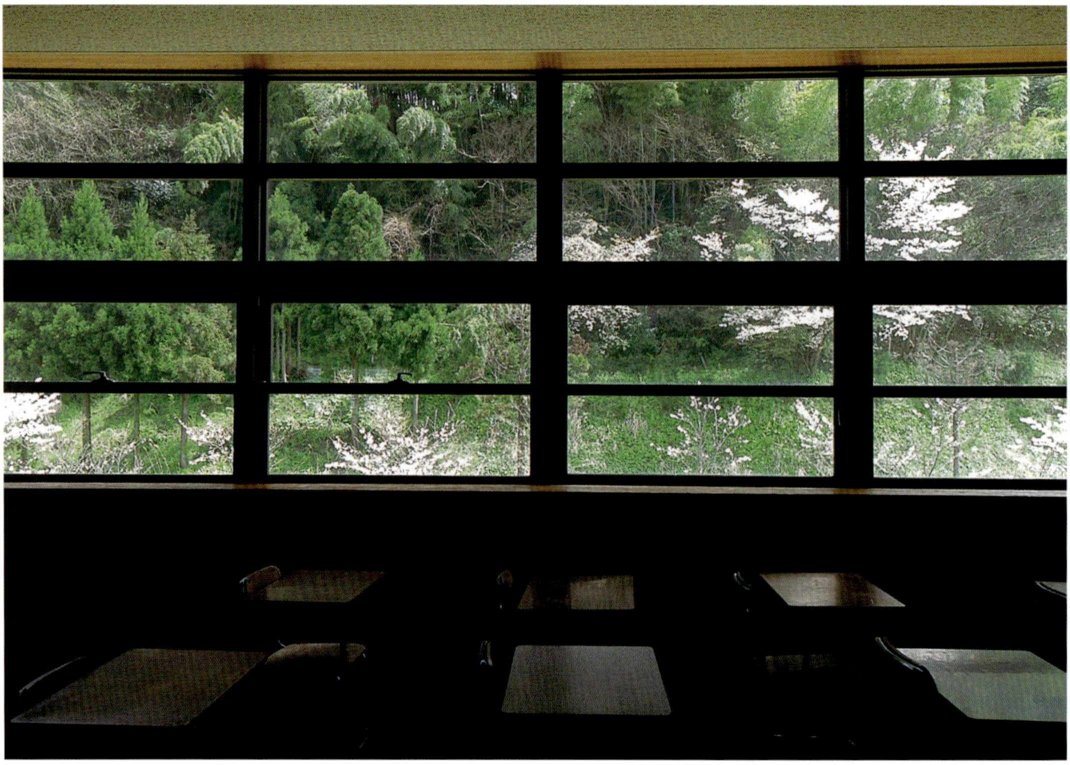

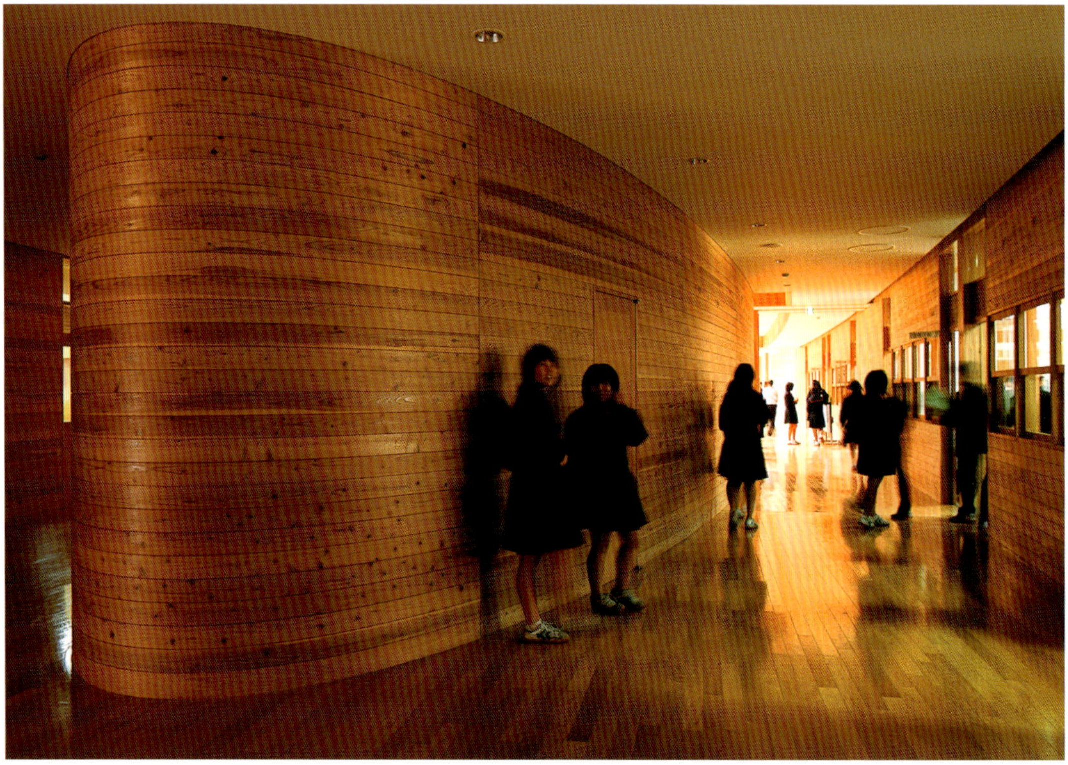

光、風、緑。随所に自然の息吹の感じられる〈木〉の学校。

Light, wind, greenery. A "wood" school in which the breath of nature can be felt everywhere.

Kinjo Junior High School

吹き抜けの底にトップライトからの光が落ちる。
Light from the skylight falls to the bottom of the void.

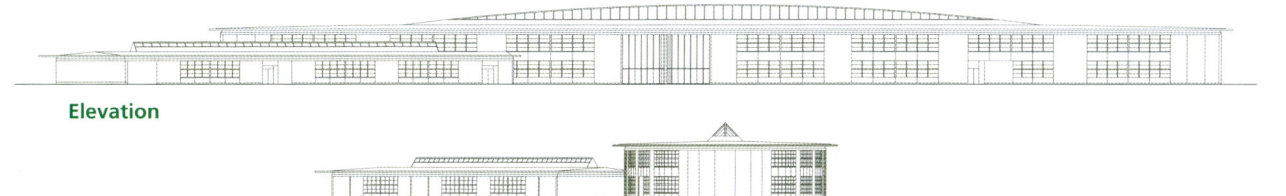

Elevation

Elevation 1:1,100

Second floor plan

First floor plan 1:1,500

1 entrance
2 faculty room
3 nurse's office
4 classroom
5 library
6 woodwork room
7 metalwork room
8 dining room
9 kitchen
10 home economics room
11 computer room
12 meeting room
13 music room
14 science room
15 fine arts room
16 void

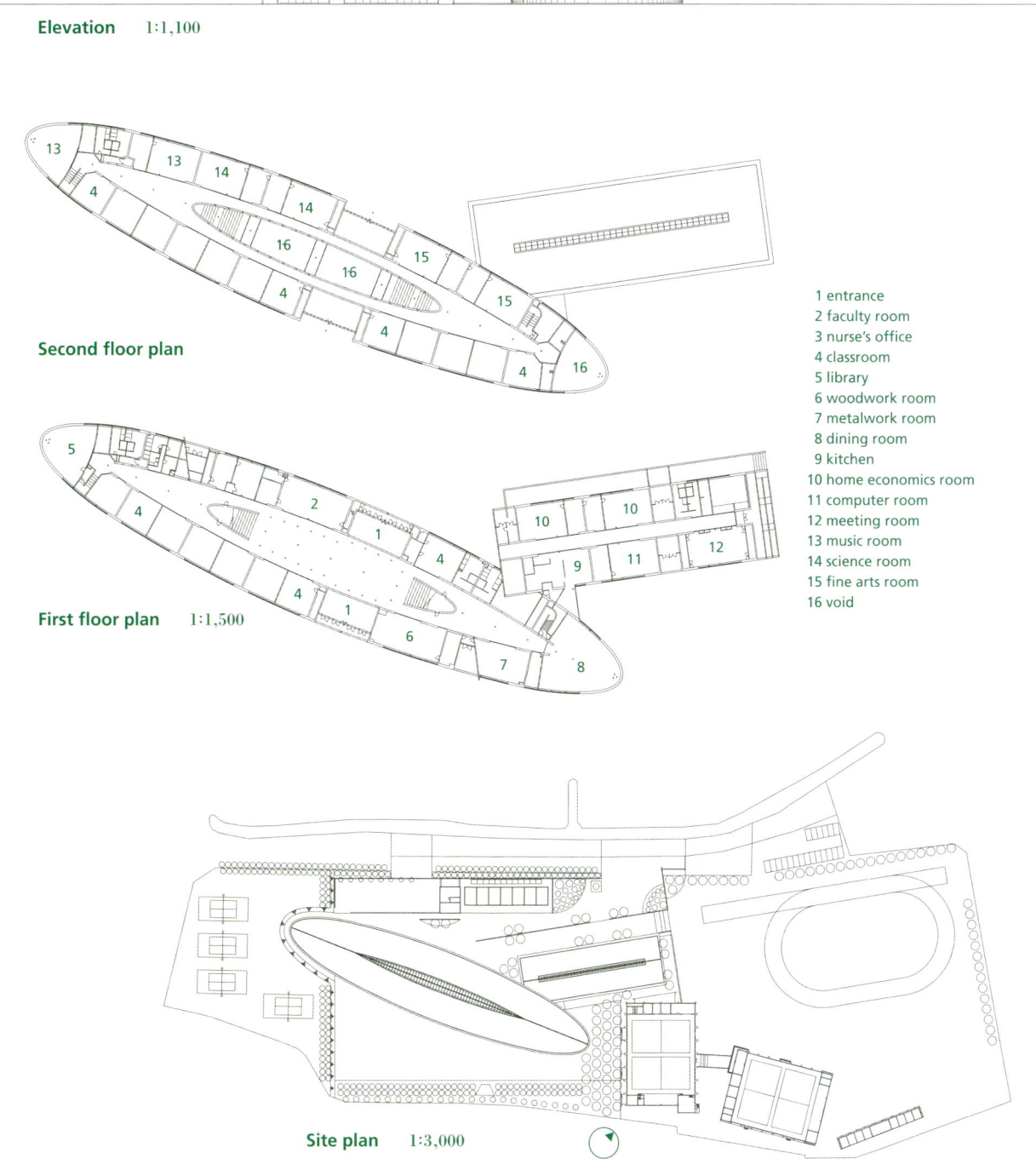

Site plan 1:3,000

359 Kinjo Junior High School

外壁仕上げは杉板目透かし貼りに対候性の塗装を施したもの。
地元産間伐材を用いている。

The exterior wall finish is openwork Japanese cedar boards with a weatherproof coating. Locally produced thinned wood has been used.

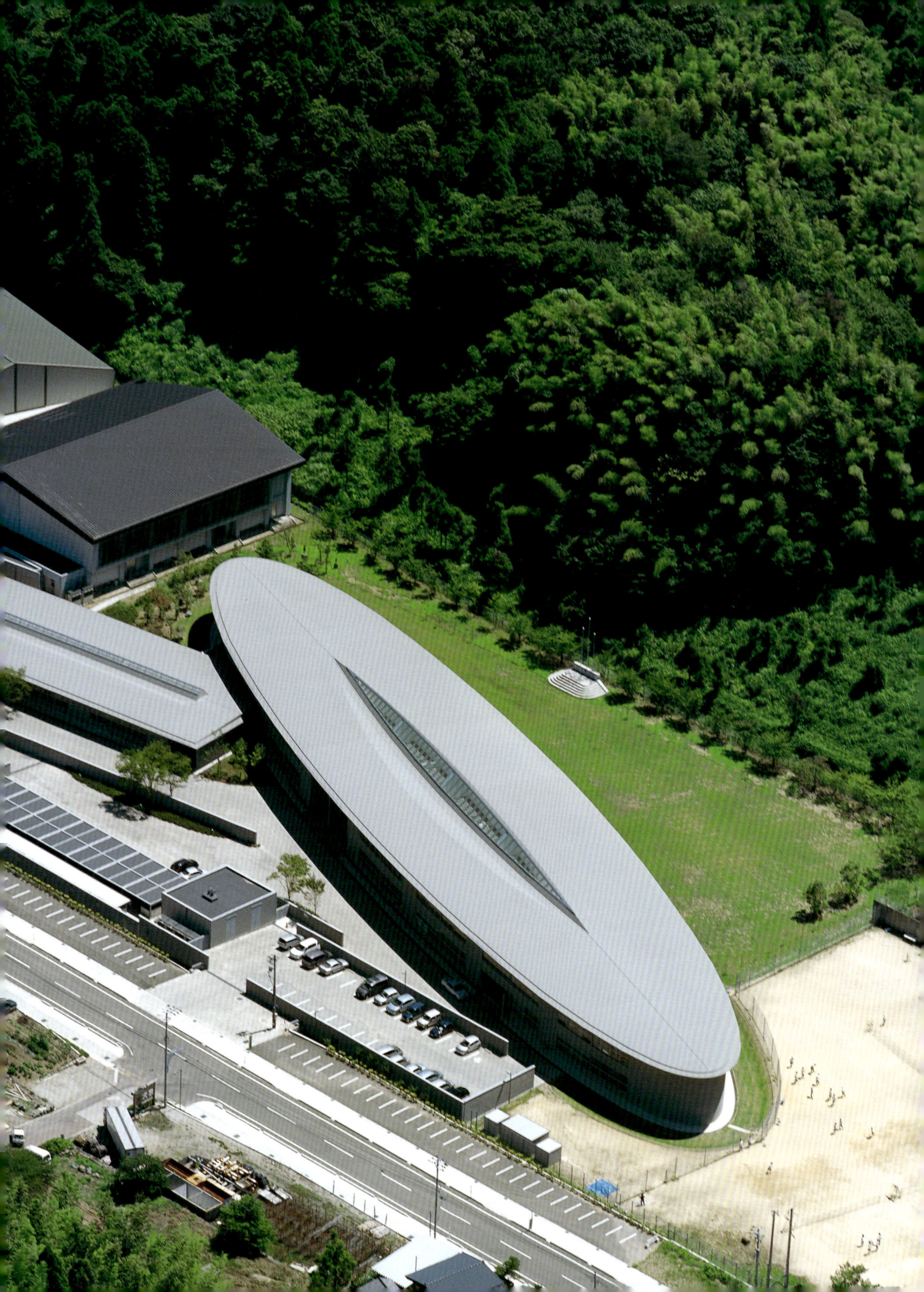

敷地は静岡県伊東市の中心部に位置する。昭和23年に開園された野間自由幼稚園の新しい園舎である。15,000m^{2}の広大な敷地は、もともと北里柴三郎の別荘のあった場所で、既存の園舎は、その美しい芝生の庭園の中、旧北里邸の洋館とともに風景に溶け込むように慎ましく建っていた。

その大らかな雰囲気を継承しつつ、より一層恵まれた敷地環境を活かした〈自然とともにある幼稚園〉を考え、生まれたのが、庭に面して思い切り開かれた〈縁側〉を中心とする構成の建物である。

1枚の大屋根の下に必要なヴォリュームを収め、そこにスリット状の動線通路を設ける。採光はトップライトにより、その光のもつ量感と方向性によって、各スペースを性格づける。さらに、ヴォリューム全体を西側に偏らせ、庭側部分を緩やかな円弧状に切り取る。これにより、芝生の庭に沿って60mの長さをもつ、奥行6mの伸びやかな〈縁側〉がつくられる。

素材については、幼稚園というプログラムを踏まえ、〈木〉を主題としている。当初は完全な木造建築を考えていたが、防災上の理由で適わず、主構造は鉄とせざるを得なかった。ただ、園児の手の触れる仕上げ部分については、すべて不燃処理を施した杉材を用いている。特に縁側の床仕上げについては、園児の素足での歩行を考慮し、再生木材のウッドデッキとした。

子どものための施設をつくる際、いつも考えるのは、明確な用途をもたない、余白の空間をどれだけ残せるかということだ。子どもの成長、自立にとって最も必要なのは、彼らが自分の頭で考え、行動できる自由な時間と場所である。野間自由幼稚園においては、全体のおよそ1/3の面積を占める半屋外の〈縁側〉が、その重要な役割を果たす。

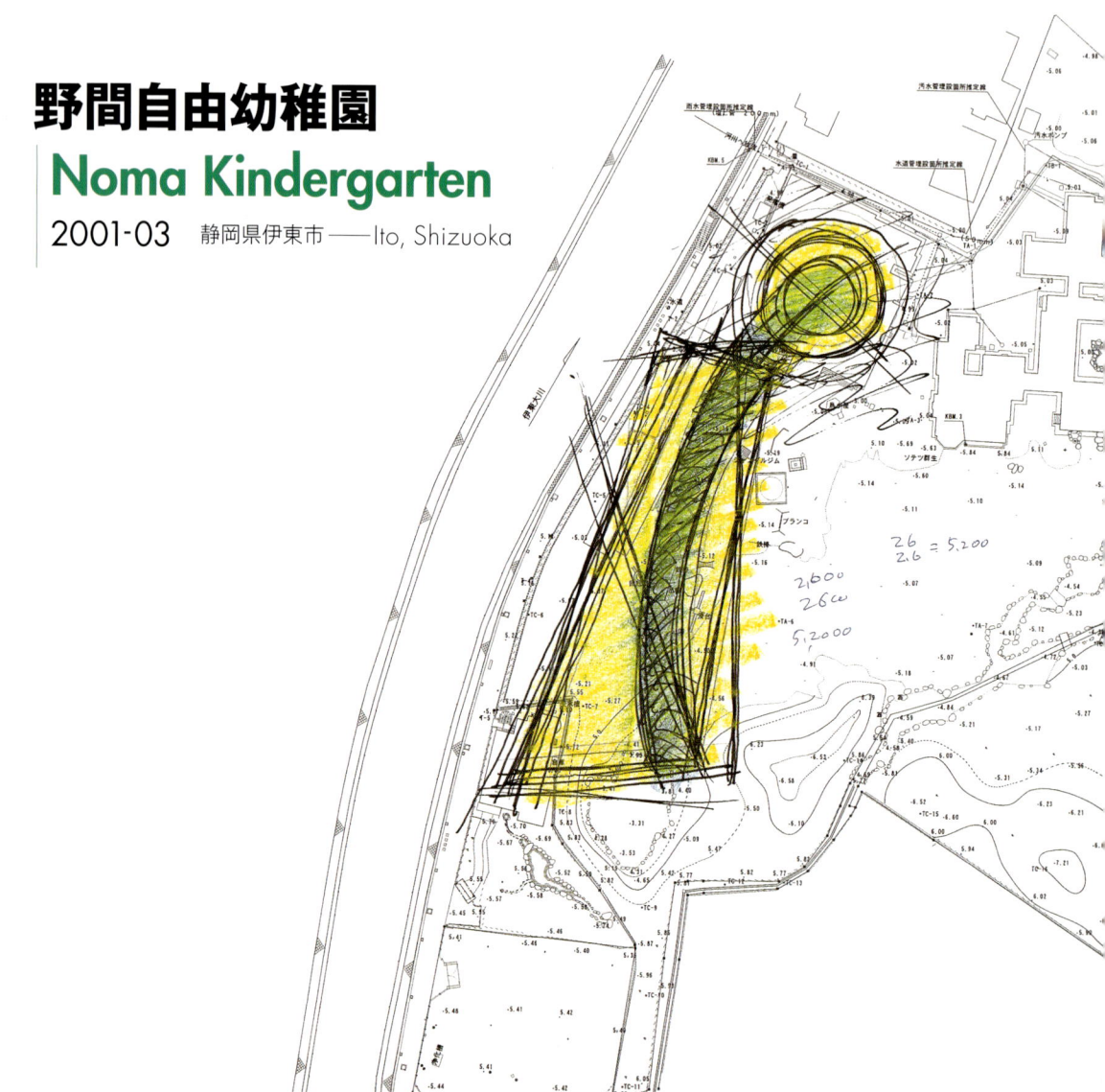

野間自由幼稚園
Noma Kindergarten
2001-03　静岡県伊東市——Ito, Shizuoka

The site is located in the center of Ito City, Shizuoka Prefecture. This is a new building for Noma Kindergarten, established in the year Showa 23 (1948). The villa of Shibasaburo Kitasato was originally located on the 15,000m^2 site, and the existing school buildings have been built modestly in the middle of this beautiful lawn park as if merging into the scenery together with the old Western-style Kitasato residence.

While inheriting this generous atmosphere, I conceived a "kindergarten coexisting with nature" that makes use of the endowments of the site's environment. What emerged is a building composition focused on an *engawa* (verandah) that is completely open toward the garden.

The necessary volume has been placed under one large roof, and slit-shaped circulation passageways established within. Illuminated by skylights, every space is given character by the directionality and quantity of light. Furthermore, the entire volume inclines to the west, and the garden area is cut by a gentle arc shape. This results in a 60m-long and 6m-wide *engawa* extending along the lawn.

Based on the program of a kindergarten, the theme for the materials is "wood." I first conceived a structure entirely made of wood, but that was unsuitable due to disaster prevention issues, and I could not avoid making the main structure of steel. However, all the finishing elements that can be touched by the kindergarten children are made of Japanese cedar with a non-flammable treatment. In particular, the floor finish of the *engawa* is a wood deck made of recycled timber that takes into account the fact that kindergarten pupils walk on it with their bare feet.

When making a facility for children I always consider how to leave empty spaces without clear usage. Free time and places where they can think and act for themselves are very important in the growth and independence of children. In the Noma Kindergarten this important role is taken by the half-exterior *engawa*, which occupies one third of the total area.

建設前の敷地現況図に重ね描かれた、サイトのイメージスケッチ。
幼稚園とあわせて円形の児童図書館も描かれている。

Site image sketch, drawn on top of a diagram of the site conditions prior to construction. The kindergarten, including the circular children's library, is depicted.

長さ60m、奥行き6mの広大な縁側空間。床材には園児が裸足で駆け回れるよう、木の再生材が用いられている。

A very large *engawa* space, 60m long and 6m deep. Reconstituted wood has been used for the floor material so that the kindergarten pupils can run around barefoot.

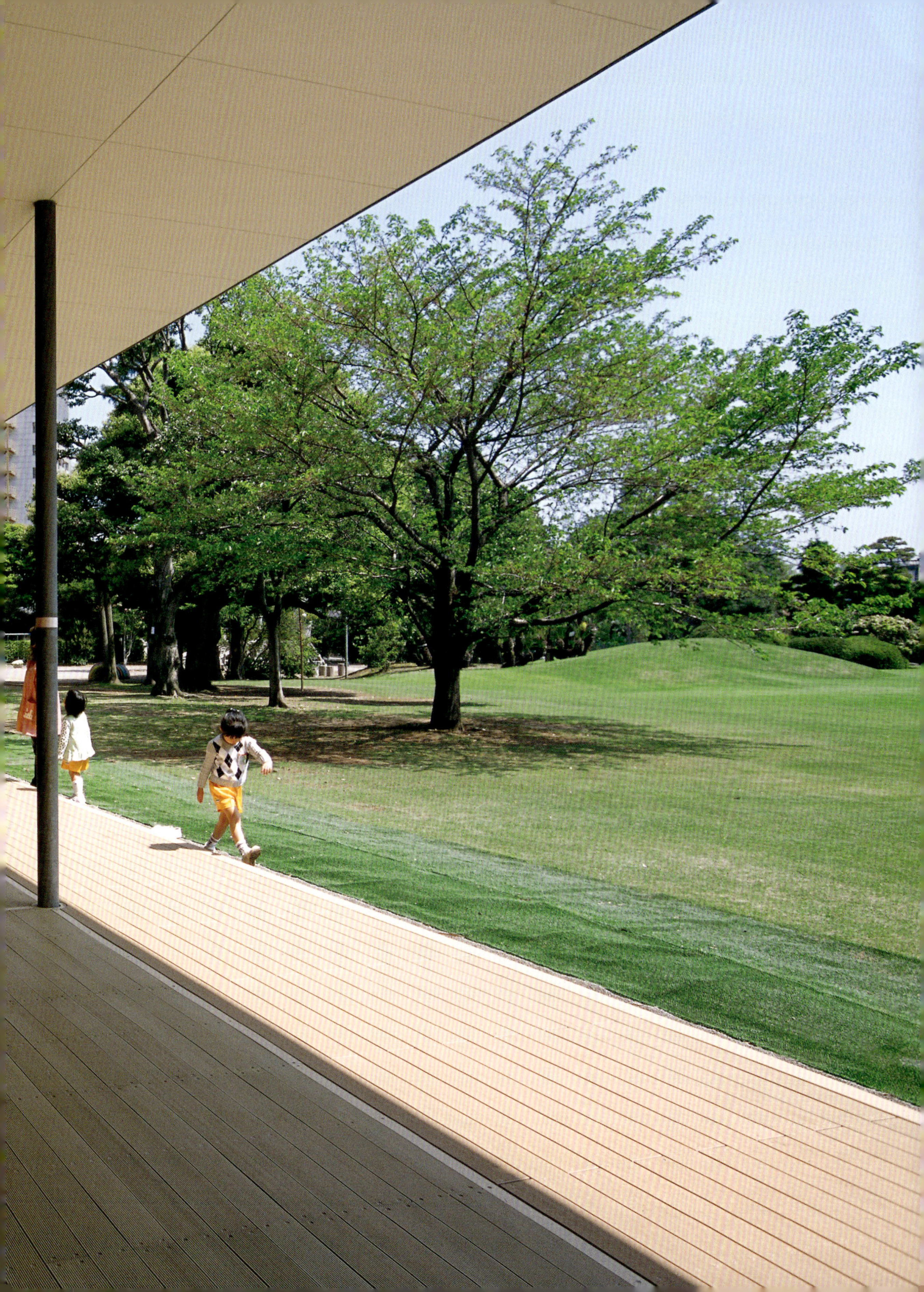

北東側外観。約3,000m²の芝生の園庭に面する縁側のある幼稚園。

Exterior view from the northeast. A kindergarten with an *engawa* facing a garden lawn of approximately 3,000m².

園庭には安田侃による彫刻作品が置かれている。
A sculpture by Kan Yasuda has been placed in the garden.

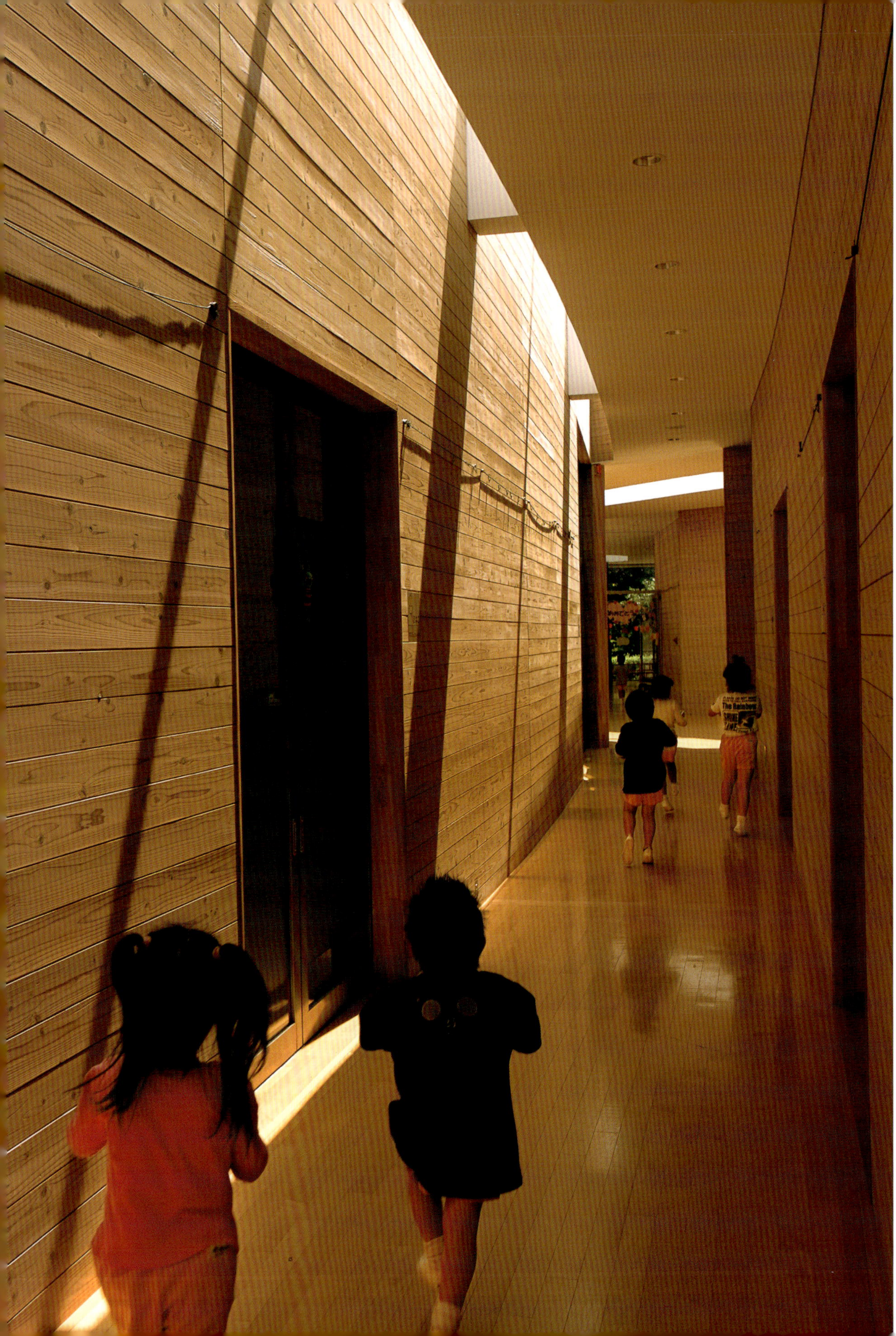
The Rainbow

平屋建ての建物内の各スペースを、さまざまなかたちで設けられたトップライトの光が特徴づける。
Illumination from skylights of various shapes gives character to each space inside the single-storey building.

建物を南北に貫く廊下に沿って設けられたトップライトの光が、
杉材で仕上げられた壁面に豊かな表情を与える。

Illumination from skylights installed along the corridor passing through the building from north to south gives a rich expression to the wall surfaces finished with Japanese cedar wood.

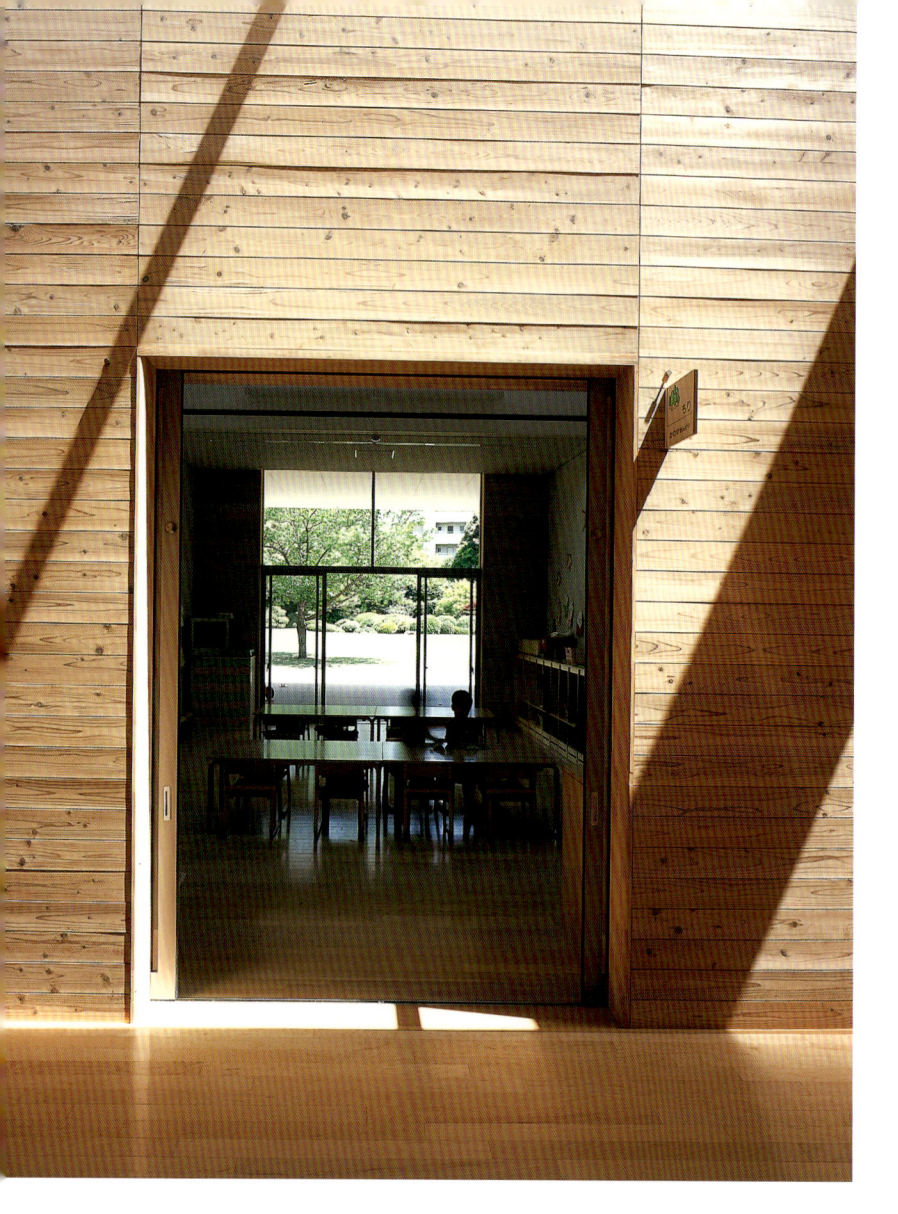

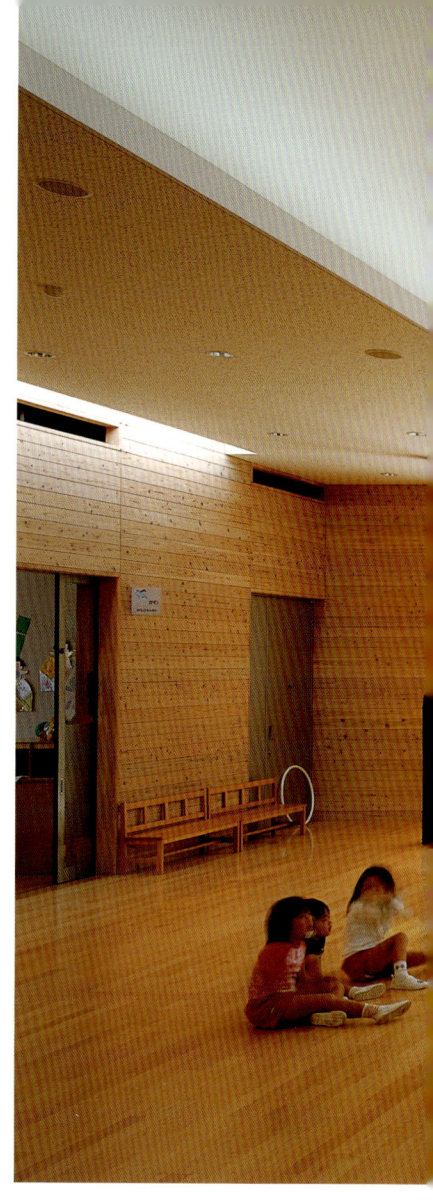

園舎内のさまざまな部分から見る園庭の風景。内外空間との連続、水平方向の空間的広がりが意図されている。

Scenes of the garden viewed from various places inside the kindergarten. The aim is continuity between interior and exterior spaces and a spatial expansiveness in the horizontal direction.

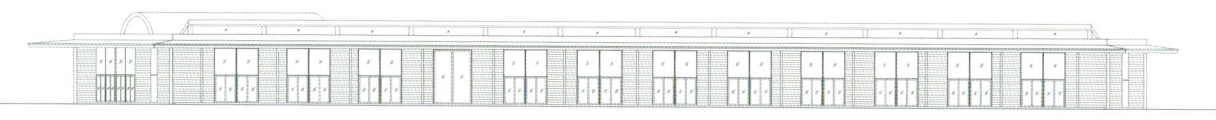

Elevation 1:500

plan 1:500

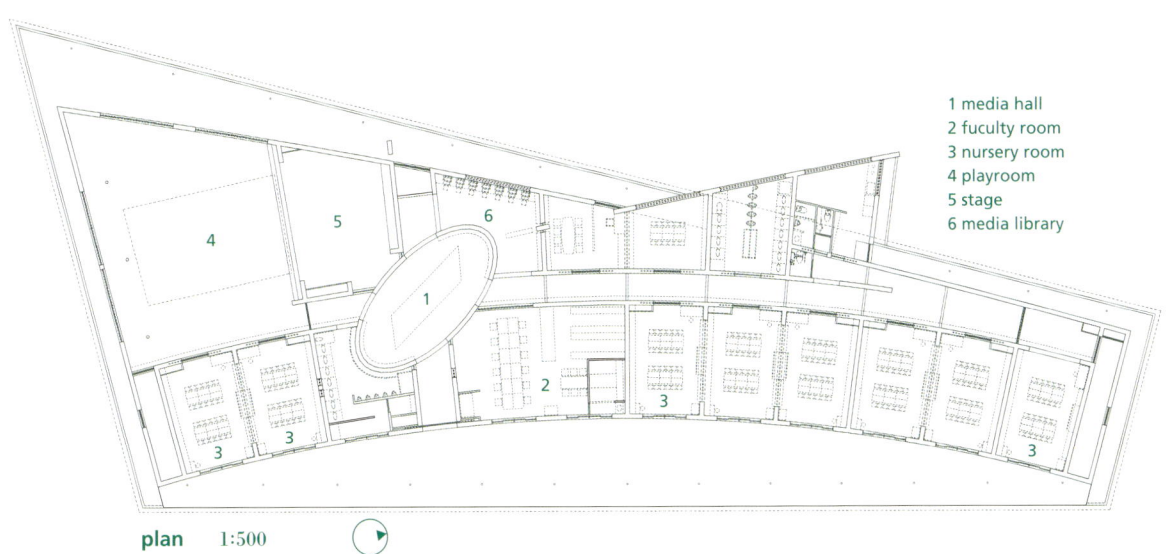

1 media hall
2 fuculty room
3 nursery room
4 playroom
5 stage
6 media library

373 Noma Kindergarten

南側より見る建物俯瞰。豊かな緑の森に包まれた幼稚園。
西側には伊東大川が流れる。

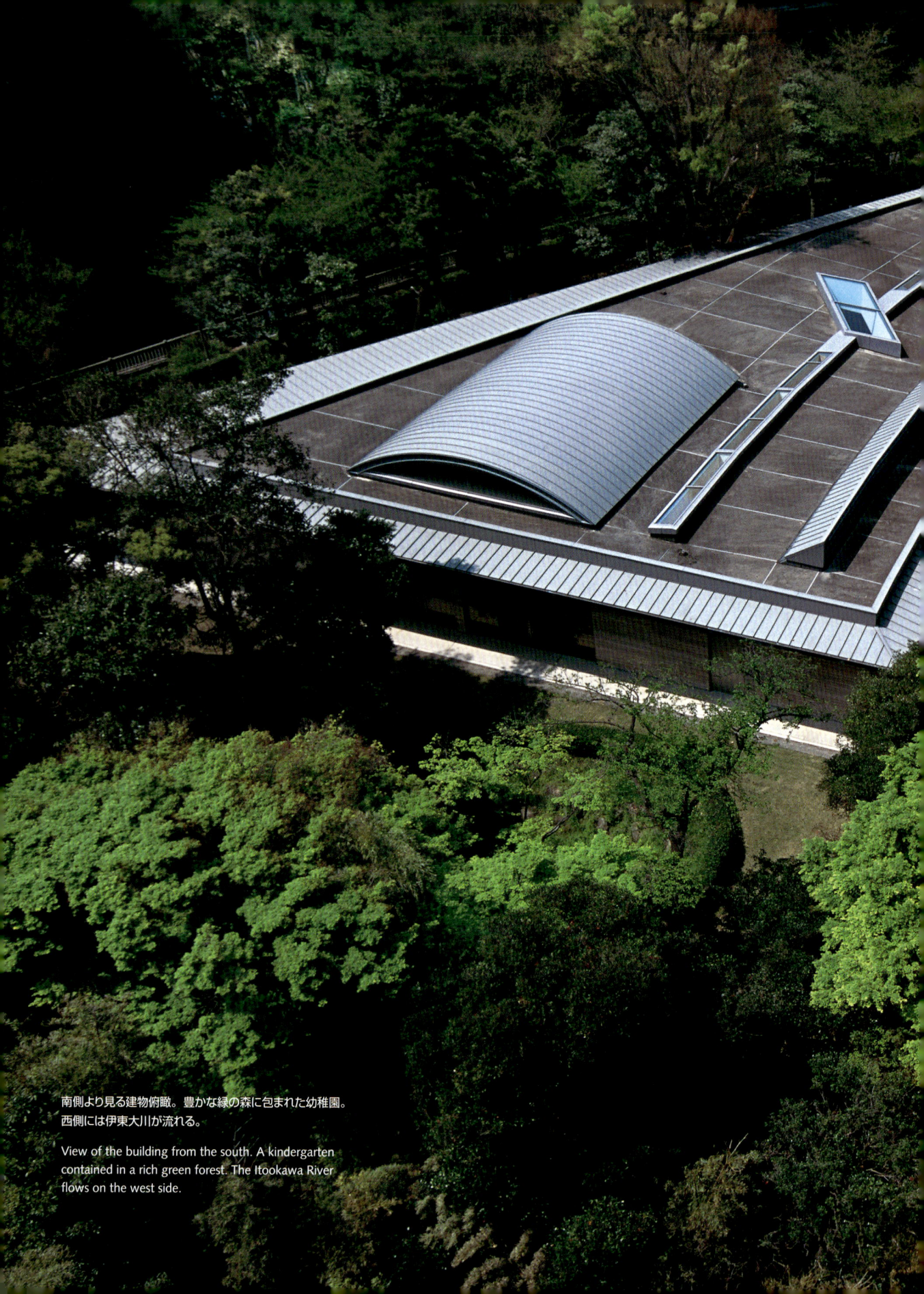

View of the building from the south. A kindergarten
contained in a rich green forest. The Itookawa River
flows on the west side.

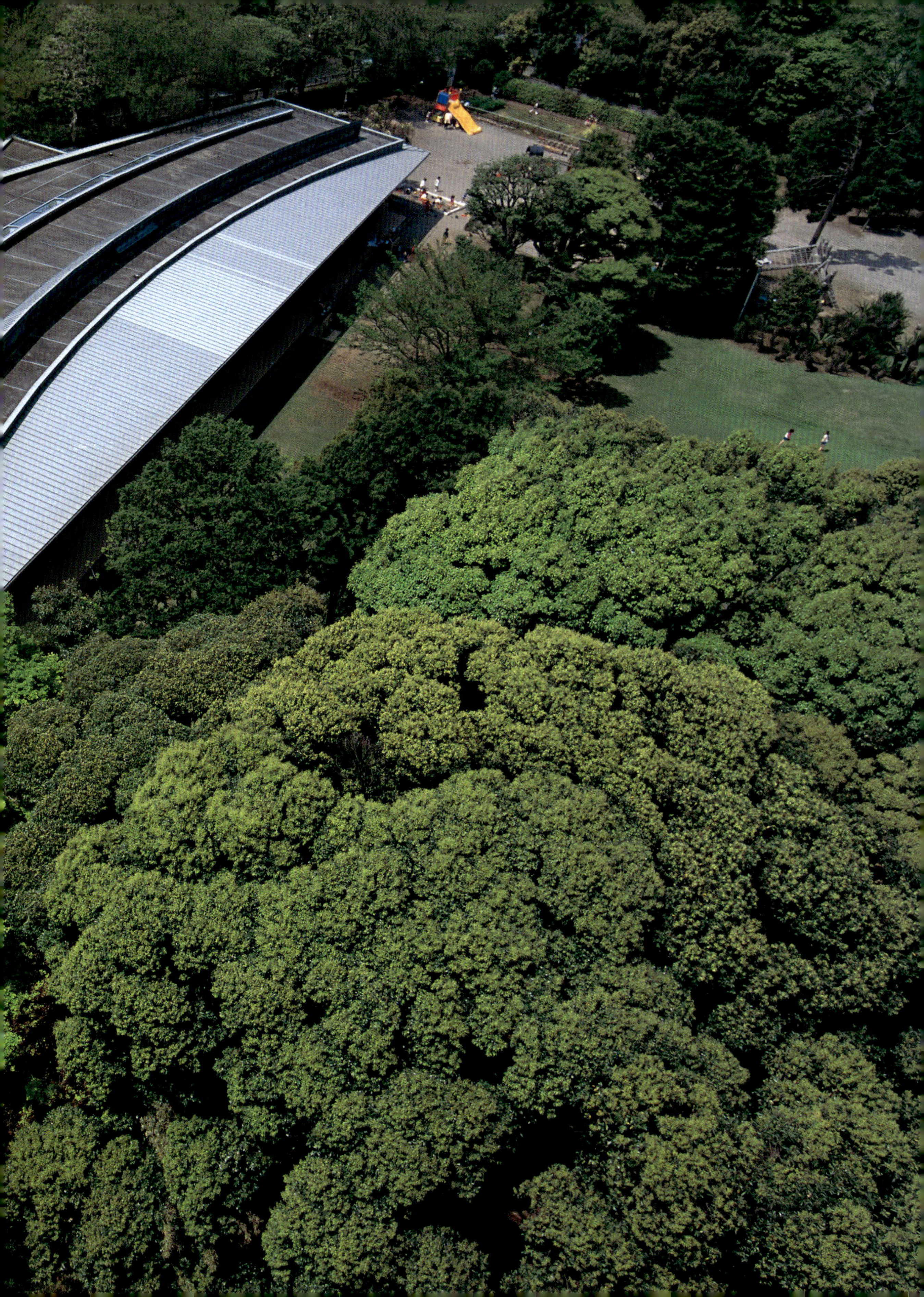

20年越しの地中

2004年、地中美術館が完成した。
建物をすべて地下に埋め込んだ、地中の建築。
建築を構築物として外部から見詰める視点は存在せず
問われるのは内部に身をおいた人間が知覚する光と闇の空間のみ。
自身の理想の建築空間の追求ともいうべき
最も挑戦精神を煽られたプロジェクトだ。

設計をスタートしたのは1999年。
しかし、構想の始まりは、その20年以上前に遡る。
1985年の渋谷プロジェクト、1988年の中之島プロジェクト（地層空間）
1994年の大谷地下劇場プロジェクト――
これら、非実現に終わったプロジェクトを通じて
ずっと私は地中の空間を心に描いていた。

地下に降り進んでいくと、地上のアクティブな空気が薄れるにつれ
静寂な闇がその深度を増していく。
その闇を形づくる壁に頭上から光が差し込んだとき、空間が現れる。
私がずっと追いかけ続けてきた、光を道標に抑揚する
かたちのない地中の建築空間のイメージ――
積み重ねてきた思考のすべてが、地中美術館に託されている。

The Subterranean Revisited After Twenty Years

In 2004, the Chichu Art Museum was completed.
This is a subterranean architecture, with all its built parts buried in the earth. Here, there is no point of view from which one gazes at this architecture as a built object from the outside. The only thing that matters is the space of light and shadow that can be perceived by those who put themselves inside. Embodying my pursuit of ideal architectural space, this was the project that provoked my spirit of challenge the most.

I started to design this in 1999. Its beginning, however, can be traced back to the three projects that are more than twenty years old: Shibuya Project from 1985, Nakanoshima Project (Space Strata) from 1988, and The Theater in the Rock in Oya from 1994. Through these unrealized projects, I have been always envisioning a subterranean space in my mind.

As one descends underground and the air of activity above the ground gradually diminishes, a silent darkness increases its depth. And when a light pours from above onto the walls that shape the darkness, a space reveals itself. I have been always chasing after this image of formless subterranean architectural space whose inflection is guided by light: all of my accumulated thinking is deposited in this underground museum.

敷地は瀬戸内海の小島、直島につくられた、もうひとつの美術館である。「地中美術館」と名づけられた建物には、印象派のクロード・モネと現代美術のウォルター・デ・マリア、ジェームズ・タレルという3作家の作品が永久展示されている。

敷地は「ベネッセハウス ミュージアム」の西方600m、段状塩田の遺構が刻まれた小高い丘の上に位置する。その場所のポテンシャルと〈空間アートの永久展示〉という特殊なプログラムを踏まえ、ここでは〈風景に溶け込む建築〉という「ベネッセハウス」での試みをさらに推し進めた完全なる〈地中建築〉を提案した。

建物は、丘の上に、海へと向かう南北の軸線に沿って穿たれた、正方形と正三角形平面を象るふたつのヴォイドを基点として構成される。海より遠い側に位置する正方形の「四角コート」の1辺に沿うかたちで、丘の中腹より地中に入り込むアプローチの坑道が突き刺さる。「四角コート」を巡る階段が導くひとつ上の地下レベルに、角度を振ってエントランスロビーが配される。

そこから空のみに開かれたクレバスのような屋外通路を経て、正三角形の「三角コート」に辿り着く。コートの3辺に沿って配された階段とスロープに導かれ、再び地下へと下降していくと、そこが地下のギャラリーゾーンの入口である。3作家のアートスペースは、「三角コート」の2辺を取り巻くかたちでそれぞれに固有の幾何学的ヴォリュームをもつ。

アートスペースへと至る一連の地中空間の主題は、〈光〉である。地下に埋め込まれた幾何学形態の連なりが生み出す暗闇の迷路——そこに差し込む光の量感と質感、その階調によって、非日常の場に相応しい、抑揚ある空間を生み出そうと意図した。

3つのアートスペースは、アーティスト及びディレクターとの妥協のないコラボレーションを経て生まれたものである。その激しい対話の痕跡が、地中の建築の輪郭として、地表面にわずかに顔を覗かせている。

地中美術館
Chichu Art Museum／Naoshima
2000-04 　香川県香川郡——Kagawa-gun, Kagawa

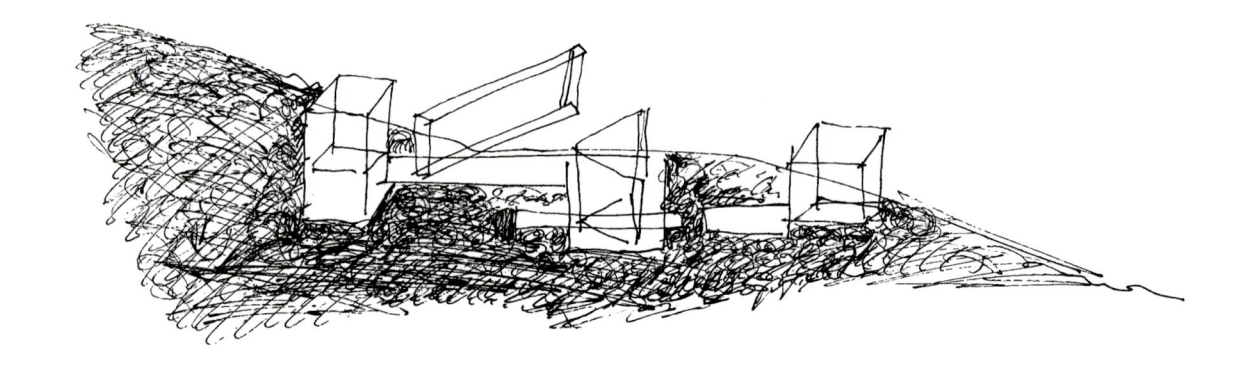

初期イメージスケッチ。地中に埋め込まれてつながる純粋幾何学空間のイメージ。

This is another art museum built on a site on Naoshima, a small island in the Seto Inland Sea. The building is named Chichu Art Museum, and contains works by three artists: the Impressionist Claude Monet, and permanent installations by the contemporary artists Walter de Maria and James Turrell.

The site is located 600m west of the Benesse House Museum, on top of a slightly elevated hill into which the remains of a stair-shaped saltpan had been carved. Based the potential of the place and the special program of a "permanent display of spatial art," I proposed a completely "underground architecture" that further develops the experiment at Benesse House of "architecture that blends into the scenery."

Excavated along a north-south axis line from the top of the mountain toward the sea, the building composition takes as its datum two voids, one with a square plan, the other an equilateral triangle. On the side farthest from the sea is a shape that follows one side of the orthogonal "square court," pierced by the underground approach tunnel. Reached by the stairs surrounding the "square court," the entrance lobby is placed at an angle on an underground level, one story above.

From there traversing a crevasse-like outdoor passage open only to the sky, one finally reaches the "triangular court." Descending once more underground, led by ramps and steps placed along the three sides of the triangle, one arrives at the underground gallery zone entrance. Enclosing two sides of the equilateral triangle, the art spaces for the three artists are contained in their own characteristic geometric volumes.

The theme of these continuous underground spaces leading to the art spaces is "light." A labyrinth of darkness produced by a succession of geometric shapes buried underground—the aim was to produce inflected spaces appropriate to an extraordinary place by means of gradations in the quantity and feeling of the light flowing in.

The three art spaces emerged from an uncompromising collaboration between the artists and the director. The traces of this intense interaction just barely show themselves above the earth as the contours of this underground architecture.

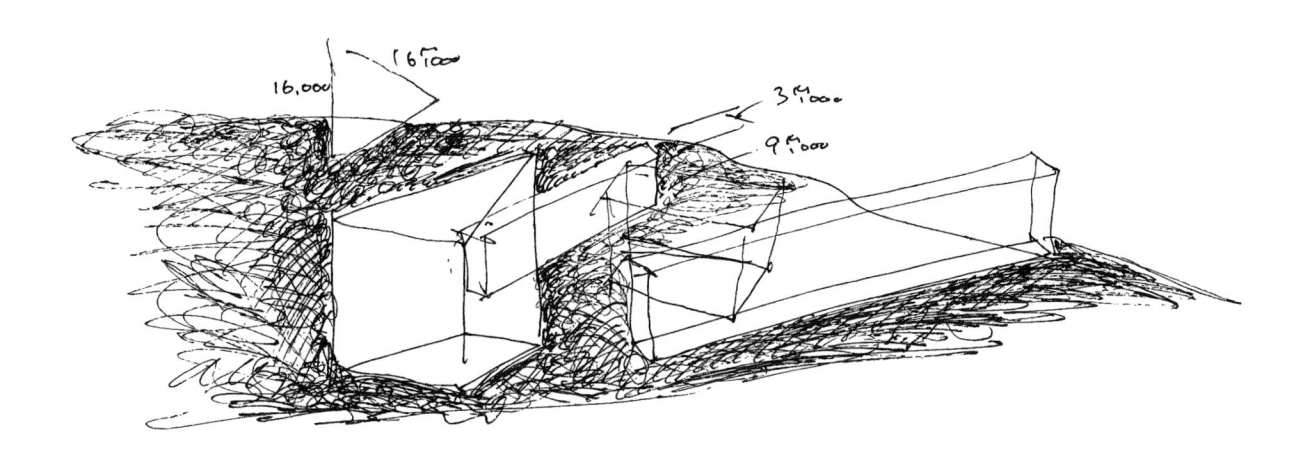

Early image sketches. Images of simple geometric shapes embedded in the ground.

瀬戸内海を見渡す小高い丘の上に現れる、地下の〈見えない〉建築の片鱗。

A glimpse of the "invisible" underground building appearing on top of a low hill with a view over the Inland Sea.

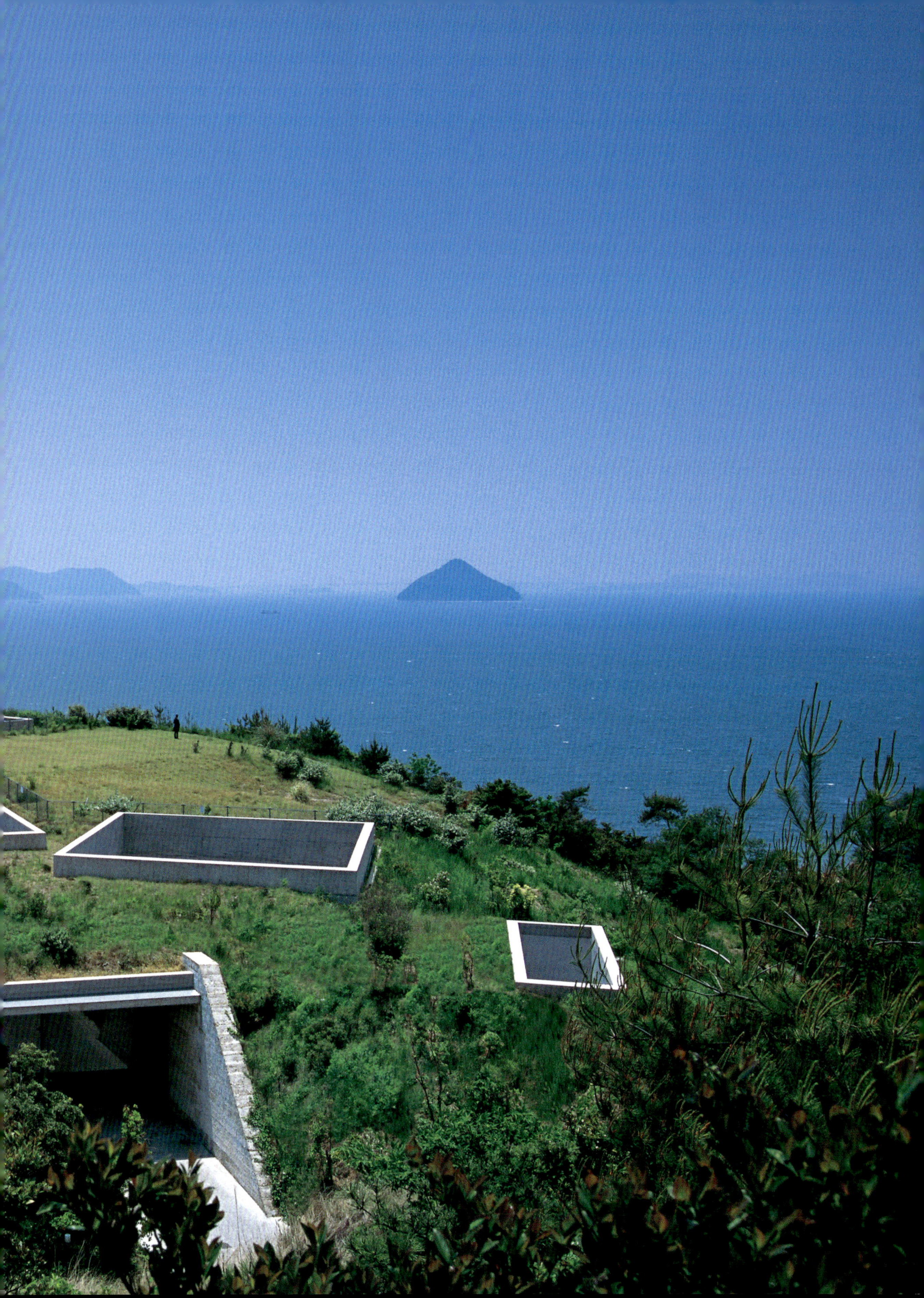

壁も床もわずかに傾いた暗がりを、スリットの光を頼りに進んでいく。光を道標とした地中建築の世界。

The walls as well as the floor are slightly inclined, and one continues in darkness, relying on light from slits. An underground architectural world with light as a guide.

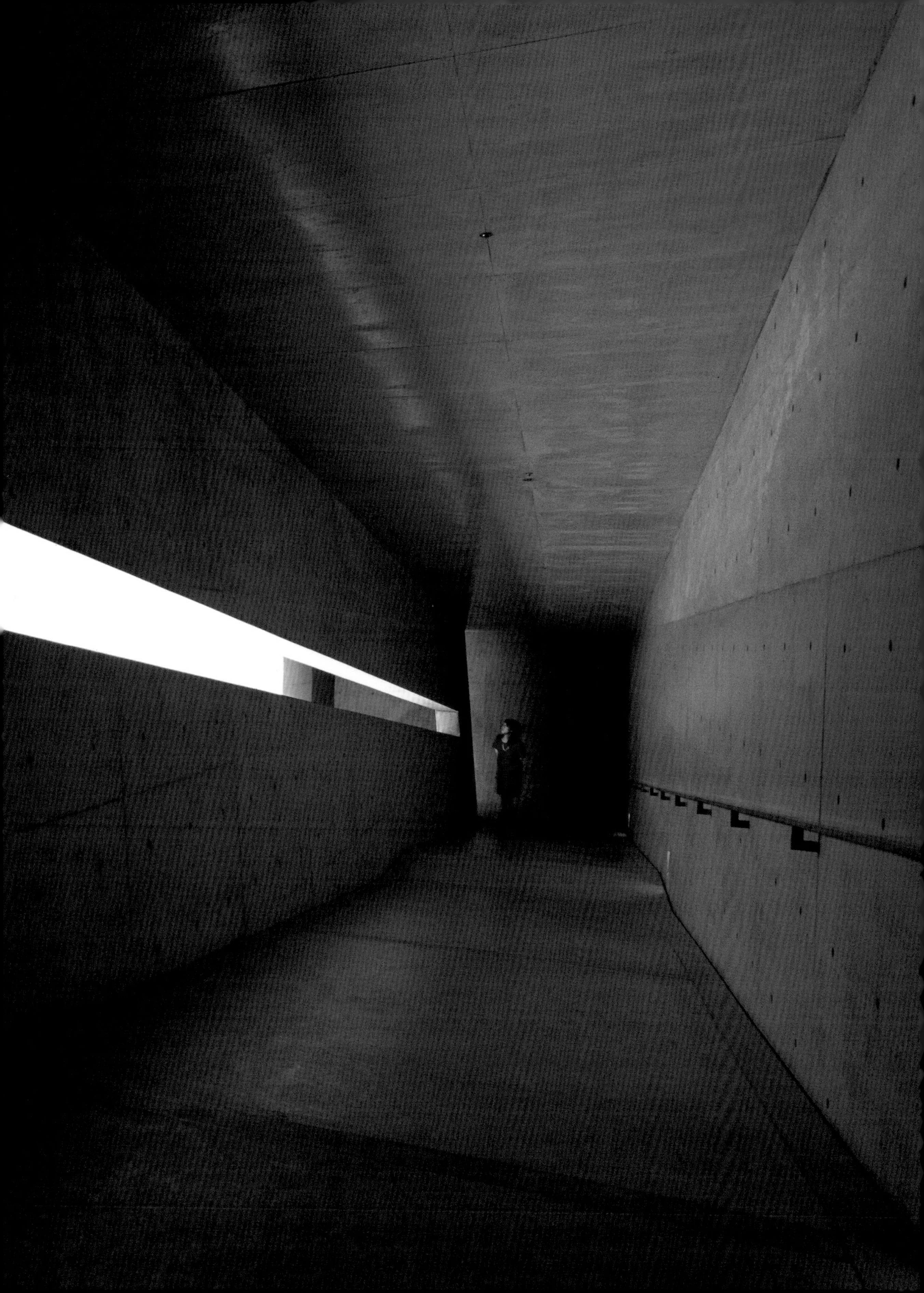

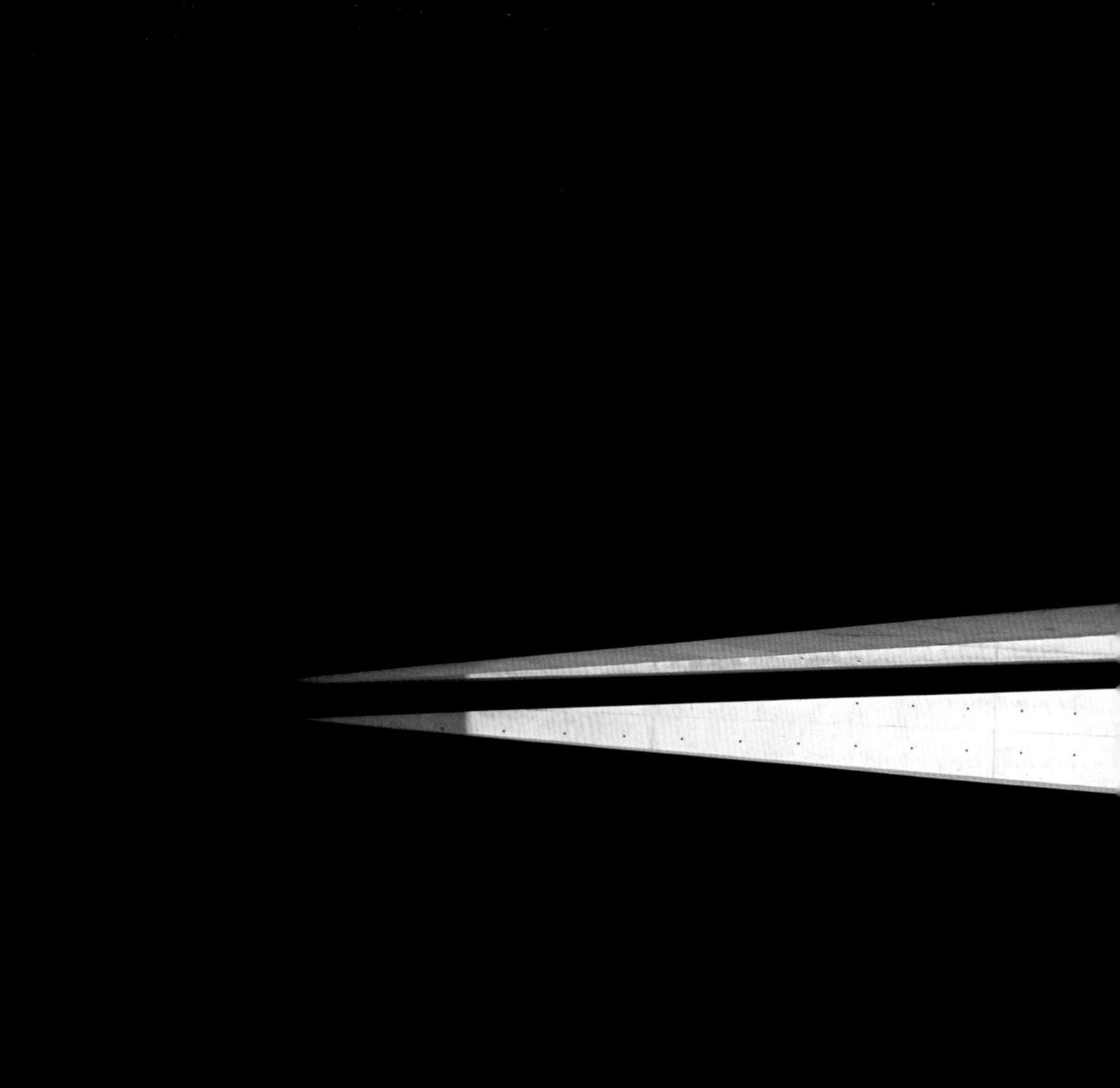

連続するスリット開口が切り取る「三角コート」の風景。
Scene of the continuous slit aperture cut into the "triangular court."

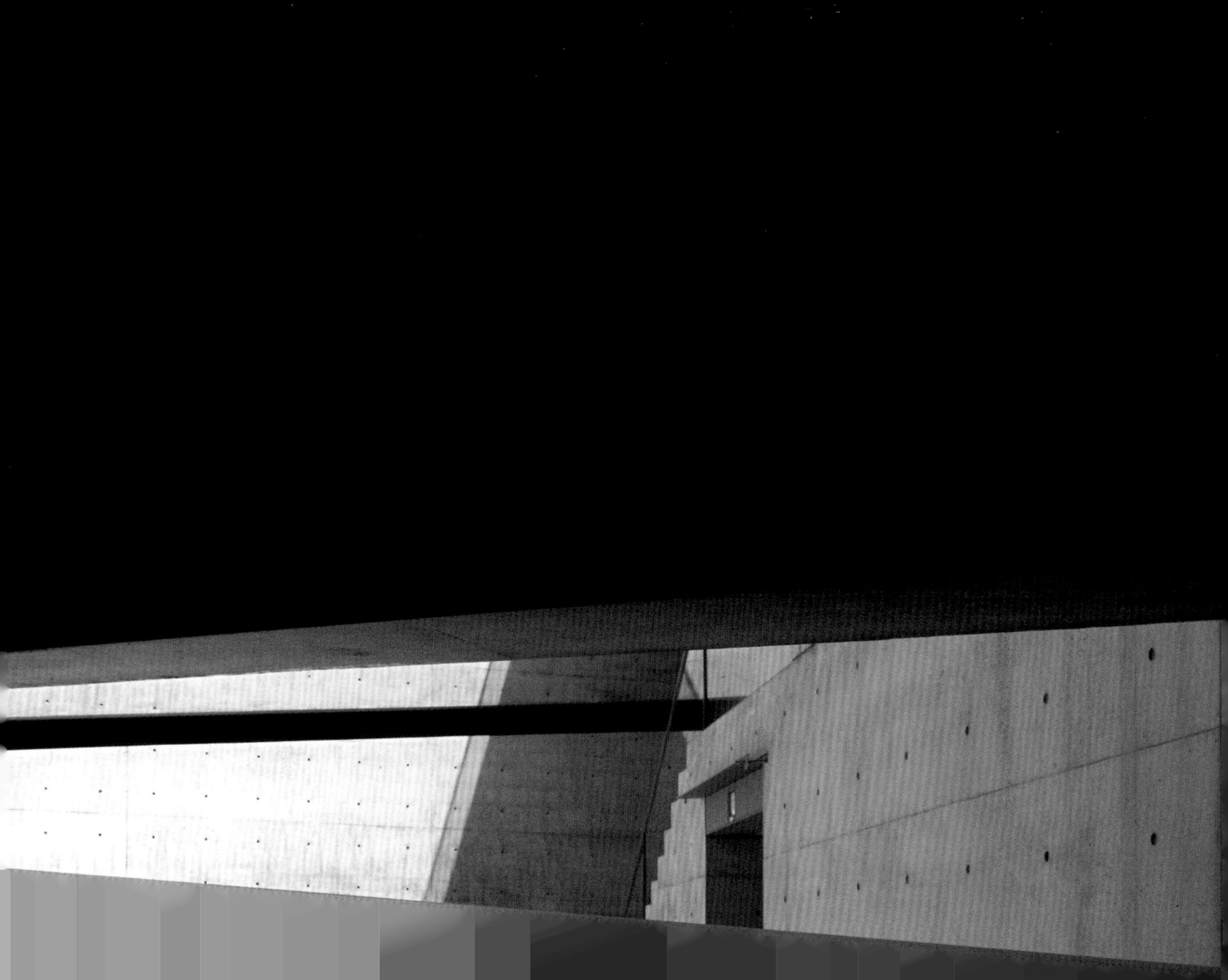

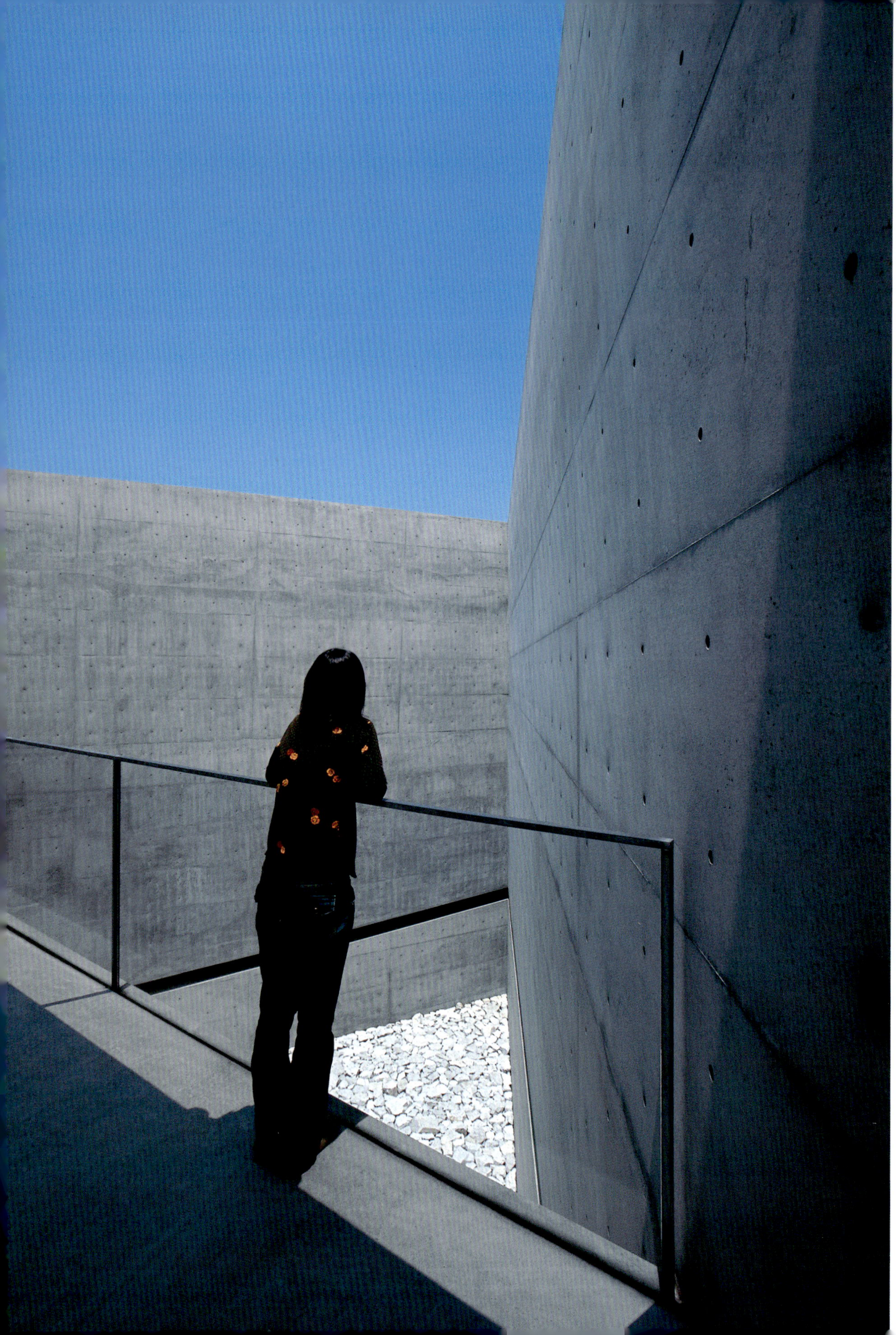

石灰岩が敷き詰められた「三角コート」の吹き抜け。
Void of the "triangular court" lined with limestone.

来訪者は、トクサを植えた「四角コート」の吹き抜けを昇り、傾いた2枚の壁に挟まれた屋外通路を通り抜け、「三角コート」を下降して、アート空間へ辿り着く。迷宮的なアプローチを進むうち、人々は日常から解き放たれ、非日常の世界へと意識を解放していく。

The visitors ascend the void of the "square court," in which horsetail grows, pass through an alley contained between two inclining walls, descend to the "triangular court," and finally arrive at the art spaces. While moving through this labyrinthine approach route, people are liberated from the everyday and their consciousness is released into an extraordinary world.

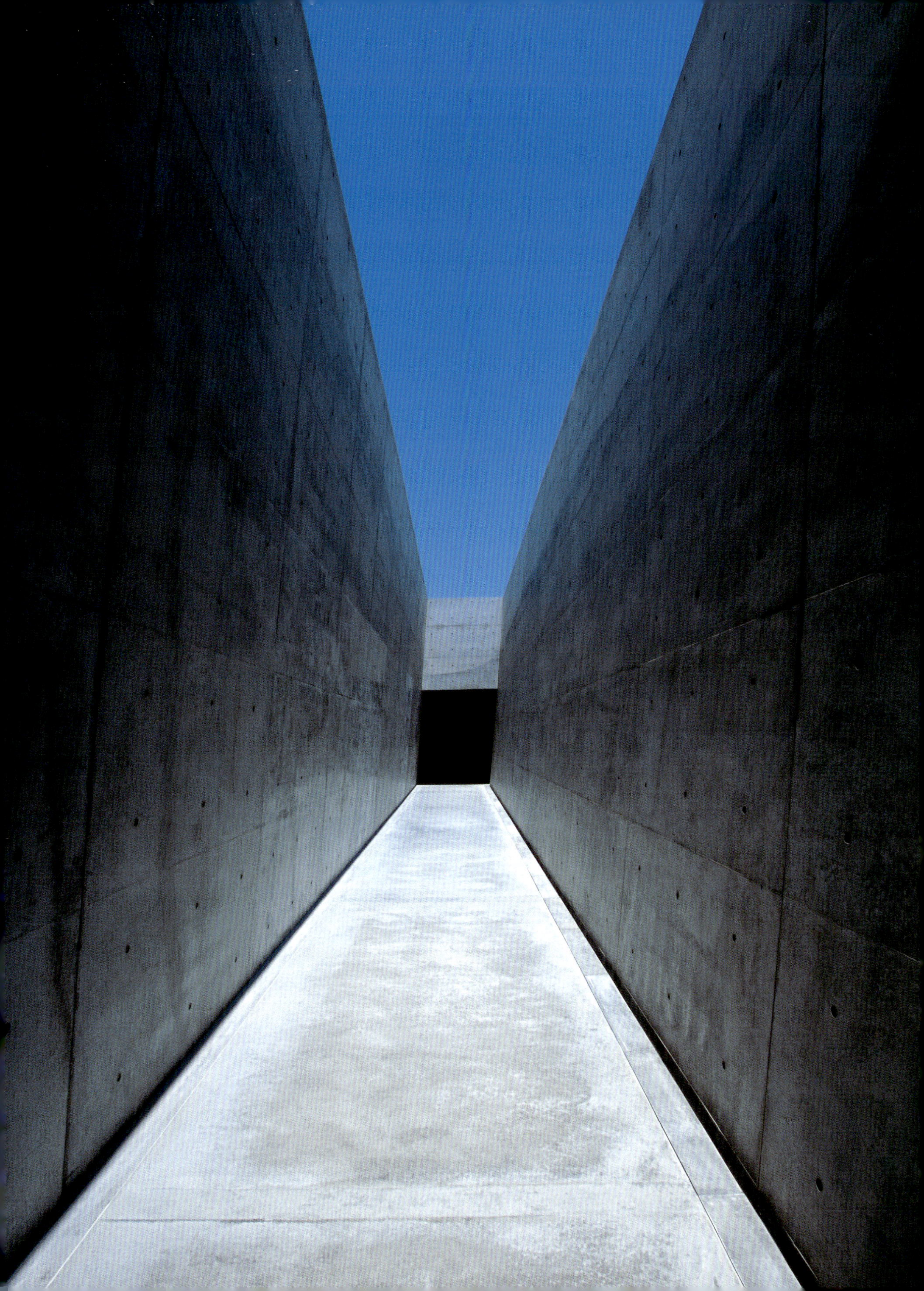

地下2階レベルのエントランスから延びる通路。
Passage extending from the entrance at the second basement level.

地下1階レベルの休憩スペース。
Resting space at the first basement level.

Axonometric

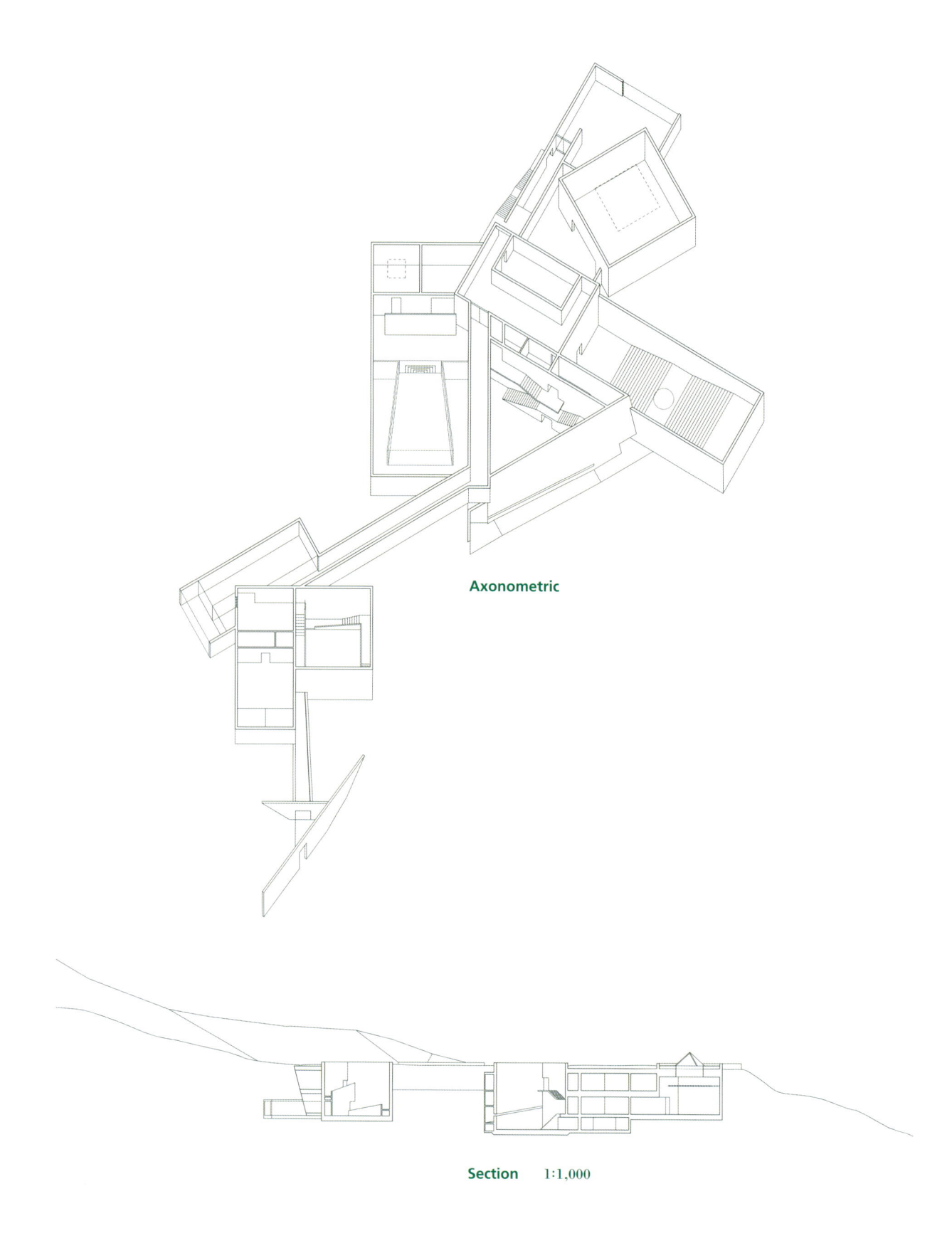

Section 1:1,000

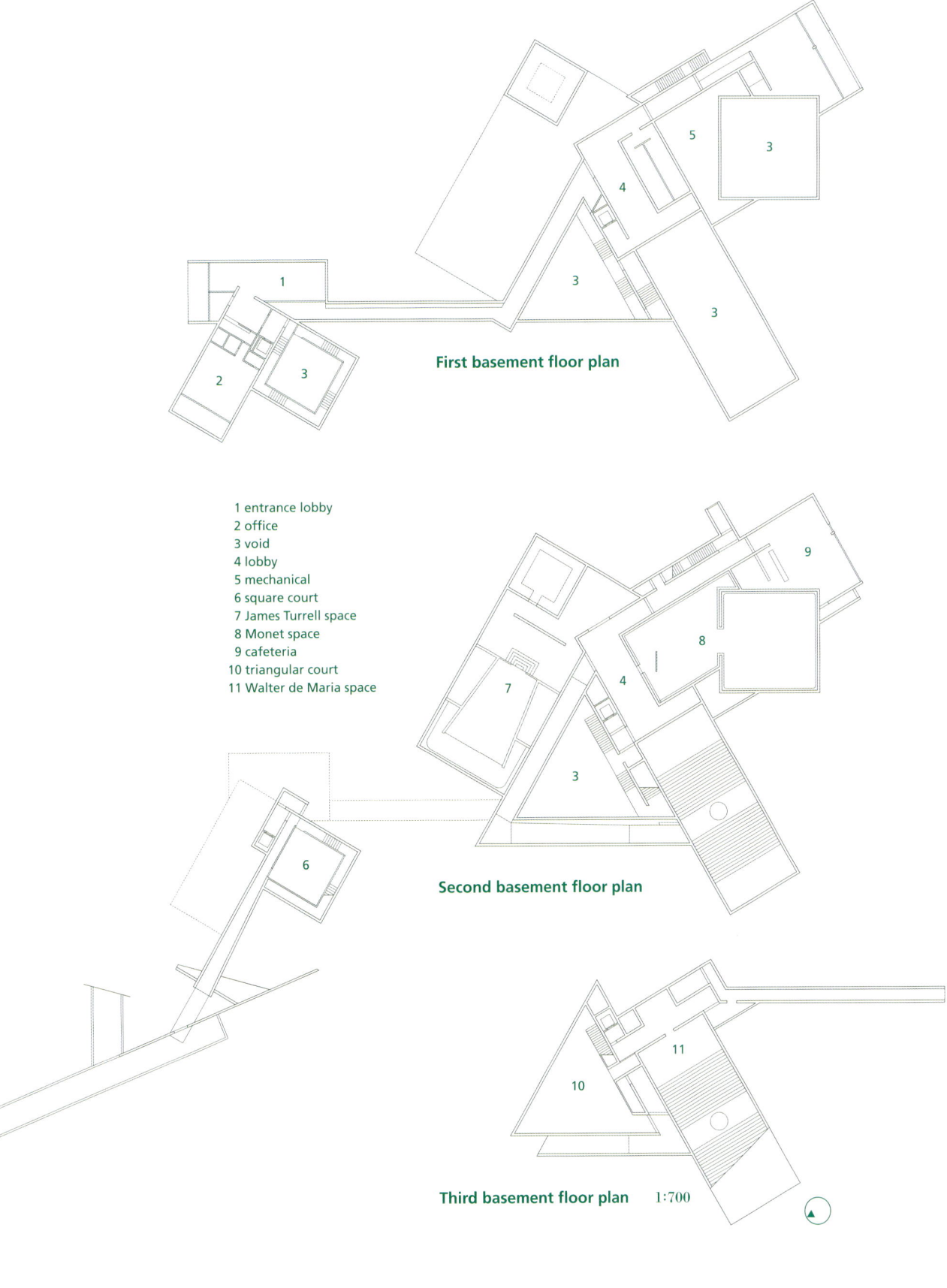

First basement floor plan

1 entrance lobby
2 office
3 void
4 lobby
5 mechanical
6 square court
7 James Turrell space
8 Monet space
9 cafeteria
10 triangular court
11 Walter de Maria space

Second basement floor plan

Third basement floor plan 1:700

393 Chichu Art Museum

ウォルター・デ・マリア・スペース。
作品名は「Time / Timeless / No Time」。東西に長い天窓から差し込む光が1日かけて室内を縦断する。数学的なデ・マリアのアートに、コンクリート、階段といった建築言語が巧みに取り込まれている。

Walter de Maria space. The name of the artwork is Time/Timeless/No Time. The illumination pouring in from a long east-west skylight slices across the interior over the course of a day. The mathematical art of de Maria is skillfully introduced to the architectural language of concrete and stairs.

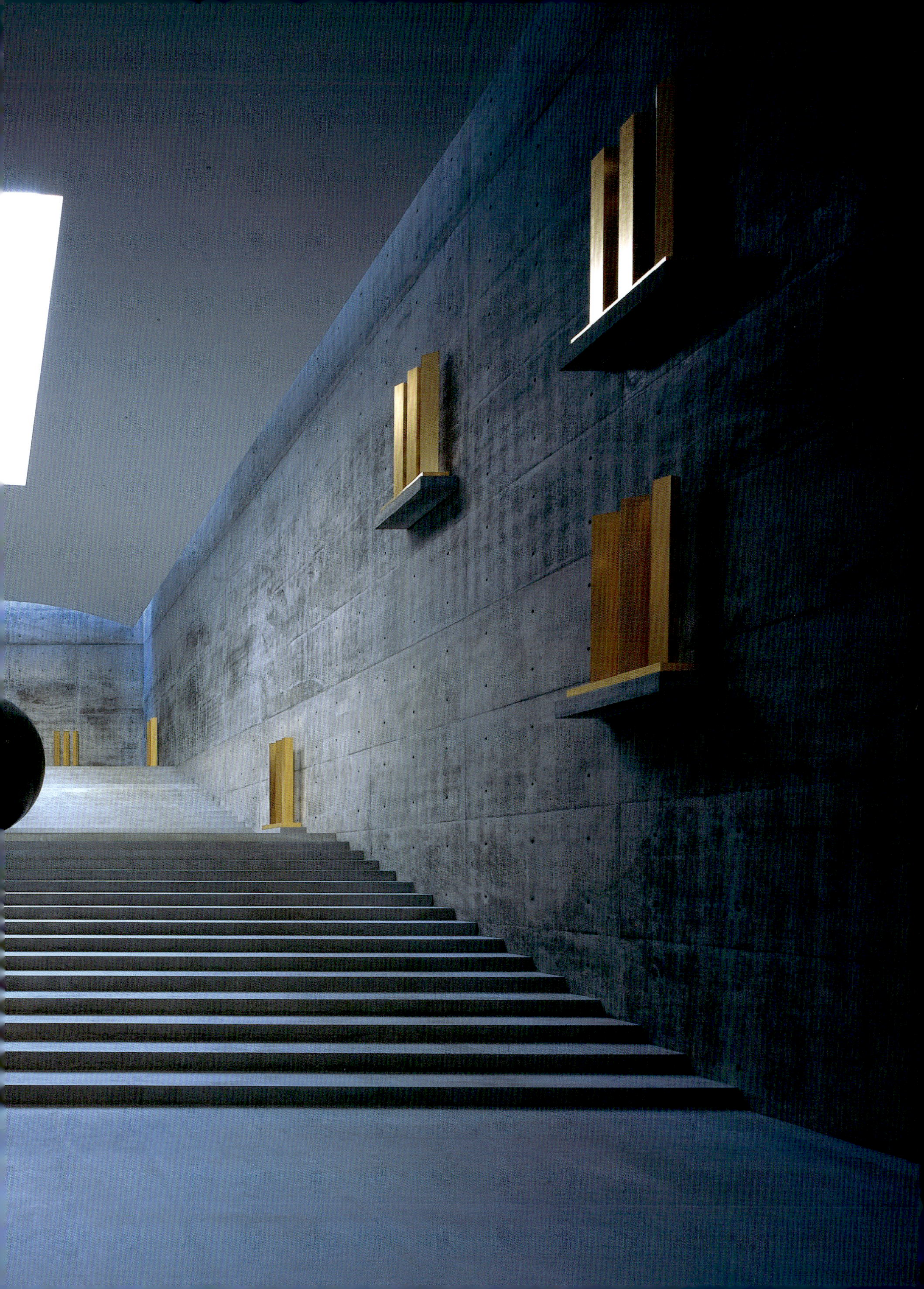

ジェームズ・タレル・スペース。光を主題とするタレルの代表作3点が収められている。上：強い光を投影する「Afrum, Pale Blue (1968)」。下：刻々と移り変わる光を体験する「Open Sky (2004)」。

クロード・モネ・スペース。5点の「睡蓮」を収める。粗めの漆喰壁と2cm角の大理石を敷き詰めた室内を、柔らかい間接光が包み込む。

Claude Monet space. This contains five works from his Water Lilies series. Soft indirect light suffuses the interior of rough plastered walls and 2cm-squares of marble covering the floor.

James Turrell space. It contains three masterpieces by Turrell, whose theme is light. Above: The strong light projection of Afrum, Pale Blue 1968. Below: Open Sky 2004 is a personal experience of light that changes from moment to moment.

大地に埋め込まれた光と闇の迷宮。地中美術館において、安藤に課されたのはアートを収める箱をつくることではない、もうひとりのアーティストとしての役割だった。

A labyrinth of light and darkness embedded in the earth. In the Chichu Art Museum, Ando did not merely make boxes to contain art, but has taken on the role of being one more artist.

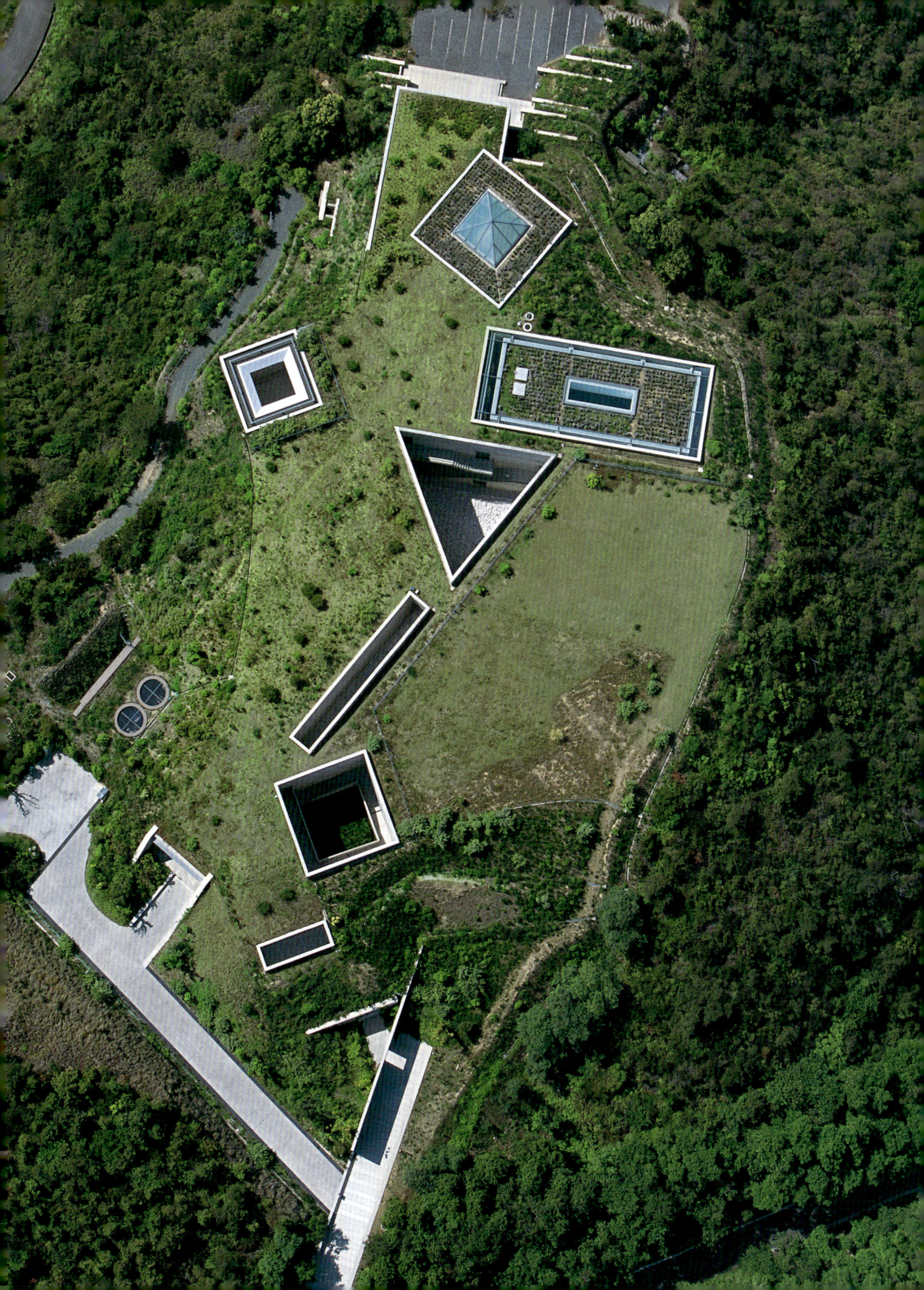

表参道ヒルズ（同潤会青山アパート建替計画）
Omotesando Hills (Omotesando Regeneration Project)
1996-2006　東京都渋谷区 —— Shibuya-ku, Tokyo

　敷地は東京のメインストリートのひとつ、青山の表参道に面して位置する。1920年代、関東大震災の復興事業として建設された同潤会青山アパートの跡につくられた、集合住宅と商業施設のコンプレックスである。

　旧アパートは、近代的な生活スタイルの礎をつくった日本のRC造中層アパートの先駆けであった。だが、その史的価値以上に、時を経たアパートのある街並みは、かけがえのない都市の原風景としての意味をももっていた。

　現状のままでの修復・再生は物理的、経済的に不可能であったが、私はその風景のエッセンスを抽出し、新たな現代建築として翻訳するという方法を試みた。要求される建物ヴォリュームの過半を地中に沈め、高さを表参道のケヤキの並木と同程度に低く抑えること。その中心にかつてのアパートが有していたような、豊かなパブリックスペースを内包すること。このふたつを新たに生まれる建築の前提とし、その上で、アパートを一部だけでも、そのままのかたちで残すことを提案した。

　建物は、表参道に約250mの連続したガラスのファサードを向ける商業施設を収めた基壇部分と、その上に浮かぶ住機能を収めたヴォリュームという、明快な図式の構成をもつ。基壇部分は、そのガラスの奥にかつてのアパートの中庭と同じ三角形の吹き抜けの広場をもつ。そのヴォイドを巡るスパイラルスロープは表参道と同じ勾配をもち、各フロアはこの〈建物内に引き込まれた坂道〉によって結ばれる。

　この建築において、最も多大なエネルギーが費やされたのは、〈記憶の継承〉という主題を巡る数多い地権者との対話のプロセスだった。市場原理の支配する都市にあって、建築はいかにあるべきか——公共性という主題をとりわけ深く考えさせられた仕事だった。

　The site is located facing Aoyama's Omotesando dori, one of Tokyo's main streets. This is a complex of housing and commercial facilities built on the remains of the Aoyama Dojunkai Apartments, which were a revitalization project constructed after the Great Kanto Earthquake in the 1920s.

　The old apartments were pioneering examples of Japan's reinforced concrete medium-rise apartments, intended as a foundation for modern lifestyles. However, beyond their historical value, the appearance of these long-standing apartments had significance as part of the irreplaceable original scenery of the city.

　Given their condition at that time, repair and regeneration was physically and economically impossible, but I attempted a method of drawing out the essence of that scenery and translating it into a new contemporary architecture. The greater part of the required building volume has been sunk into the ground, and its height has been kept to the same low level as the zelkova trees lining Omotesando dori. As if the old apartments still existed, abundant public space has been contained in the center. These were the two principles for the newly generated architecture, and I further proposed to leave at least one part of the apartments unaltered.

　The building has a clear schematic composition: a platform element devoted to commercial facilities with a continuous glazed façade approximately 250m long facing Omotesando dori, floating above which is a volume that contains residential facilities. Behind the glass, the platform element has a plaza void with the same triangular shape as the courtyard of the former apartments. The spiral ramp around the void has the same pitch as Omotesando dori, and every floor is linked by this hill road that draws people to the interior of the building.

　Most of the energy demanded by this building was for the process of dialogue with the multiple landowners around the theme of "inheritance of memory." How to make architecture in a city ruled by market principles? This is a work that above all made me think deeply about the theme of commonality.

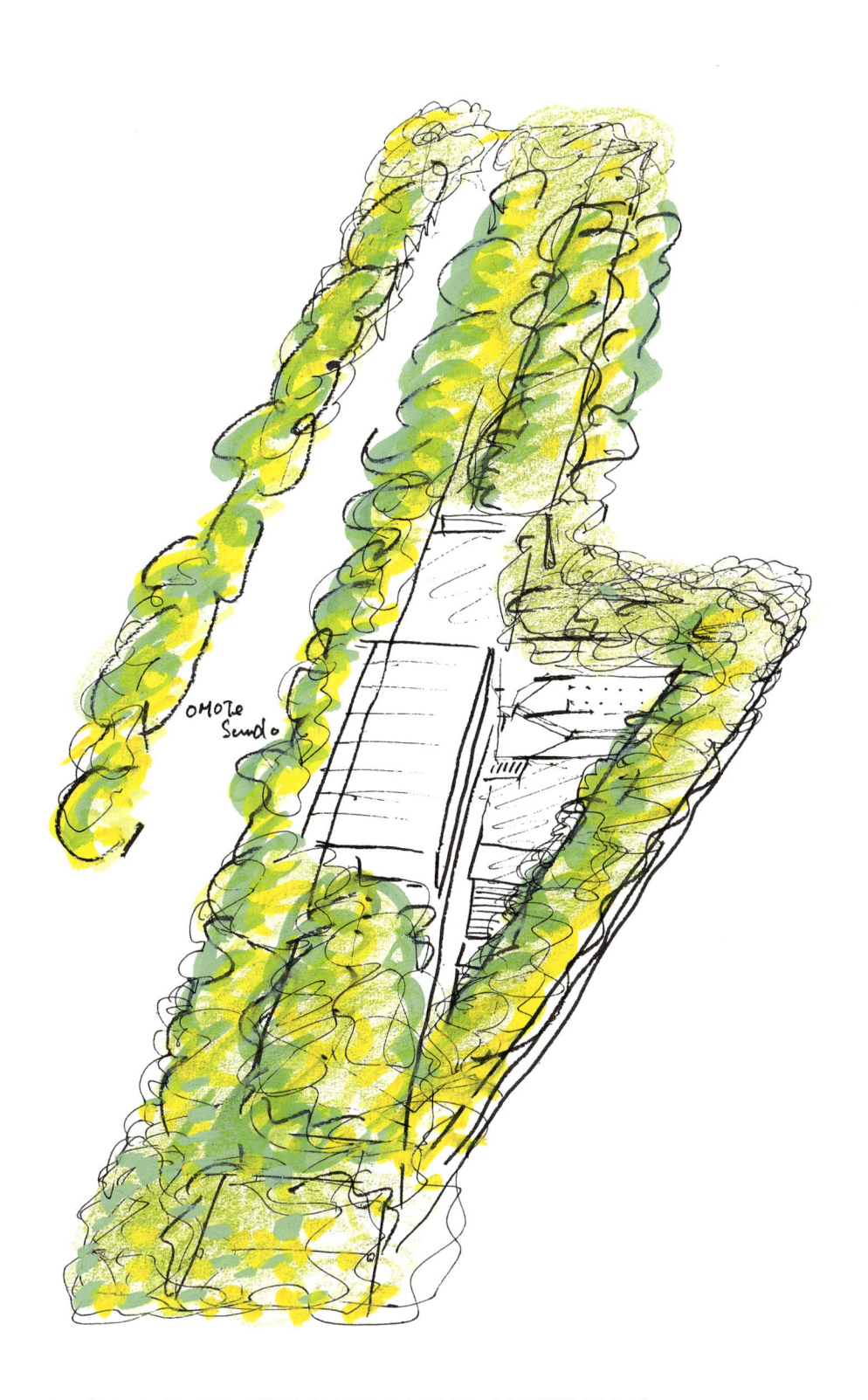

イメージスケッチ。旧アパートの輪郭をなぞりながら、ケヤキ並木と一体化する建築のイメージ。
Image sketch. An image of architecture unified with the roadside zelkova trees while tracing the profile of the old apartments.

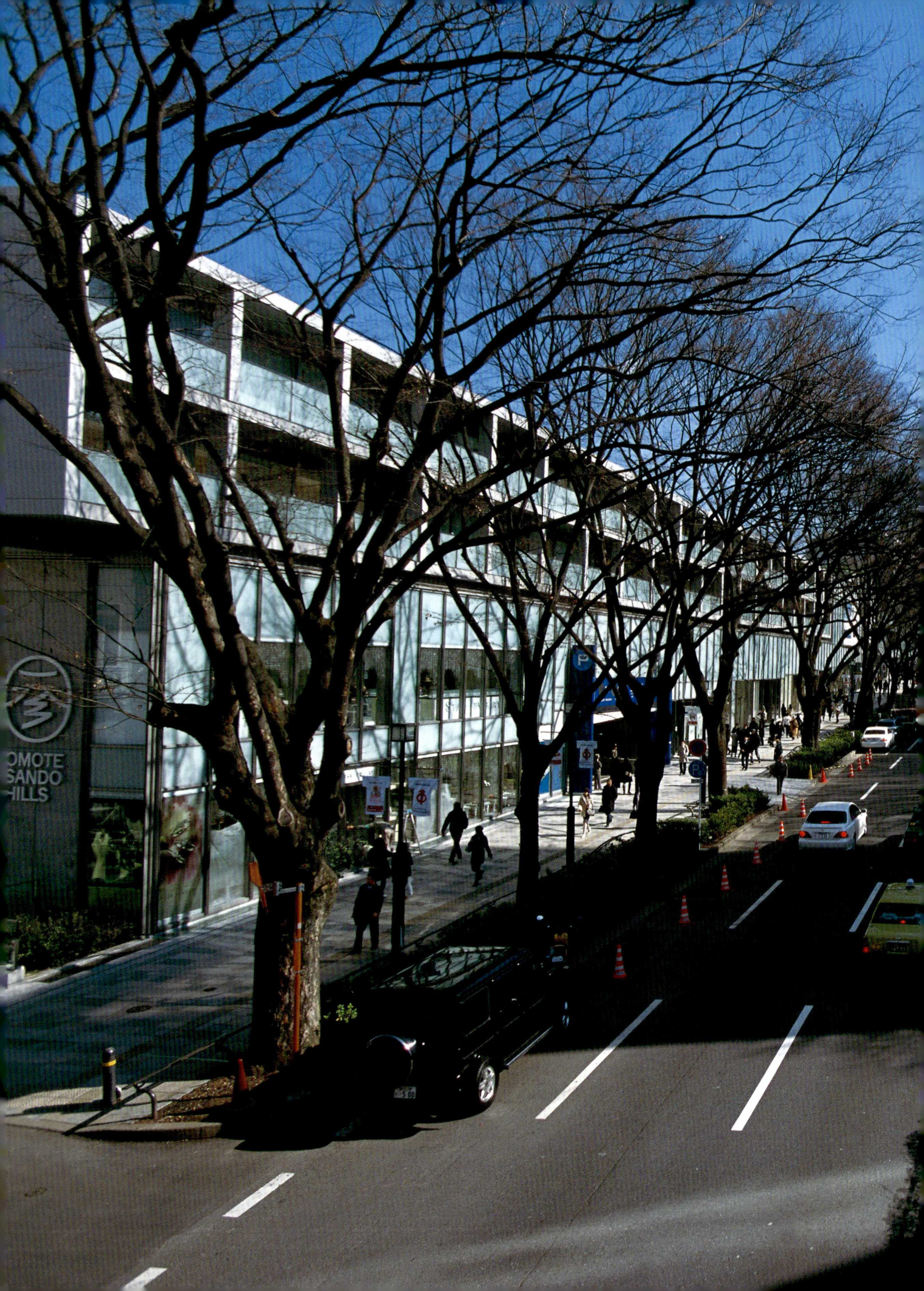
OMOTE
SANDO
HILLS

表参道越しに見るファサード。ケヤキ並木の高さに倣い、建物高さは23.3mに抑えられている。

View of the facade across Omotesando Street. The height of the building is limited to 23.3m, following the height of the zelkova trees along the road.

メインエントランスとなる、建物中央部に切り取られた三角形平面の広場。ガラススクリーン上部に住宅棟がはね出す。
A triangular plaza cut from the center of the building is the main entrance. The residential wing projects from above the glass screen.

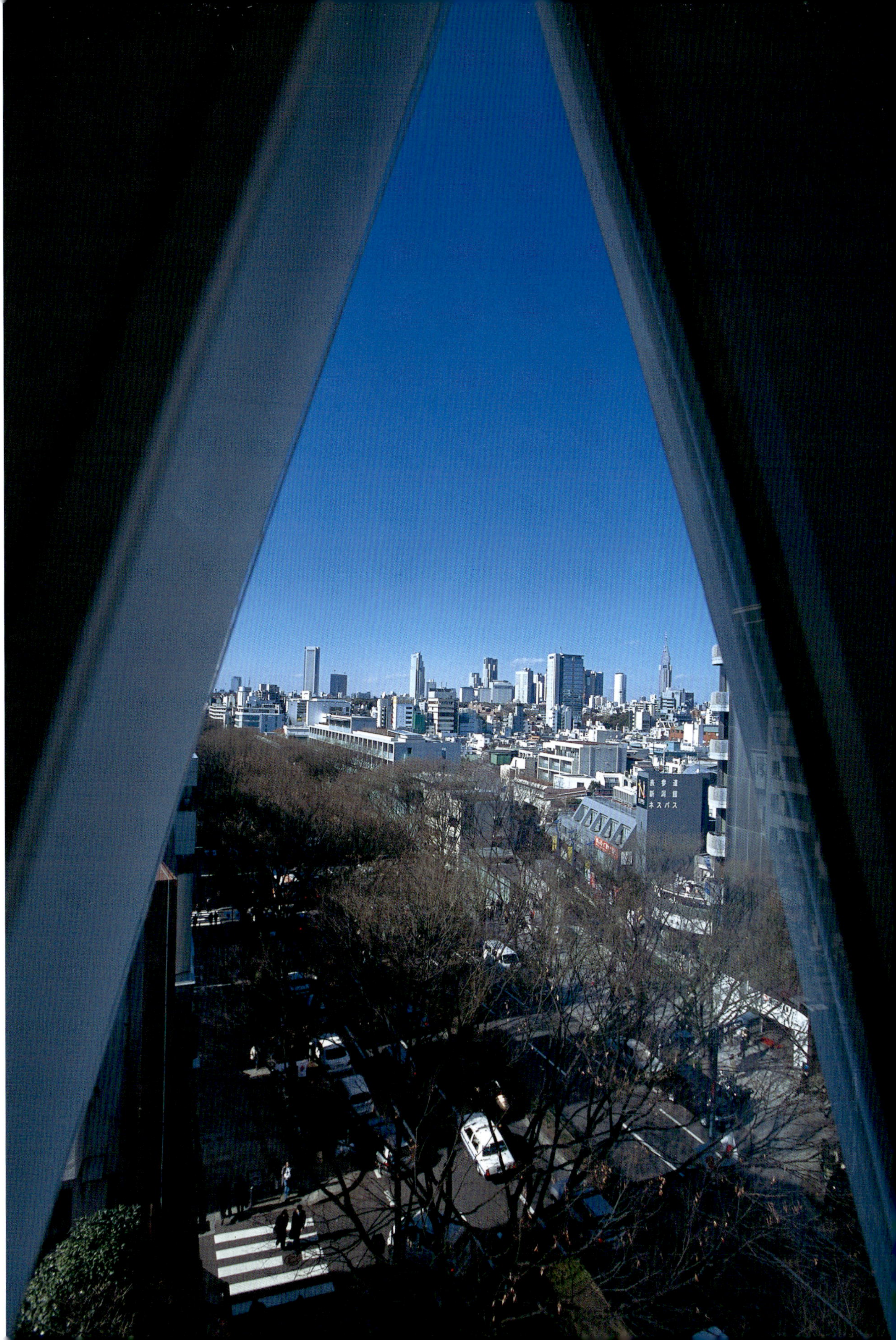
表参道
新潟館
ネスパス

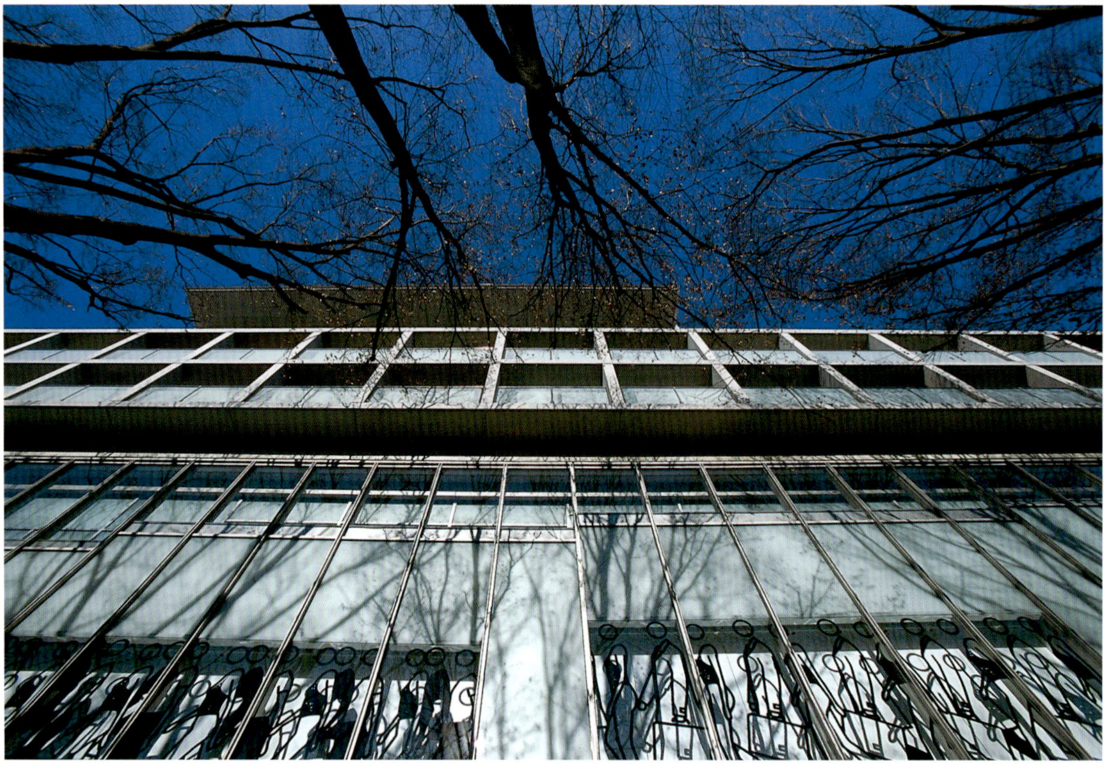

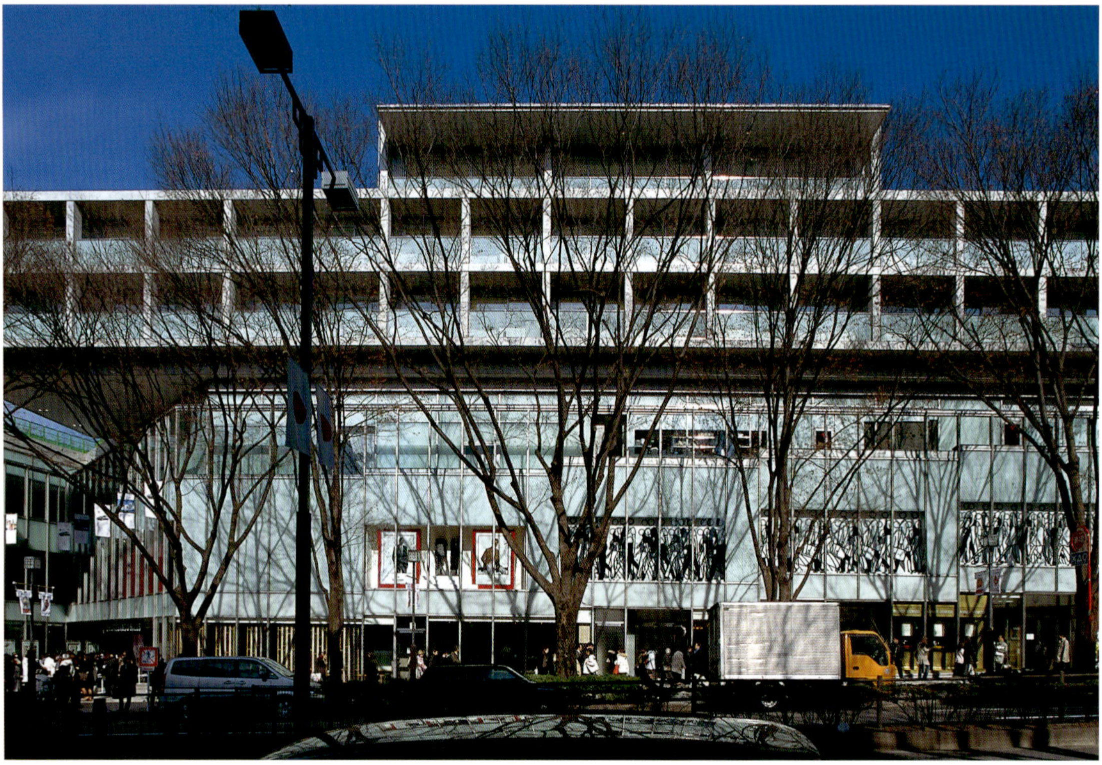

かつてのアパートの中庭を思い起こさせる、三角形の吹き抜け広場の周囲を全長700mのスパイラルスロープが巡る。店舗、レストランが連続して並ぶ斜路は、表参道と同じ1/20の勾配。

A spiral ramp with a total length of 700m follows the edge of an open triangular plaza, evoking the central garden of the former apartments. Lined with a series of shops and restaurants, this sloping path has a 1/20 pitch, like Omotesando Street.

250mの連続したガラスのファサードの背後に、地下3階から地上3階に及ぶ6層分の巨大な吹き抜け空間が潜む。

Lying behind the 250m-long glass facade is an enormous void space that extends over six levels, three floors below ground and three floors above ground.

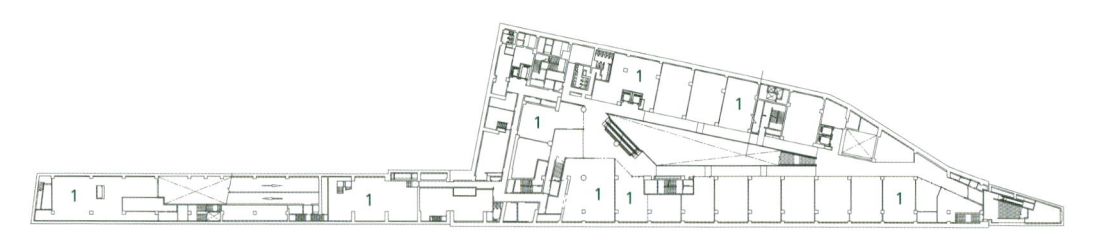

First basement floor plan

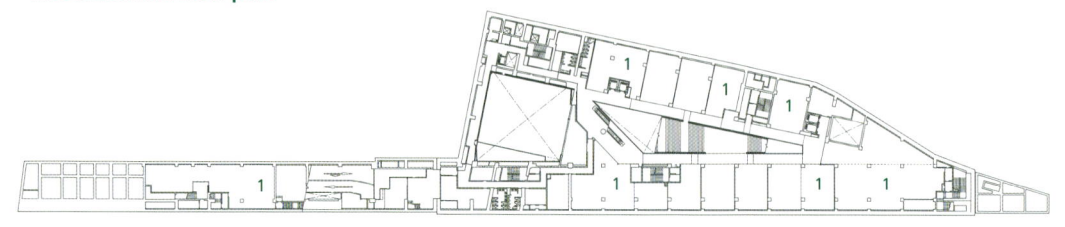

Second basement floor plan

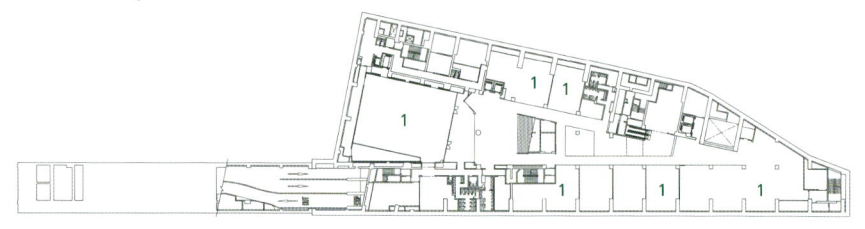

Third basement floor plan

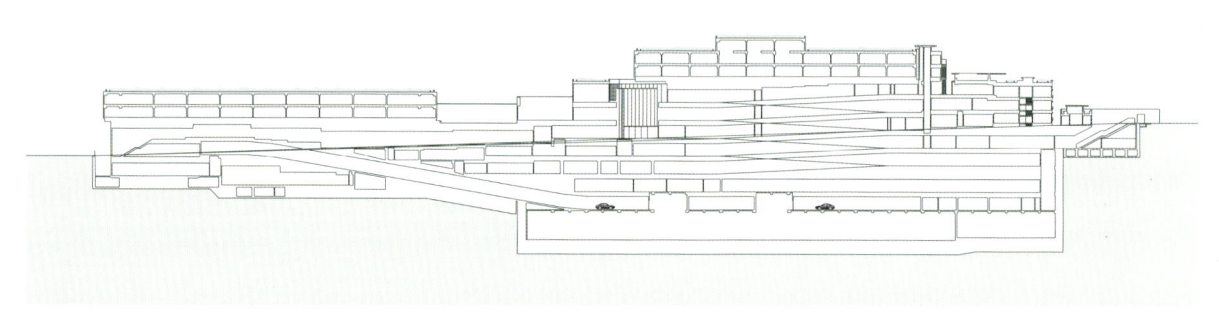

Section

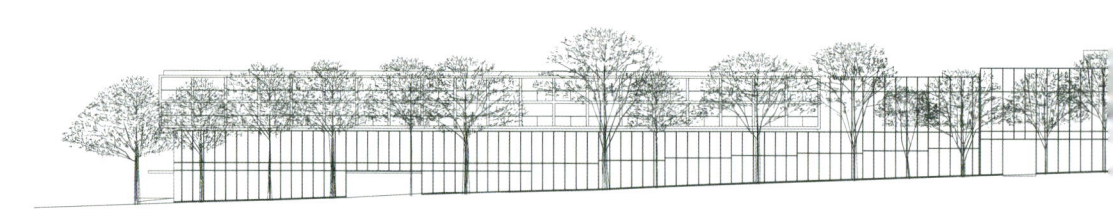

Elevation 1:900

Third floor plan

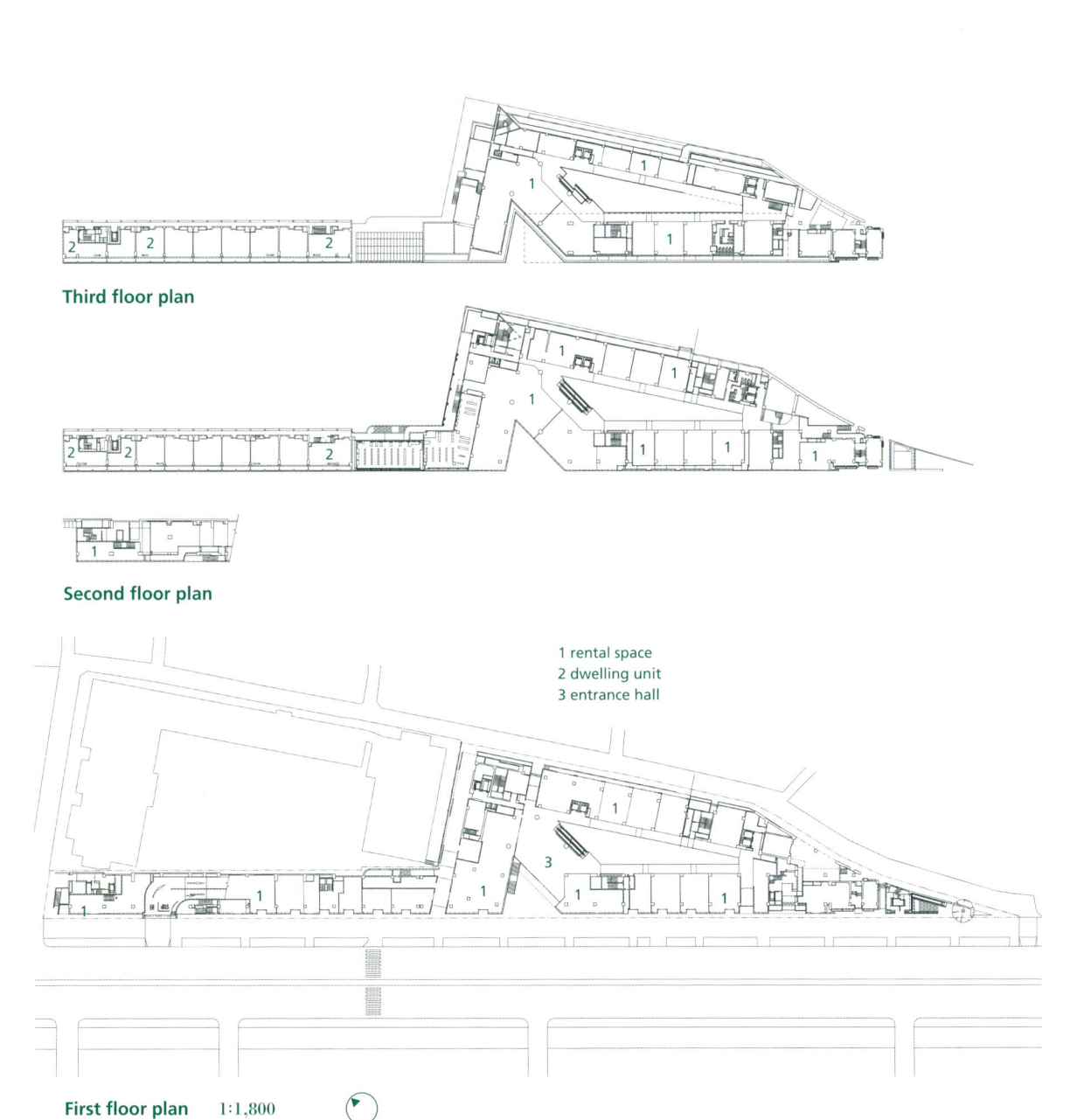

Second floor plan

1 rental space
2 dwelling unit
3 entrance hall

First floor plan 1:1,800

411 Omotesando Hills

左頁：旧アパートが存在した証として、南青山通り側に創建当時のアパートが1棟復元されている。
右頁：明治神宮の鬱蒼とした森から連続する表参道のケヤキ並木。その緑の軸線に沿って、屋上植栽を設けた建物が佇む。

Left page: As evidence of the existence of the old apartments, one section of the apartments built at that time has been restored adjacent to Minami-Aoyama Street.
Right page: The roadside zelkova trees of Omotesando Street are continuous with the dense forest of Meiji Shrine. The building stands along this green axis, with planting on its rooftop.

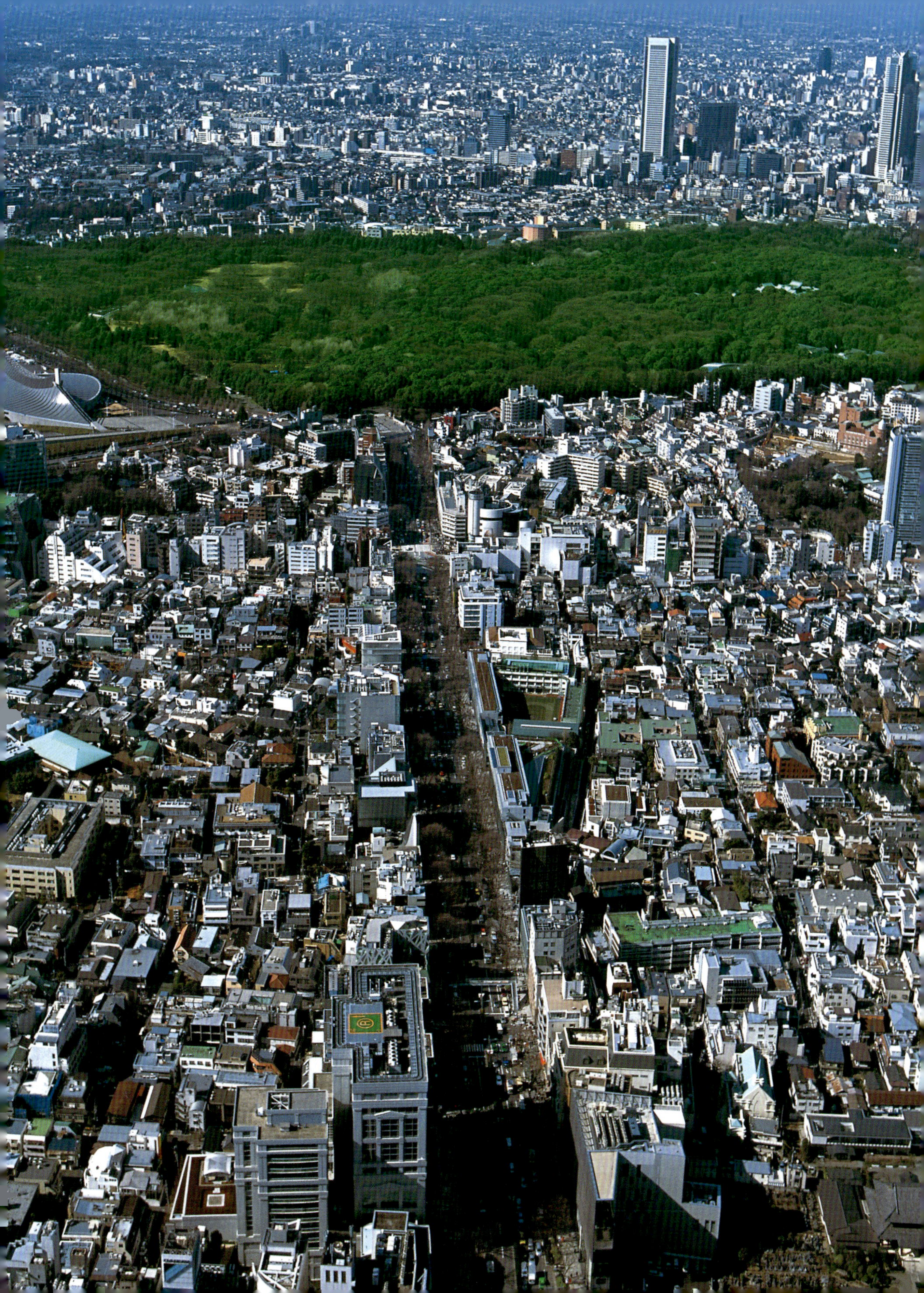

東京・六本木の旧防衛庁跡地再開発プロジェクト「東京ミッドタウン」の中につくられた、デザインをテーマとするギャラリー施設である。「21_21 DESIGN SIGHT」の企画は、国際的に活躍するファッションデザイナー、三宅一生を中心とするプロジェクトチームの発案に始まった。

　2003年の基本構想スタートから、2005年の着工に至るまで、プログラム、敷地も定まらないまま数回の計画変更を経て、最終的に落ち着いたのが、ミッドタウン北西の緑豊かなオープンスペースの敷地にふたつのギャラリーをもつ施設をつくるという計画である。設計の与条件として最も大きかったのは、都市計画に指定された公共空地という立地ゆえの建築制限であり、このため建物のほとんどのヴォリュームを地下に埋める必要があった。ならば、地下空間と連続して地上に現れる部分にいかなるかたちを与えるか——周囲の環境と一体化する〈ランドスケープとしての建築〉がひとつの主題となった。

　いくつかのバリエーションを考える中で、1枚の鉄板屋根による〈折り紙〉のようなイメージが浮かんだ。これは三宅一生がかつて提案した「1枚の布が、それを身につける身体の個性によって異なる立体のフォルムをつくり出す」という1枚の布のコンセプトに着想を得たものだ。

　建物は、敷地形状に沿って浮かぶ大小2枚の鉄板が、それぞれに一端を地面に接するよう折り曲げたかたちの、慎ましい構えをもつ。大きい方の鉄板が覆う棟の不定形な輪郭を補完するようなかたちで、内外にまたがる吹き抜けのヴォイドが穿たれている。地下に光と風を引き込むそのヴォイドを取り巻くように、大小ふたつのギャラリーが配されている。

　全長54mに及ぶ屋根を1枚の鉄板としてつくる技術的困難に加え、めまぐるしく変わる設計条件への対応に多くの時間を費やされたことで、工程は極めて厳しいものになった。現場のつくり手たちの高い技術力と、建築にかける情熱が、その難工事を可能にした。

21_21 DESIGN SIGHT
21_21 DESIGN SIGHT
2004-07 　東京都港区——Minato-ku, Tokyo

イメージスケッチ。2枚の鉄板を折り曲げてつくられる、軽やかな建築のイメージが描かれている。

Image sketches. Depicting the image of a light building made by folding two sheets of steel.

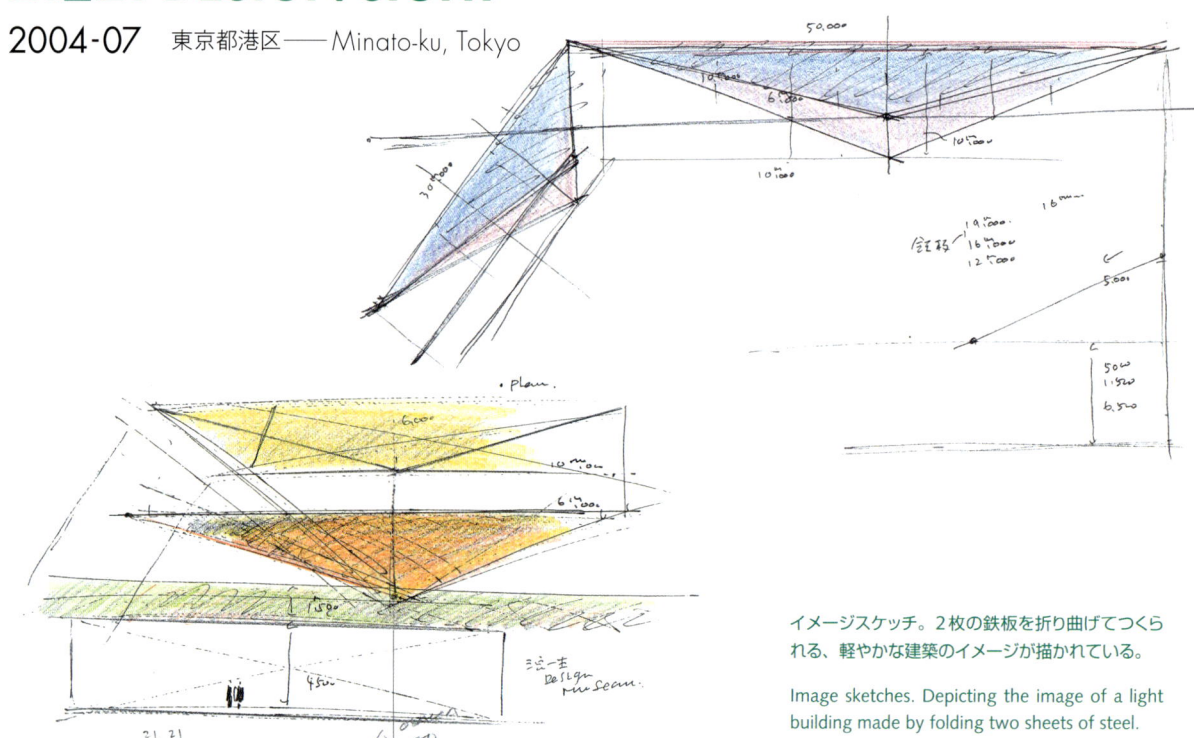

Constructed within Tokyo Midtown, a redevelopment project on the former site of the Defense Ministry in the Roppongi district of Tokyo, this is a gallery for exhibitions on the theme of design. The 21_21 DESIGN SIGHT project began as a proposal by a project team centered on the international fashion designer Issey Miyake.

From the start of the basic concept in 2003 until the start of construction in 2005, following numerous design stages in which the program and site were undecided, we finally arrived at a design for a facility containing two galleries on a site with abundant green open space located to the northwest of Tokyo Midtown. The main given conditions for the design were the building regulations on the site location, designated as public space in the urban planning, and the consequent necessity to bury most of the building volume underground. What form should be given to the part that appears above ground and is continuous with the underground spaces? One theme was "architecture as a landscape" integrated with the surrounding environment.

While considering several variations, an origami-like image appeared, with a roof comprising a single sheet of steel. I obtained this idea from the concept of Issey Miyake's A Piece Of Cloth, in which a single piece of fabric produces a different three-dimensional form depending on the personality of the body wearing it.

The building is a discrete intervention of bent shapes, as if two floating steel sheets—one large, one small—following the shape of the site each come into contact with the earth at one end. In a shape complementing the irregular contours of the wing covered by the larger steel sheet, a void is excavated that straddles interior and exterior. A large and a small gallery are arranged as if surrounding this void, which draws light and wind underground.

By increasing the technical difficulties by making a roof with total length of 54m out of a single steel sheet, and devoting a great deal of time to dealing with the rapidly changing design conditions, the construction period became very tight. This difficult construction project was made possible by the excellent technical skills of the on-site workers and their passion for architecture.

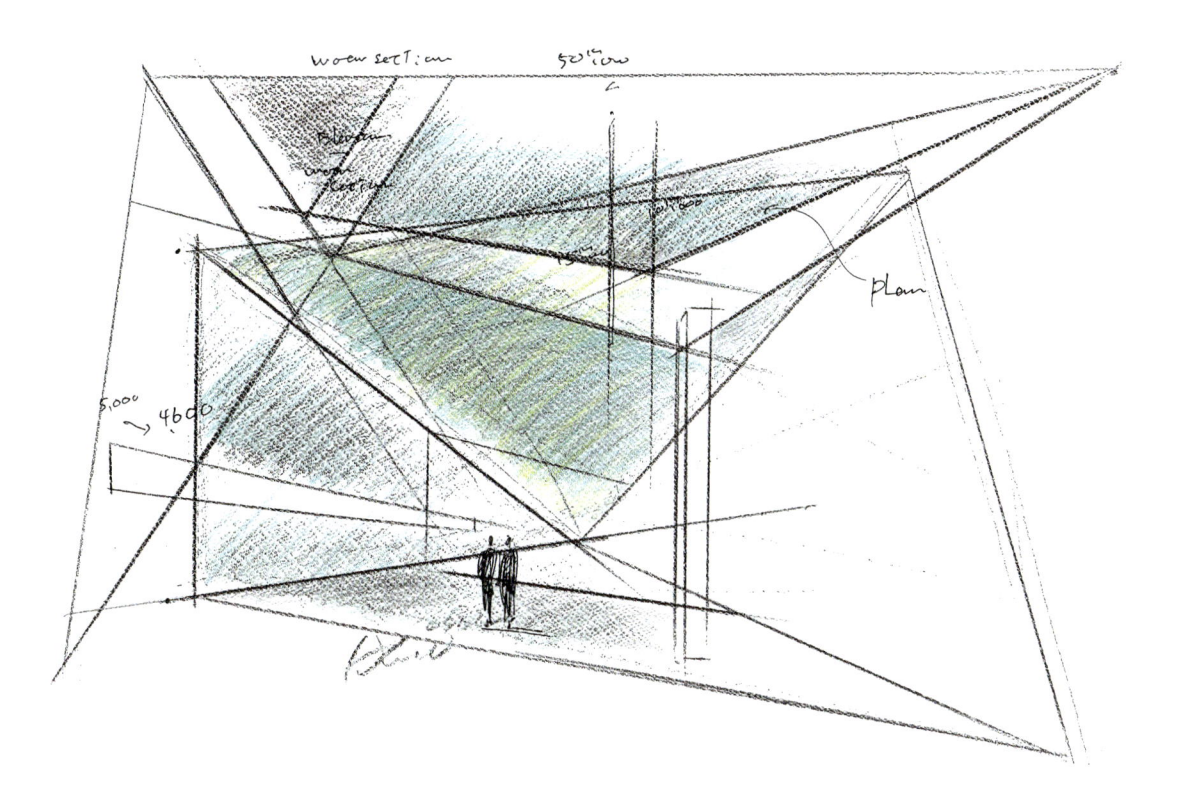

アプローチの芝生越しに建物全景を見る。2枚の平滑な鉄板の
屋根が形づくる環境に溶け込むような佇まい。
左がカフェ棟、右が地下にギャラリーをもつミュージアム棟。

Panoramic view of the entire building across the lawn of
the approach route. Formed by a roof comprising two flat
sheets of steel, it appears to melt into the environment.
On the left is the cafe wing, while on the right is the museum
wing containing the underground galleries.

417 21_21 DESIGN SIGHT

ミュージアム棟エントランスロビー。床面まで傾斜する大屋根が三角形に風景を切り取る。天井高さは最高部で4.4m。

Entrance lobby of the museum wing. The inclined roof slopes to the floor surface, framing the scenery in a triangle. The ceiling is 4.4m at its highest point.

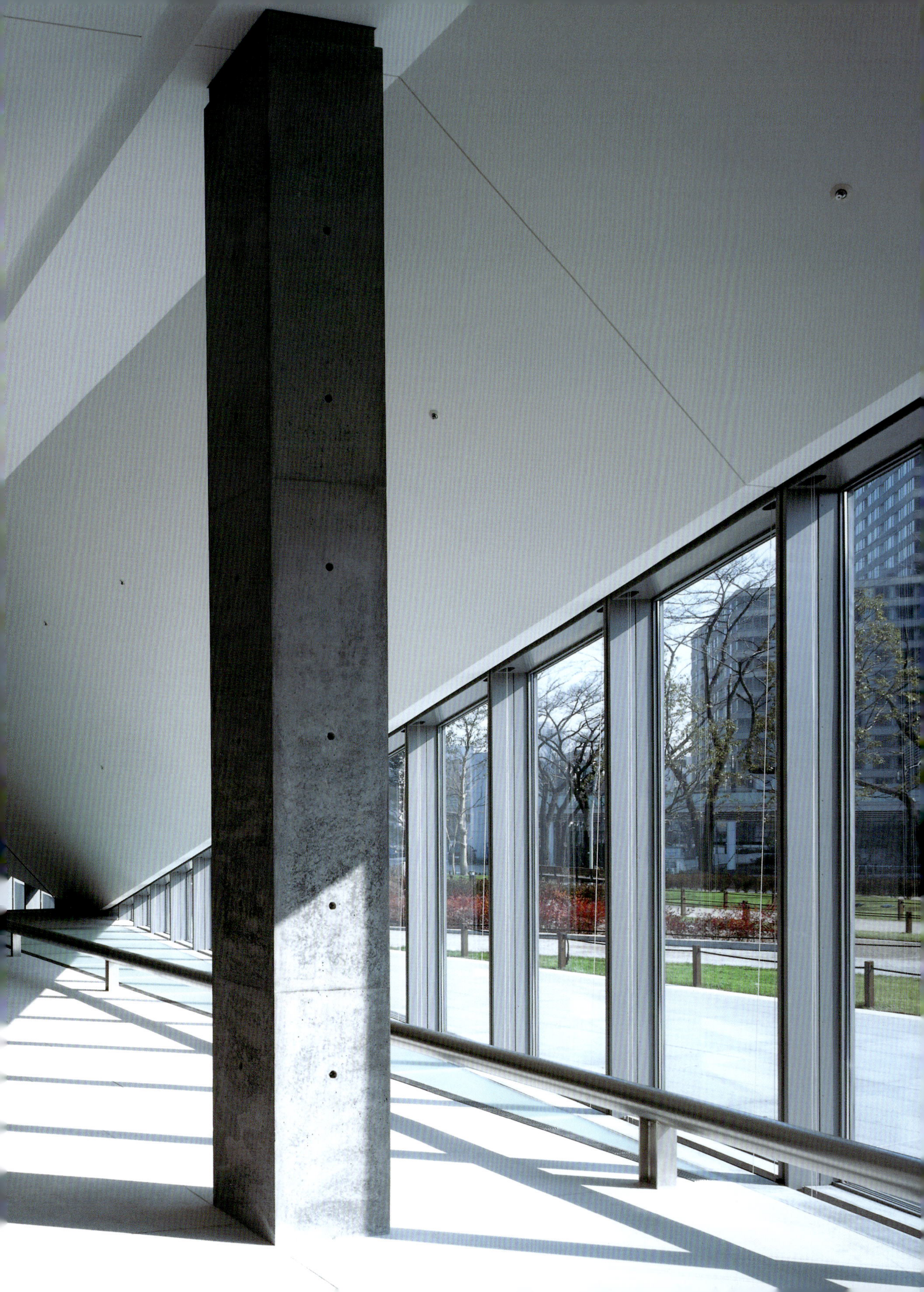

エントランスロビーから地下のギャラリーへと人々を導く吹き抜け階段。鋭角をなす建物形状を補完するような平面形状をもつサンクンコートに面して、キャンティレバーのコンクリート階段が浮遊する。

Stairwell leading people from the entrance lobby to the underground galleries. The cantilevered concrete stairs float facing the sunken court, which has a plan shape that completes the acute angles of the building shape.

三角形に空を切り取るサンクンコート。2層分の高さの
カーテンウォール越しに地下深くまで自然光が入り込む。

Sunken court framing the sky in a triangle. Natural
light penetrates deep underground through the two-
storey-high curtain wall.

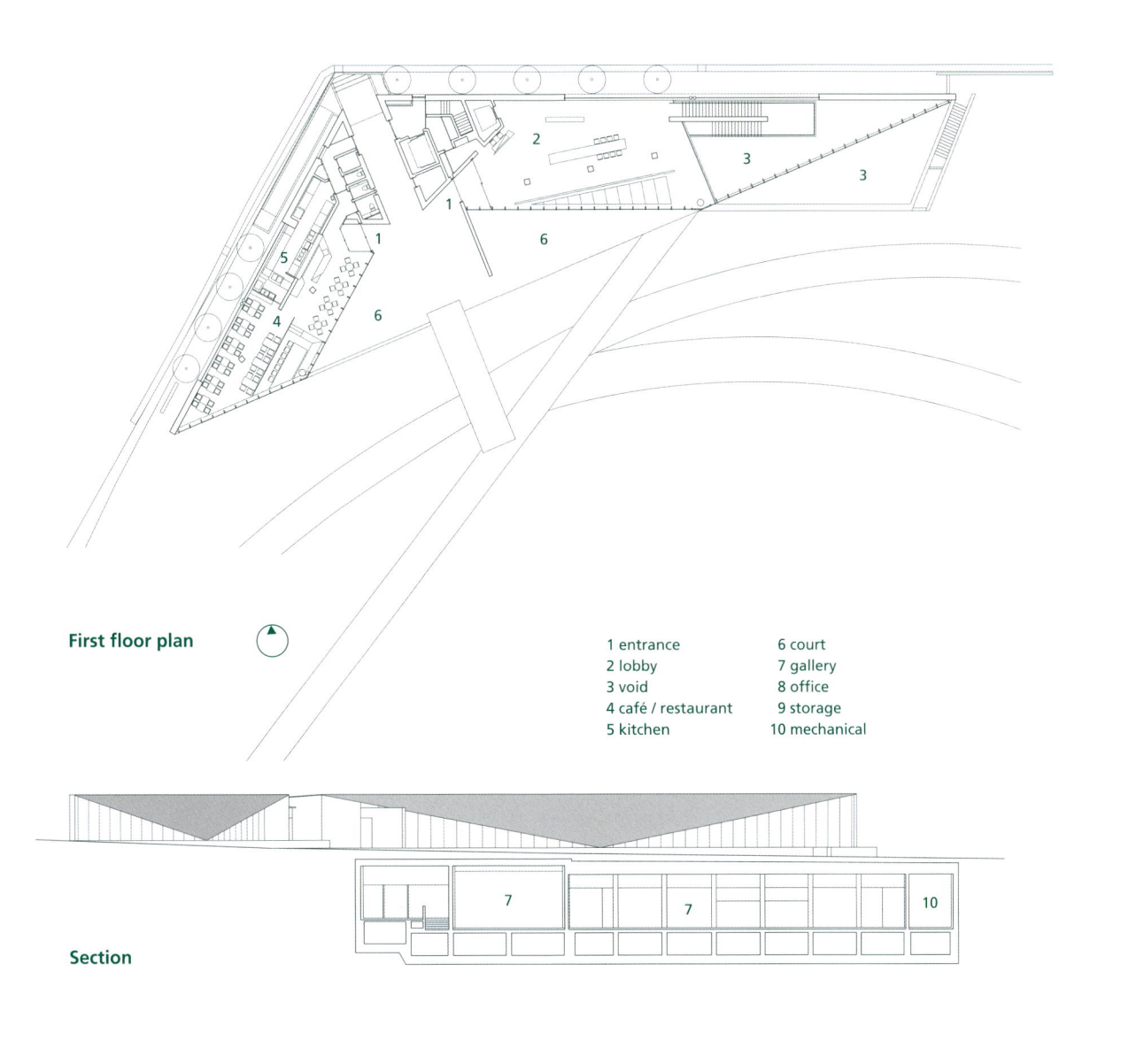

First floor plan

1 entrance
2 lobby
3 void
4 café / restaurant
5 kitchen
6 court
7 gallery
8 office
9 storage
10 mechanical

Section

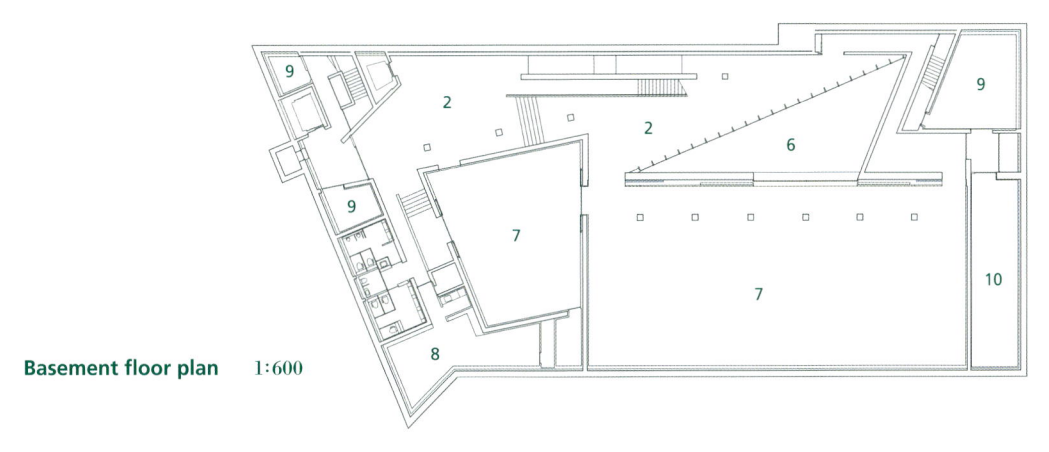

Basement floor plan 1:600

423 21_21 DESIGN SIGHT

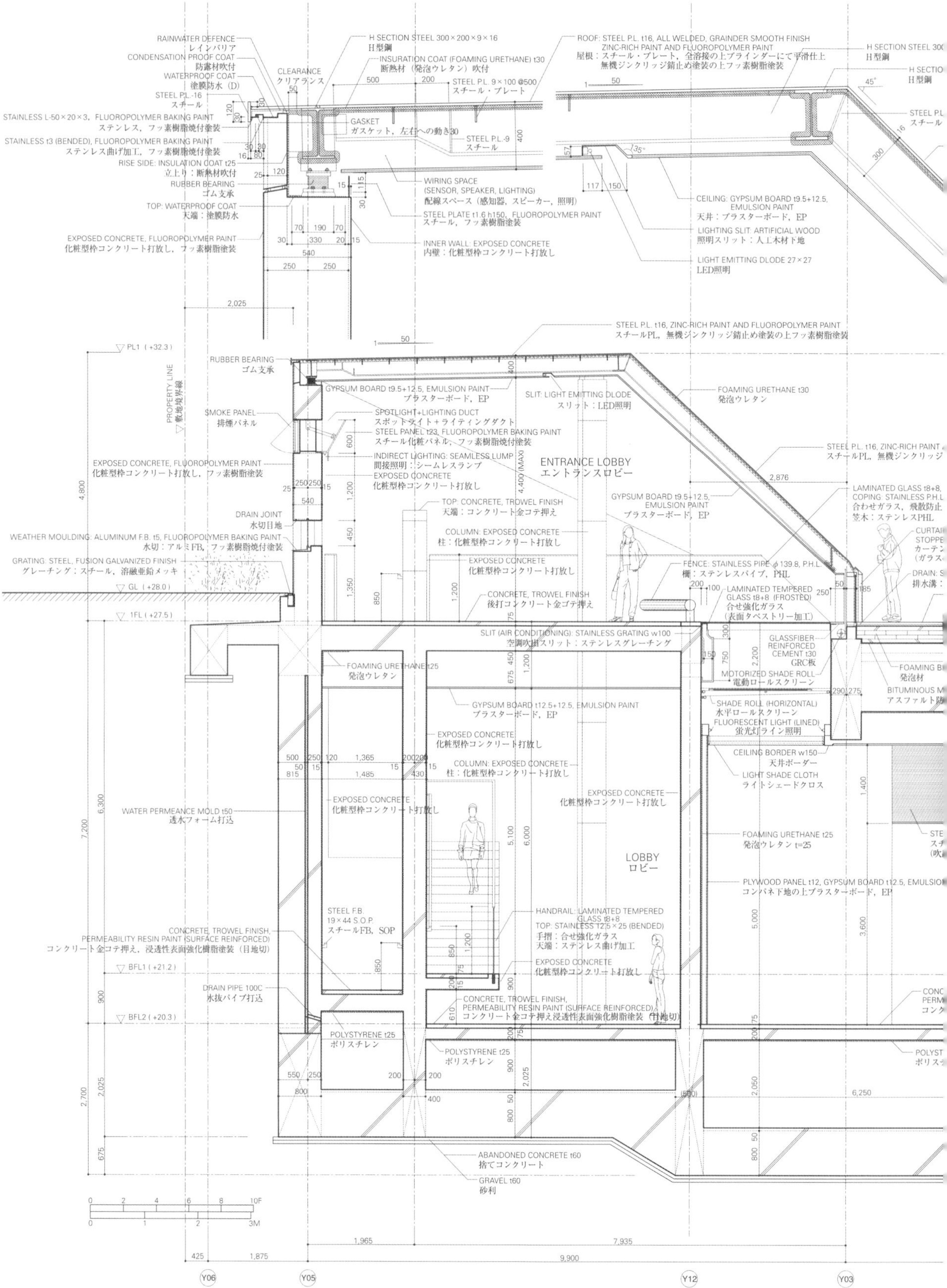
RAINWATER DEFENCE
レインバリア
CONDENSATION PROOF COAT
防露材吹付
WATERPROOF COAT
塗膜防水（D）
STEEL P.L.-16
スチール
STAINLESS L-50×20×3, FLUOROPOLYMER BAKING PAINT
ステンレス，フッ素樹脂焼付塗装
STAINLESS t3 (BENDED), FLUOROPOLYMER BAKING PAINT
ステンレス曲げ加工，フッ素樹脂焼付塗装
RISE SIDE: INSULATION COAT t25
立上り：断熱材吹付
RUBBER BEARING
ゴム支承
TOP: WATERPROOF COAT
天端：塗膜防水
EXPOSED CONCRETE, FLUOROPOLYMER PAINT
化粧型枠コンクリート打放し，フッ素樹脂塗装
CLEARANCE
クリアランス
H SECTION STEEL 300×200×9×16
H型鋼
INSURATION COAT (FOAMING URETHANE) t30
断熱材（発泡ウレタン）吹付
STEEL P.L. 9×100 @500
スチール・プレート
GASKET
ガスケット，左右への動き30
STEEL P.L.-9
スチール
WIRING SPACE
(SENSOR, SPEAKER, LIGHTING)
配線スペース（感知器，スピーカー，照明）
STEEL PLATE t1.6 h150, FLUOROPOLYMER PAINT
スチール，フッ素樹脂塗装
INNER WALL: EXPOSED CONCRETE
内壁：化粧型枠コンクリート打放し
ROOF: STEEL P.L. t16, ALL WELDED, GRAINDER SMOOTH FINISH
ZINC-RICH PAINT AND FLUOROPOLYMER PAINT
屋根：スチール・プレート，全溶接の上グラインダーにて平滑仕上
無機ジンクリッジ錆止め塗装の上フッ素樹脂塗装
H SECTION STEEL 300
H型鋼
H SECTIO
H型鋼
STEEL P.L
スチール
CEILING: GYPSUM BOARD t9.5+12.5,
EMULSION PAINT
天井：プラスターボード，EP
LIGHTING SLIT: ARTIFICIAL WOOD
照明スリット：人工木材下地
LIGHT EMITTING DLODE 27×27
LED照明
STEEL P.L. t16, ZINC-RICH PAINT AND FLUOROPOLYMER PAINT
スチールPL，無機ジンクリッジ錆止め塗装の上フッ素樹脂塗装
PL1 (+32.3)
PROPERTY LINE
敷地境界線
RUBBER BEARING
ゴム支承
SMOKE PANEL
排煙パネル
EXPOSED CONCRETE, FLUOROPOLYMER PAINT
化粧型枠コンクリート打放し，フッ素樹脂塗装
DRAIN JOINT
水切目地
WEATHER MOULDING: ALUMINUM F.B. t5, FLUOROPOLYMER BAKING PAINT
水切：アルミFB，フッ素樹脂焼付塗装
GRATING: STEEL, FUSION GALVANIZED FINISH
グレーチング：スチール，溶融亜鉛メッキ
GL (+28.0)
1FL (+27.5)
GYPSUM BOARD t9.5+12.5, EMULSION PAINT
プラスターボード，EP
SPOTLIGHT+LIGHTING DUCT
スポットライト＋ライティングダクト
STEEL PANEL t23, FLUOROPOLYMER BAKING PAINT
スチール化粧パネル，フッ素樹脂焼付塗装
INDIRECT LIGHTING: SEAMLESS LUMP
間接照明：シームレスランプ
EXPOSED CONCRETE
化粧型枠コンクリート打放し
TOP: CONCRETE, TROWEL FINISH
天端：コンクリート金ゴテ押え
COLUMN: EXPOSED CONCRETE
柱：化粧型枠コンクリート打放し
EXPOSED CONCRETE
化粧型枠コンクリート打放し
CONCRETE, TROWEL FINISH
後打コンクリート金ゴテ押え
SLIT: LIGHT EMITTING DLODE
スリット：LED照明
ENTRANCE LOBBY
エントランスロビー
FOAMING URETHANE t30
発泡ウレタン
STEEL P.L. t16, ZINC-RICH PAINT
スチールPL，無機ジンクリッジ
GYPSUM BOARD t9.5+12.5,
EMULSION PAINT
プラスターボード，EP
LAMINATED GLASS t8+8,
COPING: STAINLESS P.H.L
合わせガラス，飛散防止
笠木：ステンレスPHL
FENCE: STAINLESS PIPE φ139.8, P.H.L.
柵：ステンレスパイプ，PHL
LAMINATED TEMPERED
GLASS t8+8 (FROSTED)
合せ強化ガラス
(表面タペストリー加工)
SLIT (AIR CONDITIONING): STAINLESS GRATING w100
空調吹出スリット：ステンレスグレーチング
GLASSFIBER
REINFORCED
CEMENT t30
GRC板
MOTORIZED SHADE ROLL
電動ロールスクリーン
SHADE ROLL (HORIZONTAL)
水平ロールスクリーン
FLUORESCENT LIGHT (LINED)
蛍光灯ライン照明
CEILING BORDER w150
天井ボーダー
LIGHT SHADE CLOTH
ライトシェードクロス
FOAMING URETHANE t25
発泡ウレタン t=25
PLYWOOD PANEL t12, GYPSUM BOARD t12.5, EMULSION
コンパネ下地の上プラスターボード，EP
FOAMING URETHANE t25
発泡ウレタン
GYPSUM BOARD t12.5+12.5, EMULSION PAINT
プラスターボード，EP
EXPOSED CONCRETE
化粧型枠コンクリート打放し
COLUMN: EXPOSED CONCRETE
柱：化粧型枠コンクリート打放し
EXPOSED CONCRETE
化粧型枠コンクリート打放し
EXPOSED CONCRETE
化粧型枠コンクリート打放し
WATER PERMEANCE MOLD t50
透水フォーム打込
LOBBY
ロビー
STEEL F.B.
19×44 S.O.P.
スチールFB，SOP
CONCRETE, TROWEL FINISH,
PERMEABILITY RESIN PAINT (SURFACE REINFORCED)
コンクリート金ゴテ押え，浸透性表面強化樹脂塗装（目地切）
HANDRAIL: LAMINATED TEMPERED
GLASS t8+8
TOP: STAINLESS t12.5×25 (BENDED)
手摺：合せ強化ガラス
天端：ステンレス曲げ加工
EXPOSED CONCRETE
化粧型枠コンクリート打放し
BFL1 (+21.2)
DRAIN PIPE 100C
水抜パイプ打込
BFL2 (+20.3)
CONCRETE, TROWEL FINISH,
PERMEABILITY RESIN PAINT (SURFACE REINFORCED)
コンクリート金ゴテ押え浸透性表面強化樹脂塗装（目地切）
POLYSTYRENE t25
ポリスチレン
POLYSTYRENE t25
ポリスチレン
ABANDONED CONCRETE t60
捨てコンクリート
GRAVEL t60
砂利
FOAMING B
発泡材
BITUMINOUS M
アスファルト防
Y06
Y05
Y12
Y03
1,965
7,935
425
1,875
9,900
0 2 4 6 8 10F
0 1 2 3M

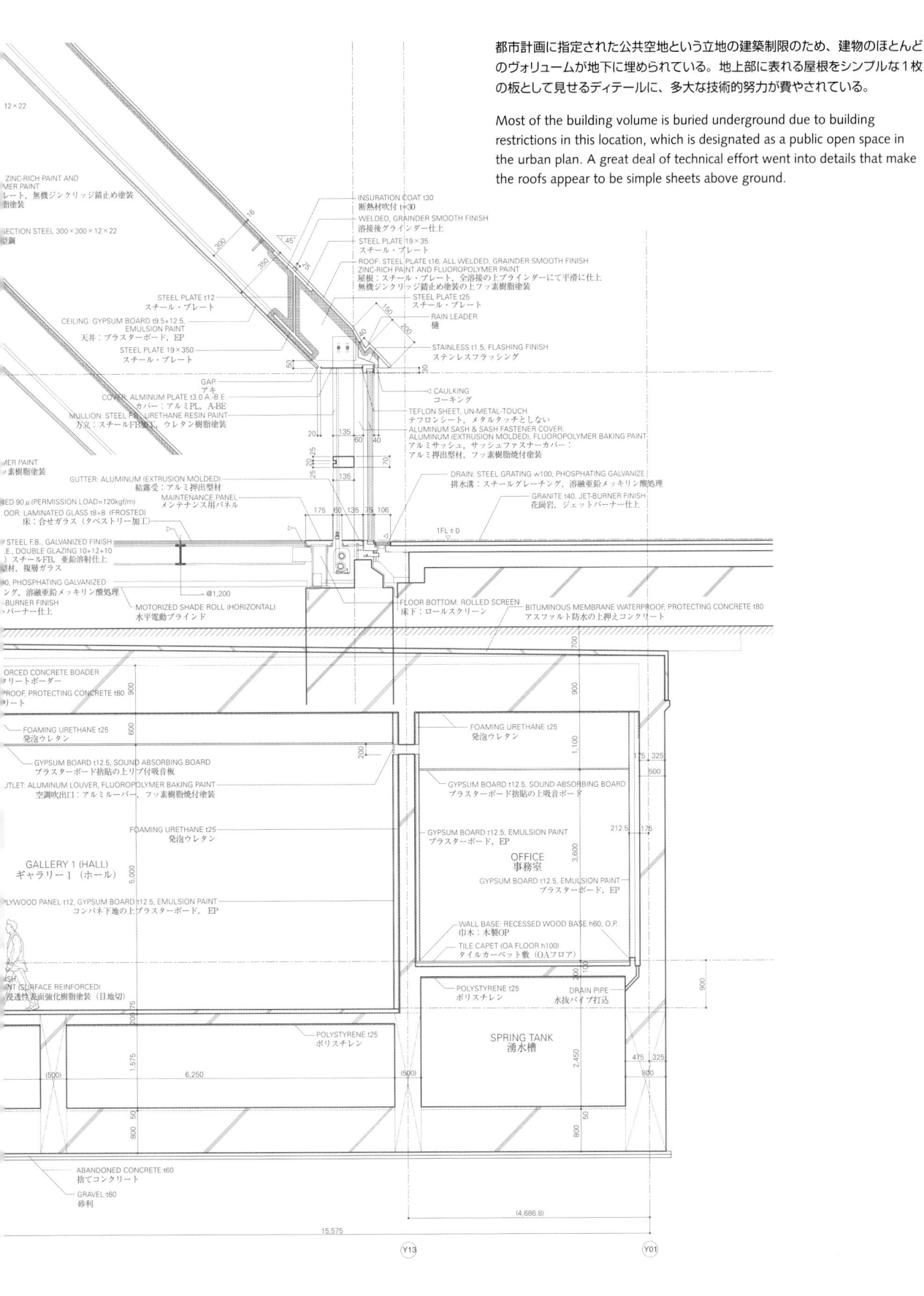

都市計画に指定された公共空地という立地の建築制限のため、建物のほとんどのヴォリュームが地下に埋められている。地上部に表れる屋根をシンプルな1枚の板として見せるディテールに、多大な技術的努力が費やされている。

Most of the building volume is buried underground due to building restrictions in this location, which is designated as a public open space in the urban plan. A great deal of technical effort went into details that make the roofs appear to be simple sheets above ground.

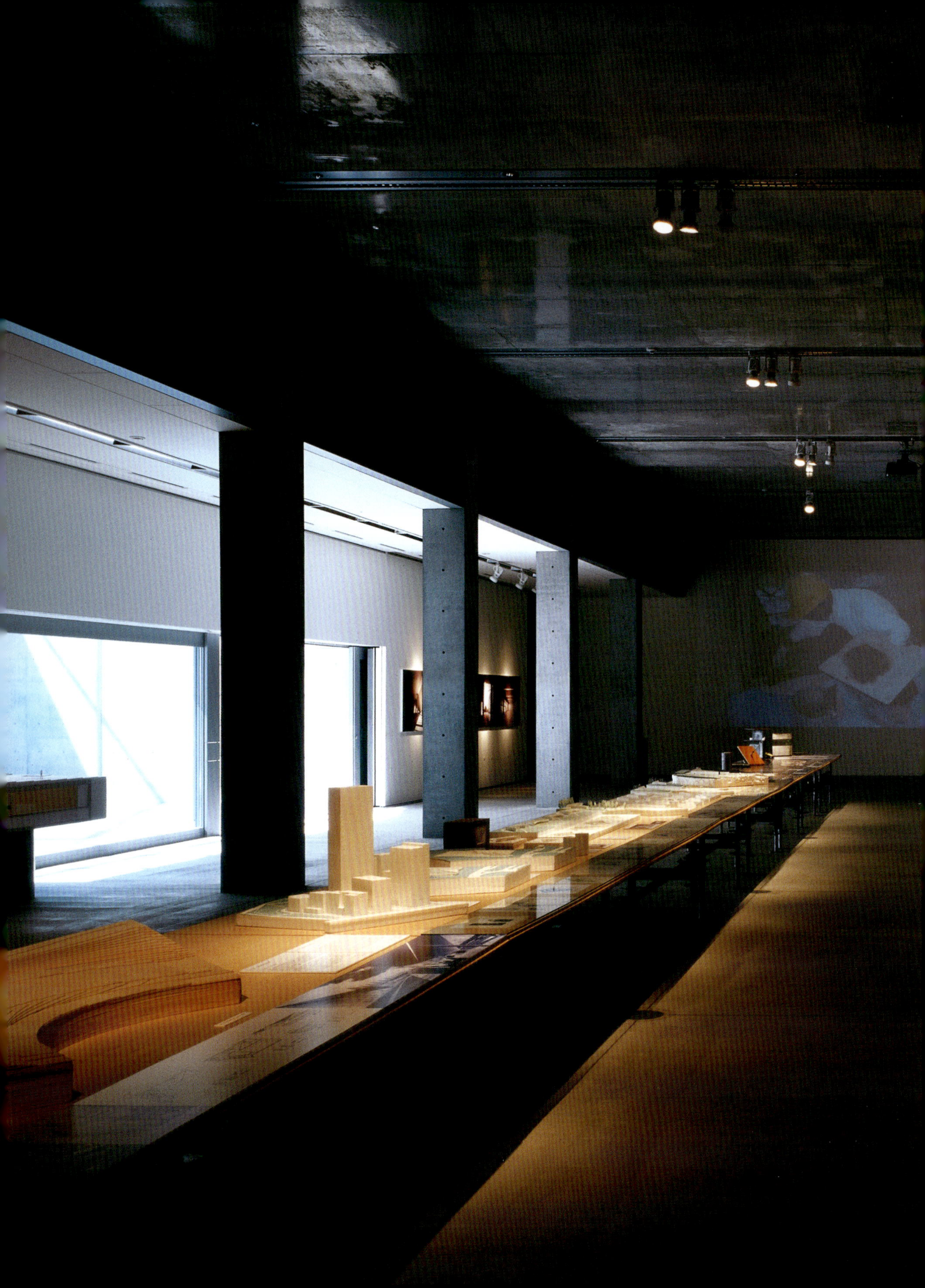

メインギャラリー。天井高は4.8m。コンクリートの列柱で緩やかに区切られた通路越しにサンクンコートの光が入り込む。

Main gallery. The ceiling height is 4.8m. Natural light from the sunken court comes in across a passageway, gently divided by a row of concrete columns.

建築の公共性

安藤忠雄

私の出発点

　私が設計事務所を開設する前年の1968年、東京大学の安田講堂が異議を唱える学生たちによって占拠された。その後1年余り、学生と大学側の対立が続き、卒業式の中止、全学部長の辞任を経て、それでも収まらない事態を収拾するために、ついには機動隊が動員された。60年の安保をきっかけに、高度経済成長の裏で激化の一途を辿っていた学園紛争がピークを迎えた事件だった。

　私は大阪にいて、その様子を遠くで見ていたに過ぎない。だが、当時の多くの若者たち同様、機動隊員に投石、火炎瓶で、必死に抵抗する学生たちの姿に、強い共感と感動を覚えていた。大学を無法地帯にした彼らの行為は〈暴力〉だったが、そこには自由で平等な社会の実現のために身を賭して闘う、まぎれもない〈個人〉の存在があった。

　日本各地で起こった学園紛争は、安田講堂事件の決着を契機に鎮静に向かい、同時にアナーキーなエネルギーに満ちた時代の空気も影を潜めていく。70年以降、日本社会は、闘争の季節の反動のように、盲目的な経済至上主義へと一気に方向転換していった。だが、60年代に20代を過ごし、社会が揺れ動く瞬間に立ち会った私の心には、抵抗する時代の精神が強く焼きついていた。

　「社会の中でいかに個としての己の意思を刻んでいくか」
　そんな時代に逆行する感情を抱えながら、私は建築家として出発した。

公共性という主題

　今回のTOTO出版の企画では、69年から今日に至る、私の建築家としての40年余りの活動を全3巻のシリーズで総括しようとしている。既に第1巻が住宅をテーマとして、第2巻が海外での仕事をテーマとして刊行された。必然的に、今回の3巻で、住宅と海外作品以外、残るすべての仕事を網羅するわけだが、問題はそれらを括るテーマである。

　京都での商業建築「TIME'S」から「光の教会」のような小さな宗教施設、「大阪府立近つ飛鳥博物館」のような公共の文化施設、あるいは「淡路夢舞台」のような環境再生を目的とした巨大な複合施設のプロジェクトに至るまで──それぞれ規模もつくられた状況も異なる仕事の連続性を、デザインの手法といった閉じた概念ではない、もっと普遍的なテーマで追いかけたい。

　「自分は一体何を求めて生きてきたのか」年月を振り返り、60年代の終わりに事務所を開設した建築家としての出発点を思ったとき、改めて自身の目指してきたものを再確認した。それは〈公共性〉という主題である。

　ここでいう建築のパブリックとは、制度的な意味での美術館や公園といった施設では

ない、人々が日常の生活の中で自身の立っている場所と時間を感じることができるしるしし、集まってともに生きていることを確認できる場とでもいうような、広い意味での建築空間のあり方だ。

当たり前に過ぎる主題かもしれない。レンゾ・ピアノが言ったように、街の中に建って否応なしに人々の目にさらされる建築とは本来的に公共的な存在だ。

だが、この当然の主題が自由主義経済の市場原理と形骸化した制度に押し潰され、人々の日常から排除されつつあったのが、私が建築の道を歩み始めたときからの日本社会の状況であり、その公共性の不在こそが、今日まで続けてきた私なりの建築における闘いの、抗うべき〈敵〉だった。

無論、大阪の片隅で、小さな点のような建築を埋め込んでいくことから都市に働きかけていこうとしていた〈都市ゲリラ〉の時代から、東京の都市計画にアドバイザーとして関わる今日とでは、社会はもちろん、私自身の立つ位置も大きく変わっている。社会の変化も甚だしく、とりわけこの10年の急激な情報化と国際化の進行によって、世界は世紀単位の変貌を遂げつつある。

しかし、いくら社会が変化し、自身を取り巻く環境が変わろうとも、建築を相手に悪戦苦闘する状況は40年前も今日も何ら変わっていない。規模が大きくなり、より深く社会と関わっていく中で問題はより大きく複雑化し、社会性を増しているわけだから、当然といえば当然だろう。

私は、建築の公共性を思い、社会と対話していく中で、自身の建築を展開させてきた。この機会に、そのプロセスを自分の言葉で整理してみたい。

丹下健三の時代

2005年3月22日、建築家丹下健三が逝去した。1941年生まれの私の世代にとって、戦後日本の建築界を牽引する世界のTANGEは、文字通りの英雄だった。

戦後間もない1949年の「広島平和会館（ヒロシマピースセンター）」のコンペを皮切りに、70年の大阪万博に至る20年間、丹下健三は時代をリードする先駆的な建築を次々と実現させた。磯崎新さんが「国家成長期の理論をもった建築家」と称した通り、それらの建築はいずれも国や地方自治体の記念碑的施設であり、つまり丹下健三は日本近代建築の礎を築いた先駆者であったのと同時に、建築の公共性という主題に真摯に向き合った最初の建築家でもあった。

伝統論争を引き起こした「香川県庁舎」を始めとする一連の庁舎建築、世界の構造表現主義の頂点をしるした「国立屋内総合競技場（現：国立代々木競技場）」、シェル構造による彫塑的空間の傑作「東京カテドラル聖マリア大聖堂」——その後の建築界に影

響を与えた丹下作品は枚挙に暇がないが、私自身が最も深く影響を受けたと思うのは、20歳のときに初めて見た広島の「ピースセンター」である。

コンクリート打ち放しによるブルータルな表現もさることながら、何より驚いたのは原爆ドームを背後に透視させる壮大なスケール感だった。そこには戦没者の鎮魂を願い、平和を祈る、共同体の意思が誰の目にもわかる風景として表現されていた。

独学で建築を始めた当時、都市という枠組みの中で単体の建築を位置づけようという建築家の意思を正確に理解できたわけではない。だが、建築が公共の存在として社会に働きかけていくことの意味、建築の可能性を、身体で感じることができた。

ゲリラの建築家

「ピースセンター」訪問から数年後、私は大阪の梅田で設計事務所を開設した。20代の10年間で、独学ながら自分なりに建築を学ぼうと努力し、数回の西欧旅行を経て、この道で生きていく覚悟は固まりつつあった。

だが、現実は甘くはない。当たり前のことだが、建築とは基本的にアカデミックな世界のものである。とりわけ官主導のかたちで都市復興が進められてきた1970年代当時においては、都市の中の重要な場所に建つ重要な（＝公的な）建築の設計は、有名大学卒のエリートが行うべしというルールが、厳然とした社会システムとしてあった。大学も出ていない独学の建築家に許されるのは、住宅以外ではよくて商業建築の設計ぐらい。いずれも、エリート建築家からは「建築にはならない」と軽視されるような仕事ばかりである。

前途揚々とはいえない厳しい状況であったが、それでも社会に対し何らかの意味のある建築をつくっていこうと腹を括り、その意思表明として論文「都市ゲリラ住居」を書いた。ゲリラのネーミングについては、キューバ革命の英雄チェ・ゲバラへの共感が多分にあった。

都市ゲリラとは、要するに例え小さなひとつの建築でも、そこに起爆剤足りうる力を秘めることができれば、その点の連なりによって、いつか都市という全体にも働きかけていくことができるだろうという、草の根の建築家ならではの姿勢だ。

ゲリラ的な小さな建築でも〈建築〉足りえると信じて前に進めたのは、丹下の活躍の傍らで、異なるアプローチで民主主義の時代の建築を切り開こうとしていた、一群のモダニスト建築家の小住宅の仕事を見ることができたからだと思う。

清家清、池辺陽、増沢洵――とりわけ鮮烈な印象を受けたのは、60年前後、リアルタイムで見た増沢洵の「自邸」である。そこには、わずか9坪に充たないスペースが、3次元的な建築の仕掛けによって、驚くべき広がりをもった住空間として実現されていた。ま

たその簡潔なディテールには、伝統に対するモダニズムの本質的な取り組みが示されており、最小限住宅というテーマに対する単なる回答以上の、建築の夢が詰まっていた。

　50年代からの小住宅を手がかりとした潮流は、ちょうど増沢洵の「自邸」をピークとして60年代に入ると急速に萎み、その後東京オリンピック、大阪万博と続く丹下健三の最盛期が始まる。それぞれの歴史的評価はともかく、50年代〜60年代にかけての日本建築が、かつてない輝きを放っていたことは間違いない。この時代に建築をスタートすることができた私たちの世代は幸運だった。

原点の建築

　都市ゲリラ住居のひとつの到達点として、私の建築家としてのデビュー作となった「住吉の長屋」もまた、極小スケールの個人住宅だった。大阪住吉区の下町、3軒長屋の真ん中を切り取ってつくった間口2間×奥行き8間のコンクリートの箱の家。本当に小さな建築ではあったが、そのスケールにそぐわぬ大きな問題を提起したために、世間の注目を集めることとなった。

　第1の問題は、四周を壁で囲って、入口以外一切の開口部がないこと。第2の問題は、内外とも、壁と天井がすべてコンクリート打ち放しでできていること。そして第3の問題は、これが一番論議を呼んだのだが、ただでさえ小さい箱を3等分して、その真ん中を屋根のない中庭としてしまっていること。

　生活動線が中庭で断ち切られるために、雨の日には傘をさしてトイレに行かねばならない。確かに、近代的な機能主義の観点からすれば、不便極まりない家である。内外コンクリート打ち放しの表現も、無愛想に過ぎるファサードも、当時の一般の生活感覚を考えれば、厳しいものだっただろう。

　だが、こうした厳しい選択は、決して生活を無視して生まれたわけではなかった。この場所で生活を営むのに本当に必要なものは何なのか、一体住まうとはどういうことなのかを真剣に考え抜いた結果、私は自然の一部としてある生活こそが住まいの本質であり、都市の限られたスペースだからこそ、無難な便利さを犠牲にしてでも、その厳しさもやさしさも含めた自然の変化を最大限獲得することを優先したのだ。

　内外打ち放しコンクリートを中心とするストイックな素材感、幾何学に従い徹底して単純化された空間構成は、厳しい敷地と経済の条件への回答であり、同時に、削ぎ落としていくことで、逆に〈無〉の空間の豊かさを実現しようという削除の美学を追及したものだった。

　モノに頼るのではなく、その場所でしか得られない空間の豊かさを目指すという主題。それを実現するための、鉄とガラスとコンクリートに限定した素材と単純な幾何学による

空間構成、そして内部空間への大胆な自然の導入――「住吉の長屋」の極限に近い諸条件が私に教えてくれたものは、実に豊かであったと思う。狭くローコストであるがゆえ、1mmの無駄も許されない。だからこそ、そこで時間を過ごす人間の精神力、体力から生活形式に至るまで、あらゆる問題を限界まで突き詰めて、自身の建築の骨格となる思想を固めることができた。

　周囲との関係を絶ったようなかたちの住吉の長屋は、一見すると、都市に閉じた完全な私的空間のように見えるだろう。だが、外に対して一切開口のない、無愛想なコンクリートの壁は、単なる公私の境界線ではない、高度経済成長の名のもとに肥大化していく都市に抗って、都市に棲み着こうとする個人の意思を表現しようとしたものだった。どんなに小さい建築であっても、主題は常に都市にあった。

商業建築から街との関わりを取り戻す

　私にとって住宅のデビュー作が「住吉の長屋」なら、商業建築でのそれは住吉の完成の翌年、1977年に完成した神戸北野町での「ローズガーデン」である。

　戦後日本の経済性一辺倒の社会は、土地も建物をも、投資の対象として扱った。商業建築に問われるのは、いかに空間効率のよい箱であるかであり、設計者にできるのは、ただ表層を飾るデザインのみ――「建築にはならない」商業建築は、建築界からは完全に見捨てられていた。

　しかし、本来、商業空間とは都市の生成とともに自然発生的に生まれ、都市の発展とともに歩んできた、スケールも機能上も街に密着したものだったはずだ。

　私は、その人々の生活の一部分としてある商業建築を、〈大文字の建築〉ではもち得ない、街の共有財産足りうるパブリックスペース創出のチャンスとして捉え、ひとつひとつの建築に全力投球で向かった。

　当時の北野町もまた、戦後日本の乱暴な都市再開発の波に呑まれようとしており、異人館の建ち並ぶかつての落ち着いた街並みも、趣味の悪い建物の乱立で破壊されつつあった。その流れに対して「ローズガーデン」では、建築としての自立性を保ちながら、建物と街を連続させることをテーマにした。既存の街並みに溶け込むようなヴォリュームの配置、切妻屋根や赤レンガのイメージの踏襲といった外側の視点による連続と、建物内に道を引き込むようにつくる回廊、アルコーブなどのパブリックスペースを媒介とした、内側の視点による建物と街の連続――。

　「ローズガーデン」の試みは、一部には認知されたようで、その後、北野町でつくられる商業建築でも、周辺に馴染んだ意匠で、中庭を設けてその周囲にテナントを配す、ローズガーデン型の構成がポツポツと見られるようになった。私自身、「北野アレイ」、

「リンズギャラリー」、「北野アイビーコート」など、その後約10年にわたって、合計8件の建築に関わっている。思えばこうした地縁的な仕事こそが、部分（＝建築）のつながりによって全体（＝都市）に働きかけていく、〈都市ゲリラ〉の目指したかたちであったように思う。

街との関わり方

「ローズガーデン」以降、個人住宅と商業建築を軸とする建築活動が始まり、80年代に入る頃には、ある程度の規模の仕事も手がけるようになっていた。高松の「ステップ」、沖縄の「フェスティバル」、京都の「TIME'S」、大阪ミナミの「BIGI」、「OXY」、「GALLERIA [akka]」、そして青山の「COLLEZIONE」。

ところで北野町の一連の仕事は、私のつくってきた仕事として、メディアなどでも例外的に扱われることが多かった。先に述べた「住吉の長屋」に始まる私の建築のストイックなイメージにそぐわない、赤レンガ、切妻屋根といった建築要素を用いているからだろう。

確かに、アーケードを切り裂くように配された、建物を垂直に貫く屋外階段を軸とした構成配置の「ステップ」、入り組んだ内外空間を一体化して封じ込める均等ラーメンのフレーム構造の「フェスティバル」、あるいは、細長い敷地の半分を占める、立体迷路のような吹き抜け空間をもつ「GALLERIA [akka]」など、強い幾何学を前面に出し、自立性の高い建築構成をもつ建築と、既存の街並みとの調和を重んじた北野町の一連の建物とは一見、デザインは大きく隔たって見えるかもしれない。だが、つくり手の意図は、人が集う建築で街を刺激するという考え方において何ら変わりはない。

北野町では、既存のコンテクストを継承することで環境に応え、逆に雑然とした都市のコンテクストの中に建つ「ステップ」、「フェスティバル」では、抑制された形式的表現で一旦周囲との連続を断ち切りながら、その内に、予想を裏切る劇的なヴォイド、都市のアルコーブとなるようなパブリックスペースを内包させることで、逆説的に都市に関わり、都市に楔していく。

「フェスティバル」では、穴あきブロックの採用により、全パブリックスペースを非空調の半屋外空間として、現代建築に沖縄の風土を組み込むことも考えていた。ファサードが閉じているか否かは、方法論の問題に過ぎない。いつも頭にあったのは、いかにして不特定多数の人が集う場をつくり出し、建築を街に〈開いて〉いくかという主題だった。

社会批評としての建築

無論、〈街との関わり〉と言って、それがすんなり受け入れられたわけではない。建築

を都市という外側の視点で捉え、構成していくことは、結果的に事業のプログラムを規制し、収益に直接結びつかないスペースをつくる結果につながる。
　「何のために、そんなに大きな吹き抜けがいるのか」
　「通路と階段の占める面積が広過ぎる」
　「パブリックスペースが半屋外空間ばかり。空調がきかず不便極まりない」
　クライアントは、黙って任せてはくれない。厄介な建築家に頼んでしまったと半ば後悔しつつ、それでも事業として成立させようと、軌道修正をはかろうとしてくる。理想の実現のためには、そんなクライアントやディベロッパーとの緊張感ある時間を最後まで耐え抜くだけの根気と体力が必要だった。
　その意味で、最も無謀な企てを試みた京都の複合商業ビル「TIME'S」が実現できたことには、大きな意味があったように思う。
　「TIME'S」で考えた街との関わりとは、即ち、建物が接する高瀬川のせせらぎとの関わりだった。当時の高瀬川は、川沿いの建物はすべて背を向けて建てられており、日常に人が近づける場所もない、現代の京都の中で完全に見捨てられた存在だった。実際、戦後の日本の経済性優先の都市化は、こうした河川など自然の犠牲の上に進められてきたといっていい。
　だが、琵琶湖疏水や市の中心を流れる鴨川など、歴史的にも水と親しい都市空間の歴史をもつ京都で、川の傍につくるならば、その水をどうしても建築に活かしたかった。
　テーマは川に向かうオープンスペース、それをいかにしてつくるか。意識したのは、川と建物の緊張感ある関係である。単なる修景というのではなく、文字通り川の流れが建物に入り込んでくるような、そんな空間の緊張感だ。
　自然と同化する建築、内外の境界の曖昧な建築——これは日本の伝統的建築の特質でもある。桂離宮や修学院、金閣寺や銀閣寺などを思い出しても、目に浮かぶのは必ず庭と一体化した建築の姿だ。水との関わりを考えてみても、宇治の平等院鳳凰堂や、厳島神社など、人工と自然の対立を前提とする西欧の建築文化では考えられない、大胆な水上の造形が実現されている。
　無論、具体的な日本の伝統建築を何か思い浮かべて設計していたわけではない。10代の終わり頃から、好きで奈良、京都の古建築巡りをしていた。そこで身体で覚えた空間感覚が、無意識に出てきたのだと思う。
　私は、各層のパブリックスペースをすべて路地状の屋外空間とし、建物内のさまざまなスペースで高瀬川と〈出会える〉建物として提案をまとめた。だが、最下層の、水面上20cmまで近づけたレベルに、一部護岸を切ってテラスをつくろうという提案は、クライアントはもちろん、行政の側からも猛反発を受けた。
　「商品もあるのに、水が溢れたらどうするのか」というクライアントの心配に対しては、

高瀬川が上流で水量がコントロールされている疎水であることを踏まえたレベル設定の技術的根拠を丁寧に説明し、納得してもらうよう努力した。だが、合点がいかなかったのは、行政の言い分である。

「いまだかつて、建築のために護岸を切り崩した前例はない。前例がないということは、やってはいけないということだ」

ルールは守らねばならないが、彼らの主張は都市を考えたがゆえの論理ではない、単なる制度の問題だった。問題となることを恐れて、規制するばかりの減点法のシステムでは、何も生み出すことはできない。これには徹底して反論し、許可が下りるまでは引き下がらないという断固とした姿勢で臨んだ。

そんな京都市との数回の交渉を経て、ついに実現した「TIME'S」は、水と接することのできる京都の現代建築として商業的にも成立し、数年後には隣接する敷地に、同じ考え方で増築を行うこととなった。北野町の「ローズガーデン」と同じように、個々の建築による街づくりのひとつのきっかけにはなったということだろう。

「TIME'S」は、「住吉の長屋」以来、囲われた領域の中に光、風という抽象化されたかたちで自然を引き込んできたのが、逆に自然の中に建築を放り出すように考えたという点において、ひとつの節目となった仕事だった。

そのプロセスを経て気づいたのは、敷地を味方につけて（＝場所の潜在力を引き出して）環境を組み立て直す建築という発想である。つくることが先行してしまい、自身の仕事を言語化することに無頓着な私はその意識を70年代に流行したコンテクスチュアリズムの一貫としてぼんやりと捉えていたが、建築評論家ケネス・フランプトンが、的確な評価を与えてくれた。クリティカル・リージョナリズム（批判的地域主義）という考え方だ。

正直、私にとって既存環境をベースに建築を組み立てていくのは、ごく自然の感覚であり、地域主義というほどに意識はしていなかったが、社会に対するクリティックとしての近代建築、という概念には非常に共感を覚えた。

近代主義の計画概念とは、即ち予測のできない、不安な要素は排除して、問題を回避する方向に向かっている。ならば、私はそうして現代社会からはじき出されるものを拾い出し、その問題を浮き彫りにするような建築をつくっていこうと、そうしてその場所にしかない、建築のあり方というものを探っていこう──。

後に、大阪天保山でつくった「サントリーミュージアム」で、与えられた美術館の敷地を超えて、前面の市の管轄の護岸から、国の管理する海上まで連続する階段広場を構想した。場所のもつ力を読み取り、それを最大限活かすことによって、環境全体を組み直す。川や海を人間の生活から遠ざけ過ぎた、現代都市の水際空間のクリティックとしての建築。その下敷きとしてあったのは、やはり「TIME'S」での試みであった。

435 The Public Character of Architecture

人の集まる場

　〈公共性〉という主題を考えたとき、すぐに思い浮かぶ建築がふたつある。そのひとつが、前述の「ピースセンター」のパースペクティブ、もうひとつがル・コルビュジエの「ロンシャン礼拝堂」のミサの光景だ。

　あれは何度目に訪れたときだったろうか。ロンシャンの彫塑的な内部空間を、光と音とが洪水のように溢れ、空間とミサに集う人々とが、文字通り渾然一体となって、凄まじいエネルギーを発散している——その光景にコルビュジエの底知れぬ才能を思うと同時に、人々が祈るために集う場所、現代社会における宗教施設の存在の重要さを痛感した。

　建築の力はその物理的な大きさに比例するわけではない。そんな可能性を感じさせる、宗教建築への挑戦は、建築を志したときからずっとひとつの目標としてあった。

　「光の教会」の依頼を受けたのは1987年、過剰な投機熱による資産価値の高騰に社会全体が沸いていたときだ。敷地はとり立てて特徴もない郊外の住宅地の一角で、規模は延べ100m²程度。予算も信者の精一杯の浄財ではあったが、教会建築をつくるにはあまりに心許なく、このような小さな仕事では施工会社を見つけるのもままならない。およそ考えうる限り最悪の条件の仕事——にもかかわらず、私がふたつ返事でその設計を引き受けたのは、その教会をつくろうという信者たちの強い意思があったからだ。

　教会建築としては、「光の教会」より前に、北海道トマムの「水の教会」、神戸の「六甲の教会（風の教会）」を既に完成させていた。ともに大自然の景勝地の中で、比較的自由に建築を考えることができた仕事であり、それまで都心の密集地での仕事が多かった私にとっては、建築と自然との関わりという新しいテーマに挑戦できた好機ではあった。

　しかし、ふたつの教会はいずれもホテル付属の、いわゆる結婚式場としての機能が主の、礼拝を目的とした純粋な宗教建築とは言えないもので、空間の意図が必ずしも宗教的動機に還元されたわけではなかった。それゆえ、建築を本気で必要とする人々がいる「光の教会」の建築は、私にとって特別な意味をもった。

　約1年間の設計期間を経て、最後に辿り着いたのは、間口6m、奥行き18mのコンクリートの箱に斜めの壁が入り込んだだけの、極めてシンプルな構成である。壁と天井の打ち放しコンクリート以外、目につく要素は祭壇に向かって段状に下降していく床と、つくり付け椅子に用いた現場足場用杉板のみ。それも真っ黒に塗りつぶした薄暗い空間に、祭壇背後の壁に穿った十字架型のスリットから絞り込まれた光が差し込むという設計だ。

　建築を徹底して簡素化したのは、ひとつには無論ローコストとせざるを得ない状況があったのだが、それ以前に、私の中には、究極まで削ぎ落とした空間の感覚に徹することで、より豊かな場をもたらしたいという意識があった。

ひとつのイメージとして抱いていたのは、ヨーロッパ中世のロマネスクの修道院である。修道士たちが、それこそ命を削りながら荒削りの石を積み上げて形づくった洞窟のような礼拝堂。その意思だけがつくらせたような禁欲的空間に、ガラスもない開口部から、強い光がダイレクトに入り込んで、床の石の表情をおごそかに照らす。あの厳しいまでの美しさをコンクリートの箱で表現しようと思ったとき、光の十字架というアイディアが浮かんだ。

　宗教建築としての象徴的空間を、光や風、水といった抽象化された自然に頼り実現しようとした点では、「水の教会」や「六甲の教会」も同じである。ただ、自然豊かな環境のもとにつくった教会では周囲に対し開いていくところから、構想をスタートしているのに対し、「光の教会」は周囲に対し空間を閉ざすことを前提に、自然との関わりをも極限まで切り詰めたかたちで考えている。

　元来、私には、理屈ではない、肉体的な感性として、光より闇の空間を求める傾向がある。それが「住吉の長屋」から2004年に完成した「地中美術館」に至るまで、一連の洞窟的建築の系譜につながっているのだが、「光の教会」は、そうした私の建築志向が、極限の条件下で、最も端的に表れた仕事であったといえる。

　最後まで限られた工費の制約に苦しんだ、この困難な工事をやり終えたのが、ここに教会堂を建てるのだという牧師、信者と、苦労を承知で引き受けてくれた建設会社の人々の素朴な熱意であったことは間違いない。

　80年代末から90年代にかけて、投機に支えられた見せかけの好景気に、社会は狂い、建築の世界もまた狂っていた。都市が市場原理に支配され、建築が商品化していく。そんな時代に戸惑いながら、〈都市ゲリラ〉の進むべき道を探していた私に、このささやかな礼拝堂の建築は、「何のためにつくるのか、誰のためにつくるのか」という、一番大切な建築の意味を再確認させてくれた。90年代以降、私は公共性のある建築へ、徐々に仕事をシフトしていく。そのひとつのきっかけが、「光の教会」であった。

枠組みを超えて、環境に働きかける

　建築を組み立てていく上で、意識して自分に課しているテーマがある。ディテールにとらわれずに問題の本質を見極め、絶えず根本に立ち返って原理から物事を組み立て直していこうという姿勢だ。これには、20代の頃に知り合った、〈具体〉の人々の影響が大きい。〈具体〉とは、関西に誕生した日本で最初で最後の前衛芸術家集団だ。

　「既成概念にとらわれるな」
　「絶対に人の真似をするな」
　「何でも自分の頭で考えろ」

こうしたラディカルな姿勢は、必然的に社会との衝突、摩擦を生じる。

　建築の世界にいて、それを特に痛感したのは、いわゆる公共事業の建築に関わるようになってからだった。

　私にとって初めての公共の仕事となる、「兵庫県立こどもの館」の設計をスタートしたのは1987年、事務所設立から約20年後である。

　「こどもの館」の敷地は姫路市郊外の桜山貯水池という人造池の側、子供たちの研究発表はじめ読書や工作などの活動が行われる施設の計画だった。依頼を受けた当初は、文字通りの公共の仕事で、子供のための施設というプログラムのもと、かつてない規模で建築が考えられると素直に喜んでいた。しかし、最初の打ち合わせで、姫路市にある計画地を見に行き、担当者の説明を聞くと、建築の敷地は全体の1/10程度の範囲で、残り9割は外構として別な人間に頼むという。それが、当時の公共事業の常識ではあったのだが、私は猛反発した。

　「そうした線引きは、あくまで行政側の都合であり、訪れる子どもにとっては何の意味もない……内外含めた敷地全体で、ひとつの場所として、トータルに考えるのが当たり前だろう……」

お役所的な前例主義と、〈具体〉譲りの前衛主義で、噛み合うわけもなく、議論は白熱した。真っ向から対立して、前に進まなくなったところで、当時の兵庫県知事、貝原俊民さんが助け船を出してくれた。

　「安藤さんの言い分は筋が通っている。思い切って、すべて任せてみよう」

　こうして「こどもの館」は、アプローチから施設まで、敷地全体を自然との出会いをテーマとするひとつの装置として捉え構想された。池に沿って配された施設を結ぶ延々とした屋外通路、その真ん中に位置する16本の柱のある中間広場、あるいは、本館をとり巻く水庭。その先には、緑深い山を背後に美しい人工池の風景が雄大に広がる。ランドスケープの一部としての建築だ。

　明確な機能をもたない、建築の仕掛けは、常識的な感覚からすれば無駄な存在である。だが「こどもの館」の目的が、子供の情操教育にあるならば、最も必要なのは、自然環境という教材であり、その面白さを子どもたちが自分で探すことができる〈あそび〉の空間である。周囲の反対を押し切り、半ば強引に実現したプロジェクトではあったが、完成から20年余りを経た今日、建物はより一層自然の風景の中に埋没して、子どもたちの遊びの場を拡張している。

　社会のストックとなりうるパブリックの建築をつくろうとするならば、建築家は建築の計画以前の、建築のあり方を決める企画段階から参加すべきだろう。

　バブル経済の崩壊以降、公共建築はハコモノという、地方自治のゆがみの象徴として批難を浴びてきた。無論、使われない箱はつくっても仕方がないが、公共建築でしかで

きないものは確かにある。いくら運営が難しいからといって、それがすべて商業資本に取って代わられてしまっては文化は育たない。

この場所で建築に何ができるのか。重要なのはつくるより前に根本を問いただしていく、建築以前のプロセスにある。

場所の建築

「こどもの館」以来、公共建築が仕事の中心を占めるようになり、とりわけ90年代に入ると美術館、博物館の仕事が目立って増えてきた。制約の多い状況を建築で克服するという図式で展開してきた、都市ゲリラにとっては、大きな転機である。

だが、無秩序に混乱した都市環境であっても、自然豊かな離島の敷地であっても、その環境に建築で応えるという方法論には変わりはない。すぐれたポテンシャルを秘めた敷地であるなら、その力を顕在化し、より価値ある場所として再生するのが、公共の建築として当然果たすべき役割だ。

場所という主題に関して、自身として与えられた枠組みを越えて提案できたと思う仕事のひとつが、「大阪府立近つ飛鳥博物館」だ。

一定のコンテクストを有する場所において、建築を周辺環境と一体的に計画していく手法は、「こどもの館」以来、「姫路文学館」や「直島コンテンポラリーアートミュージアム（現：ベネッセハウスミュージアム）」、「熊本県立装飾古墳館」など、いくつかのプロジェクトで実践していたが、「近つ飛鳥博物館」においては、その方法論をもう一歩推し進め、建築を完全にランドスケープ化することを試みた。

地形に沿って、全面ピンコロ石を敷き詰めた人工の丘陵としてつくられた、ファサードをもたない地下建築。敷地周辺に点在する古墳群に呼応するような、現代の墳墓としての博物館。訪問者は、梅林に覆われた「風土記の丘」の散策路を経て、人工の丘陵に至り、眼下の風景に刻まれた古代世界に思いを馳せる。その上で、墳墓の中に入り込み、古代の遺物に触れる。

展示物ありきの、周囲と隔絶した箱を基本とする通常の博物館建築の定石とは、ある意味で正反対の考え方だった。だが、堺の仁徳天皇陵から奈良の遠つ飛鳥へ連なる歴史街道の只中に位置し、周囲に二百数十基の古墳群が点在するこの場所において、最も重要な展示物は歴史の刻まれた環境そのものであり、博物館に求められるべきは、その歴史に対峙する時間と場所を提供する装置としての役割である。

階段広場で覆われた博物館という規格外の提案が、ともかく地方自治体の公共施設として実現したのは、やはり近つ飛鳥という場所の歴史的文脈の強さゆえのことだったのだと思う。この環境博物館というテーマは、同じ大阪の地で1994年に設計を始め、

2001年に完成した「大阪府立狭山池博物館」に受け継がれていった。

何に価値を置き、何に意味を見出すか

　槇文彦さんは、その著書の中で、ひとりの人間がデザインし得る空間の大きさには限界があると書かれていたが、実際、1993年にスタートした「淡路夢舞台」の、敷地全長600m、20万㎡という桁外れのスケールは、到底、通常の建築の概念で対応できるものではなかった。

　ひとつの全体ではない、部分の集積とならざる得ない建築。それに対して、それでも何か、パブリックな意味を見出そうとして、行き着いたのが、土砂採掘跡地としてあった敷地の、失われた自然の回復という主題である。

　「夢舞台」の敷地は、1950年代半ばから、大阪ベイエリア埋め立てなどに供してきた土砂採掘地にあった。1995年1月17日の阪神淡路大震災発生により、着工直前の状態にあったプロジェクトが一時中断されたこともあったが、そうして計画修正を繰り返しながらも、一貫して考えてきたのは、人間により破壊され傷ついた土地を、もう一度人間の手で取り戻そうという、環境再生の主題だった。

　建築より先に、掘削された30度以上の急斜面地に、50万本を超える10cmほどの苗木を植えることからスタート。広大な敷地の中に、複雑な建築複合体を組み込んでいく大工事の傍らでこの苗木から森を育てる試みは粛々と進められた。その建築の主題もまた、存在を誇示するのでなく、いかに自然と呼応して、自然の魅力を引き出せるかに集中した。

　2008年現時点で、「夢舞台」の施設のオープンから8年が経つ。10cmの苗木の連なりはいまや5m以上の高木の繁る森となり、完成当初空間のテーマパーク然としていた施設も良い具合に風化してきた。森が場所全体を包み込むまで、あと10年はかからないだろう。

　単純に公益性をもったインフラ的な施設や場所をつくっても、それが人々の生活を豊かにする公共の財産になるとは限らない。私は、建築における公共性とは、人々の心の風景として共有できる共同体の風景をつくるものであると考えている。

　それゆえ、「淡路夢舞台」においては建築を覆い隠す森の再生を主題とし、あるいは1996年にスタートし2006年に完成を迎えた「表参道ヒルズ（同潤会青山アパート建替計画）」においても、商業施設を含む全長250mに及ぶ建物が表参道のケヤキ並木の高さを超えないよう、その高さを低く抑えることを最優先事項として、10年越しの計画に取り組んだ。

　いずれも、従来の建築の枠組みからすると次元の異なる主題であったのかもしれな

い。実際、「淡路夢舞台」にしても、「表参道ヒルズ」にしても、プロジェクトの最大の難所は、建築のデザイン以前の、政治的、社会的働きかけのプロセスにあった。

　だが、私自身の中では、小さな建築のディテールを練り上げていく過程も、「淡路夢舞台」のような大規模な複合施設の計画に関わり対話を積み重ねて建築の立ち上がる状況を整えていく過程も、建築を組み立てていくという意識においては、何ら変わりはない。都市に楔していく〈都市ゲリラ〉の建築だ。

　環境全体の何に価値を置き、何に意味を見出すか——建築家として自身のすべき仕事は、その問いかけにいかに応えるかで決まってくる。

建築を育てるパトロネージ

　「淡路夢舞台」の計画が、私というひとりの建築家に依頼された経緯には、「兵庫県立こどもの館」と同じ、当時の兵庫県知事貝原さんの存在があった。計画の始まった90年代初頭、いまだバブル景気の余波で都市が浸食されていた時代に、淡路の再開発を、単純な施設の建設で終わらせたくないと考えておられた貝原さんは、ひとりの人間の舵取りの方が、方向性がぶれないという理由で、私を選び、議会を説き伏せた。その強い意思は着工直前に淡路を見舞った阪神淡路大震災を受けてもなお揺らぐことなく、逆に「これを復興のシンボルに」と奮起され、全面的な計画見直しの後、活断層の走る敷地に、文字通りの〈夢舞台〉を実現させた。この貝原さんの勇気が、日本の社会状況において、あのようなビッグプロジェクトが成立しえた最大の理由だった。

　先にも述べた通り、建築でパブリックというテーマを追求していくとき、ある意味、最大の壁はその建築のクライアント、発注者の存在だ。

　都市空間の豊かさとは、言い換えれば人々の生活空間を彩る余白の豊かさである。この非生産的な余白の部分の有無を巡って、建築家とクライアントはしばしば真っ向から衝突する。そこで大抵は雇われの身である建築家が折れて終わってしまうのが常なのだが、世の中には、少数だが、見返りを期待するスポンサーとしてではなく、建築家とともに夢を見ようと考える奇特な人々＝パトロンがいる。

　私の建築家としてのキャリアは、すべてこのパトロネージに支えられていたと、今改めて思う。

　まだ大規模文化施設の実績もなかった時期に、単なる個人的な付き合いだけで私を信じ、「サントリーミュージアム」設計の機会を与えてくれた故佐治敬三さん。佐治さんのほか、三洋電機の井植敏さん、京セラの稲盛和夫さんといった関西経済界のトップの方々と知り合うようになったのは、自前で展覧会を企画して「中之島プロジェクトⅡ（アーバンエッグ＋地層空間）」を発表した頃からだと記憶している。それぞれに波乱の人生

を歩まれてきた彼らだからこそ、誰に頼まれたのでもない、大阪の中心部を流れる川の中州の再生計画に熱を入れる私のことを面白がり、目をかけてくださったのだろう。

　そして、ベネッセ・コーポレーションの福武總一郎さん——。福武さんと、80年代の終わりから始めた、瀬戸内海の小島である直島の文化プロジェクトは、「ベネッセハウスミュージアム」から「ベネッセハウスオーバル」、「南寺（家プロジェクトNo.2）」に「地中美術館」、2006年に完成した木造の宿泊施設、さらに現在進行中の新たなギャラリーと、今日まで20年余り、継続的に進んでいる。

　マスタープランもないまま、福武さんの夢を頼りに走ってきた〈直島〉の一連のプロジェクトに参加する中で、私は美術館という建築のテーマにおける本質的な取り組みの機会を与えられただけでなく、芸術、文化という非生産的なものが、地域を活性化していく、即ち文化が場所を再生していく過程を見ることができた。

　とりわけ、直島の本村地区に残る古民家を改修して、そこに現代アートを埋め込んでいく「家プロジェクト」のもつ社会的意味は大きい。時間と空間をつなぐすぐれたアートの試みとしてあるのと同時に、従来の美術館の枠組みを越えたその企ては、風化しつつあった島の暮らしに大いに活力を取り戻し、地域振興の意味で大変な成果を挙げている。人口3,000人の、かつての名もなき小島は、今や国内のみならず海外にもその名を馳せるアートの聖地となり、年間20万人余りの観光客が訪れるまでに成長した。

　公共的な建築、場所は、必ずしも民主主義的な予定調和の中で生まれるわけではない。〈自由の空間〉を生み出す原動力は、強く激しい、個人の情熱であり、意志の力だ。私の40年の建築のキャリアが、それを証明している。

木を植えること

　公共性を主題に、自身の歩んできた道を、思いつくまま書き綴ってきた。最後は、建築ではない、森をつくる話で締め括ろう。

　現在、東京都とともに、東京湾に浮かぶ約88ヘクタールのかつてのゴミの埋立地を鬱蒼とした緑の繁る森として再生する「海の森」計画を進めている。

　「海の森」は2016年のオリンピック招致を目標とする都市再編計画の一翼をなすものだ。かつて、東京は1964年のオリンピック開催を都市整備の好機として、戦災の焼け跡から近代都市へ、劇的な変貌を遂げた。その後の日本の爆発的な経済成長は、かつてない物質的豊かさをもたらす一方で、さまざまな環境問題などを引き起こすに至ったが、そうした負の側面を抱えながらも、東京はしぶとく生き続け、今日、アジアの世界都市となるまでに成長した。その東京がこれから進むべきは、単なる発展ではなく、内在する都市問題を解消しつつ、成熟へと向かう道だ。

そのような趣旨で、東京都が作成したグランドデザインのコンセプトはあるものを活かした創造＝つくらないという都市戦略である。必要な都市機能の充実は、既存施設の最大限活用により、乱暴な再開発によって眠らされていた河川のあり方を見直すなどして、場所の風景と歴史を活かした都市の名所を再発見する。高密度に疲弊した都市空間の刷新は、街路樹を増強して都心部の緑の拠点をつなげてできる緑の回廊を軸として、建物屋上や駐車場、小中学校の校庭といった都市の隙間の緑化によって賄う。この緑のネットワークを最後に東京湾で受け止めるのが「海の森」だ。

　20世紀以来の人間の都市活動は、ついに地球の存続を脅かすまでに肥大化した。国籍を超え、文化的差異を超えて取り組まねばならない、この問題の大きさに誰もが気づき始めている。

　「海の森」は1口1,000円、50万人の寄付による市民参加形式で、少しずつ時間をかけて森を育てていくという計画だ。無論、「海の森」を含めた緑化計画が首尾よく実現したとしても、都市環境の抜本的解決にはならないことはわかっている。だが、都市の排出した産廃、ゴミの山に、市民の手で木を植えて、自然の森をつくる——このプロジェクトを3,000万人都市、東京からスタートすることは、単に森がひとつ生まれる以上の意味をもつ。人間のための都市を目指して、東京も動き始めたのだというメッセージを、世界に発信することができる。

　こうした環境運動に参加するのは、「海の森」が初めてではない。

　1995年の阪神淡路大震災復興支援として、被災地に鎮魂の白い花を咲かせる木を植えていった「ひょうごグリーンネットワーク」、産廃のシンボルとさえ言われた豊島の再生とあわせた瀬戸内の自然保護を目標として始めた「瀬戸内オリーブ基金」、大阪の河川敷に世界一の桜並木をつくろうという「桜の会・平成の通り抜け」など、いくつかの市民参加型の植樹運動に積極的に関わってきた。

　メディアに出れば、木を植える話ばかりをする私に、多くの人が「なぜ建築家が木を植えるのか」を問う。建築づくりも森づくりも、同じく環境に働きかけ、新しい価値を場所にもたらそうとするものなのだから、建築家が木を植えるのに熱心でも不思議はないと思うのだが、皆、なかなか納得してくれない。だが、ここまで公共性をテーマに、自身の歩んできた道を振り返ってきて、もっと的確な答えが見つかった。

　私にとって重要なのは、その環境への働きかけが、市民ひとりひとりの参加を前提として成立するという事実だ。

　都市が活き活きとしてあるには、豊かな余白（＝公共空間）と同時に、その余白を使いこなす成熟した市民の存在（＝公共精神）がなければない。森づくりを通じ、私が目指しているのは、人々の心にある、このパブリックの意識を刺激し、喚起することだ。

　結局、40年前から私の〈やりたいこと〉は何も変わっていない。これからも変わらずに居続けることが、今の私がすべきことなのだろう。

海の森
Umi-no-Mori (Sea Forest)

Exerting his incessant passion for architecture in engaging the environmental movement, Tadao Ando has become this project's committee chairman. A Sea Forest will be made by planting 48,000 saplings, including Japanese Chinquapin (Castanopsis sieboldii), Tabunoki (Machilus thunbergii), and Enoki nettle (Flammulina veluptipes), on approximately 88 hectares of garbage-based reclaimed land floating in Tokyo Bay, thus bringing in breezes to the heart of the city. Through a general fund-raising of 1,000 yen per person, the intention is for the provision and planting of the saplings to be a citizen-inspired undertaking.

安藤忠雄が事業委員長となり、建築と変わらぬ情熱を傾け、取り組んでいる環境運動。東京港に浮かぶ約88ヘクタールのゴミの埋立地に、スダジイ、タブノキ、エノキなどの苗木約48万本の植樹を行い、都心に風を引き込む海の森をつくる。苗木の調達・植樹は、ひと口1,000円からの一般募金により、市民の意思による事業とすることが目標とされている。

The Public Character of Architecture

Tadao Ando

My Starting Point

In 1968, the year before I opened my own architectural office, protesting students occupied Yasuda Auditorium at the University of Tokyo. The confrontation between the students and the university continued for more than a year, and when the situation remained unresolved despite the cancellation of a graduation ceremony and the resignation of deans of all university faculties, riot police were at last mobilized. The incident marked the peak of the student protests that were sparked by the signing of the Japan-US Security Treaty in 1960 and had become increasingly radical even as the economy underwent intensive growth.

I merely watched all this from my vantage point in Osaka. However, like many other youths at the time I was strongly sympathetic to and moved by the sight of the fierce resistance put up by students hurling rocks and Molotov cocktails against the riot police. Their actions, which turned the campus into an area of lawlessness, may have been violent, but they were indisputably individuals who fought with total commitment for the realization of a free and equal society.

With the end of the Yasuda Auditorium incident, the student protests all over Japan began to subside; the atmosphere of the time, which had been full of anarchic energy, began to dissipate. As if in reaction to the season of protests, after 1970 Japanese society took an abrupt turn and blindly embraced the notion of giving priority to the economy.

However, I had been in my twenties in the 1960s and witnessed a moment of social upheaval; in me the spirit of resistance of the time still lived on.

"How do I express myself as an individual in society?"

It was with a feeling of being out of step with the times that I began my architectural career.

The Theme of Social Character

This TOTO Publishing project is intended to provide in a three-volume series a summary of my more than 40 years of activity as an architect from 1969 to today. Volume 1, dedicated to houses and housing, and Volume 2, dedicated to overseas work, have already been published. This book, Volume 3, will include all works besides housing and works outside Japan; the problem is to find an all-encompassing theme for these works.

They range from the commercial building TIME'S in Kyoto and small religious facilities such as Church of the Light to public cultural facilities such as Chikatsu-Asuka Historical Museum, Osaka, and projects for enormous multifunctional facilities aimed at environmental regeneration such as Awaji-Yumebutai. I am seeking a common thread in works of different sizes and circumstances—a theme more universal than the narrow concept of design method.

"What has my life been in pursuit of?" When I look back on my starting point as an architect who opened his own office at the end of the 1960s, I recognize once more what it is I have been preoccupied with. It is the theme of public character.

By an architecture that is public in character, I am not referring to facilities such as art museums and parks that are public in an institutional sense. I am referring instead to architectural spaces that are public in a broader sense—spaces that enable people to gain, in the midst of everyday life, a sense of the place and time they live in; places where people can gather and, together, feel the vibrant possibilities of life.

The theme may be too obvious. Buildings that are exposed to view in the city are, as Renzo Piano has remarked, essentially all public.

However, when I first began to practice architecture, the market principles of a laissez-faire economy and Japan's emasculated institutions had no use for such a theme; concern for it was disappearing from everyday life in Japanese society. It is precisely the absence of public character that has been the "enemy" that I have fought against and resisted through architecture.

Of course, Japanese society and my own position in it are very different today—I am currently a city-planning advisor to Tokyo—from what they were when I was an "urban guerrilla," trying to influence the city by embedding small individual buildings in a corner of Osaka. Enormous changes are taking place in society; in particular, rapid advances in telecommunications and the internationalization of society in the last ten years are bringing about epochal transformations in the world.

Nevertheless, however much society and the environment around me may change, the conditions under which I wage my hard-fought architectural battles have not changed at all in the last 40 years. That may be only natural, since problems become more complex and take on greater significance for the public as projects become bigger in size and have greater impact on society.

My own architecture has evolved out of ideas about the public character of architecture and a dialogue I have continued to engage in with society. I would like to take this opportunity to put that process in perspective in my own words.

The Age of Kenzo Tange

Kenzo Tange died on March 22, 2005. The world-famous architect and leader of the architectural world in postwar Japan was quite literally a hero for architects of my generation. (I was born in 1941.)

Starting with the competition for Hiroshima Peace Center in 1949, immediately after the war, Tange realized a succession of groundbreaking, era-defining works for 20 years up to the Osaka Exposition in 1970. Arata Isozaki has described him as "an architect with a vision for the period of national growth," and indeed his works were monumental facilities for the central government and local governments. That is, Tange was both a pioneer who laid the foundation for Japanese modern architecture and the first architect to confront in earnest the theme of architecture's public character.

The series of local government buildings beginning with Kagawa Prefectural Government Building, which initiated the so-called Tradition Debate; Yoyogi National Gymnasium, the high-water mark of structural expressionism; and St. Mary's Cathedral, Tokyo, the masterpiece of plastic space made possible by a shell structure—the works by him that influenced the architectural world are too numerous to mention. The work that made the greatest impression on me was Hiroshima Peace Center, which I first saw when I was 20.

Although the brutal expression of the exposed concrete was impressive, what astonished me most of all was the grand scale of the composition, which incorporated the Atomic Dome in the distance. There, the communal intent to pray for the repose of the dead and to pray for peace was expressed as a landscape that could be understood by anyone.

When I first began to study architecture on my own, I was not yet able to understand fully the architect's intention to situate individual buildings in the urban framework. However, I was able to sense the significance and the possibility of buildings as public objects intended to influence society.

Guerrilla Architect

I opened my own architectural office in Umeda, Osaka, several years after visiting the Peace Center. In my twenties, I made efforts to study architecture on my own and in my own way, traveled several times to the West, and gradually made up my mind to live by this profession.

However, harsh reality soon set in. Architecture is of course basically an academic world. In particular, in the 1970s, when urban reconstruction was being carried out under the leadership of the authorities, there was an unspoken rule that important (i.e. public) buildings in key urban locations had to be designed by elite architects who were graduates of famous universities. The only things that a self-taught architect without a university education might be permitted to design, besides houses, were at best commercial buildings—the sort of work that tended to be looked down upon by elite architects as things that could not be made into "architecture."

Conditions were bleak, and my future could not be said to be promising. Nevertheless, I was determined to create buildings that were meaningful to society in some way, and it was to express that intention that I wrote an essay entitled "Urban Guerrilla Houses." I used the term "guerrilla" out of sympathy for Che Guevara, the hero of the Cuban revolution.

The urban guerrilla—able, through the design of a series of small individual buildings to eventually influence the city as a whole if they concealed in them the power to trigger a chain reaction—represented a stance that only a grass-roots architect would think to adopt.

I believe being able to see small residential works designed by a group of modernist architects who were trying to develop an architecture for an era of democracy by means of an approach different from that of Tange was what convinced me I could, in guerrilla fashion, make even small buildings into "architecture."

They included architects such as Kiyoshi Seike, Kiyoshi Ikebe and Makoto Masuzawa. What made a particularly vivid impression on me was Masuzawa's house for himself, which I saw in real time around 1960. A house of less than 30 square meters in floor area was transformed into a residence of astonishing spaciousness by means of three-dimensional architectural design. The succinct details suggested a modernist engagement with the issue of tradition and embodied a vision of architecture that made the work much more than just a solution to the problem of the minimal house.

The trend that began in the 1950s in which the design of small houses played a crucial part reached a peak with the Masuzawa House and then rapidly faded in the 1960s. That was the beginning of Tange's golden age, which covered the Tokyo Olympics and the Osaka Exposition. Whatever may be history's final judgment on those two very different lines of development, the 1950s and the 1960s were without a doubt a period of unprecedented brilliance for Japanese architecture. The members of my generation were fortunate to start architecture in that period.

My Architectural Point of Origin

Rowhouse in Sumiyoshi, a culmination of the urban guerrilla houses and my debut work as an architect, was also an extremely small private house. It was a concrete box, 3.3 meters wide and 14.1 meters deep, replacing the middle unit of three rowhouses in a "low-city" district (i.e. a low-lying area of small shops and factories) in Sumiyoshi Ward, Osaka. It attracted worldwide interest because it raised a number of issues despite its small size.

It was controversial, first of all, because of the absence of any openings on the four outer walls except the entrance. Second, its walls and ceilings on the inside and outside were made entirely of exposed concrete. Third, and this was its most discussed feature, the box, despite its already small size, was divided in three, and the middle third made into a roofless courtyard.

On rainy days the occupants must use an umbrella to go to the toilet because the path of circulation is interrupted in the middle by the open courtyard. The house is certainly quite inconvenient from a modern, functionalist standpoint. The exposed concrete used on the interior and the exterior and the unwelcoming facade were certainly severe, considering the sensibilities of most people with respect to their everyday environment at the time.

However, these choices were by no means made out of disregard for the everyday lives of the occupants. After giving serious thought to what was truly necessary for living in that place and what dwelling was all about, I decided to maximize exposure to changes in nature, whether gentle or harsh, even if it meant sacrificing some convenience, because living as a part of nature was essential to any dwelling and the site was a limited one in the city.

The stoic materiality of the mainly exposed concrete finish on the inside and outside and the thoroughly simplified geometrically-based spatial composition were responses to severe site and economic conditions; at the same time, they represented the pursuit of a minimalist aesthetic, an attempt to achieve the richness of a space of "nothingness" through the elimination of all superfluity.

The task was, not to depend on material objects, but to aim for a richness of space achievable only in that place. The nearly extreme conditions of Rowhouse in Sumiyoshi taught me that limiting materials to steel, glass and concrete, organizing space by a simple geometry and boldly introducing nature into the interior space could be enriching. The narrow site and low cost did not permit even a millimeter of extravagance. That was precisely why I was able to examine closely each and every problem, from the psychological and physical strength of the people who would be spending time there to their life style, and to develop the ideas that would become the basis for my own architecture.

Rowhouse in Sumiyoshi with a form that seems divorced from its surroundings may seem at first glance a completely private space closed to the city. However, the unwelcoming concrete walls without a single window looking out are not a simple boundary between public and private worlds but an expression of an individual's intention to resist the excessive growth of the city in the name of intensive economic growth and to cling to the city. The theme was always the city, however small the buildings may have been.

Restoring a Relationship to the City, Beginning with Commercial Buildings

If my residential debut work is Rowhouse in Sumiyoshi, its commercial counterpart is Rose Garden, completed in 1977 in Kitano-cho, Kobe, a year after the house.

Postwar Japanese society, preoccupied with the economy, treated both land and buildings as targets for speculation. All that was demanded of commercial buildings was that they be boxes with efficiently arranged spaces; all that architects could do was to design the surfaces of those buildings. Commercial buildings were neglected by the architectural world, which saw them as things that could not be made into "architecture."

However, commercial buildings had originally come into being together with cities and had developed as cities developed. Commercial buildings ought to be by their very nature closely related to the city, in both scale and function.

Seeing those commercial buildings which were a part of people's everyday lives as opportunities to create public spaces that are shared by everyone, spaces not found in buildings aspiring to be "architecture," I gave each such project everything I had.

At the time, Kitano-cho too was being threatened by the wave of reckless urban redevelopment that swept postwar Japan, and its once tranquil townscape featuring Western-style houses was being destroyed by the disorderly construction of buildings in bad taste. In Rose Garden, my theme was to make the building continuous with the city while preserving the building's autonomy. Continuity was achieved from without by means of an arrangement of volumes that allows the building to blend into the existing townscape and the adoption of features already in the existing townscape such as gabled roofs and red bricks, and from within by the creation of passageways inside the building that were extensions of the street and the provision of public spaces such as alcoves that mediated between the building and the townscape.

Some people recognized what I had tried to do in Rose Garden, and other buildings with designs that blended into their surroundings and forms of organization resembling that of Rose Garden (i.e. tenant spaces arranged around courtyards) subsequently appeared in various places. I myself was involved in a period of approximately ten years with a total of eight such buildings including Kitano Alley, Rin's Gallery and Kitano Ivy Court. Now that I think about it, I believe such regional work was precisely what I had in mind by an "urban guerrilla" approach; that is, an attempt to influence the whole (i.e. the city) by a series of connected parts (i.e. individual buildings).

Relationship to the Street

From Rose Garden, my architectural activities revolved primarily around the design of private houses and commercial buildings, and by the start of the 1980s, I was taking on projects of a certain size such as STEP in Takamatsu, FESTIVAL in Okinawa, TIME'S in Kyoto, BIGI, OXY and GALLERIA [akka] in the Minami district of Osaka and COLLEZIONE in Aoyama, Tokyo.

The media have often seen my series of buildings in Kitano-cho as an exception, perhaps because their architectural elements such as red brick and gabled roofs are not in keeping with the stoic image projected by my other buildings beginning with Rowhouse in Sumiyoshi.

Certainly, the works in Kitano-cho that emphasize harmony with the existing townscape seem, at first glance, very different in design from works that emphasize a strong geometry and possess quite independent architectural compositions such as STEP, which interrupts an arcade and is organized around an axial open stairway: FESTIVAL, which features an equal-span, rigid-frame structure that encloses interpenetrating interior and exterior spaces; and GALLERIA [akka], which is organized around a vertical, maze-like atrium that occupies half of its long, narrow site. However, the architect's intention was the same; it was to stimulate the city by means of buildings where people gather.

The buildings in Kitano-cho respond to the environment by maintaining an existing context. By contrast, in STEP and FESTIVAL, which stand in confused urban contexts, the buildings are isolated from their surroundings by their restrained formal expression but contain public spaces such as unexpected, dramatic atriums and urban alcoves; the buildings are paradoxically related to and grafted onto the city by those means.

In FESTIVAL, my idea was also to accommodate Okinawa's climate in a work of contemporary architecture through the use of perforated blocks that allow all public spaces in it to be non air-conditioned, semi-outdoor spaces. Making the facade open or closed is only a matter of methodology. For me, the question was always how to create a place where large numbers of the general public might gather and how to "open up" the building to the street.

Architecture as Social Criticism

Trying to establish a relationship to the street or neighborhood was, of course, not always welcomed. Such an attempt (to consider a building from the standpoint of the city) ultimately imposes restrictions on the building program and leads to the creation of spaces that are not directly profitable.

"Why is such a large atrium necessary?"

"Too much floor space is given over to passageways and stairs."

"The public spaces are all semi-outdoor spaces. They are quite inconvenient since they cannot be air conditioned."

A client will not entrust everything to the architect. Half regretting the selection of such a troublesome architect, he will try to change the course the project is taking so as to assure the project's financial success. The architect needs perseverance and strength if he hopes to endure the tense hours that must be spent with such clients and developers.

In that sense, the realization of TIME'S, a commercial complex in Kyoto that was a most reckless endeavor, was quite meaningful.

At TIME'S, the idea I had for relating the architecture to the city was to relate it to the Takase River, a stream flowing past the site. At the time, all buildings alongside the river turned their backs on it; people were not able to get close to the water. It was a completely forsaken place in Kyoto. Postwar urbanization in Japan, which gave priority to the economy, can be said to have been achieved at the cost of nature, including rivers such as this.

However, Kyoto has had a long history of urban spaces that are closely related to bodies of water such as the canal from Lake Biwa and Kamo River, which flows through the middle of the city. If I was going to design a building by a river in such a city, I wanted to make use of the water in some way.

The question was how to create an open space facing the river. I was interested in creating a tense relationship between the building and the river. I was interested in, not just the use of the river as something to look at, but in the creation of the sort of tension produced by the literal introduction of the flow of the river into the building.

An architecture that adapts itself to nature, an architecture of ambiguous boundary between inside and outside—that was the special character of traditional Japanese architecture. When one thinks of Katsura Detached Palace or Shugakuin Detached Palace, Kinkakuji or Ginkakuji, what inevitably comes to mind is architecture integrated with a garden. When one thinks of the relationship of traditional Japanese architecture and its relationship to water, what comes to mind are bold designs built on, or in proximity to, water such as the Hoodo (Phoenix Hall) of Byodo-in in Uji or Itsukushima Shrine—designs inconceivable in the architectural culture of the West, premised on the opposition of the man-made environment to nature.

Of course I did not design TIME'S with any actual work of traditional Japanese architecture in mind. Since my late teens, I have loved visiting old buildings in Nara and Kyoto. I think what happened is that the spatial sensibility I was exposed to through those experiences unconsciously emerged in the design of TIME'S.

On every level, the semi-outdoor public spaces are designed as narrow. mazelike passageways. TIME'S was conceived as a building with spaces that permitted "encounters" with Takase River. However, both the client and the authorities strongly objected to my proposal to interrupt the bank of the river on the lowest level, which was set only 20 centimeters above the surface of the water, and to create a terrace there.

"What will you do if the river floods? Items for sale in the building will be ruined." To allay the anxiety of the client, I carefully explained the technical reasons I had set the level of the floor where I had; it had been based on the fact that Takase River is actually a canal, whose volume of water is controlled upstream. The authorities, however, were reluctant to approve.

"There is no precedent for removing a portion of a riverbank for a building. The absence of a precedent suggests it shouldn't be done."

Rules ought to be followed, but the authorities did not rest their case on an understanding of the city; they objected simply because it presented an institutional problem. Nothing new can be produced with a system of restrictions imposed solely out of a fear that problems might arise. I refuted their argument and refused to back down until approval was granted.

TIME'S, which was realized after negotiations with Kyoto's municipal government, was successful, both commercially and as a contemporary work of architecture in Kyoto that enables people to come into contact with a body of water. Several years later, I designed a building based on the same idea on an adjacent site. As with Rose Garden in Kitano-cho, the construction of individual buildings stimulated the development of the community.

Whereas earlier works, starting with Rowhouse in Sumiyoshi, had introduced nature in the abstract in the form of light and wind into enclosed domains, TIME'S marked a change of direction, the adoption of an approach that cast buildings out into nature.

Through that process, I conceived the idea of enlisting the help of the site (i.e. making the most of the potential of a place) to reorganize the environment. I have always given precedence to the making of things and not been as attentive to the articulation of what I am trying to do. I had the vague notion that my idea was consistent with contextualism, which had been in fashion in the 1970s. However, the architectural critic Kenneth Frampton astutely described it as an example of what he called "critical regionalism."

In all honesty, assembling architecture on the basis of the existing environment came quite naturally to me, and my adoption of such an approach was not so deliberate as to warrant it being called "regionalism." However, I was quite sympathetic to the concept of a modern architecture that was critical of society.

Modernism tends to avoid problems in planning by eliminating from consideration unexpected or uncertain factors. I would like to select things that have been thus eliminated from contemporary society and create an architecture that throws that problem into relief; moreover, I would like to explore the nature of an architecture that exists only in a certain place.

In Suntory Museum, which I designed for Tempozan, Osaka, I went beyond the boundary of the given museum site and conceived a stepped plaza that extended from the coastal embankment, which was under the jurisdiction of the municipal government, to the sea, which was under the jurisdiction of the state. My aim was to understand the power of the place and, by using it fully, to reorganize the entire environment.

The building was intended to be critical of the way rivers and the sea have been cut off from everyday life in waterfront spaces in contemporary cities. It was modeled in that sense on TIME'S.

Gathering Places

There are two scenes that come immediately to mind when I think of the issue of public character. One is the perspective of the abovementioned Peace Center; the other is the sight of mass being held at the chapel at Ronchamp (Chapelle Notre-Dame du Haut) designed by Le Corbusier.

I am not certain which of my visits it was, but lights and sounds flooded the plastic interior space of Ronchamp. The space and the people who had gathered for mass were literally one and radiated tremendous energy. I thought about Corbusier's enormous talent and was reminded of the importance of places where people can gather to pray, that is, the importance of religious facilities in contemporary society.

To take on the challenge of designing a religious building that suggests that a building's power is not proportional to its size had been a goal of mine since I first decided to enter architecture.

I received the commission for Church of the Light in 1987, when Japanese society was astir over a rise in the value of assets being fueled by speculation. The site was in a corner of a suburban residential area without any particularly distinguishing characteristics. The church was to be about 100 square meters in size. Donations from worshipers were to cover the cost of the building but hardly seemed adequate; it was difficult just finding a construction company willing to take on such a small project. The conditions for this job were the worst imaginable; nevertheless, the strong wish of the worshipers to build a church convinced me to immediately accept.

At the time, I had already completed Church on the Water in Tomamu, Hokkaido, and Chapel on Mt. Rokko (aka Church of the Wind) in Kobe. I was given a free hand, relatively speaking, in designing these churches, which were both in scenic, natural settings. I had a great deal of experience working in heavily built-up districts in the middle of cities, but those commissions provided an opportunity for me to tackle a new theme, that of the relationship of architecture and nature.

However, the two previous churches had been both chapels attached to hotels, that is facilities mainly intended to accommodate wedding ceremonies; they were not pure religious buildings intended to be houses of prayer. The motives behind their construction were by no means simply religious. By contrast, there were people who truly needed a building in the case of Church of the Light, and that made the project especially meaningful to me.

What I finally arrived at after about a year of design was an extremely simple composition: a concrete box six meters wide and 18 meters deep, penetrated by a diagonal wall. Besides the exposed concrete walls and ceiling, the other visible elements were a floor stepping down toward the altar and cedar planks normally used for on-site scaffolding, painted black and used as seats. A cruciform opening in the wall behind the altar introduced light into the dim space.

I had made the building extremely simple, not just because the low budget forced me to, but primarily because I wanted to create a richer place by eliminating from the space all nonessentials.

One image I had in mind was that of a Romanesque monastery of medieval Europe, particularly the cave-like chapel, shaped by roughly hewn stones laid with enormous effort by monks. Into the ascetic space, built almost by pure will, strong light enters directly from unglazed windows and solemnly illuminates the stones paving the floor. The idea of a cross of light came to mind when I thought about trying to express that almost harsh beauty of the monastery chapel in a concrete box.

Church on the Water and Chapel on Mt. Rokko are similar to Church of the Light in that in those earlier buildings too I had relied on nature in the abstract (in their cases water and wind) to create symbolic spaces. However, in the earlier churches, built in natural environments, I began with the idea of opening them to their surroundings. By contrast, in Church of the Light, my working premise was that the space would be closed to its surroundings, and I reduced its relationship to nature accordingly to the bare minimum.

I have always tended to prefer spaces of darkness to spaces of light, not for any particular reason but simply as a matter of personal sensibility. That is evident in the series of cave-like buildings I have designed, from Rowhouse in Sumiyoshi to Chichu Art Museum, completed in 2004, but the extreme conditions under which I had to design Church of the Light can be said to have produced in that work the most straightforward expression of my architectural predilection.

Without a doubt, the simple enthusiasm of the minister, the worshipers and the people of the construction company that accepted the job in full knowledge of the effort it would require made it possible to complete this difficult construction work, which was troubled to the end by the constraints of a limited budget.

The superficial prosperity brought on by speculation that lasted from the late 1980s into the 1990s threw society and the architectural world out of kilter. The principles of the market held sway over cities, and buildings became commodities. Disoriented by such developments and searching for the path that an "urban guerrilla" should take, I found in this small chapel a chance to confirm once more the importance of this most fundamental of architectural questions: for what reason and for whom is this building to be created? From the 1990s, I gradually shifted the focus of my work to buildings that were public in character. Church of the Light was the turning point.

Transcending the Framework and Influencing the Environment

In assembling a building, there is something I always tell myself to do. Instead of being obsessed with details, ascertain the essence of the problem; always go back to the fundamentals and reorganize things according to basic principles. In this, I was greatly influenced by the people of Gutai, with whom I first became acquainted in my twenties. Gutai, which originated in the Kansai region, is Japan's first and only group of avant-garde artists.

Do not be swayed by preconceptions.

Never imitate others.

Always think for yourself.

Adoption of such a radical stance inevitably causes conflict and friction with society. I became painfully aware of this fact in architecture when I began to become involved in so-called public projects. In 1987, about 20 years after I opened my own office, I started the design of my first public work, Children's Museum, Hyogo.

The site of Children's Museum is next to an artificial pond called Sakurayama Reservoir, in a suburb of Himeji City. The facility was intended to accommodate children's activities such as reading and crafts as well as research presentations. When I first received the commission, I was pleased to be getting this project that was literally public, thinking I would be able to work on a much larger scale than I had been used to and would be designing a facility that was programmed for children. However, when I visited the site in Himeji for my first discussion with the authorities and listened to the explanation of the person in charge, I learned that the building site was approximately one-tenth of the entire site; the remaining 90 percent of the site would be landscaped and be the responsibility of someone else. That was common practice in public projects at the time, but I objected vociferously.

"Such a division of responsibility is simply a bureaucratic measure that will be meaningless to visiting children [...] The entire site, including both interior and exterior spaces, should obviously be considered as one place, as a whole."

We talked at cross-purposes, the representatives of the prefectural government agency, who set store by precedent, on one side and I, with avant-garde ideas influenced by Gutai on the other, and the argument became heated. It was when things were seemingly at an impasse that Toshitami Kaihara, who was then the governor of Hyogo, came to the rescue.

"There is logic in what Ando says. Let's be bold and give him responsibility for everything."

I was thus able to conceive the entire site of Children's Museum, from the approach to the facility itself, as a set of devices having encounter with nature as its theme. The extended outdoor path linking the facility and situated on the edge of the pond, a plaza located halfway on that path and featuring 16 pillars, and a pool-garden surrounding the main building—these architectural stratagems were conceived as part of a grand landscape centered on the beautiful artificial pond, behind which rose a wooded mountain.

These architectural devices, which had no clear function, were extravagances from a commonsensical standpoint. However, if the aim of Children's Museum was to cultivate sensibilities in children, then teaching materials in the form of a natural environment and play spaces that enable children to discover for themselves the delights of that environment were needed.

This project, pushed through despite opposition, was realized more than 20 years ago. Today, the building is even more firmly embedded in the natural landscape, and the play area for children is being expanded.

Architects must participate in projects from the conceptual stage that precedes architectural design if they wish to create public buildings that contribute to society.

After the bursting of the bubble economy, public buildings have often been criticized as containers empty of content, symbolic of a distorted system of local government. Naturally, there is no point in creating containers that are not used, but certain things can only been done with public buildings. The management of such facilities may be difficult, but if things are all left to the private sector, culture is unlikely to develop.

What can architecture do in a given place? The important thing is the process before construction, that is, the asking of basic questions before the undertaking of a project.

The Architecture of Place

Public buildings have been central to my practice since Children's Museum; in particular, museums have increased markedly since the 1990s. For the urban guerrilla who once had to overcome many constraints, it has been a sea-change.

However, my methodology continues to be to respond architecturally to the environment, whether it is a confused, disorderly urban environment or an unspoiled solitary island. It is the role of public architecture to bring out the potential of a site and to create a place of even greater value.

A work in which I myself feel I was able to develop a proposal that transcended the given framework as far as place was concerned was Chikatsu-Asuka Historical Museum, Osaka.

Since Children's Museum, I have integrated the architecture to the surrounding environment in places that possess a certain context, as with Museum of Literature, Himeji; Naoshima Contemporary Art Museum (now Benesse House Museum); and Forest of Tombs Museum, Kumamoto. In Chikatsu-Asuka Historical Museum I took that methodology one step further and tried to transform the entire building into a landscape.

It is an underground building without a facade, created as an artificial hill entirely covered with stones and built to conform to the topography of the site—the museum as a contemporary burial mound. Visitors take a stroll path on Fudoki Hill which is covered with trees of Japanese apricot and arrive at the artificial hill; from there, they are able to view a landscape on which the ancient world has left its mark. At the top, they enter the burial mound and come into contact with relics of the ancient period.

It is, in a sense, the complete opposite of a conventional museum, the kind of museum that is a box isolated from its surroundings and full of exhibits. In this place, located at midpoint on the historic highway linking the Tomb of Emperor Nintoku in Sakai to the ancient capital of Asuka in Nara Prefecture—a place where more than 200 burial mounds are scattered—the most important exhibit is the history-inscribed environment itself. The museum must be a device offering a time and a place where people may confront that history.

I believe the reason the unconventional proposal to create a museum covered with a stepped plaza was realized as a public facility of a local government was because of the powerful historical context of the place called Chikatsu-Asuka. Sayamaike Museum, Osaka, which I began designing in 1994 for another site in the same prefecture and completed in 2001, is another museum that responds to its environment.

Seeking Value and Meaning

In one of his books, Fumihiko Maki has written that there is a limit to the size of a space that a single human being can design. Awaji-Yumebutai, which I started in 1993, was in fact a project on an extraordinary scale—the site was 600 meters long and 200,000 square meters in area—and no conventional architectural concept would have been able to hold it together.

The architecture could not be a single whole but instead had to be the aggregate of parts. Trying to discover some public significance, nonetheless, I conceived the idea of restoring nature to a site disfigured by years of excavation. The site of Yumebutai had provided landfill for the reclamation of the Osaka Bay area from the mid-1950s.

The Hanshin-Awaji Earthquake on January 17, 1995 interrupted the project, which was just about to get underway. Even though there were repeated revisions of the project, I consistently believed in the goal of environmental regeneration, that is, the restoration by human hands of a land that had been destroyed and disfigured by humankind.

The project began, not with buildings, but with the planting of more than 500,000 saplings, each about 10 centimeters tall, on the steep, excavated slope of more than 30 degrees. Even as major construction work involving the building of a complicated architectural complex was being undertaken, the attempt to nurture a forest from saplings proceeded quietly on the enormous site. I focused on making the architecture responsive to nature instead of assertive; the question was how to bring out nature's attractive qualities.

As of 2008, eight years have passed since the facilities of Yumebutai opened. The ten-centimeter tall saplings have become a forest of trees over five meters tall. The facilities, which had the air upon completion of a spatial theme park, have weathered nicely. It will probably take less than ten more years for the forest to envelop the place entirely.

Simply creating an infrastructure-like facility or place in the public interest does not guarantee that it will become a public asset capable of enriching people's lives. I believe public character in architecture means the creation of a communal landscape, one that can be shared and becomes a spiritual landscape.

That is why I made the growth of a forest that will eventually cover and conceal the architecture the theme of Awaji-Yumebutai and why in Omotesando Hills (the project replacing the Aoyama Dojunkai Apartments in Tokyo), begun in 1996 and completed in 2006, I spent more than ten years developing a plan whose first priority was restricting the height of the 250-meter long building that includes commercial facilities so that it would not exceed the height of the zelkova trees lining the avenue known as Omotesando.

These themes do not fit easily into a conventional architectural framework. In fact, the most difficult aspect of both Awaji-Yumebutai and Omotesando Hills was the process of achieving political and social consensus before architectural design could begin.

However, I see both the process of working out small architectural details and the process of involvement in a large-scale multifunctional project, such as Awaji-Yumebutai, and preparing a suitable set of conditions for the construction of architecture through repeated discussions as the assembling of architecture. They are all part of the architecture of an urban guerrilla who hopes to act upon the city.

What in the total environment does one value and find meaningful? The answer to that question determines the work one ought to engage in as an architect.

Patronage for the Nurturing of Architecture

It was thanks to Toshitami Kaihara, then-governor of Hyogo Prefecture, that, as with Children's Museum, Hyogo, I was commissioned to design the entire Awaji-Yumebutai project. The project began in the early 1990s, when cities were still suffering the ill effects of the bubble. Kaihara did not want the redevelopment of Awaji to end with simply the construction of facilities. Believing that with a single person steering the project, there was less likelihood of a loss of direction, he selected me and persuaded the assembly to approve his choice. Damage inflicted on Awaji by the Hanshin-Awaji Earthquake did not dissuade him; on the contrary, he came to see the project as a symbol of reconstruction, and after a total reworking of the plan—the project lies on a fault line—he saw the project to its realization. Kaihara's courage was the biggest reason for the success of the big project under the conditions then prevailing in Japan.

In pursuing the theme of the public character of architecture, the biggest obstacle, as I have already mentioned, is in a sense the presence of clients.

The richness of urban space lies in the abundance of "blank" areas (i.e. areas without specific function) in the spaces of everyday life. The architect and the client are often in direct opposition to one another over the question of such non-productive blank areas. Usually, the architect, being in the employ of the client, gives way, but though they are in the minority, there are occasionally patrons who share the architect's vision.

My career as an architect has been supported throughout by such patronage.

The late Keizo Saji believed in me, though he knew me simply on a personal basis, and gave me an opportunity to design Suntory Museum when I had no experience as yet designing large cultural facilities. I recall that I became acquainted with leaders of the Kansai economic world such as Saji, Toshio Iue of Sanyo Electric and Kazuo Inamori of Kyocera, about the time I organized an exhibition of my own projects such as Nakanoshima Project II (Urban Egg). It was no doubt because they themselves had led tumultuous lives that they took an interest in someone like myself who was so passionate about the redevelopment of an island in the river flowing through the middle of Osaka that he developed a project for it entirely on his own initiative.

Then there is Soichiro Fukutake of Benesse Corporation. The cultural project on Naoshima, a small island in the Inland Sea of Japan, that I began with Fukutake at the end of the 1980s, is still on-going after more than 20 years and has produced Benesse House Museum, Benesse House Oval, Minamidera (Art House Project No. 2) and Chichu Art Museum; a new hotel facility was completed in 2006, and a new gallery is currently being planned.

Participating in a series of projects in Naoshima that have no master plan but Fukutake's vision, I have had an opportunity not only to explore in fundamental ways the architectural theme of the art museum but to witness a process in which the non-productive thing called art or culture has revitalized a region, that is, a process in which culture has revived a place.

In particular, Art House Projects, in which contemporary art has been embedded in restored old vernacular houses remaining in the Honmura district of Naoshima are socially quite significant. They are superb artistic endeavors that link time and space; at the same time, the projects, which transcend the conventional museum framework, have been successful in reviving the island and developing the region. This small, once forgotten island of 3,000 persons has become well-known as a sanctuary of art not only in Japan but overseas and draws more than 200,000 tourists annually.

Public buildings and places are not necessarily born of democratic, pre-established harmony. The driving force behind the creation of a "free space" is powerful, individual passion and will. That is attested to by my architectural career of 40 years.

Planting Trees

I have written about things concerning the theme of public character and the path I myself have taken. Let me conclude with a story about creating, not architecture, but a forest.

At present, I am involved in an on-going project with the Tokyo Metropolitan Government to revive a piece of reclaimed land of approximately 88 hectares in the middle of Tokyo Bay where garbage was once dumped into a thickly-wooded "Forest of the Sea."

"Forest of the Sea" is part of a project of urban reorganization aimed at attracting the 2016 Olympics to the city. Tokyo once used the 1964 Olympics as an opportunity to transform itself dramatically from the ruins of war to a modern city. The subsequent explosive growth of the economy brought unprecedented material affluence but also caused various environmental problems. Despite such burdens, Tokyo has stubbornly survived and grown into one of the world cities of Asia. Tokyo must now take not the path of simple development but the path that leads to increasing maturity as it resolves its internal urban problems.

The concept of the grand design Tokyo has prepared with that in mind is an urban strategy of putting to creative use what it already has, rather than making something entirely new. The improvement of needed urban functions requires the maximum utilization of existing facilities; rivers, which reckless redevelopment had neglected, need to be reconsidered, and famous places with scenic landscapes and historical associations need to be rediscovered. The clean-up of urban spaces exhausted by high density will be achieved through increased planting of trees along streets to create green corridors linking strategic green centers in the middle of the city and the greening of urban interstices such as the rooftops of buildings, parking areas and the grounds of elementary and secondary schools. This green network will culminate in the "Forest of the Sea" in the middle of Tokyo Bay.

The urban activities of humankind since the twentieth century have increased to the point that they threaten the survival of the Earth. To solve the problem, an effort that transcends national boundaries and cultural differences must be made. All of us are beginning to realize the scale of this problem.

"Forest of the Sea" is a project to grow a forest gradually over time through citizen participation, with donations of 1,000 Yen each from 500,000 persons. I realize of course that even if the greening project including the Forest of the Sea is successful, it will not bring about a fundamental solution to urban problems. However, to have the public plant trees on a mountain of waste produced by the city and to grow a natural forest—to begin this project in Tokyo, a city of 30 million persons—has significance beyond the creation of one forest. It will transmit to the world a message that Tokyo too has begun to act with the aim of creating a city for humankind.

Forest of the Sea is not the first movement of this kind in which I have participated.

I have been actively involved in a number of citizen participation-type movements such as Hyogo Green Network, in which trees bearing white flowers were planted in memory of the victims of the 1995 Hanshin-Awaji Earthquake, Setouchi Olive Foundation, which was begun with the aim of reviving Teshima Island, long considered a symbol of industrial waste, and protecting the natural environment of the Inland Sea, and Sakuranokai—Heisei-era Passages, a project to create cherry tree-lined paths in riverside areas in Osaka.

Seeing me always talk on the media about planting trees, many people ask, "Why is an architect planting trees?" Since the creation of architecture and the creation of forests are both actions taken to influence the environment and to add new value to places, I do not find it strange for an architect to be enthusiastic about the planting of trees, yet it is difficult to convince people who think otherwise. However, reviewing the path I have taken with respect to the theme of public character, I think I have found a persuasive answer to their question.

What is important to me is the fact that actions taken to influence the environment are premised on citizen participation.

If the city is to be full of vitality, then there must be not only an abundance of "blank" (i.e. public) spaces but mature citizens (i.e. public-spirited people) able to make full use of those spaces. My goal in helping to create a forest is to stimulate and arouse public consciousness in people.

With respect to what I want to accomplish, nothing has changed in the 40 years that have passed since I started architecture. I believe my task today is to continue to pursue my original objective.

1983年に完成した六甲の集合住宅Iから20余年。六甲の急斜面に〈その場所にしかできない住まい〉をつくる安藤の挑戦は、II期、III期へと展開し、そして今、4つ目のプロジェクトが建設途中にある。地形と幾何学、部分と全体の葛藤、パブリックとプライベート——さまざまなテーマを喚起しながら、生物のように増殖する、マスタープランなき建築の風景が、都市と建築の未来を切り拓く。

More than twenty years have passed since the completion of Rokko Housing I in 1983. Ando's challenge of making "dwellings possible only in this location" on the steep slopes of Mount Rokko led to a second and third stage, and now the fourth project is under construction. While raising various themes – topography and geometry, the conflict between part and whole, public and private – it propagates like a living thing, and this scenery of architecture without a master plan has widened the future for architecture and cities.

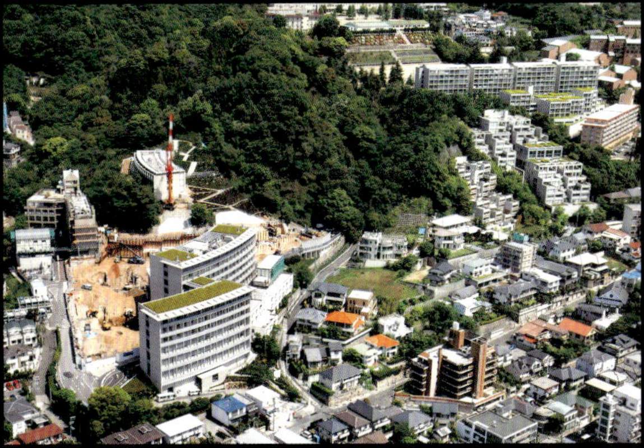
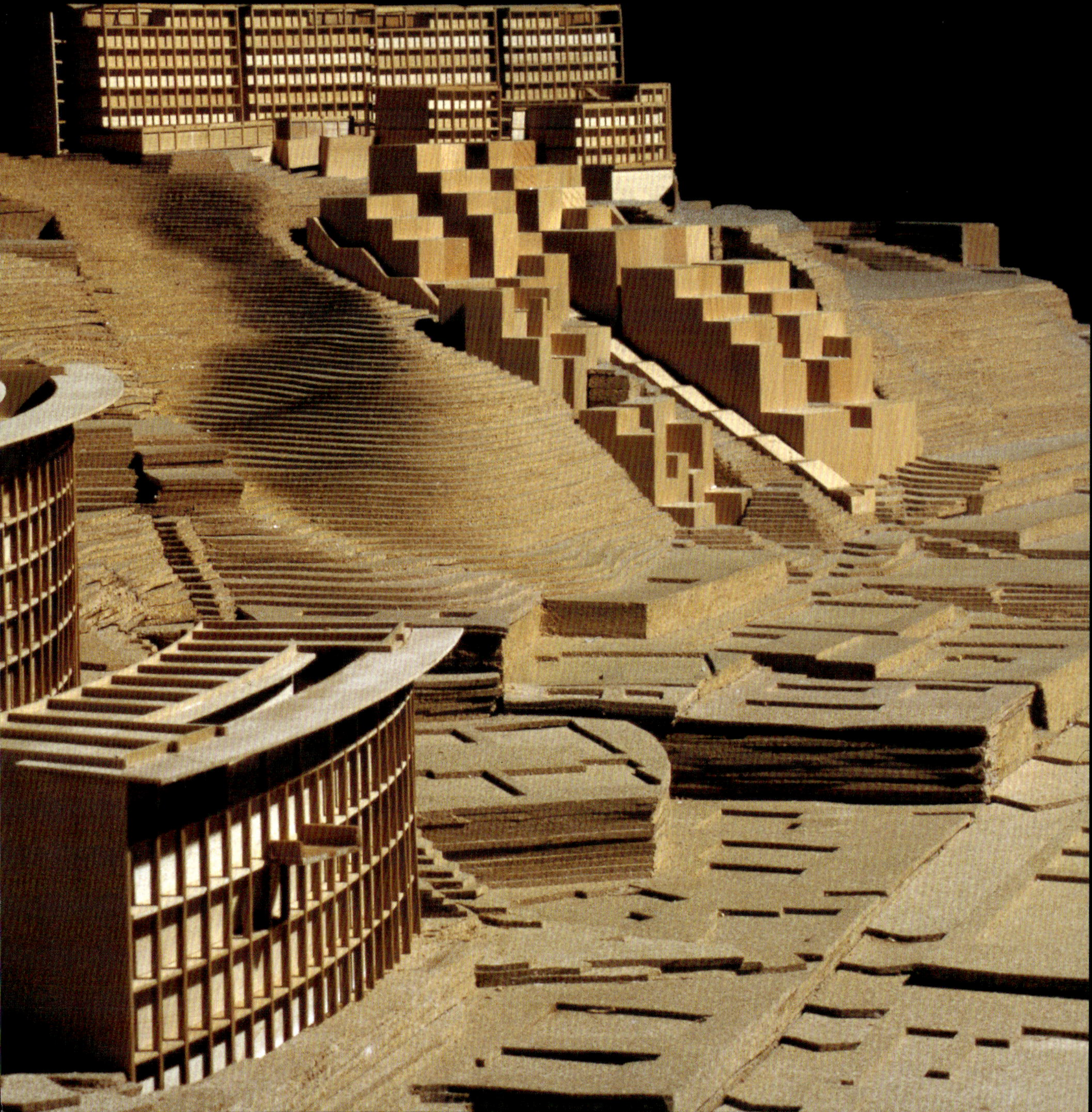

作品年表
1969-2009
Chronological Table of Projects

商業建築／公共建築
Inside Japan

専用住宅／共同住宅／茶室
House, Housing and Tea House

海外作品
Outside Japan

未完プロジェクト
Unbuild Project

完成作品は竣工年、未完プロジェクトは
設計開始年に従って配置しています。

1969-72

1969
JR 大阪駅前プロジェクト
JR Osaka Station Area Reconstruction Project

冨島邸
Tomishima House

1971
スワン商会ビル（小林邸）
"Swan" Kobayashi House

1973

ポートアイランドプロジェクト
Port Island Project

ゲリラ（加藤邸）
"Guerilla" Kato House

1974

立見邸
Tatsumi House

平岡邸
Hiraoka House

芝田邸
Shibata House

内田邸
Uchida House

宇野邸
Uno House

1975	1976	1977	1978	1979
	甲東アレイⅡ Koto Alley Ⅱ	ローズガーデン Rose Garden	甲東アレイ Koto Alley	
		北野アレイ Kitano Alley	Sunny Garden Sunny Garden	
		アートギャラリー コンプレックス Art Gallery Complex		
双生観（山口邸） "Soseikan" Yamaguchi House	住吉の長屋（東邸） "Row House in Sumiyoshi" Azuma House			ガラスブロックウォール （堀内邸） "Glass Block Wall" Horiuchi House
高橋邸 Takahashi House	貫入（平林邸） "Interpenetration" Hirabayashi House			片山ハウス Katayama Building
松村邸 Matsumura House	番匠邸 Bansho House			大西邸 Onishi House
四軒長屋 Tenement House with Four Flats	帝塚山タワープラザ Tezukayama Tower Plaza	領壁の家（松本邸） "Wall House" Matsumoto House	大楠邸 Okusu House	上田邸 Ueda House
ツインウォール Twin Wall	岡本ハウジング Okamoto Housing Project	帝塚山の家（真鍋邸） "Tezukayama House" Manabe House	ガラスブロックの家（石原邸） "Glass Block House" Ishihara House	松谷邸 Matsutani House

1980

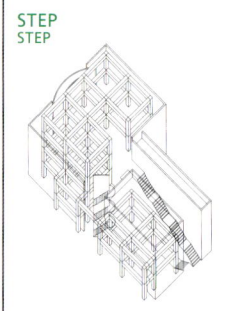

STEP
STEP

中之島プロジェクト I
（大阪市役所）
Nakanoshima Project I
(Osaka City Hall)

STEP II
STEP II

松本邸
Matsumoto House

福邸
Fuku House

北野アイビーコート
Kitano Ivy Court

大淀のアトリエ（1期）
Atelier in Oyodo (Phase I)

1981

ファッション・ライブ・シアター
Fashion Live Theater

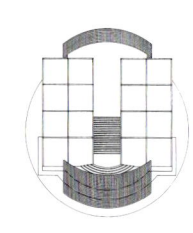

リンズギャラリー
Rin's Gallery

番匠邸増築
Bansho House Addition

小篠邸
Koshino House

児島の共同住宅（佐藤邸）
"Kojima Housing"
Sato House

泉邸
Izumi House

1982

サンプレイス
Sun Place

大淀のアトリエ（2期）
Atelier in Oyodo (Phase II)

石井邸
Ishii House

双生観の茶室（山口邸増築）
"Tea House for Soseikan"
Yamaguchi House Addition

赤羽邸
Akabane House

九条の町屋（井筒邸）
"Town House in Kujo"
Izutsu House

ドールズハウス
Doll's House

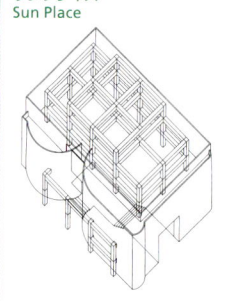

1983

ビギ・アトリエ
BIGI Atelier

梅宮邸
Umemiya House

六甲の集合住宅 I
Rokko Housing I

金子邸
Kaneko House

茂木邸
Motegi House

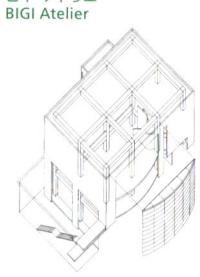

1984

フェスティバル
Festival

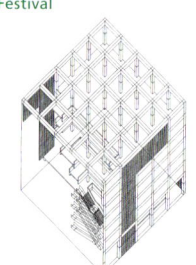

TIME'S I
Time's I

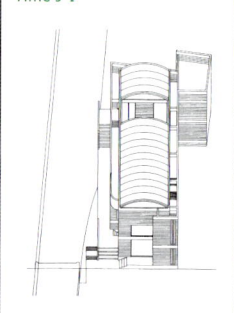

心斎橋 TO
Shinsaibashi TO

MELROSE
MELROSE

植条邸
Uejo House

小篠邸増築
Koshino House Addition

岩佐邸
Iwasa House

畑邸
Hata House

南林邸
Minamibayashi House

太田邸
Ota House

1985

青葉台アトリエ
Aobadai Atelier

青山 TO
Aoyama TO

アトリエ・ヨシエ・イナバ
Atelier Yoshie Inaba

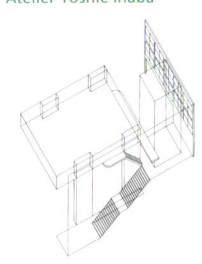

モン・プティ・シュ
Mon-petit-chou

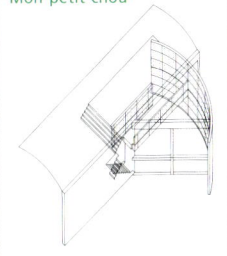

ジュンポートアイランドビル
Jun Portisland Building

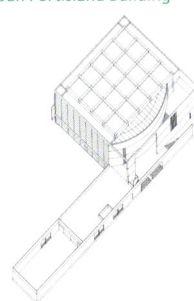

渋谷プロジェクト
Shibuya Project

中山邸
Nakayama House

大淀の茶室（ベニヤの茶室）
Tea House in Oyodo
(Veneer Tea House)

服部邸ゲストハウス
Guest House
for Hattori House

吉本邸
Yoshimoto House

1986

六甲の教会
Chapel on Mt. Rokko

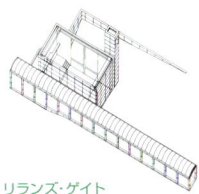

リランズ・ゲイト
Riran's Gate

北野 TO
Kitano TO

太陽セメント本社ビル
Taiyo Cement
Headquarters Building

OXY 北野
OXY Kitano

BIGI 3rd
BIGI 3rd

TK ビル
TK Building

ゲストハウス OLD/NEW 六甲
Guest House Old/New Rokko

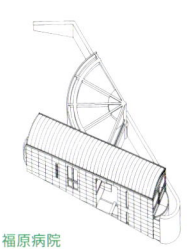

福原病院
Fukuhara Clinic

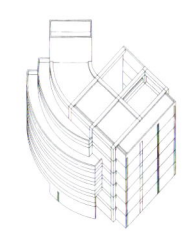

渋谷神社総合開発計画
Shibuya Shrine
Redevelopment Project

孫邸
Son House

大淀のアトリエ（3期）
Atelier in Oyodo (Phase Ⅲ)

細工谷の家（野口邸）
"Town House in Saikudani"
Noguchi House

佐々木邸
Sasaki House

TS ビル
TS Building

沖辺邸
Okibe House

城戸崎邸
Kidosaki House

大淀の茶室（ブロックの茶室）
Tea House in Oyodo
(Block Tea House)

1987

神宮前のアトリエ
Atelier, Jingumae

天王寺博覧会テーマ館
Main Pavilion
for Tennoji Fair

OXY 鰻谷
OXY Unagidani

伊豆プロジェクト
Izu Project

水の劇場
Theater on the Water

六甲山バンケットホール
Banquet Hall on Mt. Rokko

田中山荘
Tanaka Atelier

Ⅰ 計画
Ⅰ Project

1988

唐座
Karaza

GALLERIA [akka]
GALLERIA [akka]

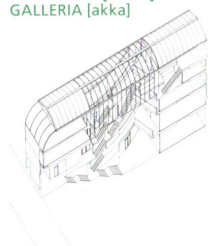

水の教会
Church on the Water

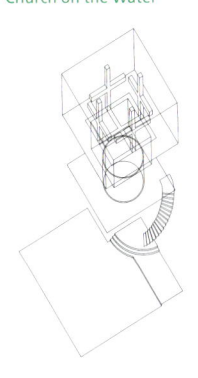

中之島プロジェクトⅡ
（アーバン・エッグ＋地層空間）
Nakanoshima Project Ⅱ
(Urban Egg + Space Strata)

小倉邸
Ogura House

吉田邸
Yoshida House

B-Lock 神楽岡
B-Lock, Kaguraoka

大淀の茶室（テントの茶室）
Tea House in Oyodo
(Tent Tea House)

Ⅰ ハウス
Ⅰ House

伊藤ギャラリー
Ito Gallery

1989

光の教会
Church of the Light

モロゾフ P&P スタジオ
Morozoff P&P Studio

兵庫県立こどもの館
Children's Museum, Hyogo

COLLEZIONE
COLLEZIONE

夏川記念会館
Natsukawa Memorial Hall

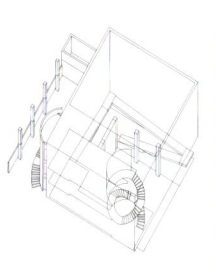

ライカ本社ビル
Raika Headquarters
Building

矢尾クリニック
Yao Clinic

城尾邸
Shiroo House

横浜ハウジング
Yokohama Housing

1990

B-Lock 北山
B-Lock Kitayama

国際花と緑の博覧会
「名画の庭」
Garden of Fine Art,
Expo'90 / Osaka

十文字美信仮設劇場
Temporary Theater for
Bishin Jumonji,
Photographer

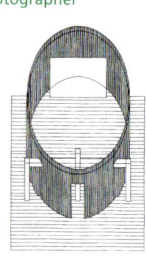

S ビル
S Building

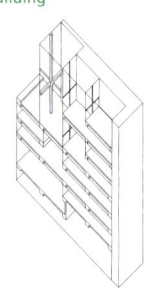

松谷邸増築
Matsutani House Addition

岩佐邸増築
Iwasa House Addition

伊東邸
Ito House

ストックホルム
現代美術館・建築美術館
国際設計競技案
The Modern Art Museum
and Architecture Museum,
Stockholm, International
Design Competition

1991

姫路文学館
Museum of Literature,
Himeji

ロック・フィールド
静岡ファクトリー
Rock Field Shizuoka Factory

播磨ヘリポート
Harima Heliport

真言宗本福寺水御堂
Water Temple

TIME'S II
TIME'S II

甲南大学
スチューデントサークル
プロジェクト
Konan University
Student Circle Project

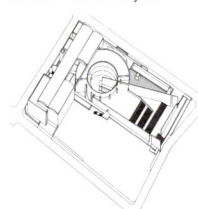

奈良市民ホール
国際設計競技案
Nara Convention Hall
International Design
Competition

JR 京都駅改築設計競技案
The Reconstruction of
JR Kyoto Station,
International Design
Competition

大淀のアトリエ II
Atelier in Oyodo II

石河邸
Ishiko House

佐用ハウジング
Sayoh Housing

ミノルタセミナーハウス
Minolta Seminar House

1992

大手前女子大学
アートセンター
Otemae Art Center

熊本県立装飾古墳館
Forest of Tombs Museum,
Kumamoto

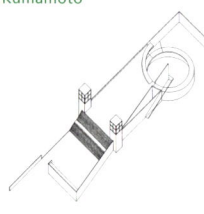

ベネッセハウス ミュージアム
Benesse House
Museum / Naoshima

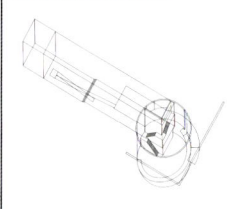

姫路市立星の子館
Children's Seminar House,
Himeji

宮下邸
Miyashita House

1992年セビリア万国博覧会
日本館
Japan Pavilion
Expo'92 / Sevilla

シカゴ美術館
屏風ギャラリー
Gallery for Japanese Screen,
the Art Institute of Chicago

1993

兵庫県立看護大学
アートセンター
College of Nursing,
Art and Science, Hyogo

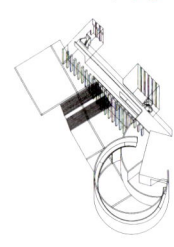

六甲アイランドプロジェクト
Rokko Island Project

垂水の教会
Church in Tarumi

ギャラリー野田
Gallery Noda

YKK 津田沼寮
YKK Seminar House

六甲の集合住宅 II
Rokko Housing II

李邸
Lee House

ヴィトラ・セミナーハウス
Vitra Seminar House

1994

大阪府立近つ飛鳥博物館
Chikatsu-Asuka
Historical Museum, Osaka

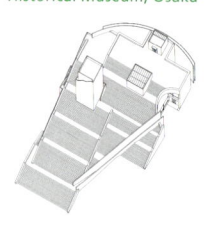

京都府立陶板名画の庭
Garden of Fine Art, Kyoto

兵庫県木の殿堂
Museum of Wood

サントリーミュージアム
+マーメイド広場
Suntory Museum + Plaza

紀陽銀行堺ビル
Kiyo Bank, Sakai Building

マックスレイ本社ビル
Maxray Headquarters
Building

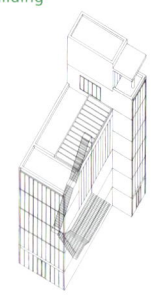

鹿児島大学稲盛会館
Inamori Auditorium

成羽町美術館
Nariwa Museum

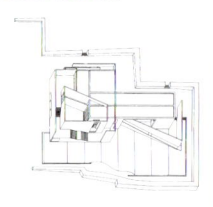

日本橋の家（金森邸）
"House in Nipponbashi"
Kanamori House

テート・ギャラリー
現代美術館国際設計競技案
Tate Gallery of Modern
Art, International Design
Competition

1995

播磨高原東小学校
Harima Kogen
Higashi Primary School

綾部工業団地交流プラザ
Ayabe Community Center

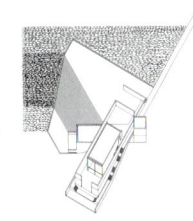

市立五條文化博物館
Museum of Gojo Culture

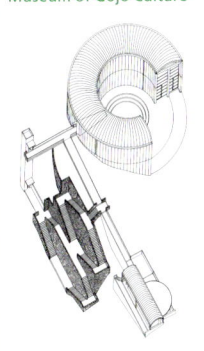

ベネッセハウス オーバル
Benesse House Oval /
Naoshima

大山崎山荘美術館
Oyamazaki Villa Museum

宇ノ気町立金津小学校
Kanatsu Primary School,
Unoke

長良川国際会議場
Nagaragawa
Convention Center

大谷地下劇場計画
The Theater in the Rock, Oya

大淀のアトリエ・アネックス
Atelier in Oyodo Annex

海の集合住宅プロジェクト
Seaside Housing Project

丘の集合住宅プロジェクト
Hilltop Housing Project

ユネスコ瞑想空間
Meditation Space, UNESCO

ローマ司教区教会
国際設計競技案
Vicariato di Roma,
International Design
Competition for the Church
of the Year 2000

1996

上海釜山航路
フェリーターミナル
Shanghai Pusan
Ferry Terminal

姫路文学館南館
Museum of Literature Ⅱ,
Himeji

白井邸
Shirai House

ギャラリー小さい芽（澤田邸）
"Gallery Chiisaime"
Sawada House

平野区の町屋（能見邸）
"Town House in Hirano"
Nomi House

マンハッタンのペントハウス
Penthouse in Manhattan

スタジオ・
カール・ラガーフェルド
Studio Karl Lagerfeld

ストーン・スカルプチュア・
ミュージアム
Stone Sculpture Museum

1997

播磨高原東中学校
Harima Kogen Higashi
Junior High School

小海高原美術館
Koumi Kogen Museum

越知町立
横倉山自然の森博物館—
横倉山・牧野富太郎展示室
The Yokogurayama Natural
Forest Museum, Ochi

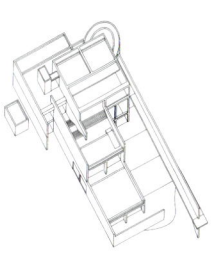

TOTO セミナーハウス
TOTO Seminar House

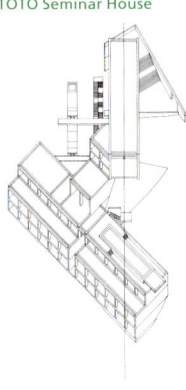

青木の集合住宅
Ohgi Housing

八木邸
Yagi House

シカゴの住宅
House in Chicago

モンテンルパ
社会復帰センター
Muntilupa
Resocialization Center

ライン世界文化博物館
The Museum of
World Cultures
on the River Rhine

1998

渡辺淳一文学館
Junichi Watanabe
Memorial Hall

ダイコク電機本部ビル
Daikoku Denki
Headquarters Building

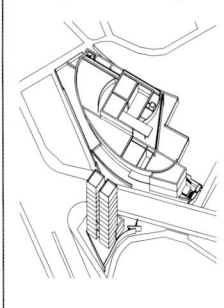

織田廣喜ミュージアム
Daylight Museum

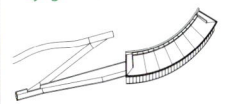

朝日新聞岡山支局
Asahi News Paper
Okayama Bureau

エリエール松山ゲストハウス
Elleair Matsuyama
Guesthouse

ネパール子ども病院
Shiddhartha Children
and Women Hospital

1999

光の教会／日曜学校
Church of the Light,
Sunday School

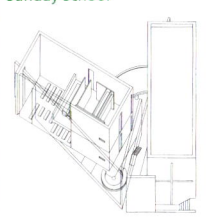

南寺（直島・家プロジェクト）
Minami Dera (Art House
Project in Naoshima)

西宮市貝類館
Shell Museum
of Nishinomiya City

淡路夢舞台
Awaji-Yumebutai
(Awaji Island Project)

六甲の集合住宅Ⅲ
Rokko Housing Ⅲ

ネルソン・アトキンス美術館
国際設計競技案
Nelson Atkins Museum,
International
Design Competition

レイナ・ソフィア美術館
国際設計競技案
Museo Nacional Centro de
Arte Reina Sofia,
International
Design Competition

パリ原始博物館
国際設計競技案
Musée du Quai Branly,
International
Design Competition

アントワープ市立博物館
国際設計競技案
Museum Aan de Stroom,
Antwerp, International
Design Competition

セント・ポール寺院聖台
デザインコンペティション
A New Font for St. Paul's
Cathedral, International
Design Competition

2000

ロック・フィールド
静岡ファクトリー
（Ⅱ期増築＋ランドスケープ）
Rock Field Shizuoka
Factory Study Center

南岳山光明寺
Komyo-ji Temple

ミュゼふくおかカメラ館
Fukuoka Camera Museum

新潟市立豊栄図書館
Niigata City Toyosaka
Library

ダラスの住宅
House in Dallas

FABRICA
（ベネトン・アートスクール）
FABRICA
(Benetton Communication
Research Center)

カルダー美術館
Calder Museum

BOSCH セミナーハウス
国際設計競技案
BOSCH Sminar House,
International
Design Competition

セント・ジョーンズ・
セミナーハウス
St. John's Abbey
Seminar House

2001

大阪府立狭山池博物館
Sayamaike Historical
Museum, Osaka

兵庫県立美術館
Hyogo Prefectural
Museum of Art

神戸市水際広場
Kobe Waterfront Plaza

国際芸術センター青森
Aomori Contemporary
Art Centre

司馬遼太郎記念館
Shiba Ryotaro
Memorial Museum

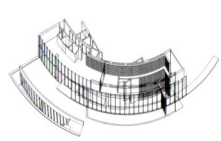

宝塚温泉
Takarazuka Onsen (Spa)

四国村ギャラリー
Shikokumura Gallery

神宮前の集合住宅
Jingumae Housing

4×4の住宅（東京）
4x4 House (Tokyo)

ピューリッツァー美術館
Pulitzer Foundation
for the Arts

アルマーニ・テアトロ
Armani / Teatro

グラウンド・ゼロ
プロジェクト
Ground Zero Project

ピノー現代美術館
François Pinault Foundation
for Contemporary Art

クラーク美術館増築計画
Sterling and Francine
Clark Art Institute
Expansion Project

2002

灘浜ガーデンバーデン
Nadahama Garden Baden

国際子ども図書館
The International Library
of Children's Literature

アウディジャパン本社ビル
Audi Japan Headquarters

西田幾太郎記念哲学館
Nishida Kitaro Museum
of Philosophy

コキュオフィスビル
COCUE Office Building

アサヒビール神奈川工場
ゲストハウス
Guesthouse,
Asahi Kanagawa Brewery

尾道市立美術館
Onomichi City Museum
of Art

加賀市立錦城中学校
Kinjo Junior High School,
Kaga

六甲プロジェクトⅣ
（病院＋老人福祉施設）
Rokko Project IV
(Hospital + Nursing Home)

マンチェスター市
ピカデリー公園再生計画
Piccadilly Gardens
Regeneration, Manchester

フォートワース現代美術館
Modern Art Museum
of Fort Worth

2003

一戸南小学校
Minami Primary School,
Ichinohe

野間自由幼稚園
Noma Kindergarten

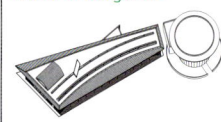

ロック・フィールド
玉川ファクトリー
Rock Field
Tamagawa Factory

4×4の住宅
4x4 House

西麻布の集合住宅
Nishiazabu Housing

マリブの住宅
House in Malibu

2004

加子母村ふれあい
コミュニティセンター
Kashimo-mura
Community Center

地中美術館
Chichu Art Museum /
Naoshima

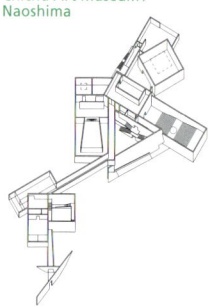

県立ぐんま昆虫の森
昆虫観察館
Gunma Insect World
Insect Observation Hall

絵本美術館
まどのそとのそのまたむこう
Iwaki Museum of
Picture Books for Children

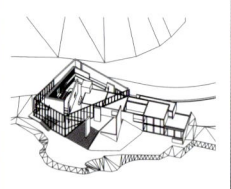

東京アートミュージアム（TAM）
Tokyo Art Museum

見えない家
Invisible House

仙川の集合住宅 Ⅰ
Sengawa Housing Ⅰ

ゴールデン・ゲート・
ブリッジの住宅
Golden Gate Bridge House

ホンブロイッヒ／ランゲン
美術館
Langen Foundation /
Hombroich

ICED TIME TUNNEL /
The Snow Show 2004
ICED TIME TUNNEL /
The Snow Show 2004

森の教会
Chapel in the Woods

上海デザインセンター
Shanghai Design Center

2005

ロック・フィールド
神戸ヘッドオフィス／
神戸ファクトリー
Rock Field
Kobe Headquarters /
Kobe Factory

hhstyle.com/casa
hhstyle.com/casa

高槻の住宅
House in Takatsuki

テアトリーノ
Teatrino

H ミュージアム
H Museum

2006

表参道ヒルズ
（同潤会青山アパート建替計画）
Omotesando Hills
(Omotesando
Regeneration Project)

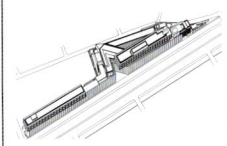

さくら広場（幕張）
Sakura Hiroba (Makuhari)

さくら広場（門真）
Sakura Hiroba (Kadoma)

ベネッセハウス
パーク／ビーチ
Benesse House
Park / Beach

坂の上の雲ミュージアム
Sakanouenokumo
Museum

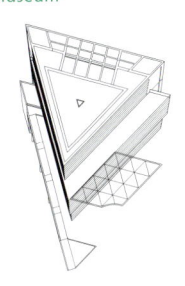

滋賀の住宅
House in Shiga

パラッツォ・グラッシ再生計画
Palazzo Grassi Renovation

アブダビ海洋博物館
Abu Dhabi Maritime
Museum

2007

21_21 DESIGN SIGHT
21_21 DESIGN SIGHT

竜王駅
Ryuo Station (JR-Line)

調布市せんがわ劇場＋
調布市立仙川保育園
Sengawa Theater + Nursery,
Chofu

曹洞宗太岳院
Taigakuin Temple

仙川の集合住宅 II
Sengawa Housing II

深井邸
Fukai House

回遊式住宅
Walk-around House

2008

東京大学情報学環・福武ホール
Interfaculty Initiative in
Information Studies,
Fukutake Hall,
the University of Tokyo

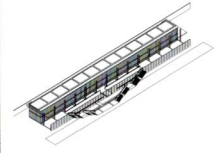

東急東横線渋谷駅
Tokyu Toyoko-Line
Shibuya Station

東急大井町線上野毛駅
Tokyu Oimachi-Line
Kaminoge Station

聖心女子学院創立100周年
記念ホール
Sacred Heart School
100th Anniversary Hall

仙川の集合住宅 III
Sengawa Housing III

2009 竣工予定

プンタ・デラ・ドガーナ再生計画
Punta della Dogana
Renovation

ノバルティス研究施設棟
Novartis WSJ-352

作品データ [掲載順] Projects Data

凡例／legend
1 所在／location
2 用途／principal use
3 設計期間／design period
4 施工期間／construction period
5 敷地面積／site area
6 建築面積／built area
7 延床面積／total floor area
8 規模／scale in building
9 主体構造／structure
10 掲載誌

東京大学情報学環・福武ホール
Interfaculty Initiative in Information Studies Fukutake Hall, the University of Tokyo

1 東京都文京区／Bunkyo-ku, Tokyo
2 学校／school
3 2005.9-2006.9
4 2006.12-2008.3
5 402,682.18 m²
6 1,454.15 m²
7 4,045.66 m²
8 地下2階 地上2階／2 basement 2 stories
9 鉄筋コンクリート造／reinforced concrete
10 『新建築』2007.6、『GA DOCUMENT』73 91、『GA JAPAN』87 89 92

東急東横線渋谷駅
Tokyu Toyoko-Line Shibuya Station

1 東京都渋谷区／Shibuya-ku, Tokyo
2 駅／station
3 2006.1-2006.11
4 2006.12-2008.6
5 28,904.57 m²
7 27,007.82 m²
8 地下5階 地上1階／5 basement 1 story
9 鉄筋コンクリート造、一部鉄骨造／reinforced concrete, partly steel frame
10 『新建築』2007.6、『GA JAPAN』86

東急大井町線上野毛駅
Tokyu Oimachi-Line Kaminoge Station

1 東京都世田谷区／Setagaya-ku, Tokyo
2 駅／station
3 2006.10-
5 3,216.85 m²
6 1,208.01 m²
  （ホーム部分を除く／except platform area）
7 2,463.31 m²
  （ホーム部分を含む／except platform area）
8 地下1階 地上2階／1 basement 2 stories
9 鉄骨造／steel frame
10 『新建築』2007.6、『GA JAPAN』86

聖心女子学院創立100周年記念ホール
Sacred Heart School 100th Anniversary Hall

1 東京都港区／Minato-ku, Tokyo
2 学校／school
3 2004.8-2007.6
4 2007.6-2008.7
5 58,640.51 m²
6 642.06 m²
7 986.75 m²
8 地上3階／3 stories
9 鉄筋コンクリート造、鉄骨鉄筋コンクリート造、鉄骨造／reinforced concrete, steel framed reinforced concrete, steel frame

TIME'S I + II
TIME'S I + II

1 京都府京都市中京区／Nakagyo-ku, Kyoto, Kyoto
2 店舗／shop
3 1983.4-1983.10 (I期／phase I)
  1984.10-1990.7 (II期／phase II)
4 1983.11-1984.9 (I期／phase I)
  1990.8-1991.9 (II期／phase II)
5 351.28 m² (I期／phase I)
  485.82 m² (II期／phase II)
6 289.45 m² (I期／phase I)
  107.87 m² (II期／phase II)
7 641.17 m² (I期／phase I)
  274.16 m² (II期／phase II)
8 地下1階 地上3階(I期)、地上3階(II期)／1 basement 3 stories (phase I), 3 stories (phase II)
9 コンクリートブロック造／reinforced concrete-block
10 『新建築』1985.2 1992.7、『建築文化』1986.9、『SD』1989.9

渋谷プロジェクト
Shibuya Project

1 東京都渋谷区／Shibuya-ku, Tokyo
2 店舗／shop
3 1985.4-1987.3
5 1,130.74 m²
6 867.10 m²
7 6,210.10 m²
8 地下5階 地上4階／5 basement 4 stories
9 鉄筋コンクリート造／reinforced concrete
10 『SD』1989.9 1992.6

中之島プロジェクト II
（アーバン・エッグ＋地層空間）
Nakanoshima Project II
(Urban Egg + Space Strata)

❶大阪府大阪市北区／Kita-ku, Osaka, Osaka
❷美術館、博物館、図書館、コンサートホール／art and science museums, library, concert hall
❸1988.1-
❿『新建築』1989.9、『SD』1989.9 1992.6

水の教会
Church on the Water

❶北海道勇払郡／Yufutsu-gun, Hokkaido
❷教会／Church
❸1985.9-1988.4
❹1988.4-1988.9
❺6,730.00 m²
❻344.94 m²
❼520.04 m²
❽地下1階 地上1階／1 basement 1 story
❾鉄筋コンクリート造／reinforced concrete
❿『建築文化』1988.7 1989.4、『新建築』1989.2 1989.4、『SD』1989.9

光の教会＋日曜学校
Church of the Light + Sunday School

❶大阪府茨木市／Ibaraki, Osaka
❷教会／church
❸1987.1-1988.5 (I期／phase I)
1997.3-1998.5 (II期／phase II)
❹1988.5-1989.4 (I期／phase I)
1998.5-1999.2 (II期／phase II)
❺838.60 m²
❻113.04 m² (I期／phase I)
116.80 m² (II期／phase II)
❼113.04 m² (I期／phase I)
148.80 m² (II期／phase II)
❽地上1階(I期)、地上2階(II期)／1 story (phase I), 2 stories (phase II)
❾鉄筋コンクリート造／reinforced concrete
❿『建築文化』1989.4 1989.9、『新建築』1989.9 1999.5、『SD』1989.9、『GA JAPAN』38

兵庫県立こどもの館
Children's Museum, Hyogo

❶兵庫県姫路市／Himeji, Hyogo
❷多目的ホール、野外劇場、美術館、図書館、工作館／hall, amphitheater, museum, library, workshop complex
❸1987.3-1988.3
❹1988.3-1989.7
❺87,222 m²
❻3,575.58 m²
❼7,488.37 m²
❽地下1階 地上3階／1 basement 3 stories
❾鉄骨鉄筋コンクリート造、一部鉄筋コンクリート造、鉄骨造／steel framed reinforced concrete, reinforced concrete, steel frame
❿『新建築』1989.2 1990.8、『SD』1989.9、『建築文化』1990.8

真言宗本福寺水御堂
Water Temple

❶兵庫県淡路市／Awaji, Hyogo
❷寺院／temple
❸1989.11-1990.12
❹1990.12-1991.9
❺2,990.75 m²
❻859.47 m²
❼417.16 m²
❽地下1階／1 basement
❾鉄筋コンクリート造／reinforced concrete
❿『新建築』1991.4 1992.7、『建築文化』1992.7

JR京都駅改築設計競技案
The Reconstruction of JR Kyoto Station, International Design Competition

❶京都府京都市下京区／Shimogyo-ku, Kyoto, Kyoto
❷駅舎、店舗、ホテル、レストラン、コンベンションホール、コンサートホール／station, shop hotel, restaurant, convention hall, concert hall
❸1990.10-1991.3
❺38,000 m²
❻34,340 m²
❼201,000 m²
❽地下3階 地上15階／3 basement 15 stories
❾鉄骨造／steel frame
❿『新建築』1991.6、『SD』1992.6

ベネッセハウス
Benesse House / Naoshima

❶香川県香川郡／Kagawa-gun, Kagawa
❷美術館、ホテル／museum, hotel
❸1988.5-1990.10 (ミュージアム／Museum)
1993.5-1994.9 (オーバル／Oval)
❹1990.10-1992.3 (ミュージアム／Museum)
1994.10-1995.6 (オーバル／Oval)
❺44,699.99 m² (ミュージアム／Museum)
53,368.99 m² (オーバル／Oval)
❻1,775.46 m² (ミュージアム／Museum)
693.10 m² (オーバル／Oval)
❼3,643.38 m² (ミュージアム／Museum)
597.79 m² (オーバル／Oval)
❽地下1階 地上3階(ミュージアム)、地上1階(オーバル)／1 basement 3 stories (museum), 1 story (Oval)
❾鉄筋コンクリート造／reinforced concrete
❿『新建築』1991.9 1993.7 1996.7、『建築文化』1993.7、『GA JAPAN』4 21

大阪府立近つ飛鳥博物館
Chikatsu-Asuka Historical Museum, Osaka

①大阪府南河内郡／Minamikawachi-gun, Osaka
②博物館／museum
③1990.4-1991.11
④1991.12-1994.3
⑤14,318.26 m^2
⑥3,407.84 m^2
⑦5,925.20 m^2
⑧地下1階 地上2階 塔屋1階／
　1 basement 2 stories 1 penthouse
⑨鉄骨鉄筋コンクリート造／
　steel framed reinforced concrete
⑩『新建築』1992.10 1994.9、『GA JAPAN』10、
　『建築文化』1994.9

サントリーミュージアム+マーメイド広場
Suntory Museum + Plaza

①大阪府大阪市港区／Minato-ku, Osaka, Osaka
②美術館、シアター、広場／museum,
　theater, plaza
③1989.8-1992.8
④1992.9-1994.8
⑤13,429.41 m^2
⑥3,983.83 m^2 (ミュージアム／Museum)
　1,362.20 m^2 (広場／Plaza)
⑦13,804.11 m^2 (ミュージアム／Museum)
　2,696.57 m^2 (広場／Plaza)
⑧地下1階 地上9階 塔屋1階(ミュージアム)、地下1階
　地上1階／1 basement 9 stories 1 penthouse
　(Museum), 1 basement 1 story (Plaza)
⑨鉄骨鉄筋コンクリート造、鉄筋コンクリート造、
　鉄骨造／steel framed reinforced concrete,
　reinforced concrete, steel frame
⑩『新建築』1992.6 1995.3、『GA JAPAN』13

大谷地下劇場計画
The Theater in the Rock, Oya

①栃木県宇都宮市／Utsunomiya, Tochigi
②劇場、美術館／theater, museum
③1995.2-1996.12
④1997.1-
⑤10,245 m^2
⑦4,750 m^2
⑧地下45m／45m under ground
⑨石造／masonry
⑩『新建築』1996.7

織田廣喜ミュージアム
Daylight Museum

①滋賀県蒲生郡／Gamo-gun, Shiga
②美術館／museum
③1997.2-1997.8
④1997.10-1998.5
⑤178,225.13 m^2
⑥210.05 m^2
⑦196.15 m^2
⑧地上1階／1 story
⑨鉄筋コンクリート造／reinforced concrete
⑩『新建築』1998.11、『GA JAPAN』35

淡路夢舞台
Awaji-Yumebutai (Awaji Island Project)

①兵庫県淡路市／Awaji, Hyogo
②会議場、ホテル、店舗、温室、野外劇場／
　conference center, hotel, shop,
　greenhouse, anphitheater
③1993.4-1994.12, 1995.10-1996.12
④1997.7-1999.12
⑤213,930.00 m^2
⑥38,429.14 m^2
⑦95,078.04 m^2
⑧地下2階 地上10階 塔屋1階／
　2 basement 10 stories 1 penthouse
⑨鉄筋コンクリート造、一部鉄骨造／
　reinforced concrete, partly steel frame
⑩『新建築』2000.7、『GA JAPAN』45

南岳山光明寺
Komyo-ji Temple

①愛媛県西条市／Saijo, Ehime
②寺院／temple
③1998.1-1999.3
④1999.4-2000.6
⑤3,221.82 m^2
⑥1,224.08 m^2
⑦1,284.09 m^2
⑧地上2階／2 stories
⑨木造(本殿)、鉄筋コンクリート造(客殿、
　礼拝堂、庫裡)／wood (main hall),
　reinforced concrete (guest house,
　place for worship and priests)
⑩『GA JAPAN』40, 48、『新建築』2001.1、
　『a+u』2001.3

大阪府立狭山池博物館
Sayamaike Historical Museum, Osaka

①大阪府大阪狭山市／Osakasayama, Osaka
②博物館／museum
③1994.6-1997.3
④1997.7-2001.3
⑤15,412.00 m^2
⑥3,773.53 m^2
⑦4,948.47 m^2
⑧地上3階／3 stories
⑨鉄筋コンクリート造、一部鉄骨鉄筋コンク
　リート造／reinforced concrete, partly
　steel framed reinforced concrete
⑩『新建築』2001.11、『GA JAPAN』53

司馬遼太郎記念館
Shiba Ryotaro Memorial Museum

①大阪府東大阪市／Higashiosaka, Osaka
②資料館／museum
③1998.9-2000.6
④2000.7-2001.10
⑤1,009.96 m^2
⑥445.86 m^2
⑦997.05 m^2
⑧地下1階 地上2階／1 basement 2 stories
⑨鉄筋コンクリート造／reinforced concrete
⑩『新建築』2002.7、『GA JAPAN』57

国際芸術センター青森
Aomori Contemporary Art Centre

❶青森県青森市／Aomori, Aomori
❷集会場、旅館、作業場／assembly hall, hotel, workshop
❸2000.1-2000.7
❹2000.10-2001.10
❺262,500 m²
❻4,277.51 m²
❼4,015.06 m²
❽地上2階／2 stories
❾鉄筋コンクリート造、一部鉄骨造および鉄骨鉄筋コンクリート造／reinforced concrete, partly steel frame and steel framed reinforced concrete
❿『新建築』2003.1、『GA JAPAN』43 60

兵庫県立美術館＋神戸市水際広場
Hyogo Prefectural Museum of Art + Kobe Waterfront Plaza

❶兵庫県神戸市中央区／chuo-ku, Kobe, Hyogo
❷美術館、広場／museum, plaza
❸1997.3-1998.3（美術館／Museum）
　1996.4-1998.3（広場／Plaza）
❹1999.3-2001.9（美術館／Museum）
　1998.9-2001.3（広場／Plaza）
❺19,000.00 m²
❻13,807.71 m²
❼27,461.41 m²
❽地下1階 地上4階／1 basement 4 stories
❾鉄骨鉄筋コンクリート造／steel framed reinforced concrete
❿『新建築』2002.9、『GA JAPAN』32 58

国際子ども図書館
The International Library of Children's Literature

❶東京都台東区／Taito-ku, Tokyo
❷図書館／library
❸1996.8-2000.3
❹1998.3-2002.1
❺5,433.76 m²
❻1,929.58 m²
❼6,671.63 m²
❽地下1階 地上7階／1 basement 7 stories
❾レンガ組積造、一部鉄筋コンクリート造、鉄骨鉄筋コンクリート造、鉄骨造／blick, partly reinforced concrete, steel framed reinforced concrete and steel frame
❿『新建築』2002.7、『GA JAPAN』57

加賀市立錦城中学校
Kinjo Junior High School, Kaga

❶石川県加賀市／Kaga, Ishikawa
❷中学校／junior high school
❸2000.9-2001.8
❹2001.9-2002.12
❺51,102.00 m²
❻5,615.31 m²
❼7,514.89 m²
❽地上2階／2 stories
❾鉄骨造／steel frame
❿『新建築』2005.11、『GA JAPAN』77

野間自由幼稚園
Noma Kindergarten

❶静岡県伊東市／Ito, Shizuoka
❷幼稚園／kindergarten
❸2001.4-2002.2
❹2002.3-2003.1
❺16,514.9 m²
❻1,478.8 m²
❼1,097.4 m²
❽地上1階／1 story
❾鉄骨造／steel frame
❿『新建築』2004.7、『GA JAPAN』59 69

地中美術館
Chichu Art Museum / Naoshima

❶香川県香川郡／Kagawa-gun, Kagawa
❷美術館／museum
❸2000.8-2002.3
❹2002.4-2004.6
❺9,990.00 m²
❻34.98 m²
❼2,573.48 m²
❽地下3階／3 besement
❾鉄筋コンクリート造／reinforced concrete
❿『新建築』2004.9、『GA JAPAN』70

表参道ヒルズ
（同潤会青山アパート建替計画）
Omotesando Hills
(Omotesando Regeneration Project)

❶東京都渋谷区／Shibuya-ku, Tokyo
❷店舗、共同住宅／shop, housing
❸1996.4-2003.3
❹2003.8-2006.1
❺6,051.36 m²
❻5,030.76 m²
❼34,061.72 m²
❽地下6階 地上6階／6 basement 6 stories
❾鉄骨鉄筋コンクリート造、一部鉄筋コンクリート造、鉄骨造／steel framed reinforced concrete, partly reinforced concrete and steel frame
❿『新建築』2002.12 2005.2 2006.5、『GA JAPAN』80

21_21 DESIGN SIGHT
21_21 DESIGN SIGHT

❶東京都港区／Minato-ku, Tokyo
❷デザイン文化交流施設／museum
❸2004.3-2005.9
❹2005.10-2007.2
❺2,653.30 m²
❻597.30 m²
❼1932.43 m²
❽地下1階 地上1階／1 basement 1story
❾鉄筋コンクリート造、一部鉄骨造／reinforced concrete, partly steel frame
❿『新建築』2005.10 2007.5、『GA JAPAN』77 86、『GA DOCUMENT』96

作品所在地
Map of Projects

東京大学情報学環・福武ホール
Interfaculty Initiative in Information Studies Fukutake Hall, the University of Tokyo

真言宗本福寺水御堂、淡路夢舞台
Water Temple & Awaji-Yumebutai

サントリーミュージアム＋マーメイド広場
Suntory Museum + Plaza

TIME'S I + II
TIME'S I + II

ベネッセハウス、地中美術館
Benesse House & Chichu Art Museum / Naoshima

織田廣喜ミュージアム
Daylight Museum

兵庫県立こどもの館
Children's Museum, Hyogo

大阪府立近つ飛鳥博物館
Chikatsu-Asuka Historical Museum, Osaka

南岳山光明寺
Komyo-ji Temple

大阪府立狭山池博物館
Sayamaike Historical Museum, Osaka

兵庫県立美術館＋神戸市水際広場
Hyogo Prefectural Museum of Art
+ Kobe Waterfront Plaza

21_21 DESIGN SIGHT
21_21 DESIGN SIGHT

司馬遼太郎記念館
Shiba Ryotaro Memorial Museum

国際子ども図書館
The International Library of Children's Literature

国際芸術センター青森
Aomori Contemporary Art Centre

表参道ヒルズ
Omotesando Hills

略歴 Profile
安藤忠雄 Tadao Ando

略歴	1941	●大阪に生まれる
	1962-69	●独学で建築を学ぶ
	1969	●安藤忠雄建築研究所を設立
受賞	1979	●「住吉の長屋」で昭和54年度日本建築学会賞
	1985	●フィンランド建築家協会から、国際的な建築賞 アルヴァ・アアルト賞（第5回）
	1989	●1989年度フランス建築アカデミー大賞（ゴールドメダル）
	1993	●日本芸術院賞
	1995	●1995年度プリツカー賞
	1996	●高松宮殿下記念世界文化賞
	2002	●2002年度アメリカ建築家協会（AIA）ゴールドメダル
		●ローマ大学名誉博士号
		●同済大学（上海）名誉教授
		●京都賞
	2003	●文化功労者
	2005	●国際建築家連合（UIA）ゴールドメダル
		●レジオン・ドヌール勲章（シュバリエ）叙勲
名誉会員	2002	●イギリス ロイヤルアカデミー オブ アーツ名誉会員
教職	1987	●イェール大学客員教授
	1988	●コロンビア大学客員教授
	1990	●ハーバード大学客員教授
	1997-	●東京大学教授
	2003-	●東京大学名誉教授
	2005	●東京大学特別栄誉教授
		●カリフォルニア大学バークレー校客員教授
	2006-	●2016年東京オリンピック招致活動の総監督を務める
主な作品	1983	●六甲の集合住宅Ⅰ（兵庫 神戸）
	1989	●光の教会（大阪 茨木）
	1992	●ベネッセハウス ミュージアム（香川 直島）
	1993	●六甲の集合住宅Ⅱ（兵庫 神戸）
	1994	●大阪府立近つ飛鳥博物館（大阪 河南）
	1995	●ベネッセハウス オーバル（香川 直島）
	1999	●六甲の集合住宅Ⅲ（兵庫 神戸）
	2000	●淡路夢舞台（兵庫 淡路）
		●南岳山光明寺（愛媛 西条）
		●FABRICA（ベネトンアートスクール）（イタリア トレヴィソ）
	2001	●ピューリッツァー美術館（アメリカ セントルイス）
		●アルマーニ・テアトロ（イタリア ミラノ）
		●大阪府立狭山池博物館（大阪 大阪狭山）
	2002	●兵庫県立美術館（兵庫 神戸）
		●国際子ども図書館（東京 台東区）
		●フォートワース現代美術館（アメリカ フォートワース）
	2003	●4×4の住宅（兵庫 神戸）
	2004	●地中美術館（香川 直島）
		●ホンブロイッヒ／ランゲン美術館（ドイツ ノイス）
	2006	●同潤会青山アパート建替計画（表参道ヒルズ）（東京 渋谷区）
		●パラッツォ・グラッシ再生計画（イタリア ヴェニス）
	2007	●21_21 DESIGN SIGHT（東京 港区）
	2008	●東京大学情報学環・福武ホール（東京 文京区）
		●東急東横線渋谷駅（東京 渋谷区）

Profile

1941	● Born in Osaka, Japan
1962-69	● Self-educated in architecture
1969	● Established Tadao Ando Architect & Associates

Awards

1979	● Annual Prize, Architectural Institute of Japan "Row House in Sumiyoshi"
1985	● The 5th Alvar Aalto Medal, The Finnish Association of Architects, Finland
1989	● Gold Medal of Architecture, Académie d'Architecture (French Academy of Architecture), France
1993	● Japan Art Academy Prize, Japan
1995	● The Pritzker Architecture Prize, U.S.A.
1996	● The 8th Premium Imperiale
2002	● Gold Medal of the American Institute of Architects, U.S.A.
	● Honorary Degree, Università Degli Studi di Roma, Italy
	● Honorary Degree, Tongji University, Shanghai, China
	● The Kyoto Prizes, Japan
2003	● Person of Cultural Merit, Japan
2005	● Gold Medal of Union Internationale des Architectes
	● Chevalier de l'Ordre National de la Légron d'Honneur, France

Affiliations

2002	● Honorary Academician, The Royal Academy of Arts in London

Academic Activities

1987	● Visiting Professor, Yale University
1988	● Visiting Professor, Columbia University
1990	● Visiting Professor, Harvard University
1997-	● Professor, The University of Tokyo
2003-	● Emeritus Professor, The University of Tokyo
2005	● Special University Professor Emeritus, The University of Tokyo
	● Regent Professor, University of California, Berkeley
2006-	● General Director, Tokyo 2016 Olympic Games Bid Committee

Representative Works

1983	● Rokko Housing I, Kobe, Hyogo
1989	● Church of the Light, Ibaraki, Osaka
1992	● Benesse House Museum, Naoshima, Kagawa
1993	● Rokko Housing II, Kobe, Hyogo
1994	● Chikatsu-Asuka Historical Museum, Kanan, Osaka
1995	● Benesse House Oval, Naoshima, Kagawa
1999	● Rokko Housing III, Kobe, Hyogo
2000	● Awaji-Yumebutai (Awaji Island Project), Awaji, Hyogo
	● Komyo-ji Temple, Saijo, Ehime
	● FABRICA (Benetton Communications Research Center), Treviso, Italy
2001	● Pulitzer Foundation for the Arts, St. Louis, U.S.A.
	● ARMANI / TEATRO, Milan, Italy
	● Sayamaike Historical Museum, Osaka-Sayama, Osaka
2002	● Hyogo Prefectural Museum of Art, Kobe, Hyogo
	● The International Library of Children's Literature, Taito-ku, Tokyo
	● Modern Art Museum of Fort Worth, Fort Worth, U.S.A.
2003	● 4×4 House, Kobe, Hyogo
2004	● Chichu Art Museum / Naoshima, Naoshima, Kagawa
	● Langen Foundation / Hombroich Museum, Neuss, Germany
2006	● Omotesando Hills (Omotesando Regeneration Project), Shibuya-ku, Tokyo
	● Palazzo Grassi Renovation, Venice, Italy
2007	● 21_21 DESIGN SIGHT, Minato-ku, Tokyo
2008	● Fukutake Hall, the University of Tokyo, Bunkyo-ku, Tokyo
	● Tokyu Toyoko-Line Shibuya Station, Shibuya-ku, Tokyo

クレジット Credits

Photography　写真

Mitsuo Matsuoka　松岡満男
pp.36, 38, 40-43, 50-51, 132-133, 168 below, 170-171, 190-191 above, 200 right, 205, 210 left, 224-225, 250-251 center & right, 252-254, 260, 261 below, 264-269, 272-273, 281, 282-283 left & center, 284-285, 288-289, 290 above, 292, 298 above, 302-305, 309, 314-323, 326-328, 330, 332-335, 338-339, 342-347, 360-361, 369, 372-373, 396, 416-422

Mitsumasa Fujitsuka　藤塚光政
pp.14-18, 20-27, 30-35, 39 right, 82-83, 86-87, 120-123, 124 below, 125-127, 162-165, 168 above, 169, 172, 186-189, 192, 196-197, 199, 202-203, 211 right, 212-215, 218-219, 274, 280, 350-358, 364-368, 370-371, 374-375, 380-391, 394-395, 397-399, 402-409, 412-413

Shinkenchiku-sha　新建築社
pp.88-89, 124 above, 130-131, 137, 139, 144-146, 150, 152, 154-155, 158-159, 166, 173, 191 below, 198, 209, 222-223, 226-229, 275, 283 right, 290 below, 294, 296-297, 298 below, 299, 306-307, 310-311, 329

Tomio Ohashi　大橋富夫
pp.92-93, 141, 147, 151 above, 178-179, 208, 232-234, 236, 238-239, 248-249, 250 left

Kaori Ichikawa　市川かおり
pp.200 left, 201

Yoshio Shiratori　白鳥美雄
pp.118-119

Yukio Futagawa　二川幸夫
pp.262-263

Yoshio Takase　高瀬良夫
p.255

Kai Nakamura　中村絵
pp.426-427

Kazuo Natori　名執一雄
pp.463 above

Courtesy of Casa BRUTUS/Magazine House Co,. LTD.
写真提供／マガジンハウス カーサ ブルータス
pp.402-409, 412-413

Other photographs courtesy of Tadao Ando Architect & Associates
上記以外の写真すべて安藤忠雄建築研究所

Drawings　図版

Tadao Ando Architect & Associates　安藤忠雄建築研究所

English Translations　英訳

Hiroshi Watanabe　渡辺 洋
pp. 52-79, 428-461

Thomas Daniell & Ellen Van Goethem
トーマス・ダニエル ＆ エレン・ヴァン・フーテム
Project descriptions and captions

Yasushi Zenno　禪野靖司
pp.112-113, 256-257, 376-377

The source of following drawings:
"TADAO ANDO DETAILS" volume 3 and 4 by
A.D.A. EDITA Tokyo
以下の図版初出：『TADAO ANDO DETAILS』3巻および4巻
（A.D.A. EDITA Tokyo 刊）
pp.143, 276-279, 424-425

Tadao Ando Architect & Associates
安藤忠雄建築研究所

Tadao Ando	安藤忠雄
Masataka Yano	矢野正隆
Fumihiko Iwama	岩間文彦
Kazuya Okano	岡野一也
Takaaki Mizutani	水谷孝明
Hironobu Wakayama	若山泰伸
Hidehiro Yano	矢野英裕
Kanya Sogo	十河完也
Yoshinori Hayashi	林 慶憲
Shimao Mori	森詩麻夫
Tatsuhito Ono	小野龍人
Takeharu Suzuki	鈴木丈晴
Tomonori Miura	三浦朋訓
Kosuke Sakai	酒井康介
Kazutoshi Miyamura	宮村和寿
Shunri Nishizawa	西澤俊理
Eiji Hayakawa	早川鋭二
Seiichiro Takeuchi	竹内誠一郎
Hiroyuki Tanaka	田中宏行
Kensuke Suto	須藤謙介
Hajime Moriyama	森山 一
Akinori Yagi	八木章徳
Gonzalo Velez Jaramillo	ヴェレス ハラミジョ ゴンザロ
Chisato Kodaira	古平知沙都
Akiko Hayashida	林田安紀子
Kaori Soneda	曽根田香
Tamao Shichiri	七里玉緒
Yumiko Kato	加藤由美子

安藤忠雄の建築 3

Tadao Ando 3
Inside Japan

2008年10月10日　初版　第1刷発行
2023年 6月15日　初版　第6刷発行

著者............安藤忠雄

発行者...........渡井 朗

デザイン..........太田徹也

プリンティング
ディレクション......髙柳 昇

印刷・製本........株式会社東京印書館

発行所...........TOTO出版
　　　　　　　　（TOTO株式会社）

〒107-0062　東京都港区南青山1-24-3
TOTO乃木坂ビル2F
[営業] tel：03(3402)7138
　　　 fax：03(3402)7187
[編集] tel：03(3497)1010
URL：https://jp.toto.com/publishing

落丁本・乱丁本はお取り替えいたします。
本書の全部又は一部に対する
コピー・スキャン・デジタル化等の
無断複製行為は、著作権法上での
例外を除き禁じます。
本書を代行業者等の第三者に依頼して
スキャンやデジタル化することは、
たとえ個人や家庭内での利用であっても
著作権法上認められておりません。
定価はカバーに表示してあります。

©2008 Tadao Ando
Printed in Japan
ISBN978-4-88706-296-2